The Modern Language Association of America
MONOGRAPH SERIES

II

DRAMATIC PUBLICATION IN
ENGLAND, 1580-1640

Dramatic Publication in England, 1580-1640

A STUDY OF CONDITIONS AFFECTING
CONTENT AND FORM OF DRAMA

BY

EVELYN MAY ALBRIGHT

Published by the Modern Language Association of America
NEW YORK, D. C. HEATH AND COMPANY
LONDON, OXFORD UNIVERSITY PRESS

MDCCCCXXVII

Approved for publication in the MONOGRAPH SERIES of the
MODERN LANGUAGE ASSOCIATION OF AMERICA

EDWARD C. ARMSTRONG
ROBERT HERNDON FIFE
JOHN LIVINGSTON LOWES
JOHN MATTHEWS MANLY
WILLIAM ALBERT NITZE
Committee of Award

PREFACE

In this essay on dramatic publication in England from 1580 to 1640, *publication* has been used in its technical sense to include the public performance, as well as the printing and selling, of plays. The aim is not to furnish a history of acted or printed plays, but to explain certain conditions of the age which affected content and form of the drama.

This study, like a companion volume on Author's Rights and Copyright in England for the same period, had its origin in a suggestion made by Professor John Matthews Manly, of the University of Chicago, in a Shakespeare Seminar in 1909. I take pleasure in acknowledging my indebtedness to Professor Manly not only for his suggestions as to materials but for his training, which has made possible whatever degree of correctness may appear in this work. Thanks are due also to Professor C. R. Baskervill for several references to sources, and to the members of the Committee on the Monograph Series for their courtesy in reading my manuscript. I am indebted to Professor Carleton Brown for much valuable editorial criticism, as well as for the reading of proofs.

Mr. A. W. Pollard, to whom I sent an outline summary of plans and materials for the two volumes in 1913, has, from time to time, kindly overseen the procuring of materials for me from the British Museum and the Public Records Office; and Mr. H. R. Plomer and Mr. George England have also assisted by furnishing transcripts.

As a number of important studies in this field have appeared between the completion of this essay (January, 1923) and the date of its going to the press, I have included references to some of them in my bibliography and in a few footnotes.

For a few works repeatedly referred to, I have used in text and footnotes short titles. The reader's attention is called to the Bibliographical Note at the end of the text for such short forms as may not be at once recognized, and to the Bibliography itself for the full titles of the works.

EVELYN MAY ALBRIGHT

Chicago, January 1, 1926

CONTENTS

INTRODUCTION.. 1

CHAPTER I. ORGANIZATION AND CONTROL OF DRAMATIC COMPANIES... 6
   1. Status of actors 6
   2. Numbers of companies.......................... 11
   3. Provincial companies and provincial visits........ 12
   4. Regulation of the drama 19
      1) Attitude of the Sovereign 19
      2) The Privy Council............................ 22
      3) Early Ecclesiastical Interest in Drama......... 22
      4) The Treasurer................................ 23
      5) The Chamberlain............................. 24
      6) The Mayor................................... 27
      7) The Master of the Revels..................... 37

CHAPTER II. LITERARY AND DRAMATIC CENSORSHIP............. 60
  PART I. Censorship of literature in general................... 60
   1. Officers of censorship: church, state, and city....... 60
   2. Aims and direction of censorship................. 71
   3. Censorship of particular kinds of books............ 72
      1) Religious works.............................. 72
      2) Seditious works.............................. 75
      3) Histories and news sheets 76
      4) Political theories............................. 82
      5) Scientific works.............................. 82
      6) Satires and epigrams 83
      7) Ballads...................................... 84
   4. Standards of propriety........................... 85
   5. Efficiency of censorship.......................... 87

  PART II. Censorship of the Drama.......................... 94
   1. Subjects considered dangerous on the stage........ 94
      1) Religious discussion.......................... 94
      2) Treatment of contemporary matters........... 101
      3) Criticism of sovereigns....................... 116
      4) Opinions on royal policies and affairs of state.... 128
      5) Satire on other nations...................... 148
      6) Satire on individuals......................... 172
      7) Seditious and treasonable utterances........... 181
      8) Impropriety................................. 188
   2. Methods of censorship........................... 193
   3. Authors' reactions on censorship of drama......... 197

Chapter III. Authorship and Ownership of Plays as
Affecting Publication.................................. 202
  1. Dramatic authorship............................... 202
  2. Attitude of the playwright toward publication......... 204
  3. Ownership of plays................................ 217
    1) Basis of stage-right before statutes............... 217
    2) Sale of plays in relation to stage-right............ 220
    3) Actors as owners of plays....................... 224
    4) Means of conserving stage-right.................. 229
    5) Copyright and stage-right....................... 233
  4. Attitudes of theatrical companies toward publication... 236
  5. Statistics on play publication....................... 249

Chapter IV. Conditions Affecting the Time of Publication of Plays.. 262
  1. Stage life of a play: revivals and revisions............ 263
  2. Restraints from acting............................. 265
  3. Prohibitions due to the plague..................... 269
  4. Status of theatrical companies...................... 276
  5. Demand for printed plays.......................... 284

Chapter V. Sources of Play Texts Printed................. 288
  1. Legitimate and illegitimate sources.................. 288
  2. Theories as to sources of play copy: Lost, stolen, and borrowed manuscripts; scriveners' copies; actors' roles; authors' manuscripts, private transcripts........ 289
  3. Characteristics of playhouse manuscripts............. 296
  4. Possible ways of pirating playhouse versions.......... 300
    1) The "traitor-actor" theory...................... 300
    2) Pirating by memory............................ 310
    3) Pirating by stenography........................ 315

Chapter VI.   and Publishing Conditions as Affecting the State of the Text............................ 317
  1. Commercializing of printing........................ 317
  2. Competition between printer and bookseller......... 318
  3. Lack of employment for printers.................... 319
  4. Use of faulty manuscripts.......................... 321
  5. Crudity of printing equipment...................... 323
  6. Work of the compositor............................ 325
  7. Kinds and causes of errata.......................... 334
  8. Work of the corrector.............................. 344
  9. Proof-reading by the author........................ 348
  10. General standards of typographical accuracy......... 356
  11. Editing by compositor, corrector, and publisher....... 369
  12. Causes and significance of variant readings........... 372
  13. Evidences of surreptitious or piratical printing........ 382

Bibliographical Note...................................... 385
Bibliography.. 385

INTRODUCTION

The purpose of this book is not to trace the history of dramatic publication from 1580 to 1640, but to discuss certain definite problems as to how, why, and when plays came into print. The control of the drama by public officials is here considered less for its own sake than for its effect upon the content of the plays, the time of their publication, and the nature of the dramatic texts. The discussion of censorship of drama is prefaced by some consideration of censorship of general literature in order to give an idea of comparative rigidity in the application of standards. The closing chapter, on printing and publishing conditions as affecting the state of the text, is intended to give the general reader such a background of information as will enable him to resist the prevalent tendency to conclude that a poor text of a play is a sure sign of piracy. How strong this tendency is may be seen from a survey of the separately edited Shakespeare texts used in the schools and colleges. In many cases the texts are declared to have been unauthorized, even though not extremely corrupt according to the standards of the day.

There has existed for about a hundred and ninety years a theory that the publication of plays in the period 1580–1640 was for the most part surreptitious or unauthorized if it took place while the plays were still in demand for the stage. The strong hold of this theory upon the public may be illustrated by a few references ranging from the early eighteenth century to the present.

In 1733 Theobald, in his edition of Shakespeare's plays (xxvii ff.), set forth the ways by which the plays might get into print:

> It was the custom of those days for the poets to take a price of the players for the pieces they from time to time finished; and thereupon it was supposed they had no farther right to print them without the consent of the players. As it was the interest of the companies to keep their plays unpublished, when any one succeeded, there was a contest betwixt the curiosity of the town, who demanded to see it in print, and

the policy of the stagers, who wished to secrete it within their own walls. Hence many pieces were taken down in short-hand, and imperfectly copied by ear from a representation: others were printed from piece-meal parts surreptitiously obtained from the theatres, incorrect and without the poet's knowledge. To some of these causes we owe the train of blemishes that deform those pieces which stole singly into the world in our author's life.

Malone, in his introduction to *Shakespeare's Works*, 1790, says of the quartos:

Undoubtedly they were all surreptitious, that is, stolen from the playhouse and printed without the consent of the author or the proprietor.

Sir Sidney Lee has made the most confident assertions as to the conditions of dramatic publication. He says:

It was contrary to the custom of the day for dramatists to print their plays for themselves or to encourage the printing of them by others or to preserve their manuscripts. Like all dramatists of his age, Shakespeare composed his plays for the acting company to which he attached himself; like them he was paid by the company for his writings, and in return made over to the company all property and right in his manuscripts.

The theatrical manager viewed the publication of plays as injurious to his interests, and until a play had wholly exhausted its popularity on the stage, he deprecated its appearance in print. But however indifferent the Elizabethan dramatist was to the reading public, and however pronounced were the manager's objections to the publication of plays, there developed among playgoers and others at the close of the sixteenth century a wish to peruse in private dramas that had achieved success in the theatre. Publishers quickly sought to gratify this desire for their own ends.[1]

In a later work, the 1916 edition of his *Life of Shakespeare* (pp. 297, 100, and 545), Sir Sidney Lee admits that the publisher usually bought (not stole) his copy from an actor, but he continues to insist on the irregularity of play publication:

The playhouse authorities deprecated the publishing of plays in the belief that their dissemination in print was injurious to the receipts of the theatre, and Shakespeare would seem to have had no direct responsibility for the publication of his plays. Professional opinion

---

[1] Int. to *First Folio*, xi.

condemned such playwrights as sought "a double sale of their labors, first to the stage and after to the press" (p. 100).

Eight or nine of these plays [Shakespeare's] were published during the period, but the publishers operated independently of the author, taking all the risks, and, at the same time, all the receipts. The company usually forbade under heavy penalties the author's sale to a publisher of a play which had been acted. The publication of Shakespeare's plays in no way affected his monetary resources. But his friendly relations with the printer Field doubtless secured him, despite the absence of any copyright law, some part of the profits in the large and continuous sale of his narrative poems. (p. 297).[2]

One infers that the author was indifferent, the manager, opposed to the publication of plays. How, then, are we to account for play publication? Sir Sidney Lee admits that printed plays were in demand, and names several possible sources. On page 100 of his *Life of Shakespeare*, he notes two ways of getting play copy. One was, through chance requisition of one of the many copies made of a play for actors or patrons, in which case "it was issued without any endeavor to obtain either author's or manager's sanction." The other method, by no means uncommon, was to take down the play by shorthand from a performance. It was so that at least four of Shakespeare's plays were secured for their publishers, according to Lee, namely: *Romeo and Juliet*, *Henry V.*, *Merry Wives*, and *Pericles* (pp. 546–7).

It is such views as Lee's that are responsible for the very general suspicion of the texts of a large proportion of the plays of the period. A similar attitude to Lee's is shown in a widely used work of reference, the *Cambridge History of English Literature* (N. Y., 1910). Mr. Ernest Walder goes so far as to assert (vol. v, pp. 289–290) that playwrights in general were indifferent to publication, and acting companies in general positively opposed to it; and that the Shakespeare quartos were alike surreptitious (although eight of them, "duplicated" in the Folio text, are entitled to rank as the only authoritative texts!).

The playwright's sole ambition was to see his play on the stage. Hardly any play was published by its author without some apology.

[2] This would seem to suggest that without friendly relations with the printer no author could expect pay—an assumption easily disproved.

Marston, in his preface to *The Malcontent*, 1604, actually complains that he is detracting from the value of his work by publishing it; and he goes on to state that his reason for consenting to this is that, if he did not publish it, others would, thus inflicting upon him still greater injury. All rights in a play were tacitly, if not legally, surrendered to the acting company, and the author's interest in it ceased. No more striking proof of this attitude could be desired than the fact that Shakespeare himself described *Venus and Adonis* as "the first heire of my invention" at a time when he had certainly written several plays.[3]

On the other hand, companies refrained from publication. They sought by this means to increase the profit from their performances. Thus Thomas Heywood speaks of some of his plays' being "still retained in the hands of some actors, who think it against their peculiar profit to have them come in print." But this short-sighted policy on the part of the companies did not prevent others from supplying the demand for printed copies which naturally existed. In the absence of any strict laws of copyright, it is not surprising that publishers were found ready to snatch a profit by the surreptitious publication of the more popular plays of so favorite a writer as Shakespeare.

This explains the origin of the quartos, in which form the text of nineteen plays first saw the light.[4]

Some modern writers go so far as to state that the acting companies were so violently opposed to the publication of plays as to destroy them to keep them out of print. Charles Read, for example, in his *The Eighth Commandment* (1860), said concerning the age of Shakespeare:

It was not the sharing author's interest to print his play, and the paid author lost the right to print his. The sharing author's parental feeling and *amour propre* made him print eventually, but only when the theatre had worn the play quite out . . . .But the sharing actors, whose vanity sided with their interest, held the bought plays tight, and kept them out of print with the keenest jealousy. They kept them under lock and key, they hid them, they destroyed them. When all their precautions were outwitted, as happened now and then by double MSS or short-hand, they applied to some great officer of state to restrain the printing, or they bought the printer off, or grinned and closed their stage-door to the author. This they did to Robert Greene.[5]

[3] Would Mr. Walder have us believe that the dramatic author tacitly, if not legally, surrendered all his rights to *remember* that he had ever written plays?
[4] Cf. also the attitude of Mr. Aldis, *Camb. Hist. of Eng. Lit.*, IV, 448.
[5] Cf. also John Coryton, *Stage-right* (1873), p. 28; Phoebe Sheavyn, *Lit. Profession in the Age of Elizabeth*, pp. 74–75; T. R. Lounsbury, *Text of Shake-*

In view of the fairly general agreement that play publication was against the desires of the author and the interests of the manager, it has seemed worth while to examine the reasons for this belief and bring together some of the facts concerning dramatic publication. I should say in advance that, if this investigation seems at one point to assume a statistical character, I am very well aware that the statistics are not, and cannot be, complete, owing to the great gaps in our records of dramatic performances, the absence of positive information as to whether plays entered on the Registers and not extant were ever published or whether the first editions extant were really the first published, and the inability to date exactly plays printed without date. But even with the incomplete evidence available, I believe that the facts readily accessible about the publication of plays will, when seen together, tend to weaken the theory that play publication was almost wholly surreptitious except when plays had been used up for the stage.

The final intention of the book is to show that it is unwise to draw a priori conclusions as to the unauthorized nature of whole groups of plays, and that each text must be fairly judged on its own evidence, and with an understanding of the typographical ideals and practices of the time.

---

peare, and H. R. Shipherd, "Play-Publishing in Elizabethan Times," *P.M.L.A.*, Dec., 1919, pp. 580–600.

CHAPTER I

ORGANIZATION AND CONTROL OF DRAMATIC COMPANIES

As it is not the purpose of this work to trace the histories of dramatic companies, I shall here present briefly only such facts as should be kept in mind in connection with the censorship of plays, the problems of stage-right and copyright in plays, the attitudes of companies toward play publication, and the conditions affecting the time of publication.[1]

The adult and the child actors were usually in separate companies, the rivalries of which are well known. What became of the child actor as actor, when he grew up, has puzzled others beside Hamlet (*Hamlet*, Act II, sc. 2, 361-8).[2] There was an attempt at a combination of adults and children when the King, in July 1622, licensed seven of those who had been comedians to Queen Anne to "bring up children in the qualitie and exercise of playinge. . . . to be called the Children of the Revels." Herbert's office-book in 1622 lists these same adults as the chief players at the Red Bull, called the players of the Revels. The combination was short-lived. (*Var.*, III, 59-60). As the problems here to be considered usually concern the adult companies, it will be understood that, when dramatic companies are mentioned, the adult companies will be meant unless it is otherwise specified.

STATUS OF ACTORS

The structure of Elizabethan society being in many respects still medieval, there are certain traditions and customs handed down from the past that vitally affected the profession of the

---

[1] For histories of individual companies, see J. T. Murray, *English Dramatic Companies*, which traces fortunes of adult and child actors in London and in the provinces from 1558 to 1642; and E. K. Chambers, *The Elizabethan Stage*.

[2] On the careers of the child actors, see John M. Manly, "The Children of the Chapel Royal and Their Masters," *Camb. Hist. of Eng. Lit.*, VI,pt.2,ch.XI;C.W. Wallace, *Children of the Chapel at Blackfriars*, 1597-1603; and C. M. Gayley, "The Fellows and Followers of Shakespeare in Comedy," *Rep. Eng. Com.*, II. xxxix ff.

actor. By far the larger proportion of acting companies, including even the greater ones that played at Court and in the main theatres of London, traveled at times from place to place. And there were numbers of companies that made a business of strolling. In so doing they escaped local responsibilities and made it difficult for any community to hold them responsible for their conduct. At a time when working people were closely organized in craft gilds, with every member responsible to the organization, it is no wonder that the unfettered life of the traveling player should seem too irresponsible to be tolerated. What happened was, that an old institution of medieval society was formally recognized by law as a cure for the otherwise masterless condition of these roving men. A nobleman was permitted to take under his patronage a group of men, who thus received their license to perform plays. The patron did not necessarily become responsible for their subsistence, but he was answerable for the conduct of his "servants." As a rule, the nobleman, besides allowing the use of his name and his livery, took an active interest in getting his men the privilege of playing in various places. This might necessitate the writing of letters to mayors or other officials or recommendations to other lords to affix their own hands and seals to the players' privileges to insure their local protection.[3]

In 1572 a statute was passed requiring traveling players to be the retainers of some "baron of this realme, or . . . . other honorable personage of greater degree," or to "have licence of two justices of the peace at the least." This statute and its revivals held for many years and became the chief support for the Puritan and other opponents of the drama. The statute was renewed in 1597–98 in the requirement that "players of enterludes belonging to any Baron of this Realme, or any other honorable Personage of greater Degree . . . . be auctoryzed to play under the Hand and Seale of armes of such Baron or Personage." The effect of the statute can be seen in an application by Burbage and his fellows to the Earl of Leicester for a licence declaring them his "household servants" in order that they might travel once a year as "other noble-mens Players do and have done in tyme past." Only the customary livery was

[3] See the documents in Murray, *E. D. C.*, II, 119 ff.

requested, with the use of his name because a "statute touching retainers" had been revived.[4]

The power of protection of noblemen over companies was largely curtailed by the statute 1 Jas. I, c. 7 (March, 1604), which deprived barons and other noblemen of power to "free or discharge said persons [the actors] from pains and punishments of said statute [that of 39 Eliz., c. 4]. At the same time there came a change of policy with reference to the court actors and the public players. There were in the time of James (1607-09) five court troupes of actors: the Chamberlain's, under patronage of the King; Worcester's, under the Queen; the Lord Admiral's, under the Prince of Wales; and two children's companies, under the King and the Queen. These facts have led to the statement that noblemen thereafter had no legal rights to be considered patrons of companies of actors. But the patent to Sir John Astley on May 22, 1622, gave him power over "every player and players, with the playmakers, either belonging to any noblemen or otherwise." (Chalmers, *Apology*, 497.) Also it is quite certain that traveling companies continued to enjoy some sort of patronage of noblemen. The statute of 1604 fixed personal responsibilities for conduct upon the individual actor, rather than the patron.

Because of the recurrent classification of strolling actors with rogues and vagabonds in the statutes, the enemies of the stage (particularly the Puritans) seized upon the idea and perpetuated it so successfully that many modern historians of the stage seriously assert that even the leading companies of Shakespeare's London were regarded by contemporaries as extremely low in the scale of society. This is a complete misconception. The strolling actor was a potential menace (1) because he strolled, and (2) because he was a masterless, and therefore irresponsible, component of the society of that day. As he could not be prevented from strolling without forbidding his professional activities altogether, and as there was a very general demand for the peripatetic drama, the next best thing was to provide him with a master. The constant insistence by the sovereigns that opportunities for practice be allowed their companies, the complimentary wordings of the patents and

[4] *Notes and Queries*, III, xi, 350.

grants of privilege, the royal patronage of the entertainments themselves, the expenditures on the dramas and the use of dramatic entertainments for the grandest and diplomatically most significant occasions in court life, as at weddings, receptions of foreign ambassadors, noblemen, etc., all go to prove what ought to need but little proof—that Elizabeth, James, and Charles were all heartily in favor of dramatic entertainments and therefore cannot reasonably be supposed to have desired to "put down" the actors who served them in this way. The dignity of the profession is further attested by its prominence on state occasions of other sorts. Five leading actors of the King's company, of whom Shakespeare and Heywood were members, marched in the triumphal procession when James I formally entered London March 15, 1604. Each received four and a half yards of red cloth for a cloak. And when James was buried, fifteen of his own players gowned in black were in the procession.[5] Also several companies marched in the funeral procession of the Queen on May 13, 1619. About 1629 it was the custom to grant every two years to fourteen players of the King's company four yards of bastard scarlet for cloaks and a fourth yard of crimson velvet for capes.[6]

When the actors got into trouble over materials of the plays, their treatment was generally much less severe than that of others guilty of similar offense. And in various ways the royal favor and the favor of the noble patrons of the drama smoothed the path of men of this profession.

Any fair consideration of the facts inevitably leads to the conclusion that the idea that actors as such were "rogues and vagabonds" and "liable to a whipping" is a mistaken inference on the part of biassed contemporary opponents of the drama; but it is one that has been so often quoted that it is now difficult for some to recognize the real situation—that a common player was "common" because he played publicly; and that he was pitied (if at all) because of the uncertainty of his income rather than because of the indignity of his profession. While not the highest, by any means, it was still, on the whole, a reputable profession, and one that was dear to the hearts of the sovereigns, the nobles, and many cultured and pleasure-loving citizens.

[5] *Trans. of the New Shakespeare Soc'y*, 1877-9, Appx.
[6] Malone, *Var.*, (ed. Boswell), III, 60, n.

The actor was usually needy. The medieval fashion of paying by refreshments when actors visited the provinces (amply illustrated in the records of the Historical Manuscripts Commission, especially Vols. V and VI) survived into the seventeenth century, though it overlapped the newer fashion of a definite gift or fee with the privilege of taking up an admission price from the spectators. On Nov. 27, 1616, the Prince's players at Coventry were given seventeen pence worth of refined sugar (one fourth of a pound) and a quart of sack, according to the warden's accounts (Murray, *E.D.C.*, II, 247). Even with the newer system of money payments, the provincial tour seems to have been on some occasions the bankrupting of a London troupe.

Few actors' contracts for this period in England survive except those found in *Henslowe's Diary*, and the contracts of Brome. The *Diary* (Greg, 204) gives an example of a contract for exclusive services. Heywood, on March 25, 1598, bound himself (by receipt of twopence) to act with the Admiral's men for two years and not to play publicly at any other house in London. The penalty was a £40 forfeit. A contract of Robert Dawes of London (*Alleyn Papers*, 75 ff.) shows a method of paying actors by the granting of shares in the proceeds of the company. It provides that Dawes "shall and will plaie with such company as the said Phillip Henslowe . . . . shall appointe, for and during the tyme and space of three yeares from the date hereof for and at the rate of one whole share, according to the custome of players."

The actor-sharers at the Globe in 1635 received half the profits from the galleries, boxes, and tiring-house, together with the money received at the outer doors; but from their share they had to pay the expenses of the actors and helpers on wages, the cost of lights, music, costuming, playbooks, etc. If the actor were a "housekeeper" he had an additional income as such, the housekeepers receiving the other half of the profits from galleries, boxes, and tiring-houses at the Globe. The plan at the Blackfriars was somewhat similar. The actor became a housekeeper partly by becoming a financial partner or part-owner of the business through a money payment, and partly through "merit and antiquity." In 1635 Burbage objected to three actors' becoming housekeepers because they had no right by antiquity, (ten, seventeen, and eighteen years representing their terms of service with the company).⁷

Numbers of Companies

No attempt has been made to discover how many companies played exclusively in the provinces. In London, however, while one cannot be sure how many companies actually played, he can be certain what number was approved by authority at some periods. On December 24, 1578, the Privy Council requested the Mayor of London to "suffer the Children of the Chapel, the servants of the Lord Chamberlain, of the Earl of Warwick, of the Earl of Leicester, of the Earl of Essex, and the Children of Paul's, and no company else, to exercise playing within the city."⁸ In 1583 the Queen's players were licensed by the Council.⁹ A letter in the registers of the Privy Council, dated February 19, 1598, informed the Master of the Revels and justices of the peace of Middlesex and Surrey that they had granted licence to two companies of players (the Lord Admiral's and the Lord Chamberlain's) in order that they might be prepared to play before the Queen, "to which ende they have bin chieflie licenced and tollerated." It was stated that there was now a third company who had not prepared any play for the Queen and were not bound to the Master of the Revels for performing orders as the other companies were. It was ordered that the third company be suppressed.¹⁰ In 1615 there are three traceable companies in London: Lady Elizabeth's, the Queen's Revels, and Prince Charles's. But at some time before 1618 the number had clearly increased. Four acting companies had formed some sort of union for the conduct of at least part of their business; for in 1618 John Heminges paid Sir George Buc "in the name of the four companys, for a lenten dispensation

---

⁷ Murray, *E.D.C.*, II, 161–62. See Professor Wallace's discussions of the Globe and Blackfriars systems 1599–1616 in *The Times* (L.) Oct. 2 & 4, 1909. Professor Thaler has an unpublished dissertation at Harvard (1918) on Finance and Business Management of the Elizabethan Theater. His book, *Shakespeare to Sheridan*, Harvard Univ. Press, 1922, also contains some discussion of financial relations in the sixteenth and seventeenth centuries.

⁸ *Acts of the Privy Council*, IX, 435-6.
⁹ *Athenaeum*, 23 Jan., 1869.
¹⁰ J. P. Collier, *Annals*, I, 298.

in the holy daies, 44 s."[11] According to Malone, "soon after his [Shakespeare's] death, four of the principal companies then subsisting made a union, and were afterwards called The United Companies; but I know not precisely in what their union consisted."[12] In another connection, he says that the office-books of Herbert show that "in the year 1622 there were but five principal companies of comedians in London: the King's Servants, who performed at the Globe and in Blackfriars; the Prince's Servants, who performed then at the Curtain; the Palsgrave's Servants, who had possession of the Fortune; the players of the Revels, who acted at the Red Bull; and the Lady Elizabeth's Servants, or, as they are sometimes denominated, the Queen of Bohemia's players, who performed at the Cockpit in Drury Lane."[13] At varying dates from 1618 to 1636 occur references in Herbert's office-books to "the four companies." On May 12, 1636, when the theatres were to be closed because of plague, Herbert sent the order to "the four companies."[14] It is, however, certain that some other companies existed, and that they sometimes played in London, because of such references as to *Come See a Wonder*, by John Day, written "for a company of strangers," Sept. 18, 1623, acted at the Red Bull and licensed without Herbert's hand to it "because they were none of the four companys."[15]

Provincial Companies and Provincial Visits

The importance of the provincial stage for the English drama has only of late years begun to be realized, and much remains to be done in the gathering, sifting, and interpreting of records. Among the older studies of local dramatic history are William Kelly's *Notices of Leicester*, Belville Penley's *Bath Stage*, and J. C. Dibdin's *Annals of the Edinburgh Stage*. The Reports of the Historical Manuscripts Commission contain many notices of companies which are not heard of in other accounts,—most of them strolling players, but often under the patronage of noblemen, as indicated by the names. These latter records are particularly useful for an insight into dramatic customs just

[11] Malone, *Var.*, III, 224.
[12] *Ibid.*
[13] *Ibid.*, III, 57-9.
[14] *Ibid.*, III, 239.
[15] *Ibid.*, III, 224.

before the age of Elizabeth. John Tucker Murray published in 1905 a preliminary survey of provincial playing in England,[16] and in 1910 devoted a volume of his excellent work, *English Dramatic Companies*, to the provincial players. Materials have recently been added by Alwin Thaler, in his "Traveling Players in Shakespeare's England"[17] and his "Strolling Players .... after Shakespeare."[18]

It should be remembered that, while the companies that traveled in the provinces were sometimes identical in composition with the London companies, they often represented a special combination. The number in these provincial playing groups ranged from four to eleven as a rule, oftener being ten or eleven than a smaller number. Even with eleven players, the necessity of doubling parts frequently arose.[19]

The significance of the provincial playing for the history of the English drama is suggested by a summary made by Thaler on the basis of Murray's investigations: that Bath had from fifteen to twenty plays a year from 1577 to 1598; Stratford on Avon had four companies in 1587; Leicester had from four to six companies a season from 1590 to 1603, and four companies a season in the reign of James; Coventry had five companies or so each year, and as many as three hundred and four official first performances between 1574 and 1642. While the list for any one place may look small, the aggregate is not. We must remember, too, that unrecorded dramatic performances probably far outnumbered the recorded.

It must be understood that not all the records of players in the provinces concern the well-known London companies. There was a flourishing provincial drama before Elizabeth came to the throne. Some of the records mentioned above concern comparatively obscure companies. The Chamberlain's accounts of Ipswich record payments in 1569 to "certain players of Lincolnshire," "to certen strange players," "to Martin the mynstrell and his companye for playinge the Fooles in the Halle." Both small and great companies often were named for a leading member rather than for a patron, as, for example,

[16] *Modern Philology*, II, 539-559.
[17] Ibid., XVII (1920), 121-146.
[18] *P.M.L.A.*, XXXVII (1922).
[19] Murray, *E. D. C.*, I, 88.

"James Camden and his company" (1569), and "Peter Moone and his companie," (1558), which are comparable with "Beeston's Boys" and "Alleyn's Company" of London. Many records exist of payments to noblemen's companies and those under royal patronage; as, in 1558, for the Duke of Norfolk's, my Lord Robert's, the Duchess of Suffolk's, and my Lord of Oxford's; or, in 1563, for the Queen's and the Duchess'.[20] By 1606–1611 the chief companies of London were performing at Ipswich: the King's, Queen's, Prince's, the younger Prince's, and the Princess Elizabeth's.[21]

The possibility of traveling through the provinces gave the London companies a chance to use plays which might be staled for the London audiences, and also opened up a playing place for them when London theatres were closed because of plague or other reasons. In 1593–94 and again in 1603 we see the importance of the provinces as an outlet for the London companies. It is pretty certain that the returns were small as compared with those in London; but they were not negligible as a supplement to the players' scanty incomes.

The visiting players' company usually went equipped with a license to play abroad. This was considered necessary even for private performances. The Hall Books of Nottingham show the imprisonment of Richard Jackson in 1603 "for allowing players to sound their trumpets and play in his house without a license to play."[22] Often the license required the town authorities to grant the use of town halls or other suitable places for acting. Examples are the license of Queen Anne's players in 1605, and those of the King's and Prince's companies.[23] The license sometimes held good for a definite number of days in any locality. Lady Elizabeth's men on March 20, 1617, had licenses permitting them to perform as much as fourteen days a year in any provincial city; and in 1633 the Red Bull Company was allowed to play in any town for forty days. But local authorities, as we shall see, learned to furnish a good reason for cutting short the stay if they found the presence of the players objectionable.

[20] Hist. MSS Comm., IX, 249.
[21] Ibid., IX, 223
[22] Ibid., I, 105.
[23] Murray, E. D. C., II, 400; and Malone Soc'y, Collections, I, 268-9, 281.

The attitudes of the towns toward the traveling players varied greatly—with the town, the season, the company of actors, and the circumstances. In normal times it was oftener favorable than not, and the approval was usually indicated definitely in such cases. It was for a long time customary for the visiting players to present their license to the mayor and aldermen, and, on receiving permission, to give an official "first performance" before them. This was often open to the public also without charge.

The licensing of plays by the aldermen seems not always to have met the approval of the citizens. The inhabitants of the borough of Kendal protested that the aldermen should not have the licensing of plays without the consent of the majority of the burgesses. They wished to have the Corpus Christi play yearly, as before.[24] But in most places the mayors treated the actors with consideration, attended their plays, and rewarded them from the funds of the town. Often "junketing and banqueting" of actors increased these rewards.

As the objections of the towns to the visits of the players always loom up more imposingly than the innumerable favors bestowed upon them, it may be well to consider some of the reasons for opposition. It will be seen that in some points the mayors' attitudes resembled that of the Mayor of London, but that there were special reasons for many of the objections made to the visits of the players in the provinces. The fact that the fees paid to the players for going away without acting were often larger than the customary first fees is probably accounted for by a desire to compensate in part for the loss of fees to be collected from the audiences. But that the townspeople or the mayors would pay such fees at all for non-performance is significant. The licenses from noblemen or royal patrons assumed willingness and were virtually a command to bestow favor. The desire to avoid antagonizing the patrons was no doubt the real reason for apparent generosity to the players when they were sent away.

It was only natural that the towns should fear the players when they came from plague-infested London; it is, indeed, a wonder that they welcomed them as often as they did in

[24] Hist. MSS Comm., (5) X, iv. 314.

times of plague. One can trace in the fees paid to players not to play in the provinces a growing appreciation of the danger from this source (there being more frequent refusals for this reason after 1630 than in similarly bad plague years before).

Danger from plague was not the only reason offered for refusal to receive traveling players from London. Some of the towns had a feeling that playgoing was inimical to the real interests of the townspeople. In Suffolk in 1597 the Whitsuntide stage plays were prohibited "because of the crowds of country folk in this time of scarcity." The stage was to be pulled down.[25] In some manufacturing towns there was a feeling that too much of the workmen's time might go into attendance at plays. The same is true of some agricultural places. Norwich furnished this objection to the Privy Council in 1623, and was permitted to forbid the plays in that year, and again in 1640.[26] At Bridport in 1630 the Sands brothers and nine companions were tried for "blasphemous" puppet shows which "lured children and servants from home day and night and threatened a dearth of corn and other crops thereby."[27]

An elaborate and serious protest from Chester under date of October 20, 1615, reminds one of some of the objections of the city authorities of London to the performance of plays:

> Moreover at the same Assemblie consideraccion was had of the common brute and scandall whiche this citie hathe of late incurred and sustained by admittinge of Stage Plaiers to acte their obscene and unlawefull plaies or tragedies in the Comon Hall of this Citie, thereby convertinge the same beinge appointed and ordained for the judicial hearinge and determininge of criminall offences, and for the solempne meetinge and concourse of this howse into a stage for plaiers and a receptacle for idle persons; and considering likewise the many disorders which by reason of plaies acted in the night time doe oftentimes happen and fall out to the discredit of the government of this citie, and to the great disturbance of quiet and well-disposed people and being further informed that men's servantes and apprentices neglecting their master's business doe resorte to Inn howses to behold such plaies and there manie times wastefullie spend their master's goodes....," it is

---

[25] *Acts of Privy Council*, 1597.
[26] Murray, *E. D. C.*, II, 347.
[27] Bridport Records, I, 56; Murray, II, 206.

forbidden to act in the Hall or anywhere in the city "in the night time or after vi of the clock in the evening."[28]

Besides the feeling that plays were an idle or undignified pastime causing the younger people to neglect their work, there were more practical reasons for objections to many of the companies. Some of the London players seemed to think that their licenses were all-powerful and entitled them to demand rather than to ask privileges of the towns. If refused, they sometimes took. For example, the Earl of Worcester's men (of whom Edward Alleyn was one) misbehaved at Leicester in 1584. They used another company's license, and, on being discovered, were refused permission to play. One of the records of the corporation of Leicester reports this incident:

Mr. Mayor did geve the aforesaid players an angelle towardes theyre dynner, and wild them not to playe at this present, being Frydaye the vi of Marche, for that the tyme was not convenyent. The foresaid playours met Mr. Mayor in the strete nere Mr. Necombe's house, after the angelle was geven abowte a ii. howers, who then craved lycence ageyne to play at thre, and he told them they shold not.
They declared they would do so. They later submitted themselves, begged pardon, and were licensed to play this instant at thre p. m.[29]

The accounts of the towns occasionally list expenses for mending chairs, tables, floors, ceilings, and windows broken by the players or the audiences. Sometimes the players contributed part of the cost of repairs. The Barnstaple accounts for 1593 show expenditures "for amendynge the seelynge in the Guildhall that the Enterlude players had broken down there this year." After that, for years to come, are entries of gifts to players "to ridd the Town." The citizens objected to Lord Morden's men's playing in the church at Syston, and gave them 12 d. not to do so in 1602. Those of Worcester objected to the breaking of glass windows in the Council Chamber at the plays in 1627.[30] Southampton, too, complained February 6, 1623, of the performing of interludes and plays in the town hall, "for that the table, benches and fourmes" intended for the King's

---

[28] Rupert Morris, *Chester in the Plantagenet and Tudor Reigns*, 353-4; quoted by Murray, *E. D. C.*, II, 235.
[29] Hist. MSS Comm., VIII, 430.
[30] Murray, *E. D. C.*, II, 402 and 410.

court are "broken and spoyled."³¹ The ingenuity in finding reasonable objections is at times amusing. One Mayor's court in 1639–1640 took exception to two men's showing "an Italian motion" as licensed by the Master of the Revels, "because he sayth his motion is noe Italian motion but made in London."

The misbehavior of the acting companies in the provinces was perhaps greater than in London because of a feeling of having escaped oversight. There was a trick by which a number of troupes evaded strict accountability. Several London companies sent special troupes made up of a few of their number with extras to tour the provinces with "exemplifications," or duplicate licenses. This abuse of the license system began as early as 1590–1591, according to the Norwich accounts.³² Such make-believe companies were two calling themselves the Queen's, one the King's Revels, and one the Prince Palatine's in 1616. On July 16 of that year Pembroke, Lord Chamberlain, sent a note to the Mayor of Norwich detailing these abuses of the license system and asking him to help reform them:

"Whereas Thomas Swynnerton and Martin Slaughter beinge two of the Queenes Majesties company of Playors hauinge separated themselves from their said Company, haue each of them taken forth a severall exemplification or duplicate of his majesties Letters patente graunted to the whole Company and by vertue therof they severally in two Companies with vagabonds and such like idle persons, haue and doe use and exercise the quallitie of playinge in diuerse places of this Realme to the great abuse and wronge of his Majesties Subjects in generall and contrary to the true intent and meaninge of his Majestie to the said Company. And wheras William Perrie haueinge likewise gotten a warrant whereby he and a certaine Company of idle persons with him doe travel and play under the name and title of the Children of his Majesties Revels, to the great abuse of his Majesties seruice. And whereas also Gilberte Reason one of the prince his highnes Playors hauing likewise separated himselfe from his Company hath also taken forth another exemplification or duplicate of the patent granted to that Company and liues in the same kind and abuse. And likewise one Chas. Marshall, Homfry Jeffes and William Parr: three of Prince Palatynes company of Playors haveinge also taken forthe an exemplification or duplicate of the patent granted to the said Company . . . . , to the end such idle persons may not be suffered to continewe in

³¹ Hist. MSS Comm., II, App. III, 28.
³² Murray, *E. D. C.*, II, 367.

this course of life. . . .," it is ordered, to confiscate the exemplifications or duplicates and send them to the Mayor and order the persons to appear at Whitehall.[33]

Some companies deliberately used the licenses of others. A Ralph Reve passed himself off as "Philip Rocester" and took a playing company into Norwich, but was discovered and expelled.[34] The players at the Fortune in 1623–24 sent to Norwich an objection stating that William Daniel "hath injuriously gotten their Letters Patents."[35] In 1630 Worcester caught a John Jones with a forged license from Henry Herbert for shows.[36] And in 1633 there was considerable trouble over the "rasing" of dates of expired licenses of the Master of the Revels, and the selling, pawning, and renting of commissions.[37] Some offenders were arrested by the Mayor of Banbury and sent before the Privy Council.

In view of these various provocations on the part of traveling players and the additional dangers of infection during plague years, it is not surprising that the townspeople sometimes paid the players to pass them by. That they permitted them to act as often as they did is a testimony to the widespread interest in the drama as a real national entertainment.

Regulation of the Drama
The Attitude of the Sovereign

Inasmuch as the drama of the reigns of Elizabeth, James, and Charles owes its existence in large measure to the desires of these sovereigns for this form of entertainment, it is only natural that occasionally some direct control by the sovereign should be found. Usually, however, the wishes of the sovereign were carried out through the Privy Council, the Chamberlain, the Master of the Revels, the Treasurer, the Mayor, or the justices of the peace, or occasionally through the ecclesiastical officers.

It is not to be supposed that there was perfect harmony of attitude on the part of all these officials. The mayor often, and

[33] Murray, *E. D. C.*, II, 343-4.
[34] *Ibid.*, II, 339.
[35] *Ibid.* II, 347.
[36] *Worcestershire County Records*, 1900, I, 470.
[37] *Ibid.*, II, 163-6.

the ecclesiastical authorities occasionally, held out against actors and plays and theaters approved by the sovereign or Privy Council or Chamberlain or Master of Revels. Some of the mayors especially, considering that the city paid a high price for the sovereign's pleasure in the trouble caused them by the theaters, showed their impatience by repeated requests for reduction and suppression of the theatres. Not all the bishops were opposed to drama, but Grindal, in suggesting to Burghley, February 22, 1564, that the theaters be closed for a year because of plague, made the grim addition, "And iff it wer for ever, it wer not amisse."[38]

The sovereign's fondness for drama is testified to in many ways: by the expenditure of large sums of money for dramatic entertainments at court, by frequent personal attendance at the performances; by patronage of companies (especially in the reign of James); by gifts to actors, by the honoring of actors on state occasions. James's fondness for theatrical entertainment brought him into conflict with the Puritans even in Scotland in 1599, because he licensed English comedians to play in Edinburgh.[39] The strong personal interest of the ruler in acting sometimes exposed him to the satire of a daring subject. A letter by Mr. Pory to Thomas Puckering (September 21, 1632) says that the Queen and some of her ladies and all her maids of honor were practising on a pastoral by Walter Montagu in which the Queen was to act a part for her recreation and the exercise of her English.[40] Justinian Paget, writing to James Harrington (January 28, 1633) traced a connection between Prynne's trouble over *Histriomastix, or the Player's Scourge* and the fact that it was published the day after the Queen's pastoral at Somerset House.[41] And this was probably the case; for another letter, of George Gresley to Sir Thomas Puckering, tells of Prynne's being brought into the Court of High Commission "for publishing a book a little before the queen's acting of her play, of the unlawfulness of plays."[42] It was rash, to say the least, to publish, when the Queen and her ladies were about

---

[38] Malone Soc'y, *Collections*, I, pt. 2, (1908), 148.
[39] James Spottiswood, *Hist. of the Church of Scotland*, p. 457.
[40] *Court and Times of Chas. I.*, II, 176.
[41] *Ibid.*, II, 222–3.
[42] *Ibid.*, II, 224.

to act a pastoral, a book containing the challenge, "Dares then any Christian woman be so more than whorishly impudent as to act, to speak publicly on a stage (perchance in mens apparel and cut hair) in the presence of sundry men and women?"

The sovereign's generally friendly attitude toward drama must always be kept in mind, as otherwise the failure of countless apparently authoritative inhibitions and suppressions of companies and theatres would be totally unexplainable. Sometimes the sovereign directly intervened, as when, in 1619, the Mayor ordered Blackfriars suppressed, but the King then gave license to his "well-beloved servants" to act "at the Globe, Blackfriars, or any town halls or Moute-halls."[43]

In the time of Mary the licensing power over plays for stage or press, like that of other works for publication, was nominally in the hands of the sovereign. A proclamation at her accession (August 18, 1553) forbade her subjects "to prynte any bookes, matter, ballet, ryme, interlude, processe, or treatyse, nor to play any interlude except they haue her graces speciall licence in writynge for the same, upon payne to incurre her highnesse indignation and displeasure."[44] This can only mean a license from someone appointed by the Queen as her representative.

On rare occasions the King or Queen was personally referred to concerning individual cases of authors or of plays. This was chiefly where sedition, heresy, or criticism of foreign policies was involved. Jonson writes of the personal anger of the King in connection with his imprisonment because of a play dealing with affairs of state (c. 1605). Massinger's *King and Subject* was referred by the Master of the Revels to the King for opinion as to dangerous remarks, and D'Avenant's *The Wits* for opinion as to the oaths. In the diplomatic questions aroused by Middleton's *A Game at Chess*, the King, as we shall see,[45] took action, though not with the promptness or severity that might be expected for this sort of offence. The usual procedure was, for the King to express himself through one of the officers entrusted with the oversight of drama.

[43] *S. P. Dom.*, 1619-23, vol. CVII, art. 56.
[44] *Proclamation against Raisers of Sedition*. . . .L. Cawode, 1553.
[45] These examples are discussed in my chapter on censorship.

The Privy Council

The Privy Council had, next to the sovereign, supreme control over the drama, when it chose to exercise it. Its function was that of an executive body which could both originate and enforce laws, and even judge particular cases reported as violating these laws. It is perhaps rash to assume that a great number of individual cases came up before the Council, but the traces we do find make it a matter of regret that so many of the records of Council procedure have perished.

The attitude of the Privy Council toward the drama could not be constant, in view of its shifting membership. It is, however, clear that the Council members were not so often inclined as were the city authorities to suppress plays or players. At least it may be said that, where interdicts are traceable to the Council as original source, there is generally an attempt to give a real reason for the prohibition. Opposition to the drama as such was not often attributable to the Council.

The orders of the Privy Council concerning drama were sent out to the actors themselves, to the ecclesiastical authorities, the mayor, the justices of the peace, the chamberlain, or the Master of the Revels,—the Council standing between these and the King.

Early Ecclesiastical Interest in Drama

In the early part of the reign of Elizabeth, the Privy Council delegated high authority over drama to the ecclesiastical commission. This was in line with their general oversight of literature (which will be discussed in connection with the censorship of literature). An order of 1557 from the Council required the actors "not to play any plays but between the feasts of All Saints and Shrovetide, and then only such as are seen and allowed by the Ordinary (i.e., the Bishop of London)."[46] The oversight of drama by the Bishop of London was not always benign. On February 22, 1563, the Bishop wrote to Cecil that nothing would renew the plague more than "the practise of an idle sorte of people which have ben infamous in all goode common-weales, I mean these *histriones*, common players, who now daylie, but speciallye on holy dayes set up boothes where-

---

[46] *Acts of the Privy Council*, VI, 169.

unto the youthes resorteth excessively, and there taketh infection."[47] Even after the Chamberlain and the Master of Revels gained the chief control over drama, a bishop occasionally intervened. For example, at the time when *Barnevelt* was played, though objectionable for purely political reasons, it was forbidden, August 14, 1619, by the Bishop of London.[48]

The Treasurer

The Treasurer had a great deal to do with patents, and was consulted on various problems connected with printed literature. The extreme trust reposed in Burghley by Elizabeth, as much as the nature of the office, perhaps accounts for the rather unexpectedly detailed connection of the Treasurer with certain problematic cases. In connection with the censorship and the recall of objectionable works he is especially conspicuous. He was occasionally appealed to in connection with the censorship of dramas where public policies were concerned.

The Chamberlain

One of the most important officials in control of the drama was the Lord Chamberlain. He was usually a peer, and at least an *ex officio* member of the Privy Council, acting often as a go-between for King and Council. He had for many years the duty of licensing the theatres of London and Westminster. At the beginning of the sixteenth century, the Lord Chamberlain had also the general oversight of revels,[49] as is seen by the order, "That Jaques Hault and William Pawne, be appointed to devise and prepare disguisings and some morisques, after the best manner they can, whereof they shall have warning by my Lord Chamberlain,"[50] for the occasion of the marriage of Prince Arthur (1501). This Jaques Haute appears several times as receiving payment for special disguisings.

Even after the development of an office of the revels, the Chamberlain continued as the real head of affairs pertaining to the drama. The Master of the Revels in the time of Elizabeth

---

[47] Thomas Wright, *Queen Elizabeth and Her Times*, I, 167.

[48] *S. P. Dom.*, 1619–23, vol. CX, art. 18. On ecclesiastical licensing of plays, see Arber, *S. R.*, III, 690.

[49] George Chalmers, *Apology*, 472.

[50] *Miscell. State Papers*, Hardwicke, I, 19.

frequently consulted him on many details of the practical work, as may be seen in numerous extracts published by Professor Feuillerat from the reign of Elizabeth (pp. 267, 277, 297, 298, 309, 341, *et passim*). For example:

Dec. 24, 1576. "For the warrant and carying a note to the Chamberlayn of alteracion of the plaies."

Nov. 4–7, 1576. "For that Mr. Blagrave [Clerk of the Revels] was sent for upon my Lord Chamberleyn his commandement, horse hire," etc.

Dec. 28, 1578. 6 s. spent for boat hire "to the Court to shew my Lord Chamberlaine A patorne for A maske."

Feb. 26, 1578. "The Master of Revels sent for by the Lord Chamberlayne about patornes of maske."

There are numerous entries of the same sort for "showing of patterns."

Certain entries suggest that the Chamberlain may have had a final word in choosing plays for court use:

1577. "John Drawater for mony by him disbursed as foloweth ffor the cariadge of the Earle of Warwick his mens stuffe from the Revelles to Whitehall and back againe to recyte before my Lord Chamberleyn."

1578–79. "Boate hier to and from the courte to carry the stuffe for the children of the chappell to Recite before my Lord Chamberleyn."

The Chamberlain was evidently the official intermediary between the King and the Master of the Revels. When a plan for reforming the office was drafted in 1573, it was stated that the Prince's commands should be given to the Master through the Chamberlain.[51]

When players were recalcitrant, the Chamberlain re-enforced the power of the Master of Revels. An example is the order issued by the Chamberlain May 3, 1640 to William Beeston's company, who had acted a new play without license from the Master of the Revels, that they cease to play anything until the Master should grant them permission.[52]

There is indeed in many respects an overlapping of jurisdiction of Chamberlain and Master of Revels. It would perhaps

[51] A. Feuillerat, *Revels*. . . .*Elizabeth*, 11, and Table I.
[52] Chalmers, *Apology*, 517.

be more accurate to say that the Chamberlain on occasions usurped the usual functions of the Master, but generally by way of co-operation rather than of opposition. Certainly he had it in his power to grant a license even when that seemed to be regularly delegated to the Master of the Revels. In rare cases one meets with a note of that in the Stationers' Registers, as in the provisional entry of *The Merchant of Venice* to James Roberts:

July 22, 1598. James Roberts "Entred for his copie under thandes of both the wardens a book of the Marchant of Venyce or otherwise called the Jewe of Venyce. Provided that yt bee not prynted by the said James Roberts or any other whatsoever without lycence first had from the Right honorable the lord Chamberlen."

In this particular case, of course, the fact that the play belonged to the Chamberlain's own company may have been the reason why the release came from him.

Over the stage performances the Chamberlain had a very definite control. Chapman, in prison over *Eastward Hoe*, wrote the Chamberlain a letter of regret that the play had been performed without his license. It was the Chamberlain who required the "motion of the tub" to be struck out of Jonson's *The Tale of a Tub*, May 7, 1633. And on numerous other occasions we find him actively engaged in censorship.

Not only playwrights in trouble, but actors appealed to the Chamberlain, who thus acquired important diplomatic functions in all matters of dispute over the contents of plays.

A "sute touching plays" to be granted to Sir Jerome Bowes and others, in which the principle of "perpetuity" was called in question, is mentioned in a letter from Robert Dudley, Earl of Leicester, April 8, 1577, to the Treasurer, Lord Burghley, as being referred by the Queen to these two and "my Chamberleyn (the Earl of Sussex).[53] The exact nature of the suit is not known; but the reference shows that the Chamberlain's interest in matters pertaining to the theatre extended back to the opening of the period under consideration.

The Master of the Revels and the Chamberlain were both concerned in the protection of the stage-right and the copyright

[53] Lans. MS no. 25, f. 38, art. 18; Malone Society, "Dramatic Records from the Lansdowne Manuscripts," *Collections*, I, pt. 2, p. 151.

of plays, the former by his official machinery, and the latter by his personal authority being, as we shall see, qualified to help the owners very effectively.

In view of the Chamberlain's power over drama, and of the fact that the city authorities were often opposed to the stage, the attitudes of the Chamberlains became a matter of importance for stage history. Lord Cobham, Chamberlain from August 8, 1596 to March 17, 1597, was of Puritanic inclination. But most of the chamberlains from 1580 to 1640 were liberal-minded, and many were noted for their patronage of letters: in particular, George and Henry Carey (the first and second Lords Hunsdon), and William and Philip Herbert (Earls of Pembroke and Montgomery). Charles, Lord Howard opposed the vigorous efforts of the city to suppress plays. William Fleetwood wrote to Lord Burghley June 18, 1584:

"Upon Sonndaye my lo. sent ij aldermen to the Court for the suppressing and pulling downe of the Theatre and Curten. All the LL agreed thereunto saving my Lord Chamberlen and mr Vizch but we obteyned a l^re to suppresse them all."[54]

There was one period when a great deal of supposedly illicit publication of plays occurred, 1598–1600, when the Chamberlain, George Carey, was ill with palsy, according to references in the State Papers;[55] but perhaps Stanhope, the Vice-Chamberlain, undertook many of his duties. The Herberts were more conspicuous than the Careys as literary patrons. The Shakespeare Folio was dedicated to the Herbert brothers. William Herbert was in the habit of sending Jonson £20 on New Year's to buy books;[56] and he was on friendly terms with other poets, among them Massinger, Chapman, Herbert (a relative), Donne, Breton, and Taylor. Many books were dedicated by their authors to the chamberlains. Not merely because of the official powers, but because of the personal tastes and interests of many of the incumbents of the office in the period we are considering, the dramatists and theatrical companies must have had in the chamberlains powerful champions of their rights. Perversions of justice, too, were less likely in the case of the

---

[54] Malone Society, *Collections*, I, pt. 2, 163 ff.
[55] *S. P. Dom.* 1598-1601, vol. CCLXXIV, art. 86, (March 29, 1600).
[56] Jonson's Conversations with Drummond; *Works* (Gifford-Cunningham, 1903), III, 483.

Chamberlain than with almost any other high official, as, unlike the Master of the Revels, for example, the Chamberlain was absolutely forbidden to accept fees for services to individuals.

Again and again we see a chamberlain extricating a player or a company of players from difficulties with the King, the Mayor, or the Privy Council. For example, one of Lady Elizabeth's players tried to play at Dover, but was checked by the Mayor with a Privy Council order of May 27, 1623. Wambus, the player, said he would risk a year in prison to "try whether the kings comand or the Counsells be the greater." He put up on a gate a notice of a performance. On being imprisoned for his obstinacy, he was set free by intervention of the Chamberlain.[57]

The Mayor

The interest of the mayor in dramatic performances was of long standing. As we have seen in connection with the traveling companies, the mayors of towns became in a sense sponsors for the plays that were performed before them and met their approval. Although in London the Master of the Revels came later on to have the special authority over both spoken and written drama, the Mayor still retained an interest. This was only natural; for, as head of the city organization, the Mayor was the overseer of the crafts and hence concerned in printing as an industry. Again, his public office gave him control over theatrical audiences, as over other public assemblies.

There was a proclamation of May 9, 1542, designed to put great power into the Mayor's hands. It is doubtful, however, whether it was completely enforced for long. Its requirement was that henceforth no printer shall issue "any English book, ballad, or play, without putting his name and the name of the author and the day of the print; and the printer shall present the first copy to the mayor of the town where he dwells two days before allowing any copy to leave his hands."[58]

---

[57] Murray, II, 348 ff. Cf. also the Lord Chamberlain's order of August 10, 1639, concerning plays at the Cockpit (Mrs. Stopes's extracts from Lord Chamberlain's office book, *Shakespeare Jahrbuch*, XLVI, 101); the order to the King's men in 1641 (Malone Society, *Coll.*, I, 364; a letter from Humphrey Moseley, 1660, in Malone, *Variorum*, III, 249.

[58] See House of Lords, *Journal*, I, 230; and Steele, *Bibl. of Royal Proc.*

A specific method of control through the Mayor is outlined in a Minute of the Court of Aldermen, for November 7, 1549:

The ij Secondaries of the Compters, Mr. Atkyns and Mr. Burnell, shall, according to the tenour of the recognysaunce lately taken before the Lorde grete Master, & remaynyng with my Lorde Mayer, peruse all suche enterludes as hereafter shalbe pleyed by eny comen playr of the same within the citie or the liberties therof. And make report of the same to the Lorde Mayer for the tyme beynge. And accordyng therunto, my Lorde Mayer to suffer them to go forwarde, or to stey.[59]

Martin Bucer, in *De honestibus ludis*,[60] while admitting the use of comedies and tragedies on certain Biblical themes, proposed to submit all plays before production to persons of sound divinity and experienced in dramatic art, who should exclude what was *leve aut histrionicum*.

About 1557 there seems to have been a tendency to introduce trouble-making material into plays. On February 14, 1557, the Privy Council ordered the Lord President of the North to command justices of the peace that "they doo in no wyse suffer any playes, enterludes, songues, or any such lyke pastymes whereby the people may any wayes be steryd to disordre, to be used by any manner personnes."[61]

On June 27, 1557, the Privy Council thanked the Mayor of Canterbury for imprisoning certain players, adding that "in the meantime their lewde play boke is committed to the consideration of the King and Queene's Majesty's learned counsell, who are willed to declare what the same waieth unto in law." What the troublesome subject-matter was does not appear, but the Mayor on August 11 was ordered to proceed against the players.[62]

On September 5, 1557, the Council directed the Mayor of London to prevent the further performance of another "lewd play," *A Sacke Full of Newes*, at the Boar's Head, outside Aldgate, to arrest the players, and send their playbook to the Council.

[59] *London Repertory*, XII, 1, f. 162.
[60] In his *De regno Christi: A New Year's Gift for Edward VI*, 1551.
[61] Lodge, *Illustrations of Shakespeare*, I, 212–13.
[62] John Brent, *Canterbury in the Olden Time* (1879), 154; cited by Murray, E.D.C., II, 232.

Licensing for public performance of plays was definitely placed in the hands of mayors, justices of peace, and lieutenants of the shire early in the reign of Elizabeth by the proclamation of May 16, 1559:

Forasmuch as the tyme wherein common Interludes in the Englishe tongue are wont usually to be played, is now past untill All Hallowtyde and that also some that haue ben of late used, are not conuenient in any good ordred Christian Common weale to be suffred. The Quenes Maiestie doth straightly forbyd al maner Interludes to be playde, eyther openly or priuately, except the same be noticed before hande, and licenced within any citie or towne-corporate by the Maior or other chiefe officers of the same, and within any shyre, by suche as shalbe Lieutenants for the Queenes Maiestie in the same shyre, or by two of the Justices of peax inhabyting within that part of the shire where any shalbe played (Steele, No. 509).

Inasmuch as the Mayor of London and other city officials frequently appear as opposed to the performance of plays, and therefore come into conflict with the sovereign or Privy Council or Chamberlain on certain issues, it may be well to note briefly some reasons for the mayor's attitude.

In the first place, it must not be assumed that all mayors were opposed to drama in general. The mayors' shows often had pageants or masques devised by playwrights; and, as we have seen above, the mayors of provinces often had an important function as patrons of drama. But there were certain duties of the Mayor that made him take precautions. The mayor must care for the public health—not only the conditions of streets and buildings, but sanitary conditions in general. In particular, as England was constantly revisited by the plague, he must guard against crowds in public places. This is evident in the payments made by mayors of the towns to traveling players to pass without playing. In London it took the form of frequent protests against theatrical performances in general. No doubt the dangers of plague were sometimes overworked by mayors who were really opposed to drama on moral or other grounds. Such seems to be the real attitude behind the protest (*c.* 1582) that "to play in plagetime is to draw the plage by offending of God upon occasion of such plays."[63]

---

[63] *Lans. MSS*, 20, no. 11.

Plays were regarded by many city officials as a nuisance. This was due in part to the location of the playing places. Whitefriars was a lawless district, and until 1608 Blackfriars also was a privileged place. Rough and immoral people tended to congregate there, and gave the theatres a bad name. There are references to this in many of the city protests against plays. This explains in part the opposition of the city authorities to the recommendations of the Privy Council, which often favored plays as furnishing honest recreation. In 1572 the Court of Aldermen heard letters read from the Lords of the Council,

> Written in the favor of certein persones to have in ther howses, yardes or back sydes, being overt & open places, such playes, enterludes, commedies, & tragedies as maye tende to represse vice & extoll vertue, for the recreation of the people, & therby to drawe them from sundrye worser exercyses. The matter theerof being first examyned, sene & allowed, by such discrete person or persons as shalbe by the Lord Maiour therunto appoynted.

But the Aldermen ordered the Town Clerk to protest against this to Lord Burghley.[64]

The triumph of the city authorities in their point of view appears in an ordinance of December 6, 1574, requiring that plays be perused by persons appointed by the Mayor and Aldermen; that the players be licensed by Mayor and Aldermen, and be bound in a penalty to the Lord Chamberlain of London; that the playing place be approved, and that the house owner be made responsible for keeping order. The reason for this was that, although plays might have a "lawful, honest, and comely use," they were now being abused. Objections were made to the multitudes of youths assembled, the quarrels, the luring of young orphans and other girls to evil, (especially in the inns where plays were given), the drawing of audiences from church services on Sundays and holidays, wasting the money of the poor, pocket-picking, and sedition, indecent speech and fights, as well as "soundrye slaughters and mayhemminges of the Quenes Subjectes" caused by "ruines of Skaffoldes, Frames, and Stages, and by engynes, weapons and powder used in plaies."[65] Like many similar proclamations, this was probably

[64] *London Repertory*, XVII, f. 316.
[65] J. P. Collier, *Eng. Dram. Poetry*, I, 208–11, (cf. Malone *Coll.*, I, pt. 2, 175).

not rigidly enforced. New attacks were made from 1580 to 1584. The Mayor, in writing to the Chancellor on April 12, 1580, of the great disorder at the theatre of that week, ingeniously made use of the statute against rogues and vagabonds, applying it, as did the Puritan writers, to players. He wrote that he thought it his duty to inform him that

the players of plays used at the Theatre and other such places, and tumblers and such like, are a very superfluous sort of men, and of such faculty as the laws had disallowed; that the exercise of the plays was not only a great hindrance to the service of God, but also a great corruption of youth, with unchaste and wicked matters, the occasion of much incontinence, practices of many frays, quarrels, and other disorders, within the City. He therefore begged that order might be taken to prevent such plays, not only within the city but also in the liberties.[66]

The city even ventured to take issue with the attitude of the crown toward encouragement of acting. They said it was not fitting to perform before the Queen plays "commonly played in open stages before all the basest assemblies in London and Middlesex." The players should "exercise" in private houses. They should not depend on acting for a living, but men who had other means of support should use acting as a recreation.[67]

The relationship between the attitude of the city and that of the Puritans toward the theatre has often been pointed out. It is undeniable, though we must not assume either that all Puritans were unalterably opposed to drama, or that all mayors and aldermen had the point of view of Puritans. London was, it is true, a stronghold of the Puritans, who on many occasions launched a pamphlet war against the stage. This reached its height 1577–87, gradually died down for a while, and revived again in the second decade of the seventeenth century. Among the attacks on the stage are: Northbrooke's *Treatise*, Gosson's *School of Abuse*, the *Second and Third Blast of Retreat*, Gosson's *Plays Confuted in Five Actions*, Stubbes' *Anatomie of Abuse* (in part), Rankin's *Mirror of Monsters*, and Rainolde's *Overthrow of Stage-Plays*, Rawledge's *Monster Lately Found Out*, and Prynne's *Histrio-Mastix*. These will give the reader a lively, if somewhat exaggerated, notion of the worst evils of the stage

[66] *Remembrancia*, I, 9.
[67] *Lans. MSS*, 20, no. 11, *c.* 1582?

of the time. It will be seen that there is a substantial resemblance as to some points made here and those in protests of mayors of London, the latter being, as a rule, rather the milder.

The Council understood the Mayor's objections as being largely on the ground of corruption of manners and morals, and in the spring of 1582, while requesting the Mayor to allow performances in London, suggested that the City appoint a censor, and that those dramas be forbidden that had "matter that might breed corruption of manners and conversation among the people." The Mayor was glad to adopt the suggestion as to censorship.[68]

As the Master of the Revels had by now power to license dramas, the enlisting of the Mayor's interest in censorship is probably to be viewed as a concession intended to mollify him. In the trouble arising over the Martin Marprelate controversy after 1589, the Mayor did appoint a representative to act on a committee of three to view all plays (see page 100).

The eagerness of the city to seize upon objections to plays is further illustrated by the interpretation of the fall of a scaffold at Paris Garden, January, 1583, in which a number of spectators were killed or injured. The Mayor attributed it to the hand of God because the performance was on Sunday. Action was taken that year against the use of city inn-yards for plays.

Brawls were a frequent excuse for prohibition of plays. In June, 1584, the Queen's men and Lord Arundel's were called before the Mayor because of disturbances over rough treatment of two apprentices near the Theatre or the Curtain. Two aldermen were sent by the Mayor to the Privy Council, and an order was passed, in spite of the opposition of Chamberlain and Vice-Chamberlain, to suppress the players and pull down the Theatre and the Curtain. It was not, however, carried out.[69]

In the period 1589–1600 again the disorders of the theatre roused the city to opposition. Aldermen on February 25, 1592, appealed to Archbishop Whitgift against theaters, listing their evils—corruption of youth by wanton and profane devices; withdrawing of apprentices and servants from work; collecting

---

[68] *Remembrancia*, 357; cf. *Acts of the Privy Council*, XIII, 404.

[69] J. O. Halliwell-Phillips, *Illustrations*, ... p. 41; cf. Thomas Wright, *Q. Eliz. and Her Times*, II, 228.

of harlots, cutpurses, cozeners, pilferers, etc. The aldermen begged that the Queen have only her private players.[70]

Again on September 13, 1595, the Mayor wrote to the Privy Council requesting final suppression of plays at the Theatre, the Bankside, and everywhere in the city.[71]

Many of the city's complaints and requests for inhibition of plays were ineffectual because of the opposition of other powers; but there were times when all were agreed on the need of such suppression. For example, c. 1589–1590, Paul's boys were suppressed because of the Martin Marprelate controversy.[72]

Some of the restrictions of plays were only in the nature of a limitation of the number of performances. On July 25, 1591, plays were suppressed on Sundays and Thursdays[73]; on Sundays because they interfered with divine service, and on Thursdays because they interfered with the bear-baiting maintained for the pleasure of the Queen.

The closing of the Rose Theatre in 1592 was presumably due to riots.[74] The more general suppression of July 28, 1597, also had for one of its main reasons the incitation to riot. The city authorities wrote the Privy Council:

Wee have fownd by th' examination of divers apprentices and other servantes whoe have confessed unto us that the saide staige playes were the very places of theire randevous appoynted by them to meete with such otheir as wear to joigne with them in theire designes and mutinus atteumptes, beeinge allso the ordinary places for maisterles men.

They requested that all plays be prohibited.[75]

The order of the Queen to the justices of Middlesex for closing (July 28, 1597) gave other reasons than riots:

Her Majestie being informed that there are verie greate disorders committed in the common playhouses both by lewd matters that are handled on the stages and by resorte and confluence of bad people, hathe given direction that not onlie no plaies shalbe used within

---

[70] *Remembrancia*, I, 9.

[71] Halliwell-Phillips, *Illustrations*, p. 20.

[72] See Lyly, *Pap with a Hatchet* for reference to the Queen's men at the Theatre, and to Paul's Boys.

[73] Chalmers, *Apology*, 379–80.

[74] *Henslowe's Diary*, (Greg), II, 50.

[75] Halliwell-Phillips, *Illustrations*, 21; *Outlines* . . . , 35.

London or about the citty or in any publique place during this tyme of Sommer, but that also those playhouses that are erected and built only for suche purposes shalbe plucked downe, namelie the Curtayne and the Theatre nere to Shorditch or any other within that county. Theis are therefore in her majesty's name to chardge and commaund you that you take present order there be no more plaies used in any publique place within three myles of the citty until Allhallowtide next, and likewyse that you do send for the owners of the Curtayne Theatre or anie other common playhouse and injoyne them by vertue hereof forthwith to plucke downe quite the stages, gallories, and roomes that are made for people to stand in, and so deface the same as they maie not be ymploied agayne to suche use.[76]

The exact cause of this very severe order is not known. There have been some guesses, such as Fleay's, that it was because of the representation of Lord Cobham as Sir John Oldcastle[77] in *Henry IV*, and Murray's, that it was because of Nashe's *Isle of Dogs*. There may have been a number of causes operating.

It was only three years later (June 22, 1600) that the Lords gave orders for the restraint of the "immoderate use and companye of playhouses", limiting the number of houses to two—one at the Bankside and the other in Middlesex. Alleyn's new playhouse was to supersede the Curtain. Plays were to be given only twice a week, and not on Sunday. The statement of the reasons for these restrictions shows a rather grudging recognition of the need of acting, to prepare the players for their court performances:

Forasmuch as it is manifestly knowen and graunted that the multitude of the saide houses and the mysgoverment of them hath bin and is dayly occasion of the ydle, ryoutous, and dissolute living of great numbers of people, that leavinge all such honest and painefull course of life as they should followe, doe meete and assemble here, and of many particular abuses and disorders that doe thereupon ensue, and yet nevertheles it is considered that the use and exercise of such playes (not beinge evill in yt self) may with a good order and moderacion be suffered in a well governed state, and that her Majestie beinge pleased at some tymes to take delight and recreation in the sight and hearinge of them, some order is fitt to be taken for the allowance and mayntenance of such persons as are thought meetest in that kinde to yealde her

[76] *Acts of the Privy Council*, July 28, 1597.
[77] Evidence of censorship appears in the cancellation leaving a fragmentary reference.

Majestie recreation and delighte, and consequently of the houses that must serve for publike playinge to keep them in exercise.[78]

The restraint was evidently not enforced.

There were temporary suppressions of acting for various reasons. Plays were prohibited for five days before and about two weeks after the death of Elizabeth. The numerous suppressions because of plague will be considered in connection with the possible effect upon the publication of plays in groups. Partial restrictions of plays are at times traceable to religious motives. At the end of the proclamation against monopolies, May 16, 1603, James I forbade "bear baiting, bull baiting, interludes, common plays," etc. on Sunday.

Many of the orders of restraint are like the requests of the city authorities in that they show a distinct tendency to blame the plays or playwrights for the behavior of the audience. For example, the order issued October 1, 1612, by a general session of the Peace at Westminster forbidding "Jigges, Rymes, and Daunces" at the end of plays, because "by reason of certayne lewde Jigges, songes, and daunces used and accustomed at the play-house called the Fortune in Goulding lane divers cuttpurses and other lewde and ill disposed persons in greate multitudes doe resorte hither at the end of everye playe many tymes causinge tumultes and outrages."[79]

On January 21, 1619, the city attempted to get Blackfriars suppressed, but the King intervened and authorized his players to perform here and also at the Globe.

The players were eager to act on Sundays and holidays, and this was a bone of contention throughout the period, especially because of interference with church services.

The universities of England fostered drama; but they usually had their own playwrights, plays, and actors. The appearance of the professional acting companies on occasions met with objections from the authorities. Thus, on June 21, 1580, Dr. John Hatcher wrote to Lord Burghley:

Reasons why the Heads of the University object to the Earl of Oxford's players shewing their cunninge in certayne playes already

---

[78] *Acts of the Privy Council*, 1600.
[79] *Middlesex County Records*, II, 71.

practysed by them before the Queenes Majestie; the like having been denyed to the Earl of Leicester's servants.[80]

Nor were there wanting objections from state officials to the appearance of public actors at the universities. The Privy Council in 1593 wrote a protest to the Vice-Chancellor of Cambridge:

Whereas the two universities of Cambridge and Oxenforde are the nurseries to bring up youthe in the knowledge and fear of God and in all manner of good learninge and vertuous educacion. . . .and like careys to be used that all soche thinges as may allure and intice them to lewdenes, follye, and vitious manners, whereunto the corrupcion of man's nature is more inclined, maie in no wyse be used and practysed in those places that are the schooles of learninge and good nurture. Wee therefore. . . .cannot but have especiall regarde of these principall places, being the fountaines from whence learning and educacion dothe flowe and so is derived into all other partes of the realme, and for that cause understanding that common plaiers do ordinarily resorte to the Universytie of Cambridge, there to recite interludes and plaies, some of them being full of lewde example and moste of vanity, besides the gatheringe togeather of multitudes of people, whereby is great occasion also of divers other inconvenyences, we have thought good to require you. . . .to take speciall order that hereafter there maie no plaies or interludes of common plaies be used or sett forthe either in the University or in any place within the compasse of five miles.[81]

A restriction by James, July 23, 1604, would limit the drama of the schools to the classical drama practised in an earlier day. The prohibition forbade "bull-baiting, bear-baiting, and common plays, public shows, interludes, comedies, and tragedies in the English tongue and games at laggets and nine holes, whereby the younger sort are or may be drawn or provoked to vain expence, loss of time or corruption of manners."[82]

It may be questioned, however, whether even this order from the king himself was effective in abolishing all the entertainments which it criticizes.

We have seen that there were several public officials and bodies of men who had some power over the English stage.

[80] *S. P. Dom.*, 1547–80, vol. CXXXIX, art. 26.
[81] *Acts of Privy Council*, 1593.
[82] T. D. Atkinson, *Cambridge Described and Illustrated*, 45; quoted by Murray, *E. D. C.*, II, 221.

REGULATION OF THE DRAMA 37

But none hitherto considered except the Lord Chamberlain made it a part of his regular duty to oversee the drama. The official most directly concerned with both the control of the actors and the regulation of the content of the plays was the Master of the Revels, whose delegated authority from the crown placed him in immediate contact with the acting companies.

The Master of the Revels[83]

The custom of appointing a Master of the Revels at the English court has been traced to various origins, especially to the Boy Bishop, the Feast of the Fools, and the Lord of Misrule. The custom of the Boy Bishop was widespread in England,[84] that of the Feast of Fools less general and enduring. But there is no very close resemblance between the functions of the Master of the Revels and those of either the Boy Bishop or the Bishop of the Feast of Fools. The Boy Bishop was appointed for a season, he made a progress, and he was sometimes accompanied by a fool in costume carrying a peculiar staff. The Bishop of the Feast of Fools presided over an adult revelry of a rather riotous character, with a feast, disguisings, and reversals of dignity involving exchange of positions between clergy or monks and laymen or fools. A slight resemblance to the function of the Master of the Revels appears in a record at Lille in the fifteenth century, where the Bishop of the Feast of Fools collected funds and offered prizes for pageants and mysteries.[85]

The Lord, or Abbot, of Misrule has more in common with the Master of the Revels, with whom for a time he co-existed. Perhaps one of the earliest references to a lord of misrule is that of the gift made by Edward III in 1334 to the minstrels "*in nomine Regis Fabae*,"[86] but we have no full account of his

[83] The appearance of Mr. E. K. Chambers, *The Elizabethan Stage* (Oxford University Press, 1923), since the completion of this study has made it desirable to cut out from this chapter most of the early history of the Office of the Revels, which Mr. Chambers covers in detail to about 1616.

[84] On the Boy Bishop, see E. K. Chambers, *Medieval Stage*; Brand, *Popular Antiquities of Great Britain*, (ed. Ellis, 1902), I, 424-25; *Collection of Ordinances for the Royal Household* (Society of Antiquaries), 1790, p. 25; Warton, *History of English Poetry*.

[85] E. K. Chambers, *Medieval Stage*, I, 306.

[86] Strutt, *Sports and Pastimes of . . . . England* (ed. Hone, 1833), p. 344.

functions at that time. By the end of the fifteenth century he was usually called "lord of misrule," or occasionally "abbot"; in Scotland he was known as the "abbot of unreason."[87] In the reign of Henry VIII[88] nearly every year a Lord of Misrule was appointed until 1520.

The function of this dignitary is thus explained by Holinshed:

What time [Christmas], of old ordinarie course, there is alwaies one appointed to make sport in the court, called commonlie lord of misrule: whose office is not unknowne to such as have beene brought up in noble mens houses, and among great house keepers which use liberall feasting in that season.[89]

Stow's account makes it equally clear that not one but many lords of misrule were to be expected at the Christmas season:

There was in the feast of Christmas in the King's house, wheresoever he was lodged, a Lord of Misrule or Master of Merry Disports; and the like had ye in the house of every nobleman of honour or good worship, were he spiritual or temporal. Among the which the Mayor of London and either of the sheriffs had their several Lords of Misrule, ever contending, without quarrel or offence, who should make the rarest pastimes to delight the beholders. These Lords beginning their rule on Allhallows eve, continued the same til the morrow after the feast of the Purificacion, commonly called Candlemas-day. In all which space there were fine and subtle disguisings, masks and mummeries.[90]

Machyn's Diary (Cotton MS. Vitellius F.v.), 1552–53, also shows that the sheriff had a lord of misrule who met and received the kings.

In the reign of Edward VI we have rather full accounts of the office of the lord of misrule, or, as he was called in a warrant of 1552 to pay George Ferrys £100, "Lorde of the Pastymes in the Kinges Majesties House."[91] He superintended the holiday amusements, including hawking, hunting, feats of arms, jousts with hobby-horses, juggling and tumbling. Collier thinks he sees in these entertainments the crude beginnings of masques and interludes (*Stage*, I, 42).

[87] See Household Accounts of Henry VII for the Christmas season.

[88] For the early history of this custom, see Chambers, *Medieval Stage*, I, 173, n. 7; 403 ff.; Brand, *Popular Antiquities*, I, 387, and bibliography; and Collier, *Annals of Stage*, I, 42.

[89] *Chronicle* (1587), III, 1067.

[90] *Survey of London*, I, 37.

[91] *Acts of the Privy Council*, n.s., IV, 181.

By 1545 there had been appointed a permanent official, the Master of the Revels, at the English court. That he is not the same as the Lord of Misrule and not an immediate evolution from him will appear from a series of extracts from the Documents of the Revels in the time of Edward VI, made by Professor Feuillerat (pp. 56–61, 77–81).

Just before Christmas in 1551, Northumberland wrote to Sir Thomas Cawarden, the Master of the Revels:

> I understand by Mr. vicechamberleyn that the kinges maiesties plesser ys for his hignes better recreation the tym of thies hollydayes to haue a Lorde of Mysrule and hathe apoyntyd apon this berer Mr. fferys, wherefor the tyme beinge so neere at hand. that he cannot prepare soche thinges for the furnishinge of that offyce as he would have don yf he had some knoledge of his hignes plesser I haue thought good to require you to Conferr with him in the better settinge fourthe of the matter to more contentacion of his maieste.

Warrants from the Privy Council follow on Christmas day and December 30, 1551, asking the Master of the Revels to furnish the necessaries for the Lord of Misrule appointed to be in the King's household for twelve days.[92] These revels accounts show a feeling of rivalry and a slight overlapping of functions of the Lord of Misrule and the Master of the Revels. It is clear that these officers co-existed, that they were not identical, and that both might be found even in a private house, as in that of the fifth Earl of Northumberland in 1522 (Percy, *N. H. B.*, 344, 346).

After the death of Edward VI the official Lord of Misrule was not revived at court by Mary, nor was it by Elizabeth, but the custom continued for a time at inns of court and at universities.[93] Lincoln's Inn had in 1455 a marshal, and under him a master of the revels, which were four in number. The Christmas revels had its special "king" or "prince." The Inns of court had officials who functioned very much as masters of revels as late as 1682 and even 1734 (Douthwaite, 243, 245).

The Master of the Revels at the court was originally intended to be the planner and supervisor of disguising, masques, etc. for festive occasions. As early as 1347 there was a regular provision

---

[92] A. Feuillerat, *Revels . . . . Edward VI*, pp. 59, 81.

[93] On Oxford custom, see Antony à Wood, *Athenae Oxon.* (Bliss), III, 480; and on Cambridge, see Cooper, *Annals of Cambridge*, II, 32.

among the expenses of the wardrobe for the *tunicae and viseres* for the Christmas *ludi* of Edward III at Guildford (*Archaeologia*, XXXI, 37). This looks like a small beginning of the Revels office. Professor Feuillerat has listed thirteen persons who organized Christmas festivities in the last quarter of the fifteenth century.[94] In the reign of Henry VII these were usually temporary officers chosen from household officials or courtiers, and this custom continued into the reign of Henry VIII.[95] One of the earliest references to the Master by title is in an order for sitting in the King's great chamber, dated December 31, 1494: "If the master of the revells be there, hee may sitt with the chapleyns or with the esquires or gentlemen ushers."[96] There was a "maister of the disguisinges" or "revills" to manage the Christmas merriments after the wedding of Prince Arthur with Katherine of Spain at Westminster Hall.[97]

Among the noblemen who held the office of master of the revels in its early history are: Edward Guilford, Earl of Essex (1510); and Henry Wentworth (the same year); Sir Henry Guildford, between 1511 and 1527; Lord Leonard Gray, 1524; Sir Anthony Browne, 1540.[98] The first use of the title with the name of the holder was with reference to Henry Wentworth in 1510.[99]

Under Guildford something like a real Office of the Revels was to be found. The distinguished nobleman could not be expected to do the actual work. He had as assistant Gibson, a royal tailor or officer of the wardrobe, who until 1534 did what was later divided among three officers. He got the directions from his superior, bought the materials, employed tailors, painters, etc., paid the bills, kept the records, and presided over the costumes.

The first person to get a real office in the Revels was John Farlyon, who on November 20, 1534, was made "yoman keper of our vestures or apparaill of all and singuler our maskes revelles and disguysinges . . . . for life," for which he was to

[94] *Le Bureau des Menus-Plaisirs*, 13; cf. Wm. Campbell, *Materials for Hist. of Reign of Henry VII*, II, 60, 63.
[95] Campbell, *op. cit.*, I, 337.
[96] *Household Ordinances and Regulations*, Soc'y of Antiquaries, 113.
[97] *Harl. MSS*, 69; cited by E. K. Chambers, *Med. Stage*, I, 399.
[98] *Letters and Papers of Reign of Henry VIII*, II, 1490–92.
[99] Feuillerat, *Bureau des Menus-Plaisirs*, 15.

receive sixpence a day, a house, livery, etc. His successor, John King, worked under the King and took orders from his Marshal.[100]

In 1545 there was appointed as a permanent officer, Master of the Revels, Sir Thomas Cawarden, his patent dating from March 16, 1544, with an annual fee of £10 (Rymer, *Foedera*, XV, 62). According to an anonymous report of the Revels (dated 1573), Cawarden, knight, "beinge of the kinges majesties pryvie Chamber, beinge skilfull and delightinge in matters of devise, preferred to that office, did mislyke to be tearmed a Seriaunt because of his better countenaunce of roome and place beinge of the kinges maiesties privye Chamber. And so he became by patent the first master of the Revelles."[101] His official title was *Magister Jocorum Revelorum et mascorum omnium et singularium nostrorum vulgariter nuncupatorum* Revells & Masks. His annual fee was £10.

Cawarden had only to care for the revels at court, and was not in control of general public amusements or of professional acting on public stages. He served 1544–59. Under him the revels office developed through the addition of a clerk comptroller, a yeoman, and a clerk, and the securing of headquarters at Warwick Inn. The office was later moved into the precinct of the dissolved Blackfriars.[102]

There are a few documents from Cawarden's time which throw light upon the management of the office. The Revels was at some times connected with the office of the "Tentes" and that of the "Toyles" and at some times separate from them. Queen Elizabeth, at the death of Cawarden, divided the office, January 18, 1560, in appointing Sir Thomas Benger Master of the Revels. Benger farmed out a good deal of his work to subordinates. It is difficult now to say whether there was any real mismanagement in his incumbency. On his death, in 1572,[103] Lord Burghley set to work to investigate the origin, powers, and methods of the office. He procured from the office

---

[100] Feuillerat, *Bureau des Menus-Plaisirs*, 17–22.
[101] E. K. Chambers, *Tudor Revels*, 2.
[102] *Molyneux Papers* (Hist. MSS Comm., VII, 603; 614).
[103] See Feuillerat, *Revels . . . . Elizabeth*, 128–29. Chambers, *Tudor Revels*, 26, and *Elizabethan Stage*, I, 80, n. 2). Fleay and others think he died years later and that there was a gap in the continuity of the office, 1573–79.

three reports. One is an anonymous history of the Revels, which is on some points probably our best source of information. There is also an account of the work of the office, and of the qualifications of the master. It looks as if Blagrave, the former clerk of Benger, who was allowed to do the work of the Master without his title and perquisites, had prepared at least some of these reports with the idea of showing his own qualifications for the office. What he got was a continuance of the opportunity to do the work without the title. He seems to have had no official appointment.[104]

On July 24, 1579, Sir Edmund Tilney was appointed to the mastership. He continued to hold office till he died, August 20, 1610, but after 1603 a considerable part of his work was done by his deputy, Sir George Buc, who held a patent for the reversion of the mastership, granted by Elizabeth and confirmed by James. (It was this, no doubt, that crowded out the claim that Lyly felt he had upon the mastership *c.* 1598.)

The conduct of the office was not greatly changed under Tilney, but the powers and dignity were decidedly increased. He raised the question of precedence on public occasions, and it was agreed that, whereas Tilney "hath the charge and direccion from her highness for all her marciall Triumphes and princlie Revells in generall . . . ," he should "mingle with Bachelorknightes according to the antiquities of the office." He was ranked with the Knight Lieutenant of the Queen's ordnance and artillery and that of the Tower of London. But more important than this is the extension of his powers by patent to give him in effect the control of public drama in England. According to a report of Henry Herbert, in reply to a complaint of Sir William D'Avenant, John Astley got a patent as Master, 3 April, 10 of Jas. I; Ben Jonson, one 5 October, 19 of Jas. I; and Henry Herbert and Simon Thelwall, Esq., patents on 25 August, 5 of Charles I. Some of these patents, however, could not be active. Buc, for example, was Master of the Revels on March 30, 1622, when Chamberlain wrote Carleton that "old Sir George Buck, Master of the Revels, has gone mad." The *Dictionary of National Biography* is mistaken in stating that he went mad two years before he gave up his

[104] Cf. Chambers, *Tudor Revels*, 52; and Feuillerat, *Revels* . . . . *Eliz.*, 443, which disagree.

duties. It was really only a little over a month between this letter and the appointment of Sir John Astley, May 2, 1622.[105] It is a pity to call attention to this, as it spoils a jest of Fowell and Palmer, who, on page 30 of their *Censorship in England*, say of Buc's madness, "This may not have been a disqualification in itself." Astley wrote Buc on May 16, 1622, to deliver up his books and other things of the office to him.[106]

The books of both Tilney and Buc have perished, but quotations made by Herbert show that an elaborate set of accounts was begun about 1571. Buc indeed made some sort of history of the office, a "particular commentary of the art of Revels, which hath a settled place within this city," according to his own statement in *The Third University of England*, written in 1612, but printed in Howe's continuation of Stow's *Annals*, 1615. When Herbert succeeded Astley in 1623, he continued his book, which runs from 1622 to 1641, when the Civil War broke up the office. Though Herbert's book has disappeared, it was examined by both Malone (*Variorum*, I and III) and Chalmers (*Apology* . . . , and *Supplemental Apology* . . . .).

The chief modern sources of information on the Revels office are: Peter Cunningham's *Extracts from the Accounts of the Revels*, published for the Shakespeare Society, 1842; Halliwell-Phillips, *A Collection of Ancient Documents Respecting the Office of Master of Revels* (1870; now rare); E. K. Chambers, *Notes on the History of the Revels Office under the Tudors*; J. Q. Adams, *Dramatic Records of Sir Henry Herbert*; the three great works of Feuillerat, *Documents Relating to the Office of the Revels . . . . of Queen Elizabeth*; *Documents Relating to the Office of Revels . . . . of Edward VI and Mary*; and *Le Bureau des Menus-Plaisirs*; and Chambers, *Elizabethan Stage*.

The early administration of the office can be reconstructed fairly well from Feuillerat's *Documents*. In the time of Cawarden the equipment was carefully inventoried and inspected by officers. Besides the master, there were a clerk comptroller, a yeoman, and another clerk. Cawarden had to supervise the arrangements for making garments for royal maskers, and have them properly kept, aired, mended, remodeled and renovated.

---

[105] *S. P. Dom.*, 1619–23, vol. CXXVIII, art. 96. The dates of the appointments above are from the Patent Rolls.

[106] Murray, *E.D.C.*, II, 193.

In the reign of Mary, the King and Privy Council gave the orders to the Master for the lending of garments and properties to gentlemen for plays. Occasionally garments were given to players as fees, or discarded ones were turned over to the Master; but the usual custom was to preserve them carefully as long as possible. Even then the expenses of the office ran as high as £865 in the fourth and fifth years of Edward VI.[107]

Perhaps the most illuminating single document is the anonymous report of 1573 produced when Burghley was investigating the office. It consisted of an historical account, together with a draft of rules for better management.[108] In the early days it was customary for the Prince to appoint a Master of Revels "such as for creditte plesaunte witte and habilitye in learnynge he thought meete to be the Master of the Revelles for that tyme." This person should, according to the report, be one "of countenance and of creditt with the Prince .... suche as the Quenes Majestye thought meetest to receyve her highnes pleasure from tyme to tyme attendant in the Courte and to delyver the same over by speache or platt to one such as followeth, videlicet,

"A Seriaunte of the Revelles learned and skilfull howe to execute the devise receyved or to invente a newe meete and necessarye with the allowance of the Master." The Sergeant is to put his whole time on seeing the device carried out in detail, "and this will much ease the Master who cannot alwayes wayte upon the Queenes pleasure and upon the devise and all the workemen." The Sergeant, with the Master and the other officers, is to attend rehearsal of plays and follow out the Master's suggestions for changes and corrections. The Clerk, Comptroller Clerk, and Yeoman are to be consulted by Master and Sergeant as to how the garments and other stuff shall be provided. The Clerk Comptroller shall stay in the office and care for the stuff, and give it out for use as ordered. He is also to keep the account books. The Clerk is to do the bookkeeping concerning names and charges of workmen, and is to oversee the workmen.

---

[107] A. J. Kempe, *Loseley MSS*, 92.

[108] *Lans. MSS*, 83, art. 59; reprinted by Feuillerat, *Revels .... Eliz.*, pp. 6 ff.

In connection with this report, certain ordinances were proposed. These concerned in part the duties of the helper, and in part those of the Master. The Yeoman should oversee the cutting and making of garments, armor, and properties, and care for them when made. Also, it was proposed that a "cunning painter limn in a fair large ledger the masks and shows last set forth" so that variety might be had.

The Master, according to the writer of the sketch (probably Blagrave, a candidate for the headship), should be "neither gallant, prodigall, nedye, nor gredye." He should be "of suche learning, wytt and experience as hable of hymself to make and devise suche shewes and devises as may best fitt and furnish the tyme place and state. . . . The mayster of the office oughte to be a man learned, of good engyne, inventife witte, and experience, as well for varietie of straunge devises delectable as to waye what moste aptlye and fitleye furnissheth the tyme, place, presence, and state." The demands of his office, according to this paper, were considerable. "The connynge of the office resteth in skill of devise, in understandinge of historyes, in iudgement of comedies tragedyes and showes, in sight of perspective and architecture, some smacke of geometrye and other thynges; wherefore the best helpe for thofficers is to make good choyce of cunnynge artificers severally accordinge to their best qualitie, and for one man to allow of an other mans invencion, as it is worthie, especiallye to understand the princes vayne."

Perhaps an example or two will best show the sort of invention the Master had to employ when the idea was furnished him by another, and he had to furnish details, especially costuming and properties. In 1552–53 Sir George Howard sent Cawarden an outline for a play (or masque) of Cupid, kindly assisting the Master's intelligence in the important particulars that "Mars must be harmed" and carry a "naket sworde," and that "Cupid shalbe a letell boy howe must be tremmed with a bow and arrows blinfelde accordenge as yow thinke hit mete other furneture I knowe of none." The Master provided, among other properties for this triumph of Cupid, "a dragons head and a dragons mowthe of plate with stoppes to burne like fier."[109] Similarly, in 1556 William Baldwin sent to Ca-

[109] Feuillerat, *Documents of Revels . . . . Edward VI, and Mary*, 108.

warden ten days in advance a crude sketch of his comedy ("love and lyve"), to last three hours and require sixty-two persons. All the players' names must begin with L (Lust, Luck, Love, Laughing, Looking, Lothyng, Lubberdly lazy, Leonard Lustyguts, Last yeres, and Little lokt for death, etc.).[110]

As a rule, however, the devising of masques was the most original part of the Master's work. The nature of these masques may be inferred from many entries in the Revels accounts. Often some degree of mechanical ingenuity was required in the devices used for show, as, e.g., when in 1552–53 "six counterfeit apes . . . . of mowlded woorke" were covered with gray cony-skins "to set upon the same bagpypes lyke minstrels." The pipes were of wicker covered with canvas and gilded. They contained pipes inserted, by means of which they were in reality played by concealed men.

As time went on, the Master of Revels, though he continued to devise some masques for the court, came to take on the function of a judge or censor of the work of others, as in selecting suitable plays for court use. Thus, in 1571, we have a record of six plays given at court, "all whiche vi playes being chosen owte of many, and founde to be the best that were to be had, the same also being often perused and necessarely corrected and amended by all thafforeseide officers."[111]

According to Cunningham, an important function of the office consisted in "calling together of sundry players and perusing, fitting and reforming theier matters otherwise not convenient to be showen before her Majestie" (p. 49). Mr. Feuillerat, I judge from his work on the revels of Elizabeth, does not consider that calling of outside companies to *rehearsal* was a function of the office.[112]

A disputed point as to the powers of the Master of the Revels is whether he licensed players. When Herbert (*c.* 1662) was making great claims for his office, a petition of D'Avenant against him produced litigation which gave rise to a decision by a London jury on the powers of the Master, which I quote, with the parenthetical remark that a jury is not necessarily qualified to determine past history. They decided that

[110] Feuillerat, *Documents of Revels....Edw. VI*, 215.
[111] Cunningham, *Revels*, 13.
[112] See also E. K. Chambers, *Elizabethan Stage*, IV, Appx. D, no. lvi.

the Master of Revels was allow'd the correction of Plaies and Fees for soe doeing; but not to give Plaiers any licence or authoritie to play, it being prov'd that no Plaiers were ever authoriz'd in London or Westminster, to play by the commession of the Master of the Revels, but by authoritie immediately from the Crowne.[113]

After the Restoration there came a question as to whether the statutory prohibition of players' wandering unless under the hand and seal of a baron or nobleman of greater rank did not nullify Herbert's assumed power of licensing traveling companies. It is certain, however, that the Master of the Revels did at times license London and other companies for tours. When the Mayor of Maidstone in 1660 raised the question as to this power, Herbert replied:

You may be asured by me that you are the first Mayor or other officer that ever did dispute the authority, or the extent of it, for to confine it to the verge of the court, is such a sense as was never imposed upon it before, and contrary to the constant practice, for several grants have been made by me, since the happy restoration of our gracious sovereign to persons in the like quality, and seriously therefore, admitted into all counties and liberties of England without any dispute or molestation.

The letter closes with threats against the mayor.[114]

It is a certainty that, in the reign of James, the Chamberlain attempted to control, through the Master of the Revels, some disorders in companies of traveling players. On November 20, 1622, Gilbert Reason, head of a provincial company of players, carried an order from the Chamberlain to provincial towns that all patents not under the seal of the Master of the Revels be seized.[115] Again, on January 29, 1625, Pembroke ordered that all the players and showmen traveling with old licenses borrowed, rented, or bought, procure licenses from the Master of the Revels.

The flexibility in the conception of the Master's powers may be due to the vagueness of the terms of the patents, as in a very sweeping commission to Tilney December 24, 1581. The most extravagant of Herbert's claims are hardly beyond the possible interpretation of this patent:

[113] Halliwell-Phillips, *Collection of Ancient Documents*, 48.
[114] MS Collection of Clement Smythe; Murray, *E. D. C.*, II, 331.

48 ORGANIZATION AND CONTROL OF DRAMATIC COMPANIES

We haue and doe by these presentes aucthorise and commaunde our said Servant Edmunde Tilney Maister of our said Revells by himselfe or his sufficient deputie or deputies to warne commaunde and appointe in all places within this our Realme of England aswell within ffranchises and liberties as without all and euery plaier or plaiers with their playmakers either belonginge to any noble man or otherwise bearinge the name or names of usinge the facultie of playmakers or plaiers of Comedies Tragedies Enterludes or what other showes soever from tyme to tyme and at all tymes to appear before him with all suche plaies Tragedies Comedies or showes as they shall haue in readines or meane to sett forth and them to presente and recite before our said Servant or his sufficient deputie whom wee ordeyne appointe and aucthorise by these presentes of all suche showes plaies plaiers and playmakers together with their playing places to order and reforme auctorise and put down as shalbe thought meete or unmeete unto himselfe or his said deputie in that behalfe. And also likewise we have by these presentes aucthorised and commaunded the said Edmund Tylney that in case if any of them whatsoever they bee will obstinatelie refuse upon warninge unto them given by the same Edmunde or his sufficient deputie to accomplish and obey our commaundement in this behalf it shalbe lawfull to the said Edmunde or his sufficient deputie to attach the partie or parties so offendinge and him or them to commytt to warde to remaine without bayle or mayneprise, etc.[116]

On the strength of this patent, Tilney not only selected plays for court and revised them, but censored other plays, licensed players, and established his right to license the building of playhouses[117] and charge the companies an annual fee for allowance. Henslowe's accounts show two kinds of payments to Tilney from 1598 to 1601: monthly payments for license of theatres, running from 10 s. a week to £3 a month, and occasional payments of fees of 7 s. for licensing of plays for performance (*Henslowe's Diary*, and *Henslowe Papers*). Buc in 1613 licensed the erection of Whitefriars, and Herbert also claimed such rights.

It is at first a little difficult to reconcile with the terms of Tilney's patent of 1581 the fact that on April 11, 1582, the Lords of the Council requested the Mayor to have the city

[115] Murray, *E. D. C.*, II, 351.
[116] Record Office, Patent Rolls, 1606 (Watson's Rolls), M. 34, n °46. Collier misinterprets this as bearing on the formation of the Queen's Company. Chambers and Feuillerat interpret it correctly.
[117] See *Remembrancia*, 352.

appoint some proper person to consider and allow such plays only as were fitted to yield honest recreation and no example of evil.[118] The discussions of plays by the Council (1582–84) do not seem to recognize the extensive powers of the Master of the Revels. This may, however, indicate only some dissatisfaction as to the efficiency of his office. At any rate, it is certain that for one company at least he had a censorship of plays some years before. For a patent granted to Leicester's men May 10, 1574, authorized them to perform in or out of London, "any act, statute, proclamation, or commaundment hertofore made, or herafter to be made, to the contrary notwithstanding," and provided that their "Comedies, Tragedies, Enterludes and Stageplayes be by the Master of our Revills (for the tyme being) before seen and allowed."[119]

The Hall papers of Leicester show, under date of March 3, 1584, an article of indenture of a company of players containing an order to all justices, mayors, *et al.* that "none shall showe forth any such playes, enterludes, tragedies, comedies, or showes in any places within this Realm, withoute the orderlye allowance thereof under the hand of the sayd Edmund." A note is affixed, that "no play is to bee played, but such as is allowed by the sayd Edmund, and his hand at the latter end of the said booke they doe play."[120] According to Kelly, a similar note is attached to a commission from Tilney to a company at Leicester February 6, 1583.

The Mayor and the Master of the Revels seemed to be cooperating in censorship when the Mayor wrote in 1589 of certain plays discussing the Martin Marprelate affair, that "Mr. Tilney did utterly mislike the same."[121] There was a necessary cooperation between Master of Revels, Mayor of London, and some representative of the ecclesiastical authorities in the work of censorship immediately after 1589; for on November 12 of that year the Privy Council wrote three letters, one to the Archbishop of Canterbury, one to the Mayor, and one to Tilney, ordering a new system of play-licensing. The

---

[118] *Remembrancia*, I, 317.
[119] *Variorum* (1821), III, 47.
[120] William Kelly, *Notices Illustr. of Drama of Leicester*, 111–12.
[121] *Lans. MSS*, 60; Collier, *Stage*, I, 265.

reason for it appears in the letter to the Archbishop of Canterbury:

There hathe growne some inconvenience by comon playes and enterludes in and about the Cyttie of London in [that] the players take uppon them to handle in their plaies certen matters of Divinytie and of State unfitt to be suffred, for redresse whereof their Lordships have thought good to appointe some persones of judgement and understanding to viewe and examine their playes before they be permitted to present them publickly.

The Archbishop was therefore requested to nominate "some fytt person well learned in Divinity" to serve on such a commission. The letter to the Mayor requested him to appoint "a sufficient persone learned and of judgement." The third letter, to Tilney, asked him to act with the other two. They were

to call before them the severall companies of players (whose servauntes soever they be) and to require them by authorytye hereof to delyver unto them their bookes, that they maye consider of the matters of their comedyes and tragedyes, and thereuppon to stryke oute or reforme suche partes and matters as they shall fynd unfytt and undecent to be handled in playes, both for Divinite and State, comaunding the said companies of players, in her Maiesties' name that they forbeare to present and playe publickly anie comedy or tragedy other then suche as they three shall have seene and allowed, which if they shall not observe, they shall then knowe from their Lordships that they shalbe not onely sevearely punished but made (in)capable of the exercise of their profession forever hereafter.[122]

Somewhat puzzling as to the jurisdiction of the licenser are a few of Herbert's entries on the plays of "strangers." On September 12, 1623, he notes that a new comedy called "the cra . . . . marchant, or Come to my Country-house" was "acted at the Red Bull and licensed without my hand to itt, because they were none of the four Companys."[123] On September 18, 1623, is a memorandum that "Come See a Wonder," written by "John Deye" for a company of strangers (possibly *Wonder of a Kingdom*, by Dekker or Day?) was licensed without his hand to it because they were none of the four companies.[124] On

[122] *Acts of the Privy Council*, XVIII, 1589–90, pp. 214–15.
[123] Chalmers, *Sup. Apol.*, 215.
[124] *Variorum*, III, 224.

November 28, 1623, he seems to have given an acting license for "The fayre fowle one, or the bayting of the Jealous knight" for a "strange company at the Red Bull."[125]

Some plays, we know, were licensed for performance by others than the Master of the Revels. The Privy Council passed on *Byron*, a censored play. The Chamberlain also seems to have had licensing power. Chapman, in prison (over *Eastward Hoe?*) wrote to the Chamberlain that nothing repented him so much "as that our unhappie booke was presented without your Lordeshippes allowance, for which we can plead nothinge by way of pardon but your Person so farr removed from our required attendance."[126] Also, some substitutes were allowed to relieve the Master. In 1624 the King's Company apologized to Herbert for playing *The Spanish Viceroy* without license under Herbert's hand, and gave this promise: "Wee will not act any play without your hand or substituts hereafter." A deputy sometimes licensed and made corrections on the plays. An example of Blagrave's work may be seen in *The Lady Mother* (Bullen, *Old Eng. Plays*, II, 200).

Samuel Daniel had for a time, by a special grant (January 31, 1604) authority to license plays for a company of "Children Revels to the Queen."[127] This did not interfere with the Master of the Revels save for this company.[128]

Not only new plays, but plays revived and modified must be licensed by the Master of the Revels. At least this was true from 1623 on. An entry of August 19, 1623, suggests that the oversight may have been less careful for the revivals:

> For the King's Players. An olde playe called Winter's Tale, formerly allowed of by Sir George Bucke, and likewyse by mee on Mr. Hemmings his word that there was nothing profane added or reformed, thogh the allowed booke was missinge; and therefore I returned it without a fee. (*Var*.III,229).

Later on a fee was required if the license of the old version had been lost. Revivals with modifications cost 10 s. to a pound for

---

[125] Chalmers, *op. cit.*, 216.
[126] *Athenaeum*, March 30, 1901.
[127] Collier, *Annals*, I, 340.
[128] See letter of Buc to Somerset, *S. P. Dom.*, 1611–19, July 10, 1615. By 1615 John Daniel seems to have taken his brother's place, according to a patent of July 7 of that year.

allowance. In 1625 *The Honest Man's Fortune* was re-allowed by Herbert, the original being lost (*Ibid.*, III, 229); and on May 13, 1629, he charged 10 s. for "allowing of a new act in an ould play" (*Ibid.*, I, 424). Adding a scene to *The Virgin Martyr* cost the owner 10 s. on July 7, 1624 (*Ibid.*). A pound was "received of ould Cartwright for allowing the Company to add scenes to an ould play, and to give it out for a new one this 12th of May, 1636." Whether because of the fees or because he felt that there was real danger that improper material would creep into revised plays, Herbert insisted that a new license was needed for revivals. In 1660 he sent a warrant for the players of the Cockpit to come before him and bring or send all old plays "that they may be reformed of prophanes and ribaldry."[129]

One who is familiar with the show-like qualities of many of the masques of Elizabethan and Jacobean times will find it less startling to consider the range of performances that, at one time or another, came under the surveillance of the Master of the Revels. Regular companies, such as Lord Strange's in 1580, had with them at times boy acrobats and tumblers (*Henslowe's Diary*, Greg, II, 71); so that feats of activity of the nature of "shows" were not, in practice, so far removed from the drama as one might suppose. As to spectacles, the masques themselves were extremely varied. In the time of Edward VI the Master of the Revels provided entertainments with tumblers apparently walking on hands with feet in air; Greek "worthies"; "medioxes, or figures half death and half men"; apes posing as minstrels with bagpipes; hobbyhorses; jousting; a mask of cats, etc. In the reign of Mary there were representations of mythological characters, goddesses, huntresses, Turkish magistrates, Turkish women, Venetian senators, gallies and galley-slaves, palmers, friars, "allmayne pylgryms and Irysshmen"; a play wherein the "kynge was ffurryd with lybardes tayles." In the time of Elizabeth there were all these and more, especial emphasis being given to portrayal of strange nations.

The Master of the Revels claimed, and at times exercised, power over matters such as these: a show of water works; an "Italian motion shewing a musicall organ with divers strange and rare motions"; a show of pictures in wax; show of a por-

[129] J. Q. Adams, *Dramatic Records of Sir Henry Herbert*, 94.

traiture of the city of Jerusalem; feats of charging and discharging a gun; tumbling; vaulting; rope-dancing; legerdemain; "sights about witches"; an elephant to be shown for a year; a live Beaver; two dromedaries to be shown by a Dutchman; a sow with six hogs; a serpent brought to town; a child born without arms (shown at Coventry, 1636); an "outlandish creature called a Possum"; a baboon that can do strange feats; "a bay nagge which can shewe strange feats"; dancing horses; a woman without hands who in 1633 traveled about with her husband "to shew diverse works &c. done with her feet." If this work of the Master of Revels seems oddly variegated, commissions such as these should be kept in mind:

(1) To an Italian, Francis Nicolini, and his company, a warrant "to dance on the ropes, to use Interludes and Masques, and to sell his powders and balsams."

(2) To "John Puncteus, a Frenchman, professing Physick, and his Company, to exercise the quality of playing, for a year, and to sell his drugs."[130]

Herbert was jealous as to the range of his power. He told the Mayor of Maidstone (1660) that rope-dancers had been licensed by him and his predecessors "time out of minde, whereof the memory of man is not to the contrary."[131] He wished to include also billiards, gaming contrary to the law, nine-pins, cock-fights and a few other trifles,[132] and by 1661 he had such power from the Chamberlain.

Writers who are unfamiliar with the previous history of the Revels office usually pronounce a violent condemnation of Herbert's grasp for power. It was greedy, but it was not without some foundation in past practice. His predecessor, Tilney, as we have seen, had a patent of very sweeping nature. And Sir John Astley had, on November 20, 1622, a warrant from the Chamberlain, Pembroke, which gave him oversight over miscellaneous popular amusements and distinctly suggested that such matters would be better attended to if licensed by the

---

[130] These examples of popular entertainments are culled from: Chalmers, *Suppl. Apol.*; *Variorum* of 1821; Halliwell-Phillips, *Collection of Ancient Documents*; J. Q. Adams, *Dram. Rec. of* . . . . *Herbert*; and Feuillerat's three books on the Revels.

[131] J. Q. Adams, *op. cit.*, 91–92.

[132] Halliwell-Phillips, *Collection of Ancient Documents*, 53–56, 59–60.

Master of the Revels than if the proprietors could secure permission from the King or from noblemen. Because of "great disorders and abuses daily committed by diverse and sundry companyes of stage players Tumblers vaulters dauncers on the Ropes and also by such as goe about with motions and shewes . . . . by reason of certaine grants Commissions and lycences which they haue by secret meanes procured both from the Kings maiestie and also from diuerse noblemen by vertue whereof they doe abusiuely clayme unto themselves a kinde of licentious fredome to travell aswell to shew play and exercise in eminent cities and Corporacions . . . . without the knowledge and approbacon of his maiesties office of the Revels . . . . and sett forth . . . . playes and shews . . . . full of scandall and offence both against the Church and state and doe lykewise greatly abuse their authority in lending, lettinge, and sellynge their said Commissions and lycences to others," it was commanded that a fresh licence from Sir John Astley, Master of the Revels, must be shown. The false licences were to be sent to the Master also.[133]

A backward glance, by Edward Hayward, deputy to Henry Herbert, in 1663, is of interest in its revelation of what he considered to be the proper jurisdiction of the office. Seeing its powers somewhat declined, he petitioned Sir Edward Nicholas to write to a Secretary of State for permission

> that hee may enjoy all ancient priuiledges at Court, the ordering of maskes in the Innes of Law, halls, houses of great personages, and societies, all Balls, Dancing schooles, and musick, except his Majestys and the priuiledges of the Corporation touching freemen, if it extend soe farre; Pageantry and other publique tryumphes, the rurall feasts commonly called Wakes, where there is constantly revelling and musick; Cockpitts, fencing and fencing schooles, nocturnall feasts and banquettings in public houses, when attended with minstrelsy, singing and Dancing, together with the ordering of all mommeries, fictions, Disguises, scenes and masking attire, all which (in the judgment of an able Lawyer) are within the verge and comprehension of the Master of the Reuells Patent, from the words Jocorum Revelorum et Mascorum.

Hayward said he had to "use his wits in an honest way" to get his expected income. He proposed to investigate how many companies of these sorts there were in England, and what ones

[133] Murray, *E.D.C.*, II, 351–52.

were out of commissions. Mountebanks, lotteries, clockwork motions, ordinary motions, dancing horses and mares, rope dancers, sleights of hand, and cockfighting, he thought, should belong to the Master of the Revels.[134]

The temptation to extend the oversight of the Revels office was largely a matter of fees. The Master depended on them more than upon his fixed income. He had his regular fee from each company for theatre allowances. Sometimes this was a winter and a summer benefit performance, amounting to £8 or £9 each time. This was the arrangement in 1628 (J. Q. Adams, *Dram. Rec.*, 43). In 1633, however, a sum was fixed by the King's Company, £10 at Christmas and £10 at midsummer in place of the two benefits (*Var.*, III, 177–78). This arrangement probably continued till the Civil War. After the Restoration, four companies of players each gave Herbert a share in their profits in addition to fees. He had also fees from licenses to traveling players and showmen.

The licensing of individual plays brought in varying sums. In the time of Tilney the fee rose from 5 s. in 1592 to 6 s., to to 6 s. 8 d., to 7 s., where it remained 1598–1600 (see Henslowe's Diary). It then rose more rapidly.[135] In Herbert's time the fees were said to be 40 s. for a new play, and 20 s. for a revived one (about 1620–21).[136] Some plays brought him £1, and others which required more revision (e.g., the *History of the Duchess of Suffolk*) as much as £2. The fee, he insisted, was not for licensing a work, but for his labor of reading and judging (*Var.*, III, 231). That is to say, he was entitled to his fee if he refused to license a play—even though he ordered it to be burned.

There were certain special fees. Citizens paid Tilney an "amity" by advice of the archbishop to induce him to be more strict in his supervision. Theatres, on the other hand, paid fees for permission to perform in Lent.

There is more than a suggestion of greed in Herbert's remarks on fees and in his grasp for fresh powers. It is hinted in D'Ave-

---

[134] Rebecca Warner, *Epistolary Curiosities*, Appx. no. 5, p. 185. Cf. Halliwell-Phillips, *Collection of Ancient Documents*, pp. 53–59.

[135] The Exchequer of Receipt Miscellaneous Order Book, 1602–04, III, 106, shows an expenditure of £66 6s. 8d. for Tilney's yearly allowance "for defraying the ordinary charges for plays."

[136] J. Q. Adams, *Dramatic Records* . . . , 106.

nant's petition in the law case against Herbert (*c.* 1662); in its request for decision for "time prescribed how long he shall keep plaies in his hands, in pretence of correcting them," and whether he can demand fees for revived plays, and "how long plaies may be laid aside, ere he shall judge them to be revived."[137] The impression one gets from Herbert's own records is that he stretched his powers to the utmost and that he was vitally interested in money-getting. It seems to me, however, that, warped as he perhaps was, he did show some signs of conscience as to the performance of duty as he saw it, and that Fowell and Palmer, in their zeal against censorship in general, have, in their portrayal of Herbert, credited to him as an individual what were, after all, defects in the system. Some of Herbert's devices as a fee hunter (on pp. 36–37 of their *Censorship in England*) are, I believe, fancifully portrayed; and it is at least conceivable that, if we had as full records of the other masters, they would show up as unpleasantly.

Fleay, in his *Life of Shakespeare* (pp. 328, 364) and in his *Stage*, (page 107), and his *Biographical Chronicle*, (II, 285–86), intimates that Chalmers and others blundered in interpreting the entries in Henslowe's Diary of payments to the Master of the Revels as licenses for acting. Fleay considers them as licenses for the press independently of the Stationers' Company. These fees are usually 5 to 7 s. Mr. Greg, in his edition of *Henslowe's Diary*, has shown conclusively that Fleay's notion is unfounded. The payments in Henslowe for particular plays are for licenses for performances, and they are few in number simply because others than Henslowe took care of the licensing of some of the plays, and because the diary does not cover the whole expenses of any company. Why or how plays could be licensed for print independently of the Stationers' Company would be difficult to explain.

So far as we now know, the Master of the Revels did not begin to license plays for the press till 1606. Certainly in 1599 the injunction concerning printing clearly states that "pamphlets, playes and balletes" were to be licensed before printing by three commissioners for religion. The Star Chamber decree of June 23, 1586 required licensing of plays by bishop or arch-

[137] Halliwell-Phillips, *Collection of Ancient Documents*, 48.

bishop. The difficulty of enforcing this was perhaps the main reason why it did not last.

Just when and how the Master of the Revels was first officially authorized to license plays for the press is still in doubt. Buc, when deputy to Tilney, licensed a comedy, *The Fleare*, November 21, 1606, but other licensers continued to authorize plays till the spring of 1607, after which Buc began. With very few exceptions, Buc licensed the plays for print from 1607 to 1615. Then other licensers appeared on the Registers. Herbert did not, immediately on taking office, appear as licenser for the press, but, with his deputies, he licensed practically all the plays regularly entered 1628–37. Shortly before the Civil War, impending changes of management of publishing perhaps broke up the custom. It is altogether likely that, when the Master of the Revels did license plays for the press, he had legal warrant for so doing, even if we do not find the record of it. On one occasion a member of the Stationers' Company entered on the Registers a play without license, and Sir Henry Herbert had the clerk of the Company forbidden to enter any "plays, tragedies, tragic comedies, or pastorals without the authority of the Master of the Revels."[138] This could not have been done without legal backing. It is a mistake to suppose that Buc, Herbert, and others merely assumed this right of licensing plays for the press. It may, however, fairly be questioned whether anything else than plays rightly came into the Master's jurisdiction over the press. Herbert did license some poetry: Ovid's Epistles translated into English; Lord Brooke's *Coelia*; "Two small pieces of verses, done by a boy of thirteen, called Cowley," (*Sup. Apol.*, 209–210). He also licensed Donne's *Paradoxes* September 13, 1632, and was summoned before Star Chamber on November 14 to tell why he allowed them to be printed.[139]

Probably Herbert convinced himself by an argument from analogy that he had licensing powers for other literature than drama. At any rate, that is what he and his deputy, Hayward, tried to do when the latter, on July 25, 1663, drew up an argument by Herbert "to prove that the Master of His Maiesties Office of the Revells, hath not onely the power of Lycencing all

[138] Arber, *S.R.*, V, lv.
[139] *S. P. Dom.*, 1631–33, vol. CCXXV, art. 20.

58 ORGANIZATION AND CONTROL OF DRAMATIC COMPANIES

playes, Poems, and ballads, but of appointing them to the Press." The argument runs that, since the design is "to have profaness, oaths, ribaldry, and matters reflecting upon church and government" obliterated before the plays are acted, "the like equitie there is, that all Ballads, songs, and poems of that nature, should pass the same examination, being argued a Majore ad Minus, and requiring the same antidote, because such things presently fly all over the Kingdome, to the Debauching and poisoning the younger sort of people, unles corrected, and regulated." This looks, however, like something cooked up by Hayward for his own benefit when he should succeed to the mastership. Hayward left a memorandum of July 27, 1663, to himself of information desired by Edward Hayward, deputy:

> To be informed by Sir Henry, whether it Doth not as equally belong to him to Lycence all Poems and Ballads as play bookes, which I may not omitt to enquire after, for the enlarging and extending of my profitts if the thing in it self proue feasable, and it wilbe the better for Sir Henry, if hee survive mee, for I intend to make a Deligent enquiry after the rights of the office and to contend soberly and cautiously for them.
>
> Memorandum. Old Mister Whitehead affirmes, that all Comedies, Tragedies, Poems, Ballads, half sides, drolleries, and all billes relating to Jokes belongs to the Revells, and were soe accompted in the times of Q. Elizabeth and K. James.[140]

It was expected that the license of a play for acting should be at the end of the manuscript submitted to the Master of the Revels, as it is, for example, in the manuscript of *Believe as You List* (B.M.), where the allowance reads: "This Play, called Believe as You liste, may bee acted this 6 day of May, 1631, Henry Herbert." Sometimes the book was submitted at the same time for licence for the press and for performance. Thus, "The Masque", licensed for performance by the Palsgrave's Company as new Dec. 29, 1624, was also licensed for the press, as is shown by Herbert's note in his office-book, "The Masque book was allowed for the Press and was brought me by Mr. Jon [son] the 29th Dec."[141]

Herbert's anxiety to be clear of offence to authorities influenced him to demand the deposit of copies with the Master of

[140] Halliwell-Phillips, *Collection of Ancient Documents*, pp. 5 and 53.
[141] Fleay, *Stage*, 305.

the Revels, that he might be able "to show what he had allowed or disallowed," (*Var.*, III,208-10), and to insist that "all ould plays ought to bee brought to the Master of the Revels, and have his allowance to them for which he should have his fee, since they may be full of offensive things against church and state, the rather that in former times the poetts took greater libertie than is allowed them by me," (*Ibid.*). One may freely admit that increase of fees may have motivated the latter suggestion in part. Herbert is perhaps a trifle more strict than Buc, in what we have to judge them by, but except with reference to profanity the difference is not great.

The Masters of the Revels were originally courtiers, and continued to be closely connected with the life of the court. They cannot reasonably be expected to have approached the work of the censorship of drama with the attitude of missionaries for the reform of public morals or manners. Their aim, as we shall see, was chiefly to guard against the publication, on the stage or in the printed play, of matters offensive to religion and government, and the satirizing of living persons.

CHAPTER II

LITERARY AND DRAMATIC CENSORSHIP

I. THE CENSORSHIP OF LITERATURE IN GENERAL

Mr. R. B. McKerrow, in his discussion of publishing conditions in *Shakespeare's England* (II,20), says: "Little or nothing in the shape of reports or discussions of the working of the censorship has come down to us. Our knowledge of it is, save for the injunctions and a few miscellaneous papers dealing with special cases, derived almost entirely from the records of the Stationers' Company." It is the purpose of this and the following section to piece together some of the scraps of evidence on the operation of the censorship, first, of literature in general, and then, more particularly, of the drama in the reigns of Elizabeth, James, and Charles.

OFFICERS OF CENSORSHIP: CHURCH, STATE, AND CITY

The attempts of governments to regulate the contents of works to be circulated dates back to classical antiquity. Satires, superstitious and heretical works, astrological treatises, and other works disagreeable to monarchs or clergy suffered suppression in the days of ancient Greece and Rome.[1] In England the censorship can be traced at least as far back as the last quarter of the thirteenth century, when the University of Cambridge secured from the Bishop of Ely (1276) the right to have the works made by its own writers and sold by its own stationers controlled by the Cambridge University Chancellor instead of the Archdeacon of Ely.[2]

Somewhat the same desire for independence of ecclesiastical oversight may be inferred from the reluctance of the University of Oxford to aid the efforts of the English bishops to suppress the Wycliffite "heresies" which had a strong hold in that university in the fourteenth century because of Wycliffe's connection with Oxford. Pope Gregory XI condemned eighteen or nineteen

---

[1] For examples of early censorship, see Johann Beckmann, *Hist. of Inventions and Discoveries*, 1846, II, 512-18.

[2] Thomas Fuller, *Hist. of the Univ. of Cambridge*, 1840, p. 48.

of Wycliffe's conclusions, and the bishops of England managed to arrange a public trial before the Bishop of London in 1377; but the results were inconclusive. The spreading of "Lollardy" by poor itinerant priests gave the heresy a more dangerous aspect, as their doctrines tended to foment class rebellion, to arouse the peasants against the exactions of the land-owning aristocracy. Lollardy came to be regarded as a menace, not only to the Church of Rome, but to the commonwealth. In 1382 an act of Parliament ordered the arrest of the itinerant priests; but this was not effectually enforced. In 1401 was passed the act *de haeretico comburendo* (2 Henry IV, c. 15). The synod at Oxford in 1410 forbade the writing of books contrary to the Catholic faith. Throughout the reign of Henry IV the Lollards continued to be an object of pursuit. The method of suppression of their doctrines may be illustrated by the searching out of a book of a well-known leader, Sir John Oldcastle (Lord Cobham) in 1413: "a volume in quires tending to the subversion of faith and holy church was discovered at a limner's in Paternoster Row where it was awaiting the process of illumination. The artist confessed that the book was Lord Cobham's."[3]

Probably because of the strong Wycliffite tendency of Oxford, Archbishop Arundel in the Provincial Constitutions provided for the re-establishment of ecclesiastical supervision of the book trade of that university. Clause 7 expressly forbids Wycliffite books and translations of the Scripture, and Clause 6 provides that "books read at universities and schools, halls, and hostels shall be read by censors appointed by the universities under oversight of the archbishop before the stationer shall be allowed to copy."[4]

After the introduction of printing, ecclesiastical control was more pronounced. In the early sixteenth century it seems to have been either required or expected that books should be presented for allowance to one of the bishops or the archbishop before printing. Mr. Reed quotes a recommendation of a devotional work of Symon in 1514 by Richard FitzJames, Bishop of London, which is in effect an *imprimatur*:[5]

[3] John Foxe, *Acts and Monuments*, 1846, III, 1830.
[4] A. W. Reed, "Regulation of the Book Trade before 1538," *Tr. of the Bibliographical Soc'y*, XV, 159.
[5] *Op. cit.*, 160.

Here endeth the Treatyse called the Fruyte of Redemption, whiche devoute Treatyse I, Rycharde unworthy Bysschop of London have studyously radde and overseen, and the same approve as moche as in me is to be radde of the true Servantes of Swete Jhesu, to theyr grete consolacyon and ghostly comforte and to the meryte of the devoute Fader Compounder of the same. Emprynted by Wynkyn de Worde, the yere of our Lorde God MCCCCC and XIIII.

When the Lutheran heresies began to circulate, an additional impetus was given to ecclesiastical censorship in England, as well as on the Continent. Cardinal Wolsey helped to enforce the Bull of Leo X (1520) requiring the burning of all Lutheran books. A prohibitory index was issued in England as early as 1526. Bishop Tunstall of London was especially active in censorship.

Mr. Reed (in the article referred to above, pp.162-3, and 170) extracts from "Foxford," a book of the records of the Biship's Vicar-General, accounts of two occasions, 12 October, 1524, and 25 October, 1526, when the London booksellers were warned against heretical books. In 1524 they were directed not to import or sell books printed in Germany, or any other books with Lutheran heresies. All books imported or printed abroad must be submitted to the Lord Cardinal, Archbishop of Canterbury, the Bishop of London, or the Bishop of Rochester. In 1526 the bishops of Norwich and London announced to thirty-one booksellers that not only Lutheran works, but all other works in Latin and English must be exhibited to the Lord Legate, the Archbishop of Canterbury, or the Bishop of London. The method of calling in forbidden works may be illustrated by the treatment of *The Image of Love*, declared heretical after it had been published by Wynkyn de Worde. Both the printer and the translator, John Gough, were ordered to collect all copies sold, even from universities and nunneries. Robert Wyer and Thomas Berthelet also got into trouble with the authorities, the latter for not submitting for inspection before publication three works by Erasmus and a sermon by Fisher against Luther.[6]

Though there seems to be a gap in the history of the licensing powers of bishop and archbishop in England, it may perhaps be accounted for by the fact that in 1535 Henry VIII, through

---

[6] Reed, *op. cit.*, 164, 166, 170.

Cromwell, delegated the control of ecclesiastical affairs to an ecclesiastical commission. This really strengthened the power of the bishops by giving them a court for the trial of offenders and putting their punishment on a legal basis. The proclamation of 1538 (chiefly directed against heresy) tightened the censorship of literature considerably. Queen Mary, because of her intense desire to force Catholicism upon England, proceeded very severely against heretics. In 1557 the twenty-two ecclesiastical commissioners were definitely commanded to proceed against heretical and seditious doctrines, whether circulated by "book, letters, tales, or otherwise", by a sort of jury trial with power of fines, imprisonment, and other penalties. These powers were confirmed by the statute of 1559 (1 Eliz., item 3) which extended the sphere of operation to include "all heretical opinions, seditious books, contempts, conspiracies, false rumours, tales, seditions, misbehaviours, slanderous works, published, invented, or set forth by any person or persons against us, or against any of the laws or statutes of this realm, or against the quiet governance and rule of our people."

The ecclesiastical commissioners were influential in securing the famous Star Chamber decrees of 1566 and 1586 for regulating publication, and they assisted in the execution of these orders.[7] The registers of the Stationers' Company show constant intercourse between the Company and the bishops and archbishops concerning the regulation of unruly stationers.

Not only were the churchmen concerned in the search for forbidden books and secret presses, the recall and burning of the books, the fine, imprisonment, or suppression of unruly printers, but they were also empowered, through a long period of time, to check the output at the source by at least partial control of licensing.[8] From 1561 on, occasional entries in the Stationers' Registers show that the Bishop of London or the Archbishop of Canterbury could license books for publication. Aylmer's name appears frequently. Whitgift had by 1588 extended his licensing power by the appointment of a group of twelve licensers, among whom Hartwell and Stallard were especially active.

[7] Strype, *Life of Parker*, I, 442; *S. P. Dom. Eliz.* 1559, vol. CXC, art. 48.
[8] See *S. P. Dom.*, 1633–34, pages 158, 412; 1635, 565; 1636–37, 546; 1637-38, 145; 1638-39, 55, 258, 547. Cf. also the decree of 1637 (July 4), Rymer, XX, 156.

64   CENSORSHIP OF LITERATURE IN GENERAL

It cannot be supposed that the pressure of the ecclesiastical hierarchy upon the national literature was at all times equally severe. The rigor depended in part upon the political and religious conditions at a given time, and in part upon the nature of the individual men in power. Mathew Parker, 1559-1575, was a scholar and at pains to promote the production of learned works. Edmund Grindal, 1576-1583, while more rigorous than Parker, was still mild and sane compared with some of his successors in power. Aylmer is known as a harsh man of some violence of temper; but, on the other hand, he is described by Strype as "a lover of and searcher after books, and especially of such as were more rare and curious . . . .a good judge of learning and languages, being an exact critic."[9]

John Whitgift began to put on the screws. The papers of the Marprelate controversy probably give an exaggerated picture of the archbishop's strenuosity,[10] but the essential facts are confirmed by history. One can trace many of them through the entries in the *Stationers' Registers* concerning Robert Waldegrave, the Puritan printer. The Hebraist, Hugh Broughton, who got along badly with the High Commission, was obliged, in 1595, to win over the Archbishop to his view that *Hades* was not hell, but the world unseen, where Christ went after crucifixion.[11]

Not only works printed in England but imported books were controlled for many years by ecclesiastical authorities. In 1564 Elizabeth ordered that importations should be examined by the Bishop of London for pernicious and heretical books. The archbishop's power to grant licences for foreign books to be imported ceased in the time of Archbishop Tillotson.[12] The ecclesiastical authorities were often assisted in their search for importations of objectionable books by the Mayor of London (*Remembrancia*).

Ecclesiastical oversight of books extended beyond religious amd political affairs; for works of pure literature were often

[9] John Strype, *Life of Aylmer*, p. 30.
[10] See John Udall, *The State of the Church of England*, 1588, Arber, *Eng. Scholar's Library*, no. 5; cf. preface to *Hay any work for Cooper*, 1589, (1880), pp. 43-46.
[11] Strype, *Whitgift*, II, 320-21.
[12] *Original Letters of Eminent Literary Men*, Camden Soc'y, pp. 231, 336.

licensed by bishops or archbishops. Edward Aldee, on Jan. 15, 1589, attempted to secure the copyright for the "first foure bookes of *Amadis de Gaule* To be translated into English," but could only get a provisional entry, "so that he first gett yt to be laufully and orderly alowed as tollerable to be printed" and show his authority at court. On April 10, 1592, the second, third, fourth and fifth books were entered to John Wolf with the memorandum "that the Lord bishop of London his hand is to euery of the said iiij French bookes seuerally for the alowance of the printinge thereof in English."

Whitgift in particular saw that pure literature could have a voice on public matters. It was during his control that the proclamation of 1 June, 1599 was made against the satires of Hall, Marston, and others, the epigrams of Davies and others, together with the command that "noe playes be printed excepte they bee allowed by suche as have aucthorytie" (*S. R.*,III,600). It may be remarked, in passing, that Fleay (*Stage*, 266) need not have been so surprised over Bullen's attributing some power over drama to the Bishop of London in connection with the suppression of the play *Barnavelt*. An interest of bishop or archbishop in the drama is by no means a "remarkable innovation," even if at the time of *Barnavelt* certain other officials usually had the spoken drama more directly under their control.

Like Whitgift, Richard Bancroft (1604-10), was severe in his oversight of printed books. A period of comparative moderation under George Abbott (1611-1633) was followed by the terrible restrictions of Laud and his co-workers (1633-1645), until Laud and the bishops fell together with the power of the High Commission.[13]

Ecclesiastical control of literature in England was in both aim and method very similar to that on the continent, the attitude and policy of the censors at any time being affected by the allegiance or non-allegiance of the ruler to the Church of Rome. The course of the censorship of the Church of Rome (particularly on the continent) has been traced by G. H. Putnam in *The Censorship of the Church of Rome*, which may be supplemented by the use of F. Reusch's *Index der verbotenen Bücher*.

[13] Commissions to archbishops of Canterbury for January 21, 1625, and December 17, 1633, illustrate the continuance of their powers over literature, (Rymer, XVII, 648; XIX, 487).

If one is inclined to consider the censorship of England peculiarly stringent, he may be interested in considering some facts contained in two monographs by G. F. Barwick: "Laws Regulating Printing and Publishing in France," (*Tr. of Bibl. Soc'y*. XIV (1916-17), 69-107); and "Laws Regulating Printing and Publishing in Spain," (*Tr. of Bibl. Soc'y*, IV, 48 ff)

In Spain a law of 1558 provided that a copy submitted to the Royal Council (a body of licensers) must have each page signed by one of its notaries, and all the *errata* entered at the end. Names of author, printer, and publisher must be published.

In France in the fifteenth century manuscripts had to be examined by the university authorities before being exposed for sale or before being put into print. This, it may be assumed, was not rigidly enforced. But the censorship tightened when, in 1515, the Lateran Council decreed that in every city books should be approved by the bishop or an ecclesisatical delegate or the inquisitor of the town. In 1521 the Theological Faculty became the licensers. And in 1539 the Crown regulated the printing trade of France. By 1566 it had become necessary to secure letters patent in order to get permission to print; also, to procure a certificate of the examiner and deposit a copy of the manuscript. The printers' copy must be signed by the examiners on every sheet. The same rule applied to reprints. In the latter part of the sixteenth century there was some relaxation of rigor, followed by a tightening again in 1624, when each page must be initialed by two censors.

It is clear that through the great crises of intellectual activity of the sixteenth century there was somewhat more freedom of expression of opinion in England than in France or Spain.

Further facts on European censorship will appear from a study of the history of the great fairs. As trade centres for book business, these were made use of by the archbishops. They furnished a means of regulating the handling of translations into the vernacular from Latin, Greek, and other foreign languages. The importation of such translations was forbidden by the Archbishop of Mainz unless passed by the censors of the University of Erfurt. The Burgomaster of Frankfort was forbidden to allow books to be sold at the Frankfort Fair unless they were properly licensed. In 1524 the Archbishop of Mainz definitely asserted his right to control the sale of books at this fair; and some sort of regulation continued to exist here until about 1648.[14]

In England, from the time of the prohibitory index of 1526, numerous proclamations, statutes, acts of Parliament, and decrees of Star Chamber (many of which are briefly summarized in the appendix to my *Authors' Rights and Copyright*) attempted to handle the problem of objectionable books,—*objectionable* being construed to mean chiefly heretical or seditious, against the fame or authority of the sovereign, the laws of the realm, the policy of officials, or tending to "corrupt manners and conversation" (as in 1582). The real aim of the censorship will perhaps be clearer from a study of the kinds of works affected and the nature of the objections raised to them.

The Court of High Commission, in carrying out its oversight of literature, worked in conjunction with the Court of Star Chamber, which had a general control of printing as a trade. Many offensive works were investigated by order of Star Chamber. For example, Sir Henry Herbert, assuming somewhat larger licensing powers than his original grant as Master of the Revels entitled him to, licensed Donne's *Paradoxes* for publication. As this work did not meet the approval of the authorities (usually fearful of satire and epigram), the King sent an order to the Master of the Revels through the Bishop of London to appear before Star Chamber and "give account why he warranted the work."[15] The two editions of 1633 are described by Edmund Gosse as "extremely odd-looking," as if a fragment were hastily printed.[16]

The experiences of Sparke, Burton, and Prynne (1633-37) illustrate the severity of Star Chamber punishments. For *Histriomastix* Prynne was fined £5000, pilloried, deprived of his ears, and imprisoned. The book was condemned by Lord Cottington, Chancellor of the Exchequer, to be burned by the hangman. But by 1637 Prynne was in trouble again, with J. Bastwick, over *Flagellum Pontificis et episcoporum Latinorum*.[17]

[14] See Beckmann, *History of Inventions*, I, 89.
[15] *S. P. Dom. Chas. I*, 1631–33, vol. CCXXV, art. 20.
[16] *Life of Donne*, I, 17.
[17] *S. P. Dom.*, 1636–37, vol. CCCLVII, articles 172–73; vol. CCCLXXI, art. 102; vol. CCCXIV, art. 35 (February 20, 1636); *Stowe MS* 159, art. 1; *Star Chamber Cases* (February 15, 1634).

Alexander Leighton was treated with even more severity when condemned by Star Chamber in 1638 for "An appeal to the Parliament or Sion's Plea against the Prelacie." This called the episcopacy anti-christian and charged the bishops with corrupting the king. Leighton was fined £10,000, and was publicly whipped and pilloried, besides having an ear cut off, a nostril slit, and a cheek branded "S.S." (sower of sedition). Such punishments represent not the norm, but the extreme of ferocity reached by the English censorship over the subject's right to utterance of his convictions.

Imprisonment and threats of imprisonment were common penalties for discussion of affairs of state. In 1567 Philip of Spain sent the Duke of Alva with a force of men to subdue the Netherlands, where there was rioting by Protestant mobs. The tribunal set up by Alva was known as the "Council of Blood" for punishment of treason and heresy. Refugees fled to Germany and to England. The oppression by Alva roused opposition among all classes. Though England later aided the Dutch in their struggle against the domination of Spain by sending men and money, the Mayor of London, Sir Roger Martyn, on October 15, 1568, wrote to William Cecil that he had committed a printer, John Aldee, to the Counter in the Poultry, together with the two Dutchmen who caused the printing of a book touching the Duke of Alva.[18] The title of the book promised an account of the horrible tyrannies, cruelties, etc. of the Duke of Alva and his council. The mayor's act in sending the printer to prison was not outside of his province, inasmuch as his general oversight of crafts presupposed an active co-operation with the Stationers' Company of London. The Privy Council made particular use of the Mayor in connection with the regulation of the drama, but it also employed him in connection with political and religious censorship of non-dramatic works.[19] For example, on September 27, 1579, J. Stubbs' "libel" referring to the proposed French marriage of Elizabeth, *A Discovery of the Gaping Gulf*, being reported to the Privy Council, the Lords ordered the mayor to "call before him the masters, governors,

---

[18] *S. P. Dom. Eliz.*, 1547–80, vol. XLVIII, art. 17.

[19] See *Acts of the Privy Council*, 1546, p. 409, for an order to search for heretical books from Flanders; and 1556–58, p. 346, for a search for Catholic books; and 1571–75, pp. 370, 389, for procedure against Anabaptists.

and wardens of the several companies, and in her Majesty's name command them to assemble in their several halls the members of their Company, and to have the proclamation openly read and published; and to charge all persons having copies of such books to bring in the same, to be delivered to the Lord Mayor with the names of the parties, etc."[20] There are in *Remembrancia* numerous examples of the mayor's activity in censorship. Imports and exports of suspicious works were sometimes examined by appointees of the mayor, through order of the Privy Council. The mayor even instituted searches about the city for persons engaged in translating "scandalous" works against the state.[21]

The treasurer also had powers of recall of seditious, treasonable, or otherwise offensive works. The exact foundation of his high authority I do not know, but assume it to have been a direct, though perhaps informal, grant from the Crown. This explanation would at least account for the Treasurer's activities in the reign of Elizabeth. William Cecil, Lord Burghley, Treasurer 1572–98 (and previously Secretary of State) was one of her most trusted and far-sighted advisers, intensely eager to guard the interests of state, and shrewd and effective in the carrying out of his policies. In July, 1573, the Bishop of London wrote Burghley to see to the calling in of the *Admonition to the Parliament* and to arrange to have the Lords of the Council "give authoritie to the Master of the Rolls, the Attorney Generall or some other" about a libel on himself.[22] The treasurer was the recipient of an apology from the Hebraist, Hugh Broughton, for a "slanderous and erroneous" work.[23] The Stationers' Registers show, too, that the Treasurer sometimes recalled works offensive to authority for other reasons, as for violation of copyright.

For the practical operation of the censorship, the Stationers' Company of London offered what was in many respects the most efficient machinery. Interested as the members were individually in the production and dissemination of books, their relations to city and state made it obligatory, as well as

[20] *Remembrancia*, I, 62.
[21] See, e.g., *Remembrancia*, I, 30 (1580); II, 450 (1582); II, 327 (1608).
[22] *Lans. MSS*, 17, art. 37.
[23] Strype, *Whitgift*, III, 360 ff.

politic, to lend aid in regulating. This they did, first of all, by endeavoring to check publication of unlicensed works. Provisional entries in the registers, jotted down in order to record the first claims made to copyright, often point out that works have not yet been properly allowed for publication. This method of making copyright depend upon authorization was a moderately effectual check upon all but the more determined printers of forbidden or suspicious books. An example of such a delay is the entry of Wither's *Motto*, 14 July, 1621, to Weaver, "provided that it be not printed until he bring further aucthority" (*S. R.*,IV,53). On 16 June, 1621 it was entered to John Marriott and John Grismond under the hands of Master Tavernor and Master Lownes, Warden, "to be printed as it is corrected by Master Tauernor."

The Stationers' Company frequently noted in the Registers the provisions attached by the Master of the Revels to a play when unsatisfactory for licensing in the form in which it was first submitted. Thus, the comedy *Holland's Leaguer*, entered 26 Jan., 1632, was entered with the note, "the reformacions to be strictly observed, may be printed not otherwise."

If offensive works slipped into publication in spite of licensers' and Stationers' precautions, the Stationers' Company had various means of recall and of punishment of offenders. Entries on the Registers could be cancelled by action of a court. We can not always assume censorship as a reason for cancellation, for trouble over copyright and other reasons may account for cases where the cause of action is not noted. A further means of control, though probably ineffectual, judging from its recurrence, was the fining of printers, publishers, and sellers of books. In 1601, twenty-eight stationers were fined by the Company for handling a reprint of the forbidden *Humours lettinge blood in the vayne* by Rowland; in 1603 many prominent members paid for handling *Basilicon Doron, or his majesties instructions to his Dearest sonne Henrie the prince*, a forbidden reprint of a work issued in a few copies abroad; and in the same year Valentine Sims was taxed for a ballad he printed which contained political allusions.

It is obvious that the Stationers' Company offered the best machinery for the recall of books to be burned or withheld from circulation. They made an approach to the enforcement of the regulation of Whitgift in regard to satires and epigrams; and they became at one time intensely active in re-inspecting ballad literature for offensive allusions and indecency after it had been allowed to go without careful oversight by the authorities.

The Registers of the Company are full of entries showing the close relationship with the courts of the archbishop and with other officials of church and state; and, while members in trouble with authorities were sometimes assisted financially because of their brotherhood in the craft, it is clear that the Company incurred a great deal of expense and went to a great deal of trouble in searches for unruly and offending members and meting out punishment to them. An example is the long and costly pursuit of Waldegrave at the time of the Marprelate controversy, and the ensuing destruction of his press and letters.[24] It must not, of course, be assumed that every printer or publisher who was temporarily suppressed by the Company was a thorough rogue. Stansby, for instance, who published the 1616 folio of Ben Jonson, was in pretty good repute; but his premises were temporarily nailed up by the Stationers for printing a seditious book.

AIMS AND DIRECTION OF CENSORSHIP

To a twentieth century reader the restrictions placed upon the utterances of subjects in the reigns of Elizabeth, James, and Charles seem inexcusably severe. They also seem, in individual cases, erratic. We should perhaps remember that it is easier for one to judge the probable effects of a work of the past than of the present. The authorities themselves were thoroughly convinced that harmony of religious and political beliefs was not only commendable but necessary to good government, and that the good order of the realm was more important than the individual's right to his views. It is difficult to understand such a position worked out into its necessary consequences. But it is possible to appreciate some of the special reasons for nervousness over the publication of upsetting ideas. Secret intrigues flourished, especially from 1580 to 1590 and early in the reign of James, as well as after his troubles with Parliament. The trial

---

[24] *S.R.*, I, 528, 556, *et passim*; and Ames, *Typ. Antiq.*, (Herbert), II, 1145.

of Mary, Queen of Scots, the conspiracy of Babington, the secretly printed Jesuit pamphlets, the menacing ambition of Philip II of Spain, native craftsmen's jealousies of foreigners, the Essex affair, the Gunpowder Plot—these are only a few of the troubles that kept the ear of authority awake for murmurs of any innovations of doctrine likely to stir public sentiment. Quantities of minor literature, such as satires, ballads, pamphlets, and tracts were rapidly produced and circulated, and many of them contained spirited discussion of affairs of the day. Attractive copy which promised to sell well was refused with difficulty by the keenly competing commercial printer and bookseller who had by this time replaced the old responsible scholar-printer or publisher. The printing press had now become a formidable force in molding public opinion, and no way had been found of controlling that force without complete suppression of what was thought to be too dangerous.

The direction and the effectiveness of the censorship can be best appreciated by the use of examples drawn from various fields of thought. Religious works were early felt to be those requiring unusually careful oversight.

Censorship of Particular Kinds of Books
Religious Works

The religious censorship under Henry VIII was largely directed against such works as the revised translation of Tyndale's New Testament.[25] Though Wolsey, regarding heresy as error rather than crime, was averse from enforcing the papal bull against Luther's works, action was taken by the King against the harboring and selling of them. R. Grafton had to appear before the Council and was committed to the porter's ward for having in his possession a copy of Melanchthon's *Epistles*. He was later sent to the Fleet.[26] It was only by allowing the multilation of his work by the censors that John Knox, the leader of the Scotch Reformation, could get an English audience.

Mary, in her endeavor to make Catholicism triumphant, threatened execution by martial law of anyone who owned

---

[25] See the proclamation of 1538 and the Act for Advancement of True Religion, 1542–43.

[26] H. Nicolas, *Proceedings and Ordinances of the Privy Council*, vii.

CENSORSHIP OF PARTICULAR KINDS OF BOOKS 73

heretical books. An example of the censorship under Philip and Mary is the search of the houses of two printers, John Kingston and Thomas Marsh, with the command for "all suche bookes corruptly sett forthe under the name of the Busshopp of Lyncolne, as all others as shall impugne the Catholyck Faithe, to be seased and sent hither." The printers also were to appear before the Privy Council.[27]

It might, at first thought, be supposed that, when Elizabeth set herself to accomplish the dominance of Protestantism in England, there would be a simple reversal of the direction of religious censorship. Jesuit and Catholic historians delight in picturing the severity of her narrow policy against the Catholics.[28] As a matter of fact, Elizabeth was interested in the consideration of a great variety of religious sects and denominations. This split the direction of religious censorship. In 1575 Elizabeth approved an act against the Anabaptists, Puritans, Brownists, and Catholics.

The opposition to the Anabaptists may be illustrated by the order in 1575 that all books on the doctrine of the "Family of Love" founded by David George, a Dutch Anabaptist, and continued by Henry Nicolae of Münster, be burned and their owners punished.

The Brownists were attacked by a special proclamation of 30 June, 1583, against the books of Robert Browne and Richard Harrison (as being seditious and schismatical).[29]

The very general anti-Catholic movement may be illustrated by a case noted in a letter sent by the Mayor to the Bishop of London 10 June, 1580, concerning a printed pamphlet, *"Truth oppressed and driven into corners,* by a self-exiled Papist, John Newman." The Mayor proposed to refer the matter to the Queen's Commissioners for Ecclesiastical Causes.[30]

Many of the offenders were brought before the authorities and punished. Cartwright, the Puritan divine, was brought before the High Commission for his preachings and his book in 1590. His *Confutation of the Rhemish Testament* was kept out of print

---

[27] *Acts of P. C.*, 1556–58, p. 346.
[28] Strype and a few earlier historians credit Elizabeth with a Catholic bias, but it is hard to see it.
[29] *S.R.*, I, 502; Steele, Proclamation no. 770.
[30] *Remembrancia*, I, 98.

for years. Udall and Penry were condemned to die for their seditious books (Strype, *Whitgift*, p. 37). William Carter, on January 10, 1584, was hanged, bowelled, and quartered for printing a seditious book, "a treatise of schisme" (Stow, *Annals*, (ed. 1600), 1176-7). Barrow and Greenwood were condemned and executed.

The secret printing of the Martin Marprelate tracts complicated the search, but it was conducted with thoroughness, and all involved were punished. "A knight of the County of Northumberland was fined in a great summe in the Starre Chamber because hee permitted a seditious book called Martin Marprelate to be printed in his house" (32 Eliz.).[31]

The long-continued prosecution of Waldegrave was largely due to his handling of Puritan books, though he was not particularly law-abiding in his other practices. In 1584 a warrant of the High Commissioners was sent to the wardens of the Stationers' Company to seize Waldegrave and his workmen, presses, and all unlicensed books. He was then engaged on *A brief declaration concerning. . . .reformation of the Church of England*, and a dialogue concerning the "strife of our church," a Puritan tract. Six weeks in prison in 1584, and twenty weeks in 1585 formed a part of his penalty. Again, in 1588 his press was seized for printing Udall's *The State of the Church of England*. The books were ordered burned, but many of the types were carried away by Waldegrave, and the prosecution therefore continued through 1588-1590.[32]

The Ecclesiastical Commission continued its activities in the reigns of James and Charles. On April 20, 1629 charges were brought against five stationers at once for handling works not licensed by the Archbishop of Canterbury or the Bishop of London according to the Star Chamber decree of 1586. Nathaniel Butter was in trouble over the printing of Henry Burton's *The Reconciler*; Michael Sparkes, for Burton's *Babel no Bethel*; William Jones, for Thomas Spencer's *Musquil Unmasked*; and Augustine Matthews and Sparke, together, for William Prynne's *Antithesis of the Church of England*.[33]

[31] *Star Chamber Cases*, L. (for John Grove, 1630), p. 29.
[32] *Works of T. Nashe*, ed. McKerrow, 184–190.
[33] *S. P. Dom. Chas. I*, 1628–29, vol. CXLIV, art. 17.

King James set himself up as an authority on theological matters. While his relations with the English church are less stormy than those with the Scottish, it is clear that he continued to regard himself as a censor of sermons, with a full right to contradict and suppress what displeased him. The estate of bishops was a bone of contention in England, as it had been in Scotland, James having in the opinion of many in both countries made too near approaches to joining hands with papistry. At the end of 1606 a minister in London was "reprimanded for some freedoms which he had taken from the pulpit with the estate of bishops. Having afterwards given out some copies of his sermon, he was publicly whipped, made to stand four hours in the pillory, and had one of his ears cut off. Two days after he was again brought out, stood four hours in the pillory, lost his remaining ear, and was condemned to perpetual banishment."[34]

Parliament occasionally took a hand in the censoring of sermons in the reign of Charles. Two of Roger Manwaring's published sermons on Religion and Allegiance were called in by Parliament June 24, 1628.[35]

The extremities of religious persecution under Archbishop Laud have been mentioned in connection with the activities of Star Chamber. They are so well known to the student of history as to need little emphasis. It is, after all, only by a stretch of the term that we can include such methods as disemboweling, slitting of nostrils, slicing off of ears, and branding of cheeks as "censorship of religious opinion."

Seditious Works

The treatment of writers who expressed seditious sentiments or who criticized current policies of the ruler was, in the reign of Elizabeth, very similar to that of heretics. Stubbes' *Gaping Gulf* criticized the French marriage projected for the Queen. A proclamation of Privy Council September 27, 1579, commanded that every copy of the "lewd seditious book dissuading hir Majesty from marriage with the Duke of Anjou" be destroyed before a public officer. Stubbes, besides being im-

---

[34] *Ambassades de M. de la Boderie*, II, 489; quoted by Thomas M'Crie, *Life of Andrew Melville*, p. 272.
[35] Rymer, *Foedera* . . . , XVIII, 1024.

prisoned, had his right hand struck off,[36] a cruelty which greatly shocked the French as well as the English. In 1594 a treatise on the succession by Parsons, advocating the claims of the Infanta, was suppressed.[37]

Books continued to be inspected through the sixteenth and seventeenth centuries for every sort of reflection upon royal personages. At some time after 1632 there came up before Star Chamber a case of Whitacres, a bookseller, "for importing and selling a French book Le Prince, wherein is some scandall conteyned against Queen Elizabeth." The Archbishop remarked: "This Basset [Balzac] the author is a deepe flatterer, a most malatious, hungry fellow. . . . It is an impudent thinge that such things should be suffered in bookes. Kingdomes cannot long stand in peace if they should." The guilty bookseller was fined 100 marks and the books were ordered to be called in and publicly burned.[38]

Histories and News Sheets

Historical works were, naturally, examined with especial care because of the possibility of their containing dangerous (i.e., unorthodox) opinion on affairs of church or state, and also because they might contain matter offensive to other nations. The Irish passages in Holinshed's *History of England* were in 1577 ordered cancelled and replaced.[39] Lewes de Mayerne Turquet's *The Generall History of Spayne* was entered to Adam Islip on the *Stationers' Registers* (November 19, 1608) under the hands of Master Etkins and the wardens, only on condition that "every sheete is to be by Master Etkins revised and by aucthority allowed."

The exact amount of censorship to which Camden's histories were subjected has not, so far as I know, been determined. Some biographers have thought that he sent the French historian De Thou materials which he did not dare publish in England. This conjecture has been made to account for

---

[36] Strype, *Annals*, II, 2, 232; Steele, Procl. no. 740. For an account of Stubbes' gallant behavior on that occasion, see Camden, *Annals of Queen Elizabeth*, an. 1581.

[37] See T. G. Law, *Essays and Reviews* (1904), p. 140.

[38] *Cases in Star Chamber* (Camden Society), pp. 305–06, 321.

[39] Later (November 3, 1590) Elizabeth wished Burghley's secretary, Windebank, to call in the Chronicle of Holinshed because it was "fondly set out."

marked differences in their treatment of Scottish affairs, on which they are known to have corresponded to some extent. It is certain that, for some reason, Camden sent part of the manuscript of his *Elizabeth*, from 1583 to 1587, to De Thou in advance; for Cotton MS Faustina F. x.f 254 has a memorandum by Camden:

The copye of this story of Queen Elizabeth from 1583 to 1587, not transcribed for myself as yett, but sent into France to Thuanus.

There may possibly be a hint of trouble over the contents of his histories in his expressed wish (Epistle 287) that no English translation of the second part of the Annals be published in his life, "knowing how unjust carpers the unlearned readers are."

Selden's work on the Court of High Commission (1618) was suppressed because it was said to have weakened the claim of divine right in the discussion of tithes.[40]

Raleigh's *History of the World*, published in 1614, was well received by many, but did not find favor with King James, who thought Raleigh should not speak slightingly of Henry VIII in his preface, and who is thought to have seen his own features in Raleigh's portrayal of Ninias, the effeminate successor to Queen Semiramis. John Chamberlain wrote to Sir Dudley Carleton, on January 5, 1614: "Sir Walter Raleigh's book is called in by the king's commandment for divers exceptions, but especially for being too saucy in censuring princes."[41] The Archbishop of Canterbury on December 22, 1614, at the King's request, wrote to the Stationers' Company to call in and suppress "all copies of the work lately published by Sir Walter Raleigh," (*S.R.*, V, p. lxxvii). There were two issues that year, one of them on March 29, according to Camden's *Annales*. No extant copy has a title-page. Hardy booksellers evidently dared to circulate the work without title or name of author. Raleigh's *Prerogative of Parliaments*, written 1615 and printed 1628, was perhaps also forbidden; but it is not the book suppressed thus in 1614, as it begins with matter of the spring of 1615.[42]

[40] J. S. Burn, *Court of High Commission*, p. 37.
[41] *Court and Times of James I*, I, 291.
[42] See *Notes and Queries*, 8 ser., V, 441–42. Cf. T. N. Brushfield, *Bibliography of Sir Walter Raleigh*, p. 93, where three issues of 1614 and one of 1617 lack title-pages.

There were some attempts in the reign of Elizabeth to comment upon current or recent events in such a way as to reflect discredit upon officials of one kind or another. The military profession came in for their share of criticism, particularly in connection with their behavior in the Low Countries. A very outspoken condemnation is that of Sir John Smith, in his *Discourse on the Forms and Effects of Divers Sorts of Weapons*, 1590. In the Proeme which he addresses to the nobility, he makes detailed complaints of the behavior of English officers abroad, and of the whole military policy in the Low Countries. The charges are various: that there was great waste of lives of soldiers; that officers gratified private malice by sending those they disliked on dangerous exploits; that they did this on a large scale just after pay-day in order to misappropriate their pay; that they treated the sick as dead, to get their pay; that, while the men were engaged in daring exploits, officers banqueted and caroused; that they allowed their men to loot their friends the "Boores"; that captains rented their insignia to lieutenants; that they used criminally ignorant methods of military assault, wrong weapons, and insufficient defensive armor; that the men were unduly exposed, that their way of living was unhygienic; that they were cheated of pay and paid in bread and cheese as if they were "naturall fooles or children"; and that thousands of lives of Englishmen were wasted in the Low Countries. In conclusion it was admitted that, after the Earl of Leicester went over at the instance of the nobility, the Queen had reformed many of the disorders.

A letter of Sir Thomas Heneage to the Treasurer, Burghley, May 14, 1590, stated that Elizabeth favored the suppression of the book on the ground that it was printed without privilege and might "breed question and quarrel."[43] Sir John Smith wrote a protest to Burghley (*Lans. MS* 64, art. 45) against his immediate suppression of the work, declaring that all he said was true and the whole realm felt with him. He insisted that no individual had been attacked, unless his own conscience were his accuser; and that other works more outspoken (such as Roger Williams' *A briefe discourse of Warre*, 1590) had been allowed. He wrote also a protest to the Queen. Both were

[43] *Original Letters of Eminent Literary Men* (Camden Soc'y, 1843), 48–65, contains a full account of the affair.

unavailing,—perhaps because, being of a choleric disposition, he allowed his anger against Burghley full vent in public talks with soldiers a little later, while under the influence of what he describes as a surfeit of food, which he endeavored to overcome by a surfeit of liquor. He was imprisoned for these treasonable utterances arising out of the censorship of his work.

An act of authority which aroused much interest in its own day was the suppression of a severe arraignment of Russia by Dr. Giles Fletcher, ambassador from Queen Elizabeth to Czar Fedor Ivanovitch, 1588. On his return from the embassy he published *The Russe Commonwealth*, 1591, picturing the state of Russia at the end of the reign of Ivan Vasilievitch, "the Terrible," and during the first few years of the following reign when the brother-in-law of the Emperor's son and successor was scheming for the headship. Fletcher's dedicatory letter to Elizabeth contrasts the lawlessness of Russia with the happy state of England.

The first complaint was made by the Muscovy traders to Burghley. They stated the case against Fletcher as frankly as he stated it against Russia:

The companie of merchauntes trading to Muskovia....doe greatelie feare that a booke latelie sett out by Mr. Doctor Fletcher, dedicated to her Majestie, intituled "the Russe Commonwealth" will turne the Companie to some great displeasure with the Russe Emperour, and endaunger both their people and goodes nowe remayninge there, except some good order be taken by your lordships honorable consideration for the callinge in of all the bookes that are printed, and some course holden therein signifyinge her Majesties dislike of the publishinge of the same. In which booke (besides the discowrse of the description of the countrie), the militarie government and forces thereof, the Emperours revenue and howe yt ryseth (which is offensive to the Russe that anie man should looke into), the person of the Emperour, his father, his brother, and the Lord Boris Federovich the Protector, and generallie the nature of the people are towched in soe hard tearmes as that, the Companie doupt the revenge therof will light on their people and goodes remayning in Russia, and utterly overthrow the trade forever.[44]

Nashe seems to be satirizing this motive for the suppressing of the comments on Russian affairs where he says, in his *Lenten*

[44] *Lans. MSS*, CXII, art. 39; printed in *The Russe Commonwealth*, (ed. Hakluyt Soc'y), appx. 14.

Stuffe,⁴⁵ that reference to a *rush*, interpreted as referring to the Emperor of Russia, "will utterly mar the trafficke into that country" unless the work is called in and suppressed.

The Muscovy Company, in their complaint, furnish a carefully prepared citation of objectionable passages, among which are: references to "a strange face of a tirannycall state," and to "intolerable exactions" of the Emperor; uncomplimentary physical descriptions of the Emperor as "meane of stature, low, grosse, sallowe . . . . enclyninge to dropsey . . . . hawcked-nosed," unsteady of gait, simple, slow-witted; the picturing of the government as "plain tyrannical," as favoring the nobles and unfair to the common people, and using no laws but the spoken law, the pleasure of prince and magistrates, as misusing the treasury and practicing strange extortions; the presenting of Russian society as intemperate, given to whoredom, adultery, and uncleanness; the portraying of the common people as oppressed and enslaved and longing for foreign invasion; the sketching of the young brother of the Emperor (six years old) as cruel and bloodthirsty like his father, and Boris Federovich as plotting against this young successor for the throne, and the Russian people in general as believing no one and unfit themselves to be believed.

In an elaborate defense to Burghley,⁴⁶ Fletcher gave his reasons for publishing the criticisms of Russia. Reduced to lowest terms, they were: the unfavorable reception given him as ambassador, and the insults to England as represented by him. It is clear that there was some personal animus. How far that affected his statements of fact is a question. It certainly colored his interpretations. One of Fletcher's missions was to get the English merchants proper protection; and in this he declares he had a measure of success. It would be interesting to know whether his companion, Sir Jerome Horsey, who for seventeen years traveled in Russia and dedicated his account of his experiences to Walsingham, met with any obstacle which prevented their publication. So far as is known, they were not printed until modern times. In Raleigh's works is listed "Answers to matters objected against Mr. Horsey by the Emperor's Counsel of Russland." Horsey's works on Danish,

---

⁴⁵ *Works*, (ed. McKerrow), III, 213.
⁴⁶ *Original Letters of Eminent Literary Men* (Camden Society), 76–85.

Polish, and German relations are non-extant, though references to them rather suggest that they were in print.

The attitude of authorities toward treatment of fresh news may very well, I believe, be largely responsible for the lagging development of the news sheet. We have few cases for study which furnish records of trouble, but such as there are show strictness of government censorship. Nathaniel Butter, one of the most persistent and enterprising of publishers of news, met with difficulties at times. On June 2, 1609 he had entered *Newes from the sea of piracies by the Turkes* "aucthorised to be printed by Master R. Etkins." A further entry reads "12 June 1609. And yet he is forbidden to prynt it in court this day." The reason is not given. Foreign news sheets were printed from time to time in the reigns of James I and Charles I, but not without strict supervision. There are several letters in *The Court and Times of Charles I* concerning news letters and "corrantoes." One from Sir George Gresley to Sir Thomas Puckering (II, 225–26) says: "I hoped to have sent you this week a very true relation which is lately come over of the King of Sweden's death and battle. But Butter having got it to his hands, and thinking to have printed it, it is there stopped from publishing it in print or copying." In times of war, reports unfavorable to certain nations were, at least temporarily, suppressed—whether because of sensationalism or for diplomatic caution we can now only guess. An instance occurred in 1632, as shown by a letter of Mr. Pory to Lord Brooke:

Yesterday was sennight, my lord keeper, my lord privy seal, my Lord of Arundel, my Lord of Kelly, my Lord Wimbledon, my Lord of London, my Lord Cottington, and Secretary Windebanke, signed an order at the council-board in these words: "Upon consideration had at the board of the great abuse in the printing and publishing of the ordinary Gazettes and pamphlets of news from foreign parts: and upon signification of his majesty's express pleasure and command for the present suppressing of the same, it was thought fit and hereby ordered, that all printing and publishing of the same be accordingly suppressed and inhibited. And that as well Nathaniel Butter and Nicholas Bourne, booksellers, (under whose name the said Gazettes have been usually published), as all other stationers, printers, and booksellers, presume not from henceforth to print, publish, or sell any of the said pamphlets, &c., as they will answer the contrary at their perils."

They say the occasion of this order was the importunity of the Spanish and archduchess's agents, who were vexed at the soul to see so many losses and crosses, so many dishonours and disasters, betide the House of Austria, as well in the Upper as in the Lower Germany; but this smothering of the Currantos is but a palliation, not a cure, of their wounds. They will burst out again one of these days.

A second letter of Mr. Pory's, this time to Sir Thomas Lucy, continued the same matter:

Since my last, Nathaniel Butter told me that a gentleman of his acquaintance having dined this day sennight in company of Mr. Taylor, the archduchess's agent, and asked him the reason of calling in the Currantos, he answered the news was so ill, as the lords would not have it known. And besides, he told me that he would (if he dare be so good as his word) complain to their lordships how much Taylor had abused them in his answer. Besides he is getting to be translated divers Antwerp Currantos, to show their lordships how they lie upon us and our friends, and we in the meantime must be muzzled and our mouths stopped. But yesternight I met him at Whitehall, after he had been in Mr. Secretary Coke's chamber; and he told me he hoped ere long his Currantos would be revived.

A letter of Mr. Pory's, dated December 13, 1632, says that "next week, Currantos shall be permitted to be published; but some men say, now that incomparable king is dead, they will buy no more."[47]

Political Theory

The sovereign's jealousy of independent opinion, even of distinguished thinkers, upon matters touching the constitution and relations between king and subject appears in a proclamation of James I (Steele, Procl. no. 1092) dated March 25, 1610, suppressing *The Interpreter*, by Dr. John Cowell, Regius Professor of Civil Law at Cambridge, 1607 (B.M. 507, d.14) because it "pried into the deepest mysteries of Kings," "mistook the true state of Parliament," and spoke "unreverently" of the common law. Censors of such books would now be appointed.

Scientific and Technical Works

Scientific texts did not escape the censor. It was only natural that works popularly supposed to deal with magic should be

[47] *Original Letters....*, 188 and 210.

treated with somewhat the same suspicion that they met in medieval days. The same is true of such technical works as taught secret writing. It is true that stenography textbooks flourished, pretending to teach secret writing; but it was rather obvious that the secret was an open secret for anyone with a little patience. On the other hand, one who handled ciphers was regarded with suspicion, as may be seen from the difficulties over the *Steganographia* of Trithemius.

Aside, however, from the classes of works which suggested secrecy or magic, the scientific and technical works were perhaps the freest from interference by public censors.

Satire and Epigram

The censor took a keen interest in personal attacks, whether humorous or malignant—one is tempted to say, because of a doubt whether the works were humorous or malignant. Not only in drama, where, in the periods of realistic comedy, there was a strong tendency to use real models, but also in other forms of literature we find examples of care to prevent personal criticism or cartooning in print. Richard Banks had the courage to print "invectives" against Thomas Smith, Clerk of the Queen's Council; but the Privy Council promptly summoned him before them.[48] The Privy Council also took action against Gascoigne's *Ferdinando Jeronymo*, among "slanderous pasquils against divers persons of great calling."[49]

In the last decade of the sixteenth century there was a definite stimulus to satirical writing, and just as definite a determination on the part of authorities, particulary Bishop Bancroft, of London, and Archbishop Whitgift, to keep it down. The most significant act was the proclamation which they secured against the satires of Hall, Marston, Guilpin, and others, the epigrams of Davies, the elegies of Marlowe and the pamphlets of Harvey and Nashe. It was a general repressive measure aimed at immorality, as well as at invectives. Marlowe's Ovid and two other works were declared immoral. Plays were forbidden to be printed unless allowed by the authorities. In executing this order, the Stationers collected and burned or

[48] *Proceedings . . . . of the Privy Council*, VII, 103–05.
[49] On the nasty libels involved, see F. G. Fleay, "Historical Allusions in Sundry English Poets," *Tr. of the Royal Historical Society*, I, 128 ff.

suppressed many satires. Marston's *The Scourge of Villainy*, three books of satires entered to James Roberts the year before, and *The Metamorphosis of Pygmalion's Image* (entered 1598) were burned. Hall's *Satires, Caltha Poetarum*, and *Willobie's "Adviso"* were "stayed." Harvey and Nashe were forbidden the continuance of their angry and contemptuous bickerings.[50] One may guess, however, that the opposition to works suppressed on this occasion had died down by 1613; for an entry of October 11, 1613, on the Registers, by consent of the Stationers' Court, turned over *The Metamorphosis of Pygmalion's Image* from its former owner (who had been obliged to submit to its being *burned*) to Richard Hawkins.

Even an offence against prominent men of the court seems occasionally to have been ignored a few years later. Sir John Harington's *Metamorphosis of Ajax* (1596), satirizing courtiers, brought its author into disfavor with Queen Elizabeth for a time only. Robert Markham wrote to Harington in 1598-99:

Your book is almost forgiven, and I may say forgotten; but not for its lacke of wit or satyr. Those whome you feared moste are now bosoming themselves in the Quene's grace; and tho' her Highnesse signified displeasure in outwarde sorte, yet did she like the marrowe of your booke. Your great enemye, Sir James, did once mention the Star-Chamber, but your good esteeme in better mindes outdid his endeavours, and all is silente again. The Queen is minded to take you to her favour, but she sweareth that she believes you will make epigrams and write *misacmos* again on her and all the courte. . . . . She did conceive much disquiet on being tolde you had aimed a shafte at Leicester. I wishe you knew the author of that ill deed; I would not be in his best jerkin for a thousand markes. . . . . I hear you are to go to Ireland with the Lieutenant Essex.[51]

There is, I believe, no evidence that in Harington's case an expedition to Ireland was intended to be a sort of banishment.

The Ballad

Even so minor a form of literature as the ballad was, perhaps because of its popularity, censored at times as a vehicle for satirical or humorous comment on affairs of the day. Political allusions in ballads were objected to. Valentine Sims was

[50] On this repressive measure, see *Stationers' Registers*, III, 677-78.
[51] Harington, *Nugae antiquae* (ed. Park), I, 239-240.

ordered to pay a fine and forfeit to Stationers' Hall (December 5, 1603) for "The Welshbate and all ballads printed of traitors lately arraigned." Religious allusions in ballads were regarded even more seriously. One was made a Star Chamber matter. Henry Goskin, at some date after 1632, was brought before the Star Chamber for the reprinting of an old ballad which "abused all the histories of the Bible." Though it was decided, after all, not worth a Star Chamber judgment, the incident furnishes a bit of news on the custom of having a man of religion inspect ballads before publication: "There was a parish clarke chosen to view all the balletts before they were printed; but he refuseth to doe it, let it be ordered that he shall undertake it by comaundment from this Court. This is not worth the sentence of the Court." The printer was sent to Bridewell, although he had merely reprinted a ballad that "was printed before he was born."[52]

Standards of Propriety

In considering the aims of early censors of literature, one who is accustomed to modern practices wonders how often, if ever, the censors of this earlier day were animated by concern for offense against public standards of morality or of taste. It may safely be said that comparatively few native English works were then barred for indecency alone. The nature of works heavily censored on other grounds is evidence enough for that; for plenty of impropriety, recognizable as such in any age, was let go. However, some censors did object to extreme indecency, the definition of indecency being individual, not to say whimsical. It should not be concluded without examination that books scored as "lewd and offensive" were obscene or indecent; for *lewd* might signify foolish, worthless, trivial, false, mistaken, or merely altogether secular. Not all the "lewd and unlicensed" books for which the Stationers' Company exacted fines were indecent, certainly. The lack of a license was sufficient cause of a fine. There are, however, some clear cases where the Stationers' Company assisted in checking indecencies of minor

[52] *Cases in the Court of Star Chamber* (Camden Soc'y), 314. A seditious song copied in a letter caused imprisonment of one man in 1600 (*Acts of Privy Council*, 1600, p. 138). The printer of a ballad by Thomas Deloney on the dearth of corn, quoting Burghley and making Elizabeth a character, was apprehended by the Mayor of London July 25, 1596, (Wright, *Q. Elizabeth* . . . , II 462-63).

literature by refusing a license or requiring revision. An example is the conditional entry to Thomas Gosson (March 7, 1591) of "a ballad of a younge man that went a wooying. . . . Abell Jeffes to be his printer hereof Provyded Alwayes that before the publishinge hereof the undecentnes be reformed." Evidently the condition was not satisfactorily removed, for a marginal entry (S.R., II, 576) runs: "Cancelled out of the book for the undecentnes of it in Diverse verses." Jeffes had a reputation for printing objectionable literature. An entry on the registers for December 3, 1595 (S.R., II, 825) states that "Abell Jeffes hath disorderly printed a lewde booke called The most strange prophecie of Dr. Ciprianus, &c. and other lewde ballads and things very offensive, yt is therefore ordered . . . . that his presses and letters and other printing stuffs which were seized and brought to the Hall for the said offenses, viz. One presse, xii paire of cases, & certen fourmes of letters shall be defaced and made unserviceable for printinge." A similar example to Jeffes's ballad entry is an order on the registers for June 25, 1600, that Edward Aldee and William White be fined 5s. apiece for a "disorderly ballad" of the wife of Bath, and Edward White, the warden, who sold this ballad, be fined 10 s. All copies of the ballad must be recalled and burned (S.R., II, 831).

Censors' objections which may have been based upon the proprieties served to keep out of English circulation for a time certain famous masterpieces, such as, for example, the "Decameron of Master John Boccace," which was at first licensed to William Jaggard by the secretary of the Bishop of London, but later had its license revoked (March 22, 1620) by the Archbishop of Canterbury. The same motive may have caused the cancellation (April 8, 1628) of an entry to Stansby of "A booke called Ovids Metamorphosis XV broken in English verse by George Sanders" (originally entered May 7, 1626). Ovid had been objected to by church authorities at an earlier date. Quarto[2] of Gascoigne's *Posies* (1575) shows cutting of passages offensive in Q[1].

As to rigidity of standards of decency, the situation was in England no more difficult for the writer and publisher than it was on the Continent. *Don Quixote* was allowed in some countries to pass with one sentence corrected; but the Lisbon index of 1624 required the cancellation of several paragraphs. And when we come to the eighteenth century, we find such books as these to be objectionable reading: La Fontaine's *Nouvelles*; Swift's *Tale of a Tub*, Richardson's *Pamela*, and Defoe's *Robinson Crusoe*, the last of which, at least, is nowadays regarded as reasonably safe.[53] A study of Reusch's *Index der verbotenen Bücher* will provide further instances.

Efficiency of Censorship

Before turning to the special problems of dramatic censorship, it may be well to consider the degree of effectiveness of the methods applied in suppression of doctrinal works and works of literature in general.

The licenser always had it in his power to delay publication indefinitely. Such procedure is occasionally complained of. In *Martin Marprelate* (p. 34) occurs a satirical comment on a catechism made by Mr. Davison and printed by Waldegrave. "He went to Canterbury to have it licensed, his grace committed it to doctor neuer-be-good [Wood] he read it over in half a yere; the booke is a great one, of two sheets of paper." A similar complaint is made by Philip Stubbes in the *Motive to Good Works*, 1593 (quoted in the preface to *The Anatomy of Abuses*, New Shakespeare Soc'y, p. 69).

Many works have doubtless perished because of the censorship. Many were indefinitely postponed or forced to appear irregularly. Cartwright's *Confutation of the Rhemish Testament* was kept from the press for thirty-five years (*S.R.*, IV, 27–28). And Foxe's *Acts and Monuments* could not be licensed at all in England, but had to be printed at Geneva and Basel. If the licenser refused to allow publication of a work and burned the first copy, there was no recourse but secret or foreign printing and underhand circulation. Herbert, as licenser of dramas, had a habit of burning particularly offensive plays—first making sure of his fee for the trouble of reading them.

If the objectionable nature of a work were not discovered until after publication, it was difficult indeed to collect and destroy all copies. This was, however, frequently undertaken. Often the printer or bookseller was first apprehended, and the author

[53] It *seems* so. One reads of the fining of an American publisher in 1922 for sending *Rabelais* by express.

then sought for, and the books ordered to be returned by all owners. For instance, a proclamation of May 14, 1637, announced that *An Introduction to a Devout Life* printed by Nicholas Oakes (who had already been apprehended) had been "falsified by translator and stationer after censure," (Rymer, XX, 144). The translator was now being sought; and the copies must be brought in to be destroyed.

In addition to the general proclamation, there was the possibility of recall through the Stationers' Company. An example of this rather common method is Michael Drayton's *The Harmony of the Church*, regularly licensed and published in 1591, but suppressed in the same year. Its author was obliged to apologize for his metrical version of the Psalms.[54] The Stationers' Registers show a note in the accounts for 1591:

Whereas all the seized Bookes mentioned in the last accompte before this were sould this yere to Mr. Byshop. Be it remembered that fortye of them, being Harmonies of the Churche rated at ii s le peece, were had from him by warrante of my lordes grace of Canterburie, and remayne at Lambethe with Mr. Doctor Cosen.

Cosen was one of the official licensers arranged for by Whitgift.

It would not be surprising if, because of the Stationers' thrifty habit of accumulating books confiscated for violation of copyright or patents, or for other reasons than censorship, and selling them, there would be some unintentional slips of copies that were intended to be permanently suppressed through the Stationers. And, as books once considered objectionable were sometimes found inoffensive a short time after, it is no wonder that the copies of many had a miraculous preservation, even if they did fall into the hands of the company.

From the diligent scurrying after satires in 1599 and the absoluteness of the prohibition, one would expect a serious shortage of that type of literature for some years to come. We find that, while Hall's *Virgidemiarum*, entered in 1597, was ordered suppressed, it now exists as printed by R. Dexter, the original owner, at the Brazen Serpent in 1599 (the year of the suppression of all satires), and in three books as printed by John Harrison for Robert Dexter in 1602. Nor must it be concluded that it was only the poorest or most disorderly printers who

[54] Burn, *Court of High Commission* (1865), p. 37.

sometimes held out against suppression. Twenty-eight booksellers, many of them prominent men, were fined for handling Rowlands' *Letting of Humour's Blood in the Head Vein* (1600) secretly reprinted without date as *Humour's Ordinary*.[55]

There were publishers and booksellers courageous enough to handle books condemned by both church and state. The Puritan printers and others played hide-and-seek with the authorities. Thomas Woodcock renewed the sale of a condemned book, *An Admonition to the Parliament*, which was said to have "depraved the Book of Common Prayer." Bishop Aylmer had him committed to Newgate in 1578.[56] Raleigh's *History of the World*, after being condemned by James, continued to circulate, but without a title-page. The persistency of these daring publishers is partly responsible for the survival of so much of the work once considered reprehensible. The eagerness of readers for condemned books was both the temptation and the justification of the booksellers.[57]

There are frequent references to the expectation of picking up a copy of a work suppressed. For example, Calvert wrote to Winwood, March 28, 1605:

> There is a Book lately published, but yet not to be had, touching the late Peace, wherein the Author, without Reservation or Respect, discovers the whole Intention, nameth the Complotters, and sheweth the Reasons why it was concluded. I will no sooner see one of them then I will take care to send it.[58]

The reading public helped the evasion of censorship considerably by failure to return all copies of forbidden works; they helped the continuance of forbidden books by buying and assisting in the circulation. There are many contemporary references to the quick and easy sale of forbidden books, which was founded on a permanent and well-nigh universal human trait—curiosity. The treasuring of the complete and uncensored

---

[55] *Rowland's Works*, ed. Rimbault, Percy Soc'y, IX, intr.; cf. S. R., II, 832.
[56] Strype, *Life of Aylmer*, 30.
[57] ~~Crites~~ remarks, in *The Dutch Courtezan* (III, 1, 44), "Those books that are call'd in are most in sale and request."
[58] Ralph Winwood, *Memorials*, II, 54.

version may be illustrated by a note in a work by Thomas Aylsworth:

> The mynes
> Of richest India shall not buy from me
> That booke one houre wherein I studye thee,
> A booke, wherin mens lives so taxed bin,
> That all men laboured death to call it in.
> What now as licens'd is dispers'd about,
> Is no true copy, or the best left out.[59]

Some books prohibited from publication got an effective private circulation. Thomas Lodge, in the epistle to *An Alarum against Usurers*, 1584, says:

About three yeres ago one Stephen Gosson published a booke, intituled, *The Schoole of Abuse*, in which having escaped in many and sundry conclusions, I as the occasion then fitted me, shapt him such an answere as beseemed his discourse, which by reason of the slenderness of the subject (because it was in defence of plaies and play makers) the godly and reuerent that had to deale in the cause, misliking it, forbad the publishing, notwithstanding he comming by a priuate unperfect coppye, about two yeres since, made a reply.

One who is acquainted with Lodge can see his tongue sticking in his cheek as he refers to the godly and reverent censors who suppressed his defense of plays. Something of the same spirit of playful malice seems to have animated the printers who put out forbidden works through hidden presses, in out-of-the-way places, even underground caves, and those who resorted to the false imprint, using false dates and foreign and imaginary localities,—sometimes with actual intent to deceive, but frequently as a bit of saucy daring. "Here I am," sings out the mocking imprint, "come and catch me." But the authorities who play the game with the mischievous printer know he will never be where he says he is.

Booksellers learned the indirect routes by which forbidden works might reach the public. When Michael Sparke was before the Ecclesiastical Commission in 1630, he declared that "when he was in the country forty-one of the books articulate were left with his servants and were sent to divers of his chapmen in Oxford and Salisbury and other parts. On his return he received

[59] W. C. Hazlitt, *Prefaces, Dedications, and Epistles*, 188.

a note to place Christ's Confession and Complaint foremost, whereupon, perusing the booke, he found it dangerous, and thereupon brought the residue of the same into the Registry of the Court. Does not know the author of the work nor can tell what to believe who is the printer or author."[60]

Condemned books were sometimes found in quantities in private houses. Richard Blagrave was imprisoned for having at his house many new Bibles of the Geneva print with the notes, as well as some books from Amsterdam. He was accused before the Court of Star Chamber of having "a stock going in the trade." This he denied, saying the books had been "sold him for an old debt."[61]

Another method of underhand sale is illustrated in a letter of Edward Rossingham to Sir Thomas Puckering, February 7, 1637, concerning a "scandalous book, News from Ipswich," supposed to be by Mr. Burton. A hundred books had been sent to a clothier of Gloucester to sell at 8 d. apiece, the money to be sent to Mr. Burton in London. Burton was brought before the High Commission and imprisoned.[62]

These are only a few of the ways of evading the diligence of the authorities and preserving works forbidden to circulate. That the censorship was evaded on the Continent, as well as in England, is proved by the checking up of extant works with the *Index generalis librorum prohibitorum a pontificiis* published by Thomas James, librarian of the Bodleian in 1627. This was a summary of the church indexes printed up to that time. The more important books which the Bodleian would need to secure because of the condemnation by the church were pointed out, so that this general index served as a guide for contemporary bookbuyers in England, and later was of service to English scholars and bookbuyers. Many of the works were not printed in England, a fair proportion being from Holland, long a refuge for those who wished to escape persecution for their opinions. The preface to the *Index generalis* states that the books listed therein as condemned by the authorities should be read with the more zeal and avidity in England. Nearly all the works are now in the Bodleian. If we consider how many books of

[60] *S. P. Dom. Chas. I*, 1629–31, vol. CLVIII, art. 49, January 15, 1630.
[61] *Cases in the Court of Star Chamber* (Camden Soc'y), 274.
[62] *Court and Times of Chas. I*, II, 274.

the period to which no objections were raised have perished utterly, we are driven to the conclusion that what the censorship usually accomplished was not complete or permanent suppression of opinion,—especially of opinion already put in print,— but delays in permission to print, recalls partially successful, and checks in dissemination.

Mr. R. B. McKerrow, summing up his impressions of censorship in Shakespeare's time, comes to the conclusion that for pure literature the loss of books is negligible:

> The influence of the censorship upon the book trade was undoubtedly bad in the main because it tended to stifle free competition among the printing houses. Success must have depended far less upon enterprise or good workmanship than on being in favor with the authorities. A printer who stood well with them would no doubt have a much better chance of getting books that had been submitted by him, or which he was known to be about to print, licensed quickly, than one who was regarded with dislike or suspicion. . . . .
>
> . . . . On the other hand, it can hardly be maintained that literature suffered at all by it [i.e., the censorship]. There is, so far as the writer is aware, not a single instance of a work of literary importance having been lost to us through the refusal to license it; though of course we cannot say what might have been written had freer criticism of current affairs been permitted.[63]

I do not myself see that the effect of the censorship upon the competition of printers was necessarily very great—except in those extreme cases where the printer lost his press or went to prison. While it is possible that high standing of a printer or publisher might tend to make authorities careless on first examination, it certainly did not seem to have much effect upon their attitude toward offensive works after publication.

It is extremely difficult to judge either the number or the probable value of works that are lost, from what evidence remains of the censorship of 1580 to 1640. We have a little more to go on for the period of Roger L'Estrange, 1637–81, when the books condemned by episcopal authority were said to list over 200.[64] Oldenburg, a licenser about 1675, declared that he had rejected more than he licensed. Undoubtedly the censorship was in some ways stricter under L'Estrange than it had been

[63] *Shakespeare's England*, 1916, II, 222.
[64] G. H. Putnam, *Censorship of the Church of Rome*, II. 262.

before. But, if we regard Milton as a competent witness, his backward glance at the censorship just before 1644 would lead us to suppose that the regulations did really suppress to some extent. We should remember, too, that the *Areopagitica* was written when the press laws were somewhat relaxed and Star Chamber had lost hold on the press. Anti-episcopal and other pamphlets circulated then without license. Protests from Parliament were not nearly as effective as had been the activities of the Stationers' Company backed by Star Chamber. Milton referred scornfully to "this whole system of Censorship and licensing of books that had prevailed so long in England and almost everywhere else; this delegation of the entire control of a nation's literature to a state-agency consisting of a few prejudiced parsons and schoolmasters seated at top, to decide what should go into the funnel, and a Company of stationers seated below, to see that nothing else came out of the funnel."[65]

Something between Mr. McKerrow's rather sanguine view and that of Milton seems to me a tenable position as to the effectiveness of suppression of books by authority from 1580 to 1640. If sedition, treason, or heresy were suspected, action was prompt and usually thorough. In lesser matters there was inconsistency and irregularity. If other Masters of Revels did as Herbert did—burned plays they thought too offensive— there can hardly be a doubt that some dramas were effectually suppressed if they were submitted before public performance, as was expected.

Considering the slips and evasions of one kind and another, it must be admitted that the strongest effect of censorship was probably repression, rather than suppression. There were some as bold as Selden, who said in the House of Commons, in 1629: "There is no *law* to prevent the printing of any book in England, but only a decree of Star Chamber"; but there were more who felt that a Star Chamber decree was worth considering. So, at a time when wrong views meant those contrary to the accepted views of church and state, and when "wrong" views might endanger the author's purse, or his freedom, the members of his body, or even his life itself (to say nothing of the fate of his published works), it is very likely that many a writer who was eager to indulge in frank discussion of contemporary matters refrained through custom or through fear.

[65] David Masson, *Life and Works of Milton*, III, 275.

II. CENSORSHIP OF DRAMA

Subjects Considered Dangerous on the Stage

The examples of dramatic censorship which we shall now consider will be found to show these as the chief offences, in the opinion of authority: indulgence in religious controversy, particularly the favorable or unfavorable exploiting of a creed or denomination; any kind of sacrilege, and (especially after 1606) the use of oaths containing the name of Christ or God or any very obvious substitute for them; the realistic portrayal of living kings upon the stage, especially their weaknesses, vices, or policies; dangerously satirical or hostile portrayal of foreign kings or of high officials of any country; discussion of foreign politics or international relations; cartooning of real persons of any rank, but especially of noblemen; seditious sentiments, or discussion of facts likely to produce popular discontent or a desire for greater civic liberty or a change of form of government; and excessive indecency, especially if a work were otherwise questionable as well.

Religious Discussion

The Catholic as a type of wicked intriguer was a popular figure on the English stage even as early as the reign of Mary, when Bishop Gardiner appeared in that role. When Elizabeth came to the throne, the treatment of religion on the stage became an important issue. Elizabeth assured the Spanish ambassador in 1559 that her own religious faith had much in common with Catholicism, but her active policy did not carry out that impression. Il Schifanoya wrote to Castellan, of Mantua, concerning the Christmas celebrations of 1558:

As I suppose your Lordship will have heard of the *farsa* performed in the presence of her Majesty on the day of the Epiphany, and I not having sufficient intellect to interpret it, nor yet the mummery performed after supper on the same day, of crows in the habits of Cardinals, of asses habited as Bishops, and of Wolves representing Abbots, I will consign it to silence.

He goes on to speak of masquerades of friars in the streets of London.[66]

[66] *S. P. Venetian*, VII (1558–80), p. 11.

Elizabeth, at some time before April 1559, gave an order prohibiting plays in derision of the Catholic religion, of the mass, of the saints, and of God. This was evidently not obeyed, for a letter of May 4, 1559, from Paulo Tiepolo, Venetian ambassador in Spain, states that in one play they brought on the stage King Philip, the late Queen of England, and Cardinal Pole, and had them discuss religion.[67]

A more rigorous and comprehensive proclamation by Elizabeth on May 16, 1559 categorically forbade political and religious problems to be discussed on the stage, charging the mayors and justices of the peace (who then had control over the plays) that they permit none to be played "wherein either matters of religion or of the governance of the estate of the common weall shalbe handled or treated: beyng no meete matters to be wrytten or treated upon, but by menn of aucthoritie, learning, and wisedome, nor to be handled before any audience, but of graue and discreet persons."

While this proclamation was not perfectly enforced, its effect was felt at times during the next fifteen years. So it is not surprising to find objection taken to all kinds of religious discussion, even that which did not oppose the belief of the sovereign.

The anti-Catholic activities of the comedians extended through several reigns, furnishing a sort of index of popular feeling, as political and religious crises arose. It was only natural that in the latter part of Elizabeth's reign there should be bound up with the ideal of patriotism a desire to oppose the Church of Rome, especially after the papal bull of Sixtus V (on February 25, 1570) branded Elizabeth a bastard and put forward Philip II of Spain as the rightful heir of England. That the issue was felt to be political, as well as religious, is clearly shown by the combined attacks upon Spain and Catholicism, as in Lyly's *Midas*, for example. Sometimes the thrust at Catholicism was only incidental to the structure, as in the allusion to the Romish anti-Christ at the end of Lodge and Greene's *A Looking-Glass for London*. Sometimes the Pope was humorously satirized, as in *Sir John Oldcastle* and *The Weakest Goeth to the Wall* (1600). There were many pronounced anti-Catholic expressions,

[67] *S. P. Venetian*, VII, 11, 80–81. Cf *S. P. Spanish*, I 375.

as in Rowley's *When you see me, you know me* (acted 1603), which carried the current opposition to popery back into the reign of Henry VIII.

The opposition to the Church of Rome continued in the reign of James, flaring up notably on three occasions. The first was about 1606–07. In the autumn of 1606 James antagonized some Englishmen by what seemed undue severity toward certain ministers of Aberdeen who had assembled without his consent and ventured to oppose his stand on episcopacy in Scotland. The frank-spoken representatives of the Scotch ministry who came over to England to present their point of view and answer for the offence were imprisoned or banished, it was thought unjustly.[68]

More specifically, the punishment of one of these Scotch representatives, Andrew Melville, was probably an occasion for sympathy from many Englishmen who appreciated the point of his offence. Melville was present at the Royal Chapel at a festival of St. Michael which was celebrated with much ceremony. "On the altar were placed two shut books, two empty chalices, and two candlesticks with unlighted candles. And the king and queen approached it with great ceremony and presented their offerings." When the service was over, the Prince de Vaudemont (son of the Duke of Lorraine, and the commander of the Venetian army), said he "did not see what should hinder the churches of Rome and England to unite; and one of his attendants exclaimed, 'There is nothing of the mass wanting here but the adoration of the host'." On returning to his lodgings, Melville composed the following verses on the scene he had witnessed:

> Cur stant clausi Anglis libri duo regia in ara,
> Lumina caeca duo, pollubra sicca duo?
> Num sensum cultumque Dei tenet Anglia clausum,
> Lumine caeca suo, sorde sepulta sua?
> Romano an ritu dum regalem instruit aram,
> Purpuream pingit relligiosa lupam?[69]

[68] Act of Secret Council, October 23, 1606; Sir John Hay's Collection; *Simsoni Annales*; Calderwood, 549; cited by Thomas M'Crie, *Life of Andrew Melville*, pp. 247 ff.

[69] An early translation occurs in *Melvini Musae*, p. 24, together with two poems by John Barclay in defence of the Royal Altar, and five by Melville in reply. The original epigram runs as follows:

SUBJECTS CONSIDERED DANGEROUS

The Chancellor and Privy Council of England devoted two solemn sessions (November 30, 1606) to this six-line epigram and one on Archbishop Bancroft, scanning them for treason. They finally contented themselves with defining Melville's offence as *scandalum magnatum*. The Chancellor admonished Melville to 'join gravity and moderation to his learning.' Melville was kept in prison in the spring of 1607. Perhaps this epigram on the royal altar may have suggested the attack on the "purple whore" in Dekker's play. I have seen no real evidence that the play was written before 1606, though critics tend to date it earlier.

There was certainly a popular outburst of feeling against the Catholics at this time. In February, 1607, a Venetian, Vincenzo Giustiniana, complained of the violently and scurrilously anti-Papist shows then in London.[70]

The Jesuit feeling against England also took the drama as a form of expression in August of the same year (1607). In the *Diary of Walter Yonge* (Camden Society, 15) is an account (dated October) of an elaborate two-day play of the Jesuits at Lyons, using a hundred actors. The plot included references to Calvin and Luther, to the "meritorious deed intended of gunpowder; the conspiracy of Babington and others, against Queen Elizabeth; all which were rewarded with the joys of Paradise." But, according to the pious recorder, another judgment was meted out. The Abbess who played the part of the Virgin and the three who were the Trinity were "stricken with the hand of the Lord" and mysteriously disappeared in a storm. The news of the play reached England promptly. There is entered on the Stationers' Registers (III, 361) October 14, 1607, "a book called

---

> Why stand there on the Royal Altar hie
> Two closed books, blind lights, two basins drie?
> Doth England hold God's mind and worship closs,
> Blind of her sight, and buried in her dross?
> Doth she, with Chapel put in Romish dress,
> The purple whore religiously express?

For an account of the incident, see Thos. M'Crie, *Life of Andrew Melville*, pp. 262–64. Cf. also John Row, *Hist. of the Kirk of Scotland* pp. 234–38 and 283–86.

[70] See E. S. Bates, "Some Foreigners in Shakespeare's England," *Nineteenth Century*, LXXII, 118.

the Jesuytes Commedie Acted at Lyons in France the 7 and 8 of August, 1607."

England experienced another wave of anti-Catholic feeling about 1618. Piero Contarini wrote that "there is mortal hatred against the pope. . . . In their theatres and public comedies they constantly speak of the papacy with contempt and derision."[71] Busino, in the same year (1618) presents a picture of the shocking state of English affairs:

> The English deride our religion as detestable and superstitious, and never represent any theatrical piece, not even satirical tragicomedy without larding it with the vices and iniquity of some Catholic churchman, which move them to laughter and much mockery. . . . . On one occasion my colleagues of the Embassy saw a comedy performed in which a Franciscan friar was introduced, cunning and replete with impiety of various shades, including avarice and lust. The whole was made to end in a tragedy, the friar being beheaded on the stage where he pretended to perform service, ordering a procession. He then reappeared familiarly with a concubine in public. He played the part of administering poison to his sister upon a point of honour, and moreover of going into battle, having first deposited his cardinal's robes on the altar.[72]

Here are suggestions of Webster's cardinal in *The Duchess of Malfi*, especially Act III, Sc. 4 and Act V, sc. 2, but the resemblance is imperfect.

On the whole, it may be said that the effort at legislative repression of anti-Catholic spirit on the English stage, if more than half-hearted, was strangely ineffective.

Though several dramatists of note (e.g., Jonson, Massinger, and Shirley) have been *said* to show at some time inclinations toward Catholicism, and many did betray an occasional poetic sympathy with its ceremonial, there was, if we may judge from what is extant, comparatively little written by dramatists for the public stage in favor of popery. It is not surprising to find that objection was made to a private performance at Christmas at the house of Sir John York in Yorkshire (July 1, 1614). The name of the play is not known, but it was reported to be "a scandalous play acted in favor of Popery." In it the Devil

---

[71] *S. P. Venetian*, 1617–19, art. 678.

[72] *Anglipotrida*, Cod. MCXXII. Bibl. di S. Marco, Venice. *S. P. Venetian*, 1617–19, no. 218.

declares that all Protestants are lost, and carries off King James on his back to hell fire. The noblemen who arranged for this performance were arrested and fined.[73] It was objected, "The greatest subject in England can have no common players, and to have them is a riot."

The dramatists' attacks upon the Jewish character and habits are perhaps too familiar now to need much comment. They have been rather fully discussed by Sir Sidney Lee in "Elizabethan England and the Jews,"[74] which interprets through these dramas the life of the Jew in England in the sixteenth and seventeenth centuries. The dramatic interest of the Jew was naturally more noticeable after the charges were brought in 1594 against the Portuguese Jew, Lopez, of being hired to poison Elizabeth. Most of the presentations of the Jew in English fiction and drama of this time show pronounced prejudice. Shakespeare's Shylock is distinctly more sympathetic than the average treatment.

Because of the narrowness and bitterness of the Puritans in their attacks upon the theatre and the drama,[75] they suffered quite as much ridicule on the stage as did the Catholics in the days of Protestantism, or as did the Jews. Playwrights of any or no religion fell upon the Puritan as a common enemy. These thrusts seem not always to have been objected to by the authorities, though Lodge had one of his pamphlets rejected by a licenser. The play *A Knack to Know a Knave* (acted as new June 10, 1592) presents a hypocritically pious priest who calls himself a pure Precisian (Puritan). A poor old man begs him for alms, but the Precisian refuses because the Holy Ghost does not so move him, and because man will not be saved by his good works. Marston and other playwrights ridicule the Puritan idea of predestination. Chapman, in *A Humorous Day's Mirth*, absurdly pictures a Puritan woman before a crucifix and a rosary. Ben Jonson dislikes the Puritan because he derides all antiquity and defies any other learning than inspiration (*Bartholomew Fair*, ed. Gifford, IV, 385). Extreme piety and a ten-

[73] *S. P. Dom.*, 1611–18, vol. LXXVII, art. 58; Hist. MSS Commission, *Reports*, III, 63. Sir Christopher Malloy acted the Devil (Burn, 119).

[74] *Trans. of the New Shakspere Soc'y*, 1887–92, pt. 2, pp. 143–167.

[75] See E. N. S. Thompson, *The Controversy between the Puritans and the Stage*, Yale Studies in English, XX (1903).

dency to harangue are frequently cartooned, as in *Bartholomew Fair*, where the Puritan, Zeal-of-the-land Busy, interrupts a puppet show with his diatribe against the worldly vanity of the theatre, against the impropriety of men's acting women's parts, etc. Mannerisms such as religious cant and a pious nasal twang are often caricatured. The nasal twang is heard in Jonson's *The Case is Altered* (*Works*, Gifford, VI, 322). Tribulation Wholesome, in *The Alchemist*, also displays a number of pious affectations.

The Puritan is usually portrayed as a precisian, a stickler for the proprieties. At the same time he is occasionally cartooned as one who, though prim and over-conscientious as to non-essential and minute details, is lax to the point of impurity in the greater affairs of life. Middleton's *The Chaste Maid of Cheapside* (pr. 1630), is a comic but severe portrayal. *The Puritaine or The Widdow of Watling-Streete*, (pr. 1607), "written by W. S.," is a farcical satire on a family of Puritans. "We dare lie," says a servant, "but we dare not swear." Marston's *The Dutch Courtesan*, (pr. 1605), shows up a Puritan (Mulligrub) as succumbing to temptation. Other instances may be found of suggestions that the Puritan is a loose liver.[76]

In the course of the Martin Marprelate controversy (1589), the Martinists (who were opposed by Archbishop Whitgift) were satirized in plays performed by the Queen's men and Paul's boys. Lyly and Nashe were on the side of the bishops, and yet, at the request of the Archbishop and the Mayor, it was ruled that plays should be examined by censors who should reform "such parts and matters as they shall find unfit and undecent to be handled in plays, both for Divinity and State."[77] Not

[76] Some of the other plays illustrating the attitudes of playwrights toward Puritans are: Dekker's *If this be not a good play, the devil is in it*, Daborne's *The Poor Man's Comfort*, Randolph's *The Muses' Looking Glass*, Barry's *Ram-Alley*, Samuel Rowley's *The Noble Soldier*, Tourneur's *The Atheist's Tragedy*, and Shakespeare's *Twelfth Night*. Chamberlain wrote to Carleton on March 8, 1623, that the Spanish and Flemish ambassadors liked their reception at Cambridge, but "declined the play on being told that the argument was chiefly about a Jesuit and a Puritan." (*S. P. Dom. Chas. I*, 1623, vol. CXXXIX, art. 64.) For comment on the ridicule of Puritans in masques, see P. Reyher, *Les masques Anglais*, 277–97.

[77] *Acts of the Privy Council*, XVIII, 214–16. Cf. R. Bond's *Lyly*, I, 52 ff, Richard Simpson and others have stated that the Archbishop engaged Marlowe. Lyly, and Greene to make these attacks, but I find no evidence for this.

only were the Archbishop and Mayor displeased over the introduction of the Marprelate affair upon the stage, but Mr. Tilney, the Master of the Revels, "did utterly mislike the plays," according to the Mayor. By his suggestion, the Privy Council ordered a temporary suppression (November 8, 1589) of all plays in London. Lord Strange's men refused to obey, and two of them were sent to the Counter.[78] Lyly, who had a strong desire to discuss contemporary politics and religion in his plays, expressed his regret over this suppression in *Pap with a Hatchet* (1589): "Would these comedies might be allowd to be plaid that are pend, and then I am sure he [the Puritan] would be decipherd and so perhaps discouraged." The use of the stage as an arena for discussion of new movements is suggested by Nashe's comment on the Martinists as being "made a may-game on the stage," in a place "where every new Bug no sooner puts out his horns, but is beaten down," (*Countercuffe*).

Ridicule of religious ceremonies of any sort was considered offensive by the authorities, partly because application might be made to the prevailing religion. A case of heavy punishment for sacrilege occurred in 1639. A letter of Edmund Rossingham, dated May 8, 1639, stated that "Thursday last the players of the Fortune were fined £1000 for setting up an altar, a bason and two candlesticks, and bowing down before it on the stage, and although they allege it was an old play revived and an altar to the heathen gods, yet it was apparent that this play was revived on purpose in contempt of the ceremonies of the church."[79]

In the order of importance, one might say that in the eyes of the censor the chief aims, so far as religion was concerned, were these: to prevent any attack upon the religion favored by the state; to suppress ridicule of religious beliefs in general; and to prohibit trouble-making satirical portrayals of particular sects and denominations—though it must be admitted that there was much laxity in the enforcement of restrictions where Jews, Puritans, and Catholics were concerned.

Treatment of Contemporary Matters

Miss Gildersleeve, in her *Government Regulation of the Elizabethan Drama,* sums up the drama of the time as essentially non-

[78] Collier, *Hist. of Eng. Drama*, I, 246-47.
[79] *S. P. Dom. Chas. I,* 1639, vol. CCCCXX, art. 109.

controversial and romantic, given to display of foibles of human nature, rather than political or social satire. Ward went much further than this in his chapter on The Political and Social Aspects of the Age, in *The Cambridge History of English Literature*. He said of the age of Elizabeth (V, 378):

> The dramatists of the age were monarchists to a man; and though, of course, their sentiments herein accorded with their interests, it would be shortsighted to ascribe the tenacity with which they adhered to the monarchical principle of government merely to a servile attachment to the powers that were: indeed, with these they were not infrequently in conflict. The steadfastness with which these popular poets upheld the authority of the crown as the pivot on which the whole state machine turned is evident from the fact that their whole-hearted loyalty was transferred, without halt or hesitation, from Elizabeth to James, as it afterwards descended from him to his successor. Its root, no doubt, was some sort of belief in the "divinity" that "doth hedge a king."

Now it is quite true that the bulk of Elizabethan drama is, as Miss Gildersleeve says, romantic, or at least it appears to be something other than realistic portrayal of affairs of the day. It is also true that the Elizabethan dramatists were fairly loyal, if not exactly "monarchists to a man," as Ward declares. But it is going too far, to lump the drama of the three reigns as lacking in contemporary satire, or the playwrights as handing down uniform loyalty by some strange process of heredity. It is certainly too much to grant that all the dramatists of the reigns of James and Charles were keenly conscious of the "divinity that doth hedge a king."

One fact is obvious, that in the reign of Elizabeth the historical dramas usually handled history of a former time—for the very good reason that the dramatists were forbidden to do otherwise. There seems to have been less daring about open breaking of such restrictions in the time of Elizabeth than in that of James. This is partly to be accounted for by the stronger personality of Elizabeth. But the fashionableness of the play which had some interesting information upon England's past, and the great vogue of romantic comedy undoubtedly helped to delay the popular demand for realistic, satirical comedy of manners and for serious plays handling problems of the day. We shall, however, see that the choice of a king who was dead or overseas was not an impossible handicap to the playwright who wished to criticize his sovereign in a play.

As to Elizabethan dramatists' being "monarchists to a man," there is surely some reason for doubt. Flattery of the monarch was expected not only by the monarch but by the audience. It was so customary as to be a recognized convention. A playwright might praise his sovereign merely because he was 'minding his manners,' just as we mechanically address even those whom we cordially dislike with "Dear Sir" and "Good morning." Praise of the powerful was so usual in literature that it is possible that even extreme flattery would not then be taken as conclusive proof of a loyal heart. Elizabeth's keen appetite for praise and what she did to those from whom she expected it in vain may account for at least a part of the admiring comment in the literature of her time. It is interesting to compare the private letters of her flatterers to their intimate friends with the printed praise in the works intended for her sight. It must, however, be admitted that the references to Elizabeth on all but a few points are more complimentary by far and have an air of greater sincerity than do those to James. But even here one must be cautious. Shakespeare's references to Elizabeth in *A Midsummer Night's Dream* have long been regarded as examples of very gracious praise; but there are certainly suggestions of keen satire in them. Ben Jonson's praises of King James to me ring hollow, though he protests greatly. Gratitude for favors past and future, conformity to the expectations of the court, and fear (if it is not a misuse of the term to apply it to one of Jonson's temperament) perhaps forced him to sing in a strain that was not quite his natural music. Certainly it seems constrained when compared with the best of his happy expressions of appreciation of the men he recognized for their individual worth. It seems, on the whole, unsafe to infer too much as to a dramatist's attitude toward a king from his compliments to him. Most of the dramatists had a wholesome desire to go on living and writing for the stage.

When an Elizabethan dramatist wished to portray the affairs or failings of his sovereign or those of other nations, he was usually careful to do it by analogy, as, by using the well-known love affairs of monarchs of the past, as in Marlowe's *Edward II* or the anonymous *Edward III*, and Heywood's *Edward IV*;

or, by picturing a tyrant king who was dead, as Richard III. Richard II proved not sufficiently dead for safety, the analogy being readily seen and long familiar to Elizabeth. It must have taken great restraint to keep from using the more spectacular aspects of the character and reign of Henry VIII during the lifetime of Queen Elizabeth. *The Life and Death of Lord Cromwell*, printed in 1602, was probably played in the life of Elizabeth. It makes slight use of Henry VIII, though there was every temptation to do otherwise. The play of *Henry VIII* (1612?), often attributed to Shakespeare in collaboration, would perhaps have offended Elizabeth if it had been staged in her life. The "All is true" produced before 1613 and usually identified with this play of Henry VIII drew criticism, but it was chiefly for the use of the actual royal costumes, etc., and for making state ceremonies too common.

Though discussion of affairs of state was forbidden very early in the reign of Elizabeth, it proved impossible to muzzle the dramatists entirely. Such questions as the succession to the throne were bound to come up directly or indirectly. Most of the dramatists, however, masked their purpose by such devices as these: by intruding a contemporary incident, situation, or problem into a story set in the past; by using type characters of the past to figure characters of their own day; by setting the action in a foreign land, with some hint to apply it to England (often in the prologue); by generalizing a tale into an allegory or morality that required intelligence or special information to interpret rightly; or by confusing criticism through the employment of a medley form commingling the purely fantastic with realistic and contemporary matters thinly veiled.

An example of picturing a situation of the past that was again applicable to the times of the play is *The Life and Death of Jack Straw* (1593). The tax situation was the main analogy. This play presents rebellion and sedition, subjects usually forbidden. The remoteness of the date—1381—made the theme safer. But the careful concealment of the aim to rouse resentment against oppressive taxes, etc., is still more effective. It is shown that the tyranny which drove the people to rebellion was unendurable; but at the same time the playwright rebukes the rebels. In this way he manages to present a situation in which taxation and imposts such as those being murmured against in the year of the play, 1592–93, figured largely as the cause of the rebellion. *Richard II* has a point in common with this play, but the treatment proved too open for safety. *Sir Thomas More* and *Barnavelt* (which we shall discuss later) show a mixture of boldness with caution. They proved "dangerous" because of their greater nearness to the times.

A typical Elizabethan treatment of an historical situation is that found in *A Larum for London* (*S.R.*, May 29, 1600), probably acted some years before it was entered for publication. The play presents the siege of Antwerp in 1576. The plundering by Spain is attributed to the indifference of the comfortable citizens who despised military preparations and neglected the defence of their country. The title points the political purpose of the analogy beyond a doubt. The printing of it in 1600 was probably due to the scare over the possible betrayal of England into the hands of Spain.

Minor problems of political and economic policy are sometimes glanced at by Elizabethan dramatists. References to foreign craftsmen intrude into the moralized *Three Ladies of London*, of Robert Wilson (pr. 1584). Heywood, in his *Edward IV* (acted 1598, pr. 1600), though an apparent loyalist in his attitude toward the sovereign's right to tax and borrow all his subjects have, insists that the monopolies are bad. He transplants the system of his day to that of Edward IV: "I like not these patents. . . . 'Tis pity that one subject should have in his hand that might do good to many throughout the land." In the time of James, the monopolist was allegorized in a hodgepodge play of medley effect permitting introduction of contemporary realistic matters under cover of fantastic conceptions mingling the unreal with the real. Thomas Dekker, under the old stock figure of a usurer, presents a contemporary salt monopolist in *If this be not a good play, the Devil is in it*. Similarly, Robert Tailor, in *The Hogge hath Lost his Pearle*, satirizes a customs fraud concerning a monopoly patent on certain wines, in which Swinnerton, Mayor of London, was involved. The method was not a new discovery, but a re-application of an old idea. Shakespeare used it to superior advantage in *A Midsummer Night's Dream*.

That the comparative scarcity of contemporary matter in the drama of the reign of Elizabeth was not due to a complete lack of interest on the part of playwrights in the questions and activities of the day is pretty clear. It is well known that in court plays and masques and private entertainments of the Queen real material from the activities of statesmen and courtiers was often made use of to win favor for them from the Queen. It is clear that Gascoigne devised such shows or masques not only for his own advantage but for his patron's. Thomas Churchyard, in *Churchyard's Challenge*, 1593, tells of some earlier works "gotten from me of some such noble friends as I am loath to offend." One he describes as "A book of a sumptuous shew in Shrovetide, by Sir Walter Rawley, Sir Robart Carey, Mr. Chidley, and M. Arthur Gorge, in which book was the whole service of my L. of Lester mencioned that he and his traine did in Flaunders and the gentlemen Pencioners proved to be a great peece of honor to the court."[80]

It is not likely that there was any attempt to conceal meanings here. The presentation was probably realistic. It was certainly so in a performance described to Robert Sidney in a letter from Rowland White, October 26, 1599:

> Two Daies ago, the overthrow of Turnholt, was acted upon a Stage, and all your Names used that were at yt; especially Sir Fra. Veres, and he that plaid that part, gott a Beard resembling his, and a Watchet Sattin Doublett, with Hose trimd with Silver Lace. You was also introduced, Killing, Slaying, and Overthrowing the *Spaniards*, and honorable Mention made of your Service, in seconding Sir Francis Vere, being engaged.[81]

It is not clear whether this was on the *public* stage or not, but instances are not lacking of regular dramas that made use of contemporary history before the death of Elizabeth. Marlowe's *Massacre at Paris* (c. 1593?) used French history up to the new ruler, Henry IV, and moralized the night of Bartholomew. The play was evidently revived about 1602; for payments for work on it are recorded in Henslowe's Diary, November, 1601 and January, 1602. The later performance gave some trouble by furnishing a precedent for the use of contemporary foreign history in plays, and was made an excuse for acting in Paris a

[80] Shropshire Archaeological Society, *Trans.*, III (1880), 1.
[81] *Sidney Papers*, II, 136.

play reflecting on Queen Elizabeth. Winwood wrote to Cecil from Paris on July 7, 1602:

> Upon Thursday last, certain Italian comedians did set upon the corners of the passages in this towne that that afternoone they would play "l'Histoire Angloise contre la Roine d'Angleterre." [Winwood entered his protest and procured an inhibition, but retorts were made.] It was objected to me before the counsaile by some Standers by, that the Death of the Duke of Guise hath ben plaied at London; which I answered, was never done in the life of the last King; and sence, by some others, that the Massacre of St. Barthelomew hath ben publickly acted, and this King represented upon the stage.[82]

An example of alertness on the part of a playwright near the end of the reign of Elizabeth in seizing upon fresh historical material may be found in a description of a journey by Professor Friedrich Gerschow (1568–1635). It contains a note on a trip to London, where he saw acted, on September 13, 1602, a comedy showing how Stuhlweisenburg (then a place of real importance) was "sacked first by the Turks and later by the Christians." Since 1553 it had been in the hands of the Turks, but it was recaptured by the imperial troops under Graf von Russworm September 20, 1601. As it happened, the place had just been recaptured by Hassan fourteen days before the play was performed. Though it is perhaps impossible that the latest turn of fate caused the performing of this play within two weeks, yet it seems quite likely that preliminary movements of the Turks were known in England and may have been the occasion for a play on the earlier history.[83]

In considering these attempts to use current problems and recent history, one must remember that the sovereign had expressly forbidden discussion of affairs of church and state upon the stage, and that few officials felt that the true aim of the drama was to hold up the mirror to the age. Walsingham is pictured as being unusually liberal in permitting the performance of *A Play of Cards* (1582), which contained some satire on existing conditions. Harington, in his *Brief Apologie of Poetry*, remarks:

[82] Winwood, *Memorials*, I, 425.
[83] There is some account of this play in an article by Bolte, in *Zeitschrift für vergleichende Literaturgeschichte*, II, 361.

Then for comedies, to speake of a London comedie, how much good matter, yea, and matter of state is there in that Comedie cald the play of the Cards? in which it is showed, how foure Parasiticall knaues robbe the foure principall vocations of the Realme, *videl.* the vocation of Souldiers, Schollers, Marchants, and Husbandmen. Of which Comedie I cannot forget the saying of a notable wise counsellor that is now dead (Sir Francis Walsinghame), who when some (to sing Placebo) aduised that it should be forbidden, because it was somewhat too plaine, and indeed as the old saying is (sooth boord is no boord), yet he would haue it allowed, adding it was fit that they which doe that they should not, should heare that they would not.[84]

This comedy was played at Court by the Children of the Chapel on December 26, 1582.

It is commonly recognized that Chapman, Middleton, and Massinger indulge in contemporary allusion; but the dramatists who got their bent in the reign of Elizabeth often show a reaching out toward fresh materials. This is true not only of the minor and anonymous writers, but of such men as Lyly, Greene, Marlowe, Shakespeare, Beaumont, Fletcher, Nashe, Lodge, Dekker, Heywood, and Jonson. In the case of the last three, the nature of their plays printed in the reign of James does suggest a greater freedom from restriction then. There was at the end of the reign of Elizabeth one play, or masque, *England's Joy*, by an actor named Fenner, or Richard Vennar, which dealt with very fresh political material. Its plot (printed in the *Harleian Miscellany*, X, 198–99) indicates that it was to be played at the Swan on November 6, 1602; and contemporary allusions would seem to show that it really was acted there in 1602–03 (though Vennar seems to have tried to trick the audience on one occasion). England's Joy is Elizabeth; the Tyrant is Spain; his victim is Belgia; Lopus is a bought creature of Spain. "The Battle at sea in 88, with England's victory" is to be set forth. Then follow the Irish rebellion, the generalship of Lord Mountjoy, etc., bringing the incidents about up to date.

There was evidently some objection to Dekker's *Whore of Babylon* as "falsifying the account of time," for his preface shows in defence that he "writes as a poet." The main events run to about 1594 or 1595. They include Elizabeth's accession, her marriage negotiations, the plots against her life, especially

[84] Feuillerat, *Documents of the Revels* . . . . *Elizabeth*, 468.

that of Lopez (executed in 1594), the Irish disorders, the death warrant of Mary Queen of Scots, and the defeat of the Spanish Armada. It is all violently anti-Catholic, attacking Rome under the figure of the "purple whore." The disguise is flimsy, Lopez being listed first as Ropus, and printed Lupus, Parry being called Parridel (as in the *Faerie Queene*), and Campion, Campeius.

Heywood, who, like Dekker, gathered up history of the reign of Elizabeth and published it in the reign of James, has in his play *If you know not me* the Armada and the plot of the fanatic papist, Parry. It seems to be strongly anti-Spanish and also anti-Jesuit.

When one considers the importance of the defeat of the Armada, one is impressed by the small amount of allusion to it in the strictly contemporary literature, and especially in the plays. But there is a strong probability that at certain periods especial efforts were made, for diplomatic reasons, to muzzle the exulting writers. There was no steadfast or permanent policy in the censorship on discussion of Spanish affairs either in the reign of Elizabeth or in that of James. One must examine the relations of the countries at a given time in order to understand the policy toward public discussion touching upon Spain.

Throughout the reign of Elizabeth there was one particularly tempting subject which the playwright could not forbear discussing—the marriage negotiations with the Queen. The more conservative scholars (among whom, with reference to political allusions in plays, we may class E. K. Chambers)[85], though admitting necessarily the political character of such a play as *Midas*, hesitate to accept such interpretations of Lyly's other plays as have been offered by Baker, Bond, and Feuillerat, connecting them with the political situations and the amours of the court and of Elizabeth. The chief objection, naturally, is that Lyly would be in danger of ruining his political career if he offended Elizabeth. We shall see, I believe, that other dramatists took such a chance in the reigns of Elizabeth, James, and Charles—the hazards being perhaps greater in the time of Elizabeth. But Lyly certainly did not succeed as well at court as he had had reason to hope; and it is entirely possible that

---

[85] See his *Elizabethan Stage* (1923), III, 415, on Lyly.

such a play as *Endymion* might have furnished the cause for the decline of his fortunes. *Campaspe* has been interpreted as associated with the suit of the Duke of Anjou, *Sappho and Phao* with the rejection of the Duc d'Alençon, and *Endymion* with Elizabeth's revived interest in Leicester. So far as the mere use of Leicester's hopes for the subject of a play is concerned, there is no reason, in view of the masques that treated the same theme, to suppose that the topic was too dangerous for mention. As to the foreign suitors, the probability is, that, if Lyly's treatment of them was not resented, it may have been because Lyly, a skilful courtier, had the knack of seizing upon the moment when Elizabeth's feelings toward a candidate were such that his play would have the effect of clever commendation of rejection.

On the important topic of the prospects for settling the succession, Sackville and Norton had set an early precedent in their allegorical tragedy of *Gorboduc*, 1561, pointing out the danger to England from having the succession undetermined. The peculiar circumstances of the first publication (1565) and the strangely worded preface of the second (1570) perhaps point to a pretended piracy used as an excuse for giving wider currency to a bit of advice which Elizabeth permitted to be given, but for which later she may have experienced a reaction of distaste. There could be no mistaking the application to Elizabeth's situation, even if Act V did not so strongly suggest contemporary England. Sackville is known to have been out of favor with the Queen, about 1563–69, but I do not know any evidence that this was caused by the play. Both authors took up the matter of determining the succession in practical political discussion as well as in the play—especially Norton, whose speech in Parliament on the subject[86] furnishes a close parallel with the conclusion of *Gorboduc*, which is obviously a contemporary political oration.

There are numerous testimonies to the skill of Elizabeth in deciphering the allegorical allusions so common to the literature of her day. Some of the allegories were fairly obvious. De Silva wrote to King Philip of Spain concerning the revels of March 5, 1565:

[86] See the *Journal of the House of Commons*, II, 62–64.

It began after supper with a comedy in English of which I understood just as much as the Queen told me. The plot was founded on the question of marriage, discussed between Juno and Diana. Juno advocating marriage and Diana chastity. Jupiter gave a verdict in favour of matrimony after many things had passed on both sides of the respective arguments. The Queen turned to me and said, "This is all against me."[87]

Playwrights continued to discuss the possible marriage of Queen Elizabeth. There seems to have been an instinctive recognition of the fact that a suitor who was rejected or at least out of favor would be a fair target for the dramatist's shafts of wit. The courtships of the King of Sweden, of Philip II, of the Duc d'Alençon, of James VI of Scotland (and even Emperor Ivan of Russia, though in this case not for Elizabeth but for a lady of her court) were subjected to ridicule on the stage in the lifetime of Elizabeth.[88]

There is ground for a suspicion of connivance on the part of Queen Elizabeth or her ministers. The Bishop of Aquila wrote to the King of Spain, August 13, 1559, that the "King of Sweden's ambassadors [for the marriage with Elizabeth] who have arrived are being treated by the Queen in a manner that does away with any doubt about her marrying their master, for they are being made fun of in masques in their own presence."[89] It seems quite possible that Elizabeth was permitting a similar treatment of Philip II, her sister's widower, and by 1559 her own rejected suitor; for on April 29 of that year the Count de Feria wrote to Philip:

> She [Elizabeth] was very emphatic in saying that she wished to punish very severely certain persons who had represented some comedies in which your Majesty was taken off. I passed it by and said that these were matters of less importance than the others, although both in jest and earnest more respect ought to be paid to so great a prince as your Majesty, and I knew that a member of her Council had given the arguments to construct these comedies, which is true, for Cecil gave them, as indeed she partly admitted to me . . . .It is very troublesome to negotiate with this woman, as she is naturally changeable.[90]

[87] *S. P. Spanish*, I, 404.
[88] One may compare the subjecting of the Spanish King and ambassador to ridicule in *A Game at Chess* in 1623, just after the breaking off of the negotiations for the Spanish marriage of Charles.
[89] *S. P. Spanish*, 1558–67, page 91.
[90] *Ibid.*, (April 29, 1559), art. 29.

Though Burghley later helped repress criticism of Spain when the relations were strained to the breaking point, it is entirely possible that he did what Feria charged. Like Robert Cecil, Burghley had a lively interest in the subject-matter of plays. In connection with a cozening case before Star Chamber June 18, 1596, John Hawarde says that "The Lord Treasurer would have those that make the plays to make a comedie hereof, and to acte it."[91]

The interest of state officials in plays presented at court has long been recognized. There is a possibility that noblemen used the public drama, as well as the masque, to express their political beliefs and to mould opinion, and, I believe, more than a possibility that they used plays with political significance in their entertainments of one another and of distinguished foreign and royal guests at their own halls.

One is tempted to wonder whether the company to which Shakespeare belonged may have been drawn, through its connection with Ferdinando Stanley, Lord Strange, for a short time, into the discussion of political questions in their plays. Patrick Collun (or O'Cullin), an Irishman, in a confession in 1594, involved not only Sir William Stanley (the adventurous Colonel in the Spanish army who had once been a hanger on in the household of Ferdinando Stanley and turned Catholic and traitor) but also Ferdinando himself. More particularly, a fellow conspirator, Hesketh, on the same occasion declared "that he had related to the said Lord Strange, then Earl of Derby, all the treasons and purposes aforesaid and persuaded him to undertake the same."[92] The plan was, for the Spanish Catholics to invade England, and make Strange King, in consideration of an oath to maintain the Catholic religion. Many historians now regard Ferdinando, however, as free from suspicion of treason, and attribute his mysterious sudden death to revenge of the Jesuit plotters for his not falling in with their plans. Another traitor, Nicholas Williamson, servant of the Earl of Shrewsbury, said to Attorney General Coke, June 21, 1595:

My lady also one day told me of the manner and forcible death of my late lord of Derby, saying that some were of opinion that my lord that

[91] *Les reportes del cases en Camera Stellata* 1593–1609 (edited by Baildon, 1894), p. 48.

[92] *Salisbury MSS*, V, 58–59.

now is, his brother, had procured him to be poisoned; "but," saith she, I "believe it not, but those foolish speeches that he spake to Mr. Fr. Hastings, saying that they two should one day fight for the crown, the shew of his great will and haughty stomach, his making himself so against my lord of Essex. I thought would be his overthrow."[93]

This passage is obscure as to at least one grammatical reference, "they two," besides being hearsay; but it shows the rumors about the Stanley brothers, Ferdinando and William. Of the other Sir William Stanley, the Colonel, we have abundant evidence as to his Catholic alliance and his plots in regard to Ferdinando and against Elizabeth.

In connection with the Jesuit plot to put Ferdinando, Earl of Derby, on the throne, another account of the same year, 1594, which mentions a "libel written by F. P." (Father Parsons?) has a note also of "Mr. Heywood, Jesuit, and Mr. Mart, R."[94] That his name was Thomas Heywood appears from a petition to Burghley in behalf of him as being mistreated by the popish recusants for giving away an attempt to break prison.[95] The name is perhaps a mere coincidence, but it may be worth noting that Thomas Heywood, the dramatist, later wrote for the Earl of Derby (William Stanley), and that he later described himself as the "creature" of a Catholic patron, Worcester. The connection with Worcester seems clear. Part of the career of Heywood is in doubt, as, for example, what he means by describing himself as the "theatrical servant" of Shakespeare's patron, Southampton, in his *Funeral Elegy upon James I* (1625).[96] He used Doctor Parry's treason in the plays on Queen Elizabeth; but these plays as we have them now are Protestant in sentiment. They seem to have been published before in a form the author was anxious to disown—but probably because of the form. He complained in the 1605 version of *If you know not me* that it had been pirated by stenography and put in print, "scarce one word true."

[93] *Salisbury MSS*, V, 252–53.
[94] *Ibid.*, 77.
[95] *Ibid.*, V, 76.
[96] Cited by editors of Heywood's *Apology for Actors*, intro., v. The statement is not in the B.M. copy of the *Apology*, but is in that in the Brown collection.

There is a possibility, but as yet no proof, that William Stanley, who succeeded Ferdinando as Earl of Derby, used his players for political discussion. On June 30, 1599, George Fenner wrote to either Hum. Galdelli or Guiseppe Tusinga, in Venice, "The Earl of Derby is busy penning comedies for the common players."[97] The career of this Sir William Stanley has unfortunately been so often confused with that of the Catholic plotter that one must proceed cautiously. Fenner knew them apart, however.

A more thorough study than has yet been made of the relations of patrons to dramatic companies, playwrights, and actors would probably reveal some interesting lines of bias in political discussion on the stage, as, for example, in many allusions to Raleigh and to Essex, and to candidates for the succession.

In the opinion of the Spanish ambassador, Elizabeth was very remiss in not checking ridicule of other rulers on the stage. This appears in a minute of a conversation (June 20, 1562) between him and the Lord Chamberlain and Doctor Wotton in regard to charges brought against the ambassador:

1. That I had sent your Majesty the leaves of a book written by the heretic Dr. Bale, in which your majesty and the Spanish nation are spoken ill of.

Answer. It is true I sent these leaves as I was tired of complaining to the Queen of the constant writing of books, farces, and songs prejudicial to other princes, and seeing that notwithstanding her promise no attempt was made to put a stop to it.[98]

It has long been known that court masques were extremely important in the entertainment of ambassadors and visitors from abroad, and that they were used almost regardless of expense for purposes of compliment and for cementing friendships. What has not been proved, but may be true, is that playwrights and actors were often tempted to indulge in presentations of foreign dignitaries on the public stage in such a fashion as would threaten to disrupt international friendships if the public plays were taken with equal seriousness.

The Spaniards seem to have been very sensitive to ridicule on the stage. A striking instance of the effect of one uncom-

---

[97] *S. P. Dom.*, 1598–1601, vol. CCCLXXI, art. 35.
[98] *S. P. Spanish*, 1558–67, no. 170.

plimentary stage presentation of their king upon his military attitude is that narrated by Hieronimo Lippomano, Venetian ambassador in Spain, in a gossipy letter of July 20, 1586, to the Doge and Senate of Venice. After remarking that His Majesty is angry over the damage done by the Queen of England in Flanders and the Indies, he goes on to say:

But what has enraged him more than all else, and has caused him to show a resentment such as he has never before displayed in all his life, is the account of the masquerades and commedies which the Queen of England orders to be acted at his expense, His Majesty has received a summary of one of these which was recently represented, in which all sorts of evil was spoken of the Pope, the Catholic religion, and the King, who is accused of spending all his time in the Escurial with the monks of St. Jerome, attending only to his buildings. . . .All this. . . . has once more stirred the King, who is naturally inclined to peace, to make vigorous preparations for war.[99]

After the defeat of the Armada, the cartoons of Philip on the public stage of London were again put forth as one of the causes of the war. A tract by Verstegan published abroad in 1592, *A declaration of the true causes of the great troubles supposed to be intended against the Realme of England*, contains the accusation that "as an introduction hereunto, to make him [the King of Spain] odious unto the people, certain players were suffered to scoffe and jeast at him on their common stages; and the like was used in contempt of his religion, first by making it no better than Turkish, by annexing unto the Psalmes of David . . . . this ensuinge meeter [some doggerel verses]."[100]

Even the English authorities at times seemed to feel that it was unwise to indulge in too much exultation over the defeat of the Armada. We have seen that in 1559 William Cecil was accused of furnishing materials to playwrights for ridicule of Spain. But in 1589 the Lord Treasurer complained to the Bishop about a "pamphlet in foolish rhyme making fun of the Spaniard, even of King Philip for defeat." He sent to the Bishop to find who presumed to print it. The first printer was found to be Joseph Barnes, of Oxford, and the second Toby Cook, a London petitioner who printed it without license.

[99] *S. P. Venetian*, 1581–91, art. 383.
[100] J. P. Collier, *Hist. of Dramatic Poetry*, I, 277. Cf. R. Bond, *Works of Lyly*, III, 111.

The complaint in the tract of 1592 shows that others than Lyly attempted to handle Spanish relations in their plays; but Lyly's *Midas* was probably one of the most direct attacks. Midas, choosing between the music of Pan and that of Apollo, decides on that of Pan (Catholicism). Folly and conceit of judgment are among his traits. He wears ass' ears. He is also cursed with the desire to turn everything into gold. He harbors ambitious designs on his neighbor's land, and attempts to conquer the island of Lesbos. In spirit he is a greedy usurper. This is a sufficiently obvious sketch of the folly of the designs of Philip II upon England. "Have I not made the sea to groan under the number of my ships; and have they not perished? . . . To what kingdom have I not pretended claim? . . . A bridge of gold did I mean to make in that island where all my navy could not make a breach."

The play *Midas* was entered for publication October, 1591, and printed in 1592 as "plaied before the Queen on Twelfth Day by the Children of Paul's." This is sometimes thought to mean 1591, but Schelling dates the composition 1589, and the reference may well be to 1590. Nashe, who is much interested in free discussion of contemporary problems, says in his *Almond for a Parrot* (January or February, 1590): For now-a-dayes a man can not have a bout with a Balleter or write *Midas habet aureas asinas* in great Roman letters, but hee shall bee in daunger of a further displeasure."[101] The Children of Paul's were in trouble near this time, but it may have been entirely on account of the Martin Marprelate discussion in their plays.

Criticism of Sovereigns

The tendency toward realism in drama which became prominent about 1600 inaugurated a much greater freedom in the discussion of political and religious matters. In the reign of James there developed a strong desire to discuss contemporary politics and problems of the day upon the stage. Criticism of sovereigns and high officials in the times of James and Charles I became more direct and open. The allegory survived, it is true, but the meaning seems to have been well understood then, no matter how it eludes us today. For example, Day's *Isle of Gulls*,

[101] Reprint by Petheram, p. 4.

because of its airy whimsicality and gay irresponsibility of manner, is generally spoken of by modern critics as if it were a pleasant and practically toothless satire. But, like some other strange medleys of that day, it seems to have had a political significance easily recognized and readily censured at the time. The Induction should hint this to us, where the three gentlemen interrupt the Prologue and one of them supposes that the play has some political libel in it because the title *Isle of Gulls* is obviously suggested by Nashe's *Isle of Dogs* (which had become a stage by-word for trouble). He goes on to ask, "Is there any great man's life charactered in't?" The Prologue vehemently denies such intention. But a letter of Sir Edward Hoby to Sir Thomas Edmondes, March 7, 1605, relating the discussions that had recently taken place in the House of Commons, said that "at this time (*c.* February 15, 1605) was much speech of a play in the Black Friars, where in the 'Isle of the Gulls' from the highest to the lowest, all men's parts were acted of two divers nations: as I understand sundry were committed to Bridewell."[102] The printed text shows signs of revision, probably for fear of censorship or as a result of it. For example, King and Queen are replaced by Duke and Duchess.[103] Both the medley arrangement of incongruous materials and the pastoral background were adopted by other playwrights as disguise for plays handling dangerous contemporary matter.

It seems quite possible that this same play, with its royal personages, its hits at the royal favorite, at the relations of Scotch and English (Lacedemonians and Arcadians), and at religion was in the mind of Calvert when he wrote to Winwood in the same month, March 28, 1605:

> Players do not forbear to present upon the stage the whole course of this present Time, not sparing either King, State, or Religion, in so great Absurdity and with such Liberty that any would be afraid to hear them.[104]

Beaumont, the French ambassador, in a somewhat pessimistic

---

[102] *Court and Times of James I* (ed. by R. F. Williams), I, 61.

[103] A similar shift appears in *Cupid's Revenge* (by Beaumont and Fletcher or by Fletcher?) where a wicked King, Queen, and Prince, are changed to duke, duchess, and marquis.

[104] Winwood, *Memorials*, II, 54.

and exaggerated survey of English affairs, wrote home, June, 1604:

The courage of the English is buried in the tomb of Elizabeth. What must be the situation of a State and of a Prince, whom the clergy publicly abuse in the pulpit, whom the actors represent upon the stage, whose wife goes to these representations in order to laugh at him, who is defied and despised by his Parliament, and universally hated by his whole people.[105]

Numerous ambassadors testify to the daring of the royal comedians in the reign of James. An ugly rumor based upon the opening of the body of Prince Henry (November 10, 1612) on account of popular gossip about his sudden death[106] gives point to a report sent by Girolamo Lando to Venice on January 10, 1620, of a play performed by the company of Prince Charles:

In connection with the subject of comedians, I ought not to conceal the following from your Serenity, owing to the mystery that it involves. The comedians of the prince, in the presence of the king his father, played a drama the other day in which a king with his two sons has one of them put to death, simply upon suspicion that he wished to deprive him of his crown, and the other son actually did deprive him of it afterwards. This moved the king in an extraordinary manner, both inwardly and outwardly. In this country, however, the comedians have absolute liberty to say whatever they wish against anyone whatsoever, so the only demonstration against them will be the words spoken by the king.[107]

The freedom of speech in 1620, however, does seem to have roused James to a prohibition. John Rushworth, in his *Historical Collections* (p. 21) concerning the year 1620, remarks of a proclamation of the King:

The relation of England to those affairs of foreign states had caused a general liberty of discourse concerning matters of state; which King James could not bear, but by proclamation, commanded all from the

---

[105] Friedrich von Raumer, *Political History of England* . . . , 1837, I, 458.

[106] *S. P. Dom.*, 1611–18, vol. LXXI, art. 31. On the nature of the gossip, see *Court and Times of James I*, I, 373–75.

[107] *S. P. Venetian*, 1619–21, p. 11. On May 21, 1621, it was reported by the same Venetian ambassador that two books were selling greatly in Paris—one of them stating that Parliament had deposed the King, beheaded his favorites, and crowned Charles (*S. P. Venetian*, 1621–23, no. 56).

highest to the lowest, not to intermeddle, by pen or speech, with state concernments, and secrets of empire, either at home or abroad; which were no fit themes or subjects for vulgar persons, or common meetings.

As early as 1612 Heywood, in his *Apology for Actors*, frankly admitted, though he did not defend, the increased tendency to use the stage for purposes of political discussion:

> Now, to speake of some abuse lately crept into the quality, as an inveighing against the state, the court, the law, the citty, and their governements, with the particularizing of private men's humours (yet alive), noblemen and others; I know it distastes many; neither did I in any way approve it, nor dare I by any meanes excuse it.[108]

Heywood's plays on Queen Elizabeth used recent history; but, as has been noted, the feeling shown in the plays as we have them is anti-Spanish and anti-Jesuit. Heywood generally played safe as to subject matter.

The greatest daring in the use of contemporary matter was the treatment of James himself on the stage. There is in the State Papers an account of a certificate by Ant. Napleton, February 14, 1617, that in a conversation in the house of Thomas Napleton, of Faversham, about a play in which a huntsman, who was intended to represent the King, said he had rather hear a dog bark than a cannon roar, Napleton said it was a pity the King ever came to the crown of England, for he loved his dogs better than his subjects."[109] The correspondence of public men of the time and other state documents show that the King spent much time and effort on dogs and hunting, and that he was devoted to the idea of peace—so devoted that Wotton was repeatedly charged with the errand of finding a way out of conflict, especially when the election of James's son-in-law as King of Bohemia made some sort of stand on the part of James a necessity.

The unwarlike spirit of James subjected him to ridicule not only in England, but also abroad. Shortly after 1618, when he sent money and men to his son-in-law Frederick, but would not take any more definite stand in Bohemian affairs for dread of disruption of the amity of nations, a farce was played at Brussels, in which "Frederick was assisted by Denmark with

---

[108] Shakespeare Society, *Publications*, III, 61.
[109] *S. P. Dom. Jas. I*, 1611–18, vol. XC, art. 66.

100,000 pickled herrings; by the Netherlands, with 100,000 butter-tubs; and by King James with 100,000 ambassadors. The King was represented with pockets turned inside out, and with a sword at his side, which many persons, in spite of all their efforts, could not draw."[110]

The King's players in 1604 performed the play of Gowry (non-extant) handling a recent conspiracy of John Ruthven, Earl of Gowrie, to depose and murder James VI of Scotland (August, 1600). Two traitors were hanged, drawn, and quartered, and the name of Ruthven extinguished.[111] John Chamberlain wrote concerning this play to Winwood, December 18, 1604:

> The tragedy of Gowry, with all the action and actors, hath been twice represented by the King's Players, with exceeding Concourse of all sorts of People. But whether the matter or manner be not well handled, or that it be thought unfit that Princes should be played on the Stage in their Life-time, I hear that some great Councellors are much displeased with it, and so 'tis thought shall be forbidden.[112]

The objection was probably not to the attitude of the playwright, as Gowry is said to have been painted in blackest colors and James, who punished Gowry and confiscated his goods, was flattered in the play. But the fact that this conspiracy was played at all suggests a change since the time of Elizabeth in undertaking to stage contemporary monarchs.

I have not been able to ascertain just when the first official act forbade the presenting of live kings on the stage. It might be understood to be implied in the statute of Elizabeth which forbade discussion of contemporary politics and religion, but it is not there explicitly. The usual statement in histories of the stage (cf. Creizenach, IV, 218) is, that in 1624 action was taken against the representation of contemporary monarchs. Chamberlain's letter quoted above indicates a feeling that it was improper to portray living kings, but does not imply the existence of any definite prohibition. The prologue to W. Smith's play, *Hector of Germanie*, written 1613, seems to

---

[110] F. von Raumer, *Polit. Hist. of Eng.*, 1837, I, 435. Cf. also the confidential directions of James to Wotton as to his embassy in the Bohemian matter, in *Reliquiae Wottonianae*. Cf. also Arthur Wilson, *History of Great Britain*, 1653, p. 192.

[111] Howell, *State Trials*, I, 1359 ff.

[112] Winwood, *Memorials*, II, 41.

indicate an awareness of some such prohibition. The play is set in the fourteenth century, but, as we shall see later, has some contemporary bearings. The prologue, which has an air of coquetting with the censorship, attempts to deny that the characters are intended to suggest any contemporaries of the playwright—a denial which the audience would know how to estimate:

> Our Author for himself, this bad me say,
> Although the Palsgrave be the name of th' Play,
> 'Tis not that Prince, which in this Kingdome late,
> Marryed the Mayden-glory of our state:
> What Pen dares be so bold in this strict age,
> To bring him while he lives upon the Stage?
> And though he would, Authorities sterne brow
> Such a presumptuous deede will not allow:
> And he must not offend Authoritye.

So far as one can now judge, this curious medley of old situation and contemporary names, if not personages, with an occasional contemporary incident, is exactly what the censor described it as being, "a harmless thinge"; but if it had not been, Authority's stern brow would doubtless have drawn into a frown over the celebration of the marriage of Frederick and Elizabeth under this transparent ruse. It is an ineffectual sort of play, in which the particularly anæmic treatment of contemporary persons was due, I imagine, to the author's unwillingness to take a real risk. The spice of the play, if it has any, is in the prologue.

After the rebuke over *Gowry*, the King's company observed more caution for a little while; but they were soon meddling in city politics (see p. 174) and international relations (as in *Biron*). Wotton, in a letter to Sir Edmund Bacon, July 2, 1613, tells of the high degree of realism they used in presenting a play of former times:

The King's Players had a new Play, called *All is true*, representing some principal pieces of the Reign of Henry the 8th which was set forth with many extraordinary circumstances of Pomp and Majesty, even to the matting of the Stage; the Knights of the Order, with their Georges and Garter, the Guards with their embroidered Coats and the like: sufficient in truth within a while to make Greatness very familiar, if not ridiculous.[113]

[113] *Reliquiae Wottonianae*, 1685, 425–26.

This is thought by many commentators to be an account of the *Henry VIII* in which Shakespeare is supposed to have collaborated. It may be noted in passing that in the same year, 1613, a similar desire to spread gorgeous spectacle appeared in a smaller way in Smith's *Hector of Germanie*, with the conferring of the Garter, an incident which occurred with splendid ceremony during 1613, while the Palsgrave was visiting in England.

If the mere detailed portrayal of kingly pomp was offensive, how much more so, may we imagine, was the hitting of royal vices or weaknesses. Such a fault was corrected in the censoring of the "Second Maiden's Tragedy," as Buc called a play without a title which reminded him of Beaumont and Fletcher's *The Maid's Tragedy*. The play was licensed October 31, 1611, "with the reformacons." We have the manuscript playbook (Lans. MSS, no. 807), and it is printed also. The manuscript shows various alterations—marks and erasures for cuts for stage purposes, as well as for censorship. Some of Buc's notes are marked in the margin with a cross. There is an opportunity to portray royal vice in telling of the lust of a usurping king who endeavors to compel the heroine to become his mistress. She loves the king he has deposed, resists the usurper, and, to escape him, commits suicide. Omission is ordered for passages such as these: "That glister in the sun of prince's favor" (act 2, sc. 1); "the lustful king"; "O thou sacrilegious villain" (addressed to the King, act V, sc. 2). The censor, Buc, seems to have regarded the King's name with almost as panicky respect as Herbert showed for the name of God after the profanity statute, for he makes a curious emendation of the dying king's speech, "Your king's poison'd" (act V, sc. 2), substituting "I am poison'd." This is not only flat, but ruins the following remark: "The king of heaven be praised for it!"

Another point is blunted where, in act IV, sc. 1, the wife of Votarius, speaking of low morals of maid-servants, says, "There's many a good knight's daughter is in service." *Knight* is altered to *man*. Regard is shown again for the presumably tender feelings of the upper classes in Act I, sc. 1, where Govianus's satirical portrait of the "third nobleman" is marked to be omitted.

Lust as a vice of kings seems to be the chief objectionable feature in this play, rather than any indecency of the whole situation. There is, however, one cancel of a savage comment on women. After the heroine has killed herself to escape the lust of the usurper, Govianus remarks that few women would do this, for "they'll rather kill themselves with lust than for it." Buc here strikes out three lines. A similar remark is edited in Act IV, sc. 3, where the usurper says of the dead woman, "Hadst thou but ask'd th'opinion of most ladies, Thou'dst never come to this." Buc slightly improves the manners, if not the metre of the playwright, by changing *most* to *many*.

Though Massinger's criticisms of contemporary conditions are many and varied, they have so frequently to do with the character of the king, his rights over the subject, and the relation between him and his subject that it will perhaps be allowable to consider several of them in one group, before passing on to plays that show more interest in policies than in the personalities from which they spring.

It requires no argument now to show that Massinger was interested in many of the special problems of his day. But the most engrossing of all subjects to him was the large vital one that runs through so many of his plays, the ideal relation between king and subject. And closely connected with that is the conception of what a king ought to be. The suggestion is critically conveyed—by showing what was wrong in the characters and policies of bad monarchs, and what the necessary results. Massinger gives us one study after another of rulers unsatisfactory to the subject because of tyranny, lust, criminal weakness, incompetence, and subjection to the rule of favorites. The plays are usually given a foreign setting, but his allegories are not obscure, and his models not very far to seek.

Massinger was thoroughly aware of the value of drama as a means of forcing home a lesson by parallels which the conscience of the playgoer may make him see for himself. This appears in his eloquent defense of the actor's art in *The Roman Actor*, Act 1, sc. 3. Paris, the actor, has been tried for treason as "libeller against the State and Caesar."

> For traducing such
> That are above us, publishing to the world
> Their secret crimes, we are as innocent
> As such as are born dumb. When we present
> An heir that does conspire against the life

> Of his dear parent, numbering every hour
> He lives, as tedious to him; if there be,
> Among the auditors, one whose conscience tells him
> He is of the same mould,—WE CANNOT HELP IT.[114]

In Act II, however, Paris himself proposes to act to the life his friend's father, the personification of Avarice and Covetousness, so as to cure him of these faults when he sees them mirrored on the stage. It is clear, then, that the Roman actors of the play were like the Jacobean: they proposed to use types in which the individuals would see themselves criticized and corrected. Massinger is pleading for free speech on the stage and for a recognition of the corrective possibilities of satirical drama for purposes of reform.

There is more than a hint of Massinger's own experiences in being muzzled, as where Æsop says (Act I, sc. 1):

> We have enemies.
> And great ones too, I fear. 'Tis given out lately,
> The Consul Aretinus, Caesar's spy,
> Said at his table, ere a month expired,
> For being gall'd in our last comedy,
> He'd silence us forever.

Paris then ridicules the senate for descending

> To the censure of a bitter word, or jest
> Dropp'd from a poet's pen.

This is probably a reference to the action of the Privy Council against actors, as, for example, in punishment for *A Game at Chess*, by Middleton, in 1624.

Massinger wishes freedom of speech on the stage, and liberty of the subject to form his own opinions on all questions. For him there is no "divinity that doth hedge a king." The Emperor of the East, in a fit of dejection caused by an uneasy conscience, confessed to his courtiers that he was, like them, flesh and blood, as much a slave to the tyranny of his passions as the meanest of his subjects, and nothing but the false flattery of sycophants and vain ambition would make him consider himself "sacred, glorious, high, invincible," (Act V, sc. 2). One may well believe that Massinger's own convictions are voiced by

---

[114] This play was acted October 11, 1626.

Camiola in *The Maid of Honor* (1632), when she says (IV, 5, 52):

> 'Twas never read in holy writ, or moral,
> That subjects on their loyalty, were obliged
> To love their sovereign's vices.

Massinger certainly cannot be accused of blind devotion to his kings. *The Maid of Honor* voices a lamentation over the lost glory of a nation. The story is set in Sicily. England was frequently called Sicily; but if one were not informed as to that use, he could still guess from the description by Bertoldo in Act I, sc. 1, which fits England much better than it does Sicily. But, to avoid any possible misapprehension, Massinger gives the exhortation,

> Look on England,
> The Empress of the European Isles:
> When did she flourish so as when she was
> Mistress of the ocean, her navies
> Putting a girdle round about the world. (Act I, sc.1)

But England has gone down. The decay is due to a weak-kneed, peace-loving king, who prefers ploughshares to swords—not for his people's good, but because he likes his ease.

At the time this play was produced, James was hesitating on the brink of deciding to do something definite in aid of the cause of his son-in-law, Frederick of Bohemia. His conscience urged him to act; his cowardice and love of ease held him back. He sent some volunteers to Gustavus Adolphus by the Marquis of Hamilton, but refused to give assurance of a definite stand.

The Bondman (acted December 3, 1623) also attacks English conditions under the thin veil of a foreign setting. It criticizes the senate house "filled with green heads"; the military and naval unpreparedness, the men untrained, the ships rotting in the harbors; the lack of good generals, and the choice of a poor admiral (who surely must be Buckingham):

> A raw young fellow
> One never train'd in arms, but rather fashion'd
> To tilt with ladies' lips than crack a lance;
> Ravish a feather from a mistress' fan,
> And wear it as a favour. A steel helmet,
> Made horrid with a glorious plume, will crack
> His woman's neck. (Act I, sc.1).

As Pembroke, Massinger's patron, was an enemy of Buckingham, it is quite possible that some bias may arise from him. There are several plays by Massinger which show contempt for undeserving favorites, as, for example, *The Emperor of the East*, *The Maid of Honor*, and *The Great Duke of Florence*.

The Bondman touches briefly upon another theme. In Act V, sc. 3, there is a deliberate justification of the revolt of slaves against their masters because of cruel usage. It is moralized as a warning against tyranny.

The tyrant king is a favorite conception of Massinger's. The extremities to which one may go if he believes in the divine right of kings are illustrated concretely in the speech and actions of Caesar in *The Roman Actor*. Caesar is lustful, and a tyrant. He takes a subject's wife (Act I, sc. iv) and defies anyone to look sullen. No fault of his may be disputed (III, ii). Parthenius says of him (Act I, sc. ii):

> As his rule is infinite, his pleasures
> Are unconfined; this syllable, his *will*,
> Stands for a thousand reasons.

As for man-made laws, what are they to a king by divine right?

> Monarchs that dare not do unlawful things,
> Yet bear them out, are constables, not kings.

He can command all, "but is awed by none." He does not need to seek the good will of his subjects, for he is absolute (Act III, sc. 2):

> Can we descend so far beneath ourself,
> As or to court the people's love, or fear
> Their worst of hate? Can they, that are as dust
> Before the whirlwind of our will and power,
> Add any moment to us?

If his desires contradict all divine decrees, they are still sacred. He has absolute power over his subjects' lives, can dispatch them at his own pleasure (II, 1):

> And with as little trouble here, as if
> I had kill'd a fly.

Caesar gives orders that anyone who sighs or murmurs at the traitor's death shall be hanged himself.

Here are many of the worst traits charged up to James by his discontented subjects. The royal prerogative and divine right are the main theoretical problems of his reign.

If Massinger wrote *Barnavelt*, we may be sure from the way it was censored that he incurred some disfavor through his outspoken criticism of conditions recognizable as English (see p. 183 ff.). And we shall see that the actors had trouble over his *The Spanish Viceroy*, which they acted in 1624 after they had been punished for acting *A Game at Chess*, by Middleton. *The Roman Actor* (performed in 1626) is suggestive of protest against muzzling by authorities. But we must not think of Massinger as entirely crushed by these repressive measures. His was a sturdy spirit. In 1631 he again attempted the hazardous subject of Spanish affairs, and had a play rejected by Herbert for fear of antagonizing Spain. Some years later, he wrote a play on Don Pedro the Cruel, named *The King and the Subject*. This is non-extant, but we know it was topical from a note made by Herbert (June, 1638). He quotes from the play, and then reacts as follows:

> Monys? Wee'le rayse supplies what ways we please,
> And force you to subscribe to blanks, in which
> We'le mulct you as wee shall thinke fitt. The Caesars
> In Rome were wise, acknowledginge no lawes
> But what their swords did ratifye, the wives
> And daughters of the senators bowing to
> Their wills as deities.

This is a piece taken out of Phillip Messinger's play, called the King and the Subject, and entered here for ever to bee remembered by my son and those that cast their eyes on it, in honour of King Charles, my master, who, reading over the play at Newmarket, set his marke upon the place with his owne hande, and in thes wordes:
"This is too insolent, and to bee changed."

Note, that the poett makes it the speech of a king, Don Pedro, King of Spayne, and spoken to his subjects.[115]

Six or eight years before this play, legal trials had been held to prove whether Charles had or had not the right to impose taxes himself without the consent of Parliament. His high-handed methods of securing money and supplies continued to be an affliction to his subjects. It was the agitation over the

[115] *Variorum* (1821), III, 240.

ship-monies that gave the special application to this portrait of the arbitrary ruler at this time.

The outstanding features of Massinger's criticism are the clear, bold, obvious hits at the chief causes of popular discontent; the insistence on the subject's right to think for himself, to criticise his ruler's vices, weaknesses, and mistaken policies for the purposes of reform.

Somewhat the same ideas are found in some of Chapman's plays, though the insistence is not so frequent. In *The Gentleman Usher* (written 1601 or 1602?) Strozza says (in Act V):

> And what's a Prince? Had all been virtuous men,
> There never had been Prince upon the earth,
> And so no subject; all men had been Princes:
> A virtuous man is subject to no Prince,
> But to his soul and honour; which are laws,
> That carry Fire and Sword within themselves
> Never corrupted, never out of rule;
> What is there in a Prince? That his least lusts
> Are valued at the lives of other men.
> When common faults in him should prodigies be
> And his gross dotage rather loath'd than sooth'd.

Again, the Countess, in *The Revenge of Bussy D'Ambois* (published 1613) instructs as to kings' behavior (Act IV, sc. 1):

> Kings are compared to gods, and should be like them,
> Full in all right, in might superfluous;
> For nothing straining past right for their right;
> Reign justly, and reign safely.

Royal Policies and Affairs of State

Plays which seemed to criticize governmental policies toward other nations were naturally open to censure by authorities in any period. In the time of Elizabeth such allusions, if they occurred, were generally rather indirect. A very interesting example of a play objected to for some such reason is that of *Sir Thomas More*, now carefully edited by W. W. Greg so as to show the censoring. The treatment of the manuscript by the censor shows that the play was quite unacceptable to the authorities. It has been pretty generally assumed that this was because of a topical reference in the riot scenes in which London apprentices showed their resentment of the encroachments of foreign craftsmen upon their livings and their liberties. In view of the censor's treatment of these scenes, one can hardly doubt that there was feared the incensing of Londoners against some foreigners (pretty certainly the French, I should say). But there are probably other, though less obvious reasons for the censor's manhandling of this play. Tilney must have been aware that the general treatment of More as a person and as Chancellor might prove offensive to Elizabeth as daughter of Anne Boleyn and Henry VIII, and as an upholder of Protestantism, in spite of the fact that the authors carefully subordinate the attitude of More as to the divorce of Catherine and the marriage of Anne, and his refusal to take the Oath of Succession, and even though a character of the play does call More's single-minded Catholicism "error." The whole attitude toward More in the play is, nevertheless, that of hero-worship. More is admirable to those of any faith, because this is a play in which, as Surrey remarked at the end, "a very learned, worthie gentleman seals error with his blood." It is a clear-cut portrait, with none of the wavering aim that one sees in the characterization of Barnavelt in the play by that name. The old lives of More (More's, Stapleton's, and others) show a close parallelism of small incident with the action of the play, as in a similar meeting of More and Erasmus *incognito*, the cutpurse incident, and many others that are not essential to the plot but serve to illustrate More's characteristics. The realism of detail, is, in fact, striking. More appears in the play as a learned and subtle diplomat, but wise, practical, and just, generous and charitable to all; brave, philosophical, witty, overflowing with good spirits even in the most trying circumstances. He is sometimes pathetic, but always dignified and courageous, able to support his own misfortunes and furnish good cheer to others.

That any sympathetic treatment of Sir Thomas More in a play would be considered offensive by Elizabeth may fairly be inferred from the fact that Topcliffe, a pursuivant, confiscated from the house of William Carter, a Catholic printer, a manuscript of about 468 pages, of which a copy survives. The account of this is dated August 23, 1592.[116] The manuscript is entitled,

[116] Hist. MSS. Comm, III, 261. Cf. Tanner. *Bibliotheca*, p. 381. Harpsfield was also author of a Life of More (cf. Christopher Wordsworth, *Eccles. Biography*, II, 45–46 and 161).

"A Treatise of marryage occasioned by the pretended Divorce of K. Henrye Eigth from Q. Catherine of Arragone. Written by Reverend Nicholas Harpsfield, LL.D., the last Catholic Archdeacon of Canterbury." It begins in this way: "Forasmuch as this matter is incident to the life of Sir Thomas More." The suppression of this work involving More, late in 1592, may have led to the conclusion that a play on his life would attract popular attention, especially as it would be possible to use his period for the suggestion of several contemporary problems, by analogical portrayal. It will be noticed that the particular cause of suppression of Harpsfield's book, the stand of More on the divorce of Henry VIII, involving as it does the question of the legitimacy of Elizabeth, is carefully evaded in the play.

The manuscript of *Sir Thomas More* (Harley 7368) was first put into print by Dyce for the Shakespeare Society. This edition is permanently valuable as showing readings of passages now illegible because of decay of paper and ink and clumsy repairs of the manuscript with thick paper. C. F. Tucker Brooke's version in the *Shakespeare Apocrypha*, according to W. W. Greg, corrects six errors of Dyce (who made 206) and introduces two new ones. A reasonably good photographic facsimile of the manuscript by R. B. Fleming in the Tudor Facsimile texts will repay the examination of those who are curious as to the look of a censored play manuscript of Shakespeare's time, with its revisions, cuts, and additions. It is, however, not legible throughout, because of the state of the manuscript. Greg's carefully edited reprint (or rather, his edition of the manuscript as collated with Dyce's text), in the Malone Society Publications, 1911, is therefore, for most readers, the best available text for study. Greg's own later conclusions and those of others as to the handwriting of portions of the text must be kept in mind in connection with the reading of his footnotes, especially where he speaks of the parts in the hand of the scribe "S."[117]

The date of *Sir Thomas More* has been speculatively placed anywhere from 1586 to 1599 or even 1604. Mr. W. J. Lawrence

[117] See W. Greg, "Autograph Plays of A. Munday," *Mod. Lang. Rev.*, VIII (1913), 89–90. Cf. also R. Simpson, *Notes and Queries*, July 1, 1871, September 12, 1872; J. Spedding, *Reviews and Discussions*, 1879, pp. 376 ff.; B. Nicholson, *Notes & Q.*, November 29, 1883, and *Shakespeare's Hand in the Play of Sir Thomas More*, Camb. Univ. Press, 1923.

has recently proposed a date of about 1589.[118] This would bring Munday's work on the play into those years when he acted as a pursuivant for Archbishop Whitgift in the Martin Marprelate affair. Exception is taken to this by Miss M. St. Clare Byrne, as very improbable for the period 1589–92. She favors 1596–97 for composition of the play.[119] The choice of a later date than 1592 is suggested by Sir E. Maunde Thompson's study of changes in Munday's handwriting. Greg in his later view favors a date as late as 1599, and Pollard, 1593–94.

The dating of the play is a matter of some interest because the nature and location of Tilney's marks on the manuscript make it quite likely that he thought contemporary analogies would be drawn. The staging of scenes from the bloody May-day of 1517 when the people of London rebelled against the foreigners was feared not for its own sake, but for some application that might be made from its rehearsal at that time.

It is not easy to establish the date from complaints against foreign craftsmen, because they appear in literature and in history at so many different times. An example of a literary reference may be found in the rather allegorical play, *Three Ladies of London*, 1584, by Robert Wilson.

A somewhat more definite point of approach is that of the riots of apprentices, though it must be confessed that several occasions might readily be found when this would apply. There is a temptation to select an occasion when it was recognized that plays might stir up such riots. On September 3, 1595, the Mayor and aldermen of London wrote to the Privy Council objecting to plays because "they move wholy to imitacon and not to the avoyding of those vyces wch they represent wch wee verely think to be the chief cause .... of the late stirr and mutinous attempt of those fiew apprentices and other srvants who wee doubt not driew their infection from these and like places."[120] It must be admitted that the objection raised seems to refer

---

[118] *London Times Literary Supplement*, July, 1920. A number of articles on this play have since appeared in *The Times*. See the index.

[119] "A. Munday and His Books," Bibliographical Society, *Trans.*, n.s. 1, no. 4 (1921), pp. 225 ff. Cf. Percy Simpson in *The Library*, January, 1917. Cf. also *Shakespeare's Hand in the Play of Sir Thomas More*, Camb. Univ. Press, 1923.

[120] *Remembrancia*, II, 103. A lively account of the troubles of 1595 is in *Salisbury MSS*, V, 248 ff. See especially June 15, 16, 17, 1595.

to a habit of playwrights rather than to a particular play containing riots and stirring up of apprentices, but the analogy is interesting and might be of value in connection with more positive evidence. It is at least worth remembering that the authorities were in 1595 particularly on their guard against the presentation of such riot scenes upon the stage. The reason for the desire to put such scenes on the stage was, no doubt, the actual apprentice riots of June, 1595. Fleay has called attention to the possible relationship of this situation to the date of composition of *Sir Thomas More*. Stow's account of the June riot shows up clearly the two dangerous topics that are in the play—insurrection of tradesmen, and jealousy of aliens:

In the year 1595 the poor Tradesmen made a Riot upon the Strangers in Southwark and other parts of the City of London. Whereupon was a presentment of the great Inquest for the said Borough, concerning the outragious Tumult and Disorder unjustly committed there upon Thursday June 12, 1595 and the Leaders were punished and also the chief Offenders. The like Tumults began at the same time within the Liberties where such Strangers commonly harboured. And upon the complaint of the Elders of the Dutch and French Churches Sir John Spenser, Lord Maior, committed some young Rioters to the Counter.

A slight resemblance may here be noted to the threat in *Sir Thomas More*, to appeal to the ambassadors representing the native countries of the alien workmen.

It is true that there are other years than 1595 which are not unlikely dates for *Sir Thomas More*, if one disregards Sir E. M. Thompson's feeling for the lateness of the handwriting. The same foreign tradesmen, French and Dutch, but especially the French, were the cause of a riot in 1586, which Sergeant Fletewood himself, in describing it to Burghley, likened to that of Ill May Day (1517):

This present daye from two of the clocke until syx, my Lo. Maior, with some of his bretherne th' Aldermen and myselffe, dyd examyne certene Apprentices for conspiringe an insurrection in this Cittie agaynst the Frenche and Dutche, but specially agaynst the Frenche; a thinge as lyke unto yll Maye daie as could be devysed in all manner of circumstances, *mutatis mutandis*, ther wanted nothinge but execucion. We have taken fyve, all of an age, yet all under xxitie; fower of them Darbishier borne; the fyrste borne in norhamshier. We are searchinge and seekinge for the principall Captayne; we hope we shall heare of him this night, for he hath been workinge all this daie in the Whythall at Westminster, and at his cominge home we truste to have him. We have this night sett a standinge watche armed, from nyne until seven in the morninge.

Tues. 6 September, 1586.
The apprentices are of the mysterie of Plasterers.[121]

In the symposium *Shakespeare's Hand in the Play of Sir Thomas More*, Mr. Pollard has made out a good case for the period 1593–94 for the play, basing it on the "complaints and libels against the Flemings and French about May, 1593" (Strype, *Annals*, vol. iv, no. 1731). I am not entirely convinced that playwrights would be frightened away by the liveness of the topic in 1595; but the play would be of sufficient interest and more use at the earlier date that he prefers. For a reason for renewed interest in More's life late in 1592, see p. 130, *supra*.

While the date, then, is still not definitely settled, it is clear that the play must have been written at some time when the riot scene was felt to be particularly dangerous; for the chief direction of criticism is against those parts which present riot and conflict among craftsmen, and enmity between Englishmen and strangers on account of the authorities' having favored these aliens at the expense of natives, and against parts of the play which present these aliens in a very unpleasant light. Next to the riot scenes, the chief matter of objection is the flaying of the vice of a prince and taxing the court with blind following of its leader. Let us examine the criticisms in more detail.

Opposite lines 1–19 (Greg's edition), Tilney crosses out the speakers' names and writes above one the note:

Leave out the insur(rection) wholy & the cause theroff and (B)egin with Sir Thomas Moore att the mayors sessions with a reportt afterwards off his good service don being Shriue off London uppon a mutiny Agaynst the Lumbards only by A shortt reportt & nott otherwise att your own perrilles.

E. Tyllney

The first 75 lines are practically wrecked by the censor. Lines 24–25, marked for omission, are probably objectionable because

---

[121] *Original Letters Illustrative of English History* (ed. Ellis), ser. 1, II, 306 (letter CCXVIII). In the play of *Sir Thomas More* some of the apprentices were carpenters—a trade allied to that of the plasterer.

they might suggest contemporary reasons for inflammation against foreigners. Lincoln says: "It is hard when Englishmens pacience must be thus ietted on by straungers." Again, lines 28–40, marked for omission by Tilney, express anger over the Lombard's insult to the carpenter's wife, and over his insolent remark, "if she were the maior of London's wife, had I her once in my possession, I would keep her in sp(ite) of him that durst say nay." Another cut, probably by Tilney, five lines below (45–75) is of a passage showing the two insolent strangers threatening to complain to their ambassador, and the English goldsmith and carpenter whom they have wronged through their wives planning to have the strangers' wickedness and insolence advertised by the preachers in the "spittle sermons."

Lines 76–106 are also marked for cutting. They would need to go if one omitted what preceded. The bill of complaints here given states that "aliens and straungers eate the bread from the fatherlesse children, and take the living from all the artificers and the entercourse from all merchants whereby pouertie is so much encreased, that euery man bewayleth the miserie of other for craftsmen be brought to beggerie, and merchants to needines." There follows a threat to make next Mayday the worst the strangers ever saw.

Some of the criticisms and cuts in *Sir Thomas More* strike us now as showing an extremity of nervousness. The mark in the margin at lines 316–23, MEND THIS, points out what seems a very general description, where Shrewsbury says:

> My Lord of Surrey, and Sir Thomas Palmer,
> might I with pacience tempte your graue aduise,
> I tell ye true, that in these daungerous times,
> I doo not like this frowning vulgare brow.
> my searching eye did neuer entertaine,
> a more distracted countenaunce of greefe
> then I haue late obseru'de
> in the displeased commons of the cittie.

Perhaps this is marked because it is in a way prefatory to the open invitation to insurrection a little further on (lines 372–85), which Tilney marked for omission:

> Surrie. But if the Englishe blood be once but up,
>   as I perceiue theire harts alreadie fu(ll)

> I feare me much, before their spleenes (be) coolde,
> some of these saucie Aliens for their pride,
> will pay for 't soundly, wheresoere it lights.
> this tide of rage, that with the Eddie striues:
> I feare me much will drowne too manie liues.
>
> Cholmeley. Now afore God, your honors, pardon me,
>   men of your place and greatnesse, are to blame
> I tell ye true my Lords, in that his Maiestie
> Is not informed of this base abuse,
> And dayly wrongs are offered to his subjects
> ffor if he were. I knowe his gracious wisedome,
> would soone redresse it.

This passage certainly suggests a play with a purpose.

Tilney's uneasiness appears in his care to change references to offensive aliens. In line 364 Shrewsbury complains that "some straunger" takes "vituals from the Catours." Tilney brackets *straunger* and interlines in its place the specific word *Lombard*. Again in line 368, where a *ffrencheman* is made to take away a carpenter's pigeons, Tilney makes the Frenchman a Lombard.

A desperate, if somewhat ineffectual effort to remove all possible cause of friction is Tilney's improvement on Palmer's report (line 351) that Bard has told him that "if he had the maior of Londons wife, he would keepe her in despight of any Englishe." Tilney bracketed *English* and substituted *Man*. However, it is questionable, even so, whether the Lombard's boast would cement the amity of nations.

Scenes of tumult and rebellion suffer throughout the play. Lines 388–93 are marked for omission. Here a messenger reports that the city is in an uproar and the mayor is threatened if he comes out of his house. The bill of wrongs has been published by the clergyman. Almost immediately following this is a riot scene (sc. 4, beginning line 410), also cancelled. Captain Lincoln here inflames the crowd against the audacious strangers, "outlandish fugitives who enjoy more privileges than natives." He proposes to fire their houses. The mayor and sheriff (More) line up against the rebels.

The next scene (5) is the prentice scene, the first part of which is canceled and imperfect in the manuscript. A row among apprentices of trades is arbitrated by More, who promises to secure them mercy if they yield. They do so, and are taken to prison. Lines 583–96 are also marked for omission, possibly by Tilney. Here the sheriff speaks of the gazing multitudes who stop up the streets in these troublous times. He orders the execution of the prisoners. The scene as a whole is surely not subversive of law and order. The leader, Lincoln, makes a fine speech, repenting of having secured his own redress as a private man, and patiently submitting to the law.

Scene viii, in which More perpetrates a merry jest upon the visiting Erasmus, is cancelled and imperfect, being revised with large insertions. The scene is based upon a story, supposed to be true, concerning the first meeting of More and Erasmus, and its only use could be as humorous relief. The revision is no doubt voluntary, for literary or dramatic reasons.

A revision of the scene (viii b) in which (lines 797–86) More gives orders for suppressing the mutinies is cancelled. My Lord of Winchester's and Ely's men were to be watched if they should come in armed.

Quite important for the plot of the play is sc. 10 (lines 1158 ff.) in which the Privy Council discuss having the Emperor fight under the English flag with them against the "perfidious French." Articles are sent in for the King and the lords to subscribe to. More asks time for consideration, and resigns his office. The Bishop of Rochester alone stands by him in refusing to sign the articles. Of this scene Tilney cancels 1247–75, including More's resignation, the king's order that he retire to his house at Chelsey, and More's invitation to other lords to visit him there and go fishing for "the great" with a cunning net. At the line where More resigns, someone (probably Tilney) writes "ALL ALTR."

A cancellation made either by the censor or through fear of him, in all probability, was that of lines 1471–1501, in a long speech by More. Lines 1491–93, at least, would give offense in an age when any criticism of a monarch's vice was dangerous:

> As for the prince, in all his sweet gorgde mawe,
> And his rancke fleshe that sinfully renewes
> The noones excesse in the nights daungerous surfeits.

There is hardly a doubt that Elizabeth would object to such a description of her father on the stage.

A good part of scene xiii (lines 1471–1516) was intended to be replaced by one of several additions to the play manuscript—that which Greg labels "I." In the new passage also a criticism of king and court, which is more general than that which it is intended to replace, suffers a cut, either because of actual or because of feared censorship. It runs (lines 5 ff.):

> The Court like heauen
> examines not the anger of the (king); Prince
> and being more fraile composde of guilded earth
> shines upon them on whom the (Prince) king doth shine
> smiles if he smile, declines if he decline
> yet seeing both are mortall court and king
> shed not one teare for any earthly thing.

In several passages nothing in the ink of the manuscript nor in the content of the passages shows certainly whether the revision is voluntary or forced. For example, near the beginning a speech is marked for omission (lines 198–201) which may be a voluntary revision. If forced, it could only be because it held up a real officer of a former age to too great ridicule. Justice Suresbie, compared with the Justice in More's *Life of More* who figures in the amusing incident of the cutpurse's gulling him under More's direction, is seen to be very like the original in essential traits: a stupid, pompous piece, verbose, repetitious, absolutely sure of himself and prone to criticise others for faults he shares with them. If he were a contemporary, one might expect a censor to object to such a realistic cartoon. As he is not, it is hard to say what caused the revision.

Clearly, the main direction of Tilney's criticism is against the staging of revolt, rebellion, popular discontent, and friction of the lower classes of Englishmen and aliens.

The state of the manuscript of the play has given rise to various theories. Until Greg pointed out what is, indeed, obvious, that the additions, substitutions, cancellations, and revisions cannot possibly be regarded as either satisfying the conditions of the censor or furnishing a text sufficiently complete and continuous for use of a dramatic company, the manuscript has been spoken of as if it showed a rough revision carrying out the censor's wishes, remodeling the play to make it actable. Even recently there has been an attempt to show that this was a playhouse copy. Fowell and Palmer, in their work on the censorship of the drama, describe it as a "book in the state in which the author sold it to the players," and one which showed how the alterations caused by censorship were carried out. Mr. Greg, on the other hand, comes to the conclusion (p. xv) that many of the alterations and additions which affect portions condemned by the censor are explicable as voluntary literary revisions, and were in the manuscript when it was submitted for license. "When it returned bearing Tilney's remarks, it became clear . . . . that it was quite impossible to comply with the demands of the censor without eviscerating the play in a manner fatal to its success on the stage. The manuscript was consequently laid aside and the play never came on the boards." The occurrence of the name of an actor of a minor part (V. 2, fol. 13) he explains as indicating no more than that the play was once cast for acting. Greg is certainly right in his position that the additions and alterations cannot be lumped. The addition which he numbers "VI" is a new scene properly inserted. The scenes dealing with Erasmus clearly show voluntary dramatic revision, whether before or after submission to the censor. A new beginning to the insurrection scene is fitted into its proper place where the earlier version was cancelled. The apprentice scene originally cancelled is dropped out, and its place taken by the guildhall scene of addition "II," which is comparatively undramatic in its report of how the prentices wounded Sir John Munday. But as this new version also suffered some crossing out (II, 68–75), Greg's contention that the revisions were there when the manuscript was submitted to the censor receives support at this point. However, as this revision does seem clearly to be an attempt to meet a previous objection along the lines of the critic's suggestions (as in addition II, where messengers report the prentices' riots, and the rebels' delivery of prisons, instead of having these acted out), is it not possible to suppose that the revision was not there when Tilney first saw the piece? Is it not possible that, in view of his very serious objections, some attempts at revision were made, including cuts, additions, and revisions both voluntary and involuntary, and the manuscript, still in an unfinished state, re-submitted to him in order to see whether it was worth while going on with —whether, indeed, it was possible to get an actable play out of the materials that would not be offensive to Tilney? The cuts

SUBJECTS CONSIDERED DANGEROUS

and revisions on revisions seem to me to favor such a theory. For example, the little passage on the prince and court as mortal and the court's blindly following the prince seems to have met two objections in its two forms.

Scenes 4, 5, and 6, which met with heavy objections from the censor, are partly revised or substituted for. The Privy Council scene marked ALL ALTR' was never satisfactorily changed; nor were the censor's directions for the opening of the play carried out. These facts alone would make it improbable that the play, after meeting such criticism, was ever acted as it stands—if indeed it could be. Whether it was ever, by any slip, acted before this censorship, is another question. At any rate the lacunae, the lack of joinings, and the bad joinings make it clear that, whether it was ever acted before or after censorship, the present composite does not itself represent an actable version. And if we took this as a specimen of the kind of playbook sold by authors to companies, we must conclude that the authors were sharpers and the companies fools.

The book of *Sir Thomas More* looks like an incomplete, and perhaps abandoned, attempt at revision, partly voluntary and partly forced by the censor, and possibly submitted to the censor a second time with discouraging results.[122]

In the reigns of James and Charles, the movements and policies of rulers were much more frequently subjected to direct comment or unmistakable reference by the dramatists. There is a very early reflection of the general resentment by Englishmen of King James's favoritism toward the Scotch in a satirical reference in *Eastward Hoe!* (by Chapman, Jonson, and Marston) to the king's grants of knighthood to Scotchmen for a fee: "I ken the mon weel, he's one of my thirty pound knights." This was an amusing bit for the jealous and resentful Englishman, but not for the resident Scot. "Sir James Murray, Scotus," so knighted by King James on August 5, 1603, resented this and another reference to the Scots—one which is extant in only a few copies, having been cancelled in the others. It is Seagull's description of Virginia (Act III, sc. ii):[123]

---

[122] Mr. W. J. Lawrence, however, believes that the play was acted, that the manuscript is a prompt copy, and that the date is as early as 1589. See *London Times Literary Supplement*, July, 1920.

[123] *Old Plays*, IV, 250.

You shall live freely there without serjeants, or courtiers, or lawyers, or intelligencers: only a few industrious Scots, perhaps, who indeed are dispersed over the face of the whole earth. But, as for them, there are no greater friends to Englishmen and England, when they are out on't, in the world, than they are: and, for my part, I would a hundred thousand of them were there, for we are all one country-men now,[124] ye know, and we should find ten times more comfort of them there than here.

Drummond's account of the matter, if reliable, would indicate that the offence was taken very seriously indeed:

He [Jonson] was delated by Sir James Murray to the King, for writing something against the Scots, in a play called Eastward Hoe, and voluntarily imprissoned himself with Chapman and Marston, who had written it amongst them. The report was, that they should then [have] had their ears cut[125] and noses. After their delivery, he banqueted all his friends: there was Camden, Selden,[126] and others: at the midst of the feast his old mother dranke to him, and shew him a paper which she had (if the sentence had taken execution) to have mixed in the prisson amonge his drinke, which was full of lustie strong poison, and that she was no churle, she minded first to have drunk of it herself.[127]

When James acceded to the English throne, his open favoring of Scotchmen in England roused active resentment on the part of Englishmen (according to Beaumont, the French ambassador, and according to various letters of statesmen of the day). In such a state of friction, ridiculing the Scotch on the stage of London was a dangerous experiment. The first passage in *Eastward Hoe* mentioned above is so slight a reference, and the second so amusing that neither would seem to us a capital

---

[124] This idea and the purchase of knighthood from James would seem to have been common talk in 1603. Between May 23 and 29, Sir Philip Gawdy wrote to his brother, "The King hath placed in all offices some Skottes and put out many Englishe, meaning to make us alle one under the name of ancient britons." And in the middle of 1603 Gawdy wrote that his uncle, Justice Gawdy, "disdaineth the manner of the making of knightes (as they are now made) and all gentlemen of worthe make a ridiculous jest of them, that bought it so dearly." He says Justice Gawdy was offered a knighthood for fifty pounds, but refused it. (*Letters of Sir Philip Gawdy*, Roxburghe Club, p. 131).

[125] This is perhaps referred to in the prologue to Beaumont's *Woman Hater* (1607?), where the author expresses his intention not to lose his ears.

[126] As these historians were both muzzled by the censorship at times, they would no doubt be sympathizing auditors.

[127] *Works of Jonson*, (ed. Gifford-Cunningham), III, 483.

offence; but we have Drummond's word for it that the authors were imprisoned because of this. To me it is questionable whether the imprisonment "without trial or hearing" referred to in a series of letters published by Bertram Dobell from a manuscript book containing copies of letters by Chapman and Jonson[128] was for this offence or for a still more serious cause. Most of the letters clearly refer to the same occasion, a joint imprisonment of Chapman and Jonson, but with no mention of the third collaborator in *Eastward Hoe*, Marston, who, according to Drummond, was with them in prison. These letters of Chapman and Jonson have been differently interpreted as referring to trouble over *Eastward Hoe* or over *Sejanus*, or over some unknown play in which Chapman collaborated with Jonson (the last being Castelain's theory). It seems to me unnecessary to suppose an unknown play, but doubtful whether the letters refer to *Eastward Hoe*, in which we know Marston to have collaborated also, or to *Sejanus*, where the "other pen" besides Jonson's is yet unidentified, but which may conceivably have been Chapman's, as, according to Henslowe, he did collaborate with Jonson on some tragedy. The dates of production of *Eastward Hoe* and *Sejanus* are so near together as to be of little service in deciding the reference. Either play might have brought the author into trouble by 1605. *Sejanus* was acted at the Globe in 1603, entered on S.R. November 2, 1604, "put over" to Thos. Thorpe August 6, 1605, and published for him in the same year with signs of trouble in the accompanying verses and the prefatory note. It is quite likely that it was held up from publication in 1604–05 either because of trouble over itself or because of imprisonment and investigation of its author or authors on some other charge. *Eastward Hoe* was entered S.R. September 4, 1605, and probably written in 1604 or 1605.

The history of the trouble over *Sejanus* is not at all clear. Drummond says of Jonson: "Northampton was his mortal enemy for beating on a St. George's day one of his attenders. He was called before the Council for his *Sejanus* and accused both of popery and treason by him."[129] The date of this appearance before the Council and its results are not known. Drummond

[128] See "Newly Discovered Documents of the Elizabethan and Jacobean Periods," *Athenaeum*, March 23, March 30, April 6, April 13, 1901.
[129] *Works of Jonson*, (ed. Gifford-Cunningham), III, 484.

is not always trustworthy, but such a serious charge would be an odd invention for which it would be difficult to find a reason. Besides, we know the play was suppressed for a time, that Jonson revised it, working alone, that he afterward referred to it as badly misinterpreted, that, in publishing, he advertised that it was changed from the stage version, and that he inserted a comment on the King which would be peculiar unless his loyalty had been called in question. This comment seems to me the nearest to an indication of fear that Jonson ever showed in a preface or postscript. He is usually vigorous and buoyant, reacting strongly against hostile criticism. Here he is almost servile in his pious postscript to his preface:

This do we advance, as a mark of terror to all traitors, and treasons: to shew how just the heavens are, in pouring and thundering down a weighty vengeance on their unnatural intents, even to the worst princes; much more to those, for guard of whose piety and virtue the angels are in continual watch, and God himself miraculously working.

The year 1605 is a mysterious one in the life of Jonson. He was once supposed to have been suspected of complicity in the "Gunpowder Plot," because he was in some way concerned in the investigation. This may have been due to the fact that Jonson was acquainted with the Catholics; and he may have volunteered his services in clearing up the plot just because of a false charge of popery against him. According to Drummond, Jonson was "12 yeares a Papist" after he had been imprisoned and had narrowly escaped hanging for killing a man in a duel.[130] But he was reconciled with the English Church, left off being a recusant, and took communion[131] at the table of Salisbury. It was to Salisbury that he offered his services, November 8, 1605, in a letter which is summarized in the *State Papers Domestic*:

Has done his best to procure a fitting person to perform a certain business but many are removed and concealed; some say they must consult the Archpriest; thinks they are all so enweaved in it as it will make 500 gent. lesse of the religion, within this weeke." Offers his own services, if a better person cannot be found.[132]

[130] *Conversations*, Bodley Head Quarto, p. 11.
[131] *Ibid.*, p. 14.
[132] *S. P. Dom.*, 1603–10, vol. XVI, art. 30.

Within two months of this date both the plays that had been giving Jonson trouble with the authorities had been entered on the Registers for publication. There are other puzzling aspects. Drummond implies it was Northampton who accused Jonson of popery and treason for *Sejanus*. Northampton was one of the three commissioners appointed to investigate the Gunpowder plot.[133] And later Northampton was himself accused by an enemy before the Council of covering the crimes of the guilty in this plot.

Jonson's interpretation of *Sejanus* as a "mark of terror to all traitors and treasons" seems to fit in with Drummond's account of the accusation. The accompanying verses of Hugh Holland, though guarded in their denial of parallelism of the ancient story of Sejanus with contemporary history, show clearly that there is a moral in the play applicable to the favorites of King James.[134] The verses of "Philos" show, too, that the noting of the resemblance was not altogether unreasonable. For instance:

> For thou has given each part so just a style,
> That men suppose the action now on file.
> ....
> And others are so quick that they will spy
> Where later times are in some speech unweaved.

That the imprisonment of Jonson referred to in the letters mentioned above is for at least a second offence supplies no

---

[133] *S. P. Dom.*, 1611–18, vol. LXX, art. 61 (August, 1612). A little before his death, according to Thomas Lorkin, Northampton declared himself of his old religion (popery), (Letter to T. Puckering, July 2, 1614, *Court and Times of James I*, I, 331).

[134] It is interesting to note here an application of the Sejanus parallel made by Charles. In the proceedings against Sir John Eliot and other members of the Commons by Charles in 1629, Charles was particularly angry with Eliot. "The implication of the King's connivance with Buckingham in the affair of the plaister and potion given to James I, as I think, was so understood at the time, when Eliot abruptly broke off with an invidious quotation from Cicero in a like case, 'which he feared to speak and feared to think' was not likely to be forgotten by the King. Charles asserted that, in comparing Buckingham to Sejanus, Eliot, by implication, must mean that he was Tiberius." (Disraeli, *Commentaries* .... *Chas. I*, I, 325.) There was some reason for this touchiness of Charles. Dr. George Eglisham, a physician, published at Frankfort in 1626, a charge that Buckingham caused the death of James, *Prodromus Vindictae in Ducem Buckinghamiae*, etc., later published in English as *The Fore-runner of Revenge* (John Row, *Historie of the Kirk of Scotland*, 347).

decisive evidence as between *Eastward Hoe* and *Sejanus*; for the earlier imprisonment might be that of Jonson just before October 8, 1597, when, according to a note discovered by E. K. Chambers, Jonson, with Gabriel Spencer and Robert Shaa, was discharged from the Marshelsea.[135] Or Jonson may even have been imprisoned in connection with a threatened libel suit over the *Poetaster*, according to a hint in the 1616 dedication.

The two strongest bits of evidence for a reference to *Eastward Hoe* are: first, the known collaboration of Chapman and Jonson in that play; and, second, Chapman's plea to the King for himself and Jonson, "whose chief offences are but two clauses, and both of them not our owne; much less the unnaturall issue of our offenceless intents." This applies better to *Eastward Hoe* with its two references to the Scots than to *Sejanus*, at least so far as we can judge of the old play by its rewritten form. The trouble with *Sejanus* was probably a large one—of central conception, a supposed parallelism of the favorite and the tyrant with persons of his own day.

On the other hand, it is hard to account for Marston's not being in prison (as Drummond said he was for *Eastward Hoe*), and for his not being mentioned in the letters of either Chapman or Jonson, unless indeed he is being referred to as the scapegoat who is guilty of the errors. That those responsible for the two clauses in *Eastward Hoe* concerning the Scots were players is a bit improbable because the passages are in a few printed copies of the first edition. Chapman may have meant to suggest actors' interpolations by way of evasion, however.

Although the bulk of the evidence does seem to favor Dobell's view that the letters of Chapman and Jonson that he publishes refer to their joint imprisonment over *Eastward Hoe*, I find it difficult to agree that all do so refer, because some of Jonson's describe so inaptly that quite obvious offence of ridiculing the Scotch, about whose importance there might well be two opinions (say, that of an Englishman and that of a Scotchman), but about whose meaning there could not well be. But Jonson writes to "Excellentest of Ladies":

I am commytted and with me a worthy Friend, one Mr. Chapman ....and our offence a Play, so mistaken, so misconstrued, so mis-

---

[135] *Acts of Privy Council*, n.s. XXVIII, 33. Cf. *Mod. Lang. Rev.*, IV, 511.

applied, as I do wonder whether their ignorance or Impudence be most, who are our adversaries. It is now not disputable, for we stand on uneven bases, and our cause so unequally carried, as we are without examininge, without hearinge, or without any proofe but malicious Rumor, horried to bondage and fetters; The cause we understand to be the Kinges indignation.

What has "malicious Rumor," or ignorance, or misapplication to do with the offence of *Eastward Hoe*?

Again, Jonson's letter to Pembroke, and that to a "most honorable Lord" (printed by Dobell) seem to refer to very grave charges, such as would question Jonson's loyalty as a subject. I cannot see that making fun of the Scotch does that, exactly— though a Scotch king might feel differently about it. The letter to the "honorable lord" turns largely on his loyalty:

Though the imprisonmente itselfe can not but grieve mee (in respect of his Majesties high displeasure, from whence it proceedes, yet the manner of it afflicts me more, being commytted hether, unex-amyned, nay unheard (a Rite not commonlie denyed to the greatest offenders) and I made a guiltie man longe before I am one, or ever thought to bee: God I call to testimonye what my thoughts are, and ever have bene of his Majestie: & so may I thrive when he comes to be my Judge & my kinges as they are most sincere: And I appeale to posteritie that will hereafter read and judge my writings (though now neglected) whether it be possible I should speak of his Majestie as I have done without the affection of a most zealous and good subject. It hath ever been my destinye to be misreported and condemn'd on the first tale.

In his letter to the Chamberlain, an authority to whom playwrights frequently appealed for sympathy when in trouble over the contents of their plays, Jonson writes as if the imprisonment had endured a while and the anger of the King were grave:

The anger of the Kinge is death (saith the wise man) and in truth it is little less with mee and my frend, for it hath buried us quick. And though we know it onlie the propertie of men guiltie, and worthy of punishment to invoke Mercye; yet now it might relieve us who have onlie our Fortunes made our fault; and are indeed vexed for other men's license.

Jonson's letter to Salisbury, printed in the Gifford-Cunningham Memoir, as well as by Dobell, could refer either to *Sejanus* or to *Eastward Hoe*. It states that Jonson has been, "unexamined and unheard, committed to a vile prison" with George Chapman because of a play falsely construed by others.

I protest to your honor, and call God to testimony, since my first error, which, yet, is punished in me more with my shame than it was then with my bondage) I have so attempered my style, that I have given no cause to any good man of grief; and if to any ill, by touching at any general vice, it hath always been with a regard and sparing of particular persons .... Let me be examined both by all my works past and this present; and not trust to rumour but my books.... whether I have.... given offence to a nation, to a public order or state, or any person of honor and authority; but have equally laboured to keep their dignity as mine own person, safe.

He begs Salisbury to intercede with the Chamberlain, to whom he has written.

Additional clues to the situation are these points in the series of letters published by Dobell: Chapman's apology for having the play performed without submitting it to him for license because of his inaccessibility; and the suggestion that the imprisonment lasted a while, because the two friends' "habilities and healths fainte under their yrcksome burthens"; and the statement that Lord "Dawbney" has interceded for one of them. It was through Aubigné, the friend and patron of both Jonson and Chapman, and through the Chamberlain that the release was effected. One of the letters from Chapman, who was helped out of his difficulties over *Byron* by the same patron, thanks Aubigné, through his secretary, for a shelter in the "austeritie of the offended time." Jonson, on his visit to Drummond of Hawthornden (1619) said he had lived with "my Lord Aulbanie" for five years; and rather implied he had been "in my Lord Aubanies house" in 1604.[136]

Esmé Stuart, Lord d'Aubigné, as patron of these two Jacobean dramatists who repeatedly got into trouble over the use of political materials, arouses some interesting speculations. He was the cousin of James's father, and he went from France to Scotland soon after James became the Scottish king. He was a great favorite with James,[137] but was accused of filling the

---

[136] *Conversations*, Bodley Head Quarto, p. 12 and p. 6.

[137] James wrote an epithalamium on the marriage of Henrietta Stuart, daughter of Esmé Stuart (then Duke of Lennox) July 21, 1588 (A. F. Westcott, *New Poems of James I*, 1911).

court with Papists. He was himself suspected of being an emissary of the Pope, in spite of a public renunciation of popery.[138]

If the imprisonment of Jonson and Chapman was for *Eastward Hoe*, what of Marston, whom some think more responsible than either Jonson or Chapman because of their insistence on their innocence, and some because the few offensive passages remaining seem to them more like Marston than either of the other authors? I have seen but one hint that Marston may have been punished for a part in *Eastward Hoe*. In Anthony Nixon's *The Black Yeare* (1606) is a suggestion that the sales of Jonson's and Chapman's works (if one may guess them to be the "good wittes") have suffered from collaboration with Marston for a play reminding one of *Westward Hoe*:

Some booksellers this yeare shall not have cause to boast of their winings, for that many write what flowe with phrases and yet are barrein in substance, and such are neyther wise nor wittye; others are so concise that you neede a commentarie to understand them, others have good wittes but so criticall that they arraigne other men's works at the tribunall seat of every censurious Aristarchs understanding, when their owne are sacrificed in Paules Churchyard for bringing in the Dutch Courtezan to corrupt English conditions, and sent away westward for carping both at court, cittie, and countrie. For they are so sodaine witted that a flea can no sooner friske foorth but they must needs comment on her.[139]

Sending away westward means to the gallows at Tyburn, as where Touchstone in *Eastward Hoe*, Act II, sc. 1, line 108, says, "Sir, Eastward hoe will make you go westward ho." Similarly Greene, in the *Art of Connycatching*, part 2, says: "Westward they goe, and there solemnly make a rehearsal sermon at Tiborne." *Eastward Hoe*, in Act II, sc. 3, and elsewhere contains

---

[138] Such renunciations were regarded with suspicion because letters were intercepted from Rome carrying dispensations to those believers who, under stress, professed Protestant tenets for a time. (Strype, *Annals*, II, 630–31; Spottiswood, 308.) See "Notes proving that the Duke of Lennox and Arran sought of old the wrack of Religion, the king, and commonwealth," where his associates are named "papists by profession . . . . obstinate enemies to the king's crown and amitie," (*MSS Bibl. Jurid. Edin.* M. 6.8.; quoted by Thomas M'Crie, *Life of Andrew Melville*, p. 424).

[139] See C. M. Gayley, *Representative English Comedies*, II, 411, for comment.

references to the age as "wittie," and to satire of both court and city.

If all the letters published by Mr. Dobell must be construed as referring to the same offence, I must admit that the preponderance of evidence seems to favor an imprisonment for *Eastward Hoe*; but there are some parts of it which do not seem to fit that offence very well, and it is hard to believe that this play could cause so much trouble. The offences against the Scottish knights are duplicated in Chapman's references to the "strange knights abroad," *Widow's Tears*, IV, 1, 28 (between 1603 and 1609?), and to Jacobean knights in *Monsieur d'Olive*, I, i, 263; I, ii, 124; IV, ii, 77 (*c.* 1604?). The latter play refers to costly embassies, and both plays criticize monopolies (*W.T.*, I, 1, 125; and *M. d'O.*, I, i, 284). Again, Barry's play *Ram Alley* (1607–08) also refers to the Jacobean knightings of 1603–05 (Dodsley, p. 272). If such reference were a capital offence, it seems strange that we hear so little of punishment.

Satire on Other Nations

Closely connected with criticism of royal policies is satire on foreign nations, when that satire is anything more barbed than genial ridicule such as humorists of any nation tend to heap on other nations for pure fun. Throughout the reign of Elizabeth one may find instances of innocuous ridicule of foreigners. For example, Elizabeth was generally friendly to the Welsh; but their language was tempting to parody in comic dialect. *Patient Grissell*, *Satiromastix*, *Northward Ho*, *Henry IV*, and *Merry Wives of Windsor* all show humor at the expense of the Welsh. On March 13, 1599, Henslowe described a play by note of payment to Drayton and Chettle for "a booke wherein is a part of a Welshman." Other outlandish dialects are used for humorous portrayal of foreigners, as in William Haughton's *Englishmen for My Money*, where three discomfited suitors talk Dutch-English, Italian-English, and French-English. French jargon was very commonly used for humor, as in *Henry V*, or as in the talk of Dekker's French doctors. *Shoemaker's Holiday* and *The Roaring Girl* show a similar use of Dutch dialect.

All this is very innocent. But the three nations which came into real rivalry in any way with England—Spain, France, and Scotland—came in for a more serious type of satire on the

English stage, a satire probably intended to influence public opinion. The nervousness of officials with regard to thrusts against a foreign nation at critical times shows that the effect of such thrusts was feared. In censoring *Sir Thomas More*, Tilney changed a number of lines to avoid abuse of the French. He substituted *Lombard* for *Frenchman* where a passage seemed insulting; and he struck out the taunt of "any English" made by the insolent Bard (as noted above), though he cannot be said to have removed the insolence by so doing. Letters written by foreign ambassadors resident in London show how they watched the plays for such satires. The French ambassador took action on Chapman's *Byron*; the Spanish, on Middleton's *A Game at Chess*; and James himself took a hand in punishing for *Eastward Hoe* and its slight on the Scotch. And still it is quite clear that there was, in spite of this watchfulness, considerable of such satire on other nations.

The claim of James to the succession aroused much popular discussion from the time when he first showed a desire to marry Elizabeth to make his claim sure.[140] There was a very strong anti-Scotch feeling shown in drama, as well as in other forms of literature, from that time to the accession. One of the earliest examples of this feeling is in Greene's *Scottish History of James IV* (written before 1592 and perhaps as early as 1585 or 1586), where the playwright goes out of his way to include a critical satire on court policies and manners and the customs of professional classes. There is one remark which would probably be construed as referring to the time when the play was performed, and not the time of the play: "In the year 1520 was in Scotland a king over-ruled with parasites, misled by lust and many circumstances too long to trattle on now, much like our Court of Scotland this day." Not only Greene, but Peele, Dekker, Shakespeare, Jonson, and Chapman display anti-Scotch feeling in greater or less degree. Traces of it appear, for example, in *George-a-Greene, Edward III, The Famous History of Sir Thomas Wyatt, A Midsummer Night's Dream*, and the Folio version of *Henry V*.

The period 1594–1601 contains most of the uncomplimentary references to Scotland. The relations between Elizabeth and James were strained. On April 13, 1594, James sent am-

[140] See *S. P. Scotland*, II, 964 and *S. P. Foreign*, 1584–85, p. 161.

bassadors to Elizabeth "upon weighty and urgent occasions, importing no less than the break of the amity so long and happily continued between the two crowns."[141] The cause of the threatened break was the harboring in England of the Earl of Bothwell, who was plotting against the person of James. Elizabeth had similar complaints to make of James for failing to act against three popish earls, Angus, Errol, and Huntley, who found favor in Scotland at this time, though they were recognized enemies of Elizabeth.

On June 18, 1595, George Nicolson, the Scottish agent, wrote to William Bowes: "In the conclusion of a book called Rich his Farewell [to the Military Profession], printed in 1594, such matter is noted as the king is not pleased with; he says little but thinks the more."[142] In the last of Rich's book, he tells of a king of Scotland somewhat resembling Machiavelli's Belphegor. As Rich was a crown servant after 1598 and also prospered under James, he was perhaps not proved guilty of intent to offend.

A William Leonard was accused of speaking slander to the dishonor of the King and the Queen of Scotland his mother, but was acquitted on August 14, 1595.[143]

In the following year (November 12, 1596) James brought complaint against Edmund Spenser for his satire on himself and his mother in *The Faerie Queene*, books iv–vi of which were published then. The affair is recorded in the *Register of the Council of Scotland*, vol. V, p. 323, and also in the *Calendar of State Papers of Scotland*, II (1509–1603), vol. LIX, art. 66. In the latter record, Bowes's communication to Burghley is thus summarized:

> Great offence conceived by the King against Edmund Spenser, for publishing in print, in the second part of the Fairy Queen, chapter 9, some dishonorable effects, as the king deemeth, against himself and his mother deceased. He [Bowes] has satisfied the king about the "privilege" under which the book is published; yet he [the King] still desireth that Edmund Spenser, for his fault, may be duly tried and punished.

---

[141] W. B. Devereux, *Lives and Letters of the Devereux*, I, 311–312. Cf. an entry for Nov. 3, 1594, in *Salisbury MSS*, vol. V, on James's anger over harboring traitors.

[142] *S. P. Scotland*, II (1509–1603), vol. LVI, art. 13.

[143] *S. P. Dom. Eliz.*, 1595–97, vol. CCLIII, art. 83.

In a transcript of Bowes's letter furnished by Henry R. Plomer[144] one point comes out more clearly:

> He alledged that this booke was passed with previledge of her majesties Commission(er)s for the veiwe and allowance of all wrytinges to be receaued into Printe. But therin I haue (I think) satisfyed him that it is not given out with such p(ri)viledge: yet he still desyreth, etc.

This evasion of official responsibility was on purely technical grounds, apparently, as it would be easier to suppress the book and punish the author if unprivileged than if privileged. Bowes's explanation merely relieved English officials of deliberate complicity in the insult.

The complaint no doubt refers especially to the false Duessa as she appears in Canto 9 of Book V. One reason for the remonstrance at this time was that Elizabeth had just complained of Buccleuch's offence in the famous rescue of "Kinmont Willie" Armstrong. The relations between the two countries were strained, largely, no doubt, because of the tension over James's hopes for recognition of his claim to the English throne.

An eloquent Irishman, Walter Quin, took it upon himself to reply to Spenser's *Faerie Queene*. His first approach to James was in 1595, through a "treatise of poesie" containing *anagrammata in nomen Jacobi sexti . . . . variis linguis inventa*. There were four epigrams in four languages. The English verses were sonnets inscribed "Charles James Stewart claims Arthur's seat," and "Charles James Stewart, ceas letts I am Arthur." One poetical composition in French was entitled *Discours sur le mesme anagramme en forme de dialogue entre un zelateur du bien public et une Dame laquelle represente le royaume d'Angleterre*. Quin also made an oration to the King about his title in January, 1596.[145] And on February 25, 1598, George Nicolson sent word to Robert Cecil of an attempt through the agency of James to force Waldegrave (a publisher often disciplined by the Stationers' Company of London for unruly behavior) to publish a defence of the title of James to the throne of England. I quote from Mr. Henry Plomer's abstract of Nicolson's letter,[146] which

---

[144] See F. I. Carpenter, *A Reference Guide to Spenser*, p. 41.

[145] *S. P. Scotland*, II (1509–1603), vol. LVII, art. 9 (December 4 and 5, 1595).

[146] See F. I. Carpenter, *A Reference Guide to Spenser*, p. 42.

is fuller than the summary in the *Calendar of State Papers of Scotland* (II, 747):

> Mr. Davyd Fowlis in the K[ing's] name and in great hast hathe pressed Robert Walgrave the K[ing's] printer to print a booke in Latyn made by Walter Quin the Irishman & corrected by Monseur D'Amon, concerning the K[ing's] title to England, that it may be dispersed to forrayne Princes: But Robert Walgrave deferred to do it untill the Actes of Perliam[e]nt almost don should be ended. And with great grief and sorrow I assure yo[ur] honor told me thereof: lamenting his hard fortune, that ether he must printe it, stayenge here, or be undon, and he feares quarrelled for his life if he refuse it, and printing it greve his conscience, offend her Majestie & utterly loose his contry: allmost weping, and wishing that for avoyding of this he might have libertie to returne to his owne contrye; wh[i]ch being granted to him he wold returne and leave all here to themselues to printe as they coulde. Of w[h]ich I have thought it my dutie to advertise yo[ur] honor, that you might take what course herein you please, w[hi]ch upon your honors warrant to him shalbe secretly and surely obeyed. Quyn is also answering Spencers book whereat the K[ing] was offended.

To this is added in the summary in the State Papers, "And Dixon that taught the Art of Memory in England, is answering Doleman," i.e., the Jesuit, Parsons, who advocated the claims of the Infanta of Spain.

This agitation over the succession probably contributed to Elizabeth's irritability. Several quarrelsome letters passed between her and James from January to August, 1598. An especially threatening one from Elizabeth is dated January 4, 1598.[147]

Some English writer seems to have offended James again in the spring of 1598 by references to his mother; for on March 16 the Scottish agent from England, Nicolson, received instructions from Elizabeth that "her Majesty will have that part left out which mentions the burning of the body of the King's mother, and that her Majesty grants the King £3000 a year only, whatever the King hath received above that sum having been presented as a gift."[148]

---

[147] *S. P. Scotland*, II (1509–1603), vol. LXII.

[148] *Ibid.*, II, vol. LXII, art. 2. Cf. the complaint concerning an English comedy, by Nicolson to Burghley, because it ridiculed the Scotch, p. 156 *infra*.

The personality and the claims of James to the English throne are discussed or glanced at in military and genealogical treatises, in poetical allegory, oration, anagram, sonnet, chronicle history, and comedy—this in spite of a censorship of literature for meddling in affairs of state. In the matter of James's claims to the crown of England, perhaps the very agents of literary censorship set no good example of restraint of opinion. When Andrew Melville was tried before the Council of England for high treason for his little epigram against Romish rites in James's chapel in 1606, he melodramatically turned the charge upon Richard Bancroft, who had been left by James to preside over the trial in his place. Denying his own guilt, Melville turned to the Council, saying, "But there is one Dr. Bancroft (for so he was called when he wrote his booke) in England who is a great traitour; let him be searched for and punished as a notorious traitor." He then put his hand in his pocket, pulled out a book. "There, sayeth he, is Dr. Bancroft's booke whilk he hes written against our King's right to the Crown of England, whilk Mr. John Davidson, our brother minister at Prestonpannes, hes ansuered; then I am sure he is a traitor."[149]

Calderwood has an account of the same incident, in which he pictures Melville as bringing all sorts of charges against Bancroft. "Taking him by the whyte sleeves of his rotchet, and shaiking them, (he) called them 'Romish rags' and 'a part of the Beast's marke.' He told him if he was the author of the booke entituled English Scotizing, he esteemed him the capitall enemie of all the reformed kirks in Europe."[150]

[149] John Row, *History of the Kirk of Scotland, 1558–1637* (Edinburgh, 1842), pp. 283–87. This account is not in the 1650 MS., but in one of the others. It is inserted out of chronological order in the printed history. Cf. pp. 220, 233, 236; and cf. also Thos. M'Crie, *Life of A. Melville*, pp. 264–65.

[150] David Calderwood, *History of the Kirk of Scotland* (Ed., 1845), pp. 597–98. *English Scotizing* is the title of Books II, III, and IV of an anonymous work usually attributed to Bancroft, *Dangerous Positions and Proceedings* (see *The Presbyterian Movement in the Reign of Queen Elizabeth*, Royal Hist. Soc'y, 1905, pp. 82–84). As Book II is *English Scottizing, for discipline by rayling*, it is probably a later version of a sermon preached by Bancroft at Paul's Cross, February 9, 1588, which was replied to by I. D. (John Davidson?) of the Church of Scotland in *D. Bancrofts rayling against the Church of Scotland noted in answere to a letter of a worthy person of England*, 1590 (see B. M. catalogue for the last two items).

Scotchmen were naturally astonished that James should forgive and raise to favor one who had so opposed him. John Forbes remarks:

Not only was he maid to favour the Estate of Bischops, bot, against his resolution uttered at his first coming ther, to tak be the hand that pest both of Kirk and Commonwealth, Bishop Bancroft, his own particular enemie, and in his heart a knowen enemie to the trueth, notwithstanding he had before oppenlie spoken and wrytten against his Majestie's undouted right to the Crown of Ingland; who shortlie after, by flatterie and bribes, did get himselff maid Primat of England, to the great greiff of all guid men and unspeakable hurt of the Kirk.[151]

Not only were there numerous attacks upon James during his candidacy for the English throne; but after his accession there was even an increase of boldness in criticism. This freedom of speech was doubtless due largely to James's notorious pusillanimity. Long before he came to the throne, he was known to be cowardly and vacillating. His emotional reactions were fleeting, often unexpected, sometimes ridiculous. He would fly into quick rage over an insult to himself or his mother, but the rage might go off with a mere frothing at the mouth. The weakness of his rages was well known to ambassadors from other countries. James's failure to follow up his complaint of Spenser's offence in portraying Mary Queen of Scots as Duessa, after the flimsy excuse of the English agent, illustrates this phase of his character. It is in line with his behavior on the death of his mother, as it may be gathered from an extract "out of Monsieur Courcelles Negociation in Scotland from 4th October, 1586 to 28 September 1587 in possession of the Right Honourable the Marquess of Lothian." Courcelles' tone in writing to the French King of James is that of one speaking of a person whom he regarded as child-like, if not indeed positively irresponsible. On October 4, 1586, Courcelles wrote about an inquiry made by James of the Earl of Bothwell as to what he should do if Elizabeth asked his consent to proceed against his mother. Bothwell replied that "yff he did suffer it he were worthie to be hanged the nexte daye after; whereat the King

[151] *Certaine Records Touching the Estate of the Church of Scotland since the Reformation*, (Edinburgh, 1846), pp. 374–75.

laughed[152] and said, he would prouid for that." A letter from Courcelles on November 30, 1586 hints at a secret intelligence between Elizabeth and James, the King's Secretary and Gray being in the secret. This opinion is confirmed by the Master of Gray's embassy, according to a letter of December 31. Courcelles goes on to predict "that the King of Scots will not declare himselfe openly against her [Elizabeth] though his mother be put to death, unless the Queene and the Statts would deprive him of his right to that crowne, which himselfe both uttered to Earle Bothwill and Chevaleire Seaton." A further letter of February 10, 1587, contains the news that Alexander Stewart, sent in the company of the ambassadors "with more secret charge," had said to Elizabeth, "were she [Mary] even deade, yf the king at first shewed himselfe not contented therewith they might easily satisfy him in sending him dogs and deare." On being informed of this, however, "the king was in marvilose collore, and sware and protested before God that yf Steward came he would hang him before he putt off his bootes, and yf the Queene medled with his mother's life, she should knowe he would follow somewhat else than dogges and deare." But in spite of this "marvilose collore," in his next letter, of February 28, 1587, Courcelles voiced the expectation that, if Mary should be executed, James would "digeste it as patiently as he hath done that which passed betwene the Queene of England and Alex. Stuard, whose excuse he hath well allowed, and useth the man as well as before." When news came of the execution, James was "greatly affected." But when Gray was banished, the Queen's death was not mentioned as a reason, "lest he should have accused others," (Letter of March 8). And when the Estates twice requested the King to avenge his mother's death and offered their lives and fortunes in the cause, he merely thanked them and said he "would open his intentions afterward."[153]

Making all due allowance for the character of Mary Queen of Scots, one still feels that there was a marked instability in the

---

[152] James is described as laughing, frisking, and capering boyishly about while still "in mourning" for his mother, thus tempting Melville to one of his sharp epigrams, on the unreality of his grief. (See Thomas M'Crie, *Life of Andrew Melville*, p. 132.)

[153] Quoted by Thomas M'Crie, *op. cit.*, pp. 429-30.

emotional reactions of James on this occasion, with some symptoms of a general inability to let a resolve go over into action. It was this, as much as his pleasure-loving nature,[154] that made him in the eyes of foreign ambassadors a particularly futile sort of king. Their letters are full of slights. Is it strange if some Englishmen should have a similar impulse to expression?

The attitudes of English playwrights and actors in this critical period (1594–1601) are still problematic. It is clear that some company of English players performed in Scotland under the protection of King James on several occasions, and that a company of English actors was very highly favored by him. It seems, however, that they took some advantages of the easy-going nature of James where drama was concerned, and ridiculed his personality or his pretensions in their comedies.

According to an entry in the Register House, Edinburgh, February, 1594, the Scotch Treasurer paid by the King's orders to the "Inglis comedianis the sum of iii c. xxxiii l. vi s. vii d."[155] The leading player, Fletcher, seems to have got into some trouble in connection with his experiences of 1594; for George Nicolson, the English agent in Scotland, wrote to Bowes March 22, 1595: "The king heard that Fletcher, the player, was hanged, and told him and Roger Aston so, in merry words, not believing it, saying very pleasantly, that if it were true he would hang them also."[156]

In 1598 the English actors entered the political arena with derision of King James, presumably in Scotland. George Nicolson wrote to Burghley:

It is regrated to me in quiet sorte that the Comedians of London

---

[154] James Howell wrote to Christopher Jones, October 8, 1621 (*Epistolae Ho-Elianae*, Bk. 1, sec. 1, xl) that he had recently in Rome met with a pasquil against the Scots, so witty that James would laugh if he saw it. He went on to say: "As I remember, some years since, there was a very abusive Satire in Verse brought to our King; and as the passages were a-reading before him he often said, That if there were no more men in England, the Rogue should hang for it; At last being come to the Conclusion, which was (after all his Railing)—
  Now God preserve the King, the Queen, the Peers,
  And grant the Author long may wear his Ears;
this pleas'd his Majesty so well, that he broke into a laughter, and said, By my sol, so thou shalt for me: thou art a bitter, but thou art a witty knave."
[155] J. C. Dibdin, *Annals of the Edinburgh Stage* (Ed., 1888), 20.
[156] *S. P. Scotland*, II (1509–1603), vol. LV, art. 59.

should in their play scorn the K[ing] and people of this land and wished that it may be spedely amended and staied: lest the worst sort gitting understondinge thereof should stier the K[ing] and Contry to anger thereat. A matter which beinge thus honestly and quietly deliuered unto me by Mr. Arnott, sometyme Provost of this Towne and a very substantious honest man, I haue thought mete to commend to your Lordships considerations [to] put stay of these courses.[157]

The English players' tour in Scotland in 1599 involved James in a fresh outbreak of their standing feud, the players profiting by James's settled antipathy to the clergy. A letter from George Nicolson to Robert Cecil, on November 12, 1599, told of the performances of English players, Fletcher, Martin, and their company, by the King's permission; of the enactment of the Town Sessions and preaching of the ministers against them. "The bellows blowers say that they are sent by England to sow dissension between the King and the Kirk." Nicolson enclosed James's proclamation in behalf of the players.[158]

Calderwood, in his *History of the Kirk of Scotland* (V, 765–67), gives some details of the controversy:

Some English comedians came to this countrie in the moneth of October. After they had acted sindrie comedeis in the presence of the king, they purchassed at last a warrant or precept to the bailiffes of Edinburgh, to gett them an hous within the toun. Upon Monday, the 12th of November, they gave warning by trumpets and drummes through the streets of Edinburgh, to all that pleased, to come to the Blacke Friers' Wynd, to see the acting of their comedeis. The ministers of Edinburgh, fearing the profanitie that was to ensue, speciallie the profanatioun of the Sabboth day, convocated the foure sessiouns of the kirk. An act was made by commoun consent, that none resort to these profane comedeis, for eshewing offence of God, and of evill example to others; and an ordinance was made, that everie minister sould intimate this act in their own severall pulpits. They had indeed committed many abusses, speciallie upon the Sabboth, at night before. The king taketh the act in evill part, as made purposelie to crosse his warrant,

---

[157] *MS State Papers of Scotland, temp. Eliz.*, vol. LXII, f. 19; quoted by Sir Sidney Lee, "Topical Side of the Elizabethan Drama," *Trans. of the New Shakespeare Society*, 1887–92, pt. 1, p. 8.

[158] See *S. P. Scotland*, II (1509–1603), vol. LXV, art. 64. Cf. a letter from Sir John Carey to Robert Cecil, November 23, 1599, *Cal. of Border Papers*, II (1595–1603), art. 1126; and David Calderwood, *History of the Kirk of Scotland*, (Edinburgh, 1844), V, 765–67.

and caused summon the ministers and foure sessiouns, *super inquirendis*, before the Secreit Counsell.

Several of the clergy were sent for to appear before James and the Council. Robert Bruce was one of the spokesmen. He declared they had fulfilled the King's warrant when they let the English comedians have a house; but the King replied that he wished the people to resort to their comedies. Bruce charged that the acts of parliament were a warrant to stay them from their plays. The King would not yield. On leaving, Bruce remarked, "Sir, please you, nixt the regard we ow to God, we had a reverent respect to your Majestie's royall person, and person of your queene; for we heard that the comedians, in their playes, checked your royall person with secreit and indirect taunts and checkes; and there is not a man of honour in England would give suche fellowes so muche as their countenaunce." The clergy, on being requested to rescind their acts, consulted with advocates as to the application of the king's acts forbidding "slanderous and offensive" comedies. The elders voted to rescind the act, but many of the clergy stubbornly held out against it. Robert Bruce the next day preached in justification of the action of the clergy in forbidding the plays, and was not punished for it.

The clergy at length yielded, and on November 10, 1599 the four sessions prepared an act and proclamation withdrawing the opposition to the English comedians "in respect of the pruif quhilk they have evir had of his Majestie, that his Hienes hes not commendit nor allowit ony thing careying with it ony offence or sclander."[159]

The accounts of the Treasurer of Scotland show that money was given the English comedians in October, November, and December of 1599, once to buy timber to prepare a house.[160] And Fletcher visited Edinburgh and Aberdeen in October,

---

[159] The last quotation is from the *Register of the Privy Council of Scotland*, II, pp. 39–41. The account here is largely based on Calderwood. Tytler, in noting this incident under the year 1599, said that Fletcher visited Scotland in 1594 and "received such attentions from King James as to have been in some trouble on that account after his return to England." Possibly this interesting but vague comment refers to the report of King James's remarks on the rumor of the hanging of Fletcher.

[160] J. C. Dibdin, *Annals of the Edinburgh Stage* (1888), p. 21 ff.

1601, with special letters from the King recommending the company to the magistrates. The freedom of Aberdeen was conferred upon Laurence Fletcher and each of his company.[161]

The make-up of this traveling company has not been ascertained, though there are probably some records in Scotland which would throw light on it. Fleay (*Stage*, 136) assumed that it was Shakespeare's company. Murray (*E.D.C.*, I, 104) took issue, pointing out that Martin was not one of the Chamberlain's men, and that Fletcher was not one in 1599. Murray thinks it would be strange if Fletcher should be head of the company in 1601. Whoever this Fletcher was, he seems to have had the favor of James from 1594 on (see page 156, *supra*). Possibly further evidence will sometime show a certain number of the Chamberlain's men grouped with other actors for foreign travel.

There is at least a possibility that some of the actors who toured in Scotland were of Shakespeare's company. If so, the situation is piquant enough in its dramatic implications in 1599. It would be interesting to know what sort of 'checks and taunts' at the person of James the company would dare to use in Scotland.

Edith Rickert, in an extremely interesting article on *A Midsummer Night's Dream*,[162] has made out a strong case for the existence of a pungent satire, in the person of Bottom, on the traits and claims of James VI of Scotland. The play was probably written in 1594 or 1595, when the relations between Elizabeth and James were severely strained. And in the years 1598–1601, critical for the establishment of the succession, there appeared two quartos of *A Midsummer Night's Dream* and one of *Henry V*, as well as two of *Richard II*. The last-named play was performed on the eve of the Essex rebellion. It had already suffered the cut of the deposition scene, which was not put into print in the lifetime of Elizabeth. I believe that all these plays were topical, concerning themselves with vital issues of the day. There is a touch of this also in *King John*. Less seriously, there is a handling of royal policy and international relations in *Love's Labour's Lost*. My reasons for believing that *Love's Labour's Lost*, *Richard II*, and *Henry V* had

[161] William Kennedy, *Annals of Aberdeen* (1818).
[162] "Political Propaganda and Satire in *A Midsummer Night's Dream*," *Modern Philology*, XXI, no. 1 (1923), 53–89, 133–55.

special meanings for contemporaries I shall present in separate articles, as they require too much space for inclusion in this chapter.

We have no clue to any trouble over a performance of *A Midsummer Night's Dream*, unless it should at some future date appear that Fletcher was already in Shakespeare's company, and that this was the play for which King James heard the false rumor that he was hanged (March, 1595). The date would, in my opinion, fit well the probable time of first performance of *A Midsummer Night's Dream* in England.

After the accession of James, we see, besides occasional thrusts at the Scotch, the use of matters connected with French and Spanish rulers and their policies in English plays. If Scotch royalty is made ridiculous in Bottom in *A Midsummer Night's Dream*, so is French royalty, in a milder way, in Chapman's *Byron*. Some have thought that this is the same play as the *Berowne* or *Burone* acted, according to Henslowe, by Worcester's men September-October, 1602—just two months after the execution of Byron. It is true that some of the materials are timely for this date, particularly the circumstantial account of the visit of the ambassador Byron to England in 1601, and the parallel drawn between the fate of Byron and that of the "matchless Earl of Essex."[163] But students of Chapman now trace part of the matter of the play to Grimeston's *General Inventorie of the Historie of France*, 1607. We have no record of any trouble over the old Byron play in Henslowe. But when Chapman's *Byron* was performed, the French ambassador, Antoine Lefevre de la Boderie, made a complaint, in a letter of April 8, 1608, that, although he had forbidden certain players to act the history of the Duke of Biron, when they saw the whole court had left town, they persisted in acting it. According to his account,

they brought upon the stage the Queen of France and Mademoiselle Verneuil. The former, having first spoken very harshly to the latter, gave her a box on the ear. At my suit three of them were arrested; but the principal person, the author, escaped .... One or two days before

---

[163] On the French origin of this parallel, see *Letters of Cecil*, Camden Society, p. 118 (July, 1602).

they ridiculed their own King and his Scotch mine[164] in a very strange fashion. They made him swear over the theft of a bird, and beat a gentleman because he had called the hounds off the scent.[165] They represented him as being drunk at least once a day .... He has made an order that there shall be no more comedies played in London, for the repeal of which prohibition four other companies there have offered 1000,000 francs, which perhaps will regain their permission; but at least it will be on condition that they shall represent no modern history nor speak of affairs of the day on pain of death.[166]

Though Chapman probably escaped, it seems clear that James did give a very sweeping order of repression because of the French offence and the reference to the Scotch mines. Sir Thomas Lake wrote to Salisbury on March 11, 1608:

His Majestie was well pleased with that which your lordship advertiseth concerning the committing of the players that have offended in the matter of France, and commanded me to signifye to your lordship that for the others who have offended in the matter of the Mynes and other lewd words, which is the children of the blackfriars, That though he had signified his mynde to your lordship by my lord of Mountgoumery, yet I should repeat it again, that his Grace had vowed they should never play more, but should first begg their bred and he wold have his vow performed. And therefore my lord Chamberlain by

[164] This was probably the silver mine near Edinburgh which attracted the attention of Londoners in 1607. Thomas Hamilton, the King's advocate, discovered it on his lands and got a grant of the whole profit to himself except ten per cent which was to go to the King. When it seemed that the mine was important, "the advocat was sent for, and renounced, as was reported, his infestment of the said minerall. The king sent certain English and Scotish men, to bring a great quantitie of the ore to Londoun to be melted and tryed. How it proved, it is not weill knowne to manie; but after that the myne was closed till his majestie advised farther." (Calderwood, *History of the Kirk of Scotland*, VI, 688–89.)

[165] Possibly this elicited a reply. There is in *Sloane MSS* (No. 3543 ff. 19^v, 49) *A Treatise Apologeticall for Huntinge*, which contains a reference to James's being taxed on the stage for his devotion to the sport. See R. Simpson, in *Trans. of the New Shakespeare Soc'y*, 1874, p. 375.

[166] J. J. Jusserand prints the French text of this letter from *Bibl. Nat. MS Fr.* 15984, in *Modern Language Review*, VI, 203. Friedrich von Raumer, in his *Political History of England* (sixteenth and seventeenth centuries) has wrongly attributed the letter to Beaumont as ambassador, and has been widely followed in this error. A recent version of the incident may be found in E. K. Chambers, *Elizabethan Stage*, III, 257–58.

himselfe or your lordships at the table should take order to dissolve them, and to punish the maker besides.[167]

Chapman's escape from punishment was probably due to protection by the same powerful favorite of James, Aubigné, who helped Jonson and Chapman out of prison a few years before. Chapman's letter to "his right worthie and exceedinge good friend Mr. Crane: Secretarie to my lord Duke of Lennox," thanking him for a shelter in "the Austeritie of this offended tyme," has been referred to above, in connection with *Eastward Hoe*.[168]

Chapman was naturally anxious to get the Byron play in print; but he was refused a license to publish. His letter of complaint, presumably to Buc, is spirited and independent, not the least conciliatory:

Sir—I have not deserv'd what I suffer by your austeritie; if the two or three lines you crost were spoken: my uttermost to suppress them was enough for my discharge: To more then whych no promysse can be rackt by reason: I see not myne owne Plaies; nor carrie the Actors Tongues in my mouthe .... If the thrice allowance of the Counsaile for the Presentment gave not weight enoughe to drawe your after for the presse, my Breath is a hopeles adition: if you say (for your Reason) you know not if more then was spoken be now written, no, no; nor can you know that, if you had both the copies, not seeing the first at all: Or if you had seene it presented your Memorie could hardly confer with it so strictly in the Revisall to discerne the Adition .... I desier not you should drenche your hande in the least daunger for mee: And therefore (with entreatie of my Papers returne), I cease ever to trouble you.[169]

Chapman, like some other playwrights, was willing to escape from difficulties by shifting blame upon the actors.[170] But here it is not a question of interpolation. The author simply charges that they did not observe the cuts made by the censor in his manuscript.

[167] *S. P. Dom.*, 1603–10, vol. XXXI, art. 73.
[168] See Dobell's collection of letters, *Athenaeum*, 1901, I, 433.
[169] Published by Dobell, *Athenaeum*, April 6, 1901.
[170] A notable example of this subterfuge is Nashe's disclaimer of more than the inception and one act of the *Isle of Dogs*. See his disowning of the monstrous birth in *The Praise of Red Herring, Works* (ed. McKerrow), III, 153–54. Note his strictures on the legions of "mice-eyed decipherers."

By June 5, 1608, Chapman was able to get the two parts of *Byron* licensed for the press, but at some expense to the integrity of the plays. His dedication refers to "these poor dismembered poems." As Act II is omitted, it was probably the part most offensive to the French ambassador. Extensive recasting is shown in Act IV, giving the effect of a summary of scenes dealing with the English court in the time of Queen Elizabeth, who seems to have been required to discuss the politics of her day. Naturally, the scene in which the jealous queen of France boxed the ears of her rival, Madame de Verneuil, had to be left out. The effect of the cut remains in that a masque later on has Cupid bring together the two women who have been at odds for the love of the King and are now to be reconciled for love of him. The point is blunted when the women have not been shown as at odds.[171]

Another play which was objected to because it would wound the sensibilities of the French was an "interlude" concerning the Marquis d'Ancre, the favorite of the Queen of France. He was killed in Paris in April, 1617. On June 22 of the same year, the Privy Council of England sent this order to Sir George Buc:

> We are informed that there are certeyne Players, or Comedians, we know not of what Company, that goe about to play some interlude concerning the late Marquesse d'Ancre, which for many respects wee thinke not fitt to be suffered: We do therefore require you upon your peril, to take order, that the same be not represented or played in any place about this city or elsewhere where you have authority.[172]

The condemnation of Concini in 1617 for treason and sorcery seems to have been a tempting subject for English playwrights. Only a few years later (1621) there was printed anonymously a play by Fletcher and Massinger(?), *The Tragedy of Thierry, King of France and His Brother Theodoret* (c. 1617?), which does trace the career of the Marquis d'Ancre. The play was said to have been "diuerse times acted at the Blacke-Friers by the Kings Maiesties servants." The name De Vitry and

---

[171] By 1634, if not earlier, Samuel Rowley was able to get in print his *Noble [Spanish] Soldier*, with an account of the love of Henry IV for Madame de Verneuil.

[172] J. P. Collier, *Hist. of Eng. Dram. Poetry*, I, 391–92. Cf. *S. P. Dom.*, 1611-18, p. 461.

Lacure's astrology point the reference to Concini's condemnation.

From the time of Elizabeth on through the reign of Charles, the desire of writers to comment on Spanish relationships brought occasional conflict with the authorities. National rivalry, feeling over contemplated alliances, and some association of Jesuit intrigue with the thought of Spain seem to have combined to produce an inclination to picture the Spanish on the stage in a more or less unfavorable aspect.

In April, 1621, the dislike of Spain reached such a height that apprentices attacked Gondomar, the Spanish ambassador, in the street.[173] A royal proclamation forbade citizens to meddle in Spanish affairs—"a proclamation," says Lando, "which rather loosens men's tongues than restrains them."[174] There seems to have been a popular outburst against Gondomar in several forms of literature. James Howell wrote to Sir John North (August 15, 1623):

> I am sorry to hear how other Nations do much tax the English of their Incivility to public Ministers of State, and what Ballads and Pasquils and Fopperies and Plays were made against Gondomar for doing the King his master's business.[175]

Many of these flings in the popular literature seem to be lost. The antipathy made itself felt also in court circles. Valaresso wrote to the Senate of Venice on January 19, 1624, "The usual verses written for the Masque containing some rather free remarks about the Spaniard, they were altered by his [James's] command."[176] This is supposed to refer to Jonson's mask, *Neptune's Triumph*, which was postponed and later abandoned.[177]

The most striking example of antagonism toward Spain after Lyly's *Midas* (unless we should make exception for the unknown comedies that the Venetian ambassador charges with responsibility for England's warlike mood) was Middleton's *A Game at*

---

[173] *S. P. Venetian*, 1621–23, no. 25.
[174] *Ibid.*, p. 108.
[175] *Epistolae Ho-Elianae*, Bk. 1, sec. 3, no. 20.
[176] *S. P. Venetian*, 1623–25, no. 246.
[177] See R. Brotanek, *Die engl. Maskenspiele*, 359; and P. Reyher, *Les masques anglais*, 305.

Chess, 1624.[178] This was originally allowed for acting by Herbert, the Master of the Revels, but ultimately suppressed. By the autumn of 1623 the marriage projected between Prince Charles and the Infanta Maria had been broken off, to the great satisfaction of the English people. Middleton, under the very thin allegory of a game at chess, portrays this situation, even to the visit of Charles to Madrid. Charles is usually thought to be figured by the White Knight, Buckingham by the White Duke. The ridiculous Fat Bishop stands for the Archbishop of Spalato (later Dean of Windsor). The Black Knight is a gross caricature of Gondomar, the Spanish ambassador recently at London. Gondomar was popularly identified with Jesuit intrigue. He was thought to be planning to turn to the use of Spain Queen Anne's secret conversion to Catholicism. An explicit reference to this occurs in the play (Act IV, sc. iv):

> You aim'd at no less person than the Queen,
> The glory of the game; if she were won,
> The way were open to the master check.

How daring the cartoon was, and how attractive to the London public may be judged from a contemporary account, in a letter from Chamberlain to Carleton on August 21, 1624:

I doubt not but you have heard of our famous play of Gondomar, which hath been followed with extraordinary curiosity, and frequented by all sorts of people, old and young, rich and poor, masters and servants, papists, wise men, &c., churchmen and Scotsmen, as Sir Henry Wotton, Sir Albert Morton, Sir Benjamin Rudyard, Sir Thomas Lake, and a world besides .... I would willingly have attended her [Lady Smith] but I could not sit so long, for we must have been there before one o'clock at farthest to find any room .... They represented him to the very life, and had his cast off apparel and litter, but they depicted

---

[178] The idea of using the chess game for a teaching in regard to the state of the commonwealth is an old one. In 1474 Caxton printed *The Game and Play of the Chesse*, translated from the French (presumably of Jehan de Vignay, from an earlier Latin version of Jacobus de Cessolis; Ames, *Typ. Antiq.*, ed. Dibdin, III, 28–29). Caxton's book was dedicated to the Chamberlain of England. It closes with a pious prayer that England's king may rule virtuously and wisely, defend the realm, punish malefactors, and reward the good. The third chapter in an account of the game of chess contains the information that the play was founded and made "to correct and reprove the king."

some one else too, and therefore are forbidden to play at all during the king's pleasure .... and may be glad if they so escape.[179]

He says the wonder lasted only nine days. The titles were changed to avoid the interruption of the performance by objectors.[180]

Marvelous tales were told of the financial success of the play. Sir Francis Nethersole wrote Carleton that a new play, the plot of which is a game of chess in which the whole Spanish business is taken up and Gondomar brought on the stage was so popular that the players gained £100 a night.[181] Salvielli has it that the players gained 300 gold crowns at each performance.[182] And an old manuscript copy has a note, says Bullen, stating that the proceeds were £1500. Certainly the play passed into stage history as an extraordinary stage success. D'Avenant's *Playhouse to be Let* (acted 1663) has an actor say, "There's such a crowd at doors as if we had a new play of Gondomar."

In spite of the great concourse of people of all classes, including even Wotton the ambassador, we learn with some surprise that the play ran without interruption nine days, and the King first had his attention called to it by the Spanish ambassador, Coloma, the successor of Gondomar (who had left England in June, 1622). James ordered Secretary Conway to write to the Privy Council (August 12, 1624) that the Spanish ambassador had informed him of a very scandalous comedy acted publicly by the King's players,

wherein they take the boldness and presumption, in a rude and dishonorable fashion, to represent on the stage the persons of his Majesty, the King of Spain, the Conde de Gondomar, the Bishop of Spalato, etc. His Majesty remembers well there was a commandment and restraint given against the representing of any modern Christian kings in those stage-plays; and wonders much both at the boldness now taken by that company, and also that it hath been permitted to be so acted, and that the first notice thereof should be brought to him by a foreign ambassador, while so many ministers of his own are thereabouts, and

---

[179] *Court and Times of James I*, II, 472–73; and *S. P. Dom. Jas. I*, 1623–25, vol. CLXXI, art. 66. Valaresso, the Venetian ambassador, thought the play much more injurious to the dignity of James than to that of Gondomar.

[180] *S. P. Venetian*, 1623–25, art. 557 (p. 425).

[181] *S. P. Dom. Jas. I*, 1623–25, vol. CLXXI, art. 49.

[182] *British Museum Add. MSS*, 27962 C.

cannot but have heard of it. His Majesty's pleasure is; that your Lordships presently call before you as well the poet that made the comedy as the comedians that acted it: And upon examination of them to commit them, or such of them as you shall find most faulty, unto prison, if you find cause, or otherwise to take security for their forthcoming; and then certify his Majesty what you find that comedy to be, in what points it is most offensive, by whom it was made, by whom licensed, and what course you think fittest to be held for the exemplary and severe punishment of the present offenders, and to restrain such insolent and licentious presumption for the future.

On August 21 the Council replied that they had called before them the chief actors and inquired by what authority they acted it. In answer "they produced a book being an original and perfect copy thereof (as they affirmed) seen and allowed by Sir Henry Herbert, Knt., Master of the Revels, under his own hand, and subscribed on the last page of the said book: We demanding further, whether there were not other parts or passages represented on the stage than those expressly contained in the book, they confidently protested they added or varied from the same nothing at all." The poet, "one Middleton," had "shifted out of the way," but he would be sent for. The others had been reproved and forbidden to act until the King's pleasure was known. The playbook with the license by the Master of the Revels was being sent to the King with the suggestion, "Call Sir Henry Herbert before you to know the reason of his licensing thereof."

The Lord Chamberlain (Pembroke) wrote to the President of the Council on August 28, 1624, that the whole company had been interdicted from all playing during the King's pleasure on account of this play, which had "passages in it reflecting in matter of scorne and ignominy upon the King of Spain, some of his Ministers and others of good note and quality." The company had been put under bonds of £300, and the punishment, if not satisfactory, was, at least, "such as, since it stops the current of their poore livelyhood and mainteanance, without much prejudice they cannot longer undergoe." In view, then, of the players' need, the King directed that this play "bee not onely antiquated and sylenced, but the Players bound as formerly they were, and in that point onely, never to act it agayne."[183]

Edward Middleton, the poet's son, appeared before the Board on August 30, 1624, but the playwright himself seems to have escaped punishment. The King was evidently not so shocked as he sounded in his first letter to the Council, which was probably severe for diplomatic reasons. At any rate, he forgave; for he had Conway write the Council on August 27 to ascertain who was responsible for the impersonation of Gondomar and others, and to punish only these. 'His Majesty is unwilling to punish the innocent or utterly to ruin the Company.'[184] A foreign ambassador, Valaresso, said that James passed the matter over to the Privy Council for this reason: "He willingly refers such cases to them, in order to give them some employment and rid himself of the odium of such decisions."[185]

If Herbert had been called to account for licensing the performance, it was useless to expect him to license the play for the press, especially as it was "antiquated and silenced" by order of the king. But it was printed surreptitiously in 1625, without entry on the Stationers' Registers. Two other extant editions, undated, were also in all probability surreptitious. It is not unlikely that the author took the precaution to revise somewhat before the publication. Mr. Bullen, in his edition of Middleton's works (VII, 3), notes a bookseller's advertisement (about 1866) of a manuscript copy of *A Game at Chess* with a dedication to "the Worthelie Accomplished Mr. Wm. Hammond," which contained these lines:

> This, which nore Stage nor Stationer's Stall can showe,
> The Common Eye may wish for, but ne're knowe.

The King's men were not too repentant for their behavior. They ventured on a Spanish theme again in Fletcher's *Rule a Wife and Have a Wife* in 1624. The prologue shows an awareness of the danger:

[183] *Egerton MSS*, 2623, f. 28. The correspondence was printed in Chalmers' *Apology*, 497 ff., for the most part, and is reprinted with comment in Bullen's *Middleton*, I, lxxviii–lxxxi (cf. VII, 3). Cf. also *S. P. Dom. Jas. I, 1623–25*, vol. CLXXI, art. 64, art. 75, art. 66, *et passim.*
[184] *S. P. Dom. Jas. I, 1623–25*, vol. CLXXI, art. 75.
[185] *S. P. Venetian*, 1623–25, no. 568.

Do not your looks let fall,
Nor to remembrance our late errors call,
Because this day we're Spaniards all again,
The story of our play, and our scene Spain:
The errors, too, do not for this cause hate;
Now we present their wit, and not their state.

In the same year, without attempting to get a license for it, the company acted a new play, *The Spanish Viceroy, or The Honour of Women.* Herbert probably rebuked them; for they wrote him a letter of apology on December 20, 1624, promising good behavior for the future.[186]

If one wonders that this company of actors were not more severely treated for their Spanish offenses, it should be recalled that by the middle of March, 1624, war was declared against Spain. The Spanish match was off already, Gondomar in disrepute, and Buckingham in somewhat general favor for his part in breaking off the alliance.[187]

Two examples of "dangerous" dramatic comments on Spanish affairs may be found in the reign of Charles. One is Massinger's *Believe as You List*, which Herbert, on January 11, 1631, according to a note in his office-book, refused to license, "for it did contain dangerous matter, as the deposing of Sebastian, king of Portugal, by Philip II, and there being a peace sworn 'twixt the Kings of England and Spain."[188] Massinger, however, changed part of the action and some of the names, and got it licensed on May 6. It was not printed until 1653, but the second manuscript draft with Herbert's license survives. It was edited for the Percy Society in 1849, and has been published in facsimile by the Tudor Society. A discussion appears in an article by Sir George Warner, *The Athenaeum*, January 19, 1901. The corrections and additions in the manuscript appear to be in the same hand. The assumption is, that this draft is the author's revised copy of the manuscript criticized by Herbert. Halliwell-Phillips regarded it as one of only a few copies that are obviously

---

[186] Shakespeare, *Variorum* (1821), III, 209–10. Murray (*E. D. C.*, II, 348) calls attention to a performance at Norwich, April, 1624, of *The Spanish Contract* by the "Princesse Servants." It was forbidden, and Wambus, an actor, arrested.

[187] See S. R. Gardiner, *History of England* (1883), V, 160 ff. *et passim.*

[188] Shakespeare, *Variorum* (1821), III, 229–30.

playhouse versions. It is now known to be an autograph MS by Massinger. The setting of the play was changed from the contemporary one appropriate to the incidents to an ancient one. There are evidences of haste not only in the writer's literary revisions but also in the incomplete substitutions of names. Sebastian's name is left in two places (e.g., at II, 2, 368, Cunningham's ed.). Under *Carthage* is a deleted word, probably *Venice*. In III, 1, 22, *To the good King Hiero* is deleted for *To the pro-consul Marcellus*. In IV, 1, 45, below *Enter Flaminius* is another deleted name, probably Ferdinand. In IV, 3, 1, *Sampayo* is deleted, and *Berecinthius* written in. In V, 2, 59, *Marcell* is deleted before *King Antiochus*. As is the case with many censored plays, the prologue intentionally recalls to the minds of the hearers the thing for which the censoring was done. Considerable cleverness is sometimes shown in the use of the prologue or epilogue to make the audience look for a contemporary application in spite of the fact that its obviousness has been edited away. This prologue begs pardon if

> What's Roman here,
> Grecian, or Asiatic, draw too near
> A late and sad example.[189]

We do not know the fortune of two earlier plays, non-extant, but mentioned in Henslowe: a 1601 *Sebastian of Portugal*,[190] by Dekker and Chettle, just when the pretender, Marco Tullio, was passing himself off for Sebastian; and a 1602 *Philip of Spain*, written four years after the death of Philip II.

Even though the form of allegory was employed or the play set at another time or in another place, the handling of contemporary affairs in plays was prevailingly realistic in the reigns of James and Charles. The desire to refer to persons and events of the day was persistently present, in spite of efforts to repress it. There was clearly a recognition of the fact that drama could be, like the sermon, a powerful influence in forming public opinion.

[189] S. R. Gardiner ("Political Element in Massinger," *Trans. of the N. Shakespeare Soc'y*, 1876, p. 321) would make this refer to the fate of Frederick of Bohemia.

[190] Non-extant, I believe, but described by Mary Hunt (*Thomas Dekker*, p. 45) as based on Munday's translation of a French account.

An example of a very deliberate plan to utilize drama to stir up popular sentiment was one reported by Locke in a letter to Carleton on February 21, 1625, concerning the troubles of the English East India Company and the Dutch one after a massacre of Englishmen at Amboyna.

The East India Company have ordered Greenbury, a painter, to paint a detailed picture of all the tortures inflicted on the English at Amboyna, and would have had it all acted in a play, but the Council was appealed to by the Dutch ministers, and stopped it for fear of disturbance this Shrovetide.[191]

Five days later Chamberlain wrote to Carleton on the same matter:

We are sadly fallen in the esteem of other nations, or the chief instrument of such notorious cruelties would not be permitted to walk up and down Amsterdam unpunished. Wilkinson has printed a sermon, with a bitter preface, against them, and a play is written on the Amboyna business, and also a large picture of it made for the East India Company, but both are suppressed by Council, and a watch of 800 men set to keep all quiet on Shrove Tuesday.[192]

A very interesting article by Frederick S. Boas, entitled "Stage Censorship under Charles I" appeared in the *London Times Literary Supplement* for December 14 and December 21, 1917. It gives an account of a censored manuscript of a play entitled *The Lanchinge of the Mary; or, The Seamans Honest Wife*, written in 1632 in the interests of the East India Company to prove that they were in harmony with the best ideals of political economists of the time. Professor Boas points out that the play shows the use of a pamphlet, *A Discourse of Trade from England into the East Indies*. It has, however, other interests. Herbert, in 1633, subjected it to censure. His note

---

[191] S. P. Dom. Jas. I, 1623–25, vol. CLXXXIV, art. 22. An unsatisfactory settlement between the English merchants and the Dutch had been reached two months before the play. Redress for the Amboyna grievance was often sought, but not gained until 1654. (See Thurloe State Papers, II, 592; and see F. H. Durham, *Relations of the Crown to Trade under James I*, Royal Historical Society, *Trans.*, n.s. XIII (1899), pp. 224–27.) *The Devils Law Case*, published in 1623, refers (Act IV, sc. 2) to some trouble with the Dutch in the East Indies, but possibly the case is an earlier one (August, 1619). The reference in *The Faire Maide of the Inne*, licensed January, 1626, is to the Amboyna massacre.

[192] S. P. Dom. Jas. I, 1623–25, vol. CLXXXIV, art. 47.

on the matter mentions chiefly the oaths, and these are rigidly censored. But the other cuts and changes are more significant. The manuscript preserved has the passages marked by the censor for omission or change, and shows the reformations written in with the hand of the dramatist. A few slips are pasted in for longer corrections.

Anger against the Dutch for the Amboyna injury was one of the main points censored. Though Charles was treating with Spain against Holland, tentatively, the situation was not ripe for public discussion. Even references to Dutchmen are cut here and there. And, as Charles was reaching out toward Spain, the censor naturally cut out a reference to the Armada. Extreme diplomatic caution appears in the cut of six lines on the recent increase of England's navy. Insults to professions as by presentation of a lustful vicar and an immoral army captain are cut out. A reference to this severe censorship appears in the prologue intended for the second performance: "H'as been before the Tryers" and "lost a limb to save the rest."

Satire on Individuals

About the beginning of the seventeenth century, an outburst of individual satire on the stage caused a vigorous resistance by the authorities. An example of partially effective censorship is the attempt to eliminate the Oldcastle name from *Henry IV*, Part I. The leaving in of the reference to "my old lad of the castle" (I, 1, 149) in Part I, and the abbreviation of *Old.* in Part II for one of Falstaff's speeches, as well as making Falstaff (like Oldcastle) page to Sir Thomas Mowbray, of Norfolk (Part II), III, 2, 27 ff., Q. of 1600), all serve to keep the Oldcastle name from being forgotten. It seems, indeed, likely that at least the First Part may have been played once uncensored; for there are several references implying the use of the name, as that of Field, who speaks of "the play where the fat knight, hight Oldcastle, did tell you truly what his honor was."[193] It is not usually supposed that Shakespeare was interested in satirizing the Lollard martyr at all, if such a thing *could* be done in the person of Falstaff. The slight is probably to the family name, and perhaps directed at a descendant, William, Lord Cobham, who, besides objecting to the use of the name, signed the

---

[193] *Amends for Ladies*, 1619.

petition against the players in Blackfriars.[194] He was of Puritanic temper, and unpopular among frequenters of the stage. As he died early in 1597, his son Henry may be the target.

A somewhat similar objection to a slight on ancestors was that written to Sir Robert Cecil by Richard Hadsor July 25, 1602. He speaks of the attainder of the Earl of Kildare's grandfather 'by the policy of Cardinal Wolsey as it is set forth and played now upon the stage in London.'[195] Henslowe's Diary[196] shows the run of a Wolsey play 1601–02. Chettle had a *Life of Cardinal Wolsey*, June-August, 1601. Later there was prefixed a play on the Rising of Cardinal Wolsey, by Chettle, Drayton, Munday, and Smith, written August–November, 1601. Again, Chettle was mending the *Life* in May–June, 1602. It is perhaps this latest version that preceded the complaint.

There was an attempt to deal summarily with such satire when the persons were prominent. On May 10, 1601, for example, the Lords wrote to the Justices of the peace of Middlesex County:

We do understand that certaine players that use to recyte their playes at the Curtaine in Moorefildes, do represent upon the stage in their interludes the persons of some gent. of good desert and quallity that are yet alive under obscure manner, but yet in such sorte as all the hearers may take notice both of the matter and of the persons that are meant thereby. This beinge a thinge very unfitte, offensive, and contrary to such direccions as have bin heretofore taken, that no plaies shoulde be openly shewed but such as were first perused and allowed, and that might minister no occasion of offence or scandall, wee do hereby require you that you do forthwith forbidd those players to whomsoever they appertaine that do play at the Curtaine in Moorefieldes to represent any such play, and that you will examine them who made that play, and to shew the same unto you, and as you in your discrecions shall thincke the same unfitt to be publiquely shewed to forbidd them from henceforth to play the same eyther privately or publiquely, and if upon viewe of the said play, you shall find the subject so odious and inconvenient as informed, wee require you to take bond of the chiefest of them to aunswere their rashe and indiscreet dealing before us.[197]

[194] See Charlotte Stopes, *The Life of Henry, Third Earl of Southampton*, p. 102, and Stopes, *Burbage and Shakespeare's Stage*, p. 66.
[195] *Hatfield MSS*, XII, 248.
[196] II, 218 and elsewhere.
[197] Halliwell-Phillips, *Outlines of the Life of Shakespeare*, ed. 4, p. 416.

Censors tend to condemn satire wholesale because it is hard to tell innocent humor from barbed wit. In the sixteenth and seventeenth centuries any form of personal ridicule, whether of officials, noblemen, or private individuals of lower rank might give offence, though more attention was paid if the aggrieved person were prominent.

In 1605 a city alderman was put on the stage. The Mayor of London made the simple request that the theatre be put down or removed for this reason:

Lenard Haliday, Maior, 1605.—Whereas Kempe, Armyn, and others, plaiers at the Blacke Fryers, have again not forborne to bring upon their stage one or more of the worshipfull aldermen of the City of London, to their great scandall and to the lessening of their authority, the Lords of the right honorable the Privy Counsell are besought to call the said Players before them, and to enquire into the same, that order may be taken to remedy the abuse, either by putting down, or removing the said Theatre.[198]

Another objection to the satirizing of a prominent city official on the stage was the application of the figure of the Hog in Robert Tailor's *The Hog hath Lost His Pearl* (acted at Whitefriars, 1613) to the Mayor of London, Sir John Swinnerton. Sir Henry Wotton, in a letter to Sir Edmund Bacon on a Tuesday of 1612–13, tells how some sixteen apprentices learned secretly a new play without book, under this title, but were interrupted by the sheriffs and played the last act in jail. "Now it is strange," wrote Wotton, "to hear how sharp-witted the City is, for they will needs have Sir John Swinnerton the Lord Mayor be meant by the Hog, and the late Lord Treasurer by the Pearl."[199]

The play had a stormy time, was "toss'd from one house to another," according to the cautiously mischievous prologue printed in the quarto of 1614. But at length it got a "knight's license," i.e., a license from the Master of the Revels. The whole tone of the induction, in spite of its half-denial of intention of contemporary satire, is such as to confirm suspicion that it is

---

[198] From the city archives: quoted by Collier, *Hist. of Eng. Dram. Poetry*, III, 352. The University of Cambridge was obliged to deny "misusing the free burgesses and magistrates" of Cambridge in plays, April 23, 1601 (*S. P. Dom.*, 1601, CCLXXIX, art. 66).

[199] *Reliquiae Wottonianae*, 1685, p. 402.

intended, but that the point has been somehow missed by the authorities. Hence the mocking escape and triumph. I cannot take space here to discuss the reasons for my belief, but I am convinced that the hog is Swinnerton in intention, and equally convinced that the Hog's "treasure" could not, by any stretch of allegory, be made into the Treasurer who had recently died. The ludicrousness of the latter idea is, no doubt, what provoked the hilarity of the writer of the induction, and what amused Wotton in his comment on the sharp wits of the City. I wonder whether it may not have been in Ben Jonson's mind when he wrote in his induction to *Bartholomew Fair*, the year after, that someone might "apply" his pig-woman's wares to some person. If, as I think could be fairly well established, the hog is Mayor Swinnerton, this figure of the usurer is sufficiently uncomplimentary to warrant him in stopping the performance.

Another play which ridiculed city officials came up before King Charles in Council on September 29, 1639. It was called *The Whore New Vamped*.

> Complaint was this day made that the stage players of the Red Bull [the Prince's men] many days together acted a scandalous and libellous [play in which] they have audaciously reproached and in a libel [represented] and personated not only some of the aldermen of the [city of London] and some other persons of quality, but also scandalized and libelled the whole profession of proctors belonging to the Court of [Probate] and reflected upon the present government. Ordered that the Attorney-General be hereby prayed forthwith to call before him, not only the poet who made the play and the actors that played the the same, but also the person that licensed it, and having diligently examined the truth of the said complaint, to proceed roundly against such of them as he shall find to have been faulty.

The particular objections urged were these:

> In the play called The Whore New Vamped, where there was mention of the new duty on wines, one personating a justice of the peace says to Cain: 'Sirrah, I'll have you before the alderman, whereto Cain replies, 'The alderman, the alderman is a base, drunken, sottish knave, I care not for the alderman, I say the alderman is a base, drunken, sottish knave.' Another says, 'How now, Sirrah, What alderman do you speak of?' Then Cain says: 'I mean Alderman [William Abell] the blacksmith in Holborn.' "(He is then referred to as a vintner.). One player, speaking of projects and patents he had, named "a patent for

12 d apiece upon every proctor and proctor's man who was not a knave."[200]

For a few years some of the rival dramatists made use of the stage for personal thrusts at one another. From 1598 on, a number of plays show this sort of personal animus. *The Scourge of Villainy, Satiromastix, The Case is Altered, Jack Drum's Entertainment, Cynthia's Revels, The Poetaster,* and *What You Will* are some of the works which have been supposed to satirize contemporaries as individuals in a spirit of rivalry or jealousy or malice. Fleay and Penniman have speculated considerably as to the particular applications, and Roscoe Small has studied at some length a smaller nucleus of plays—what he finds to be the real stage quarrel.[201] From the widely varying interpretations of references one may select as pretty commonly agreed upon, that Marston in some play represented Jonson on the stage; Jonson ridiculed Marston and Dekker in *The Poetaster* as Crispinus and Demetrius; and Dekker replied in *Satiromastix*. The probable reason for their freedom to abuse one another was that the attacks involved little else than the direct objects—the feelings of the rival dramatists, the conservation of which cannot have been a matter of extreme importance in the eyes of the authorities. It was not quite the same thing as attacking the aldermen, or city proctors, or justices, or soldiers, or lawyers. If the literary men resented such treatment, let them bring a libel suit.

Jonson's personalities were so caustic as to provoke severe reaction from classes as well as individuals who saw, or thought they saw, their portraits on the stage. He frequently refers to the danger of libel; and it is not unlikely that at least one of his troubles in court was a libel suit by some offended person or group. The note at the end of the 1602 edition of *The Poetaster* shows that Jonson was restrained from publishing his apology for putting the play before the public. But in the folio of 1616 that play is dedicated to Richard Martin, a lawyer friend who helped him out of difficulties incurred by the severe satire—probably that directed at the law and lawyers in this play, "for whose innocence, as for the author's, you were once a noble and

[200] *S. P. Dom.*, 1639, vol. CCCCXXIX, art. 51, 52.
[201] *The Stage Quarrel between Ben Jonson and the Poetasters, 1899.*

timely undertaker to the greatest justice in this kingdom."[202] Again, there is added in 1616 a Dialogue between Horace and Trebatius in which Trebatius gently dissuades from satire, and Horace defends his innocence, admitting that *libels* "aimed at persons of good quality" are wrong, but insisting that his verses are not of that sort:

> But if they shall be sharp yet modest rhimes,
> That spare men's persons and but tax their crimes,
> Such shall in open court find current pass,
>   Were Caesar judge.

The particular charge made against the *Poetaster* on its first appearance was probably that quoted by Polyposus in the Address to the Reader, at the end: "They say you taxed the law and lawyers, captains and the players, by their particular names."

Perhaps Jonson felt more at ease in 1616 in bringing out a play which ridiculed lawyers because in March, and again on May 20 of that year King James had enjoyed a Cambridge play, by Thomas Ruggles, called *Ignoramus*, whose title role represented, under the figure of a common lawyer, Francis Brakin (or Brakyn), Recorder of the town of Cambridge.[203]

Jonson frequently denies that he is guilty of naming, or even of sketching, individuals. He is, however, often guilty of the latter, and occasionally of the former, offence. But he has some justification for his feeling that his habit is to satirize the individual by use of a type character which hits off his one or two most conspicuous traits. This is what makes Jonson able to believe that he writes impersonal satire, and what makes his victims who see themselves readily in the types wince as at a personal thrust.

An odd error of misinterpretation, probably of the passage in *Epicœne*, V, i, 17, where La Foole speaks of "the Prince of Moldavia, and of his mistris, Mistris Epicœne," seems to have been made, by which "his mistress" was read as referring to

---

[202] The prologue to Day's *Isle of Gulls* (1606) disclaims satirizing lawyers' fees. Markham's *The Dumb Knight* (1608), according to the preface, was misconstrued, probably as attacking lawyers.

[203] On James's enjoyment, see *S. P. Dom.*, 1611–18, vol. LXXX, art. 102. On the local satire, see letter of J. Chamberlain to Dudley Carleton, *Court and Times of James I*, I, 304; 306–7; Fuller, *Church History* (1655), X, 70.

the Prince of Moldavia's, though the passage preceding refers it to Daw as his mistress, and she is further named as Mistress Epicœne. Lady Arabella Stuart in applying the reference to herself seems to have gone out of the way looking for trouble; but the error probably arose out of sensitiveness over slanderous association of the names of Bogdan, the Moldavian pretender, and the Lady Arabella by the ambassador Boderie early in 1610. It was threatened to air the matter in Parliament (as was done occasionally with satires on prominent persons). Francesco Contarini wrote to the Doge and Senate of Venice on February 18, 1610:

> Lady Arabella complains that in a certain comedy the playwright introduced an allusion to her person and the part played by the Prince of Moldavia. The play was suppressed. Her Excellency is very ill pleased and shows a determination in this coming Parliament to secure the punishment of certain persons we don't know who.[204]

The play was acted in 1609, and seems to have been printed in the same year; but, as no copies of that edition are extant, it may have been suppressed. At any rate, echoes of trouble appear in later versions. The second prologue says,

> If any yet will, with particular sleight
> Of application, wrest what he doth write;
> And that he meant or him, or her, will say:
> They make a libel, which he made a play.

Also, the dedication, in the 1616 Folio, is to a kinsman of the Lady Arabella, Sir Francis Stuart, a man of literary tastes, who seems to have been Jonson's protector and the judge to whom he appealed for a fair reading of his lines. He says in his address, "Read therefore, I pray you, and censure. There is not a line, or syllable in it changed from the simplicity of the first copy. And when you shall consider, through the certain hatred of some, how much a man's innocency may be endangered by an uncertain accusation; you will, I doubt not, so begin to hate the iniquity of such natures, as I shall love the contumely done me, whose end was so honourable as to be wiped off by your sentence."

[204] *S. P. Venetian*, 1607–10, art. 794. Mr. Graves has discussed this in "Jonson's Epicœne and Lady Arabella Stuart," *Modern Philology*, XIV, 141.

Jonson's several thrusts at the vanity and self-importance of the distinguished stage architect and designer, Inigo Jones, who wished his work to be regarded as more important than the poet's in the production of a masque, are an example of his severe and obvious caricature—obvious, i.e., to everyone but Gifford, who is apoplectic with rage if one suggests anything not gentle and sweet in Jonson. Inigo's father was a cloth-worker. *The Tale of a Tub*, from Act IV, sc. 2 on, is the re-working of an older play, satirizing from this point In-and-In Medlay, a joiner or architect, son of a weaver. There are some indications that Jonson's intentions in this play were well known before it was submitted for publication, and that it was by no means his only attack on Inigo Jones. There was at least a temporary check put upon Jonson. Mr. Pory wrote to Sir Thomas Puckering, January 12, 1632, that the inventor of a certain masque was Mr. Aurelian Townshend, "Ben Jonson being for the time discarded, by reason of the predominant power of his antagonist, Inigo Jones, who this time twelvemonth was angry with him for putting his own name before his on the title-page, which Ben Jonson made the subject of a bitter satire or two against Inigo."[205]

Jones had appealed to the Chamberlain, as is shown by an entry in Herbert's office-book for May 7, 1633, noting a receipt of £2 "for allowinge of the Tale of the Tubb, Vitruvius Hoop's part wholly strucke out, and the motion of the tubb, by commande from my lord chamberlin; exceptions being taken against it by Inigo Jones, surveyor of the king's workes, as a personal injury unto him."[206] The play was produced at court January 14, 1634, and "not liked," according to Herbert. The printed version contains, near the end, a fairly large amount of personal ridicule of Inigo Jones. It is possible that the King and Queen did not, like the Chamberlain, object to a laugh at Inigo. At any rate, Jonson dared to satirize him again before them in the masque *Love's Welcome*, July 30, 1634. Here Inigo calls himself a supervisor, an overseer. "I am a busy man!" he says, "and yet I must seem busier than I am! as the poet sings, but which of them I will not now trouble myself to tell you." Here the humor is mellower than in the earlier satire.[207]

[205] *Court and Times of Charles I*, II, 158–59.
[206] *Variorum*, 1821, III, 232.
[207] Cf. also *An Expostulation with Inigo Jones; Epigram of Inigo Jones;* and *To Inigo Marquis Would-be*.

Inigo Jones, by virtue of his office in the king's household, took the easiest way of checking Jonson—by appeal to the Chamberlain. In private life, recourse was probably had rather to libel suits or threats of libel suits. Jonson was not referring to imaginary dangers of charges of libel in connection with *The Poetaster* (acted by the Children of the Revels in 1601). The prologue to Day's *Isle of Gulls* (1606) complains that the poet who strikes at abuses or sins is charged with libelling (see p. 117). As Fleay has pointed out (*Eng. Drama*, I, 108–10), *King* and *Queen* have been changed in the extant version to *Duke* and *Duchess*, giving evidence of danger of application to real persons. There is an account of a libel suit in Star Chamber for slander and sacrilege by Henry Earl of Lincoln against Sir Edward Dymock and others, who had a stage play on a Maypole green which contained "scurrilous and slanderous matter" against the Earl of Lincoln. The sacrilege charge was based upon the "vain and scurrilous" preaching of an actor who impersonated a minister. Sir Edward Dymock was committed to the Fleet and fined £1000 for instigating the offense. The three chief actors were whipped, pilloried, and fined £300 apiece.[208]

About 1630–34 the desire to indulge in recognizable satirical portraitures on the stage gave Herbert considerable trouble. An entry in his office book for November 18, 1632, concerning *The Ball* "written by Shirley and acted by the Queen's players," states that "there were divers personated so naturally, both of lords and others of the court, that I took it ill, and would fain have forbidden the play, but that Biston [Beeston] promiste many things which I found faulte with all should be left out, and that he would not suffer it to be done by the poett any more, who deserves to be punisht; and the first that offends in this kind, of poets or players, shall be sure of publique punishment."[209]

Probably the most obnoxious of the personalities were eliminated before the printing of the 1639 edition (as "by Chapman and Shirley"), where, in IV, 3, and V, 1, *Lionel*, *Stephen*, and *Loveall* replace *Travers*, *Lamount*, and *Rainbow*.

[208] Hudson, *Star Chamber*, p. 101.
[209] *Variorum* (1821), III, 231–32.

Herbert again exercised his censorship in October, 1633, when, as he says, "exception was taken by Mr. Sewster to the second part of the City Shuffler [non-extant] which gave me occasion to stay the play till the company [of Salisbury Court] had given him satisfaction."[210] It was in the same year that *The Tale of a Tub* was censored.

These are only examples of what appears to have been a pretty common dramatic tendency. Jonson was not the only dramatist who had an "armed prologue," in effect. But by their very disclaimers the prologues, inductions, and prefaces bear witness to the frequency of contemporary personal allusion.

Sedition and Treason

Plays suspected of being seditious naturally caused the most commotion. A conspicuous example is *The Isle of Dogs*, of which Nashe was part author. This was not published, but it was played by the Admiral's men between July 19 and August 10, 1597. It resulted in the seizure of Nashe's papers at his lodgings for examination, the arrest of several players, and the examination of Nashe himself. A letter to several justices of peace on the Privy Council Register under date of August 15, 1597, shows the gravity of the offense:

Upon informacion given us of a lewd plaie that was plaied in one of the plaiehowses on the BanckeSide, contanynge very seditious and sclanderous matter, wee caused some of the players to be apprehended and comytted to pryson, whereof one of them was not only an actor but a maker of parte of the said plaie. For as moche as yt ys thought meete that the rest of the players or actors in that matter shalbe apprehended to receave soche punyshment as theire leude and mutynous behavior doth deserve, these shalbe therefore to require you to examine those of the plaiers that are comytted, whose names are known to you, Mr. Topclyfe, what ys become of the rest of theire fellowes that either had theire partes in the devysinge of that sedytious matter or that were actors or plaiers in the same, what copies they have given forth of the said playe and to whome, and soch other pointes as you shall thincke meete to be demaunded of them, wherein you shall require them to deale trulie as they will looke to receave anie favour. Wee praie you also to peruse soch papers as were fownde in Nash his lodgings, which Ferrys, a Messenger of the Chamber, shall delyver unto you, and to certyfie us th'examynacions you take.[211]

[210] *Variorum* (1821), III, 172.
[211] *Acts of the Privy Council*, XXVII, 338.

Nashe was not the only one arrested. Ben Jonson, it will be recalled, was one of the men discharged. Several players are said to have been apprehended. This was not uncustomary even when they were not regarded as joint-authors. But here Nashe escaped in part by insisting that the first act was the only one he was responsible for, and the other four were supplied by the players (see his *Lenten Stuff*, 1599). Henry Porter, an actor by profession, was regarded as guilty of part-authorship, according to an entry of a loan by Henslowe of 10s. on August 23, 1597, to Henry Porter "now at this tyme in the fflete for the wrytinge of the eylle of Dogges."

On July 28, 1597, the Privy Council ordered all the theatres closed, because "there are verie great disorders committed in the common playhouses both by lewde matters that are handled on the stages and by resorte and confluence of bad people."[212] There are some who attribute this action to the *Isle of Dogs* as a cause (cf. Greg's *Henslowe*, fol. 232, 12).

The accusation of "popery and treason" which Drummond says was lodged against Ben Jonson because of his *Sejanus*, probably between 1603 and 1605, has been discussed above in connection with *Eastward Hoe*. Unfortunately no definite conclusions can be reached yet.

Samuel Daniel's *Tragedie of Philotas* was acted 1604-05 by the Queen's Revels Company, but was suppressed at some time after January 3, 1605—the same year in which Chapman and Jonson were in so much trouble over one of their plays. The story and the chief character of Philotas were construed as referring to Essex, and the author was obliged to dèny this charge before the Privy Council.[213]

Feeling the need of support, Daniel involved the Earl of Devonshire as having heard the play in advance. An apology to the Earl is in the *State Papers Domestic* (1603-10, vol. XI, art. 4). Daniel says he is "sorry for having offended him by pleading before the Council when called in question for the tragedy of Philotas, that he had read part of it to the Earl;

---

[212] *Acts of the Privy Council*, XXVII, 313.

[213] Philotas is a popular courtier who boldly criticizes his sovereign, Alexander the Great. He feels himself greater than the unworthy courtiers who are his jealous rivals. He refuses to do what they do, to secure advancement; hence his fall.

had no other friend in power to help him; knows he shall live *inter historiam temporis*: and will vindicate his innocence." To clear himself more fully, Daniel had the play entered on the Registers in the first year of its acting, November 29, 1604, and printed in 1605 with a prefatory letter to Prince Henry stating, by way of apology, that Acts I to III had been written "near half a year" before the execution of Essex. The only resemblance, he said, was to Essex's weakness, which he would to God might be buried. His explanation hardly accounts for Acts IV and V, nor for his "allowing" this play as censor of his company.

The play *Sir John van Olden Barnavelt*, written for the King's men acting at Blackfriar's in 1619, is particularly interesting because of its bold attempt to deal with contemporary foreign politics in such a way as to extract from them a truth or two of universal application, and even to suggest a particular analogy for an English audience to carry out in imagination. The hero of the play, Barnavelt, was the advocate of Holland, who, on May 13, 1619, was executed on the charge of having conspired with the Arminian faction to break up the religion and the unity of the state of Holland,[214] to degrade the Prince of Orange, and, if necessary, to take assistance of foreign potentates to these ends. He was, however, popularly regarded as a martyr to his country who died to save it from the yoke of Spain. He was well known in England, having been five times extraordinary ambassador to England and France. The death sentence of Barnavelt contained the charge that he "had injured some of their mightiest allies by his secret practices, namely, by calumniating the King of Great Britain, as though he had been the author of these troubles in the Low Countries."[215] A letter from Chamberlain to Carleton (*S. P. Dom.*, May 31, 1619) remarks that "Barnavelt is thought to have had hard measure, no conspiracy being proved against him."

The extant manuscript of the play, which was not put into print in its own day, but has been published by Bullen (*Old English Plays*, vol. II), shows corrections and criticism by the Master of the Revels, who signed the initials G. B. (George Buc)

[214] See John Motley, *Life of John of Barnaveld*.
[215] Arthur Wilson, *History of Great Britain* (Jas. I), 1653, p. 127.

to a marginal note in Act I, sc. 3. Miss W. Frijlinck's critical edition of this play (Amsterdam, 1922), I have not yet seen.

The Prince of Orange appears frequently in the play—too frequently to suit Buc's taste. The authors seem to have taken pains, at least in the first three acts, to sketch the Prince in an inoffensive way. He is sweet, gracious, humble—too humble and forgiving, perhaps, for a kingly character. The offence is to royalty rather than to a particular representative. It arises from the treatment accorded a prince—a treatment very undesirable to portray before an audience not altogether pleased with the relationship between James and his Parliament.

In Act II, sc. 1, Barnavelt speaks against the tyranny of the Prince of Orange. Six lines suffer a cancel because of this. The Lords of the Council accuse him of pride, insolence, and ambition. The end of the fourth act draws an analogy between the Prince and the emperors of Rome. Buc's most outspoken objection to the treatment of the Prince was to the passage in Act 1, sc. 3, where the guard politely but firmly refused to allow the Prince of Orange to enter the Senate then in session. Buc wrote in the margin: "I like not this; neither do I think that the prince was thus disgracefully used, besides he is too much presented." It is rather interesting to note, at this point, that what Buc did not wish suggested to the subjects of James actually occurred just ten years later, when the Parliament, unwilling to be prorogued, ordered Hobart to lock the doors and refused to admit the royal messenger. Charles commanded the guard to force the entrance. (Also, Elliott is said to have likened Buckingham at this time to Sejanus, and by implication, thought Charles, likened the king to Tiberius.)

In censoring *Barnavelt*, Buc took pains to reduce the number of times that the Prince of Orange was specifically named. Twice he substituted "the valiant Prince" or "this Prince that contemns us."[216] In other passages the name is left. It looks as if Buc would have preferred to cut out more of the matter pertaining to the Prince, but found it difficult to do so because of the care taken to make him an inoffensive character.

An important feature of the play is that the Senate is elevated in dignity at the expense of the prince. Barnavelt speaks eloquently of the servility of bowing down to a king—"to one

[216] Bullen, *Old English Plays*, II, 218, 231.

that only is what we have made him," and urges that the Senate show that it is not beneath the king in power. The Prince is made to voice respectful sentiments concerning the "mighty powerful princes" of the Senate, whose functions are really greater than a monarch's.

Also, the divine right of kings and the monarchical form of government are hit at more than once. The most "dangerous" speech of all is one of Barnavelt's at the trial (end of Act 4):

> Octavius, when he did affect the Empire
> And strove to tread upon the neck of Rome
> And all hir ancient freedoms, tooke that course
> That now is practised on you; for the Catos
> And all free sperritts slaine, or els proscribd
> That durst have stird against him, he then sceasd
> The absolute rule of all. You can apply this.
> And here I prophecie I, that have lyvd
> And dye a free man, shall, when I am ashes,
> Be sensible of your groans and wishes for me;
> And when too late you see this government
> Changed to a monarchie youll howle in vaine
> And wish you had a Barnavelt againe.

Buc's marks here show him at first desirous of making the modifications as slight as possible. "That now is practisd on you" was cut, doubtless because the English audience would sit up and watch for an English analogy at such words. "All free sperritts slaine or els proscribed" might readily suggest the execution of the enemy of James, Sir Walter Raleigh. The desire for absolute rule which characterized Octavius would not require much acumen to place.

The reason why such sentiments were likely to be applied to the English situation was, very simply, that absolutism was the chief bone of contention between James and his people. James called no Parliament between 1609 and 1620 except the very brief one in 1614 which he impulsively dissolved.[217] At the time when Barnavelt was produced (summer of 1619), there was probably a feeling that there was urgent need of parliamentary consideration of public questions. Royal prerogative and the relations between King and Parliament were constantly

---

[217] See Wotton's letter to Bacon, June 8, 1614, *Reliquiae Wottonianae* (1685), p. 431, on the friction between James and his Parliament.

being called in question. And when, the following year, 1620, Parliament did meet, the accumulated feeling burst into expression in the declaration that Parliament (after a special meeting at which only part of the members were present) caused to be entered on the Journal of the House of Commons:

The privileges and rights of Parliament are an ancient and indubitable birthright and inheritance of the English, and all important and urgent affairs in Church and State as well as the drawing up of laws and the remedying of abuses, are the proper subjects of the deliberations and resolutions of the parliament. The members are free to speak upon them in such order as they please, and cannot be called to account for them.[218]

On November 20, 1621, James forbade Parliament to meddle in affairs of state, and himself struck their declaration out of the Journals publicly on December 31, 1621. He dissolved the next Parliament January 6, 1622, because the members spoke disrespectfully of foreign sovereigns and wasted time, he thought, in arguing about their privileges and the rights of the King. Many of the boldest speakers in both houses, according to von Raumer, were sent out of England on one pretext or another, and others were imprisoned. The "free sperritts slaine or else proscribed" proved prophetic of the immediate future of those who in England protested against the absolutism of James's government.

One can hardly doubt that, in spite of any close analogy in situation, many passages in *Barnavelt* would be interpreted by an English audience as intended to picture English conditions. Barnavelt as hero was dangerous because he voiced an earnest desire for civil liberty. His dread of a monarchy for his people was not allowed to go unchallenged in the play. "Changed to a monarchie" in the passage quoted above was converted into "changed to another form." Then Buc either saw how flat this was or realized that minor operations could not cure the general intent of the whole passage, and so marked the whole twelve lines for omission.

These are the principal matters that seem to have met Buc's censure in *Barnavelt*: passages voicing a desire for civil liberty; protests against the absolute tyranny of kings; admiration for

[218] F. von Raumer, *Polit. Hist. of Eng.* . . . . I, 443.

other than a monarchical form of government. A minor item whose omission may also have been due to Buc is the scoring out of thirteen lines by a sea-captain at the end of Act I, sc. 1. The passage is illegible, but probably concerned the number of wenches available as a bribe to a young lord's son. This cut, which leaves one person with two speeches in succession, may have been made in the interests of decency.[219]

The stage history of *Barnavelt* is not fully known. It is, however, clear, from a letter of August 14, 1619, from Locke at London to Carleton, the English ambassador at the Hague, that the play was temporarily prohibited by the Bishop of London, but later allowed for performance—whether with or without alterations does not appear. The letter says:

> The Players heere were bringing of Barnevelt upon the stage, and had bestowed a great deale of mony to prepare all things for the purpose, but at th' instant, were prohibited by my Lo: of London.[220]

Locke wrote again, on August 27:

> Our players have found the meanes to goe through with the play of Barnevelt, and it hath had many spectators and receaved applause; yet some say that (according to the proverbe) the diuill is not so bad as he is painted, and that Barnavelt should persuade Ledenberg to make away himself (when he came to see him after he was prisoner) to prevent the discoverie of the plott, and to tell him that when they were both dead (as though he meant to do the like) they might sift it out of their ashes, was thought to be a point strayned. When Barnavelt understood of Ledenberg's death, he comforted himself, which before he refused to do, but when he perceaueth himself to be arested, then he hath no remedie, but with all speede biddeth his wife send to the French Ambassador.....[221]

The wavering treatment of Barnavelt's character here complained of may very well have been due to excess of caution not to make him too attractive a character in comparison with the Prince.

[219] Thrusts at women's morals and manners seem to have been fairly common at this time. A letter of Chamberlain to Carleton February 12, 1620, says: "The pulpits ring continually against the insolence and impudence of women; the players and ballad singers also take them to task." (*S. P. Dom.*, 1619–23, vol. CXII, art. 82.)
[220] *S. P. Dom. James I*, 1619–23, vol. CX, art. 18.
[221] *Ibid.*, art. 37.

Antagonism to James was probably the cause of Herbert's objection to a play called *The History of the Duchess of Suffolk*, in 1624, "which being full of dangerous matter was much reformed by me; I had two pounds for my pains: Written by Mr. Drew."[222] It was not until the reign of Charles that Herbert licensed this for the press (November 13, 1629), and it was not printed until 1631. The matter was, no doubt, "dangerous" because of certain historical facts: that the will of Henry VIII had favored the line of the heirs of his youngest sister Mary, Duchess of Suffolk, skipping over James, the descendant of the eldest sister, Margaret, who married James IV of Scotland.[223]

In spite of the censoring of manuscripts and the prosecution of authors and actors, the desire to discuss contemporary matters on the stage continued even to the closing of the theatres. In March, 1640, Charles was planning a journey to Scotland. Shortly after, Beeston's players, or "The King's and Queen's Young Company," acted without license a new play. The Chamberlain transmitted from King to Master of Revels the order for punishment. Beeston was "committed to the Marshalsey." Herbert's note of the matter is:

"The play I cald for, and, forbiddinge the playinge of it, keepe the booke, because it had relation to the passages of the King's journey into the Northe, and was complaynd of by his Majestye to mee, with commande to punishe the offenders."[224] Herbert suppressed the company, but pardoned them four days later. Beeston soon after gave offense again, and the Chamberlain appointed D'Avenant in his place.[225]

Impropriety

If the city authorities or the Puritans had succeeded in regulating the drama to suit their tastes, we might possibly

[222] Chalmers, *Sup. Apol.*, 217.

[223] There was once a play (non-extant) by Haughton, *The English Fugitives*, touching on the Duchess of Suffolk in the time of Mary. It is recorded in *Henslowe's Diary* for 1600. Possibly it was never published. Books on the succession generally proved unlucky for their authors. Hales was in the Tower of London in 1564 for a book he wrote on the succession, in which he showed his fear of a Scotch queen if Elizabeth should die childless (Strype, *Life of Sir Thomas Smith*, 91–93). Dudley wrote to Cecil and Sir John Mason that he had consulted Queen Elizabeth about delivering Hales' book to the Judges (*Cecil Papers*, I, 418).

[224] *Var.*, III, 241.   [225] *Ibid.*

have seen censoring earnestly applied in the direction of propriety. Certainly the Puritans objected zealously to the indecencies of the drama, often confusing these with practices more properly to be charged against the stage customs than against the drama itself. An order for the perusal of plays by the mayor and aldermen (December 6, 1574) required, among other things, censoring of "unchaste, uncomely, and unshamefaced speeches." It is needless to inform a reader of Elizabethan drama that this regulation was not strictly enforced—that is, if the standards of uncomeliness of that age and of this have any points of contact. One may, however, find some examples of censorship by the Master of the Revels in the interests of decency.

"On Friday the nineteenth (18th) of October, 1633," says Herbert, "I sent a warrant by a messenger of the chamber to suppress *The Tamer Tamed*, to the King's players for that afternoone, and it was obeyd; upon complaints of foule and offensive matters conteyned there in." The order, "to Mr. Taylor, Mr. Lowins, or any of the Kings players at the Blackfryers," commanded them to "forbeare the actinge of your play called the Tamer Tamed, or The Taming of the Tamer." But the play was permitted after revision. Herbert says, "On Saterday morninge followinge the booke was brought mee, and at my lord of Hollands request I returned it to the players the monday morninge after, purgd of oaths, prophaness, and ribaldrye" (October 21, 1633). This play was Fletcher's *The Woman's Prize*, which was "very well likt," according to Herbert, when it was performed at court on November 28, 1633.[226] Profanity was the chief objectionable feature.

In the play that Buc named *The Second Maiden's Tragedy*, 1611, part of the censoring seems aimed at impropriety; in *Barnavelt* there is possibly a trace of such aim; and a careful search would doubtless reveal other instances of similar treatment. It would, however, be an error to assume that passages equally objectionable would inevitably be censored, whenever met. In regulation of the drama, the attitude was very liberal as to matters of good taste and propriety. Herbert's model play which he holds up to the admiration of playwrights for its propriety is Shirley's *The Young Admirall*. It is to him an ideal

[226] J. Q. Adams, *Dram. Records of* .... *Herbert*, pp. 20–21.

play because "free from oathes, prophaneness or obsceanes." A study of this and of other plays that Herbert seems to have passed without objection will show that, however fussy he was about an oath, unless a play were otherwise offensive, obscene speech and broad vulgarity of general situation had a fair chance of passing without comment. His treatment of D'Avenant's *The Wits* illustrates his attitude. He hunts down the oaths to the very death, but leaves untouched the broad indecencies.

Buc and Herbert have both furnished some amusement to this generation by the excess of zeal with which they expurgated even the more harmless expletives along with the really questionable oaths. They should not be seriously charged with originating this attitude toward profanity in spoken or written drama. They merely applied, in accordance with their own standards of propriety, the regulations which as public officials they were bound to observe. The statute of 3 Jac. I, c. 21 (January, 1606) provided for a fine of £10 for profaning the name of God, Christ, the Holy Ghost, or the Trinity in play, show, pageant, or May-game. A statute of 21 Jac. I, c. 20 (February 19, 1623) ordered that "no person or persons shall from henceforth prophanely swear or curse," providing a small fine, or a whipping, or the stocks as penalties. Again, on July 26, 1635, a proclamation provided for the "suppression of prophane swearing and cursing" in conformity with old statutory prohibition.[227]

An example of the application of the profanity statute by Buc may be seen in the *Second Maiden's Tragedy*. Here he sometimes cancels, and sometimes lets slip *Life*. *'S life*, however, is cancelled, as is *'Sheart* and even *Heart*. *By the mass* is, of course, expurgated. *Faith* he allows, differing therein from Herbert, who is more fastidious.

In August, 1623 (following the new profanity statute) an entry in Herbert's office-book made the license of *A Tragedy of the Plantation of Virginia* to the Company at the Curtain conditional—"the profaneness to be left out, otherwise not tolerated."[228] A similar condition appears on the last page of the manuscript of William Methold's *The Launching of the Mary*, or the *Seaman's Honest Wife* (Egerton MS 1994):

[227] Rymer, *Foedera*, XIX, 647.
[228] Chalmers, *Suppl. Apol.*, 214.

This Play called the Seamans honest wife, all the Oaths left out in the action as they are crost in the booke, and all other Reformations strictly observ'd, may bee acted, not otherwise. This 27 June, 1633. Henry Herbert. I commaunde your Bookeeper to present mee with a faire Copy hereafter and leave out all Oathes, prophaness, & publick Ribaldry, as he will answer at his perill.[229]

This last requirement suggests some of the censor's difficulties: that the parts might already be distributed to the actors for study while the play was in the censor's hands; and that the the small reformations might be (intentionally or unintentionally) overlooked for that reason; and that irresponsible actors might even interpolate new oaths impromptu. Expletives, by their very nature, are likely to be improvised at times; and the marked extra-metrical quality of many such remarks in blank verse dramas may sometimes be accounted for in this way.

The danger that the actors' roles might be distributed from the uncensored version was provided against in Fletcher's *Woman's Prize*, or *The Tamer Tamed*, by the order sent to the company's book-keeper, Mr. Knight:

Purge there partes, as I have the booke, And I hope every hearer and player will thinke that I have done God good servise, and the quality no wronge; who hath no greater enemies than oaths, prophaneness, and publique ribaldry, which for the future I doe absolutely forbid to bee presented unto mee in any playbook, as you will answer it at your perill. 21 Oct., 1633.

Three days later the players apologized and were pardoned.[230] The actors had, however, stirred up some discussion, and Herbert made note of this, adding:

The Master ought to have copies of their new playes left with him, that he may be able to shew what he hath allowed and disallowed. .... All ould plays ought to bee brought to the Master of the Revells, and have his allowance to them, for which he should have his fee, since they may be full of offensive things against church and state; the rather that in former times the poetts tooke greater liberty than is allowed them by mee. The players ought not to study their parts till I have allowed of the booke.[231]

[229] J. Q. Adams, *Dram. Rec. of Henry Herbert*, 35.
[230] *Var.* (1821), III, 208–10.
[231] J. Q. Adams, *Dram. Rec. of H. Herbert*, 20–21.

Herbert was nervously anxious to clear himself of blame for profanity in plays. 1633 was a very trying year for him. In October Jonson's *The Magnetic Lady* was acted with a good deal of profanity. When this was reported to the Court of High Commission, objections were raised. The actors shifted the responsibility upon the author (who was then ill), and also upon the censor; but in their second petition, says Herbert, "they did mee right in my care to purge their plays of all offense, my lords grace of Canterbury bestowed many words upon mee, and discharged mee of any blame, and layd the whole fault of their play, called The Magnetick Lady, upon the Players. This happened the 24 of Octob. 1633 at Lambeth" (the archbishop's court).[232]

Jonson's induction to *Bartholomew Fair* has a sly dig at the censoring of profanity: *"I' fac's* no oath." It may not be to Jonson, but Herbert had some deep convictions as to what is or is not an oath. He examined D'Avenant's *The Wits* so microscopically for oaths that the author, with the aid of Endymion Porter, appealed to the King to moderate Herbert's censorship. The King's decision was dutifully recorded by Herbert, and his own opinion just as dutifully annexed:

> The king is pleased to take faith, death, 'slight for asseverations and no oaths, to which I do humbly submit as my master's judgment; but under favour conceive them to be oaths, and enter them here to declare my opinion and submission.

The play was licensed for the King's Company on January 10, 1634, as "corrected by the King."[233]

The effect of the elimination or alleviation of oaths upon the text may be conveniently observed in the Shakespeare Folio, in the Jonson folio of 1616, and in the Variorum edition of plays of Beaumont and Fletcher. Greg's edition of *Merry Wives of Windsor* contains a list of oaths changed from the quarto to the folio version. In Jonson's *Every Man in His Humour, by Jesus!* of Q¹ becomes *by Heaven!* or *by Jupiter!* in F¹, *O God!* becomes *O manners!* and *by Heaven* of Q¹ becomes (perhaps for variety) *by the bright sun! 'Sblood, s'wounds,* and *'sbread* are all eliminated, but *'slid, 'sdeins* remain. *St. Mark!* is eliminated, but *St. George*

[232] *Var.* (1821), III, 233.
[233] Ibid., III, 235.

remains. In Q⁴ of *Philaster* even *faith* is cut out. In some plays *faith* is toned down to *indeed* or *marry*, neither of which expressions, for some reason, seems to have struck Herbert as sacrilegious. *By the gods* might be rendered as *by all that's good*. *By my life* and *by my sword* were also considered harmless. *By Heaven* could safely be translated as *by these hilts*. And if one were so much moved that he was tempted to exclaim *by Jesu*! he might say instead, *believe me*! Many emendations which we may suppose were made by the authors themselves exhibit haste and carelessness as to suitability of phrase, so that a passage which gains in reverence, when cleansed to meet the censor's taste, does not always gain in effectiveness. As many of the oaths, however, did not originally convey profound emotion, but slight damage is done by the occasionally ludicrous or feeble substitutes.

Methods of Censorship

We have seen that various methods were employed in the censorship of drama. The Bishop of London, the Treasurer, the Privy Council, the Court of High Commission, the Chamberlain, and the Master of Revels all on occasion suppressed the performance of objectionable plays. The city officials, especially the Mayor, could appeal to any of these authorities. The most regular procedure for restraint of acted drama in London was by order of the Master of Revels, though frequently he merely carried out the orders of the Chamberlain or the King himself or the Privy Council. The Master of the Revels, by virtue of his censorship, had it in his power to destroy a play copy absolutely and refuse to license it for stage or for press; or, he could grant a license, noting certain conditions which must be met before the grant should become effective. Note of these conditions might be made in the back of the playbook submitted, or in Herbert's office-books, or, in case the drama was to be printed, in the registers of the Stationers' Company. A number of play manuscripts extant show such provisos at the back. One is Glapthorne's *The Lady Mother* (B. M.) in which Blagrave, deputy to Herbert, wrote that it might be acted, "the reformacons observed" (1635). The Master of the Revels could forbid the distribution of the parts of a play to the actors until it had been revised, and could insist upon having a revised version submitted for his approval before rehearsal. Whether he could effectively carry out such a prohibition is another question.

The method by which the Master of the Revels indicated his objections in detail may be observed in a number of plays, such as *The Second Maiden's Tragedy*, *Barnavelt*, *Sir Thomas More*, and *The Seaman's Honest Wife*. Though other alterations than those due to censorship appear, enough are clearly distinguishable as censor's changes to make the methods clear. We find crossing out of words, of lines, and of long passages for cutting, indication of insertions to be made, interlining, rewording, and adding of marginal comments on both matter and form. Sometimes, as in *Sir Thomas More*, the censoring would require a pretty complete reorganization of the whole play.

The Master of the Revels might attach similar provisos in licensing for the press, in which case it was probably necessary to convince the Stationers that the required reforms had been made. Although the Stationers' Company occasionally censored other literature themselves in licensing, they do not seem to have meddled much with dramatic censorship on their own initiative.

Besides these checks by delay, cancellation of parts, requirement of rewriting, etc., the authorities over drama had the right to recall licenses for either spoken or written drama afterward discovered to be objectionable.

There was always a chance that the changes required would not be carried out, and that new matter might be interpolated after the license. Herbert, as we have seen, recognized this, and insisted that he ought to have a copy of just what he had licensed. This was not a problem peculiar to the drama. As early as 1538 it was found to be important for religious censorship to protect against sly interpolations made after the license was secured. The proclamation made by Henry in 1538 provided penalties for such changes. Still the difficulty was not met squarely until the stricter requirement of the Licensing Act of 1637 provided, in item 4, that two copies of every book be provided, with the "titles, epistles, prefaces, proems, preambles, introductions, tables, dedications, and other things whatsoever thereunto annexed; that one copy be kept by the licenser, and no alterations made in the other (Rymer, *Foedera*, XX, 156).

This regulation solved Herbert's problem so far as printed drama was concerned, but did not help for spoken drama. The only way of discovering interpolations in acted drama was by the chance report of tale-bearers who took exceptions to certain parts recognized by the censor as not in the licensed version; and the only way to discover the offenders was to summon authors and actors and examine them to fix responsibility. The examinations were not always productive of results. Some of the prominent writers of the day were called in person before the authorities, such, for example, as Daniel, Jonson, Chapman, Marston, Middleton, and Nashe. Jonson's *The Magnetic Lady* and Nashe's *The Isle of Dogs* were two cases in which actors were held responsible to authorities for their interpolations. In studying the cases of Chapman's *Byron*, Jonson's *The Magnetic Lady*, Middleton's *A Game at Chess*, Nashe's *Isle of Dogs*, and Chapman, Jonson, and Marston's *Eastward Hoe*, one is tempted to infer that there was a collusive slipperiness as to who was to be held chiefly responsible for offensive matter, and that whoever was first caught might, so long as he could conveniently, blame the absent one. If the actor gets more than his share of blame, perhaps it is because he as an individual is comparatively irresponsible. This is doubtless the reason why whole companies had sometimes to be temporarily suppressed for the fault of one or a few. For example, the Admiral's Company is shown by a contract of Henslowe's with William Borne, August 10, 1597, to have been under a restraint for playing the *Isle of Dogs*. This lasted till October 11.[234] There was a similar restraint in connection with *A Game at Chess*, as we have seen above. Imprisonment, usually brief, was a punishment inflicted upon either author or actor. We have in the censorship of the drama little or no record of the extremely severe physical penalties occasionally suffered by writers in other fields of literature. It is true that Drummond in the *Conversations* (Gifford, IX, 390) said it was rumored in connection with the "voluntary" imprisonment of Jonson with Chapman and Marston for the offensive references to the Scots in *Eastward Hoe!* that "they should then have had their ears cut and their noses"; but this was only a rumor. Actors were

---

[234] *Henslowe's Diary*, ed. Greg, I, 203; cf. *Lenten Stuff; Works of* . . . . *Nashe*, ed. McKerrow, III, 153, and *Acts of P. C.*, August 15, 1597.

often threatened with much more severe penalties than they were obliged to undergo. Apologies and promises to reform often forestalled punishment. It is true that Jonson and Chapman complain (in the letters quoted ~~from~~ above) that they were imprisoned without examination or hearing, and that their play had been altogether misconstrued; but in Jonson's case, at least, it was not the first offence. His pronounced inclination to cartoon contemporary types so definitely as to suggest individuals signified by the types may have stimulated the authorities to over-watchfulness of his plays for criticism of royal policy and affairs of state. In spite of his denials, he was at times a personal satirist, even naming individuals, as where he poked fun at the maddening genealogies of the Hebraist, Hugh Broughton (*Alchemist*, Act 2, sc. 1) or in his many satires on Inigo Jones.

In judging the amount of contemporary reference in the printed drama of the sixteenth and seventeenth centuries, we should always remember that local hits were not usually printed in plays (as is the case even today); that the most "dangerous" dramas were no doubt revised even before submission to the Master of the Revels or other authority for permission to print; and that the most daring comments on forbidden topics were perhaps not committed to writing, but either actually interpolated extemporaneously or made to seem so. Kempe and Tarleton, in particular, had a reputation for extemporaneous insertions of a pungent nature. There is an anecdote to the effect that Tarleton pointed at Raleigh while saying, "The Jack commands the Queen." (E. Bohun, *Character of Q. Elizabeth*, 352.) Harmless words accompanied by significant expression, gesture, and inflection were made to convey dangerous ideas. A play that had nothing whatever in the text to offend a person or a nation might be made offensive by the manner of delivery. The farce mentioned on page 95.n. presented Elizabeth in an offensive light by mere dumb show. A pageant of Middleton's in 1617, *The Triumphs of Honour and Industry*, 1617, written for the mayoralty of George Howles, has an innocuous text. But the ambassador, Busino, reported that it had in it a Spaniard who "kept kissing his hands right and left, but especially to the Spanish ambassador, who was a short distance from us, in such wise as to elicit roars of laughter from the multitude."[235] Even the clergymen who wished to introduce politics into their sermons used the actor's art to make their allusions clear within the limits of safety. Chamberlain, on March 5, 1600, wrote a letter saying that Babington, Bishop of Worcester, "made many proffers and glances on behalf of the Earl of Essex, then in disgrace, as he was understood by the whole auditory and by the Queen herself, who presently calling him to a reckoning for it, he flatly forswore that he had any such meaning." The same ingenious method was employed in 1620 by a chaplain of King James, who preached before him on the text of the devil taking Jesus to the top of a mountain and showing him all the kingdoms of the world.

He pictured the Devil as a great monarch of many kingdoms, with viceroys, council of state, treasurers, secretaries. He gave a character of every officer fit to be the Devil's servants, running through the body of the Court .... In telling of the Devil's Treasurer, he fixed his eye on Cranfield and said, "That man that makes himself rich and his Master poor, he is a fit Treasurer for the Devil.[236]

Authors' Reactions on the Censorship of the Drama

The prefaces, inductions, prologues, and epilogues to plays, especially such as were printed some years after the play was produced, often contain authors' reactions upon the censorship. Sometimes these are in a humble and conciliatory tone. The prologue to the 1637 edition of Brome's *The English Moor* mentions a restraint of actors, and promises that they "will utter nothing may be understood offensive to the state, manners or time." Often these prologues show a genuine anxiety to be cleared of suspicion. Daniel's explanation of *Philotas*, though somewhat lame, really tries to explain. So, too, Nashe's comments take a serious turn, for once, when he speaks of the *Isle of Dogs* and its fate, in his *Summer's Last Will and Testament*. And so do Jonson's explanations at beginning and end of *The Poetaster*, and his conspicuously loyal addition of devout thanks for the King's preservation from his enemies, placed before the published *Sejanus*, the performance of which is said to have caused Jonson to be accused of treason. Not all the protests of

[235] *S. P. Venetian*, 1617-19, art. 103A (p. 62).
[236] Arthur Wilson, *History of Great Britain* (1653), pp. 151-52.

innocence in the prologues and epistles can be taken seriously, but still they furnish testimony to the existence of a rather active censorship on matters of state and religion, as well as of allusions to real persons of the time.

The dread of spies and reporters is expressed, sometimes seriously, sometimes mischievously, but so frequently as to convince one that the informer is no mere bogie. Nashe says, in his *Strange Newes* (1592): "Now a man may not talk of a dog, but it is surmised that he aims at him that giveth the dog in his crest; he cannot name straw, but he must pluck a wheat-sheaf in pieces."[237] The epistle to *Christ's Teares* (1594), contains a similar remark: "Let one but name bread, and they will interpret it to be the town of Bredan, in the Low Countreyes." He may have had in mind here the suppression of Sir John Smith's book criticizing the military operations in the Low Countries discussed above (p. 78). In 1594 he again protests against the interpreters who construe mutton and pottage as kings and princes, beer as Count Biron, and bad weather or a shower of rain as referring to someone who would reign next.[238] He pursues the same theme in a later pamphlet: If the unlucky writer, driven by necessity to write in haste, does not explain carefully,

"out steps me an infant squib of the Inns of Court, catcheth hold of a rush and absolutely concludeth, it is meant for the emperor of Russia, and that it will utterly marre the trafficke into that country if all the Pamphlets bee not called in and suppressed wherein that libelling word is mentioned."[239]

This is a daring reaction, I imagine, upon the recent suppression of Giles Fletcher's *The Russe Commonwealth* (see page 79), which used rather more than a rush to signify Russian affairs. Marston's preface to *The Malcontent*, 1604, shows that he had had trouble with "application." "Some," he says, "have been most advisedly over-cunning in misinterpreting with subtlety as deep as hell."

Jonson frequently satirizes the tattling spy, reporter, and decipherer who make trouble for writers. In the dedication to *Volpone* he says: "Application is now given a trade with many,

---

[237] *Works of Nashe* (ed. McKerrow), I, 260. The reference is to Shrewsbury and Burghley. On a possible reference to *Midas*, see p. 116, *supra*.
[238] *Ibid.*, II, 182.
[239] "Lenten Stuffe," *Works*, (ed. McKerrow), III, 213.

and there are that profess to have a key for deciphering of everything." The idea recurs in the second prologue to *Epicœne* (acted 1609):

> If any yet will with particular sleight
> Of application, wrest what he doth write;
> And that he meant or him, or her, will say,
> They make a libel, which he made a play.

A bolder reaction is his induction to *Bartholomew Fair* (acted 1614), in which he ridicules the official attitude toward profanity in plays, and still more sharply the misinterpretation of contemporary allusions by ignorant informers:

> It is agreed by the aforesaid hearers and spectators, that they neither in themselves conceal, nor suffer by them to be concealed, any state-decipherer, or politic picklock of the scene, so solemnly ridiculous as to search out who was meant by the ginger-bread woman, who by the hobby-horse man, who by the costard-monger, nay, who by their wares. Or that will pretend to affirm on his own inspired ignorance, what Mirror of Magistrates is meant by the justice, what great lady by the pig-woman, what concealed statesman by the seller of mousetraps, and so of the rest. But that such person, or persons, so found, be left discovered to the mercy of the author, as a forfeiture to the stage, and your laughter aforesaid. As also such as shall so desperately, or ambitiously play the fool by his place aforesaid, to challenge the author of scurrility, because the language somewhat savours of Smithfield, the booth, and the pigbroth, or of profaneness, because a madman cries, *God quit you*, or *bless you*.

A great deal of this is clearly reminiscent of Jonson's own painful experiences over *The Poetaster*, *Eastward Hoe*, and *Sejanus*. There may be a little side-thrust in the seeking of reference to a person in the pig-woman's wares at the city's stupid interference in regard to *The Hog hath Lost His Pearl*, a play inhibited the year before *Bartholomew Fair* was produced. The Hog's treasure, or pearl, was ludicrously mistaken for a reference to the Lord Treasurer recently deceased, an explanation which would make utter nonsense of the other parts of their interpretation even if there were any conceivable analogy between the gold and silver of that play and the Treasurer.

As Jonson was not of an unusually timid nature, a study of his references to the attitude of the authorities will, I believe, convince any doubter that the fear of censure on the part of so many dramatists was no invention of their own, but a natural reflection of serious troubles growing out of their attempts to treat contemporary characters and problems on the stage. The censorship did not succeed in keeping such matter out of the drama as spoken on the stage, but it undoubtedly did bar much of it from publication in print. Also, it necessitated an allegorical or roundabout portrayal of people, places, events, and problems which dramatists longed to present more realistically to the public. And, doubtless, the censorship had much to do with the choice, by more timid authors, of old or foreign themes which would not get them into trouble with the authorities. In the reign of James, particularly, one feels that there was definite repression of a genuine impulse to treat realistically the actual problems of the day.

In *Eastward Hoe!*, a play which got its authors into serious trouble because of the satire on the Scots, there is a reference (Act III, sc. 2, lines 61 ff.) to the use of real persons as characters in plays. Touchstone says:

> I hope to see thee one o' the monuments of our city, and reckon'd among her worthies, to be remembered the same day with the Lady Ramsey and grave Gresham, when the famous fable of Whittington[240] and the pusse shalbe forgotten, and thou and thy actes become the posies for hospitals; when thy name shall be written upon conduits, and thy deeds plaid i' thy life-time by the best companies of actors and be call'd their get-peny.

Lady Ramsey was a noted benefactress, the wife of a Mayor of London. Like Gresham, the founder of the Royal Exchange, she was characterized in plays of the time. Heywood made use of such materials as here suggested in a very innocuous manner. It is the innocent nature of this sort of contemporary allusion, doubtless, that is emphasized in the burlesque prologue to *The Knight of the Burning Pestle*, published in 1613, the year when criticism of the city officials was receiving special attention in London (see page 174), but possibly written earlier along with the rest of the play. It is clearly a bit of good-natured satire on the city's anxiety to gag the actor on matters of contemporary interest, and at the same time a sly reminder of what happened to Jonson and Chapman when they handled contemporary topics and indulged in local hits:

This seven years there have been plays at this house. I have observed it, you still have girds at the citizens: and now you call your play 'The London Merchant.' Down with your title, boy, down with your title.
Prol. We intend no abuse of the City.
Cit. No, Sir? Yes, Sir,—for if you were not resolved to play the Jacks, what need you study for new subjects purposely to abuse your betters? Why could you not be contented, as well as others, with the legend of Whittington, or the life and death of Sir Thomas Gresham, with the building of the Royal Exchange, or the story of Queen Eleanor with the rearing of London Bridge upon Woolsacks?

The City, presumably, would tolerate no mention of its important characters that was not adulatory.

CHAPTER III

AUTHORSHIP AND OWNERSHIP OF PLAYS AS AFFECTING PUBLICATION

Dramatic Authorship

Sir Sidney Lee, in discussing the attitudes of playwrights and theatrical companies toward the publication of plays, states that "a very small proportion of plays acted in the reigns of Elizabeth and James I—some 600 out of a total of 3000—consequently reached the printing-press, and the bulk of them is now lost."[1] I do not know on what he bases his statistics; but, assuming them correct, one might still inquire whether, if one-fifth of the plays now listed as being produced on the stage in the year 1923 are in the year 2270 generally known to have been put into print, it will not be a matter of surprise.

It is not to be expected that, in any age, all plays suitable for the stage should be put into print. But if, after making due allowances for lost plays and plays of ephemeral interest, the proportion of extant ones published between 1580 and 1640 should seem unusually small, perhaps a consideration of some of the conditions of production and disposal of plays will help to explain why even some of the successful stage-plays were not, apparently, published in their own day.

In the first place, there was a very free appropriation of the plots of older plays. Reputable authors took over not only plots, but whole lines from earlier plays. An example of this very common practice is Davenport's *King John and Matilda*, expanded from *Robin Hood*, part 2, which had a run in 1598.[2] Even the best writers, such as Shakespeare, remodeled old plays; and the second-rate writers constantly did hack-work at revision, as we see from the numerous entries of payments in *Henslowe's Diary* for the altering and mending of old plays, for additions, prologues, epilogues. The desire to see a play in print as one of his "collected works" must have been considerably lessened if an author and his readers were alike aware that his own contributions were but slight.

[1] *Life of Shakespeare* (1916), p. 100.
[2] *Henslowe's Diary*, (ed. Greg,) II, 191.

Again, collaboration with contemporary playwrights would often tend to destroy the feeling of individual ownership in the product. This would not necessarily be true of a firm partnership such as that of Beaumont and Fletcher, but there seem to have been far more shifting than steady partnerships at this time. If one follows through Greg's table of authorship in his edition of *Henslowe's Diary* (II, 365) for the years 1597-1603 the co-operation of Chettle, Dekker, and Drayton with various playwrights, he will begin to wonder how it would be possible to have a feeling of ownership in the results of such collaboration. To take a very simple example, whose play would this be? Henslowe on Dec. 3, 1597, paid for the Admiral's men £1 to Ben Jonson "upon a boocke which he showed the plotte unto the company at crysmas." The next autumn Chapman wrote a tragedy "on bengemens plot." There was, it is true, somewhat more hackwork, more farming out of piece-meal reconstruction among Henslowe's playwrights than was entirely typical of stage practices; but there is outside of Henslowe abundant evidence that remodeling of old plays and miscellaneous collaboration were common practices.

Another check upon a playwright's desire to have his plays published under his own name was the extraordinary speed at which many of the dramas were written. There was a pretty general appreciation of the fact that a play which went off successfully on the stage would still need considerable furbishing up for a more critical audience who might read it in print. Whether because the pay was so low or because the demand was so great, the average dramatist of the period was a rapid producer. Heywood, in 1633, referred to the *English Traveler* as "being one reserved amongst two hundred and twenty in which I have had either an entire hand or at the least a main finger." Could we expect Heywood to have a pride in seeing all those plays in which he had a "main finger" in print under his own name? Or take the prolific Chettle. Imagine him attempting to see through the press all the plays in which he had any part.

The conditions of production being what they were, one would expect that only those authors who worked alone or in steady partnerships or those who had great literary ambitions or a strong sense of ownership would tend to cherish their plays as permanent contributions to literature. From this brief survey of the customary methods of production of plays, let us turn to some evidence of fact as to what the playwrights really did wish as to the putting of their plays into print.

ATTITUDE OF THE PLAYWRIGHT TOWARD PUBLICATION

One reason for the very general belief in wholesale piracy of plays has been the assumption that all playwrights were entirely indifferent toward the publication of their works. This assumption is as old as the mid-eighteenth century, but still flourishes today. Sir Sidney Lee says:

> It was contrary to the custom of the day for dramatists to print their plays for themselves or to encourage the printing of them by others or to preserve their manuscripts. Like all dramatists of this age, Shakespeare composed his plays for the acting company to which he attached himself; like them he was paid by the company for his writings, and in return made over to the company all property and right in his manuscripts.[3]

The same position was taken by Professor Wendelin Foerster in a speech (8 June, 1913) before the Hauptversammlung des Sächsischen Neuphilologenverbandes in Chemnitz:

> Ein drama drucken zu lassen, daran dachte damals kein dramatiker, zumal der gewinn an büchern fast einzig und allein dem verleger nicht dem verfasser zufiel. War der dichter, wie das bei Shakespeare der fall war, zugleich noch schauspieler und mitaktionär der bühne, so hatte er sogar zunächst ein direktes interesse daran, seine annahmen aus den aufführungen seiner stücke nicht durch druckausgaben beeinträchtigt zu sehen.[4]

Such statements have been made so often that they are usually accepted as truisms. As we shall see, it does seem to have been the custom for the author to sell his copyright together with the play-right, doubtless for the double purpose of giving the company a chance for better control of the property in a play for stage use and giving them some security that it would not be put into print without their knowledge or consent. It was perhaps at this time regarded as unfair that an author should be in a position to take a financial advantage of a stage success which might be in part attributable to the work of the theatrical

---

[3] Int. to First Folio, xi.
[4] Sonderabdruck aus *Die neueren Sprachen* (1914), p. 4.

company which had purchased the stage-right. Anyone can see that there are questions arising in regard to copyright in plays which do not arise in regard to other literary works. I do not know what evidence Sir Sidney Lee has for his statements as to Shakespeare's contracts for his plays—I have myself found none whatever,—but the possibility of private arrangements for publication of plays that were acted may be conclusively demonstrated, as well as the fact that authors were frequently able to see their plays through the press. A number of Elizabethan and Jacobean dramatists did arrange for the publication of their own works.

Miss Charlotte Porter refers to Ben Jonson's signature, "The Author, B.I." in the 1616 Folio as "moving toward the innovation of the authorization of the publication of plays," an "exceptional innovation" which she attributes to the fact that Jonson did not, like Shakespeare, share in the proceeds of the company. But by 1616 authorization of play publication was, as we shall see, not an exceptional innovation. And the fact that Ben Jonson wrote for so many different companies and yet put his plays into print when he wished is certainly significant.

Among the authors who oversaw publication of some of their own plays are: Chapman, D'Avenant, Day, Ford, Glapthorne, Heywood, Jonson, Marston, Massinger, Middleton, Shirley, and Webster. Chapman wrote dedications for *Byron*, 1608, for *All Fools*, 1605, *The Widdowes Teares*, 1612, *The Revenge of Bussy D'Ambois*, 1613; Day (with collaborators) for *Travailes of the Three English Brothers*, 1607, and for *Lawe Trickes*, 1608; Glapthorne oversaw the publication of a volume of his poems in 1639 and of three plays (equipped with dedications) in 1640. Ford, Heywood, and Marston, with what has been construed as unwillingness, *allowed* their works to appear in print. Massinger dedicated a great many of his plays: *Duke of Milan*, 1623, *The Bondman*, 1624, *The Roman Actor*, 1629, *The Renegado* and *The Picture*, 1630, *The Emperor of the East* and *The Maid of Honor*, 1632, *A New Way to Pay Old Debts*, 1633, *The Great Duke of Florence*, 1636, and *The Unnatural Combat*, 1639. Many of D'Avenant's plays were printed in his lifetime, and in 1763 an edition of his works advertised that it contained the plays formerly printed and "those which he designed for the press now published out of the author's original copies."

Shirley may fairly be called a professional writer of plays. He oversaw the publication of many of his works; among others, *The Wedding*, 1629, *The School of Complement*, 1631, *Love in a Maze*, and *The Witty Fair One*, 1632, *The Traitor*, 1635, *The Lady of Pleasure*, 1637, *The Maid's Revenge*, 1639, *The Opportunity*, 1640. Jonson, as all know, frankly published many plays, singly and in collections. Middleton, in his preface to *The Roaring Girl*, 1611, shows that he expects a reading audience and is writing for them, as well as for an audience at the theatre. After commenting on the fashion of play-making as calling for "single plots, quaint conceits, lecherous jests drest up in hanging sleeves," he goes on to say:

Such a kind of light-colour summer stuff mingled with divers colours you shall find this published comedy; good to keep you in an afternoon from dice at home in your chambers, and for venery, you shall find enough for sixpence, but well couched, and you mark it . . . . The booke I make no question but is fit for many of your companies, as well as the person itself, and may be allowed gallery-room at the playhouse, and chamber room at your lodging.

That many other authors oversaw publication of plays is certain. The list above includes only writers of some prominence selected somewhat casually from my own reading, on the basis of a single indication, the presence of an author's dedication or a preface obviously by the author. Before the close of the period under consideration, it is probable that a large proportion of works published by authors' direction had no dedications. Though Massinger himself persistently dedicated plays,[5] he says in his dedication of *The Unnatural Combat* to Anthony Sentleger, 1639:

That the patronage of trifles, in this kind, hath long since rendered dedications and inscriptions obsolete, and out of fashion, I perfectly understand, and cannot but ingenuously confess that I walking the same path may be truly argued by you of weakness or wilful errour.

It might be expected that, at least in the age of Elizabeth, some dramatists would share the attitude of other authors in the matter of backwardness about publication. But only occasionally do we find such apologies for publicity in itself; for

[5] See *The Bondman, The Duke of Milan, A New Way to Pay Old Debts, The Great Duke of Florence, The Renegado, The Picture, The Maid of Honor, The Roman Actor, The Emperor of the East.*

most dramatists even then were recognized as professional writers for the stage, and were known to live by the publicity of their productions. The apology usually made by a dramatist for publishing his works is, what is often a very sensible admission, that the play was written for the stage and therefore loses something through the lack of scene and voice and action. A similar apology might be made by almost any successful playwright today—but this is not a day of apologies.

We should not conclude from the apology of a playwright that he was disinclined to publish. Ford, in his dedication of *The Lover's Melancholy* to some gentleman of Gray's Inn, 1629, clears his reputation of the blemish of professionalism:

> My presumption of comming in Print in this kind, hath hitherto been un-reprooueable. This Piece, being the first, that euer courted Reader; and it is very possible, that the like complement with Me, may soone grow out of fashion.

Because of this dedication and of the prologue in which he declares

> It is Arts scorne that some of late have made
> The Noble Use of Poetry a Trade,

it has been inferred that Ford was disinclined to publish his plays. But how can we believe this when Ford himself dedicated seven of his eight extant plays?

Heywood's practice is equally inconsistent with his views, repeatedly expressed. In his case, it becomes a simple question as to whether we shall attach more importance to what he says, or to what he does, in the matter of publication. He distinctly states, in his prologue to the *Play of Queen Elizabeth*, for revival at the Cockpit, that

> Some by Stenography drew
> The plot: put it in print, (scarce one word trew:)
> And in that lamenesse it hath limp't so long,
> The Author now to vindicate that wrong
> Hath tooke the paines, upright upon its feete,
> To teach it walke, so please you sit, and see't.[6]

And because of this statement many have been ready to believe that in all the prefaces in which Heywood expresses reluctance

---

[6] *Pleasant Dialogues and Drammas*, 1637, p. 28.

about publication we have evidence of a perpetual fear of pirates.

We should take into account Heywood's exaggeratedly apologetic attitude about appearing in print; his desire to avoid censure by the more critical audience of readers; his nervousness as to the reception of a work by readers; his irritability over typographical errors and his constitutional unwillingness to see to it that none appeared in the works he oversaw; and the thinness of the excuses he made when he directed the publication of his plays. We may find illustrations of these traits in his prefaces. After *nine* of his works had been published, Heywood, in his *Apology for Actors*, 1612, assured the reader:

> My pen hath seldome appeared in presse till now: I have beene ever too jealous of mine owne weaknesse willingly to thrust into the presse; nor had I at this time, but that a kind of necessity enjoyned me to so sudden a businesse.

If one is looking for pirates at every corner, he may find them in "a kind of necessity."

In *The Golden Age*, printed by William Barrenger under the oversight of Heywood in 1611, we have a preface, by the author to the reader, the sincerity of which is somewhat open to question. At any rate, the promise at the end shows that the author is not honestly disinclined to publish his plays, however he may feel about proposed surreptitious publication:

> This Play comming accidentally to the Presse, and at length hauing notice thereof, I was loath (finding it mine owne) to see it thrust naked into the world to abide the fury of all weathers, without either Title for acknowledgement, or the formality of an Epistle for ornament. Therefore rather to keepe custome, then any necessity, I haue fixt these few lines in the front of my Booke: neither to approue it, as tastfull to euery palat, nor to disgrace it as able to relish none, onely to commit it freely to the generall censure of Readers, as it hath already past the approbation of Auditors. This is the Golden Age, the eldest brother of the Three Ages, that haue aduentured the Stage, but the onely yet, that hath beene judged to the Presse. As this is receiued, so you shall find the rest: either fearefull further to proceede, or encouraged boldly to follow.

The promise was fulfilled by the publication of *The Silver Age*, through Nicholas Okes, 1613, with preface by Heywood; of *The Brazen Age*, through Okes in 1613, with a similar preface (containing complaint of misuse of certain translations of Ovid by a pedagogue Austin); of *The Iron Age* by Okes in 1632. In the preface to *The Iron Age*, Heywood apologizes for these plays, being then out of fashion, but anticipates a collection of all four:

> If the three former Ages (now out of Print) bee added to theese (as I am promised) to make up an handsome Volumne; I purpose (Deo Assistente) to illustrate the whole Worke, with an Explanation of all the difficulties, & an Historicall Comment of every hard name, which may appeare obscure or intricate to such as are not frequent in Poetry.

Evidently by 1632 Heywood was a calloused author.

Possibly a little light on the excuse for the appearance of the first "Age" in 1611 may be got from a similar excuse for the publication of *Four Prentises of London with the Conquest of Jerusalem* (printed at London for I.W. 1615). Here the intended piracy is less plausible, first, because of the greater age of the play, and second, because of the obvious use of such a plea for excusing the play as crude and old-fashioned:

> None but to you (as whom this Play most especially concernes) I thought good to Dedicate this Labour, which though written many yeares since, in my Infancy of Judgment in this kinde of Poetry, and my first practise: yet understanding (by what meanes I know not) it was in these more exquisite and refined Times to come to the Presse, in in such a forwardnesse ere it came to my knowledge, that it was past preuention, and then knowing withall, that it comes short of that accuratenesse both in Plot and Stile, that these more Censorious dayes with greater curiosity acquire. I must thus excuse. That as Playes were then some fifteene or sixteene yeares agoe it was in the Fashion.[7]

That Heywood was not indifferent to the glory a dramatist might win from publication may fairly be inferred from his preface to the reader, in Cook's *Green's Tu Quoque; or the City Gallant* (printed in 1614, acted as late as 1624):

> To gratulate the love and memory of my worthy friend the author, and my entirely beloved fellow the actor, I could not choose, being in the way just when this play was to be published in print, but to prefix some token of my affection to either. For the gentleman that wrote it, his poem itself can better speak his praise, than any oratory from me.

---

[7] Heywood's sensitiveness to fashion in play-making appears in the Epilogue to the reader in *Royal King and Loyal Subject*, 1637.

Nor can I tell whether this work was divulged with his consent or no; but howsoever, it hath passed the test of the stage, with so general an applause, pity it were but it should likewise have the honour of the press.

For himself, however, he continues to apologize. When he can no longer deny appearing in print of his own volition, he modestly calls attention to the "small noise" he is making in having his works appear singly in quartos rather than in folios:

My Plaies have not been exposed to the publike view of the world in numerous sheets and a large volume; but singly (as thou seest) with great modesty, and small noise. These Comedies, bearing the title of *The Fair Maid of the West*: if they prove but as gratious in thy private reading, as they were plausible in the publick acting, I shall not much doubt of their successe.[8]

In 1633 he revives the excuse that the play has come accidentally to the press, and again calls attention to his modesty about appearing in print:

If Reader thou hast of this Play beene an auditour? there is lesse apology to be used by intreating thy patience. This Tragi-Comedy (being one reserued amongst two hundred and twenty, in which I haue had either an entire hand, or at the least a maine finger, comming accidentally to the Presse, and I hauing Intelligence thereof, thought it not fit that it should passe as *filius populi*, a Bastard without a Father to acknowledge it: True it is, that my Playes are not exposed unto the world in Volumnes, to beare the title of Workes, (as others) one reason is, That many of them by shifting and change of Companies, haue beene negligently lost, Others of them are still retained in the hands of some Actors, who thinke it against their peculiar profit to haue them come in Print, and a third, That it neuer was any great ambition in me, to bee in this kind Voluminously read.[9]

In 1636 Heywood published *Loves Maistresse, a Masque*, dedicated to the Lord Chamberlain, with the extraordinary admission, "For this Dramaticke Poem, I neede not much Apologie." But a revised edition of *The Rape of Lucrece*, in 1638, repeats the preface of the 1608 quarto which admits that the publication is by consent (of the Company?) and of his own volition, but also suggests as a motive the fear of piracy:

[8] *Fair Maid of the West*, 1631.
[9] *The English Traveler*, L. R. Raworth, 1633, dedicated by the author to Sir H. Appleton.

It hath been no custome in me of all other men (courteous Readers) to commit my Plays to the Presse; the reason though some may attribute to my owne insufficiency, I had rather subscribe, in that, to their seveare censure, than by seeking to avoyd the imputation of weakenesse, to incurre greater suspition of honesty: for though some have used a double sale of their labours, first to the Stage, and after to the Presse: For my owne parte, I here proclaime my selfe euer faithfull in the first, and never guilty of the last: yet since some of my Playes have (unknowne to me, and without any of my direction) accidentally come into the Printers' hands and therefore so corrupt and mangled, copied onely by the eare) that I have been as unable to know them, as ashamed to challenge them, This therefore I was the willinger to furnish out in his native habit: first being by consent, next because the rest have been so wronged, in being publisht in such savage and ragged ornaments.[10]

After Chapman's *All Fools* had been on the stage for six years, he published it voluntarily in 1605; but in apologizing for it as "the least allow'd birth of my shaken brain," in his dedication to Sir Thomas Walsingham (which does not appear in all copies of the impression), he gave his reason for publishing thus:

> Lest by others' stealth it be imprest,
> Without my passport, patch'd by others' wit,
> Of two enforced ills, I elect the least.

But we should note that he published (apparently of his own accord) at least three other plays: *Byron*, 1608, *The Widow's Teares*, 1612, and *The Revenge of Bussy D'Ambois*, 1613. His attitude toward the printed play may be inferred from his remark in dedicating *The Widow's Tears*: "Other Countrymen have thought the like worthy of Duke's and Prince's acceptations."[11] Ford expresses a similar sentiment in his dedication of *The Fancies*, (1638) to Lord Randal MacDonnell.

Sir Sidney Lee states that Marston was obliged to protect himself against threatened piracy, and uses *The Malcontent* to prove it.[12] Ernest Walder also uses Marston as his chief example

[10] Fifth impression by J. Raworth for Nathaniel Butter, 1638. This is advertised as having "the copy revised," including "songs which were added by the stranger that lately acted Valerius his part."

[11] This preface, like several others, seems to be used by H. R. Shipherd in his "Play-publishing in Elizabethan Times," *P.M.L.A.*, December, 1919, to prove the direct opposite of what it says.

[12] *Life of Shakespeare* (1916), p. 546.

of the playwright whose sole ambition was, to see his play on the stage:

Marston in his preface to *The Malcontent*, 1604, actually complains that he is detracting from the value of his work by publishing it: and he goes on to state that his reason for consenting to this is that, if he did not publish it, others would, thus inflicting on him still greater injury.[13]

But he is not merely consenting to the publication of *The Malcontent*: he is eager to vindicate himself against the charges of satirical personal allusions:

Some have been most advisedly over-cunning in misinterpreting me, and with subtlety as deep as hell, have maliciously spread ill rumors, which springing from themselves might to themselves have heavily returned.

He goes on to say that he would have preferred not to put the play in print:

Only one thing afflicts me, to think that scenes, invented merely to be spoken, should be enforcively published to be read, and that the least hurt I can receive is to do myself the wrong. But, since others would otherwise do more, the least inconvenience is to be accepted. I have myself, therefore, set forth this comedy; but so, that my enforced absence must much rely upon the printer's discretion; but I shall entreat slight errors in orthography may be as slightly over-passed, and that the unhandsome shape which this trifle in reading presents, may be pardoned for the pleasure it once afforded you when it was presented with the soul of lively action.

It will be seen that, if one studies the whole dedication and the circumstances, it becomes clear that what Marston feared was not piracy, but the attacks of censors. He apparently did not care to publish this play, but the reason assigned is, that the true life of a play is on the stage. His disinclination to publish, however, was overcome by a stronger motive—the desire to get the matter of the play before the public, because of the false interpretations that had been made of it. He was willing, therefore, to put the play into print himself—but he shirked the accurate oversight of textual details, preferring to apologize.

Almost identical is the attitude expressed in the preface to "the Equal Reader" in one edition of *The Faune*, 1606 (first staged Jan., 1606):

[13] *Camb. Hist. of Eng. Lit.*, (N. Y., 1910), V, 289–90.

If any shall wonder why I print a comedy, whose life rests much in the actor's voice, let such know that it cannot avoid publishing; let it therefore stand with good excuse that I have been my own setter out.

He speaks of the malice and detractions of a few, and goes on to say: "For mine own interest for once, let this be printed."[14] He declares the other impression faulty, but does not say it was surreptitious. Possibly he left details in the printer's hands, as in the case of *The Malcontent*, and was dissatisfied with the results. Or perhaps relation of copyright to stage-right was involved (See p. 227). In the second quarto of *The Faun*, Marston pronounces the issue authoritative, and at the same time promises future publication of a more perfect work:

Reader, know I have perused this copy, to make some satisfaction for the first faulty impression: yet so urgent hath been my business that some errors have still passed, which thy discretion may amend. Comedies are writ to be spoken, not read; remember the life of these things consists in action; and for such courteous survey of my pen, I will present a tragedy [*Sophonisba*, a marginal note in Q.²] to you, which shall boldly abide the most curious perusal.

It is beyond question that Marston was not opposed, or even indifferent to having his work in print. When W. Sheares, his bookseller, dedicated six of his plays in 1633 to Lady Falkland (Dodsley, *O. P.*, IV, 4), he said, "Were it not that he is so far distant from this place, he would have been more careful in revising the former impressions, and more circumspect about it than I can."

Other authors seem at times to have been actuated, as Marston was in publication, by the desire to clear up misunderstandings or to answer attacks based on the stage presentations. Daniel, though apparently willing to appear in print, apologizes for the publication of *Philotas* (and more particularly for its presentation on stage). The play was taken as referring to Essex; but Daniel defended himself by declaring that it was begun before the Essex affair:

But by reason of some occasion then falling out, and being called upon by my Printer for a new impression of my workes, with some additions to the ciuill Warres I intermitted this other subject. Which

---

[14] There were three quartos of this play in this year. One was, according to Mr. E. E. Stoll, (*Eebster*, p. 17), a pirated text.

now lying by mee, and driuen by necessity to make use of my pen, and the Stage to bee the mouth of my lines, which before were never heard to speake but in silence.[15]

A similar motive seems to have influenced Lewes Machin to publish *The Dumb Knight* in 1608, which he wrote in collaboration with Gervase Markham. He says, "Rumour, that Hydra-headed monster, with more tongues than eyes, by help of his intelligencer, Envy, hath made strange constructions of all sharp critical censures, which heretofore have undeservedly pass'd upon him." *Eastward Hoe*, *Sejanus*, and *Byron* were published for similar reasons.

In not a few instances the author set out his play to get, if possible, a better judgment from the readers than had been given it by the audience at the theatre. Thus Webster, in his preface to *The White Devil* (1612), candidly expressed his opinion of his audience at the theatre as judges:

In publishing this tragedy, I do but challenge to myself that liberty which other men have ta'en before me: not that I affect praise by it, for *nos haec novimus esse nihil*; only, since it was acted in so dull a time of winter, presented in so open and black a theatre, that it wanted (that which is the only grace and setting-out of a tragedy) a full and understanding auditory, and that, since that time, I have noted most of the people that come to that playhouse resemble those ignorant asses who visiting stationers' shops, their use is not to inquire for good books, but new books.

Jonson, especially in his latter days, showed the same spleen over unfavorable reception of his plays on the stage. In a fit of anger he published *The New Inn*, "as it was never Acted, but most negligently Played by some, the KINGS SERVANTS, and more squeamishly beheld and censured by others, the KING'S SUBJECTS, 1629. Now at last set at Liberty to the Readers, his MAJESTY'S Servants and Subjects, to be judged of, 1631." To the reader he said, "If thou canst spell and join my sense, there is more hope of thee than of a hundred fastidious impertinents who were there present the first day."

The same attitude toward the judgment of play-readers, as compared with that of play-goers, is shown in Beaumont's verses to Fletcher, on his *The Faithful Shepherdess*:

[15] Letter to the Earl of Devonshire, 1604, in Daniel's *Works*, ed. Grosart, I, xxiii.

But since it was thy hap to throw away
Much wit, for which the people did not pay,
Because they saw it not, I not dislike
This second publication, which may strike
Their consciences, to see the thing they scorn'd,
To be with so much wit and Art adorn'd.
Besides one vantage more in this I see,
Your censurers now must have the qualitie
Of reading, which I am afraid is more
Than half your shrewdest Judges had before.[16]

The appearance of plays in collections, as, for example, a folio of Jonson's plays in 1616, one of Shakespeare's in 1623, and an octavo volume containing six of Lyly's court comedies in 1632, seems to indicate a real audience of play-readers. There

---

[16] Positive failure to get a play staged might be expected to result in publication of drama that was judged unactable. But the stationers, though eager enough to print plays that had roused positive objection when performed, seem not to have cared to print much drama that was unable to get even a hearing on the stage. "Acted with great applause" was one of the chief advertisements used. There is an occasional instance of publication of unacted drama; but this is clearly regarded as unnatural. For example, Thomas Nabbes put in print "The Unfortunate Mother; a tragedie never acted; but set downe according to the intention of the author" (1640), referring to it in his dedication as "a piece that (undeservedly, I hope) hath beene denied the credit which it might have gain'd from the stage." "E. B." (Edward Benlowes ?), in his prefatory verses to the author, laments its non-appearance on the stage:

Printed before 'tis Acted! such a tricke
As fewe men will judge to bee politike.
But little reason for it wee can see,
Profit should grow contemptible with thee.
I read it, and it hath my vote for good;
Sure 'twas not by some others understood;
By whom I wish action might added be,
For that's the best life of a Tragedy.
Sure, though they tyrant-like did sentence give
Upon thy Mother, she deserves to live.

Another friend, "C. G.," applies a stronger salve to the author's wounded feelings:

But I commend the wisedome of thy Fate
To sell thy labours at a better rate,
Then the contempt of the most squeamish age;
Or the exactest Roscii of the stage.

Nabbes also had *Covent Gardens* published with a dedication by himself, and *Tottenham Court, Hannibal and Scipio,* and *The Bride.*

seems also to have been gradually growing a conviction among a few of the dramatists and their friends that a work might have a double character—that of a play to be seen and heard, and that of a dramatic poem, to be enjoyed in the reading. A few there were, even in this playgoing age, who frankly declared that in their opinion the final judgment of merits rested with the wider and more critical circle, of readers of plays in print. A keen appreciation of the importance of critical judgment of plays by readers is shown by the dedication by Shirley of *Hyde Park*, 1635, and the prefatory poem by his friend, James Merwyn.

A more extreme expression of the desire that a play be preserved to the reading world is that contained in the verses prefixed by Edward Fraunces to Thomas Randolph's revised comedy, *The Jealous Lovers*, 1632:

> The more I this thy masterpiece peruse,
> The more thou seem'st to wrong thy noble Muse
> And thy free Genius. If this were mine,
> A modest envy would bid me confine
> It to my study or the critics' court,
> And not make that the vulgar people's sport,
> Which gave such sweet delight unto the king.
> Who censur'd it not as a common thing.
> Though thou hast made it public to the common view
> Of self-love, malice, and that other crew,
> It were more fit it should impaled lie
> Within the walls of some great library;
> That if by chance, through injury of time,
> Plautus and Terence, and that fragrant thyme
> Of Attic wit should perish, we might see
> All those reviv'd in this one comedy—
> The Jealous Lovers.

Richard Brome even suggests, in his verses prefixed to Fletcher's *Monsieur Thomas*, that posthumous fame through publication is the only real fame, even for a writer of plays:

> And yet perhaps it did participate
> At first presenting but of common fate;
> When ignorance was judge, and but a few
> What was legitimate, what bastard, knew.
> The world's grown wiser now; each man can say
> If Fletcher made it 'tis an exc'lent play.

Thus Poemes like their Authors may be sed,
Never to live 'till they have first beene dead.[17]

Ownership of Plays

We have seen, then, that for various reasons an author of a play might desire to see his work in print, as well as on the stage. The question naturally arises, Could he honestly gratify this desire? When he sold his play to the acting company, did he sell with his manuscript not only acting rights, but printing rights as well? The answer depends in part on what sort of stage-right, if any, existed at the time.

Basis of Stage-rights before Statutes

Perhaps because of the customary assertions by historians of English law that no stage-right existed before its statutory recognition, many writers on the history of the English stage assume an entire absence of protection of exclusive rights in the performance of plays purchased by the companies, and when they meet actual instances of such protection, try to explain it away as an unusual instance, due perhaps to the power of the patron or some similar advantage. Nobody has ever attempted to explain how the King's Company kept the acting rights of an extremely popular play, *The Merry Devil of Edmonton*, from 1608 to 1661, or to account for hundreds of other examples of successful maintenance of exclusive rights. The extremely few proved thefts are of infinitely more importance, in their judgment. Fowell and Palmer, in their *Censorship in England*, say, (pp.39-40):

---

[17] This attitude naturally became more common in the later period, during the interdicts of plays. In the 1647 folio of Beaumont and Fletcher, "John Web." elevates the judgment of the press above that of the theatre:

> What though distempers of the present Age
> Have banish'd your smooth numbers from the Stage?
> You shall be gainers by 't; it shall confer
> To th' making the vast world your Theater.
> The Presse shall give to ev'ry man his part,
> And we will all be Actors; learne by heart
> Those Tragick Scenes and Comicke straines you writ.

Cf. also Thomas May's poem on the publication of Shirley's plays in the period of the interdict.

In those days the best copyright in a play [by which, I think, they must mean the stage right] was secured simply by guarding the copies of it. Rival players had no scruples against purloining any stray copy and thus securing a first performance. Several cases are on record of a copy of a play produced at a rival establishment, and in this fact lies the probable explanation of the comparative rarity with which early plays were printed.

Miss Virginia Gildersleeve, though admitting a sort of stage-right, thinks there was still a necessity of guarding copies of the playbook, and that printing necessarily endangered stage-right:

Though the players or manager who purchased a play from its author seem to have had a property right in it, there was difficulty in enforcing this, except by careful guarding of all copies of the play-book, so that none might be available for performance by others. This was an urgent reason, of course, for avoiding of the printing of plays. Probably the prominent London companies had some agreement binding them to respect each others' property, but at times of hostility between the theaters thefts of plays occasionally occurred.[18]

She goes on to suggest that the simplest way to avoid such thefts was, to get the Master of the Revels to forbid the performance of plays by other companies, as did the King's Company in 1627, in having the Red Bull Company restrained from acting Shakespeare's plays, which were then in print.

Miss Gildersleeve's attitude is much more reasonable than the usual conclusion on this subject. But it may be questioned whether, if the copy had to be absolutely guarded and a play kept out of print, or else a special injunction secured against the acting of plays in print, the so-called right in the property of a stage play amounted to anything worth the having. It degenerates thus to the right of immediate possession of an article, the written copy,—which is far from being a legal right to exclusive performance.

The only bit of evidence I have myself run across that favors such a view (if one wishes to interpret it so) I here present to the holders of this theory. In connection with a play to be given at New Romney, an agreement was entered into by "the Mayor, Jurats, and commoners":

[18] *Government Regulation of the Drama*, p. 83. Cf. also Phoebe Sheavyn, *Lit. Profession in Eliz. Age.*, p. 75.

That all the players, or the moste part of them, shall enter into sufficient boundes of 40 s. to Mr. Wallishe, at or before the next day of rehersalle .... with condicion effectually to prosecute the playe the same; otherwise every player having .... shalle presently surrender all their partes up again into the hands of Arthur Bee; and so to be no more spoken of, or any more repetition of rehersall therof had or made.[19]

This may have been merely intended to prevent some local or amateur company from deserting and running off with their roles, because of the inconvenience of such action rather than because of fear of loss of stage-right. I do not consider that this has any special bearing on the practices of the London companies; but I mention the item in passing merely because it does not favor the conclusions I have reached in regard to stage-right in London theatres.

Against the opinion that the ability to guard the copy was the basis of stage-rights in the time of Elizabeth, are the following considerations. The well-established system of sales, contracts, tradings, and gifts of play manuscripts could not exist without a fairly clear recognition of exclusive acting rights. If loss or theft of manuscript gave a right to perform, the known cases of such transfers would be almost innumerable instead of occasional. And the number of plays put into print and still handled successfully by their rightful owners on the stage would be quite unexplainable.

Absence of statutory recognition of stage-right does not prove absence of right at common law. The statutes on this subject were naturally late to appear in copyright legislation, because, so long as the plays were in manuscript, they were probably held as any private property, the infringements of rights being no doubt punishable at common law, in case of theft. And when plays were in print, recourse to the Master of the Revels or the Lord Chamberlain to secure observance of stage rights when there was any special need for such interference was no doubt quite as effective as lawsuits in the days after statutory protection. Indeed, settlement of stage rights out of court whenever possible must have been a real blessing, if we may judge from the erratic and even extraordinary decisions rendered at times in the eighteenth and nineteenth cen-

[19] *Records of New Romney*, fol. 148, Hist. MSS Comm. V, 553, 10 Eliz.

turies through the somewhat doubtful aid of stage-right statutes.[20]

Sale of Plays in Relation to Stage-right

Without a fairly safe property in plays, the systems of sales and contracts for plays used in this period would be difficult to explain.

The contract discovered by Wallace between Brome and the Salisbury Court Theatre in 1635 is, very probably, a fair ex-

---

[20] Long after statutes protected stage right, cases were settled without hearings in court, or were referred to Chancery for the quicker relief of equity. Mr. J. A. Morgan, in his *The Law of Literature* (II, 336–37), says: "Dramatic manuscripts, from the fact of their immediate availability, without tarrying for the expensive and laborious processes of printing and manufacture, no less than because of the attractiveness of the drama, which has been for three hundred years the favorite amusement of the civilized world, have become, perhaps, the most valuable of all literary compositions; and mainly, too, because their value depends upon a season or a 'run,' the cases in which the law is called upon to interfere in reference to them, make very little show in the reports or in the digests, and very seldom get beyond a mere motion or two at a special term or in chambers. If the plaintiff obtains his preliminary injunction, defendants are usually permitted to settle, and the case ends." Brackett explains more fully the reason why some equitable arrangement of dramatic rights is always preferable to actions on the case:

"The impecunious manager who pirates another's play or opera is often financially unable to satisfy a judgment for damages, and if he was, the amount recovered would seldom reflect the real loss such injury occasions, it being a matter incapable of adequate money compensation.

"A play is a property of a peculiar nature; its handling and production, its novelty, its success in some well-known locality, its favorable comments, its originality, all contribute to make its peculiar and indefinable value. The manager often spends large sums before his production is accepted by the public, his experiments in cast, scenery, situations, and advertising are of great expense, and he looks to its future success for financial profit. To pirate his play, allow its use by others and merely give an action for the injury sustained would be manifestly unfair, for no rule of damages could adequately measure the real injury done, as it is incapable of any absolute, certain proof.

. . . .

"The rule of damage in an action at law is one which must be entirely arrived at by actual definite proof; it is not a matter of speculation or belief; no damage is assessable unless distinctly established by evidence. It must be capable of definite ascertainment. Such rigid measurement applied to the vague and intangible questions of dramatic rights and their invasions affords little satisfaction and leaves many real sources of injury uncompensated for. No other rule at law can obtain; its very inadequacy gives rise to the protective measure of injunction in chancery." (*Theatrical Law*, p. 420.)

ample of the method of employing a popular playwright to give his exclusive services for a term of years at a definite rate. Another method is illustrated by numerous entries in Henslowe's Diary. As the work of Henslowe has been variously interpreted, it is perhaps worth while to summarize his functions. As the owner and part manager of the Rose Theatre (opened in 1592) he had certain relationships with the companies that played there, and some of these transactions appear in the Diary. He was also interested in the pawnbroker's business from 1593 to 1596, and he lent money to actors on apparel, etc., and also sold apparel and ornaments to actors. In his capacity as moneylender he no doubt succeeded in getting many reputable but needy authors in a position to do what he wished. Ben Jonson received numerous advances from him. Henslowe was in some ways a great convenience to the authors. Though he drove sharp bargains, he frequently lent money to get actors and playwrights out of prison, and still oftener made advances on plays merely begun or perhaps thought of. He had a keen eye for the main chance, and these loans were expected to be returned when due, often at an usurious rate of interest. His chief virtue was, that he had cash to lend to company or actor for immediate needs. Occasionally Henslowe was the means of arranging contracts for playwrights to write for a particular company at a fixed rate; but his more usual service to the author was that of acting as a go-between for dramatic company and authors, engaging one or more playwrights to write a work and furnishing the necessary advances to pay for the composition.

The rate of pay through Henslowe to the author was from £5 to £7 (usually £6) from 1598 to 1599. Chapman got as much as £8,10 for *The World Runs on Wheels*, and Dekker and Jonson got £8 for *Page of Plymouth*. Dekker had £10 for *Patient Grissell*, which became a popular play. By 1602, £8 was not an unusual price for plays; and by 1612 Daborne could command from Henslowe £10 to £20, and he declared that he could get elsewhere £25 for a play. The probability is, that Henslowe was a shrewd bargainer for the plays as he was in other financial matters, and that his prices represented something considerably lower than the best market prices for plays otherwise disposed of. In addition to the price for the manuscript, the author generally had a benefit performance (between 1625 and 1641, on the second day of production.)[21]

A note in the *Diary* (Greg, 1, 176) for 1603 shows that Henslowe may have been a useful person in arranging for the renting (or possibly sale?) of stage right in plays owned by individual actors:

Memorandum that I Robert Shaa have receaued of mr Phillip Henchlowe the some of forty shellinges upon a book Called the fower sones of Aymon which booke if it be not played by the company of the fortune nor noe other company by my (apoynt) leave I doe then bynd myselfe by theis presentes to repay the sayd some of forty shellinges upon the delivery of my booke att Cristmas next which shall be in the yeare of our Lord 1603 & in the 46th yeare of the Raigne of the queene.

The whole business of Henslowe presupposed the protection of stage-rights. No companies would have been willing to buy or rent plays from him unless somehow assured of ownership. Nor would he venture to pay dramatic authors unless he had hope of selling or renting the stage-rights in their plays. Once he seems to have got into trouble with a company he made up from other companies, over refusing them the complete rights (as I take it) in the books they purchased of him. In the "articles of oppression against Mr. Hinchlowe" (1615?) the eighth item is the complaint, "Alsoe wee have paid him for plaie bookes £200 or thereaboutes and yet hee denies to give us the Coppies of any one of them."[22] It is barely possible, but, I think, wholly unlikely, that Henslowe had refused to deliver any copies in the ordinary sense of the term. The meaning is in all probability either copyright or exclusive stage-right. For anyone who knew Henslowe would be unlikely to hand over £200 for playbooks before a copy was forthcoming. Nor, we may suppose, would any company pay that much without a hope of some exclusive rights of acting.

It is clear, too, that, if the author disposed of them directly, the acting rights were expected to be sold exclusively to one company. In a pamphlet, *A Defence of Coney-Catching*, 1592, Greene is charged with double-dealing:

[21] Malone, *Var.*, III. 158. Cf. Alwin Thaler, "Playwrights' Benefits," *Studies in Philology*, XVI (1919), pp. 187–97.

[22] See Greg, *Henslowe Papers*, pp. 89–90; *Alleyn Papers*, p. 78; Malone, *Var.*, xxi, 416.

Maister R. G. would it not make you blush—if you sold Orlando Furioso to the queenes players for twenty nobles, and when they were in the country, sold the same play to Lord Admiral's men, for as much more? Was not this plain coney-catching, M. G.?[23]

But if there were no stage-right, double sales might well be an every-day occurrence. The competition between rival companies was so keen that a lack of recognized and defensible stage-right would inevitably have resulted in their seizing upon attractive plays, indiscriminately, as soon as they were put upon the stage. For, if there were no other means of getting copy, it could certainly be acquired by shorthand. Now if there had been any great number of double sales, or any wholesale seizures of plays by rival companies, we should certainly expect to hear even now the noise of the ensuing stage quarrels. Actors, playwrights, Henslowe, stage-managers, satirists on stage customs,— how shall we explain their silence?

The known cases of trouble in Elizabethan and Jacobean England over *stage-right*, strictly speaking, are so few that they should be regarded as a remarkable testimony to efficiency of protection by officials before the statutes on the subject, or else as indicating a fairly high ethical standard or a common-sense business attitude toward respecting a neighbor's common-law property rights. The familiarity of the public with the facts as to the original ownership of a play was doubtless one of the chief safeguards, though, as we shall see, the protection of stage-right by certain public officials in emergencies was of some importance.

[23] The entry of this play on the Stationers' Registers is somewhat irregular, and suggests the possibility of some compromise as to ownership, such as might have arisen from a double sale of the work. Danter, on December 7, 1593, "entred for his copie under thandes of the wardens, a plaie booke, intituled, *the historye of orlando ffurioso*, one of the xii peeres of Ffrance." In the margin is a note, "This copie is put over by the consent of John Danter to Cuthbert Burby ut patet 28 Maii 1594." The latter entry contains an agreement that Danter is to do the printing for Burby. The title-role of this play, which Alleyn had, is reprinted in his papers. (See *Henslowe Papers*, 155; Creizenach, IV, 555). W. W. Greg has a new theory as to the nature of this "double sale" in his *Two Elizabethan Stage Abridgements* (Clarendon Press, 1923), of which I have as yet seen only Mr. Chambers' review.

Actors as Owners of Plays

Who should be regarded as the true owner of a particular play was the real crux. It is clear, in the first place, that the author customarily parted with his rights, i.e. unless, by virtue of a place in the company as an actor of a certain standing, he was also a sharer in the ownership of the plays which, as author, he sold to the company. It is, of course, entirely possible that playwrights who were also sharers in the company had private contracts by which they did not permanently lose the stage rights in their plays. But no instance of such an arrangement, so far as I know, has been found; and we tend to assume that the actor-authors followed the usual custom and parted with the stage-rights of the plays they sold to the company.

The acting company as a body usually owned the plays. As we shall see from a contract of the sharers in the Whitefriars Theatre in 1607-8, the company could make regulations for the conservation of the rights in the plays they owned in common which would prevent the disposal of such rights by any individual member of the company. Whether this was specified by contract or not, it was doubtless the understanding among members of companies, as business partners.

This does not, however, preclude the possibility of occasional ownership of plays by individual actors. It is certain that several enterprising actors were on the lookout for plays, and that they bought and for a time kept the rights in some plays. It is possible that they rented them to the companies instead of selling. Where actors bought and sold plays, it is not always possible to be sure whether they did so as individuals or as representatives of their companies. Heminge and Condell in publishing the Shakespeare Folio are generally assumed to be representing the whole company in the matter of ownership of the plays. A few documents, however, prove the possibility of an individual actor's purchasing the rights in a play previously owned by a company. Such was the case with Edward Alleyn. He was for some years before 1589 in Worcester's Company, but in 1589-90 he left to go to the Admiral's. On January 3, 1589 he entered into an agreement with Richard Jones for Jones' share in plays and other properties, which Alleyn and his brother and Jones and Robert Brown had owned in common:

Be it knowen unto all men by theis presentes that I Richard Jones of London, yoman, for and in consideration of the somme of Thirtie Seaven poundes and Tenne shillinges of lawfull mony of Englande to me by Edward Allen of London, gent, well and trulie paid, have bargayned, and solde, and in playne and open market, within the citie of London, have delivered to the said Edwarde Allen all and singular suche share, parte, and portion of playing apparalles, play bookes, instrumentes, and other commodities whatsoever belonging to the same, as I the said Richard Jones nowe have or of right ought to have, joyntly with the said Edward Allen, John Allen, citizen and Inholder, of London, and Robert Browne, yoman, To have and enjoye .... for evermore without let, clayme, or disturbance of mee.[24]

As Alleyn's brother was one of the sharers, and as Robert Browne shortly afterward was planning a European tour with Jones (1592; see Murray *E. D. C.*, I,49), the probability is that Edward Alleyn was able to follow up the matter of getting control of the plays he wanted, presumably for the use of the Admiral's Company which he was about to join.[25] Alleyn was probably the means of transfer of a number of plays from one company to another. *Henslowe's Diary* (ed.Greg,II,155), shows that Edward Alleyn sold *I. Tamar Cam* to the Admiral's men for a revival for £2 on Oct. 2, 1602. It had been played by Strange's men in 1592-3, and by the Admiral's men as "new" in 1596. Just how it came into Alleyn's hands between 1596 and 1602 is not known. Alleyn is thought to have left the Admiral's men in the fall of 1602, and the disposition of this play is perhaps a prelude to his departure.

Martin Slaughter, like Alleyn, was an owner of plays. He left the Admiral's company on July 18, 1597. On the eighth of March, 1598, he was engaged in a lawsuit against Birde, Downton, and Spenser. This probably concerned the division of properties at his departure. An entry of Henslowe's in the *Diary* (Greg, F45ᵛ, 30) shows the intent of the Admiral's men to purchase from Slaughter five old plays which they had previously acted:

Lente unto the companye the 16 of maye 1598 to bye V boocks of martine slather called ii ptes of hercolus & focas & pethagores & elyxander & lodicke which laste boocke he hath not yet delyuered the some of vii£.

[24] Collier, *Memoirs of E. Alleyn*, Shakesp. Soc'y, 1841, p. 198.
[25] *Alleyn Papers*, Shakesp. Soc'y, Publ., 1853, pp. 4-5.

Another payment of 20 s. for "elexsander & lodwicke" is entered on July 18 (F47ᵛ, 16).

It may be of some interest to note an analogous example of contemporary purchase of the stage-rights in a group of plays by the actor-manager of a Spanish company in his own right, and a subsequent transfer of these stage-rights along with the histrionic services of himself and his wife. In 1602 Jerónimo Lopez de Sustaya, manager of a company, made an agreement for himself and his wife, with another manager of a company, Antonio Granado, to act in the company of the latter for two years for a definite sum. At the same time he agreed to give Granado "the comedias which they may have, and among them the following four: *San Reymundo, Los Caballeros nuevos, La Fuensanita de Cordoba,* and *El Trato de la Aldea,* all of which he said he had "bought from the poets who had written them, paying his money for them, so that the said Antonio Granado may use them as to him may seem best."[26]

A study of Murray's *English Dramatic Companies* will convince any reader that the personnel of an acting company was very shifting. The provincial companies were notoriously evanescent as to organization. In *Histriomastix* (1599),II,251, a strolling player says:

> Once in a week new masters we seeke
> And never can hold together.

There were sudden and frequent changes even in the make-up of the London companies. In 1583 the Queen's company was drafted largely from other companies, and numerous other changes equally upsetting can be traced. Whether the consecutiveness of ownership in playbooks was maintained through a majority of members clinging to one company, or whether it rested with a few leading members is not yet definitely solved, though it is quite clear that not all actors were sharers in properties of any sort. It would become a matter of some importance when leading members split off from their companies and formed new groups for provincial tours, as did Martin Slaughter, for example. And when companies went on the rocks financially and were temporarily disbanded and recomposed, there

---

[26] Perez Pastor, *Nuevos Datos,* p. 64; cited by H. A. Rennert, *Spanish Stage in the Time of Lope de Vega,* 190.

must have been recurring necessity for adjustment of property rights in plays.

The contract with Brome (discovered by Professor Wallace) and his subsequent relations with companies show that he got into trouble over the ownership of a play when he terminated a contract to write for one company and began work for another. And, as we have seen, Slaughter was involved in difficulties over ownership of plays when he left one company for another; Alleyn took a quit-claim from Jones when there was some breaking up of the company, he bought up plays from Worcester's men when they were in financial straits and good actors were leaving, and he later sold plays to companies he joined. In the transfer of services of an author from one company to another, and more largely in the transfer of the actor from company to company may be sought, I believe, the true explanation of most of the bits of evidence hitherto interpreted as indicating a lack of the possibility of conserving stage-right save through the special intervention of high officials. It is entirely possible also that what have usually been regarded as unauthorized versions of plays reached the press for the same reason that imperfect or unrevised copies remained in the hands of an old company after the original or authorized version was transferred to a new company,—because the controlling interest in the property was held by one or more individuals who were making a transfer of their services.

If this is the case, many instances apparently demonstrating a lack of any true stage-right will be seen to resolve themselves into quarrels as to who is at a particular time the rightful owner of the property. Slight as is our knowledge of the fortunes of the various companies, it will suffice to show that a few striking instances of trouble over stage-right can be so explained.

Take for example a much cited stage quarrel—a clear case of reciprocal theft of stage rights,—the acting of Marston's *The Malcontent*, by the King's Men in 1604, in retaliation for the filching of "*Jeronimo.*" *The Malcontent* had belonged to the Children of the Chapel. The induction as given by the King's men shows that the theft was inspired by the Children's misappropriation of *Jeronimo*. By this is probably meant the play performed twenty-two times in 1592 by Lord Strange's men and later passed on to the Chamberlain's men and hence to the

King's. The Chapel Children perhaps took advantage of the shift of properties, etc. that went with changes of personnel in the Strange-Chamberlain combination, and thus got hold of a copy of *Jeronimo* and proceeded to play it. Those who believe that the play-books must be rigidly guarded or else stage-right would be lost will pounce upon this as evidence. But it was not regarded as the right, the usual, or the expected thing. The King's men, in retaliating by a return theft, simply gave them a dose of their own medicine. They did not attempt to gloze over the fact of the theft. On the contrary, they took pleasure in pointing out, in the induction, the absurdity of the notion that *finding is having* in the matter of a lost play-book. The induction shows a consciousness of professional ethics in its obvious satire on the justification of performance of another company's play because they had got hold of the book:

Sly. I would know how you came by this play?
Condell. Faith Sir, the book was lost; and because 'twas pity so good a play should be lost, we found it, and play it.
Sly. I wonder you would play it, another company having interest in it.
Condell. Why not Malevolo in folio with us, as well as Jeronimo in decimo sexto with them? They taught us a name for our play, we call it, *One for another*.
Sly. What are your additions?
Burbage. 'Sooth, not greatly needful; only as your sallet to your great feast, to entertain a little more time, and to abridge the not-receiv'd custom of musick in our theatre.

The stage-right quarrel over *The Malcontent* is reflected in the publication. There were, in the year of its acting, three editions, all by the same publishers, one being advertised as "augmented by Marston, with the additions played by the Kings Maiesties servants. Written by John Webster, 1604."

The loss of play-books when companies broke up must have been not infrequent. Heywood, in his address to the reader of *The English Traveler* (1633) explaining why so few of the two hundred and twenty plays he had worked on had come into print, remarked: "One reason is that many of them by shifting and changing of companies have been negligently lost; others of them are still retained in the hands of some actors who think it against their peculiar profit to have them come into print." If many were lost, the chances are that a few were found. It is to be observed that Heywood does not here complain that either stage-rights or copyrights were violated because of this loss of copies in the confusion of the re-forming of the companies. And Heywood was interested in authors' rights and companies' rights in plays. It is reasonably evident that there was no general assumption that it was right to stage or to print a play picked up, and that when, by a shift of personnel, the wrong individual got a copy and made such use of it, he was violating recognized property rights.

It is possible that the publication of the second quarto of Marston's *Faun* in 1606 (referred to above, pp. 227) was occasioned by some trouble over a shift of ownership due to ill fortunes of a company. The play was acted at the Blackfriars by the Children of the Queen's Revels; but, according to Fleay, this company lost the Queen's patronage in 1605. The play was transferred to Paul's Boys, presumably by some actor or actors who went over. The entry of the play on the Stationers' Registers to Cotton 12 Mar., 1606 contained a proviso that "he shall not put the same in prynte before he gett alowed lawfull aucthoritie." It was printed by Pavier for Cotton "as it hath beene diuers times presented at the Blacke Friars by Children of the Queenes Maiesties Revels." The second edition, in the same year, by the same publishers, added "and since at Poules," with the note, "and now corrected of many faults which by reason of the authors absence were let slip." Marston's preface to the second edition criticises the first but does not say positively that it was against his wish (see pp. 213, above). It is possible that either the author or the company (more probably the author) forced the publication of the second edition, and that the first edition in some way was the result of the shift in the make-up of the companies concerned in the transfer of the stage-rights and thus came prematurely into print.

Means of Conserving Stage-right

Those who believe that stage-right as such did not exist before the statute usually declare that the only possible protection was by intervention of a high official such as the Chamberlain or the Master of the Revels, and that this was to be regarded as a mark of special favor. They cite the fact that the King's men paid, through John Hemminge, on April 11, 1627, the sum of £5 to Sir Henry Herbert, Master of the Revels, to forbid the playing of Shakespeare's plays by the Red Bull company (*Var.*, III, 229). There is usually more than a suggestion that only a powerful company like the King's could hope for the favor of such protection of their stage rights in their own plays, and that even they could not get it without the payment of a fee amounting to a bribe. It has even been suggested that the necessity of this action of Hemminge's arose from his having (unwisely) arranged for the publication of the plays in the First Folio. As the plays were in print, any company, presumably, might act them unless a special restraint were invoked.

But this is surely a misconception. The company of Prince Charles I acted at the Red Bull as early as August, 1623. In 1625, when Charles I came to the throne, he took under his patronage his father's company, known as the King's men. Three of the Prince's own men then joined with the King's old company now taken under the Prince's patronage (See Cunningham, *Revels*, xlii). But others of the Prince's old company joined the company of the King's provincial players. This latter group was thereafter known as the Red Bull Company in London (because of taking over the Red Bull for their customary playing-place), but, when traveling in the provinces, it used the name of the King's Company as heretofore. The new King's company of London (whose composition I described above as of the old King's London company and a few of the Prince's men) took the Globe and the Blackfriars for their playing-places. With such a splitting up and re-formation of companies, problems of ownership were almost inevitable (See Murray, *E.D.C.*, I, 271 on the change of companies). It is very likely that the remnant of the old King's Company that went into the "Red Bull" imagined they still had a right in the Shakespeare plays which had been part of their old repertoire, and that they therefore continued to act them. The intervention of Sir Henry Herbert, then, far from being a typical case of the only sort of protection possible for stage rights, would seem to be a nice decision on equitable grounds under rather unusual circumstances. It was no simple case of stage-right, but one involving the law of partners, or joint ownership in a property. As for the fee of £5, it is not excessive, compared with fees in legal trials;

nor is it out of line with customs of the day. It does not by any means imply that stage-right was non-existent save by purchase from an official. Herbert got a good part of his income from his fees. He was the man who had the best chance at records of original ownership and was a power in dramatic circles. It was, according to standards of the day, but natural that he should have something for his pains.

Another example of special intervention to conserve stage-right is often similarly misinterpreted. It is found in a document dated Aug. 10, 1639, in the Lord Chamberlain's office, entitled "Cockpitt playes appropried," for the protection of acting rights in 45 plays:

> Whereas William Beeston, gent., governor of the kings and queens young company of players at the Cockpit in Drury Lane, has represented unto his majesty that the several plays hereafter mentioned, viz.... [Here are listed 45 plays] .... doe all and every of them properly and of right belong to the said house, and consequently that they are all in his proprietary. And to the end that any other companies of actors in or about London shall not presume to act any of them to the prejudice of him the sayd William Bieston and his company, his majesty hath signified his royal pleasure unto mee, thereby requiring mee to declare soe much to all other companies of actors hereby concernable, that they are not any wayes to intermeddle with or act any of the above-mentioned playes. Whereof I require all masters and governors of playhouses, and all others whom it may concerne, to take notice and to forbeare to impeach the said William Bieston in the premises, as they tender his majesties displeasure, and will answer the contempt.[27]

It is not to be supposed that a number of acting companies contemplated an invasion of Beeston's stage rights in 45 plays, and that he had no possible protection except by getting out a sort of injunction from the highest official charged with oversight of the drama. There is in the restraint itself a clear hint of a special reason for anticipating difficulties as to ownership. Here again it seems to be the delicate question of deciding in whom the ownership of the repertoire resides when the company breaks up. The plays had belonged to the Queen Henrietta's men, with whom Beeston was from 1625 to 1637. By February, 1637 the Queen's men had abandoned the Cockpit to the newly

[27] *Var.*, III, 158.

formed company of Beeston's boys. Many of the Queen's men had joined with the Revels company at Salisbury Court by October, 1637,[28] the joint company being known thereafter as the Queen's company.

It would be difficult to trace now all the streams of descent of the plays in that protected list. Some were written directly for the Queen's men. Some were perhaps transferred from the Queen's Revels' boys when they joined the Lady Elizabeth's in 1613, and some probably came over when Middleton and Samuel Rowley joined the Lady Elizabeth's men in 1623. But, whatever the sources, the plays seem to have passed from the Queen's company to Beeston's boys when he took over the management of the new company. Whether he secured adjudication in favor of himself as manager and representative of the company or whether the majority of owners transferred along with him, or whether, like the Spanish actor cited above, he paid cash for the plays on transferring his services, does not appear. At any rate, he proved to the king that the plays "of right belong to the said house" and "are all in his propriety." The reason for this injunction may have been that The Queen's company continued to act some of the plays (as the remnant of the King's old company did with Shakespeare's plays at the Red Bull in 1627). At any rate, the history of Beeston's own transfer makes it quite clear that this also is a special case of adjustment of property rights under unusual circumstances. It is unsafe to infer that in normal conditions such methods would need to be resorted to. Beeston's boys and the King's new company, by invoking extraordinary aid, accomplished somewhat the same purpose that Alleyn achieved more simply by personal contract with previous part-owners which gave him the right to transfer the plays to a new company he was to join. The effect was in each case that of a quit-claim (voluntary or involuntary) from previous joint-owners.

Out of the situation that arose when Beeston went over to the new company (Beeston's boys) in 1637, there grew, in all probability, a trouble of another sort. The Chamberlain, Philip Herbert, on June 10, 1637, ordered the Stationers' Company not to let plays of the King's men or the King's and Queen's young

[28] Herbert's office-book has an undated entry, but seemingly referred to the date given above. Cf. also Murray, *E.D.C.*, I, 267.

boys come into print without the written consent of Lowen and Taylor[29] for the King's company and Beeston for the young company. Here, then, we see both copyright and stage-right difficulties caused by the break-up of companies and the transfer of a manager.

When troubles such as these arose, undoubtedly the records at the Revels office were invaluable for tracing ownership of both stage-right and copyright, inasmuch as the licenses for both acting and publishing must be secured from the Master of the Revels. There seems to have been through many years a recognized practice of filing lists of plays in the stock of a company with the Master of the Revels. On Aug. 30, 1660, Moseley, the publisher, wrote to the Master of the Revels to insist that he held the stage-right as well as the copyright in the plays he published (*Var.* III, 249). And when the Red Bull company was under the management of Killigrew (1660-1663), the manager of the company filed a list of its plays, which has been found among Sir Henry Herbert's papers. Among those plays are: Jonson's *Silent Woman*; Shakespeare's *Henry the Fourth, Merry Wives, Othello*; Fletcher's *Humorous Lieutenant, Beggars Bushe, Wit without Money, Elder Brother*; Beaumont and Fletcher's *Maid's Tragedy, Philaster, A King and no King*; D'Avenant's *The Unfortunate Lovers*; Shirley's *The Wedding, The Traitor, Love's Cruelty; The Tamer Tamed; Rollo, Duke of Normandy; Dumboys (Bussy D'Ambois?); The Widow*; and Killigrew's *Claricella*.

Copyright and Stage-right

There are extant some printed plays laying claim to authority as being "printed by the original copy" and prefaced or edited by actors, which bear witness to the occasional ownership of plays by individual actors. But usually the company or its main business representatives seem to have owned the copyright, as well as the stage-right, of plays. Some authors may have had special agreements to retain privileges of publishing either at their own discretion or by agreement with the company (the

[29] These men, with Robinson and Benfield, continued to represent the King's company. See the 1647 folio of Beaumont and Fletcher. The folio of 1652 names only Lowen and Taylor. In view of the complete temporary disbandment of companies caused by the Civil War, and the wavering combinations of struggling companies after, it is interesting to note how well the King's men held on to their copyrights.

latter being more probable). The acting companies, presumably, after the first novelty of the play had worn off or at some later stage in the history of a play when it seemed to the advantage of the joint owners to do so, sold the copyright to a stationer or employed one to print the play for their benefit. That the members of a company owned the copyright of a play jointly was an excellent reason for the failure of many plays to come into print while current on the stage—a better reason, in my opinion, than those usually ascribed, most of which assume the killing of interest in the spoken drama or the endangering of stage-right. If an individual owned the copyright in a play, and particularly if that individual were the author, one might reasonably expect a fairly early appearance of a successful play in print. But there must be special reason for the trouble of securing agreement of a company and for making the necessary arrangements for the oversight of publication. If the playwright was an actor in the company, it was a simpler matter. Jonson, however, seemed to have no difficulty in getting his plays into print as soon as he liked, though he wrote for several companies, and though he was often at odds with the actors. He was pretty well aware of his rights and may have taken precautions to stipulate in advance. A clear hint as to the ethics of the matter, so far as disposal of rights of control of the copy for the press is concerned, appears in the preface of Heywood's *Rape of Lucrece* (first printed in 1608), where he refers to the dishonest practice of some who "have used a double sale of their labours, first to the stage and after to the press," and assures the reader that the company have consented to the publication of this play.

It is hardly fair to assume that, even if a contract with a company should explicitly forbid an author to publish his play without the company's consent, he would necessarily have to give up all hope of publication under his own oversight. Professor Wallace's discovery of a contract in 1635 between Richard Brome and the Salisbury Court Theatre[30] throws some light upon the circumstances of the publication, in 1640, of his *Antipodes*, acted 1638, and particularly upon the author's

[30] See his "Shakespeare and the Blackfriars," *Century*, LXXX (Sept., 1910). Cf. also C. E. Andrews, "Richard Brome," *Yale Studies in English*, XLVI, N. Y. Holt, 1913.

preface to the reader. The contract of 1635 requires Brome to write three plays a year, for which he is to receive 15 s. a week and the benefit of the first day's profits of each new play. There was in 1638 a proposition that the rate be raised to 20 s. a week for exclusive services for a seven year term. But the Cockpit Company seem to have offered something more attractive; for Brome went over to them in 1638. He may have been still under the obligation of his previous contract with Salisbury Court when he wrote *The Antipodes* in 1638, and this may explain why what "properly appertained" to Beeston's new company of boys at the Cockpit was first played instead by the company at Salisbury Court. The latter company took some liberties in the matter of cutting the play that displeased the author. In publishing it two years later, Brome said in his address to the reader:

You shall find in this booke more then was presented upon the stage, and left out of the presentation, for superfluous length (as some of the players pretended) I thought good al should be inserted according to the allowed original; and as it was, at first, intended for the Cock-pit stage, in the right of my most deserving friend, Mr. Wm. Beeston, unto whom it properly appertained; and so I leave it to thy perusal, as it was generally applauded, and well acted at Salisbury Court.

It is interesting to note that the contract with Brome provided that he should not publish any of the plays without the consent of the company. His previous record shows a desire to publish. *The Northern Lass*, acted by the King's men at the Globe and Blackfriars *c.* 1630 (Fleay) was entered on the S.R. 1632 and printed the same year with dedication and prefatory verses. And a revision by Brome of an old play of Heywood's, *The Late Lancashire Witches*, acted by the King's men at the Globe in 1634, was entered and published in the same year. After the contract Brome continued to publish. *Sparagus Garden* (acted 1635), which was highly successful, bringing the company an estimated profit of £1000 (according to C. E. Andrews, *Richard Brome*, p. 14), was published in 1640. And the *Antipodes* over which there was evidently some trouble, and which the Salisbury Court players certainly acted, was published under the author's oversight in 1640, with remarks on the acting of the play. Also it, like *The Mad Couple,* was somehow taken over by

Beeston's boys, later. In the same year, 1640, four other plays of Brome's were entered on the Registers, but possibly only with intent to reserve copyright, as editions do not seem to have followed until 1658-9. Just how Brome vindicated his rights in his plays is not clear. But his putting into print two plays that had belonged to the Salisbury Court actors and the entering of four others on the Registers are significant. These and six other plays were published after Brome's death by Alexander Brome. Incidentally, as Mr. Andrews points out (*Richard Brome*, p.15), the Salisbury Court company may have brought a law-suit, though the reference in *The Court Beggar* (?1640) is casual: "Here's a trim business towards, and as idle as the players going to Law with their Poets." (II,1,215). In Brome's case the actors seem not to have prevented the author and his assigns from publishing, though they may have caused delay.

Attitudes of Theatrical Companies toward Publication of Plays

The attitude of the acting company toward the publication of their plays has been argued chiefly upon theoretical grounds. The manager should be, and therefore was, in general, opposed to the publication of a good play. Why? First, because gratifying the curiosity of the reading public would lessen the interest of possible spectators, or even keep them from going to the play at all. This is, I think, questionable even as a theory. Nowadays many people prefer to read a play before they see it acted; and others find a real satisfaction in going over a play in print after they have seen it. Have we any assurance that Elizabethan audiences had only the childish curiosity as to how the story turned out, and were totally devoid of esthetic enjoyment in the quality of the acting? Is it not likely that, in this age of drama, there was a pretty general appreciation of the difference between plays read and plays seen and heard; and that publication, far from being a drawback from the point of view of the stage, would in some cases serve to advertise the plays and attract play-goers? The only true test would be, to examine actual play-receipts before and after publication. Henslowe's *Diary* furnishes the means for the study of a few plays, but the number is insufficient for a fair test. Some light may be thrown on the question by an elaborate comparison of dates of new editions of plays and the revivals of plays on the stage. It is obvious that the inclusion of new scenes, interpolations, etc. in new editions indicates an eagerness on the part of the stationers to keep up with the newest version on the stage. Their frequent success in doing so raises the question whether managers may not have willingly co-operated, for advertising purposes.

Though there may be some force in the theory of objection to early publication because it would satisfy curiosity and so dull the interest, it is clear that, after a play had become generally known and talked of because of a few performances, there might come a time in its fortunes when publication through print would stimulate and revive the interest in it as a play, rather than satiate the reader. Again, the profit to be gained by selling copyright, though probably small compared with proceeds from the stage, might eventually prove an incentive to the company to publish, as stage receipts began to diminish.

In the attempt to prove that companies of actors were unwilling to have plays put into print, there has been much misapplication of evidence. A glaring example occurs in Coryton's *Stage-right*, p. 28. He remarks, concerning the Chamberlain's restraint (Aug. 10, 1639) of other companies' acting of plays belonging to Beeston at the Cockpit (see page 231, above):

"For the printing of bought plays restrained by the Lord Chamberlain's Office entitled Cockpit places (*sic*) appropried. .... Nor was this, I think, a mere jealousy of the press. Five playgoers out of six could not read, but printing enabled other theatres to play their pieces." He adds in a footnote:"Any theatre could play a play once printed. This defect in literary property lost us the true text of two hundred plays at least .... The better the play, the less likely were the sharers to let it escape into print. No poet's work, unless he was a sharer, was safe. If Shakespeare had sold his plays out and out to a theatre, we should have lost many of them."

But the warrant is not against "printing of bought plays" at all: it is a restraint from acting a company's repertoire. It does not indicate that companies were opposed to publication of their good plays, but rather the reverse—that they thought it possible and worth while to protect the stage rights in plays already published. For, although nine of the forty-five plays listed were not published until after 1650, four were published shortly after the protest, i.e., in 1640, three were in print in 1639 and two more entered for publication, while twenty-seven were certainly printed before the protest. The period of time that elapsed between the dates of publication of these twenty-seven plays and the time when the company thought it desirable to assert their stage rights in them in this formal way may interest such readers as suppose that publication of plays in that day meant either abandonment of stage rights or unfitness of the plays for further use on the stage. We find one of the plays published either in 1595 or 1599, one in 1608, one in 1613, one in 1615, one in 1617, one in 1620, one in 1624, one in 1629, two in 1630, one in 1631, one in 1632, five in 1633, two in 1635, two in 1636, four in 1637, and three in 1639. Two more were entered in 1639,[31] and one was published in 1640.

There are three bits of evidence which do seem to favor the supposition that theatrical companies were opposed to publication of their plays. One is, the somewhat vague allusion in the preface to *Troilus and Cressida*, "Thank fortune for the 'scape it hath made amongst you; since, by the grand possessors' wills, I believe, you should have pray'd for them rather than been pray'd." So little is known of the circumstances of this publication that it is impossible to determine the true significance of this remark; and, as the titlepage contains what is in effect a lie—that the play was 'never staled with the stage,' the reliability of any conclusions based upon statements of the publishers is somewhat shaken.

Heywood's reference, however, is more explicit. In his address to the reader of *The English Traveler*, 1633, he comments on the small number of his plays that have appeared in print:

> True it is that my plays are not exposed to the world in volumes, to bear the title of works (as others). One reason is that many of them by shifting and changing of companies have been negligently lost; others of them are still retained in the hands of some actors who think it against their peculiar profit to have them come into print; and a third that it was never any great ambition in me in this kind to be voluminously read.

[31] One of these was Shirley's *Love's Cruelty*, entered S. R., April 25, 1639, to Crook and Cook. It was later entered (November 29, 1639) to J. Williams and Francis Egglesfield, with a marginal note, "Loves Cruelty is entered before to Master Crooke." Evidently the first entry held, for the work was issued in 1640 by Thomas Cotes for A. Crooke.

It will be observed that, although the objection is here positively stated, it is not referred to as if it were a universal attitude; and the addition of two other reasons shows that even in this case it was regarded as insufficient to account for failure of so many plays to come into print.

The strongest evidence of objection to publication is contained in two items of a contract between sharers in the Whitefriars' theatre, 10 Mar., 1607-8:

5) Item, it is also covenaunted, graunted, concluded and fully agreed betweene all the said parties, That if, at any time hereafter any apparell, bookes, or any other goods or commodoties shalbe conveyed or taken awaye by any of the saide parties without the consent and allowance of the residue of his fellow-sharers, and the same exceeding the value of twoe shillinges, that then he or they so offending shall forfeite and loose all benefitt, profitt, and comoditie as otherwise should arrise and growe unto him or them by their shares, besides the loss of their places and all other interest which they may claim amongst us.

8) Item .... That all such apparell as is abroade shalbe imediatly brought in, And that noe man of the said company shall at any time hereafter put into print, or cause to be put into print any manner of playe booke now in use, or that hereafter shalbe sould unto them, upon the penaltie and forfeiture of ffortie pounds starlinge or the losse of his place and share of all things amongst them. Except the booke of Torrismount, and that playe not to be printed by any before twelve months be fully expired.[32]

It is not usually noted that this was but a temporary arrangement of one company which broke up shortly after. By April 12, 1608, their plays are being entered on the Registers for publication.

The fifth item, by requiring consent of the company to publication, simply protects common property in the interests of the whole company as against any individual disposed to use it to his own private gain. And possibly the eighth item should be read in the light of this, with the emphasis upon the "noe man of the said company" selling to his own gain. This seems a reasonable interpretation, as it is a contract between sharers, concerning the disposal of their common goods (the penalty of the individual who usurped the common property being "loss of his

[32] Greenstreet, "Law-Suit about the Whitefriar's Theatre in 1609," *Trans. of N. Shaks. Soc'y.*, I, 3, 269.

place and share of all things amongst them.") Perhaps the clause most significant for publication of the drama is the exception of "Torrismount," which is "not to be printed by any before twelve months be fully expired." This does suggest what Heywood mentions, the attitude of the actor who does not want a new play published. The twelve month interval may be the allowance for a "run"; it could not, however, represent the whole stage life of a successful play.

Two prohibitions of unauthorized publications of plays have been construed as indications of a desire on the part of the companies to keep plays out of print. The first is a letter to the Stationer's Company, dated June 10, 1637, from Philip, Earl of Pembroke and Montgomery, then Lord Chamberlain:

Whereas complaint was heretofore presented to my dear brother and predecessor, by his majesties servants, the players, that some of the company of printers and stationers had procured, published, and printed, diverse of their books of comedyes and tragedyes, chronicle historyes, and the like, which they had (for the special service of his majestye and for their own use) bought and provided at very dear and high rates. By means whereof, not only they themselves had much prejudice, but the books much corruption, to the injury and disgrace of the authors. And thereupon the master and wardens of the company of printers and stationers were advised by my brother to take notice thereof, and to take order for the stay of any further impression of any of the playes or interludes of his majesties servants without their consents: which being a caution given with much respect, and grounded on such weighty reasons both for his majesties service and the particular interest of the players, and soe agreeable to common justice and that indifferent measure which every man would look for in his own particular, it might have been presumed that they would have needed no further order or direction in the business, notwithstanding which, I am informed that some copies of playes belonging to the king and queenes servants, the players, and purchased by them at dear rates, having been lately stollen or gotten from them by indirect means, are now attempted to be printed; which, if it should be suffered, would directly tend to their apparent detriment and prejudice, and to the disenabling them to do their majesties service; for prevention and redresse whereof, it is desired that order be given and entered by the masters and wardens of the company of printers and stationers, that if any playes be already entered, or shall hereafter be brought unto the hall to be entered for printing, that notice thereof be given to the king and queenes servants, the players, and an enquiry made of them to whom they do belong; and that none bee suffered to be printed until the assent of their majesties' said servants be made appear to the Master and Wardens of the company of printers and stationers, by some certificate in writing under the hands of John Lowen and Joseph Taylor, for the kings servants, and of Christopher Beeston for the king and queenes young company, or of such other persons as shall from time to time have the direction of these companies; which is a course that can be hurtfull unto none but such as are about unjustly to peravayle themselves of others' goods, without respect of order or good government; which I am confident you will be careful to avoyd, and therefore I recommend it to your special care. And if you shall have need of any further authority or power to enable you in the execution thereof, upon notice given mee either by yourselves or the players, I will endeavour to apply that further remedy thereto, which shall be requisite. And soe I bid you very heartily farewell.[33]

Dramatic companies were, then, not without some means of protection against unauthorized publication. The Lord Chamberlain called confidently upon the Stationers to exercise what he evidently believed to be a real power of control. This seems to tell against the theory that the stationers granted copyright regularly to all applicants for licenses, without any challenge as to sources of copy. The language expressing the nature of the damage done the players by unauthorized publication is very vague—"to their apparent detriment and prejudice"; and so is the reference to the "particular interest of the player" and the "much prejudice" sustained by the infringement. The language concerning the wrong done the author is unmistakable—the books had "much corruption, to the injury and disgrace of the author." This might be interpreted as meaning that publication of plays lessened attendance at the theatre, or that it depreciated the property of the owners by corrupting it, or that it deprived them of a financial benefit to which they were entitled, whenever they chose to avail themselves of it. The last is probably the true significance. Certainly the requiring of the company's consent to publish cannot rightly be regarded as equivalent to a determination not to publish. As a matter of fact, both companies did publish a large number of plays near this date which bear no indications of surreptitiousness.

[33] *Prolegomena* (Malone), III, 160–61. A new company had been formed under Beeston before February 7, 1637.

This is ignored by F. Robinson Shipherd in his article on "Play-publishing" cited above, where he says (p. 598 ff.), in connection with the unwillingness of theatrical companies to have plays published, that this document "shows the Lord Chamberlain taking the part of the companies in their efforts to keep their plays unpublished, against the Stationers' Company." In the first place, the effort is not to keep the plays unpublished, but to prevent their publication by others than the owners. In the second place, the action is not in any true sense "against the Stationers' Company." It is rather a direction by a high official of state that the Company, whose natural function it was to control such matters, should exercise its regulating authority. There is, it is true, a rebuke for negligence in inquiry as to certain printers' authority for publication of copies got by stealth. At the same time there is an assumption that the matter will be righted by means of the Stationers' Company. Fairly construed, the order does not indicate utter lawlessness in printing. To say so is almost as unreasonable as to assume that it is now quite lawful to hurl a brick through a shop window, from the fact that the window is seen to contain a printed copy of an injunction restraining from repetition of the offense.

We have seen above that, in the transfer of the head of the company there arose a question as to who owned the repertoires once the Queen's and later belonging to the King's and Queen's Young Company (Beeston's boys); so that, so far as one half of this matter is concerned, it is really an assertion by the players that they were the true owners of the copyright and they wished it to be safeguarded by prevention of invasion; or, more exactly, it is an order from the Chamberlain, that the Stationers' Company investigate play ownership and watch out for authorization by the right representatives of the companies concerned.

A second objection to unauthorized publication of plays is to be found in a warrant of the Lord Chamberlain in behalf of the King's Company, Aug, 7, 1641:

To my very loving friends the Master and Wardens of Stationers' Company:

The players which are his Ma^{ts} servants haue addressed themselves unto mee as formerly to my pr'decessors in office, complaining that some Printers are about to Print & publish some of their Playes which hitherto they haue beene usually restrained from by the Authority of the Lord Chamberlain. Their Request seemes both just and reasonable as onely tending to preserue them Masters of their proper Goods, which in Justice ought not to bee made comon for another mannes profitt to their disadvantage. Upon this Ground therefore I am induced to require your care (as formerly my Predecessors haue done) that noe Playes belonging to them bee put in Print w^tout their knowledge & consent. The particulars to which they now lay claime are contained in a List inclosed, and if any of those Playes shall bee offered to ye Presse under another name then is in the List expressed, I shall desire yor care that they may not bee defrauded by that meanes but that they may bee made acquainted wth it, before they bee recorded in ye hall & soe haue Oportunity to shew their right unto them. And thus not doubting of y^r ready care herin I bid you hartily farewell & rest

Yor very loueing friend
Essex.

To my very loueing friends
the Masters and Wardens
of ye Company of Printers & Stationers.[34]

This warrant is followed by a list of sixty plays—not, of course, the company's repertoire, but the unprinted plays which were to be kept out of print until authorized for publication. It should be noted that it is not stated or suggested that the company is opposed to publication; so that it is unfair to assume from this that, if a play passed out of the possession of these men, it was invariably by some surreptitious procedure.[35] The point is simply that the players, as owners, are entitled to all profits. How far back we may suppose the predecessors' activity in protection to have gone is a matter of speculation. Explicit reference takes it to 1616, when William Herbert entered office.

It will be observed that the Chamberlain's prohibition in regard to the sixty plays listed in 1641 was apparently not with-

---

[34] Chamberlain's Warrants, vol. 96; printed by E. K. Chambers, in "Plays of the King's Men in 1641," Malone Society, *Collections*, parts 4 and 5, p. 367.

[35] Of these sixty plays, thirty-eight were still in the acting repertoire of the King's Company after the Restoration, as is shown by a catalogue "of part of His Majesties Servants Playes as they were formerly acted at the Blackfryers & now allowed of to his Majesties Servants at the New Theatre," 1668–69, (Pub. Record Office, L.C. 5/12, p. 202). If we allow for some transfers, such as a few known ones to a rival company under D'Avenant, and also for changes in public taste in almost three decades, we shall see that the stage rights were very well conserved, especially if we take into consideration the closing of the public theaters and the greatly changed public of Restoration days as helping to account for the missing plays from the list of 1641.

out effect. The copyrights of many were conserved for years. The plays went off in small lots, some eleven, twelve, or thirteen years after this prohibition, some few not till thirty-two years later. Moseley (or Robinson and Moseley) and Herringman were often the chosen publishers, both being very reputable firms. Moseley's entries on the Stationers' Registers on September 4, 1646 and in 1653 contain not only titles of plays actually published but titles of eleven or twelve plays apparently not printed during the seventeenth century. Here there is a possibility that a trusted publisher was holding copyright by agreement with the company, but without immediate intention of publishing.

In an article some years ago on the "staying" entry of certain plays on the Stationers' Registers in 1600, I tried to show[36] that the intention was not to forbid the publication of these plays, but rather to hold them for certain stationers who brought the copies for entrance, the order thus amounting to a reserving of first claim to copyright. It left untouched the date when the plays might go into print. That, I judge, was a matter of release by the company, to be satisfactorily indicated to those overseeing play publication. I pointed out also the probability that the "staying" of *Patient Grissell* arranged for March 18, 1600, by a loan from Henslowe (see *Diary*) was another case of reserving copyright through a stationer (Burby) who was favored by the company that owned the play. These acts, I take it, are not to prevent publication, but to control the copyright for the benefit of the true owner, and to determine the time when the work shall go into print. It was no doubt one of the recognized means of protection. There are probably many examples of such entries on the Stationers' Registers for conservation of copyright with no intention of immediate publication. Roberts' entry of the *Merchant of Venice*, July 27, 1598, with the proviso that it be not printed without license from the Lord Chamberlain, as well as the entries of *A moral of Cloth Breeches* and of *Allarum to London* with provisos in 1600, were perhaps of this nature. Some of the plays Brome got into his possession in 1640 and registered for publication may have been entered only to conserve copyright, as he was having trouble over ownership of plays shortly before this.

[36] "To be Staied," *P.M.L.A.*, XXX, 3 (1915), pp. 474 ff.

In leaving the subject of the relationship of copyright and stage-right, it must be admitted that much remains to be ascertained, especially as to the rights of the dramatic author in connection with the publication of his plays. If he did indeed barter away all right to consideration, it is, to say the least, surprising to see how frequently he was permitted to see his own plays through the press. The facts would seem to argue an unexpected display of courtesy on the part of the purchasers.

If the dealings of Moseley with theatrical companies are ever fully worked out, they should throw some light on the relations between stage-right and copyright. In 1660 he evidently regarded himself as sole owner of both in the plays he purchased; for he protested to the Master of the Revels that the Cockpit players and those at Whitefriars had no right to act his plays. The letter is found in Sir Henry Herbert's books, and is dated Aug. 30, 1660:

> Sir,
>
> I have been very much solicited by the gentlemen actors of the Red Bull for a note under my hand to certifie unto your worship what agreement I had made with Mr. Rhodes of the Cockpitt playhouse. Truly, Sir, I am so far from any agreement with him, that I never so much as treated with him, nor with any from him, neither did I ever consent directly or indirectly, that hee or any others should act any playes that doe belonge to mee, without my knowledge and consent had and procured. And the same also I doe certify concerning the Whitefryers playhouse and players.[37]
>
> Humphrey Moseley.

Full allowance must be made, in interpreting this document, for the fact that the plays concerned were doubtless picked up by the stationers during the official discontinuance of stage companies, when the sale to the press was practically the only means of a profit. In such a case, when public acting in London was forbidden and only occasional and semi-surreptitious performances were given, stage-right might be made a corollary, in a sale, to copyright, whereas under normal circumstances, as before the Civil War, the reverse was no doubt the usual practice.[38]

[37] Malone, *Variorum*, III, 249. (For protest against violation of their copyright, see *Beggars Bush*, 1661.)

[38] Since this was written, a brief article by Allardyce Nicoll, "The Rights of Beeston and D'Avenant in Elizabethan Plays," has appeared in *The Review*

One thing is quite clear—that, as acting licence and printing licence were both to be secured through the Master of the Revels for the greater part of the period, the records of the Revels Office should be a protection to both stage-right and copyright. And the Stationers' Company was expected to aid in requiring proper licensing of plays for publication. Old plays were often re-licensed. This would serve as a protection if there were any fear that a play would be taken over by another company because it was in print. Thus, *The Renegado or The Gentleman of Venice*, licensed for the Cock-pit April 17, 1624, was printed 1630 as acted by the Queen's men. On October 30, 1639 it was re-licensed by Herbert under its subtitle; and it appears in Beeston's list of Cockpit plays whose stage rights are to be conserved for his new company in 1639. This simple method of protection was open to all. *A Winter's Tale* was re-licensed by Herbert on August 19, 1623, just about the time of the first appearance of the First Folio. It was acted at court April 7, 1618 and again January 18, 1624.

It is not unlikely that, when there was any special reason for so doing, a company filed an entire list of its repertoire with the Master of the Revels (see the case of the Red Bull Co., p. 233), and so provided for an accounting that was up to date. Transfers from other companies, or radical changes in the constitution of the companies might occasion such a move.

The special interventions of the Master of the Revels or of the Chamberlain to help conserve the stage rights in published plays, properly construed, will, I think, eventually be seen to be

---

of English Studies, I, 1 (January, 1925), pp. 84–91. It concerns post-Restoration rights in Elizabethan plays. The reader of his article should keep in mind that the 1641 list of plays which he discusses has to do with copyright in plays, and the 1668–69 catalogue with stage-right. The relation between copyright and stage-right in plays is not taken up by Mr. Nicoll. A point in Mr. Nicoll's conclusion invites inquiry. It is that D'Avenant, of a company rivalling the King's players, during the period of suppression of theatres, "secured the possession of a number of prompt-books belonging originally to the King's men, and by virtue of the possession of these the former contrived to get a royal warrant in 1660, declaring that he might have those dramas as the property of his company" (p. 91). If this means that the King construed physical possession of copies of plays as bestowing stage-right, against the interests of his own players, it seems to me very improbable, especially so if these were merely prompt copies.

emergency measures arising out of the problems caused by the peculiar fortunes of a company on a special occasion. Normally, a play might go into print with every expectation that its stage-right would remain intact. And such a measure as the forbidding of the playing of Shakespeare's plays by the Red Bull Company is certainly not an indication of a fatal blunder on the part of the actor-editors who put their own play-copies into print in the Folio. There was, as has been shown, a special reason why the Red Bull Company might suppose they had a right to play them. If stage-right were not generally safe when a play went into print, extreme opposition to publication would be the only sane attitude for any company in regard to its successful plays. But what are the facts, so far as we can now discover them, concerning the publication of plays while still useful for the stage?

A complete and accurate statistical account is beyond hope, particularly as one can seldom be absolutely certain as to the date of first performance of a play; but, on the basis of what evidence I have been able to accumulate in the course of a few years, I have put together some partial lists which, even though incomplete, will, I trust, serve to convince the reader of the improbability that the objection to the publication of plays still good for use on the stage was as strong as is commonly supposed. Some of these issues were no doubt unauthorized; but it is inconceivable that all or most of them should have been. I list first those plays which are known, from external evidence, to have been published before, during, or shortly after their performance on the stage; next, those revived after publication (a list obviously incomplete); next, plays whose title-pages give evidence of the date of acting, as acted "now," "lately," or at a definite date named in the title (with a caution that the "now" and the "lately" are not always reliable); and finally, some plays entered on the Stationers' Registers near the time of their performance. These lists will be followed by some illustrations of the practice of getting out new editions of plays with additions and alterations, to keep up with the new stage versions.

If the records of performances on the public stages of London were even as complete as those of the Court performances, doubtless there would be added many examples to the lists of early printed plays, plays printed while having a run, and plays frequently revived after being printed.

CONCLUSION.—It will be seen that many plays were published while they were still being acted on the public stage or at Court; that many were revived after publication, both on the public stage and at Court; that stage-right in printed plays could be, and was, protected (even for a longer term than would be possible under modern statutes); and that in case of any special trouble, companies could invoke the aid of the Master of the Revels, the Chamberlain, or the Stationers' Company. Both stage-right and copyright in plays were based upon the common law; yet, in spite of the absence of statutory protection of stage-right, there is a remarkable infrequency of apparent violation of stage-right, considering the keen rivalry of companies and the accessibility of the plays. In the case of printed plays, there were, it is true, some piratical and surreptitious publications; but the attitude of the playwright and that of the acting company were apparently not such as to make us suspect that plays printed while they were still popular on the stage were necessarily issued without allowance. There does seem to have existed an unwillingness on the part of some actors and some companies to let a play get into print during its first "run"; but there is no evidence even that this objection was general. And we must not suppose that the first run represented more than the infancy of a really good play. The periods elapsing between first acting licences and the dates on which stage-right was protected by Beeston for the Cockpit (1639) will show that in many cases, although records of dramatic performances are totally lacking, they apparently took place from time to time, or the Company would hardly have thought it worth while to keep the plays in their repertoire and insist upon the protection of performing rights in them. So that we cannot safely say of the plays put into print soon after their first appearance on the stage that this was because their usefulness for the stage was over. The records of performances are very incomplete. Entries of plays on the registers apparently in advance of intent to publish them seem to suggest that this was a measure taken to protect copyright or stage-right (more probably the former) from possible invasion. And finally, the corrupt condition of the text of a popular play, while it may properly lead to an investigation of the circumstances of its publication, cannot, as we shall see, be taken as proof positive that a play was surreptitiously or piratically issued.

Statistics on Play-Publication

1. *Plays Acted and Printed in the Same Year.*

Aglaura, 1638. Acted at Cockpit by King's Co. Apr. 3, 1638 (*Jo. of Brit. Archaeol. Ass'n*, 1860). Revived Feb. 27, 1661 (*Var.* III, 273); Dec. 28,1661.

(the) Alchemist, 1612. Acted 1610, 1612–1613. Revived, 1622, Jan. 1, 1623, 1631, Dec. 16, 1661 (*Var.* III, 147; 273). *S. R.*, Oct. 3, 1610.

All Fools, 1605. Acted, Court, Jan. 1, 1605 (Cunningham, 203).

Barnavelt, 1619. Acted, Aug. 14–27, 1619, by King's Co. (Barnavelt was executed May 13, 1619. Play censored.)

(the) Bondman, 1624. Acting license, Dec. 3, 1623 (*Sup. Apol.* 216). Acted at Court Dec. 27, 1623 (Murray, I, 261). Lic. for press, Mar. 12, 1624; *S.R.* Mar. 12, 1624. Stage right protected, 1639 list. Revived by King's at Red Bull, May, 1661 (*Var.* III, 273).

Byron, Conspiracie and Tragedie of Charles Duke of, 1608. Acted and suppressed on stage, in 1608. (Censorship.)

(the) Changes, 1632. Acting license, Jan. 10, 1632. (Revived after Restoration.) *S.R.*, Feb. 9, 1632.

Cleodora, Queen of Arragon, 1640. Acted first at Court, Apr. 9, 1640, and later at Blackfriars by King's Co. (*Var.* III, 240–41.) *S.R.*, April 2, 1640.

Eastward Hoe,1605. Written in winter of 1604–05? Later acted at Court, Jan. 25, 1614. Suppressed and censored on first acting. *S.R.*, Sept. 4, 1605.

(the) Elder Brother, 1637, "as acted by King's Co." at Blackfriars. Acted at Court Jan. 5, 1637 (*Var.* III, 239; Murray, I, 177). Revived by King's Co. at Red Bull, 1660–61 (Nov. 23, 1660), (*Var.* III, 273). *S.R.*, Mar. 29, 1637.

(a) Fair Quarrel, 1617. Re-issued same year, with additions, as acted before the King. Stage right protected, 1639 list.

? (the) Fleire, (or Fleare), 1607. ? Acted 1605–06 (Fleay). *S.R.*, May 13, 1606, provisionally; assigned Nov., 1606, with authorization noted.

(old) Fortunatus, 1600. Acted as "old," 1595–96. Pd. in full Nov. 9–30, 1599; for altering, Dec. 1, 1599; for properties, Dec. 6–12, 1599 (Henslowe). Acted at Court, Dec. 27, 1599 and Jan. 1, 1600 (Murray, I, 138). *S.R.*, Feb. 20, 1600, Old Fortunatus in his new lyverie.

Friar Bacon and Friar Bungay, 1594. Acted as old, 1591–92; Feb. 19 to Jan. 29, 1592–93, Apr. 1 and 5, 1594 (Henslowe). At Court, 1602. *S.R.*, May 14, 1594.

(the) Honest Whore, 1604. Paid "in earnest," by H., Jan. 1–Mar. 14, 1604, £5. Pt. 1 was acted at the Fortune between 1603 and 1612, according to Fleay. *S.R.*, Nov. 9, 1604.

? Jack Drum's Entertainment, 1601. Acting licence, as already acted, July, 1600. ? Acted. *c.* May, 1600. *S.R.*, Sept. 8, 1600; transferred Oct. 23, 1600.

(a) Knack to Know an Honest Man, 1596. Acted as new Oct. 23, 1594–Nov. 3, 1596 (H.). *S.R.*, Nov. 26, 1595.

250   AUTHORSHIP AND OWNERSHIP OF PLAYS

Knight of the Burning Pestle, 1613; "as now acted," 1635. Acted at Court by Henrietta's men Feb., 1636, and publicly at Cockpit, 1635. Stage-right protected, 1639 list.
(the) Late Lancashire Witches, 1634. Acted at Globe, 1634. *S.R.*, Oct. 28, 1634.
(the) Lost Lady, 1638. 1639. Acted at Court Mar. 26, 1638 (*Jo. Brit. Archaeol. Ass'n*, 1860). Revived by King's Co. Jan. 19, 1661 (*Var.* III, 273).
? Love's Labour's Lost. (See list of dated title-pages.)
? Love's Metamorphosis, 1601, as acted by the Children of Pauls, "and now by the Children of the Chapel." *S.R.*, July 31, 1607.
(the) Malcontent, 1604; 1604, the second issue "augmented by Marston, with additions played by the King's Majesty's servants written by John Webster".
Monsieur Thomas (or, Father's Own Son), 1639, "as now acted." Stage right protected, 1639 list. Revived, by King's at Red Bull, Apr. 19, 1662 (*Var.*, III, 273). *S.R.*, Jan. 22, 1639.
Oldcastle, pt. 1, 1600. Pd. Oct. 16, 1599 for pt. 1, in earnest, and in earnest of pt. 2, £10; Dec. 17–26, for pt. 2, £4 (H.). Pt.1, first acted Nov. 1–8, 1599. Pt. 2, properties, May 12, 1600. Additions (to which part?) Sept., 1602, £2, 10 s. Properties (for which part?) Aug. 21 and 24. A play called "ould Castel" was acted at Cockpit May 29, 1638 (*Jo. Brit. Arch. Ass'n*, 1860). *S.R.*, 2 pts., Aug. 11, 1600.
Parasitaster, or The Fawne, 1606, as played at Blackfriars; re-issued 1606 as played at Blackfriars "and since at Paul's," "and now corrected of many faults." (Perhaps acted first as early as 1604? Fleay, *Chr. H.*, II, 79.) *S.R.*, Mar. 12, 1606, provisional entry.
Romeo and Juliet, 1597; 1599, "newly corrected, augmented, and amended." Allusions: Marston, Scourge of Villainy (*S.R.*, Sept. 8, 1598), in Centurie of Prayse, 27: "What's play'd today? . . . . Juliet and Romeo," (at the Curtain).
(the) Royal Master, 1638. Acting licence, Apr. 23, 1638 (*Var.*, III, 232). *S.R.*, Mar. 13, 1638.
(the) Taming of a Shrew, 1594. Acted as old, June 13, 1594. *S.R.*, May 2, 1594.
Travailes of the Three English Brothers, 1607. Founded on Nixon's Tract, June 8, 1607? Acted by Queen's Co. June, 1607. *S.R.*, June 29, 1607. Printed "as now" acted, with dedication signed.
Titus Andronicus, 1594. Acted as new by Sussex' men Jan. 23 (24), 1593–94 and Jan. 28 (29), and Feb. 6, 1593–94; acted by Chamberlain's men and Admiral's, June 5 (7) and 12 (14), 1594 (corrections of dates by Greg). *S.R.*, Feb. 6, 1594. Printed as acted by Derby's (i.e. Strange's), Pembroke's, and Sussex' men. Ed. of 1600 adds Chamberlain's men.
(Twelfth Night, Folio of, 1623. Acted perhaps as early as Feb. 2, 1602 (*Diary of John Manningham*). Acted at Court, Feb. 2, 1623).

2. *Plays Printed within One Year of Acting Date*

Blind Beggar of Alexandria, 1598. Acted Feb. 12, 1596–Apr. 1, 1597; May-June 4, 1601. *S.R.*, conditionally, Aug. 15, 1598.
Cynthia's Revels, 1601. Acted publicly, 1600; at Court, 1600–01. *S.R.*, May 23, 1601.

? Dutch Courtesan, 1605. ? Acted, *c.* 1604 (Fleay, *Chr.*, II, 77). Acted at Court Dec. 12, 1613 (Murray, I, 261); also June 21, 1614 (Collier, *Actors in S's Plays*, 61). S.R., June 26, 1605, "as yt was lately presented at the Blackefryers Provyded that he gett sufficient aucthoritie before yt be prynted.' Note, allowing it later.

Emperor of the East, 1632. Acting license, Mar. 11, 1631 (*Var.*, III, 230). (Fleay says Mar. 4 in *Chr. H.* and Mar. 20, *Stage.*) S.R., Nov. 19, 1631. Pr. with author's dedication.

Every Man out of His Humour, 1600. Another issue, 1600 (one pirated). Acted, 1599; at Court Jan. 8, 1605. S.R., (to Holmes), April 8, 1600.

(a) Game at Chess, 1625. Acted and suppressed, 1624. Censored. "Seen and allowed," by Herbert, Aug. 21, 1624.

(the) Grateful [Faithful] Servant, 1630. Acting licence, Nov. 3, 1629. Stageright protected, list of 1639.

Henry IV, pt. 1, 1598. Probably acted 1597. Acted at Court, 1612–13 (Murray, I, 175); and on Jan. 1, 1625 (I, 176). Revived, at Red Bull, Nov. 8, 1660 (*Var.*, III, 273). S.R., Feb. 25, 1598.

Henry V, 1600, by Creede, for Millington and Busby; 1602, by Creede, for Pavier; 1608. ? Acted at Globe, by Chamberlain's, 1599 (July, 1599, Murray, I, 100); at Court Jan. 7, 1605 (*Ibid.*, I, 173). S.R., "to be staied," Aug. 4, 1600. Aug. 14, 1600, with other copies, "formerlye printed and sett over" to Pavier, by warden's direction.

(Note: Creede in 1598 printed The Famous Victories of Henry V, a Queen's play, entered to him S.R., May 14, 1594. Henry V was acted as new by Admiral's men Nov. 28, 1595–July 15, 1596 (H.).)

(the) Hog Hath Lost His Pearl, 1614. Acted, 1613 (letter of Sir H. Wotton, *Reliq. Wott.*, ed. 4, p. 402). S.R., May 23, 1614. Criticized by city authorities.

Holland's Leaguer, 1632. Acted 6 days at Court, Dec. 1631. Lic. Dec. 7, 1631 (*Var.*). S.R., Jan. 26, 1632.

Hymen's Triumph, 1615. Acted Feb. 3, 1614. S.R., Jan. 13, 1615. An "occasional" play.

(the) Just Italian, 1630. Acting lic. Oct. 2, 1629 (*Var.*, III, 284). S.R., Jan. 10, 1630. Pr. with author's dedication.

(King) Lear, Pide Bull ed., 1608; "for Nathaniel Butter, 1608," really 1619; acted at Court, Dec. 26 and 29, 1606 (Murray, I, 173). S.R., Nov. 26, 1607.

(a) Knack to Know a Knave, 1594. Acted as new, 1592–Jan. 24, 1593 (Henslowe). (Possible revivals, "1. Knaves", Court, Mar. 2, 1613. 2. Knaves, Mar. 5, 1613.) S.R., Jan. 7, 1594.

(the) Lady's Trial, 1639. Acting license, May 3, 1638. First acted, Cockpit, May, 1638 (*Var.*, I, 424). Revived, 1669. S.R., Nov. 6, 1638.

Lover's Melancholy, 1629. Acted, Nov. 24, 1628. S.R., June 2, 1629.

? (the) Massacre at Paris, "Printed *c.* 1595 or 1594" ("The Guise," Fleay). Acted as new Jan. 26, 1593–Sept. 27, 1594. Properties, 1598 and 1601 (H.).

? Perkin Warbeck, 1634, with author's dedication. ? Acted *c.* 1633 (Fleay). S.R., Feb. 24, 1633, provisionally, with a caution.

(the) Phoenix, 1607. Acted at Court, by Children of Paul's, 1606. S.R., May 9, 1607.

(the) Picture, 1630. Acting license, June 8, 1629 (*Var.*, III, 230).

(the) Platonic Lovers, 1636. Acting license, Nov. 16, 1635. *S.R.*, Feb. 4, 1636, as licensed by Herbert.
(the) Poetaster, 1602. Acted, 1601. *S.R.*, Dec. 21, 1601.
? (the) Puritan, 1607. ? "written 1606" (Fleay). *S.R.*, Aug. 6, 1607.
(the) Rival Friends, 1632. Acted Mar. 19, 1631. *S.R.*, June 13, 1632.
(the) Roaring Girl, 1611. ? Acted, 1610; see prologue; cf. Day's account of Moll Cutpurse, *S.R.*, Aug. 7, 1610, and entry *S.R.*, Feb. 18, 1612.
Satiro-Mastix, 1602. Acted, 1601. *S.R.*, Nov. 11, 1601, conditionally.
(the) Silver Age, 1613. Acted at Court, Jan. 12, 1612 (Murray, I, 174; Cunningham, 210).
Two Angry Women of Abington, 1599, as lately acted. Pt. 1 or pt. 2 was acted 1598–99. Properties, Feb., 1599 (H.). 2d issue, 1599.
Two Merry Milkmaids, 1620. Acted after Mar. 2, 1619 (Greg). *S.R.*, May 22, 1620.
(the) Virgin Martyr, 1622. "Reformed and licensed" by Buc, Oct. 6, 1620. *S.R.*, Dec. 7, 1621. Revived, Red Bull, Jan. 10, 1662 (*Var.*, III, 273).
Wit in a Constable, 1640. "A Comedy written in 1639," (title-page). Revived, 1662.

Doubtful

"(the) Bewties," by Jas. Shirley, lic. by Herbert, Jan. 21, 1633. Fleay identifies this with The Bird in a Cage, pub. 1633.
Fair Maid of the West, 1631. Acted 1617 and *c.* Christmas, 1630? (Murray, I, 266.) *S.R.*, June 16, 1631.
(the) Woman Hater, Beaumont and Fletcher, 1606? *S.R.*, May 20, 1607. Q¹ & Q², 1607.

Note.—To this one-year list belong some of the plays listed below as having "now," "lately," and references to special seasons of acting on their title-pages.

3. *Plays Printed within Two Years of Acting Date.*

Antipodes, 1640. Acted at Salisbury Court, 1638. *S.R.*, Mar. 19, 1640. Revived by King's at Red Bull July 6, 1662 (*Var.*, III, 273).
Antonio and Mellida, 1602. Acted at Paul's, 1600. *S.R.*, provisionally, Oct. 24, 1601.
Bartholomew Fair, Folio of 1616. Acted at Court, Nov. 1, 1614 (and Oct. 31; Murray, I, 261). Revived, by King's at Red Bull, Dec. 17 or 18, 1661 (*Var.*, III, 273).
(the) Bloody Brother, 1639; another ed., Rollo, Duke of Normandy, 1640. Acted at Court, Jan. 5, 1637 (Audit Off. Doc.); Jan. 24, 1637 (Murray, I, 177; *Var.*, III, 239); and revived, Red Bull, Dec. 6, 1660 (*Var.*, III, 273). *S.R.*, Oct. 4, 1639.
? Blurt, Master Constable, 1602. Acted by Paul's boys, 1600–01 (Fleay). *S.R.*, June 7, 1602.
(the) Bride, 1640. Acted at Cockpit, 1638.
Cupid's Revenge, 1615. Acted by Children of Queen's Revels, Jan. 5, 1612 at Court; by Children of Chapel Jan. 1, 1613 (Murray, I, 363); at Court by Queen of Bohemia's, Dec. 28, 1624 (Murray, I, 261); at Court by Beeston's

Boys, Feb. 7, 1637 (Murray, I, 370); revived after Restoration; protected on the Cockpit list of 1639. S.R., Apr. 24, 1615.

(the) Duke's Mistress, 1638. Acting license, Jan. 18, 1636. Acted at Court Feb. 22, 1636 (*Var.*, III, 232 and 238). S.R., Mar. 13, 1638.

Hannibal and Scipio, 1637. Acted in Drury Lane, 1635. S.R., Aug. 6, 1636.

(the) Heire, 1622, "as it was latelie acted"; 1633, as it was acted in 1620.

Hector of Germany, 1615. Written 1613. S.R., Apr. 24, 1615 ("occasional").

(a) Lady of Pleasure, 1637. Acting license, Oct. 15, 1635. Acted Dec. 8, 1635 (MS diary of Sir Humphrey Mildmay, Collier, II, 5). Stage-right protected, list of 1639. S.R., Apr. 13, 1637.

? Merchant of Venice. See list of revivals.

(the) New Inn, 1631. Acting license, Jan. 19, 1629 (*Var.*, I, 421).

? Ram-Alley, or Merry Tricks, 1611. ? Acted 1609 (Murray). S.R., Nov. 9, 1610.

(the) Royal Slave, 1639. Acted at Court Aug. 30, 1636; and with additions, as new, on Jan. 12, 1637 (*Var.*, III, 239; Murray, I, 177).

Sappho and Phao, 1584. Acted after Feb. 6, 1582, and on Mar. 3, 1584 (Wallace, *Evolution*, 209). S.R., Apr. 6, 1584, "yf he gett the comedie of Sappho lawfully alowed."

Sejanus, 1605. First acted after May 17, 1603. S.R., Nov. 2, 1604. (Censored.)

(a) Trick to Catch the Old One, 1608. Another issue, as presented before his Majestie on New Yeares night last. Murray and Fleay, however, make this Jan. 1, 1606, not 1607. Acted on public stage, 1605. S.R., Oct. 7, 1607.

Volpone, or The Fox, 1607, with author's dedication. First acted, 1605. Reprinted, 1616. Acted at Court Dec. 27, 1624 (*Var.*, III, 228), and revived after Restoration.

Wit without Money, 1639. Acted at Court Feb. 14, 1637; protected on list of 1639; revived, 1660–62 (*Var.*, III, 272–73) by the King's.

(the) Wits, 1636. Acting license, Jan. 19, 1634 (*Var.*, III, 284). Acted at Court, Jan. 28, 1634 (*Var.*, III, 236).

4. *Some of the Plays Continued or Revived on the Stage after Publication*

(1) Not Included in Other Lists

Bussy D'Ambois, 1607, 1608, 1616, 1641, 1646. Written, c. 1600? (Stoll, *M.L.N.*, Nov., '05). Acted by King's Co. at Cockpit Apr. 7, 1634 (*Var.*, III, 237); and Mar. 27, 1638 (*Jo. Brit. Archaeol. Ass'n.*, 1860); and at Red Bull Dec. 30, 1661 (*Var.*, III, 273). S.R., June 3, 1607.

Cymbeline, 1623 Folio. Acted at Court Jan. 1, 1634 (*Var.*, III, 234; Murray, I, 177).

Epicœne, Folio of 1616; 1620. Acted, 1610 and at Court on Feb. 18, 1636. (*Var.*, III, 237); and revived at Red Bull Nov. 10, 1660 (*Var.* III, 273), S.R., Sept. 20, 1610.

Every Man in His Humour, 1601. Acted, 1598; at Court Feb. 2, 1605; revived Feb. 18, 1631 (Herbert). Entered S.R., Aug. 4, 1600, "to be staied," and re-entered Aug. 14, 1600. (See Collier, *Actors* . . . . , 25; Cunningham, *Rev.*; Murray, I, 173.)

Faithfull Shepeardesse, c. 1610?; 2d ed., 1629; 3d ed., 1634, with additions Acted at Court Jan. 6, 1634, and possibly Apr. 8, 1634 (*Var.*, III, 234–35, and Murray, I, 177).

Faustus, 1604; with new additions, 1619; as now acted, 1663. Acted by the Admiral's 1594–97, 1598; Pembroke's, 1597. Additions paid for Nov. 22, 1602 (Henslowe).

Green's Tu Quoque, or City Gallant, 1614. Acted at Court 1611 and Jan. 6, 1625 (*Var.*, III, 228; Murray, I, 261; Cunningham, 210).

Hamlet, 1603, 1604, 1605, 1611, etc. Stage history uncertain because of references to the old Hamlet. The Hamlett at Hampton Court Jan. 24, 1637 probably Shakespeare's (*Audit Office Doc.*, E. Law). Entered to Roberts on *S.R.*, July 26, 1602. 1603 Hamlet is "for N. L. and John Trundell", 1604 is "by I. R. for N. L."

Henry IV, pt. 1, 1598, 1599, 1604, 1608, 1613, 1623, 1629. Acted at Court May 20, 1613 (Stanhope's Acc'ts.); Jan. 1, 1624 (*Var.*, III, 228); on Red Bull list of King's Co. 1660–62, (*Var.*, III, 263).

Julius Caesar, 1623. Acted at St. James Jan. 31, 1637 (*Var.*, III, 239); and acted Nov. 13, 1638 (*Jo. Brit. Archaeol. Ass'n*, 1860).

(a) King and no King, 1619, 1625, 1631, 1639. Allowed for acting and printing, 1611. Acted at Court Jan. 10, 1637 (and also 1612, 1613, Murray, I, 175). *S.R.*, Aug. 7, 1618.

(the) Maid's Tragedy, 1619, 1622, 1630, 1638, 1641, etc. Acted at Court 1612–13 and Nov. 29, 1636 (*Audit Off. Doc.*, E. Law); at Red Bull Feb. 25, 1662 (*Var.*, III, 273). *S.R.*, Apr. 28, 1619.

(the) Malcontent, 1604. New editions of the same year show augmentations from stage versions.

Merchant of Venice, "I. R. for Thomas Heyes, 1600"; "J. Roberts, 1600" (really 1619). Acted at Court by King's men Feb. 10, 1605 (Murray, I, 173; Cunningham, *Rev.*, Oct., 1605.) [Feb. 12, Fleay, *Stage*, 171.] Provisionally entered on *S.R.*, to Roberts July 22, 1598; on Oct. 28 entered to T. Hayes with Roberts' consent; on July 8, 1619, the year of Jaggard's piracy, entered to Lawrence Hayes "by consent of a full court" as a copy of his father's. Pr. by M. P. for Lawrence Hayes, 1637.

(the) Merry Devil of Edmonton, "as sundry times acted by the King's at the Globe," 1608, 1617, 1626, 1631, 1655. Acted at Court Apr.–June, 1612–13 (Murray, I, 175); at Court, by King's Nov. 6, 1638 (*Brit. Archaeol. Ass'n*, 1860); revived at Red Bull, Jan. 6, 1661. *S.R.*, Oct. 22, 1607. This play was in possession of the King's Company for over 53 years.

Merry Wives of Windsor, 1602. Acted at Court, Oct. 1605 (Cunningham, 203) or Nov. 4, 1604 (Murray, I, 173; at Court, 1613, (Murray, I, 175); and Jan. 1, 1625 (Murray, I, 176); at Court Nov. 15, 1638 (*Brit. Archaeol. Ass'n*, 1860); at Red Bull, Nov. 9, 1660 (*Var.*, III, 272). *S.R.*, Jan. 18, 1602, with immediate assignment of copy.

Mucedorus, 1598, 1606, 1610, 1611, 1613, 1615, 1618, 1619, 1626, 1631, 1634, 1639, 1663. Edition of 1610 advertises additions as acted on Shrove Tuesday. Acted at Court 1605–06 (*c.* Christmas, Murray, I, 173). No entry on *S.R.*, but an assignment from Jones to Wright Sept. 17, 1618.

Much Ado About Nothing, 1600. Acted at Court as Benedicite and Bettris, 1612–13 (Murray, I, 175); May 20, 1613 (Stanhope's Accounts). S.R., Aug. 4, 1600, "to be staied." Aug. 23, entered to Wise and Aspley, with name of author and of company, probably a stage version.

Northern Lass, 1632. Acting license, July 29, 1629 (*Var.*). Acted, 1629; Nov. 29, and Dec. 28, 1638 (*Jo. Brit. Arch.*, 1860).

(Oldcastle. See list of plays acted and printed same year.)

Othello, or the Moor of Venice, 1622. Winter benefit for Herbert, Nov. 22 1629 (J. Q. Adams, *Herbert*, 44); at Hampton Court Dec. 8, 1636 (*Audit Off. Doc.*, E. Law); acted at Red Bull Dec. 8, 1660 (*Var.*, III, 272–73).

Parasitaster, or The Faun, 1606. Ed. 2 of the same year adds note of later acting version of that year.

Pericles, 1609. Pd. Mr. of Revels £3, 10 s. to perform at Globe June 10, 1631 (*Var.*, III, 177). S.R., 1608.

Philaster, 1620, 1622, 1628, 1634, 1639. Acted at Court 1612–13 (Murray, I, 175) and Feb. 21, 1637 (*Var.* III, 239); at Red Bull Nov. 13, 1660 and Jan. 11 1662 (*Var.*, III, 272–73). S.R., Jan. 10, 1620.

Rape of Lucrece, 1608, 1609, 1630, 1638. Acted at Court Jan. 13, 1610; 1628. Protected for Cockpit 1639. S.R., June 3, 1608.

Richard II, 1597, 1598, 1608. Acted at Globe Apr. 30, 1611 (Forman, *Book of Plays*). Summer benefit of £5, 6 s. 6 d. pd. for King's men by Shank on June 12, 1631 (Herbert). The 1608 edition has the Parliament scene (probably cut out from the earlier ed.). S.R., Aug. 29, 1597. (Probably acted on the eve of the Essex conspiracy.)

Richard III, 1597, 1598, 1602, 1605, 1612, 1622, 1623, 1629, 1634. Acted at Court Nov. 16, 1633? (*Var.*, III, 233–34).

? Robert, Earl of Huntington, 1601. Revived later? *Henslowe's Diary*, Appx.

Romeo and Juliet, 1597, 1599. Acted at Curtain, 1598 (Marston, *Scourge of Villainy*).

(the) Scornful Lady, 1616, 1625, 1630, 1635, 1639, 1651. ? Acted 1609–10, (Murray); but 1613–16, Chambers, *E. Stage*, Oct. 18, 1633 (*Var.*, III, 208–10); at Court Jan. 6, 1642 (*Var.*, III, 241); at Red Bull, Nov. 21, 1660 (*Var.*, III, 273). S.R., Mar. 19, 1616.

Sir Giles Goosecappe, 1606. See edition of 1636 for changes.

(the) Spanish Tragedy, undated ed. 1592?; 1594, 1599, 1602, 1602, 1610, 1615, 1618, 1623, 1623, 1633. Acted as new Jan. 7–Oct., 1597. No additions show up till edition of 1602. Jonson was pd. 40 s. for additions Sept. 25, 1601, and June 22, 1602. S.R., Oct. 6, 1592.

Tamburlaine the Great (1 & 2). 1 was printed 1592, 1605 (S.R., Aug. 14, 1590). "Almost certainly acted 1587" (Greg). 1605 text "about same as 1590." "j" (new ?) in *Diary*, Aug. 10–14, 1594–Nov. 12, 1595 (Greg). Pt. 2 (*S.R.*, Aug. 14, 1590); extant in ed. of 1606. Acted as old Dec. 19, 1594–Nov. 13, 1595. (Greg lists pt. 1 in Q. of 1590 in *H.D.*, but not in *Handlist.*)

Taming of the Shrew, Folio of 1623. Acted at Court Nov. 26, 1633 (*Var.*, III, 234).

(the) Virgin Martyr, 1622, 1631. Licensed by Buc Oct. 6, 1620; with added scene, by Herbert July 7, 1624. S.R., 1621.

Volpone, 1607. Acted in 1605; at Court, Dec. 27, 1624 (*Var.*, (III,228; Murray, I, 176); at Cockpit Nov. 8, 1638 (*Jo. Brit. Arch.*, Jan., 1860), and after Restoration. Pr. with author's dedication.

(the) Widdowes Teares, 1612, with author's dedication. Acted at Court Feb. 20, 1613 (Murray, I, 363). *S.R.*, Apr. 17, 1612.

(the) Winter's Tale, F. of 1623. Acted May 15, 1611 (Forman, *Bk. of Plays*). Licensed for revival by Herbert Aug. 19, 1623. Acted at Court Jan. 18, 1624, and Jan. 16, 1634 (*Var.*, III, 236).

(2) OVERLAPPING OTHER LISTS

Alchemist, 1612. Acted 1612-1613, 1622, Jan. 1, 1623, and Dec. 1, 1631 (Herbert, Office Bk.).

Catiline, 1611. Acted 1635, and again printed.

Blind Beggar of Alexandria, 1598. Acted May–June, 1601.

Cupid's Revenge, 1615. Acted 1612, 1613; at Court, Dec. 28, 1624 and Feb. 27, 1637. Stage-right protected for Cockpit, 1638. *S.R.*, Apr. 24, 1615.

Dutch Courtesan, 1605. At Court, Dec. 12, 1613 (Murray, I, 261).

Eastward Hoe! 1605. At Court Jan. 25, 1614 (Murray, I, 261).

Every Man out of His Humour, 1600. At Court, Jan. 8, 1605 (Murray, I, 173; cf. Cunningham, *Rev.*, 203).

Friar Bacon, 1594. "For the Corte," Dec. 14, 1602 (Henslowe). See also ed. of 1630.

Henry IV, 1598. At Court Jan. 1, 1625 (Murray, I, 176); also Feb. 17, 1601 (which part ?). See *S. P. Dom. Eliz.*, 1598–1601, vol. 278, art. 78.

Henry V, 1600. At Court, Jan. 7, 1605 (Murray, I, 173; cf. Cunningham, 203).

Knight of the Burning Pestle, 1613; and "as now acted," 1635. Acted at Court Feb. 28, 1636, and at Cockpit, 1635. Stage-right protected for Cockpit in 1639 (see Brome's *Sparagus Garden*, II, 2 and Murray, I, 269). Revived at Red Bull May 5, 1662 (*Var.*, III, 273).

Love's Labour's Lost, 1598. At Court, Jan. 2–6, 1605 (Murray, I, 173; Cunningham, 203).

Richard III, 1597. At Court Nov. 16, 1633 (Murray, I, 177).

Sappho and Phao, 1584. "Afterwards played at Blackfriars" (Haz., *Man.*, 202).

(a) Trick to Catch the Old One, 1608. New ed., 1608, shows acting continued.

NOTE. A long list of plays might be added which were revived, so far as the history of the stage can prove, only after the Restoration. I have added such notes of late revivals only where the play continued to be acted after publication and before the Restoration. The Red Bull lists of 1660–62, however, are interesting as showing the ability to conserve stage-rights for a long time under unusually difficult conditions.

5. *Extant Plays Printed by 1639, Protected as to Stage-right, 1639*

All's Lost by Lust, 1633, as acted "now lately." *S.R.*, 1632. Revived by King's Co. at Red Bull, 1661 (*Var.*, III, 273).

Bloody Banquet, 1620.

Bondman, 1624. Acting license, Dec. 3, 1623. At Court, 1623–24. Publication authorized. *S.R.*, Mar. 12, 1624. Revived by King's at Red Bull, May, 1661 (*Var.*, III, 273).

Chabot, 1639. Acting license, as altered by Shirley, Apr. 29, 1635.
Coronation, 1640. Acting license, Feb. 6, 1635.
Cupid's Revenge, 1615. Acted 1612, 1613; at Court, Dec. 28, 1624 (*Var.*, III, 228); at St. James Feb. 7, 1637 (*Var.*, III, 239); and revived after Restoration.
Example, 1637. Acting license, June 24, 1634. *S.R.*, Oct. 18, 1637.
Fair Quarrel, 1617. Three new leaves added, 1617, "with new additions."
George a Greene, pr. 1595?; 1599, as acted by Sussex' men. Acted as old Dec. 28, 1593–Jan. 23, 1594; with alterations, as late as 1662 (Haz., *Man.*, 94). *S.R.*, Apr. 1, 1594.
Grateful Servant, 1630. Acting license, Nov. 3, 1629. *S.R.*, Feb. 26, 1630. New ed., 1637.
Great Duke of Florence, 1636. Acting license, July 5, 1627. *S.R.*, Dec. 7, 1635.
Hyde Park, 1637. Acting license, Apr. 20, 1632. Revived by King's Co. 1668. *S.R.*, Apr. 13, 1637.
Knight of the Burning Pestle, 1613, 1635, "as now acted." Acted at the Cockpit, 1635; at Court Feb. 28, 1636; revived by King's at Red Bull, May 5, 1662 (*Var.*, III, 273).
Lady of Pleasure, 1637. Acting license, Oct. 15, 1635. *S.R.*, Apr. 13, 1637.
Love's Cruelty, 1640. Acting license, Nov. 14, 1631. *S.R.*, Apr. 25, 1639 to Crook and Cook, and Nov. 29 to Williams and Egglesfield (cancelled). Revived by King's at Red Bull, Nov. 15, 1660 (*Var.*, III, 273).
Love's Mistress, or the Queen's Masque, 1636; 1640, "corrected by the author." *S.R.*, Sept. 30, 1635. Revived by King's at Red Bull, Oct. 26, 1661.
Love's Sacrifice, 1633. *S.R.*, Jan. 21, 1633.
Maid of Honor, 1632. Author's dedication. *S.R.*, Jan. 16, 1632.
Maid's Revenge, 1639. Acting license, Feb. 9, 1626. *S.R.*, Apr. 12, 1639.
Monsieur Thomas (Father's Own Son), 1639. *S.R.*, Jan. 22, 1639 "as now."
New Way to Pay Old Debts, 1633, author's dedication. *S.R.*, Nov. 10, 1632.
Nightwalker, 1640. (The Little Thief.) Acting license, May 11, 1633. Acted at Court, Jan. 30, 1634; revived by King's at Red Bull, Mar. 15, 1662 (*Var.*, III, 273). *S.R.*, Apr. 25, 1639.
Opportunity, 1640. Acting license, Nov. 29, 1634. Revived at Red Bull, Nov. 26, 1660 (*Var.*, III, 273). *S.R.*, April, 1639.
Rape of Lucrece (Lucretia), 1608,* 1609, 1630, 1638. (* With the company's consent.) Acted at Court Jan. 13, 1610; revived, 1628 (*Athenaeum*, Oct. 18, 1879). *S.R.*, June 3, 1608.
Renegado, 1630 (or, the Gentleman of Venice). Acting license Apr. 17, 1624. On Oct. 30, 1639, Herbert licensed it as The Gentleman of Venice (*Var.*, III, 230–32). *S.R.*, Mar. 22, 1630.
Schoole of Complement, 1631, 1637. Acting license, Feb. 11, 1625; and revived, 1667. *S.R.*, Feb., 1631.
[Sun's Darling (a masque) 1656. Acting license, Mar. 3, 1624.]
'Tis Pitty She's a Whore, 1633, with author's dedication. Acted *c.* 1626? (Fleay.)
Traitor, 1635. Acting license, May 4, 1631; revived at Red Bull, Nov. 22, 1660 (*Var.*, III, 273). *S.R.*, Nov. 3, 1634.
Trick to Cheat the Devil (Middleton's Trick to Catch the Old One?).
Wedding, 1629. Acting license, May 31, 1626. Acted at Court, May 31, 1626.

Wit Without Money, 1639. Acting license for Court, Feb. 14, 1637 (*Var.*, III, 239); revived at Red Bull, Nov. 5, 1660 (*Var.*, III, 273).
Witty Fair One, 1633. Acting license, Oct. 3, 1628. *S.R.*, Jan. 15, 1633.
Young Admirall, 1637. Acting license, July 3, 1633. Acted at Court, Nov. 19, 1633 (*Var.*, III, 234). *S.R.*, April 13, 1637.

NOTE. These plays listed above were protected for the players at the Cockpit in 1639, though already in print. Many of them continued in the possession of the same company until after the Restoration and were then revived.

6. *Plays Printed "As Now Acted," According to Title-Page*

(1) THOSE NOT INCLUDED IN OTHER LISTS

Catiline, "and now acted by his Majesties Servants," 1635. The first edition was in 1611.
Love's Metamorphosis, "first played by the Children of Paules and now by the Children of the Chapel, 1601 (first edition). *S.R.*, Nov. 25, 1600.
Miseries of Inforst Mariage, "as it is now played by his Majesties Seruants," 1607 (first ed.). *S.R.*, July 31, 1607.

(2) OVERLAPPING PREVIOUS LISTS

Knight of the Burning Pestle, "as it is now acted by her Majesties Seruants," 1635 (first ed. was in 1613). Acted at Court Feb., 1636. Stage rights protected in 1639 for Cockpit.
Monsieur Thomas, "formerly acted at the Private House in Black Fryers; And now at the Theatre in Vere Street by His Majesties Servants, 1639." Sheets of 1639 edition issued also by Thos. Harper for John Waterson. The other issue was for Robert Crofts. Stage-right protected (as Father's Own Son) for Cockpit, 1639.
Travailes of the three English Brothers, "as it is now play'd by her Majesties servants, 1607. Acted by Queen's Co. June, 1607. *S.R.*, June 29, 1607. Signed dedication by authors. Revived July 6, 1662? (*Var.*, III, 273).

NOTE. This list is obviously capable of extension by study of the title-pages of successive editions of the plays. The samples above are included for their illustrative value.

7. *Plays Printed as "Lately Acted," According to Title-Page*

(1) THOSE NOT INCLUDED IN OTHER LISTS

(the) Deserving Favorite, 1629.
(the) Heire, 1622, with author's name to dedication.
Herod and Antipater, 1622, with author's dedication.
Humour out of Breath, 1608.
If it be not good, the Diuel is in it, 1612; "a new play," lately acted at the Red Bull.
Look about you, 1600. *S.R.*, 1600.
(a) Mad World, My Masters, 1608 (by Children of Paul's). *S.R.*, Oct. 4, 1608.
Match Me in London, 1631.
Richard III, by Chamberlain's men, 1597.
Trial of Chivalry, 1605. *S.R.*, Dec. 4, 1604, as Life and Death of Cavaliero Dick Bowyer.

(A) Warning for Fair Women, by Chamberlain's men, 1599. *S.R.*, Nov. 17, 1599.
(the) Wedding, as lately acted by the Queen's Co. at the Phoenix, 1629. Acted at Court *c.* May 31, 1626. Stage-right protected for Cockpit, 1639. Acting license, May 31, 1626. Acted at Red Bull, Jan. 9, 1661 (*Var.*, III, 273).
(the) Woman Hater, 1607, two issues, "as sold by J. Hodgets," and "printed by R. R. and sold by J. Hodgets."

(2) OVERLAPPING OTHER LISTS

All Fools, 1605.
All's Lost by Lust, 1633.
Byron, Conspiracie and Tragedie of . . . . , 1608.
Fair Maid of the West, 1631.
Hollands Leaguer, 1632. Twice noted as licensed by Herbert, *S.R.*, Jan. 26, 1632, "reformacons to be strictly observed."
(the) Just Italian, 1630.
(the) Late Lancashire Witches, 1634.
Oldcastle, 1600.
Patient Grissill, 1603.
(the) Rival Friends, 1632.
(the) Roaring Girl, 1611.
(the) Scornful Lady, 2d ed., 1625.
Trick to Catch the Old One, 1608. Acted 1605–08; revived later; protected 1639? *S.R.*, Oct. 7, 1607.
Two Angry Women of Abington, 1599.
Wit in a Constable, 1640.

NOTE. This list, like the above, is easily extensible.

8. *Plays Printed with Dates of Acting in Title*

(1) THOSE NOT INCLUDED IN PREVIOUS LISTS

Albumazar (at first a college play, 1615). Acted at Trinity College before King, Mar. 10, 1615; later on public stage. *S.R.*, Apr. 28, 1615.
Divils Charter, "upon Candlemas night last," 1607; augmented for the reader. *S.R.*, Oct. 15, 1607.
Campaspe, on "New Yeares day at night," 1584, before Queen. Same sheets, with new title, "A moste excellent comedie of Alexander and Campaspe, & Diogenes, Played before the Queenes Majestie on Twelfe day at night . . . . 1584."
Endimion, before Queen at Greenwich "on Candlemas day at night," 1591.
Gallathea, before the Queen at Greenwich "on New Yeeres day at night, 1592. *S.R.*, Tityrus and Galathea, Apr. 1, 1585. Bond (*Lyly's Works*, I, 427) thinks this was acted Jan. 1, 1586, 1587, or 1588, probably 1586.
Midas, before the Queen "upon Twelfe day at night," 1592. Fleay thinks this was played Jan. 6, 1590 (*Chr. Hist.*, II, 42).
Shoemaker's Holiday (The Gentle Craft), before the Queen "on New Yeares day at night last," 1600. Author not named. Paid for July 15, 1599; for Court use, Dec. 12, 1599; played Jan., 1600 (Henslowe).
(Faithful Shepherdess, before King and Queen "on Twelfe night last," edition of 1633. Edition of 1634 had new additions. The play was written in 1608. Acted at Court Jan. 6, 1634, and **Apr. 8, 1634.**)

260   AUTHORSHIP AND OWNERSHIP OF PLAYS

(2) OVERLAPPING OTHER LISTS.
(Old) Fortunatus, before the Queen "this Christmas," 1600.
(King) Lear, "as it was played before the King at Whitehall upon St. Stephans night in Christmas Hollidayes," 1608.
Love's Labour's Lost, before the Queen "this last Christmas," 1598.
Sappho and Phao, before the Queen "on Shroue-tewsday," 1584. Hazlitt says, "afterward played at Blackfriar's."
Trick to Catch the Old One, one issue of 1608 "as on New Yeares night last." Fleay and Murray think it 1606, not 1607, however.

NOTE. There is in every case a possibility that the wording of the title-page may be older than the date of a particular issue; so that other evidence is needed for the reliability of dates on this list.

9. *Some Early Entries of Plays on Stationers' Registers*

There are on the registers numerous entries of plays of which we have no extant copies, as, for example:

Bellendon, *S.R.*, Nov., 1595. Acted as new June 10, 1594; June 15–25, 1597. 24 performances (Henslowe).
The Colonel, by Davenant, licensed for the King's Co. July 22, 1629. (*Var.*, III, 284). *S.R.*, Jan. 1, 1630, to Ephraim Dawson.
Godfrey of Bulloigne, *S.R.*, June 19, 1594, to Danter. Is this perhaps the play acted as new at the Rose by the Admiral's men July 19, 1594–Sept. 16, 1595?

There are other entries, corresponding to which we have no extant editions near in time, as the following:

Anthony and Cleopatra, entered to Blount May 20, 1608.
Jew of Malta, *S.R.*, May 16, 1594. Acted as old, 1591–93, 1593–94, 1594–96. Properties, May 19, 1601 (Henslowe). At Cockpit, *c.* 1625. Henslowe records 36 performances.
Leir. *S.R.*, Apr. 6–9, 1594, to A. Islip; crossed out, and E. White entered below. The edition of 1605 is by Stafford for Wright. Acted Apr. 6–9, 1594.

In some cases, the delay was of only a few years' duration:
Patient Grissill. 40 s. paid to the printer for "staying" it Mar. 18, 1600. Entered on *S.R.*, Mar. 28, 1600, to C. Burby. Printed for Rocket (who had been apprentice of Burby), 1603. Written late in 1599. Acted *c.* Feb.–Mar., 1600.
Philotas, *S.R.*, Nov. 29, 1604. Acted, 1604–05. Printed, 1607.

10. *Plays Printed and Not Acted*

There are a few known examples of plays which were read in print and not acted on the stage:
Adrasta, by John Jones. "A Tragicomedie never Acted," for R. Royston, 1635. Author's dedication.
Albovine, King of the Lombards, by Wm. D'Avenant, 1629. "Could not be personated by copper-laced Christians." (Howard's commendatory verses.)
(the) Unfortunate Mother, by Thos. Nabbes. "A Tragedy, never acted." J. O. for Frere, 1640.

11. *Plays Printed before Being Acted*

There are a few instances of plays printed first and later put on the stage. A problematic case is that of Troilus and Cressida. There were two issues of this play in 1609 for the same publishers. One states that the play was "acted by the Kings Majesties Servants at the Globe. The other has a preface stating that the play has never been "staled with the stage." Early writers (Halliwell-Phillips, *e.g.*) made the one containing the notice of the acting a correction on the other. But bibliographical proofs (the use of a new half sheet with a new signature) indicate the "never staled with the stage" as the later statement. There is more than a hint of trouble between the publishers and the acting company, but the facts are not known. The play was regularly entered to its publishers Jan. 28, 1609, with consent of Buc and the wardens.

CHAPTER IV.

CONDITIONS AFFECTING THE TIME OF PUBLICATION OF PLAYS

Unless the claim to the acting rights were uncertain, as might be the case with a very old play only slightly modified for revival and with no clear title to the original version, it would seem to have been quite unnecessary that a play should be kept out of print by theatrical companies because of danger to stage-right. Possibly some companies or members of companies believed that it dulled the interest of a playgoer to have read their version of the play in advance. In every age there are some persons who entertain the childish idea that the plot of a play should be new to the playgoers. One must admit, however, that much of the material used on the stage in Shakespeare's day must have been familiar in its broad outlines to many in the audience, so that any freshness must lie in the treatment of the tale. Heywood's statement that certain actors thought it against their peculiar interest to have a play in print, and the provision in the Whitefriars contract against putting one play ("Torrismont") into print before the expiration of a term of months, suggest a disposition to withhold plays from publication in order not to dull their interest.

We are confronted with the fact that a large number of plays were put into print, many of them with every evidence of authoritativeness, when there was a manifest intention to continue them upon the stage. Shirley, a professional playwright, evidently did not think publication of his play, *The Royal Master*, would kill the interest of the London public. The play was entered on the *Stationers' Registers* March 13, 1638, and published the same year. An acting licence was taken out after the entry for printing was made (*Var.*, III, 232). The play appeared as acted at the new theatre at Dublin, with the explanation: "Tis new and never yet personated; but expected with the first, when the English stage shall be recovered from her long silence, and her now languishing scene changed into a welcome return of wits and men." This advance publication was no doubt due to the plague, but there was no suggestion of giving up the performance because of previous publication.

Stage Life of a Play: Revivals and Revisions

In considering the relation of the newness of plays to their publication, the tendency has been to take into account chiefly, if not solely, the career of the plays upon the public stage of London. According to Greg, a run of twelve performances was up to the average record for a new play. But it would be absurd to regard this as the stage life of a play. Henslowe's *Diary* alone shows that runs were repeated after intervals of quiet; and the records of court performances add further evidence. There is no reason to believe that a really successful play was more than temporarily "staled" by a run, if it can fairly be said to have been staled at all. Possibly twelve successive performances of a play might exhaust the expected London audience for a season; but there were repeated seasons for good plays. We have, it is true, a suggestion in connection with the playing of *Richard II*, in 1601 that one of the players objected "that the play was olde and they should have losse in playing it because fewe would come."[1] But, on the other hand, we have the fact that the best companies produced the fewest plays in a year and ran them for the longest time. And the plays produced at Court were so frequently revivals that one cannot doubt the value attached to plays that had stood the test of the stage. Revised versions of plays were, for stage purposes, apparently, new plays. The prologue to *The Lover's Progress* (Beaumont and Fletcher), claims for the revision the merits and the valuation of a new play:

> Some may object, why then do you
> Present an old piece to us for a new?
> Or wherefore will your profest Writer be
> (Not tax'd of theft before) a Plagiary?
> To this he answers in his just defence,
> And to maintain to all our Innocence,
> Thus much, though he hath travell'd the same way,
> Demanding and receiving too the pay
> For a new Poem, you may find it due,
> He having cheated neither us, nor you;
> He vowes, and deeply, that he did not spare
> The utmost of his strength, and his best care
> In the reviving it.

John Chamberlain wrote to Sir Dudley Carleton concerning the plays at court (Jan. 5, 1614):

---

[1] *Declaration of practises and treasons attempted and committed by Robert late Earl of Essex and his complices.* L. Barker, 1601, next to last page.

They have plays at Court every night, both holidays and working days, wherein they show great patience: being for the most part such poor stuff that, instead of delight, they send the auditory away with discontent. Indeed our poets brains and inventions are grown very dry, insomuch, that of five new plays there is not one that pleases; and therefore they are driven to furbish over their old, which stand them in best stead and bring them most profit.[2]

The revivals of old plays at court throughout the period are so frequent as to make it very certain that for use at court an old play was often quite as desirable as a new.[3]

In addition to the chance of revival of a successful play in a new run at London, there was, as we shall see, an outlet for it on the provincial stage. While the proceeds here were less than at London, they would no doubt exceed the returns from printed plays. A play old to the London stage might be fresh in the provinces. This should be kept in mind in connection with play publication.

In the face of the large number of plays which appear to have been legitimately published in the midst of their stage careers, those who assume an inalienable opposition on the part of theatrical companies to the publication of live plays are obliged to seek compelling forces to account for the publication. Some of the theories are worth examining.

Among the most conspicuous today are those theories which seek reasons for publication of plays in Puritan and other official restraints of actors and closing of theatres. Some of these restraints are on moral grounds; some for avoiding of disturbances of citizens, some for punishment of actors and playwrights for the use of forbidden materials of contemporary significance; and some on grounds of public health. Whatever the motive, the effect, the temporary closing of the theatres or suppression of a

[2] John Nichols, *Progresses* . . . . *James I*, III, 26.
[3] An example of the way plays revived may be had in the history of *Longshanks*, in all probability the same as Peele's *King Edward the First, surnamed Longeshank. Longshanks* was acted as new by the Admiral's men August 29, 1595, and again acted July 14, 1596. Peele's play was entered on the Registers October 8, 1593, and printed by Abel Jeffes in 1593. It was reprinted in 1599, practically without change. If there were important additions or changes which made the play rank as "new" in 1595, they do not appear. *Longshanks* ran through thirteen or more performances in 1595–96. It was owned by Alleyn, who sold it to the Admiral's men August 8, 1602, for £4. (Greg's *Henslowe's Diary*, 12b, 15b, 21b, 187a.)

company from acting, is interpreted as a reason for publication of their plays. There is in this general theory a superficial reasonableness which entitles it to consideration.

Play Publication as Affected by Restraints from Acting

The opposition of the Puritans, who from time to time came into power in London, together with that of the city authorities, who usually favored some restraints of playing, may be thought to have had some influence upon the publication of plays by tending to discourage the players about the future prospects of the stage and driving them to sell manuscripts when temporarily thrown out of work. There are a few bits of evidence concerning the publication of particular plays following the suppression of plays by a certain company or of plays in general. For example, the Children of Paul's were dissolved between Sept. 29, 1590 and Oct., 1591. It has been stated by some, though on no positive grounds, that they did not come back into favor until 1600-1. *Endymion*, printed by Charlewood for the Widow Brome in 1591, contains the following note on the source of the copy: "Since the Plaies in Paules were dissolved, there are certaine Commedies come to my handes by chaunce, which were presented before her Majestie at severall times by the Children of Paules. This is the first, and if in any place it shall dysplease, I will take more paines to perfect the next." In the same year, probably before her husband's death (though a note in the Registers would seem to date that event in 1588, S.R., II, 210), new editions of *Campaspe* and of *Sappho and Phao* were issued for Brome. *Galathea* followed *Endymion* in 1592, being printed by Charlewood for the Widow Brome, and *Midas* in the same year, being printed for her by Thomas Scarlet. It looks as if the restraint from playing had affected the publication of plays in this instance.

The Puritan opposition to plays extends well on into the beginning of the seventeenth century. Particular efforts were made, from time to time, to restrain playing. On April 12, 1580, the Mayor of London wrote the Chancellor concerning the great disorders at the theatre on Sunday, begging for a suppression of Sunday playing in the city and also in the liberties, (*Remembrancia*, I, 9). A renewed complaint concerning the evil effect of the theatres upon the youth was made 25 February, 1592, with a suggestion that the Queen keep only a company of her own private players. In 1593 the Privy Council forbade, on moral grounds, the representation of common plays within a radius of five miles of the universities of Oxford and Cambridge. A more stringent measure was the letter from the Privy Council 28 July, 1597, suppressing plays in general for the summer in London or about the city, because of their evil effects, and requiring the destruction of such theatres as The Curtain and The Theatre near Shoreditch, which were built only for such purposes as public plays. There was at this time a definite prohibition of plays within three miles of London until Allhallowtide. While there seems to be a rather lively shifting of the make-up of companies from 1592 to 1598, with transfers of ownership of plays as a natural result, I do not see any profound influence of the restrictions of 1592 and 1597 upon play-publication.

On June 22, 1600 the Privy Council again gave order for the restraint of "the imoderate use and companye of playhouses and players." In this the performing of plays was conceded to be not in itself an evil; it was granted that the Queen should be permitted to enjoy their representation; and order was given for the limitation of the houses to two, one on the Bankside and one in Middlesex. The plays were to be given only twice a week, and never on Sundays. Historians of the stage do not regard this order as entirely effective, but it probably had some temporary results through the limitation of the number of performances.

There are many puzzling problems concerning the publication of plays in 1600. Two companies, the Chamberlain's and the Admiral's, had certain of their plays "stayed" by the Stationers' Company. And Henslowe lent £2 for the "staying" of Patient Grissell, an Admiral's play, on March 28, 1600. On a fly-leaf of the Stationers' Registers (Arber, *S.R.*, III, 36) are a note, "My Lord Chamberlains mens plays entered," and three memoranda, two of May 27 entering to James Roberts *A Moral of Clothe breches and velvet hose,* and *Allarum to London,* and one of 4 August, 1600 entering as "to be staied" these plays: *As You Like it, Henry V., Every Man in His Humor, and Much Ado about Nothing.* This "staying" was, I believe, a reserving of copyright for the first claimant. It may possibly indicate that the Chamberlain's men were taking precautions against theft of their copyrights in plays by having a chosen publisher reserve the rights by official entrance on the Hall books of the stationers. There are some indications of a wave of piracy or threatened piracy near 1600, when a number of unusually poor texts appeared, *Henry V.* being one of the most conspicuous examples. There are also certain irregularities as to entries on the Registers and peculiarities of publication. There were two quartos of *Every Man out of His Humour* in 1600, one definitely a piratical reprint. The 1600 Q. of *Oldcastle*, (the one not ascribing it to Shakespeare), the 1600 *Midsummer Night's Dream*, and the 1600 *Merchant of Venice* were piratically reproduced in 1619. About 1600 a number of unscrupulous stationers like Pavier, Danter, Ferbrand, and Ling were handling play texts: and, while it is unsafe to infer that a text printed by one of the poorer or more unruly stationers is necessarily illegitimate, it is at least worth while to investigate their output. Shortly before 1600 some of the Admiral's plays had been published under suspicious circumstances. In 1598 Chapman's *Blind Beggar of Alexandria* was published in a very short version, seemingly from the playhouse, but without dedication by Chapman or mention of a theatre. The entry, of Aug. 15, 1598, on the Registers, to William Jones, is "upon condition that it belong to no other man." The play was not dead for the stage, because, according to Henslowe, it was acted in May or June of 1601. There may have been good reasons for the Admiral's and Chamberlain's men to take special precautions by "staying" entries of their plays, though it is of course possible, on the other hand, that both companies resolved to put some of their plays into print because of a bad outlook for stage receipts, and that they wished to make sure that they got exclusive returns from the copyrights. It is noteworthy that of the fifteen plays printed in 1600, eleven belonged to these two closely related companies, the Admiral's and the Chamberlain's. The distribution of ownership of the fifteen is as follows: seven belonged to the Chamberlain's (*Henry IV, pt. 2, Henry V, Merchant of Venice, Midsummer Night's Dream, Much Ado, The Weakest Goeth to the Wall,* and *Every Man out of His Humour*; four belonged to the Admiral's (*Old Fortunatus, The Shoemaker's Holiday, Sir John Oldcastle,* and *Look about You*); three to the Children of Paul's (*Jack Drum's Entertainment, The Wisdom of Doctor Dodypoll,* and *Maydes Metamorphosis*); one belonged to Derby's (Heywood's *Edward IV*). The companies are good, the authors mostly well known, and the plays often in the height of stage success. At least eleven, possibly twelve, are entered on the Registers. The dates of entry may have some significance. *Shoemaker's Holiday,* bought from Dekker July 15, 1599 and played Jan., 1600, was apparently not entered, though it was regularly transferred in 1610. *Look about You* was not entered, and was published by Ferbrand, who in 1599 had published another Admiral's play without entry,—*Two Angry Women of Abington.* Dekker's *Old Fortunatus,* an old play remodeled for use at court on 12 December, 1599, was entered as early as February, 1600. Ten of the entries of the fifteen plays of 1600 are made at dates after the decree of the Privy Council restricting plays. They are: 24 July; 11, 23, 23 August; 7, 8, 23, 28, 28, October. Now it is to be noted in this connection that, according to Henslowe, dramatic production ceased July-November, 1600. There was clearly a depression as to the immediate future of the stage. As eleven of the fifteen plays belonged to the closely connected Admiral's and Chamberlain's men, it is possible that the need of putting so many plays into print may have arisen from a peculiarly bad outlook of these companies. One fact, besides the order of the Privy Council, that may have affected them was that in the summer of 1600 the Chamberlain, George Carey, a powerful patron not only of his own company but of players in general, was ill with palsy.[4]

It is not possible, nor, I think, necessary to find special reasons for the publication of each of the fifteen plays of 1600; but I incline to believe that most of them were voluntarily released by the companies for the sake of additional income because of the prospect of a bad year; but that there was in a few cases special precaution taken against theft, and in a few others perhaps actual piracy. *Henry V.* can hardly be regarded as a legitimate text on any explanation of its defects. I do not believe that at this date (or at any other) fear of piracy drove a company to publish a large number of plays that they earnestly desired to keep out of print.

When we examine the statistics of publication of plays during the period 1580-1640, we see that there are, from decade to

---

[4] *S. P. Dom.,* 1600, vol. CCLXXIV, art. 86.

decade, marked variations in the numbers of printed plays: 1580-1590, 7 (or 8?); 1590-1600, 56; 1600-1610, 100; 1610-1620, 39; 1620-1630, 26 (counting the Shakespeare Folio as *one*); 1630–1640, 106. A glance at the table of publications arranged by years will show that one cannot trace an immediate and constant effect of the Puritan and other restraints of playing upon the output of printed plays. The significant periods for publication seem to be, 1594, 1600-1609, 1631-41; and if we are to look for special influences bringing about increased publication, we should find them operating during or shortly before these times. We shall be forced to conclude that for any really satisfactory study of causes of publication, the fortunes of the various companies owning the plays, as well as the attitude of authorities toward plays in general, should be taken into consideration.

The Effect of Plague upon Play Publication

Inasmuch as many recent writers follow Fleay in assigning the plague as a chief cause of play publication in certain years, it seems worth while to collect from C. Creighton's *History of Epidemics in Britain*, from Rymer's *Foedera*, from various proclamations and acts of state and orders of Privy Council, and from Bell's *London's Remembrancer* (1665) a series of notes on the plague years between 1580 and 1640 and observe what was the actual relation between plague and the publication of the drama. The table of plays which follows is, with but slight variation, based upon Greg's list of extant plays. In considering the effect of the plague (or, indeed, of any restraint of playing) one must take into account the year following, as well as the current year of play publication.

I have indicated by from one to four asterisks the years when the plague, according to public proclamations, seemed the most repressing. Before 1575-6 theatres were usually closed when the plague deaths were fifty a week. After 1575-6 they were to be closed when the number of all deaths came to fifty a week, though in the provinces the old regulation held. A patent to the Queen's company in 1603 and a Privy Council order of 9 April, 1604 ordered that thirty weekly deaths from plague in London and the liberties should close the theatres. At some time after 1608 the limit rose to forty.[5] A licence to the King's company

---

[5] An allusion in *Ram Alley* (printed 1610), Act IV, sc. 1, confirms this number.

270 CONDITIONS AFFECTING TIME OF PUBLICATION

in 1619 shows forty as the limit, as does a similar licence on June 24, 1625 (Henslowe, II, 145 and Rymer, XVIII, 20). This arrangement probably continued until 1640. Entries in Herbert's office-book for 1636-7 show the limit to be fifty.[6]

DATE	PLAYS PUBLISHED	REMARKS ON SEVERITY OF PLAGUE
*1579		No week above fifty deaths; yearly deaths, 629 (Murray).
*1580	0	Weekly death list low. May 1, P. C. forbade plays. Not enforced?
*1581	2	74 a week, August 31; in 45 weeks, 987. Plays restricted July 10 till Michaelmas (*Remembrancia*, I, 221). Allowed, November 18, 1581.
**1582	0	Plays allowed in spring of 1582 (Steele). Plague severe August to February, 1583; 70 a week, August 16; in 51 weeks, 2976.
*1583	0	Plague, April to December. Mayor protested against plays, April 27 (Collier, I, 238). Walsingham protested against plays May 3 (*Remembrancia*, I, 583). Queen's Company obliged to travel.
*1584(?)	4	All theatres suppressed for a time, June, 1584.
1585	1	
*1586(?)	0	Privy Council asked Mayor to restrain plays May 4.
*1587	0	Theatres probably closed for a while about Bartholomewtide?
1588	0	
1589	1	
1590	1	
1591	1	
*1592	5	Stow says theatres were closed July-September; but this may be because of riots. Plague severe in autumn (Creighton, 351). Court adjourned for plague September, October, and November. The Rose theatre reopened December 29 to February, 1593.
***1593	2	Yearly deaths, 10,662 to 15,000 estimated. P. C. forbade plays January 28. Henslowe entries ceased and Rose closed, February 1 (Greg's Henslowe, 16; II, 157) Theatres probably closed February to December 22 (see Creighton, *Hist. of Epidem.* I, 352 ff.). Traveling licenses to Sussex', Admiral's, Strange's men, and others.

[6] See Murray, *E.D.C.*, II, 171 ff. for a discussion of Fleay's handling of plague statistics.

EFFECT OF PLAGUE UPON PUBLICATION

**1594	19	Plays forbidden by P. C. February 3.
1595	5	
*1596	2	Plays forbidden by P. C. July 22.
1597	4	Order for demolition of theatres. The interdict of this year, July–November, was not due to plague (Halliwell-Phillips, *Illustrations*, 2).
1598	8	
1599	9	
1600	15	(Another restraint of plays, not due to plague, June 22, 1600. No. of performances limited).
1601	5	
1602	12	
****1603	3	Plague very severe June to September and continued to December. 2495 deaths in one week. Theatres closed May 26 (Murray) and opened some time between December and April, 1604. King's Co. and others traveled.
1604	5	
*1605	11	Brief restriction, October 5–December 15.
**1606	10	30 deaths a week July–November; 2124 a year.
**1607	22	Over 30 deaths a week in January, February, March, April, July, August, September, October, November. Murray, however, thinks (*E.D.C.*, I, 151) theatres were open January 8–July 9. Severe plague July 9–November 19.
**1608	11	Plague severe July 28 through December; 2262 deaths in year. Allusions in *Your Five Gallants* (*S.R.*, Mar. 22, 1608) to closing of theatres for plague (IV, 2). Interdict April 12.
***1609	6	Plague high January 5–December 18; 4240 deaths in year. Theatres reopened in December.
*1610	7	Plague high July to December; 1803 deaths in year.
1611	2	
1612	6	
1613	7	
1614	2	
1615	6	
1616	2	
1617	1	
1618	3	
1619	3	
1620	3	
1621	1	
1622	4	
1623	5	publications, 24 new plays in all (20 in Folio).
*1624	2	Norwich refused to receive the Prince's players in May for fear of plague. Parliament prorogued October 1 (Steele).

272   CONDITIONS AFFECTING TIME OF PUBLICATION

****1625	1	January 22, public thanksgiving for cessation of plague. Over 40 deaths a week, May 12–November 24; in one week of August, 4463. Court, parliament, and fairs interrupted. Fairs reopened December 30 (Steele). Provincial towns hostile to those fleeing London plague.
*1626	0	June 30, general fast ordered because of plague.
1627	2	
1628	2	
1629	6	
*1630	8	Over 40 deaths July 8–October 21. "No play this summer on account of the plague," (Herbert); Bartholomew Fair forbidden August 3; Law courts adjourned September 9. King's Company impoverished.
(?)1631	13	Theatres opened June 10, 1631. Herbert received a fee from the King's men for playing at Globe on cessation of plague.
1632	14	
1633	14	
1634	5	
*1635	3	Trade ceased for six months between 1635 and 1636 (*Remembrancia*, VII, 162).
***1636	6	Orders for precaution April 22 (Steele; Rymer). Theatres closed May 12, 1636 (*Var.*, III, 239). King's men traveled in provinces. Bartholomew Fair forbidden July 26 (Rymer); all fairs forbidden August 20. (10,400 deaths in a year.)
**1637	12	Theatres opened February 24, but soon closed (March 1). Plague high January to August 17. Fairs forbidden July 23 (Steele) and August 21 and September 3. Theatres opened October 2. (3082 deaths in year.)
(?)1638	13	Plague increasing September 2 (Steele, No. 783).
*1639	18	Plague high July to October.
*1640	24	Theatres closed September 11; probably open in November. 1450 deaths in year.

Mr. Fleay, in commenting on the letter of the Chamberlain to the Stationers June 10, 1637, prohibiting publication of plays of certain companies without consent, says its peculiar significance has not been noted, for "it was in the confusion of plague years that the players' consequent poverty induced them to sell to dishonest printers copies of plays made for prompters' use or special Court performances, which, being thrown aside after

⁷ *Stage*, 361.

their immediate purpose was fulfilled, were appropriated by needy actors and surreptitiously issued. Such years were 1625 and 1637." Mr Fleay refers to a future volume on authors for "abundant instances" and also to his list of play entries in his *Life of Shakespeare*, p. 328.[7] To begin with the years he has selected for illustration, we find issued, without entry on the Registers, in 1625, *one* play, Middleton's *A Game at Chess*, which was undoubtedly published because of the sensational interest of its material and because author and company had got into trouble over the censorship with it. The following year *no* extant play was published. Nor was any play entered on the Registers during the year 1625-6. It is true, the output of plays, except for the one year 1623, when the Shakespeare Folio came out, had been small since 1616; but it was the smallest for a decade in the very year mentioned by Fleay and the year after it, when, according to his theory, we might expect plays bought to come into print. Again, in 1637 we find no unusually large output of plays, though there is a larger number than in 1636. Of the twelve plays published in 1637, none is by King's or Queen's players. Five are Shirley's, two Nabbes's, and one Heywood's. The probabilities are that there was nothing extraordinary about the publication of plays in that year. Just as a matter of theory, it seems quite reasonable to suppose that, when the theatres were closed because of plague there would be a tendency to throw plays into print. We do not lack testimony as to the poverty of the players during some plague seasons. On September 29, 1593 Henslowe wrote to Alleyn concerning Pembroke's men (of the Curtain), "They are all at home and have been there 5 or 6 weeks for they can not save their charges to travel, as I hear, & were fain to pawn the 'parel."[8] In 1594 they disposed of some plays to the Earl of Derby's men (afterward the Chamberlain's). Three of their plays found their way into print in 1594. It is, of course, possible that in 1594 the outburst of dramatic publication was in some way influenced by stage restrictions: but we can evidently not extend this as a general principle, for it will not work. There were many other years when plague raged and the theatres were closed, and all but necessary business was at a standstill. Why was there not a

[8] Collier, *Alleyn*, p. 32. Beeston in 1637 in one petition after another for permission for his company to act, spoke of their poverty due to plague.

great output of dramatic literature in these or the years immediately following? One reason may have been, that plays were not at these seasons so much in demand as at others because the tastes of the reading public suddenly veered to medical treatises on the cure of the plague and to spiritual remedies for the cure of souls. If the reader doubts the force of this suggestion, let him read the entries on the Stationers' Registers during the seasons when plague was raging. Let him observe also that the book business in general, like other industries, was somewhat crippled by the plague. A reference to the table on pages 270 ff. will, I believe, show that the plague did not have the influence on dramatic output that Fleay supposes and that one would, at first thought, expect. (I have indicated, in my table, by a single asterisk the years in which the plague was bad enough to cause restraints of public performances in London, and by added asterisks the years when plague was most severe). In using the table, it should be remembered that the year following the bad plague year should also be observed.

Several reasons may have conspired to prevent the expected effect of plague upon dramatic output. One was, that the financial conditions of all companies were not equally affected by each epidemic, and the less successful companies would often sell plays to the more successful, who could afford to wait over. We must remember that, however appalling the statistics of plague years seem to us today, having the plague was with London for some time almost a habit, and working people had to learn to adjust themselves to it. There are always many whose craving for public entertainment will overcome the dread of epidemic contagion. And so we find Elizabethan actors hanging around hopefully, living on expectation of better days. One outlet often provided them was a traveling license which permitted them to play in such of the provinces as would receive them. The custom of touring the small towns and rural districts was evidently much more general than is usually recognized by historians of the English stage. As early as 1576 John Northbroke, in his "Against Dicing, Dauncing, Playes, and Enterludes," (Shakespeare Soc'y, *Publ.*, XII, 84) makes Youth say he wishes to talk of "stage plays and enterludes, which are nowe practised amongst us so universally in towns and country." And throughout the period 1580-1640 many references may be found to the traveling of the better, as well as the minor, companies of players. As might be expected, we find that licences were issued to some of the companies in the plague years 1592–96 to travel in the provinces. The Rose Theater was closed for a part of 1592. Strange's men were obliged to travel because of plague (*Henslowe's Diary*, 15). They visited Canterbury, Bath, Gloucester, and Coventry. Again in 1593 they had a license from the Privy Council to play anywhere seven miles away from London. They visited Chelmsford, Bristol, Bath, Shrewsbury, Coventry, and Leicester (Murray). The Lord Chamberlain's men in 1592 declared: "Our companie is greate and thearbie our chardge intollerable in travellinge the countrie, and the contynuance therof wilbe a meane to bring us to division and separation" (Murray, I, 88: II, 127–28). This company also had a license to travel in 1593. In May of the same year Henslowe records the loan of £15 to Francis Henslowe "for his share to the Quenes players when they broke and went into the contrey." (*Diary*, I, 4.) Murray's records show that the Queen's players in 1593 visited Leicester, Coventry, Stratford-on-Avon, Southampton, Plymouth, Bath, York, Canterbury, Maidstone, and Norwich: and in 1594 they were at Coventry, Leicester, Gloucester, Bristol, Bath, and Barnstaple. In 1593 the Admiral's men visited Coventry, Norwich, York, and Shrewsbury, and in 1594 played at Bath. Pembroke's were at Bath in 1593. The companies of Sussex and Worcester were also traveling in the provinces 1593–94.

The question may arise, whether the provinces were always willing to receive the refugees from plague districts. The attitude seems to have varied. There are numerous provincial records of sums paid to players "not to play." Some of these are traceable to puritanic bias, but many are definitely due to fear of infection.[9] But of course in many cases the actors might be able to prove that they had not been exposed. At any rate, we have records of London players performing in the provinces during bad plague years. Kelly's *Notices of the Drama in Leicester* (pp. 227ff.) shows two payments to the Queen's players in 1593, besides payment to the Earl of Derby's, Wor-

[9] See the appx. to Murray, *E.D.C* for entries showing attitudes of provinces at various times.

cester's, Darcy's, and others. In 1594 there was not much playing at Leicester. In 1595 the Queen's men were paid twice. Fleay and Murray both say that there are no records of the King's men's playing in the provinces in 1625, one of the very bad years mentioned by Fleay: but in Kelly's *Notices of the Drama in Leicester* we find (p. 260) records of one pound given to the King's men on Oct. 15, and fifteen shillings to the Earl of Pembroke's. In the next year, also a great plague year, four items concerning players in Leicester appear. In the equally bad years 1636–37, the King's men were permitted to act in the provinces, and were also granted a weekly allowance of £20. The Children of the Revels, as well as the King's men, played at Leicester in 1637. Thus, by gifts and special privileges to play outside of London, many of the companies tided over these crucial times. When companies actually went bankrupt or disbanded, we should expect the disposal of their plays to take place, preferably by sale to another company, or, as second choice, by sale to a stationer. Sufficient evidence as to the fortunes of the various companies has not been brought together to enable one to trace with accuracy the break-up of the companies in relation to the publication of their plays. Nor can one hope for accuracy until the existing provincial records have been exhausted. A good beginning has been made by Murray, in his *History of the English Dramatic Companies*, in which records of a sufficient number of provincial performances have been brought together to convince the most skeptical that the life of a play was by no means confined to the London court and the London public stage.[10]

STATUS OF THEATRICAL COMPANIES
Evidences of Poverty

To account for the publication of plays in batches, A. W. Pollard and J. Dover Wilson have made an elaborate study of the plays traceable to 1594 (either published then or going back to manuscripts probably intended for use at that time).[11]

[10] Since this was written, additional references to provincial acting have appeared in Alwin Thaler's "Travelling Players in Shakespeare's England," *Mod. Philol.*, XVII (1920), 489–515.

[11] See "The 'Stolne and Surreptitious' Shakespeare Texts," *The Times Lit. Suppl.*, Jan. 16, 1919, and the 1917 and 1920 editions of Pollard's *Shakespeare's Fight with the Pirates*, the latter of which has further references.

Their theory I shall consider more particularly in connection with the sources of play copy for publication. Stated briefly, the gist of the proposed explanation is, that a flood of playhouse manuscripts came on the market, especially from companies in low water. "Many of them bear obvious traces of having been shortened for provincial playing." These abridged manuscripts, "which would be useless for London performances, were less carefully guarded than the complete texts." The low financial status of the companies seems to me an entirely reasonable assumption. I am a little suspicious as to the careless guarding of abridged manuscripts because useless for London.

Before passing to a consideration of the circumstances affecting publication of plays in 1594, it should be noted that the number of plays (18 or 19) was not strikingly in excess of other years. 1600 (with an output of 15), 1602 (12), 1605 (11), 1606 (10), and 1607 (22) might be thought also to call for explanation. 1600 and 1607 expecially would need interpretation. 1607 has a particularly interesting assemblage of plays— by Barnes, Beaumont and Fletcher, Chapman, Day, Dekker, Heywood, Jonson, Marston, Middleton, Sharpham, Tourneur, Wilkins, besides three anonymous plays and one pseudo-Shakespearian. It is just possible that the plague had something to do with the output of 1607; but 1606 and 1608 show no more than 1605 when there was no plague, and 1607, on the other hand, doubles the record.

But to return to the "batch" of plays of 1594. The effect of the plague as at least an indirect cause is rather likely, but as a cause which would affect certain companies more than others because of their comparatively tenuous hold on public favor, or because of the low state of their finances, or weakness in organization, or lack of good actors or good authors, or other handicaps. Twelve of the plays printed in 1594 were entered for publication between January and July of 1594. Four of the plays printed in that year belonged to the Queen's players. From 1584 to December of 1591 the Queen's men had been in high favor at Court, the Admiral's being their one rival. After 1591 Strange's men appear at Court in place of the Queen's, for some reason, though the Queen's men continue to act in the city and also in the provinces. The greatest actors of the Queen's men were dead or retired by 1591, and the company show symptoms of decline thereafter. They played at the Rose with Sussex' men in 1594, but did not appear in London after May 3, 1594. They perhaps acted in the provinces, but they may have needed to dispose of old versions of some of their plays (See *Henslowe's Diary*, ed. Greg, 4, and Murray, *E.D.C.*) Three of the four Queen's plays printed in 1594 were Greene's. One was *Orlando Furioso*, printed as "played before the Queenes Maiestie." *The Defence of Coney-Catching* (*S. R.*, 21 April, 1592) accuses Greene of selling *Orlando Furioso* to the Queen's men for 20 nobles and then to the Admiral's for as much more when the Queen's were in the country. The play was acted by Strange's men as "old" 22 Feb., 1592. It was entered on the *Registers* Dec. 7, 1593 and published by Danter for Burby in 1594. The text is a short version "as played before the Queen." The question is, whether it really is a court version, or, as Greg thinks, (*Henslowe's Diary*, II, 150) a short version used by the Queen's men for provincial tours. The so-called double sale of Greene's work may conceivably have been due to a shifting of actors and to a pretty complete revision of the manuscript. If Strange's men were practically the same as the Admiral's 1589-1594, as Greg once believed, and Chambers still believes, possibly that company owned it before the Queen's did, as Strange's acted it in 1592 as old. Another play of Greene's, *Friar Bacon and Friar Bungay*, was played by Strange's men as old, 19 Feb., 1592- 30 (29) Jan., 1593. It then was acted by the Queen's men, who, after a partial dissolution, had joined with Sussex' men. These united companies gave 9 performances of it 1-5 April, 1594. The play was then entered on the *Stationers' Registers* May 14, 1594 and printed the same year. It was later revived for court use for the Admiral's men 14 Dec., 1603 with a prologue and epilogue by Middleton (Henslowe). The similarity of history here in two plays of Greene's,—Strange's, Queen's, Admiral's,—suggests some regular arrangement for transfer of copy. "Jeronimo" also, played by Strange's 1591-3, passed by 1597 into the Admiral's hands and by 1601 into Alleyn's, so that the Strange-Chamberlain combination seems to have been intimate. A third play of Greene's belonging to the Queens' men and put into print in 1594 is *The Tragical Reign of Selimus*, of which the stage history is obscure. The *True Tragedy of Richard III* (anon.) was also a Queen's play put into print in 1594 after being entered on the Registers on June 19. It seems likely that the Queen's Company voluntarily disposed of some of its plays because of its weakened condition of organization and finance.

Dissolution and Re-combination

The effect of dissolutions and recombinations of theatrical companies would probably, if we could get at the evidence, go far toward explaining why at definite times the plays of a certain company were thrown upon the market in groups. Some facts appear concerning one association of companies that have bearing on the publications of 1594.

There was an intimate relationship between Pembroke's men and the Chamberlain's, Pembroke's and the Admiral's, and the Admiral's and the Chamberlain's. The Admiral's and Chamberlain's men acted at Court together in 1586 (Murray, *E.D.C.*; and Halliwell-Phillips, *Ill.*, p. 31). Again in 1589 and from 1592 to 1598 they continued their co-operation, playing together at Newington Butts in June, 1594. Alleyn played in both companies, the Chamberlain's having been Strange's men up to 1594. Greg once believed (*Henslowe's Diary*, II,150). that for a part of the time the Admiral's men and the Chamberlain's were identical. There were naturally frequent transfers of players and also of plays. The Admiral's company suffered some temporary dispersion 1592-4 (Greg, *Henslowe's Diary*, 83). In 1594 the Admiral's and Chamberlain's men gave performances together at London. Any passing of plays between the Admiral's and Chamberlain's men (or the former Strange's) is explainable by the customary co-operation of the companies and the interchanges of players. In a similar way, the inheritance by either company of plays belonging to Worcester's men before 1589 is explainable as possibly through Edward Alleyn, a share-holder in Worcester's who, when (after the death of Somerset, Earl of Worcester, in 1589) the company lost its leading men to the Admiral's, bought up shares of others of the company in certain plays, doubtless for the use of the company to which he was going.

More definitely traceable is the effect of the friendly relations of Pembroke's men with these companies. In the summer of 1593 Alleyn, then traveling with his company in the provinces, wrote to Henslowe inquiring how Pembroke's men were getting along. Henslowe replied on September 29, 1593, "They are all at home and have been these 5 or 6 weeks, for they cannot save their charges to travel, as I hear, and were fain to pawn the 'parel' " (*Henslowe's Diary*, II, 161). The records show that Pembroke's men left the city about February, 1593, and visited Ipswich, Leicester, Coventry, York, Shrewsbury, Ludlow, and Bath. But, as they could not pay expenses, they went back to London and pawned their properties and wardrobe (Collier, *Alleyn*, 32). The company then drops out of sight from 1594 to 1597. A natural result of this poverty and apparent dissolution was a double disposal of the plays. They seem to have put into print Marlowe's *Edward II*, *The True Tragedy of Richard, Duke of York*, and the anonymous *Taming of a Shrew* (1594-5), all of which were published as acted by Pembroke's. At the same time they disposed of the stage-rights in these and perhaps other plays to their friends the Earl of Derby's men, known first as Strange's, and later as the Chamberlain's. That there was co-operation between these companies is shown by the fact that in 1593 the list of characters in the *True Tragedy of Richard Duke of York* showed two of Pembroke's men to be acting with the Strange-Chamberlain company.[12] This is one indication of what I believe to be a fairly normal situation,—that a theatrical company could be persuaded to take over the stage-right and revise and continue to perform a play in spite of the fact that the old version as played by the former owners was being put into print at the time of the transfer. It happened too often to make reasonable the assumption of piracy. *The Taming of A Shrew* entered on the Registers as acted by Pembroke's on 2 May, 1594, was acted by the Admiral's and Chamberlain's together 11 (13) June, 1594.

The history of *Titus Andronicus* will illustrate this splitting of copyright from stage-right in times of stress. It was played by Sussex' men as "new" 24 Jan., 1594 and 6 February, perhaps having been retouched after it was acquired from Pembroke's men who had previously performed it. On the day when the Sussex men last performed it (Feb. 6, 1594), it was entered on the Registers, and it was printed as having been acted by

[12] Murray, *E.D.C.*, I, 62–63 on *Sinkler*, and I, 66, on *Spenser* and *Jeffes* and their shifts.

Derby's, Pembroke's, and Sussex's men. But the stage-rights passed on to the Chamberlain's men, who succeeded also to the rights in several other plays formerly Pembroke's. *Titus Andronicus* was then acted by the Admiral's and Chamberlain's men in June, 1594. The 1600 Quarto, which has the same text as that of 1594, adds the new company to the former list of three. This split in disposition of copyright and stage-right is another instance of arrangement to make the most of the property when there was an impending break-up of a company. Sussex's men played with the Queen's at the Rose in April, 1594, but presumably dispersed soon after (see Murray, *E.D.C.*, and *Henslowe's Diary*, II, 161). They had never been a great success, and they did not reappear till 1602-3 in London or the provinces. Doubtless in this case, as in *Hamlet* and *The Taming of a Shrew*, the Chamberlain's Company had the play freshened up by securing soon a revised version.

Probably at the same time the Chamberlain's company acquired the stage right in *The True Tragedie of Richard Duke of York, and the death of good King Henrie the Sixt*, which, so far as we know, did not get into print until 1595, but which then appeared as acted by the former owners, Pembroke's. The names of actors inserted for characters show that two of Pembroke's men acted it along with the Strange-Chamberlain company. It also was probably re-worked by Shakespeare (cf. the 3 *Henry VI.* of the 1623 Folio), though just when and how often he worked on it is still a problem. The "T.P." quarto of *The Whole Contention* (1619) acknowledges Shakespeare as the author, and it may possibly be an early Shakespearian revision (say about 1594).

One of the Strange-Chamberlain plays, *A Knack to Know an Honest Man*, was published in 1594 in what may well be a stage version, "with Kemp's applauded merriments." It was acted 10 June, 1592- 24 January, 1593, and entered on the *Registers* 7 January, 1594. No special reason for publication appears.

Transfers of plays from Pembroke's to Admiral's men continued after 1594. The two companies played together in 1597. Henslowe bought two plays for them to use in common. Accounts for Pembroke's men in *Henslowe's Diary* cease soon after (by January, 1598). A number of plays that belonged to Pembroke's in 1597 passed into the stock of the Admiral's company, presumably at this time. Henslowe lent them £7 to buy five books from Slaughter, who was probably leaving or preparing to leave in 1597. Within a year, Alleyn left the Admiral's. And, as Alleyn and Slaughter were owners of play copies, their exit would probably necessitate a filling-up of repertoire.

If we had a full history of the "union" of four principal companies, afterwards called "the United Companies," which came into existence at some time after Shakespeare's death, (*Var.*, III,224), we should probaply have cleared up some problems of play ownership in that later period. The obscurity of much of the history of the companies leaves many of the transfers of rights in plays untraceable.

Summing up what evidence appears as to causes of publication of plays in 1594, it may be said that of the nineteen plays, only two, Marlowe's *Edward II* and Greene's *Orlando Furioso*, were entered on the Registers during the months of 1593 when Henslowe's accounts show a stoppage of stage business (i.e. 1 Feb.- 27 Dec., 1593). Most of those entered were at dates after the resumption of playing in 1594. Also, we know that a number of the plays continued to be performed by friendly companies after they had been put into print, presumably by the consent of their former owners. In the cases of three companies, Sussex's, the Queen's, and Pembroke's, poor success in general, loss of leaders among actors and writers, and poverty, occasioning temporary disbanding, seem to have resulted in transfers of stage-rights, with an occasional splitting off of the copyrights for the sake of increased funds. The new owners in several cases had the plays whose stage-rights they had thus acquired revised and expanded. (Marlowe's *Edward II* and *The Spanish Tragedy*, besides those mentioned above, enjoyed such revivals). While there may have been a piracy or two at this date, there are certainly no evidences of any general wave of piracy in play publishing. On the other hand, there are several obvious cases of friendly agreement as to disposition of plays of a dissolving company.

The "moral" I would draw is this: if we find in print the plays even of a solvent company shortly after their appearance on the stage, we are not driven to conclude *a priori* that they were discarded for the stage. And if they are obviously not so discarded, we need not infer that the printed text was necessarily pirated. And if the text happens to be good, say, obviously a playhouse manuscript, we need not assume that the company published it through fear of a pirate. If plays of the companies were from time to time put into print while still useful for the stage, the commonsense conclusion is that, unless there is in the plays themselves clear evidence of piracy, the probability is, that there was no such widespread and constant objection to publication as has been supposed. Yet even the very best of Shakespeare critics still assume this frequently. For example, Mr. A. W. Pollard, who has, in his *Shakespeare Folios and Quartos* done so much to clear away false impressions as to the texts of the early quartos, allows himself in his more recent work to fall in line with this assumption. In his *Shakespeare's Fight with the Pirates* (1917, pp. 50-51), which is an admirable book (even if Shakespeare cannot be shown to have fought any pirates), he says, after commenting on Danter's certain piracy of *Romeo and Juliet* and probable piracy of *Love's Labour's Lost*, "Finding themselves thus attacked, the players, lest more plays should go the same way, sold to Andrew Wise the right to print three of Shakespeare's Chronicles, *Richard II*, *Richard III*, and *Henry IV*, part 1." But surely it would not be necessary to go to the length of publication to protect the copyright, when entry on the Registers would apparently be as effective. Mr. Pollard goes on to say (p. 53) concerning the 1608 Quarto of *Lear* published from a playhouse copy by Butter and Busby:

It seems clear that the King's players consented to this, and yet as John Busby (if it was Busby senior who entered the play, as seems agreed) had robbed him twice before, and their policy was clearly against printing, it seems improbable that they did so willingly. I venture to hazard the suggestion that Busby may have been in a position to annoy them by reprinting the old play of 'King Leir' which Simon Stafford, a printer frequently in trouble, had entered and printed when Lear was first being acted in 1605.

Again, on page 54, Mr. Pollard says: "After five years' immunity we find them in 1608 and 1609 selling 'King Lear' (perhaps to a blackmailer), once more resorting to precautionary entries, losing Pericles . . . ."

This motivation of the publication of *Lear* is certainly fanciful and difficult to entertain without some sort of evidence.

There are numerous examples of obviously authorized publications of plays by other than thoroughly honest stationers, as Mr. Pollard is entirely aware. Why go so far afield for a reason? Only because of the assumption of an entire opposition to publication of plays. But from 1597 to 1609 there are numerous plays of the Chamberlain's company put into print, and it would require infinite invention to assign motives for all if the policy is to be shown as absolutely against publication. As a matter of fact, the policy of this company was, I believe, that of any other self-respecting group of actors, to make acting the main business, and editing only a side-line, and to protect themselves, if they had to, against having copyrights *stolen*. They wished to choose their own seasons for publication; and they were a little slower than the other companies about putting their plays into print.

The Demand for Printed Plays

The custom of selling plays at the theatres had certainly not yet risen.[13] But an examination of the entries on the Registers and of Greg's list of extant plays cannot fail to convince one of a real demand for printed plays. Miss Phoebe Sheavyn says: "Plays sold well if published in the height of their popularity on the stage; otherwise they were less certain of a market in London and had to be 'vented by termers and country chapmen,' "[14] citing as authority the preface to Middleton's *Family of Love* (1608), in which he regrets the decline in public interest since the representation. But is not this play somewhat exceptional in its dependence upon current interest in the subject-matter? Certainly the numbers of editions through which successful plays ran (see, for example, *Mucedorus*) would seem to indicate that popular interest in a printed play did not rest wholly upon its freshness on the stage. Richard Hawkins, in his address to the reader, prefixed to the third (1628) impression of *Philaster* (five editions of which were published in nineteen years) confidently counted on the interest of readers:

[13] It has been said that *The Anatomist, or, The Sham Doctor*, a comedy by Ravenscroft (1697) was the first play to be sold at the theatres; but I do not know whether this is true. (See Hazlitt, *Manual*, 13.)

[14] *Lit. Profession in the Elizabethan Age*, p. 74.

This play so affectionately taken, and approoved by the Seeing Auditors, or Hearing Spectators (of which sort, I take, or conceive you to bee the greatest part) hath received (as appeared by the copious vent of two Editions,) no less acceptance with improovement of you likewise the Readers, albeit the first impression swarmed with Errors, prooving it selfe like pure Gold, which the more it hath beene tried and refined, the better is esteemed; the best Poems of the kind, in the first presentation, resemble that all tempting Minerall newly digged up, the Actors being only the labouring Miners, but you the skilfull Triers and Refiners: Now considering how currant this hath passed, under the infallible stampe of your judicious censure, and applause, and (like a gainefull Office in this Age) eagerly sought for, not onely by those that have heard and seene it, but by others that have meerely heard thereof: here you behold me acting the marchant-adventurer's part, yet as well for their satisfaction as mine own benefit.

In 1632 Edward Blount ventured to publish *Sixe Court Comedies*, by Lyly, which, as he said, were "acted by none but worms."

One should remember, too, that the habit of reviving and rewriting plays meant much for the possibility of sale of the old plays. Sometimes the publisher trickily pretended that he had, and sometimes he took the pains really to secure, innovations from recent stage versions. In either case it was customary to advertise the freshness of the version on the title-page. Either those who had recently attended the plays or their associates were depended on as the audience of the printed text. Greg's hand-lists are full of evidence of this effort to keep up to date with the stage. Even first editions advertise it. A few examples will suffice. In 1594 *A Knack to Know a Knave* was published "with Kemps applauded merriments." Middleton and Rowley's *A Fair Quarrel*, printed 1617, came out in a new issue the same year with three extra leaves and a new title-page, "with new additions of Mr. Chaughs and Trimtrams Roaring, and the Bauds Song. Never before Printed."[15] Heywood's *Rape of Lucrece* in 1638, in a note to the reader at the end, shows that it is keeping up with the stage version: "Because we would not that any mans expectation should be deceived in the ample Printing of the Book: Lo (Gentle Reader)we have inserted these few Songs, which were added by the stranger that lately acted Valerius his part." "Arise, arise, my Juggie, my Puggie,"

---

[15] W. Greg, A List of English Plays. . . . .

forms one of these valuable additions, and "The Cries of Rome" is the other.

The testimony of the Puritan writers who so vigorously attack the stage is all to the effect that plays were very popular in print as well as on the stage. Prynne, in the dedication to his *Histriomastix* (1633), says:

I saw the number of Players, Playbooks, Playhaunters, and Playhouses still increasing, there being above forty thousand Play-books printed within these two yeares (as Stationers informe mee,) they being now more vendible than the choycest Sermons."

And again, in his preface "To the Christian Reader,"

Some play-books since I first undertooke this subject are growne from Quarto into Folio; which yet beare so good a price and sale, that I cannot but with griefe relate it, they are now newprinted in farre better paper than most Octavo or Quarto *Bibles*, which hardly finde such vent as they: .... Besides, our Quarto Play-bookes since the first sheetes of this my Treatise came unto the Presse, have come forth in such abundance, and found so many customers, that they almost exceede all number, one studie being scarce able to holde them, and two years time too little to peruse them all.[16]

During the period 1580-1640 about 355 plays are known to have been printed for the first time, not counting school plays and masques. [Lee estimates the whole number as 600.] Can we suppose them all to have been either dead plays or surreptitious?

A suspicion of illegality has been attached to many plays because of the corrupt state of the text (a matter which will be considered in the chapter on the text), and to many other plays because they were printed for publishers who were not of high repute. It must be admitted that small publishers and publishers of low repute (I believe these terms should not be used as synonymous) did publish plays. Miss Charlotte Porter attributes this fact to the decree of 1599 which required "that noe English historyes be printed excepte they be allowed by some of her Majesties privie Councell," and "noe plays be printed except they be allowed by suche as have aucthorytie." She goes on to say, "The natural result could be no other than that such parlous wares were open to publication by the feeblest and

[16] W. C. Hazlitt, *Prefaces, Dedications, and Epistles*, pp. 333, 346.

least reputable, and scorned by them." This, then, is her reason why "at the foot of the list of books thought desirable by the 'honest' or conservative stationer were political pamphlets and plays." In what sense the stationers scorned the plays is not made clear, for Miss Porter admits that, although "on the playwright's side there was no inducement to seek publication, on the printer's side was every inducement to steal copy and print it as secretively as possible."[17] It is apparent from printers' prefaces that they did not all scorn plays. Creede, for example, says in his preface to the reader of Fletcher's *Cupid's Revenge*, 1615: "It is a custom used by some Writers in this Age to Dedicate their Playes to worthy persons, as well as their other works; and there is reason for it, because they are the best Minervaes of their braine, and expresse more puritie of conceit in the ingenious circle of an Act or Scaene, then is to be found in the vast circumference of larger Volumnes." While plays probably had not, in the eyes of most publishers, the dignity of privileged works, it is clear that they were in demand. They were popular; and they were comparatively small investments. Men who could get the larger privileged works would naturally prefer these because of a surer market for the class of works represented and because the margin of profit was probably larger. Stationers with small capital would naturally be interested in smaller works (if unable to secure the privileged ones). And, as the market for plays was apparently fluctuating, depending on the whims of public taste, the speculative feature of play-printing naturally attracted some of the stationers of the lower class. But this is not the same as admitting that all plays published by such men were surreptitious or piratical. When we find a play printed by a Danter, Pavier, Ward, or Jaggard, we have reason for suspicion, for investigation—but certainly not for an assumption, without proof, of irregular or illicit printing.

[17] Int. to Folio ed. of *Richard III*, pp. xx–xxi.

CHAPTER V.

SOURCES OF PLAY TEXTS PRINTED

Legitimate and Illegitimate Sources

It must be admitted at the beginning that many editors, bibliographers, and critics of literature are still approaching early printed texts of plays with the assumption that they must necessarily be illegitimate, unauthorized. The reasons for this attitude have been discussed. It is true, we do not now, like Pope, refer to the various editions of Shakespeare as "whole heaps of trash," but we have still too many broad generalizations, such as the declaration by Hon. D. H. Madden in *Shakespeare and His Fellows* (p. 58):

Of the thirty-six plays included in the First Folio, sixteen had been published in quarto from 'diverse stolen and surreptitious copies, maimed and deformed by the frauds and stealthes of incurious impostors that expos'd them.'

It is refreshing to contrast with such generalizations the discriminating and scholarly classifications of Mr. A. W. Pollard in his *Shakespeare Folios and Quartos*, which seems to me his most important and most permanent contribution to Shakespeare literature. In his more recent work, *Shakespeare's Fight with the Pirates*, Mr. Pollard concludes that the players handed to the printers the texts of fourteen plays of Shakespeare for quarto publication, three of them being improved versions for re-issue.

Mr. Pollard's "bad quartos," *Romeo and Juliet*, *Henry V.*, *Merry Wives*, and *Hamlet*, are pretty generally regarded as open to suspicion. As to Q. 1 of *Hamlet*, there has been of late some change of attitude. Mr. F. G. Hubbard's study of the text[1] even presents it in the light of a possibly legitimate issue on the basis of playhouse copy.

Favoring the assumption of legitimacy of a text are: an author's dedication or preface, an actor's dedication or preface,

---

[1] *Univ. of Wis. Studies in English*, 1920; his study is continued in *P.M.L.A.*, XXXVIII (1923).

the printing of the author's name, and of the exact stage history of the play, the good repute of the stationer (difficult to ascertain reliably), the entry of the play to this publisher on the Stationers' Registers in the regular manner, the purity of the text (again a matter to be decided only by one who knows texts of the period), and the presence of marks indicative of origin in a playhouse manuscript. These marks differ in value, of course. Not one alone could safely be taken as a mark of legitimacy or the opposite, though judgments are often based upon as little evidence.

Theories as to Sources of Play Copy

The legitimate means of acquiring copy for texts of drama are conceivably three. (1) The printer might purchase from the author if he in any way retained the right to have his play put into print, or if he later made arrangements with the acting company for the publication of his works. But this was perhaps not often done even when, as in the case of Jonson, Middleton, Brome, Marston, and Heywood, for example, the authors saw their plays through the press.[2] (2) The stationer might purchase from the company as a whole, or, more commonly, from its manager or its authorized representative the copyright for a play. The Shakespeare Folio and the Beaumont and Fletcher Folio illustrate normal methods of acquisition of copy. (3) The stationer might buy copy from a single actor as an individual, who had bought up the copyright with the stage-right of a play. According to available evidence, this happened occasionally but not usually. Alleyn and Slaughter and Beeston as managers of companies bought many play copies. There is some evidence that Allen and Slaughter, at least, also purchased as individuals.

Various illegitimate means are suggested by which play manuscripts might be acquired by enterprising publishers: picking up stray manuscripts which belonged to the author or his friends, or to the actor or his friends, or to the whole company; hiring scriveners to make copies of playhouse manuscripts; hiring shorthand reporters to secure the text from performances, or hiring memorizers for part or all of the matter;

[2] Sir Sidney Lee (*Life of Shakespeare* (1916), p. 297), says: "The companies usually forbade under heavy penalties the author's sale to a publisher of a play which had been acted." I have no evidence for this statement.

patching up a play from the roles of one or more actors, with the aid of a hack poet, it was thought, in the old days, and nowadays, with the editorial and creative artistry of an actor-pirate turned text-maker. One of the most recent theories is of a pirate-actor playing from one to six roles renovating an old abridged acting version (as, of one of the four "bad quartos"), furnishing his own new parts more or less accurately, and in some mysterious fashion remodeling the others to resemble the latest stage version, all the while being handicapped by lack of exact knowledge of any of the new version except as he found it in his own roles. Let us consider briefly the plausibility of some of these theories.

First, as to lost, stolen, or borrowed manuscripts. If one were to accept the idea that finding was having, this would no doubt be the largest source of illegitimate play copy. It is, however, impossible for one who faces the facts to regard this as an *allowed* procedure. That it happened on occasion may be readily granted. That it happened oftener then than nowadays may also be conceded, but that it was considered a right or normal source of play copy for the printer is an untenable position. Miss Sheavyn, in *The Literary Profession in the Elizabethan Age* (p. 78), says: "No complaint is so often met with as that of the theft and illicit sale of manuscripts," but, so far as drama is concerned, I have seen *very few*. The notion that, if a manuscript were to be lost, some pirate would inevitably print it has given rise to that fiction of the close guarding of the manuscript, the destroying of manuscript, etc. to keep it out of print.

In view of the common practice, among authors, of allowing manuscripts to circulate, with no intention of abandonment of rights in them, I cannot believe in the extreme inaccessibility of even play manuscripts that is insisted upon by various writers, from Charles Reade to Sir Sidney Lee. There were too many loop-holes of escape to make it possible to believe that the retention of manuscripts was the sole, or even chief, safe-guarding of theatrical companies' rights in plays. Of course, if a company resolved firmly that a certain play ought not to be printed, they would naturally tend to limit unnecessary multiplication of copies, so as not to expose its stage rights unduly to dishonest persons. But, so far as I know, not a scrap of evidence has ever been produced to prove that it was the custom of the companies to keep all manuscripts under lock and key, or that they ever wilfully destroyed manuscripts to keep the plays out of print. A great many statements abut the treatment of dramatic manuscripts are ventured upon without proof. For example, Sir Sidney Lee declares:

> No genuine respect was paid to a dramatic author's original drafts after they reached the playhouse. Scenes and passages were freely erased by the managers, who became the owners, and other alterations were made for stage purposes. Ultimately the dramatist's corrected autograph was copied by the playhouse scrivener; this transcript became the official "prompt copy" and the original was set aside and destroyed, its uses being exhausted.[3]

This scrivener's copy was, according to Lee, often the copy used for publication (p. xii.). In view of the frequent revivals of plays and their representations before various audiences of city, town, and court, one would assume that a manager who had good sense might be glad to have on hand more than one version of a successful play, especially if the extra version happened to be the original document. We have in print so many widely varying versions of plays that it looks as if some of them are, as they make claim, really adapted stage versions, and others, as the authors or editors assert, the original versions. Of course the preservation of originals might in such cases be attributed either to the company or to the author; but it is generally assumed that the author's draft had to be used by the company in getting it licensed if it were a new play. If it were not, the Master of the Revels would be supposed to have required a clean copy for legibility, as he does seem to have required on occasion. At any rate, it is safe to assume that the company owned the author's draft, as a rule, when it got the license; and why it should destroy it is difficult to imagine.

The scrivener's copy figures largely as a source of the printed text with Sir Sidney Lee:

> More frequently the publisher would hire a scrivener, or perhaps an actor, into procuring for him a rough copy of the play which had been carelessly transcribed for some subordinate purpose of the playhouse. Such a transcript seldom proved faithful to the author's intention. In most instances it was unsparingly abridged, or it was defaced by actors'

[3] Int. to First Folio, xvii.

interpolations, and by ignorant errors of the copyist which the printer's reader made little effort to amend.[4]

Copies of this copy also, he believes, were often used as sources.

Many copies of a popular play were made for the actors or their patrons, and if one of these copies chanced to fall into a publisher's hands, it was issued without any endeavour to obtain either author's or manager's sanction.[5]

It is a fact that the companies, or some of them, had bookkeepers, and that they might see to copies being made when original manuscripts had to be subjected to too great alterations. Henry Herbert wrote an order (June, 1633) in regard to *The Seaman's Honest Wife*: "I command your Bookeeper to present me with a faire Copy hereaft. and to leave out all oathes,[6] prophaness, & publick Ribaldry as he will answer it at his perill."

It is true also that there were split off parts, or actors' roles, in use, and that the book-keeper revised them or had them revised when corrections necessitated this. Herbert, in connection with the censoring of *The Woman's Prize, or the Tamer Tamed*, ordered Mr. Knight, the book-keeper of the company: "Purge ther partes, as I have the booke." (*Var.*, III, 208-210). Daborne, writing to Henslowe in regard to his delay on the play *Machiavel*, for which he had been mostly paid in advance of completion, said he had taken great pains with the end and altered a scene. "This they have now in parts." (*Henslowe's Diary*, ed. Greg, II, 142). An example of an actor's part may be seen in Alleyn's title role of Orlando Furioso (*Ibid.*, Appx. III). It is entirely possible that some of these "parts" may have been secured and used by an unscrupulous printer in bringing an old version up to date in a portion of the work; and this may account for the great inequalities of some puzzling texts. It should not, however, be pushed too far or assumed as explaining anything if there is not in the text some special evidence of such an origin of the copy.

[4] Int. to First Folio, *xii*.   [5] *Life of W. Shakespeare* (1916), page 100.

[6] Bullen, *Old Plays*, II, 32. See also, on the bookkeeper as playhouse scrivener (1620–40), W. W. Greg, "Prompt copies, Private transcripts," etc. "Tr. of the Bibliogr. Soc'y,"n.s., VI 2(1925), 148ff. Cf. F. P. Wilson, "Ralph Crane, Scrivener", *Ibid.*, VII. 2 (1926), 194.

As to the throwing aside of manuscripts of special versions, such as those for court performance, when the immediate uses were fulfilled, (see Fleay, *Stage*, 364), this does not fit in with the other notions held by those who believe there was no stage-right. It is not necessary to suppose that all playhouse manuscripts were kept locked up and each actor could know only his role or roles (an idea which would not appeal to one who had ever acted much, I fancy); nor, on the other hand, do we need to imagine that manuscripts of plays were strewn thick about the theatre. A reasonable degree of precaution was no doubt taken to preserve the manuscripts.

Middleton was able, many years later, to get back the manuscript of his play *The Witch* (presumably from the King's players) to send it or a copy of it to a friend. He wrote to Thomas Holmes:

Noble Sir,
As a true testimony of my ready inclination to your service, I have, merely upon a taste of your desire, recovered into my hands, though not without much difficulty, this ignorantly illfated labour of mine. Witches are, ipso facto, by the law condemned, and that only, I think, hath made her lie so long in an imprisoned obscurity. For your sake alone she hath thus far conjured herself abroad.[7]

The authors' manuscripts of Beaumont's and Fletcher's plays seem to have been preserved, in many cases. The Folio published, apparently by consent of the company, in 1647 contains an assurance of the stationer to the reader (dated Feb. 14, 1646): "I had the Originalls from such as received them from the Authours themselves." All the plays are here, he says, except the "Wildgoose Chase, which hath beene long lost, and I feere irrecoverable; for a Person of Quality borrowed it from the Actours many yeares since, and (by the negligence of a Servant) it was never return'd; therefore now I put up this *Si quis*, that whosoever hereafter happily meets with it shall be thankfully satisfied if he please to send it home." He goes on to explain the origin of the new matter in the reprinted texts as being traceable to the author's original versions:

One thing I must answer before it bee objected; 'tis this: when these *Comedies* and Tragedies were presented on the Stage, the *Actours*

[7] Bullen, *O. E. Plays*. *The Witch* was not published until 1778. The MS is at the Bodleian.

omitted some *Scenes* and Passages (with the Authours' consent) as occasion led them; and when private friends desir'd a copy, they then (and justly too) transcribed what they Acted. But now you have both All that was Acted and all that was not; even the perfect full Originalls without the least mutilation; So that were the Authours living, (and sure they can never dye) they themselves would challenge neither more nor less than what is here published.

Apparently, original manuscripts were carefully preserved in this case; but, on the other hand, there was no locking up or denying access to stage versions. Free circulation, rather, is implied.

An example of such circulation is found in a manuscript of *The Humorous Lieutenant* (*Wynn MSS* at Peniarth) dated Nov. 27, 1625, written by Ralphe Crane and dedicated by him to "Sir Kelham Digbie, Knight." Crane says he knows that to a man of Digby's religious nature a "divine argument" would be more welcome, but hopes that after so sad a season the comedy will not be inopportune. The play was not printed until 1647.[8]

Another extant illustration of the private transcript is a copy of *The Tell-Tale*, a five act comedy (*Dulwich MSS*, no. 20). A "fair copy" made for the licenser, Herbert, of Beaumont and Fletcher's *Honest Man's Fortune* (acted 1613) is in the Dyce Library.

Sir Sidney Lee believes that original manuscripts were lost in the Globe fire, and that private transcripts or licenser's copies helped out in the printing of the Shakespeare Folio. It is as well, I suppose, to burn the author's manuscripts in the Globe fire as to "throw them aside." It really seems more sensible if they must be got rid of.

As to Sir Sidney Lee's "scrivener," it may be said that though one might be employed at times to copy manuscripts for the licenser if he required "fair copies," we are not driven to assume a playhouse scrivener for preparing all manuscripts for the company unless for copying separate roles. There are extant manuscripts of plays with licenses for acting appended, which appear to have been made use of later for prompt copies without re-copying.

[8] Beaumont and Fletcher, *Works*, Cambridge series, II, 508–09. See also a note of manuscript copies of plays, Sir Sidney Lee, *Life of Shakespeare*, (1916,) p. 558. Often in such transcripts stage directions are omitted.

Examples of extant autograph manuscripts of plays are: Anthony Munday's *John à Kent and John à Comber*, Dec., 1596; *Sir Thomas More* (by Munday, Dekker, and others, c. 1600)[9] and Massinger's *Believe as You List*, 1631. An examination of the facsimile of *Sir Thomas More* with all due allowance for ravages of time will convince one that the complaints made of illegibility of manuscripts by the Master of Revels were not unfounded, and that one must always, in considering the errors of a printed text, keep bad handwriting, cancels, changes of location of passages, etc., in mind as a possible cause.

Mr. A. W. Pollard has recently developed a somewhat elaborate theory, based in part upon the bibliographical facts found in the texts, that certain of the manuscripts handed to the players were in Shakespeare's autograph, and in other cases an autograph manuscript was used as a prompt copy and eventually reached the press. The reader should consult Mr. Pollard's chapter in *Shakespeare's Fight with the Pirates* on the manuscripts of Shakespeare's plays for his own statement of this theory, because in such an argument the skill in presentation counts for much. As in his large earlier work, Mr. Pollard here makes use of his known bibliographical data, but there is in the recent work a larger superstructure of theory. This is true also of the recent *Times* articles by Pollard and Wilson on sources of Shakespeare texts. An example of the necessity of building up such theory may be found in Mr. Pollard's edition of *Richard II*. He thus reasons out the source of the copy (pp. 96-97):

> A clean copy may have been made at the same time for the use of the prompter, or .... the author's own manuscript may have been taken for the purpose..... It seems probable .... that the clean copy made by the scrivener would have been considered better worth keeping than the author's draft, and that thus, whether there was one complete copy or two, it was probably the one in Shakespeare's handwriting which (with the Deposition scene cut out) reached the printer.

Mr. Pollard then produces examples of "sound errors" to show that the printer, Sims, probably dictated the text to a com-

---

[9] See Greg's edition of this for the Malone Society, 1911, and his article, *Mod. Lang. Rev.*, VIII, 89. Cf. Sir Ed. Maunde Thompson, "The Autograph Manuscripts of Anthony Munday," Bibl. Soc'y, *Tr.*, XIV (1915-17), 325-57, and *Shakespeare's Hand in 'Sir Thomas More,'* Camb. Univ. Press, 1923. A list of MS plays is in E. K. Chambers, *Elizabethan Stage*, IV, appx. iv.

positor (contrary to the usual custom of compositors). Having reached this conclusion, he finds the cause of such procedure in the fact that the manuscript was probably "not written in a specially clerkly hand." This not very good hand we must then assume to be Shakespeare's. "Finally," he says, "we really want to get rid of Shakespeare's autograph at the very earliest possible moment, because if it remained in existence for any length of time many people must be seriously blamed for not having made much better use of it."

Now although this theory may be absolutely right, and is certainly ingenious and interesting, I would call attention to the necessity under which the modern editor labors of resorting to successive hypotheses in his effort to solve the puzzle as to the derivation of a text.

Characteristics of Playhouse Manuscripts

As a good many problems turn on the nature of the manuscript supposed to underlie a text, students find it of interest to examine extant playhouse manuscripts to determine their chief characteristics. The B. M. Egerton MS 1994, a folio of about 350 pages, contains 15 manuscript plays. Three have been printed by Mr. Bullen. They are *The Lady Mother*, *Dick of Devonshire*, and *The Captives*. Halliwell-Phillips in 1870 reprinted *A Tragedy of King Richard the Second*. Mr. Boas has been studying others with a view to editing. The manuscript is supposed to have been the property of an actor, William Cartwright, who bequeathed it to Dulwich College. Of the plays contained in it, *The Lady Mother* and *The lanching of the Mary* are obviously original playhouse manuscripts, and Mr. Boas also regards the following as being of the same origin: *The Captives*, *Edmond Ironside*, the Charlemagne romance play, *Richard II*, and *Two Noble Ladies*.[10] Among the reasons which

---

[10] See F. S. Boas, "A Seventeenth Century Repertoire," *The Library*, VIII (1917), 225–240. For signs of playhouse origin, these plays are interesting for comparative study: *Barnavelt*, *Believe as You List*, *Love's Pilgrimage*, *The Spanish Curate*, and *The Custom of the Country*. Mr. Boas has an account of *The Lanchinge of the Mary* in "Stage Censorship under Chas. I," *London Times*, *Lit. Sup.*, December 14, 1917 (614) and December 21 (636). On the significance of actors' names in the text, see Allison Gaw, "Actors' Names in Shakespearean Texts," *P.M.L.A.*, XL (1925), 530 ff.

Mr. Boas gives for his opinion are: many bracketings and cancels, some of which are due to criticism by the Master of the Revels; some cuts to shorten as if for stage adaptation; the insertions of extra notes of entries and exits; the provision of properties, as of thunder, etc. Such a note as "storm continued" would be a clue to this type of manuscript. The advance provision of the properties is a very good evidence. In one play pen and ink are called for, and sixteen lines above the point where they are needed appears the note, "Ink: paper ready." Actors' names are also inserted in many plays of this group. Necessary directions for music, shouts, knocks, etc., appear, and some for change of properties. "Bed put forth" (*II Henry VI*, III, 2) somewhat suggests playhouse origin, but it could be a reporter's description of what was done. By comparing several such notes, one can usually see whether they are imperative directions in the practical and condensed forms suitable for the stage, or whether they are descriptive or literary comments. This is not saying that a manuscript of genuine playhouse origin might not very well be so edited that these directions in a printed text would be transformed into literary (descriptive) notes, such as, say, in Shakespeare's *The Tempest*. But if one has the manuscript itself or a facsimile or a very slightly edited text like some of the early quartos, the marks of the playhouse manuscript are often clear enough.

A clear example of these marks may be found in Robert Yarington's *Two Plays in One* (1601) edited by A. H. Bullen (*O. E. Plays*, IV, 1885). Here the stage directions precede actual entry of characters. In the middle of a speech, in the Induction by Avarice is the direction, "Enter Trueth." Fourteen lines below she is pointed out as being present, and nineteen lines below, begins to speak. In Act 1, sc. 1 Merry's speech is interrupted by such directions as "Enter Beech and a friend" and "sit in his shop". In the midst of other speeches are such orders as, "Kiss, embrace;" "strive curtesies;" "Maister Beech drinkes; drinke Neighbour;" "goe up the lather;" "then Merry must passe to Beeches shoppe, who must sit in his shop, and Winchester his boy stand by;" "Beech reading;" "Then being in the upper Rome Merry strickes him in the head fifteen times;" "when the boy goeth into the shoppe, Merrie striketh six blowes on his head and with the seaventh leaves the hammer sticking in his head; the boy groaning must be heard by a maide who must crye to her maister;" "brings him forth in a chaire with a hammer sticking in his head; they survey his wounds." The asides are here often labeled "To the People."

In some plays known to derive from playhouse manuscripts actors' names are inserted for the characters. Because of this fact and because this seemed to be the most natural inference to draw from their presence, it is frequently declared that actors' names are an infallible sign of a playhouse manuscript. But an absent-minded author writing with a well-known actor in mind might accidentally make such a slip, and the error might be copied in other than true playhouse versions. Also it is entirely possible that a shorthand reporter might be more familiar with a player's name than with the part he took in the play, and therefore insert the name of the player either by accident or with intention of looking up his role later. Examples of the insertion of actors' names may be found in *Romeo and Juliet*, Q^2, 1599 (IV,5); "Enter Will Kemp," in place of Peter a servingman; in *Much Ado*, Q. of 1600 (IV,2), Kemp and Cowley inserted for Dogberry and Verges; *3 Henry VI* (1623), Gabriel (Spenser) and Sinklo (John Sinkler?) and Humfrey (Humphrey Jeffes), actors, named in the stage directions. In *George a Greene, the Pinner of Wakefield*, (ed. J. C. Collins, 1905) stage directions give the name John. The Earl of Kendal says to John, "Say, John Taylor, what news with King James?" As John is a servant, the use of the full name is unusual. In sc. 13, George says, "Here, Will Perkins, take my purse." Will Perkins is not in the stage directions. *George a Greene* is a peculiarly confused text of very problematic origin, with its cuts, its jumble of prose and verse, and its confusion (as in Act IV, sc. 3). It is worth some study by one interested in origin of texts of printed plays.

A fairly large proportion of the dramatic texts printed between 1580 and 1640 will be found either to put forth a claim or to give external evidence of playhouse origin (whether with or without editorial revision). I think it will eventually be recognized that, in spite of their manifold imperfections of text, the rule, rather than the exception, was that these playhouse manuscripts were acquired by the stationers in some legitimate fashion. I have attempted to show some reasons why this may be so.

Some support for this opinion may be found in the history of the changes that the play texts undergo in the new issues. We have numerous examples of successive revisions by authors, as in plays of Jonson and Heywood, or as in John Day's *Parliament of the Bees*. The presence of interpolations in re-issues, as in the 1616 Q. of Marlowe's *Doctor Faustus*, which, imperfect as it is, seems to have some of Marlowe's changes as well as additions by others, would seem to indicate a close relationship between stage and press in the matter of keeping editions of plays up to contemporary stage versions. Some of the much advertised additions of new matter are no doubt improvised actor's stuff rather than changes by the author. Brome in his *Antipodes*, 1638, lets Letoy, in advising actors for his private stage, discuss the practice of actors' interpolations.:

> But you Sir are incorrigible and
> Take licence to your selfe, to adde unto
> Your parts, your owne free fancy; and sometimes
> To alter, or diminish what the writer
> With care and skill compos'd; and when you are
> To speake to your co-actors in the scene,
> You hold interloqutions with the Audients.
>
> *Bip.* That is a way my Lord has bin allow'd
> On elder stages to move mirth and laughter.
> *Letoy.* Yes, in the days of Tarlton and Kempe,
> Before the stage was purg'd from barbarisme,
> And brought to the perfection it now shines with.

Cuts, as well as insertions in new editions of a play, must also be considered as possibly emanating from a new stage version instead of being made by the author freshly for publication. The additions, however, are more relevant to our purpose. When the Parliament scene is restored to *Richard II* in 1608, we need not, certainly, assume a fresh piracy unless the more corrupt text of that portion requires such explanation. Play-titles of new editions often advertise the acting by other companies after the original quarto appeared. This could be, and probably was occasionally, an advertising hoax intended to deceive the buyer into thinking he was going to get the latest version. But, inasmuch as the works so advertised often do contain new matter, we must consider each case in itself. At any rate, it is clear that in some way it was entirely possible for an enterprising publisher to get many a printed play altered to keep up with the stage version. And the custom was so prevalent that I cannot believe the company was heartily opposed to it except when it meant cheating them out of the purchase price. Rightly considered, it would be a means of mutual advertising for the actors of the new version and the printers.

Possible Ways of Pirating Playhouse Versions

The usual method of accounting for this obviously close relationship between the drama text and the recent stage version is by assuming some kind of piracy that permits of securing the most recent version as it is given on the stage. One of these theories is, piracy by a traitor-actor. In the old days, he was the poor or wicked actor who stole the playhouse manuscript and sent it to the press for his private profit. He is a rather appealing character, but now out of the fashion. The traitor-actor, new style, is oftener a minor, than a major, one, but an actor who has perhaps several roles owing to the smallness of the acting company. The new theory, of course, is of but limited application and would work best (if at all) with plays which are very "spotty" as to correctness, and whose spots are pretty regularly in harmony with the actor's supposed roles. One of the beauties of the theory will immediately suggest itself. The theorizer may examine the text and then pick out the roles he wishes to assign to his pirate actor. One can imagine a text where this might be done convincingly. The question is, whether it can be worked with any extant play-texts so as to convince others than the theorizer. There are, as we shall see later, some difficulties.

The other method commonly used to explain derivation of early printed texts from playhouse versions is that of hiring someone to secure them by memorizing or by stenographic reporting, the latter being the more usual assumption. This theory also is of limited application. Attempts are made to apply it only to corrupt texts, on the assumption that the stenography of the time could not give the basis for a goood text.

The "Traitor-Actor" Theory

Let us consider first some phases of the pirate-actor theory Greg's handling of this in the *Merry Wives of Windsor* is one of the most elaborate and careful studies. It appears in the introduction to his edition of the 1602 Q. of that play for the Clarendon Press in 1910 (Tudor and Stuart Library). The text is generally admitted to be very corrupt and to show essential differences in both matter and order, as well as wording, from the text of the Folio (the second quarto, a Jaggard reprint of 1619, being negligible). Even the Folio text is a bit unusual in the style of its editing for the press. Exits and entries are left out and lists of characters head the scenes of the Folio text, as in the 1616 Jonson folio. The oaths have been toned down as if in conformity with the statute. The Folio text still shows some gaps and evidences of reconstruction of plot incompletely carried out. Both the nature of the play and its reception may have something to do with the leaving of the text in a somewhat unsatisfactory condition. On the whole, however, the Folio text is a markedly better version, the last act in particular showing vital differences.

The early editors of the *Merry Wives of Windsor* made the Quarto a crude early sketch of a play later elaborated. Daniel attributed the quarto text to a shortened stage version based on the same original text as the later revised Folio, and reported by a literary hack who rewrote the product of his memory and longhand notes, with perhaps the aid of short-hand notes here and there. Most of the editors recognize the existence of a shortened stage version which the Quarto may represent, though very imperfectly. Several have assumed that this shortened stage version was pirated by stenography to give the quarto text.

Greg rejects the stenography on the ground that a memorizer could report the play as satisfactorily as is here done. This position may be correct, but it is still worth while to test the play for possible reporting by stenography, as a bad stenographer might give as bad a text as a bad memorizer. Mr. Greg, however, considers that the Quarto represents in part, at least, the work of some sort of reporter of the spoken drama. The question is, how to isolate his work. He proposes, very wisely, to consider the differences between the Folio text and the Quarto which may properly be attributed to an authorized reviser of a text which also underlies the Quarto version; and also, the differences which might be attributed to a stage adapter cutting and rewriting the play in parts for acting on special occasions. This is, of course, the only intelligent way to proceed in dealing with the work of a reporter where one is comparing two widely differing versions of a text; yet, strangely enough, it is disregarded by many theorizers as to sources of text.

Mr. Greg's theory of the derivation of the Quarto text of *Merry Wives* is that Busby (who entered the text for publication but promptly transferred it) got it surreptitiously through a pirate or traitor-actor who played the part of the Host, and reported with a fair degree of correctness those scenes in which he was on the stage (eight in number according to the Folio text). He picked up a good deal of the other actors' parts by hearing them on the stage, remembering best those most interwoven with his own. The versions, according to Greg (p. xxxix),

spring into substantial agreement when he comes on and lapse into paraphrase when he quits. But when he disappears for good and all at the end of Act IV (and the actor very likely went home or to the tavern) we find what remains of the play in a more miserably garbled condition than any previous portion.

In considering this theory, it must be kept in mind that our only way to test the accuracy in the Host's reporting is by the resemblance of the Quarto at certain points to the Folio text, which at other points diverges so widely that any comparison is frankly impossible. Mr. Greg assumes that the pirate actor "learned his part imperfectly and very probably by ear, substituting passable makeshift if he forgot the actual words." With this much allowance, it is exceedingly difficult to check on such a theory.

As to the last act, Mr. Greg assumes that a reviser supplied two alternative versions, one for court use and one for the public stage. If this is so, is it absolutely necessary to send the Host home or to the tavern? And why did a business man like Busby (or Creede) hire an actor to report a play if he had no source of information as to the lines of his fellow-actors except by hearing them and memorizing them in the course of his own acting in scenes with them, and if he was known to be out of the last act altogether? It seems unbusinesslike, that selection of the Host.

Another difficult assumption is that, when a new fifth act was substituted, the actors became lazy and made a poor attempt to learn the new dialogue. "They possibly felt some resentment at the interference which threw extra work on their shoulders, and introduced bits of gag containing sly allusions to forbidden matter." Unless one can prove extremely short time given the actors to learn new parts, this seems a bit forced. Plays were revamped in those days at such a rate that actors of a good company must have been thoroughly broken in to the necessity of learning new parts.

The difficulties in tracing resemblances between the Folio and Quarto versions of the scenes where the Host is on the stage may be suggested by the following instances: II, iii, 19 ff, the cue for the host to enter is entirely different; III, i, 65, the cue differs, a different speaker even preceding the Host; IV, iii, the cue and the first speech of the Host differ; IV, v. 1, the cue from the preceding scene is quite different. I am not at all sure that we should expect close verbal resemblances in these texts, but, as Greg's theory depends on them, let us examine a few instances where the Host is on the stage and there is sufficient resemblance in the action to justify a comparison of the wording of Folio and Quarto. II, i shows only occasional resemblances when the Host is on stage. Again, in Act II, sc. 3, line 23 of the Folio, the Host's speech runs:

> To see thee passe thy puncto, thy stock, thy reverse, thy distance, thy montant: Is he dead, my Ethiopian? Is he dead, my Francisco, ha Bully? What saies my Esculapius? My Galien? My heart of Elder? ha? is he dead bully-stale?—is he dead?

The pirate-actor renders this speech of his own in this fashion:

> .... the punto. The stock, the reverse, the distance: the montnce is a dead my francoyes? Is a dead my Ethiopian? Ha what says my gallon? my escuolapis? Is a dead bullies taile, is a dead?

The whole scene is badly reported. Some of the Folio speeches of this scene are stuck into an earlier one in the Quarto (II, 1); speeches of Caius are omitted, and two of the Host's own speeches are assigned to the Doctor. The Host was clearly not at home nor at the tavern in this scene, but if he was hired to act as reporter, he was not "on his job." The errors do not seem to me to be such as an actor would be likely to make (nor yet all a compositor's), and there are differences extending throughout the scene. The imitation French is thicker in the Quarto. The *alon, alon, alon* of the Doctor which, as Greg says, may have originated in "a bit of gag," corresponds to the Host's

'Let us wag' and Caius 'Come at my heels' of the Folio. One may remark in passing, that *if* the Host reported this scene, he seems to have tried to report what he heard rather than what he saw in MS. The *tarche un pettit, tarche a little* (296 of the Quarto) which Mr. Greg explains as based on a mishearing or else "some corruption of an actor's gag," is probably someone's effort to spell an actor's rendering of the Old French word *targe*, wait, a command addressed to the messenger about to take the letter. If not that, it must have been made from some corrupt form such as *tarde*, with the *de* of the MS read as *che*. Numerous readings occur which indicate that a very illegible manuscript underlay the quarto text. This fact causes little trouble for Mr. Greg, but is not properly allowed for by those who attribute the text to stenographic report.

A scene which would put a severe strain on Mr. Greg's theory is III,1 after the Host appears (lines 65-103). In the first 10 lines after his entry, Page's speech is attributed to Shallow, the Host's own speech split between Host and Shallow, Caius' two speeches combined and re-worded, and Evans' dropped out. There is certainly not much to argue from to prove that the Host reported thus. This scene, it is true, is probably cut in the Quarto; but even in the speeches of the Host himself where there is some resemblance, one wonders why there would not be more if he were the reporter. For example, the Host says:

What say you to young Mr. Fenton? He capers, he dances, he has eies of youth: he writes verses, he speakes holliday, he smels April and May, he wil carry 't, he will carry 't, 'tis in his buttons, he will carry 't.

It is fair to compare with this an obvious attempt to reproduce substantially the same passage in the Quarto:

But what say you to young Maister Fenton? He capers, he dances, he writes verses, he smelles all April and May; he wil cary it, he wil carit, Tis in his betmes he wil carite.

Let the Host write as badly as you like, and there is still something suggested as a further cause of such corruption—haste in the grasping of oral delivery, which need certainly not have troubled the Host, who had both memory and manuscript of that part.

[11] *Mod. Lang. Rev.*, X (1915), 171–80.

Again, IV, v, 64 ff., after the entry of Bardolph, when the Host speaks:

Host. Where be my horses?
　　　Speake well of them varletto.
Bar. Run away with the cozoners, for so soon as I came beyond Eaton, they threw me off from behind one of them in a slough of myre; and set spurres and away: like the Germans divels: three Doctor Faustasses.

The Quarto has this reading:

Why man, where be my horses? Where be the Germanes. Rid away with your horses? After I came beyond Maidenhead, they flung me in a slow of myre and away they ran.

It omits the next speech of the Host. The reference to Germans is quite clear in the Folio, but not in the Quarto. This whole scene is little indicative of the use of Host as reporter. In the Folio Evans speaks of "three cozen-Jermans that has cozend all the Hosts of three places of horses and money," and then Caius comes in and tells that there is no "Duke de Jarmaine that the Court is know." In the Quarto the Doctor mentions a German duke who has come to court and cosened the hosts of two places. And then Sir Hugh comes in and refers to "three sorts of cosen garmombles that have cosened in two places." In the Folio the Host then cries out, *Huy and cry (villaine)* etc. In the Q. the Host says *Hugh, and coy Bardolfe.* The last error may be due to manuscript (for *hu. and cry*, perhaps); but the rest is difficult to explain as indicating any close resemblance of texts suggestive of report by the Host.

A scene which is much more rapid in the Quarto (IV,vi) reduces 46 lines to 13 and makes changes of content. This, too, shows scant resemblance where the Host is on stage.

On the whole, the verbal resemblances of the Host's own speeches in quarto and folio are perhaps a little more striking than those of any other character, though single speeches of Falstaff show a more marked similarity. But resemblances of speeches of other characters when the Host is on stage do not seem to me to be sufficient to support Mr. Greg's theory. The reader, however, may base his conclusions upon his own comparisons. Even if one is not convinced by Mr. Greg's pirate-actor theory, his analysis of the text remains of great value.

On common-sense grounds, the pirate-actor theory has many a priori difficulties. Two appear pre-eminently in Mr. Greg's study. One is that, though the actor had his own part, presumably, in manuscript, he seems to prefer to give a garbled text of his own speeches from memory. Why would not a businesslike stationer buy the use of his role, rather than his memory? And the actor's parts do not seem to have been used. Another difficulty appears in every application of this theory. It is, the unwisdom of the stationer's hiring an actor to report from memory the scenes when he was on stage, if it were understood that he could not get hold of the scenes where he was not to appear. If these amount to one-fifth or more of the whole play, the difficulty is great; but it is there in any case. Any person in the audience equipped with a pencil and paper or even a fair memory would make a better pirate than an actor who frequently had less opportunity (according to the holders of the theory) than the audience to hear the whole play. If an actor is a useful pirate, it is because he has or can get roles or whole play manuscripts. As a reporter, editor, or hack poet, he has, as a type, no special advantages that I can see. When he is acting, he should have his mind on his lines and his actions, not on reporting others' speeches from memory. One can imagine what a play text might look like if reported from memory by an actor who had not taken pains to memorize the whole play and who used no manuscripts; but I never saw a text which looked to me like such a product.

As a matter of fact, I suppose the Elizabethan actors had no such severe handicaps as the holders of this theory make them work under. Aside from neglecting to use manuscripts of their own roles, the pirate-actors are usually supposed to be out of hearing of the parts of others except when on stage with them or waiting in the wings. This presupposes that an actor did not read the whole play through or see other scenes than his own acted or hear his fellow-actors deliver their lines. This would certainly produce an extremely bad lot of actors. Are we to suppose Elizabethan actors had no wish to understand the whole play and act in keeping with its spirit? This bogie of fear of piracy of stage-right or copyright in a play has led to very strange conclusions as to the customs of the Elizabethan theatre.

Mr. Henry D. Gray has another variety of pirate-actor theory in "The First Quarto Hamlet."[11] Here again the vast differences between the first and second Quartos and the Folio make comparison very difficult. The relationship of the texts must first be disposed of. Mr. Gray says that it is inconceivable that the uneven Q¹ represents Shakespeare's treatment, but the text is "not like the shorthand plays, because these are fairly even throughout." The one difficulty here is that nobody has yet proved which are "the shorthand plays," and so their evenness is a little difficult to pass upon.

On the basis of a comparison of Q¹ and the F¹ text, Mr. Gray concludes that Q¹ was pirated, and "based upon a very corrupt version of the acted play supplied to the publisher by the player who acted the part of Marcellus." This was filled in by a "hack poet." This is made to account for the fact that Act I has a fuller and better text, and that Marcellus' own speeches are better than others in Q¹. Marcellus gives the lines of others much better when in the scene himself, according to Mr. Gray. In every part but his own "there are many extreme and absurd blunders." As in the cast of the Host in *Merry Wives*, so the actor of Marcellus in Hamlet is assumed to have been "a man of considerable ignorance." A questionable example of this is the error of *invelmorable* for *invulnerable*, which is very likely as a manuscript error and very unlikely as an actor's misreporting. According to Mr. Gray, Marcellus had a good memory for indecencies and for rime tags. It was his promise to supply the text that led Roberts to enter the play, "and it was the following year before the manuscript was put into shape by the hack poet."

An investigation of Roberts's relationships with this company will, I believe, convince anyone that he would be unlikely to need or wish to get a play from a pirate-actor. If Marcellus could supply satisfactorily only those parts when he was on stage, a year is perhaps not too much time to allow the hack poet to work up the rest of the text. It is unlikely, however, that the company of actors would refrain from taking any action for an entire year after the entry was on the Registers in the name of the man who did the printing of their playbills.

In this theory of Mr. Gray's, Marcellus is allowed to hear the scenes when he is not on stage, but he reports them badly. The hack writer fills in deficiencies as needed. "He may very possibly

[11] *Mod. Lang. Rev.*, X (1915) 171–80.

have been materially aided in his task by attending a performance of the play." Why not several performances? And why not memorize or take notes? Mr. Gray's theory is interesting, but leaves unsolved a number of important textual problems; and those which it does account for are open to other solutions.

Certain characters might become fixed conceptions in the mind of the author early in his work on a play. Their lines may have been developed until they were felt to be satisfactory, even essential to the portrayal of these characters. Again, in reworking a play, there is always the possibility that the changes in plot will not affect some character enough to necessitate a change in his lines. These very simple facts may possibly explain the presence of better speeches for one or a few characters in a corrupt setting. Still another possibility is that, if a reporter in the audience took down the play or even memorized it, he may have followed one or a few actors (perhaps the roles of the same actor) better either because they were more interesting to him or because the actor talked better for the purpose of the note-taker or memorizer. Strikingly better speeches for one or a few characters might be a good argument for the employment of the actor's role in manuscript, but are not a proof that an actor *reported* the play so unevenly.

A new turn is given the pirate-actor theory by J. Dover Wilson and A. W. Pollard in "The 'Stolne and Surreptitious' Shakespeare Texts," *Times Lit. Suppl.*, Jan. 16, 1919. In connection with a theory accounting for a "flood of playhouse manuscripts" shortened for provincial playing and reaching the press about 1594, these scholars suggest that the success in selling these shortened versions based on partly revised manuscripts would depend on their resemblance to revised versions then in use on the stage. The shortened texts, were, it is supposed, touched up by a competent pirate—an actor. Leading players would not do for such work, because, as share-holders, "they would be cutting their own throats by turning pirate." But an actor of several small parts scattered rather evenly through the scenes would be a useful procurer of copy. He would fill out these shortened texts from his memory of what took place when he was on stage. This, they say, will explain all the phenomena of the bad quartos, if one grants the history of the 1593 transcripts as it is carefully worked out by Pollard and Wilson. The pirate-actor had to "fill up the 'cuts,' substitute up-to-date matter for the non-Shakespearian scenes, and generally make the old text look as much like the latest theatrical success as he could." They admit, however, that at times he leaves untouched "scenes which are glaringly pre-Shakespearian or gaping with the shortener's 'cuts'." Their reason for this is, that he cannot report these scenes because he is not on the stage when they are being played. He must, of course, change costume often, as he plays several small parts. An example is used from *Henry V.*, where he changes costume while thirty lines are spoken in the middle of a badly reported scene. The beginning and ending are done better because the pirate-actor is hanging around the stage-door to get them. "Loitering at the stage door is not likely to have been tolerated, except immediately after an exit or before an entry .... and too great an interest in the play on the part of an inferior actor might awake unwelcome situations." The player pirate could at times "copy out his 'player's part' and take it to the printer. For some reason, he does not often avail himself of this resource, and then only in the case of brief, detached speeches."

The test of the worth of this theory will be the detailed application to one or more texts. It has some a priori difficulties. For an actor of perhaps four or five small parts to fit his roles into the play with only cues overheard at the stage-door to go by would require that this actor of small parts have unusual histrionic talents. If there were such actors then, perhaps it is not going too far to endow them with the additional gifts of poets, playwrights, and editors of dramatic texts. They had their own roles in manuscript, but preferred to trust their memories, which were evidently feeble. They were hired to report plays in which they were known to be off-stage very frequently, though, according to this theory, anybody in the audience would have better opportunity of reporting those scenes in which they were off. For, being actors of small parts, they were regarded with suspicion if they tried to learn what the play was all about. One is inclined to wonder how an actor ever managed to rise in his profession and become a player of great parts in those dark days in the history of acting.

Now it is well-known that actors often had their own parts in manuscript in the time of Elizabeth. It is reasonable to suppose that they often heard the whole play—at least in rehearsal. It is also reasonable to suppose that in their association with fellow-actors outside the theatre, they could hear or read their lines on occasion. It is possible that many actors had access to a playhouse manuscript or a transcript of the entire play. We know that transcripts were sometimes made for the actors' friends. It is, then, quite probable that in every company there were a number of actors who had it in their power to furnish a stationer with a reliable text representing the current stage version. But the question is simply, was it worth while for an actor to risk his standing with the company by doing so without their consent? If we can now trace the guilty person by guess-work when we do not know the distribution of parts, would it not be quite easy for the company, who knew what each man played, to discover who had turned traitor? If so, it is unlikely that many pirated texts could be accounted for by such a theory.

Pirating by Memory

A possible source of many corrupt portions of texts obviously based in some way upon the actual performance but just as obviously not based on an authentic playhouse manuscript is the paid memorizer in the audience. Few modern Shakespeare critics are inclined to admit the possible significance of such a person as a source of text. The chief reason is, that the verbal memory of the average modern scholar is not so good that he would think he could reproduce a play himself from memory even as well as it is done in the corrupt texts that puzzle him. Mr. Greg, however, in editing *Merry Wives of Windsor*, gives the memorizer his dues. He says that, with no previous experience in dramatic piracy, he was able, after four visits to *John Bull's Other Island*, to reproduce all the material parts of the dialogue with sufficient accuracy to convey an idea of the play which was not seriously modified by subsequent reading. He believes he could easily have made new dialogue for the forgotten parts which would approximate the real text as closely as the Quarto of *Merry Wives* does the Folio. There are doubtless today many persons quite inferior to Mr. Greg in intellectual ability who could surpass this feat of memorizing. Moreover, the Elizabethans, as is well known, placed much more reliance upon verbal memory than we do today, and trained it better. It is but natural to suppose that it would be entirely possible for memorizers of the sixteenth and seventeenth centuries to supply a part or the whole of a play text with a fair degree of accuracy after several visits to the performance, if there were no better way of procuring a text.

The memorizer, however, does not seem to me a very plausible source for whole play texts. He may perhaps account for some apparently unauthorized attempts to bring old editions up to date by adding new matter being used on the stage.

The memorizer, like the hack-poet, is regarded as an old-fashioned creature, and is practically discarded by many of the Shakespeare critics of today. It seems reasonably certain, however, that the two did combine to pirate plays from the Spanish stage at the beginning of the seventeenth century. Lope de Vega, in the prologue to *El Peregrino en su Patria* (1603) and in the prologue to part XIII of his *Comedias* (1620) and elsewhere, alluded to the pirating of his plays by such means. In the latter prologue he remarks:

> To this must be added the stealing of *comedias* by those whom the vulgar call, the one Memorilla, and the other Gran Memoria, who, with the few verses which they learn, mingle an infinity of their own barbarous lines, whereby they earn a living, selling them to the villages and to distant theatrical managers; base people these, without a calling, and many of whom have been jail-birds. I should like to rid myself of the care of publishing these plays, but I cannot, for they print them with my name while they are the work of the pseudo-poets of whom I have spoken. Receive, then, Reader, this Part corrected as well as it was possible to do it, and with my good will, for the only interest it has is that you may read these *comedias* with fewer errors, and that you may not believe that there is anyone in the world who can note down a *comedia* from memory, on seeing it presented; and if there is such a person I should praise him and esteem him as standing alone with this power, even though he should lack understanding.[12]

Professor Rudolph Schevill in his study, *The Dramatic Art of Lope de Vega*, states (p. 126) that there is in the Biblioteca Nacional a manuscript copy of the first third of the seventeenth century, "apparently a copy made by Luis Ramírez de Arellano, who, according to both Cristóbal Suárez de Figueroa and

---

[12] H. A. Rennert, *The Spanish Stage in the Time of Lope de Vega*, 175.

Vicente Espinel, had the reputation of being able to reproduce a play which he had heard but three times in the theatre: among the plays he is reported to have thus reproduced was the *Dama boba.*"[13]

To digress for a moment from the memorizer-pirate as source of text, it may be remarked that a study of this text of Lope de Vega's *La Dama boba* has some interest for students of English drama in that it shows that the author allowed to go to the press a copy which was not his autograph manuscript, that he signed this copy, and that he did no careful editing of the text, as is clearly to be seen in the appearance of typographical errors, worse diction, and cuts in the printed texts as compared with the extant autograph manuscript. This tends to confirm the idea that a dramatic author who positively objected to having his plays pirated might still be a very careless editor of his own text when publishing them himself. In 1604 Lope de Vega declared he wrote his *comedias* for money, not for fame, but in 1617 he did supervise the publication of some of them. A comparison with Heywood at once suggests itself. He objected vigorously to the piracy of his plays by stenography because of the inaccuracy as well as the violation of his rights, but when he himself saw them through the press, he was very slovenly and inaccurate in many instances.

As to the possibility of preventing the piracy of a play by memory in Shakespeare's time, we have no positive evidence. One who was notorious as a reporter by memory might conceivably, on being recognized, be interfered with by authorities at the theatre. Suárez de Figueroa has an anecdote concerning the great memorizer said to have pirated Lope de Vega's plays, which would seem to indicate that public sentiment in the theatre was chiefly relied upon to check such piracy when it was discovered going on. He says:

There is at present in Madrid a young man of remarkable memory, named Luis Remirez de Arellano, a native of Villaescusa and the son of noble parents. This person takes from memory an entire comedia on hearing it three times, without the slightest variation either in plot or verses. The first day he devotes to the general disposition of the plot, the second to the variety of the composition, and the third to the exactness of the verses. In this manner he commits to memory any comedia

[13] Univ. of California Press, 1918.

he desires. He thus noted down in particular *La Dama boba, El principe perfeto*, and *La Arcadia* [all by Lope de Vega] besides others. Being present on one occasion, listening to *El Galan de la Membrilla* [also by Lope de Vega] which was being represented by the Company of Sanchez, the latter began to interrupt the argument and cut short the speeches so obviously that, being questioned as to the cause of this hastening and mutilation of the play, he replied publicly that someone was present in the audience (and he pointed him out) who in three days took down any comedia, and that he recited the comedia thus badly for fear that he might wrongfully get possession of it. Hereupon there was great excitement among the auditors, who requested that the play be stopped until Luis Ramirez left the theatre.[14]

Public sentiment might perhaps apply moral pressure in the English theatre, if the memorizer were known and recognized. Whether there was any strictly legal basis for interference, one may well doubt, in view of later legislation and interpretation of laws pertaining to the theater. As recently as 1793 reporting and reproducing by memory was held lawful by J. Buller in the case of Coleman *v.* Wathen (5 T. R. Durnford and East, p. 245). Again, a decision in equity was made in the case of Keene *v.* Wheatley and Clarke (Circuit Court of U. S., E. D. Pa., Phila. *Reports*, 4, vol. xvii, p. 349) that, if the piracy in question had been accomplished by the memorizing of the play, there would be no case,—not even a breach of confidence to be pleaded as in the case of misuse of others' manuscript. As recently as 1882 a play was pirated by making a number of visits to a theater and memorizing a bit at a time, then dictating these bits after leaving the theater. This case received an elaborate hearing in full court, and many precedents were cited. The outcome was the decision that a manager of a theater has a right to prevent stenographic or phonographic report, but he could not restrain "the privileges of listening and of retention in the memory." "Where the audience is not a select one, these privileges cannot be limited in either their immediate or ulterior consequences."[15] This seems, of course, to an ordinarily logical and non-legal mind, to typify blind justice, as the reasons for the decision sound like solemn nonsense. A common-sense

[14] *Plaza universal de todas Ciencias y Artes*, Perpiñan (1615), 1630, pp. 254–55; quoted by H. A. Rennert, *The Spanish Stage in the Time of Lope de Vega*, 176.
[15] Tompkins *v.* Thomas E. Hallock, 133 Mass., p. 32.

decision would naturally recognize the fact that the author's and the company's rights in a play suffer much greater injury from a garbled report by memory than from a fairly accurate stenographic report such as might well have been produced by 1882. But in most matters of law, as in matters of fashion, not what is logical but what has managed to be regarded as customary rules the decision. This is one reason why the oversight of the drama by the Master of the Revels and the chamberlain in Elizabethan and Jacobean England may not have been such a poor substitute for modern judgments based on statutes as most people are inclined to think.

In all likelihood, common law protection of dramatic manuscripts was sufficiently developed in Shakespeare's day to insure reasonable safety from piracy by theft if the rightful owner cared to trouble himself to invoke the law. The whole history of legislation pertaining to drama shows that protection of manuscript has always preceded protection of any kind of spoken discourse delivered in public audiences. The safest way to pirate a lecture, sermon, or play in Shakespeare's time was —as it continued to be for centuries later—to take it down by memory, by longhand, or by shorthand notes. I have seen no evidence that these latter methods had been dealt with in English law at that time. In 1544 Conrad Lagus, a lawyer and lecturer on law at Wittenberg, protested against a theft of certain of his public lectures on law piratically issued on the basis of class-room notes by Christian Egenolf. Several possible charges, such as theft, plagiary, piracy, and fraud upon the purchaser were suggested by the lawyer in his threat to bring a law-suit; but perhaps the very number of these charges may suggest a little uncertainty in the great lawyer's mind as to the proper legal classification of this type of literary theft, based on notes from public discourse.[16] Though there is abundant evidence that such theft of sermons, lectures, or plays was considered by Englishmen as reprehensible, I have seen no similar threat of law-suit in England at this early date. Legal control of such thefts has always lagged far behind public sentiment. That there was not an orgy of such piracy indicates either that the pirates of Shakespeare's day never fully realized

---

[16] See my article, "Notes on the Status of Literary Property," *Mod. Philol.*, December, 1919.

their privileges or else that public sentiment was a powerful check and was several centuries ahead of the law.

Pirating by Stenography

Some piracy, by stenography, of sermons, lectures, and plays undoubtedly existed in Shakespeare's time. Mr. F. G. Hubbard, in his recent edition of the first Quarto of *Hamlet*, says:

> There is no evidence to show that either the systems or the shorthand writers who used them were equal to the task of reporting a play as accurately as the text of even the worst Shakespearian quarto is given.[17]

The study of a few contemporary sermon texts known to have been so derived might change Mr. Hubbard's opinion. The same sort of statement is, however, often hazarded by historians of shorthand and inventors of more modern shorthand systems. It is quite true that the older systems were comparatively clumsy and inaccurate, and that they taxed the memory more than do some of the modern ones. Nevertheless, if they were actually used as the source of printed texts in their day, we must face the facts.

It can easily be shown that stenography was taught in the public schools of England, in the universities, and in private lesson-courses; that there were many systems used between 1580 and 1640; and that, however we may condemn these systems, users continued to employ them for recording sermons, lectures, plays, law cases, parliamentary debates, as well as in private diaries and postal service business. References to note-taking by "charactery," "brachygraphy," "stenography," and "shorthand" occur in plays of the period. One of these references, in the prologue to Thomas Heywood's *Play of Queen Elizabeth*, Part I, (as it was revived at the Cockpit), specifically charges that

> some by Stenography drew
> The plot: put it in print (scarce one word trew:).

And the preface to his *Rape of Lucrece* (1608) declares that his plays have "accidentally come into the Printers hands, and therefore so corrupt and mangled (coppied only by the eare) that I have bin as unable to knowe them, as ashamed to challenge them."

[17] *Univ. of Wis. Studies in English*, 1920, p. 27.

But, in view of the fact that no one has yet succeeded in making out a sure case for the actual piracy of any particular play by stenography, the confident assertions by many of our best editors of Shakespeare's plays that such and such a play was put into print from stenographic notes are open to challenge.

Only one of several possible systems has received careful study,—that of Timothy Bright's *Characterie*, used as early as 1586 (if not earlier) and printed in 1588. At least two other systems should be considered with equal care: Peter Bales, *The Art of Brachygraphy*, printed January, 1590, and entered for publication December, 1589; and John Willis, *The Arte of Stenographie*, 1602. To discuss these and to point out the various other systems used in England from 1580 to 1640 would require too much space for this chapter. In a separate article, I shall attempt to show some reasons why those who have applied any stenographic system to a particular text, from the time of Dewischeit (1898) to the present, have failed to produce an absolutely convincing argument for the derivation of any particular text through stenographic notes; and what points of method in the works of these investigators are worth repeating.

There is a possibility that some play texts were secured for publication through the use of stenography; but no case has yet been proved by scientific methods. Certainly there is no justification for assuming that every badly corrupted text must come from stenography: (1) because it has not been clearly shown what sort of text would result from the systems of that day; and (2) because there were, as we shall see, several other reasons for corruptions in the texts.

CHAPTER VI.

PRINTING AND PUBLISHING CONDITIONS AFFECTING THE STATE OF THE TEXT

It seems to be the common opinion that the typography of the period 1580-1640 was poorer than that of the preceding period. The most commonly noted causes of this inferiority are: first, the "monopoly system," which made the printing of pure literature (rarely falling in the class of privileged works) a comparatively profitless undertaking; and, second, the control of the output by authorities of church and state, resulting, in the opinion of many critics, in a poorer quality of work. Thus, Mr. H. R. Plomer, in two of his articles on the printers of the period, explains the decline of typography:

Pick up what one [play] you will, and its distinctive features will probably be bad paper, wretched type, and careless and slovenly press work. This was largely due to the low condition to which the printing trade had been reduced by the monopoly system, which put all the best paying work into the hands of half a dozen men, while the majority of the printers, whose numbers were increasing year by year, found it nearly impossible to make a living by their trade. The printers were thus compelled to seek work that was out of the reach of monopolists. Of such a nature were plays.[1]

With such fetters [as the Star Chamber decrees of 1566 and 1586] hampering the freedom of the men by whose means whatever was noblest and best in the nation's language was given to the world, it is not surprising to find that the work of Spenser and Shakespeare and their contemporaries was put forth in a totally unworthy form. Take as a whole the books printed between 1560 and 1600, and they tell the same tale. No attempt whatever was made at artistic workmanship. The type is wretchedly cut, printers' errors abound, and carelessness in both setting and printing is only too evident. But worse was yet to follow.[2]

COMMERCIALIZING OF PRINTING

It is no doubt true that monopolies and state regulation of printing worked hardships upon some of the stationers, and so,

[1] "Printers of Shakespeare's Plays and Poems," *Library*, n.s., VII, 149-166.
[2] "Notices of Printers and Printing in the State Papers," *Bibliographica*, II, 214.

directly or indirectly, affected the state of the text. Throughout the period under consideration, printing continued to be a costly venture, and the market more or less unsure. The large works, such as folios and collected works in general, involved a risk. The oversupply of printers, the lack of sufficient work, and the resultant cut-throat competition were a still greater cause of inferiority of workmanship. There can be no doubt in the mind of a student of the period that, in spite of an increasing number of book-readers and book-buyers, the trade was, in some respects, in a worse financial condition than in the early days of printing. Poverty often prevented the acquisition of the best materials and tools, as well as of skilled workmen and learned correctors; haste of production in order to seize upon a market meant carelessness of workmanship; and the discontent common among the minor printers (many of whom were engaged in the publication of what we call "pure literature") because of their inability to get sufficient work also tended to lower the ideals of the printers concerning accuracy of text. Printing was no longer an art, where the printer-publisher found his reward for loving care in the artistic workmanship itself: it was a trade, a business badly over-run.

COMPETITION BETWEEN PRINTER AND BOOK-SELLER

According to Christopher Barker, Warden of the Stationers in 1582, one of the chief symptoms, if not indeed the cause, of the degeneration of the art of printing, was the rise of the bookseller at the expense of the printer:

> The Bookesellers, being growen the greater and wealthier number, haue nowe many of the best copies and keepe no printing howse, neither beare any charge of letter, or other furniture, but onlie paye for the workmanship, and have the benefit both of the imprinting and the sale of all Commentaries of the Scriptures, and (till of late yeres of all Schoole bookes, Dictionaries, Chronicles, Histories,) Bookes of Phisick, and infinite others; most whereof are generally free to all; so that the artificer Printer, growing every daye more and more unable to provide letter and other furniture requisite for the execution of any goode worke, or to gyve mayntenaunce to any such learned Correctours as are behovefull, will in tyme be an occasion of great discredit to the

professors of the arte, and in myne opinion prejudiciall to the Common wealth.[3]

This was a shrewd prophecy of Christopher Barker's in 1582. Robert Barker was the defendant in a Star Chamber suit by the King's advocate "for false printeing of the Bible in divers places of it, in the edition of 1631,"and for printing it "in very bad paper."

The Bishop of London shewed that this would undoe the trade, and was a most dishonorable thing; that they of the Church of Rome are soe carefull, that not a word or letter is to be found amisse in their Ladie's Psalter and other superstitious bookes; and that we should not be so carefull in printinge the sacred Scriptures; and that they in Holland, at Amsterdam, had gott up an English presse, and had printed the Bible in better paper, and with a better letter, and can undersell us 18 d. in a bible.

Barker and his partners tried to lay the blame on the workmen, but such excuses were rejected. The Archbishop of Canterbury remarked:

The Printers that print for his Matie have a very profitable place, and therefore should be more carefull. I knew the tyme when greater care was had about printeing, the Bibles especiallye, good compositors and the best correctors were gotten being grave and learned men, and the paper and letter rare and faire every way of the best; but now the paper is naught, the composers boyes, and the correctors unlearned: There is a farmer and he makes the benefit, and careth for nothing about it. They heeretofore spent their whole time in printeing, but these looke to gaine, gaine, gaine, nothing els.[4]

Lack of Employment for Printers

Attention has already been called to the lack of sufficient employment for the large number of journeymen printers as one

---

[3] *Lans. MS* 48, No. 82. On the rise of the bookseller, cf. Wither's satirical remark in his *Schollers Purgatorie* (pp. 9–10): "The retailer of bookes, commonly called Booke-seller is a Trade, which being well gouerned, and lymited within certaine bounds, might become somewhat seruiceable to the rest. But as it is now (for the most part abused) the Bookeseller hath not onely made the Printer, the Binder, and the Clasp-maker a slaue to him: but hath brought Authors, yea the whole Commonwealth, and all the liberall sciences, into bondage. For he makes all professors of Art, labour for his profit, at his owne price, and utters it to the Commonwealth in such fashion, and at those rates, which please himselfe."

[4] *Cases in . . . . Star Chamber*, Camden Society (1886), pp. 296–97 and 305.

of the menacing conditions of the trade. The poverty of the journeymen is insisted upon repeatedly in petitions to Parliament such as this, which states that the laws of the kingdom permit all persons that have served an apprenticeship according to statute to use that trade:

But the petitioners are deprived of that benefit by ordinances of the masters of their company. And made perpetuall bondmen to serue some few of the rich all their liues upon such condissions, and for such hire and at such times, as the masters thinke fit; for their trade of Printing (but as seruants) they must not use, so as they take all possibilitie of Aduancement (be they neuer so exquisite in their qualitie) from the petitioners, and make them uncapable of maintenance for them their wiues and posteritie.[5]

Often the desperation of these journeymen drove them to invade the rights of patentees. Though occasional concessions were made by privileged men and other measures of relief were taken by the authorities, the condition evidently remained serious even beyond the period under our consideration, if we may judge from the recurring protests and petitions of the workmen, and from such comments as Richard Atkyns's (in 1664) on the results of the Stationers' failure to restrict their numbers. He says:

There are at least 600 Booksellers that keep Shops in and about London and Two or three Thousand free of the Company of Stationers; the Licensed Books of the Kingdome cannot imploy one third part of them. What shall the rest do? I have heard some of them openly say, They will rather hang than starve, and that a man is not hang'd for stealing but being taken.[6]

For at least a part of the period 1580-1640, the situation was complicated by the necessity of competing with foreign printers. On March 1, 1636-7 the journeymen, according to their petition to Sir John Lambe, were reduced to carrying plague corpses to get something to live on. The petition states that they "have suffered great misery through want of employment in their mystery, one special reason whereof is the multitude of bibles and other books printed in Scotland and transported hither, as may appear from a note stated to have been annexed." The

[5] *S.R.*, IV, 525. Arber dates this petition *c.* 1614.
[6] *Original and Growth of Printing* (1664), p. 15.

petition asks for prohibition of importation of all sorts of books from Scotland.[7]

The lack of employment inevitably resulted in a willingness, on the part of the poorer and more reckless printers, to undertake unlicensed, surreptitious, and piratical printing, and thus became of great significance both for the literary output and also for the state of the text. In "Notes for the Journeymen Printers," under date of June 14, 1637 in the *State Papers*, (which is a set of minutes endorsed by Sir John Lambe), "it was observed that no seditious pamphlet had been printed, but some journeymen printers had been the directors therein." If this statement is correct, it will be seen that, but for the existence of this poorer class of printers, the activities of political and religious censors would have more narrowly restricted the output of various kinds of literature. Of rather more lasting importance, however, was the temptation that led these poverty-stricken printers to break down the property distinctions which were perhaps best conserved at such a period by these very stringent measures which the Stationers endeavored to enforce.

There is another point of view from which we may consider the condition of the trade as affecting the state of the text. If we may believe the charges of the journeymen, the very security of the leading stationers in their monopoly of printing privileges tended to lower the bigger stationers' standards of printing. In the petition noted above (*c.* 1614?) the journeymen complain to Parliament:

Besides the Masters of the Company have raised the prizes of bookes, Print in worse Paper, and with dimne and bad Letters....

Further, the Stationers by an agreement among themselues will retale no new Copies unlesse they be of their owne.

Use of Faulty Manuscripts

But the poor state of the texts is not due solely to the general trade conditions mentioned. In considering the texts, we must remember that many of them were printed from single manuscripts chosen from among several in circulation among the authors' friends. Where the chosen manuscript was given by

[7] *S. P. Dom. Chas. I*, 1636–37, Vol. CCCXLIX.

the author or by some one commissioned to act for him, we assume that to be the authoritative version, whether or not its readings are best suited to a modern taste. Unfortunately, owing to the shyness of some young authors and their occasional practice of arranging for an apparently reluctant entrance before the public, we are often left in doubt whether a given text is really authorized and intended for publication, or whether it is but one of several versions picked up, as it pretends to be, by some well-wisher of the author or philanthropic benefactor of the reading public.

Even legitimately acquired manuscripts may often have been to blame for errors that are hastily charged to the printers' account. A study of sixteenth and seventeenth century *errata* will show a fair proportion of the errors to be due to misreading of manuscripts. Nor is this surprising when we have examined these old manuscripts, with their eccentric handwriting, interlinings, erasures, marginal notes for insertion and correction, their slighted punctuation, frequent contractions, and various other pitfalls.[8] Punctuation and italicising were, as we shall see, often left to the judgment of the compositor. The very common use of abbreviated forms offered abundant opportunity for errors of interpretation. And not the least of difficulties was the condition of English spelling; for it was at this time in that delightful state of anarchy which Mark Twain longed for, when every man "might spell according to his own conscience." A modern reader would naturally assume that it was the compositor's conscience that dictated variety at all hazards; but the manuscripts of the period are rich in inconsistencies of spelling. And if the spellings in a manuscript vary, how could one expect of a compositor faithful adherence to the copy? As a matter of

[8] On Elizabethan handwritings, see Hilary Jenkinson, "Elizabethan Handwritings," *The Library*, 4th Ser., vol. III, no. 1 (1922), pp. 1–34, and other works on handwriting by the same author; M. St. C. Byrne, "Elizabethan Handwriting for Beginners," *Review of English Studies*, I, 198. On misreading of manuscript as a source of text corruption, see Leon Kellner, *Restoring Shakespeare: A Critical Analysis of Misreadings in Shakespeare's Works*, Allen and Unwin, 1925; and a valuable review of this by W. W. Greg, *Review of Eng. Studies*, I, 4 (1925), pp. 463–78. A standard work is E. Maunde Thompson, *Shakespeare's Handwriting*, 1916. A careful study of several possible causes of errors in texts is C. J. Sisson, "Bibliographical Aspects of Some Stuart Dramatic Manuscripts," *Review of English Studies*, I (1925), 421 ff.

fact, the Elizabethan compositor seems not to have been expected to live up to an ideal of absolute fidelity to copy. Often he varied spellings merely to space out or condense a line; and oftener yet with no apparent reason. The illegibility of manuscripts, the use of contractions, and the possibility of several spellings of a word, taken together with the liberties customarily granted to the compositor, will perhaps account for many an invention of a "likely" reading of a passage. Some printers, in apologizing for *errata*, mention pathetically their difficulties with the manuscripts; but, on the whole, the early printers seem to have been singularly patient with careless manuscripts.

Crudity of Printing Equipment

The bad appearance of the pages of many texts was not due solely to carelessness of the workmen. It was caused in part by inferior equipment. Trade conditions favored increasing haste of production; but the materials and appliances of printing remained so crude as not to favor haste. Indeed, if we are to believe the statements of many printers of the period, the tools were poorer than they had been—or, at least, many printers could afford only the poorer furnishings.

In the seventeenth century (and, indeed, in some places almost to the nineteenth) types were inked by beating them with balls of some soft material such as wool, cotton, or hair covered with skin or leather. The ink was spread out on a flat surface, usually a stone in the sixteenth century. The balls were dabbed on the ink, and then on the type. The occasional damage to the the text from this method can be imagined. A hasty worker, or a bad ball, or gummy ink might cause loose types to be picked up from the form, and wrong ones might be inserted carelessly in their places.[9]

The uneven blackness of the letters in many texts printed between 1580 and 1640 has been attributed to mere laziness on the part of the man who inked the types in the forms by beating them with sheep-skin balls dipped in ink. It may be due in part to the use of uneven types, and it is very probably due in large measure to the use of inferior inks by English printers. The popular impression that the inks of that time were brighter

[9] On the ink-ball, see *Trans. of the Bibliographical Society*, XII, 233, 283.

and blacker than modern inks because of the bold black lettering of many prints has been dealt with by De Vinne, who calls attention to the fact that "weak ink applied to a bold type, and printed on wet paper against a spongy impression, seems blacker in print than a better ink printed on dry paper against an unelastic impression."[10]

Not only the appearance of the printed page, but, to some extent, the typography is dependent upon the accuracy of the press. The printing-press in most common use in England was simply the old wooden press of early times, with its screw acting with a direct downward pressure upon the forms of types in wooden or stone beds, which were run under the screw by hand. According to De Vinne and others, the press was often a shackling affair, clumsily put together, but, in spite of its crudeness, capable of producing good results provided that the pressman worked with care and deliberation. Apparently two pulls were required for the printing of a full sheet on one side by all English presses up to 1800.[11] A better press was devised c. 1620 by an Amsterdam printer, J. W. Blaew. It contained a device for rolling the bed of types in and out, and an iron hand lever to turn the screw. Also, greater accuracy of pull was insured by passing the spindle of the screw through a block which

---

[10] Moxon's *Mechanick Exercises* (1683), ed. by De Vinne, II, 413. (Cf. Charles T. Jacobi, "Printing Inks," *Library*, n.s. VII, 70–77.) In his *Invention of Printing* (ed. 2), De Vinne tells of the testing of some of the old inks by Mr. Ticheborne with a weak solution of ammonia, which fairly floated the characters off the pages. Moxon's own description of the art of ink-making in England in his day [though his book was dated 1683, his experience extends back much earlier] should convince us that the English inks were far from perfect. He says that the English printers, "to save the Press-Man the labour of Rubbing the Blacking into Varnish on the Inck-Block, Boyl the Blacking in the Varnish, or at least, put the Blacking in whilst the Varnish is yet Boyling-hot, which so Burns and Rubifies the Blacking that it loses much of its brisk and vivid black complexion. Fifthly, because Blacking is dear, and adds little to the weight of Inck, they stint themselves to a quantity which they exceed not; so that sometimes the Inck proves so insufferable Pale, that the Pressman is forc'd to Rub in more Blacking upon the Block; yet this he is often so loth to do, that he will rather hazard the content the colour shall give, than take the pains to amend it; satisfying himself that he can lay the blame upon the Incke-maker." (II, 75.)

[11] De Vinne, Moxon's *Mechanick Exercises*, p. 410. Cuts of early European presses may be seen in F. Madan, "Early Repr. of the Printing-Press," *Bibliographica*, I, 223–49; 449; and in *Tr. of Bibliogr. Soc'y*, XII, 231.

was guided in the wooden frame. The platen hung from this block by wires or cords. The block served to prevent the platen from twisting, and also to regulate the motion of the screw. (Cf. De Vinne, *The Invention of Printing*, ed. 2, and Bamford, *Essays on Subjects of Mechanism and Literature*, 1838, p.29). But, according to Moxon, the Blaew press was not in common use in England even in 1683:

> The old fashion is generally used here in England; but I think for no other reason than because many Pressmen have scarce Reason enough to distinguish between an excellently improved Invention, and a make-shift slovenly contrivance, practiced in the minority of this Art.
>
> The New-fashion'd Presses are used generally throughout all the Low-countries.[12]

From the crudity of the press and the difficulties of wedging up movable types into pages might result such purely typographical errors as the misplacing of letters, syllables, or even whole words. Other varieties of textual errors may be traced to the distribution of a work to several compositors; to the compositor's methods of setting-up; to the press-correcting; to the author's attitude toward his share of the proof-reading; to unwise editing by compositor, printer, or publisher; to accidental degeneration of texts in the course of successive reprints; and to the customs in regard to the gathering and binding of printed sheets corrected and uncorrected. One is not prepared to study Elizabethan and Jacobean texts without at least a general knowledge of the printing and publishing customs of the time, in so far as they affect the accuracy of the text.[13]

The Work of the Compositor

Undoubtedly the richest source of error is faulty composition: for to this we may trace mis-spellings (by which is meant not phonetic mis-spellings or such as are due simply to lack of

---

[12] *Mechanick Exercises*, pp. 37–38.

[13] The best single source of information on many of these points is R. B. McKerrow's *Notes on Bibliographical Evidence for Literary Students and Editors of English Works of the Sixteenth and Seventeenth Centuries*, reprinted from the *Transactions of the Bibliographical Society of London*, 1914. The original draft of this chapter was written two years before Mr. McKerrow's work was accessible in America; but I have inserted a number of references to his excellent discussion, in the course of my revision.

uniform standards, but real mis-spellings, *e.g.*, *candle* for *caudle*); omission, addition, and transposition of letters; omission of whole passages; repetition of letters, syllables, words, and passages; wrong collocations of letters, sometimes resulting in different words; line-shiftings; and errors in capitalization and punctuation. The question then arises as to how types were set at this time.

There is a fairly general belief that in the sixteenth and seventeenth centuries it was customary to dictate from the copy to compositors. Thus, Miss Sheavyn, in her study, *The Literary Profession in the Elizabethan Age* (p. 84), says: "The common practice of dictating to compositors was doubtless responsible for many errors." Similarly, Furness, in his preface to *Much Ado* (p. xi), sets forth this theory:

When it is asserted that the Folio follows the text of the Quarto, we assume that the compositors of the Folio had before them, as copy, the pages of the Quarto, either printed or in MS. If this assumption be correct, there will remain an unexplained problem. At the present day, when compositors set up from printed copy, they follow that copy slavishly, almost mechanically. Surely, the same must have been true of the less intelligent compositor of Shakespeare's time, and we might justly expect that the printed page of the Quarto which had served as copy would be exactly reproduced in the Folio, in spelling, in punctuation, in the use of capitals, and of italics. Yet this is far, very far, from being the case; 'don Peter of Arragon' in the Quarto of the present play becomes '*Don Peter of Arragon*' in the Folio, in italics, and with a capital D; with "happy" before him in print, it is almost unaccountable that the compositor of the Folio should take the trouble of adding another type[14] and spelling the word "happie;" or that he should change "4 of his fiue wits" into "foure of his fiue wits" or "lamb" into Lambe" with a needless capital and a needless *e*; and so we might go on in almost every line of the play. And yet it is incontestable that the Folio was printed from the Quarto,—the very errors of the Quarto are repeated in the Folio, such as giving the names of the actors, Kemp and Cowley, instead of the characters they impersonated.

The solution of the problem is to be found, I think, in the practice of the old printing-offices, where compositors set up types not from copy before them, which they themselves read, but by hearing the copy read aloud to them. We now know that in the printing offices of aforetime,

---

[14] On the use of changed spellings as an aid in "justifying," see McKerrow, *Notes on Bibliographical Evidence. . . . .*" p. 8.

it was customary to have a reader whose duty it was to read aloud the copy to the compositors.

Again, in the preface to *A Midsummer Night's Dream*, Mr. Furness remarks, "I am inclined to regard all the spelling in Fisher's Quarto of *A Midsummer Night's Dream*, archaic and otherwise, as the result of composing by the ear from dictation, instead of by the eye from MS." Another reference to this theory occurs in *Antony and Cleopatra*, p. viii.

Because of the extensive use of the Variorum edition, it is worth while to examine the theory in some detail. Mr. Furness's reasons for holding it are of three kinds: (1) a remark quoted by De Vinne in his *The Invention of Printing*, as made by Conrad Zeltner, of the eighteenth century, to the effect that it was customary to employ a reader to dictate to the compositors (perhaps to three or four compositors working at the same time);[15] (2) in cases of texts apparently based on earlier editions, the presence of such departures as seem to Mr. Furness unaccountable on the supposition that the copy is before the compositor's eye; and (3) the ease with which the dictation theory explains errors apparently arising from confusion of sounds.

The first of Dr. Furness's reasons is elaborately refuted by Guy M. Carleton, of Columbia University, in an article entitled "The Elizabethan Compositor."[16] He first denies the authority of Zeltner, calling attention to a note at the end of vol. 2 of the second edition of De Vinne's *The Invention of Printing*, to this effect:

Dr. Madden says Zeltner was not a printer but a Protestant minister (born in 1687), ... the author of a curious book entitled "The Gallery of Learned Men who have excelled in the honourable Art of Typography" printed at Nuremberg in 1716, in which he shows so much knowledge of the usages of printers and the technicalities of printing that he deserves to be regarded as at least an uncommonly well qualified theoretical printer.

[15] 2d ed. (N. Y., 1878), p. 524. But cf. the note on Zeltner at the end of the volume.

[16] Columbia University, *English Graduate Record*, I–III (January–February, 1906), pp. 7–24. Cf. a review of the Variorum *Antony and Cleopatra*, by Professor Neilson, *Atlantic Monthly*, March, 1908, pp. 424–27.

The passage in which Zeltner stated that it was once the custom to dictate to compositors occurs in the second edition of his *Theatrum Virorum Eruditorum* . . . .(Nuremberg, 1720), p. 408, in an account of Henry Pantaleon, the Swiss historian who in 1537 was employed at Basle in Michael Isengrin's printing-house:

> Aliquandiu in Isengrinii officina lectorem egit. Olim enim diverso a nostris more præ ceteris unus eligebatur, qui sonora voce praelegeret e manuscripto typothetis, quae imprimenda essent. Quo facto prompti erant, qui verba ex ore recitantis excepta componebant, idque ex tribus vel quattuor schedis totetiam praelegebatur compositoribus. Nostro vero ævo, ut nemini ignotum est, is, qui munus componendi elementa sibi impositum habet, schedam manuscriptam ante oculos positam inspicere solet. Qui modus haud dubie propter ignorantiam typographorum mutatus, cum temporis rationem habet et hallucinationibus minus est obnoxius, maxime mihi arridet.

J. P. A. Madden, in translating and commenting on this passage from Zeltner, adds: "On designait ce lecteur par le mot grec 'anagnostes,' " and assumes that both terms refer to one who reads to a compositor. Mr. Carleton examines Madden's three authorities: (1) Melchior Adam's *Vitae Germanorum philosophorum*, 1615,[17] which may be rejected because the passage on the *anagnostes* does not define his duties; (2) the passage from Zeltner noted above, which is no more trustworthy because of the lateness of its date (1720), the profession of its author, and the vague time reference concerning the old custom ("aliquandiu"); and (3) the account of the *anagnostes*, or *lector*, in the Enclyclopædia of Johann Heinrich Alsted (Herborn, 1610, pages 1914ff.). Mr. Carleton quotes passages from the Encyclopædia which he thinks necessarily imply setting up copy by the eye. For example, the compositors are defined as "quaedam mechanicae, quoniam imitantur exemplar typis, quos colligunt et componunt, compositores vulgo." The copy is to be imitated in the setting up of types ("Ergo curandum, ut typi per se, imitatione exemplaris colligantur"). Mistakes in forms are to be corrected on proof-sheets; but every formal emendation of the letters themselves belongs to the correctors and the

---

[17] See Madden, *Lettres d'un Bibliographe* (1868–86), ser. 5, letter 1; cf. also ser. 1, letter 3, p. 11.

readers ("Emendatio autem quaedam formalis, correctorum et lectorum propria, in ipsis typis").

It is reasonably clear that the *anagnostes*, or *lector*, of the early seventeenth century was not a dictator to compositors but an assistant to the corrector of proofs.

That the setting up from a written or printed copy under the eye of the compositor was very common appears from the twenty-nine engravings listed by Falconer Madan, in his "Early Representations of the Printing-Press,"[18] the dates ranging from 1499 to 1600. Several of the engravings are negative; but nineteen show distinctly the use of the *visorium*, or copy-holder, by the compositor. A very clear example is that of a sixteenth century printing office (*c.* 1600) from the *Nova Reperta* of Johannes Stradanus (of Antwerp), where three compositors have *visoria* above their cases.[19] Another (1564) is a cut from Jost Amman showing two compositors with *visoria* at the frames.[20]

Unfortunately, none of the engravings listed by Madan as showing the *visorium* is of an English house; and English usage in matters of printing was not in all respects the same as that on the continent. Moxon's account (begun in 1677, but not published till 1683) ignores any custom of dictating to compositors, though many old printing customs do receive mention. The "reader" is very clearly a reader of copy to the corrector of the proofs.[21] According to Moxon, "Some compositers use the Visorum."(There is nothing to imply that others do not do so because they set up from dictation.) He gives the following directions for the use of the *visorium*:

> Therefore pricking the point of the Visorium most commonly upon the Border or Frame of the Case on the Left Hand about the E-Box they fold the Leaf of the Copy they compose by, so as the bottom of it may rest upon the Square-Shoulder near the bottom of the Visorum; then with the pieces of Sca-board tyed together at one end, they clasp

---

[18] *Bibliographica*, I, 223–49, 449. See also *Transactions of the Bibliographical Society* (1898), IV, 239; and Silvestre, *Marques Typographiques*, 1853–67. Madan's examples are discussed by Carleton in the article cited.

[19] See plate 12, opposite p. 223 of Madan's article in *Bibliographica*, vol. 1.

[20] Plate 40, opposite p. 188, De Vinne, *Notable Printers of Italy during the Fifteenth Century*.

[21] *Mechanick Exercises*, II, 260–61.

both the Copy and Visorum between these two Scaboards, which two Scaboards pinch the Copy and Visorum fast enough to keep the Copy in its place, and at the same time also serves for an Index to direct the Eye to every Line, as the Compositer moves it downward.[22]

Indeed, all Moxon's remarks about composing imply having a copy before the eye:

The Compositer now addresses himself to Composing: And looking a little over his Copy to see how it pleases him for he runs different fortunes, either of good or bad Copy, *viz.* well or ill writ, if it be a written Copy, or much Italick, Latin, or Greek, or marginal Notes, or few Breakes &c., for this he likes not in his Copy: But a Printed Copy, or a fair Written Hand, and full of Breaks pleases him well .... The compositor falls to composing. But first reads so much of his Copy as he thinks he can retain in his memory, till he have composed it, as commonly is five or six words or sometimes a longer sentence. And, having read, he falls a spelling in his mind: yet so, that his Thoughts run no faster than his Fingers.[23]

While it may be objected that Moxon's work was not begun till 1677, and that he does not deny dictation to compositors, but is only silent on the subject, yet to one who has read the whole of the *Mechanick Exercises* such silence is significant; for Moxon is in the habit of discussing old and new processes and appliances and commenting upon their comparative effectiveness. The evidence of engravings of printing-houses is, as has been sufficiently pointed out, in favor of the use of *visoria* at a very early date.[24]

If there ever was such a practice as that described by Zeltner, it was apparently neither wide spread nor long continued. This is but natural; for the inconvenience and confusion arising from reading to several compositors from several manuscripts, alternately, make it impossible to suppose such a custom could long exist. Even if but one manuscript at a time were handled, the greater difficulty in securing fidelity to copy by the dictation method, and the delays necessary for indicating punctua-

[22] *Mechanick Exercises*, II, 212.
[23] *Ibid.*, II, 211.
[24] Even Madden, in spite of his interpretation of the passage from Zeltner (which, if authoritative, would carry the custom only up to 1537), admits that Paris printers used *visoria* in 1510, (*Lettres d'un bibliographe*, ser. V, letter 1, p. 2).

tion, spelling, capitalization, and italicization of many words would make it unreasonable to assume the practice of dictating, without very positive proof. It is altogether improbable that the unlearned compositors of England from 1580 to 1640 set up from dictation, when the *visorium* had long been in common use in other countries.

We come now to Dr. Furness' remarks concerning the "almost unaccountable changes" in spelling, punctuation, capitalization, etc. in the Folio of *Much Ado*, from the readings of the Quarto, from which it is "incontestable that the Folio was printed." Mr. Furness comfortably concludes that the Folio compositor departed from the Quarto text because he had it read to him and did not see it. This would account for variations of detail and at the same time explain the preservation of such errors as the substitution of the actors' names for the characters.

But the variations from copy that troubled Mr. Furness are accountable without such an assumption, if we bear in mind that it is now, was in Moxon's time, and probably also much earlier, the custom of a compositor to memorize a short passage before setting it up. Whether in writing or setting up types, memories of individuals differ in reliance upon visual, auditory, and muscular images of words. But words are primarily vocal signs; and it is only natural that most people should have a fairly lively auditory image of the words they are using. That spelling from sound is a very common procedure of compositors I am thoroughly convinced by the testimony of experienced printers; and, if I had still any doubt, it would be dissipated by a study of modern printers' proofs. Like students' themes, they abound in mis-spellings based on sound.[25]

We should bear in mind also that, while the Elizabethan

[25] Cf. Blades, "Common Typographical Errors . . . . ," *Athenaeum*, Jan., 1872, p. 114: "Every compositor when at work reads over a few words of his copy, and retains them in his mind until his fingers have picked up the various types belonging to them. While the memory is thus repeating to itself a phrase, it is by no means unnatural, nor in practice is it uncommon, for some word or words to become unwittingly supplanted in the mind by others which are similar in sound. From the time of Gutenberg to now this similarity of sound has been a fruitful source of error among printers." Among the examples given are: mistake—must take (*Hamlet*, III, sc. 1); idle votarist—idol (*Timon*, IV, sc. 3); long delays—longer days (*Titus*, IV, sc. 2). The first of these is perhaps not an error.

compositor who had a *printed* copy before him would find it much easier to justify his lines by guaging the longest line of the printed copy and allowing for the others in accordance, and to order pagination by adhering closely to that of the original, in the matters of spelling, punctuation, and capitalization such slavish adherence to the copy would require additional strain of eye and mind, besides taking more time than if these details were managed to suit the taste of the compositor. I hope to show that the ideal of accuracy in the following of copy was in the sixteenth and seventeenth centuries very much lower than it is today; so that a man who varied spelling, capitalization, and punctuation from his copy was not necessarily considered a bad compositor in that period. Indeed, as we shall see, the compositor was then expected to exercise some judgment in such matters. It would have seemed a bit meticulous to insist upon exact observance of copy in spelling, capitalization, and punctuation, when the rules were so lax even among the best writers.

In order to see to what extent a compositor setting up a text from a printed copy before his eye might depart from his exemplar, I compared, line by line, Ling's "1600" Q. and Holmes' second[26] 1600 Q. of Ben Jonson's *Every Man out of His Humour*, using the texts printed in *Materialien zur Kunde des älteren englischen Dramas*. Ling's quarto is, I think, undeniably set up from Holmes' and probably without permission. Evidence that Ling is following Holmes may be found in the use of identical catch-words, even to the division of a word into syllables, and also in the presence of unusual errors in both texts, such as the following:

   390. Hee cannot lightly after [alter] the scene.
   437. Yon'd sackbut's mouth (cf. also elixi'r, p. 15)
   720. Mistaken use of ? for . at end of line
   821. feed with disgestion [digestion]
 1272. gueuener [Gueneuer]

The priority of one of these texts may be determined by pagination and line-numbering. On page 14 of the text,

---

[26] Mr. Greg has shown that the Bodleian-Dyce Q. of Holmes is a second edition, the first of Holmes being in the B.M., (*Tr. of Bibliogr. Soc'y*, n.s. I, 3, 153).

Holmes spaced out line 425 so that the word *againe* makes line 426. Ling failed to imitate the wide spacing, got *againe* into the line, and so had one line lacking at this point. Again, on page 70, Ling set up the letter with so much wider spacing between the words that he required an extra line ("2440 *bis*"). To make up for the extra line and recover the pagination of his copy, Ling economized at the foot of the same page by eliminating line 2482, composed of a single word, *done*, which he set in a parenthesis above the line. Except for these variations, numbering and pagination are identical.

But, though Ling very evidently had Holmes' quarto before him, [27] there are frequent variations of spelling in his reprint; as, for example, *Bir Lady* for *Byr Lady*; *bankroutes* for *bankruptes*; *yenough* for *ynough*; *predominate* for *predominant*; *Pomardo* for *Pomander*; *fleame* for *flame*; *malancholly* for *melancholly*; *mounsier* for *monsieur*. Capitals and punctuation depart still more widely from those in the copy. Contractions are sometimes expanded; and, again, the full form is contracted. There is now a slavish adherence to copy, even to the repetition of the most absurd blunders; and, again, such wide departure that, unless we knew, we should never guess that the compositor had seen the copy. Almost every kind of familiar typographical error that a compositor could commit is illustrated in the work of this compositor setting up from a copy before his eye. Consequently variations of the text in matters of detail cannot be made to prove that the compositor of the Folio text of *Much Ado* set up from dictation without the Quarto before him, as Mr. Furness would have us believe.

It is true that the assumption of the custom of dictating to compositors in this period accounts very satisfactorily for an important class of textual inaccuracies—those where there is a substitution of a word or part of a word similar in sound to the word or syllable desired. But there are two other possibilities

---

[27] A recent article by W. W. Greg, "An Elizabethan Printer and His Copy," *Trans. of the Bibliographical Society*, n.s. IV, no. 2 (1923), 102–18, will throw light on compositors' habits. Incidentally, it tends to destroy confidence in some recent assumptions that we can safely infer authors' spelling habits where plays are set up from authors' manuscripts. Cf. McKerrow, "Elizabethan Printers and the Composition of Reprints," *Tr. of the Bibliogr. Soc'y*, n.s. V, no. 4 (1925), 357 ff.

of accounting for such errors. One is, that the *manuscript* was either dictated to a scribe, or taken down in short-hand or otherwise from a public rendering. An oral transcript is the most probable explanation of the two errors noted by Richard Grant White, from the French scene of *Henry* V. as "showing that the copy was written by the ear." *Il est appellé* is twice printed with the character *&* for *est*;[28] and in Act IV, sc. 4, *a cette heure* is transformed into *asture*. Though I have seen many astonishing spellings by sound rather than sight when the writer or compositor could see the copy, I cannot stretch my imagination to include these errors in that class. But there are many reasons for believing that the text of *Henry V* had been illegitimately secured from an acting version; and it seems altogether likely that these are garblings by a stenographer (or even a taker of notes in long hand) who was ignorant of French and did not catch the words. *Asture*, in particular, is better regarded as a derivative from the actor's hasty utterance than from the probable articulation of the hypothetical reader to a compositor in an English printing-house.

Mr. White, in his discussion, gives two interesting examples of type-setting from auditory images: "the lash of philom" (a mispronunciation of *film* comparable with the modern vulgar "ellum" for *elm*) in two quartos and the first folio of *Romeo and Juliet*, I, iv; and "that test of eyes and ears" for "th 'attest," in the folio of *Troilus and Cressida*, (V, ii, 122).

A similar explanation to that of "that test" would account for two of the errors which puzzled Furness: "thou should'st tow me after," which becomes *stowe*; and "shall well gree together," which becomes *greet together*, in the first Folio of *Antony and Cleopatra*.[29] It is entirely reasonable to suppose that an absent-minded compositor might carry over these sounds, even with the copy before him, if he simply worked from the memory of the sound-images.

Kinds and Causes of Errata

While the compositors' errors in Elizabethan and Jacobean texts seldom differ in kind from those of modern compositors,

---

[28] Interchanges of *et* and *est* in copying or composing, Professor E. C. Armstrong assures me, may occur in the work of a French scholar, because of the auditory image. To account for the use of the & for the *et* is harder.

[29] See the preface to the Variorum edition, 1898, pp. xxiv ff.

yet they are of more importance for a study of texts, simply because they more frequently escaped the proof-readers. For that reason it is worth while for a student of texts of the period to consider the kinds of errors that may be due to the setting-up. In the classification which follows, I do not claim certainty as to the actual causes of the errors noted, but assign what appear to be the most probable causes.

First, we may consider errors due to false visual perception of the words in the manuscript or the printed copy used as exemplar. The desirabilty of an editor's being familiar with manuscripts of the period, as well as with manuscripts of the text he is working on, so far as these are accessible, is now so well recognized as to require no comment. Many misreadings seem to have arisen from mistaken visual impressions of the copy. For example, when setting up from manuscript, it would be easy to misread, "This time goes manly" as "This tune" (*Macbeth*, Act IV, sc. 3). In setting up from printed copy, false visual perception is less likely to occur, but still entirely possible. Ling's reading, "Their wits are refined and ratifi'd," for "rarifi'd" in his 1600 reprint of Holmes's quarto of *Every Man Out of His Humour* (l.1286) may have been due to faulty distribution of types (the r's and t's were often interchanged in Ling's text); or, it may have been due simply to false visual perception of the copy. The same alternative appears in the case of Ling's rendering of "A rude tongue will profane Heaven," (l.1415) as "a rude rogue;" but it seems to me likely that *tongue* was misread *rogue* because it was preceded by a word beginning with an r. "A most odious and fiendlike disposition" seems to have been misread as friendlike" in Ling's quarto (l.933). One of the errors which Miss Sheavyn thinks needs to be explained by the theory of dictation to compositors is easily explainable as an error of visual perception; *i.e.*, "impudent and bedrid" for "impotent and bed-rid;" for *impudent*, whether in manuscript or print, resembles *impotent* as closely in appearance as it does in sound. A knowledge of the handwritings of the day will sometime be recognized as a prerequisite for certain kinds of text-criticism.[30]

[30] It is to be hoped that the "Facsimiles of English Literary Autographs," 1550–1650, projected by W. W. Greg and others, will serve to rouse interest in such study on a larger scale.

False perception of a word in a written or printed copy may take the form of the unconscious substitution of a more usual word than that which occurs in the text. Such might be the explanation of the change from "so much uncurbable her garboils" to "uncurable." Another probable instance of substitution of a more familiar combination of words occurs in lines 4385-6 of the Ling quarto of *Every Man Out of His Humour*:

> And with discerning thoughts measure the space
> Of our straunge Muse in this her maze of Humor.

The Holmes quarto has *pace*, which, though less usual, certainly makes better sense. (Ling's reading, however, is the one furnished in the foot-note to the Gifford and Cunningham text of this play, p. 139). Holmes and Ling both make lines 4400ff. read:

> and like guiltie children,
> Publish their infancie before their time,
> By their own fond exception.

This reading also is retained in the footnote to p. 139 of the Gifford and Cunningham edition; but it is likely that *infancie* is an error for *infamie*, and that the compositor was led into false perception by the marked similarity between *ncie* and *mie* in loose handwriting,—an error which would be aided by the association of ideas with the word *children* just before. (I take it that *infamie* would mean naughtiness, misdoing of these guilty children whose self-consciousness betrays them).

Wrong endings of words may sometimes be due to the fingers' unconscious selection of some familiar combination of letters for the close of a word whose sound-image or visual image was but hazily in mind. For example, in the Ling quarto we have *Frenchefield* for *Frenchified*; *predominate* for *predominant*, though the reprint was from a printed copy.

Anticipation of a somewhat similar word occurring further on or repetition of one that goes before is a common cause of false perception or false memorizing of a word. Thus, Ling, in his quarto of *Every Man Out of His Humour*, sets up *affection* for *affliction* (l.4343), probably because he caught a glimpse of *affection* in the line below.

Where words are repeated in the copy, there is a very common tendency to omit them, either through failure to perceive the doubling, or because picking up the types once satisfies the compositor's mind and makes him forget to double. An example of this reduction of the text may be found in Ling's line 3815, "I heard him," for "I, I heard him" of his copy; and another in line 2151, "frying pan to the Crest had no fellow" for "had had." The opposite error,-of repetition,-is no doubt often due to interruption of the compositor's work, or to simple lapse of memory. Erroneous repetitions, however, are not so important as some other errors, because they are usually obvious.

One of the commonest errors made by compositors is that of skipping a passage and resuming just after a word which is identical with the last word copied. The reverse error, of repeating a passage because of identity of wording between the rightful close of the passage and an earlier part of the same passage, is almost equally common, because of the difficulty in finding one's place after glancing away from the copy. Like other errors of repetition, this will usually correct itself.

It is hardly necessary to observe that the sense of a passage can be completely changed by the dropping out of letters, as well as words and lines, and also by the insertion of letters or the substitution of wrong ones.

A wrong letter might occur in a word because the compositor had a false perception of the letters in his case; but that is not a very likely cause of error on the part of trained compositors, who rely largely on their muscular memory of the location of boxes. A slip in the muscular memory—a wrong reach—is more probable than an error of sight. Confusion of the types through visual error is more likely to occur in the course of "distributing" them at a high rate of speed to the boxes.[31] Types are often accidentally dropped into wrong boxes; and again, even if they are correctly distributed, there is often an overflow from a neighboring box which is too full—usually from a higher box in

---

[31] In Moxon's time (*Mechanick Exercises*, De Vinne, II, 198) the compositor's distributing is thus described: He takes up in his hand about an inch or an inch and a half of types, "squabbles the shanks askew," reads the letters, "and remembering what Letters he read he nimbly addresses his Hand with a continued motion to every respective Box, which his Fingers, as they pass by, let a Letter drop into, till this Taking off be quite Distributed."

the slanting case to one directly beneath, less often to a box on the same level.

This latter cause of error is one example of what the printers call "foul case." To faulty distribution might be due "who *falling* there to find his fellow forth," for *failing*, in *A Comedy of Errors*, as the *l* type is easily mistaken for the *i*. The same cause may account for *piercel* instead of *pierce!* in Ling's text of *Every Man Out of His Humour*. And while a *t* does not usually bear quite so close a resemblance to an *r*-type, yet in many Elizabethan fonts there is enough similarity to cause confusion in the haste of distributing perhaps three types a second. At any rate, Ling's compositor has *fathet* for *father*; *thar* for *that*; *rhat's* for *that's*; *ttue* for *true*; *gteat* for *great*; *dureous* for *duteous*, *sir* for *sit*. Ling's spellings, *Jocob's, ond, obsurd*, and *fovour'd* are no doubt due to an overflow of *o*'s into the *a*-box directly underneath, as represented in old arrangements of cases.

Blades in his article, "Common Typographical Errors . . . .,"[32] illustrates the error of foul case by the following examples, some of which are open to reasonable doubt:

1. "Were they not *forc'd* with those that should be ours," (*Macbeth*, Act V, sc. 5)
2. "Make *Liuers* pale and lustyhood deject," (*Troilus and Cressida*, Act II, sc. 2)
3.   "We must away,
Our Wagon is prepar'd, and time *revives* us." (*All's Well*, Act IV, sc. 4, 33).

In the first example, while it is possible that Shakespeare meant *farced* and not enforced, it is, as Professor J. M. Manly points out, quite reasonable to assume that he would write it *forc'd*, in accordance with a common usage. And even if the manuscript had *farc'd*, a misreading of *a* as *o* in manuscript is as likely a cause of error as the slipping of an *o* into an *a*-box. In the second example, many will agree with Blades in preferring the more ordinary reading, *make lovers pale*, on the ground that

---

[32] *Athenaeum*, Jan., 1872. His representation of cases of the seventeenth century is based on Moxon's *Mechanick Exercises*, the arrangement of boxes being "undoubtedly the same as in 1632," according to Blades, and remaining without change until the abandonment of the long *s* and its combinations, i. e. until the beginning of the nineteenth century.

the *i*-box is just above the *o*-box; but we cannot be certain that *livers* is incorrect (cf. Shakespeare's "lilly-liver'd boy," *Macbeth*, V, iii, 15 and his "Lily-livered . . . .slave," *King Lear*, II, ii, 17). In the third example, *revives* is in all probability an error for *reviles*, and the cause may have been foul case; but here we have to assume a *v* to have got into an *l*-box *above* it. Mr. Blades explains the *booke* in "I came to thee for charitable license to booke our dead," (*Henry* V, Act IV, sc. 2), as an error for *looke*, due to foul case, the *b*-box being just above the *l*-box. He says *booke* in such a sense as we must give it in this passage is a modern commercial phrase. But the *New English Dictionary* notes, under the meaning "enter in a book, record, register," these earlier examples: 1393, Gower, *Conf.*, I, 3, "Some newe thing I shoulde boke;" and 1594, Nashe, *Unfort. Trav.* 9, "I haue done a thousand better jests, if they had been bookt." The erroneous reading in *Julius Caesar* (Act IV, sc. 1, lines 36-7),

> A barren-spirited fellow; one that feeds
> On objects, arts, and imitations,

may possibly be due to foul case; but it seems more likely that it was due to false visual perception of the words because of the greater familiarity of *objects*, *arts*, as compared with *abjects*, *orts*.

Even when types are correctly picked up, many mistakes may result from permutations of letters within words and from faulty collocations. Richard Grant White illustrates the possibilities of permutations in producing puzzling forms by an error in G. W. Curtis's *Nile Notes of a Howadji*:

> I muse as a traniuce, whene'er
> The languors of thy love-deep eyes
> Float on me.[33]

A traniuce easily resolves itself into *in a trance*. Strange words in an old text need careful scrutiny: they must be looked at piece-meal, even upside down. A good many textual difficulties might become simpler if a student who lacks imagination would take in his hands the types represented and see what other possibilities of arrangement lie in them. Very small blunders in handling types can make nonsense of a passage. For example

---

[33] *Works of Shakespeare* (1898), I, xxiv.

note Ling's "Blad-rid Macilente" for "Bald-rib,"[34] involving only a permutation of two letters and perhaps a false distribuion of the d-type because of its resemblance to the b-type.

Attention has already been called to a very important class of errors resulting from false recall of words by sound, by an absentminded compositor. This may take on several forms. There may be, first, the carrying over of sounds, as in the cases noted above: *must take, mistake; th' attest, that test; should'st tow, stowe;* and *a rivall* for *arrivall* (conversely). Or, a homonym may be used, as *sight* for *cite*, or *site*; *right* for *write* or *rite*. This is a common error even among educated people. Somewhat similar is the substitution of a different word somewhat resembling the right word in its sound. This is a common error, and often a troublesome one to perceive and to correct. Perhaps the Folio reading of line 133 of *Richard III*, "While kites and buzzards *play* at liberty," is such an error, for the quarto reading, *prey*. One cannot be sure, in this case, as *play* is a possible reading. The Folio reading, "the lady" in line 138 for "thee, lady" can be paralleled by changes made in Ling's quarto of *Every Man Out of His Humour*, where the compositor had the copy before him but sometimes set up sounds regardless of sense. For example, line 459 is made to read, "Gentles al, I can say for him," though it is correctly punctuated in the copy of Holmes. And line 4809 is so set up that, because of indention and period, Carlo is made to be the speaker instead of the person addressed: "Carlo. did I offer any violence."

An error directly traceable to habits of memorizing is that of line-shifting. It will be observed that Moxon remarks of the seventeenth century compositor that he memorizes a group of words, as many as he can hold in mind,—usually five or six words. The number would naturally vary with the compositor, and might not even be constant with the individual. Some people in copying tend to arbitrary chopping into units of a given length, while others are more dependent, for memorizing, on the thought groups. If one were little interested in the subject matter or were copying as a business, he would, I suppose, tend to the more mechanical division into units of suitable length for memorizing. In setting up a play in blank verse,

[34] *Every Man Out of His Humour*, Ling, "1600."

the natural unit would be the normal blank verse line. The
adoption of such a unit would help explain the cutting off of
extra words from long lines, the filling out of broken or incomplete lines, and also the setting up of prose as if it were
blank verse. The lines in *The Famous Victories* seem to be
compositors' units for memorization (*e.g.* lines 67–88 of sc. ix,).
The "Roberts" (1619) quarto of *Merchant of Venice* (practically a reprint of Hayes's) turns the prose of lines 50–55
of Act II, sc. 2 to blank verse. Conversely, blank verse lines
are often jumbled up into lines too long or too short, or are
printed as if they were prose. Thus, the Folio printer turned
Hamlet I, i, 9–13 into prose.[35] A compositor naturally tends
to close with a full stop; hence the many lines of blank verse
broken at full stops occurring near their rightful close. Again,
the introduction of a new speaker seems to have tempted
the Elizabethan compositor to assign to him a new line, even if
the blank verse line were incomplete. That so many texts were
published in this faulty shape indicates that not only compositors, but publishers, editors, even authors must then have been
somewhat indifferent to the accuracy of line-division.[36]

It remains to note an error which is sometimes not recognized
as a possible error of a compositor—the substitution of a
synonym. This has been variously explained: as caused by the
mistaking of a stenographic symbol—which might very well
happen in such a system as that of Bright; as due to variant
readings (not necessarily mistakes) in different manuscripts.
One of these causes may be necessary to explain some cases; but
if it cannot reasonably be assumed, it is still possible to explain
the error or departure of one text from another by supposing
that the compositor was not then working from an auditory
image at all, but grasped the thought and retained it, forgetting
both the sound and the appearance of the words. We find

[35] B. A. P. Van Dam and C. Stoffel, *Wm. Shakespeare: Prosody and Text*
contains other examples of such line-shiftings, pp. 293–302.

[36] Line-shifting, according to Van Dam and Stoffel, is an indication that an
author did not see his proofs. Yet there are passages of verse set up as prose in
Chapman's *The Widow's Tears,* 1612; and at the same time there are variations
in the copies of the 1612 edition which suggest a sporadic revision by Chapman
(see Dodsley's *Old Plays,* 1825, VI, 115). His dedication showed that he considered a printed play of some importance; and there is no indication that
Chapman did not see the proofs.

preserved in literature numerous examples of substitution of synonyms which do not call for the theory of revision by the author or variant readings in different manuscripts. Ling's compositor, copying Holmes's 1600 quarto of *Every Man Out of His Humour,* made the following substitutions of synonymous or similar words, or of opposites:

1. 645, *peaceable* for *placable.*
   767, *there's* for *here's*
   979, *turnes* for *runnes*
   1218, *those inward virtues,* for *innated*
   2534, *overslipt my expectation,* for *outstript.*

The inadvertent substitution of synonyms because of the lack of any auditory image of the words will, I think, explain some of the errors noted by Van Dam, in "High-handed Ways of Elizabethan and Jacobean Printers."[37] I choose some examples which contain unmistakable errors, as betrayed by the rime-scheme of the passages:

> 1. My Voice is like unto the raging wind,
>   Which roareth still and never is at *rest.*
>   The divers thoughts that tumble in my mind
>   Are restless like the wheele that wherles alway.
>   —Watson, *The Tears of Fancie,* 1593.

Stay is quite certainly the word intended; and it is natural to suppose the change a simple case of thought-memory *vs.* sound-memory.

> 2. In seate of judgement, in th'Almighties *place.*

Stead is clearly the word of the original, to rime with *aread, dread, read, (Faerie Queene,* V, Pr. 11, 2)

> 3. Were I with her, the night would post too soone,
>   But now are minutes added to the houres:
>   To spite me now, ech minute seemes an houre
>   Yet not for me, shine sun to succour flowers.
>   —*The Passionate Pilgrim* (1599), ll. 205-8.

In this example, the substitution of the flat *an houre* for *a moone* is explained partly by its readiness of occurrence as a fixed formula and partly, no doubt, by the "minutes-hours" combination in the line above.

[37] *Anglistische Forschungen,* IX, (1902).

4. Numbers so like the gods in elegance
As this man flowes in. By the morn's first light.
—Chapman, *Homer's Iliad*, (1616).

Here again, the substitution of the usual phrase, *morn's first light* for the rarer *glance* is doubtless due to customary association of ideas, and not to deliberate change by compositor or editor.

The tendency to mis-perceive rare words as words more familiar, or to substitute sound-images or ideas of more familiar ones, resulting in the one case in words similar in sound but not in sense, and in the other case, in words similar in sense but not in sound, is so common that it is now a generally recognized principle of textual criticism that, of two doubtful readings, the rarer or harder one is to be preferrrd, if it makes a real meaning and there are no valid objections against it on other grounds. In a few instances the application of this principle might cause mistakes; but at least it may be said that it is oftener right than wrong, and that it should always be taken into consideration as a probability.

I have dwelt at length upon compositors' habits in setting up because I believe them to be of very great significance to a student or an editor of sixteenth and seventeenth century texts. One or two other matters connected with composition need detain us only for a word of comment.

The theory that the composition was done in the homes or private work-rooms of journeymen compositors has already been discussed, with the conclusion that there is no sufficient evidence for supposing this to have been the custom. Common-sense favors the assumption that the composing was done in the main printing-house because of the better facilities for work and the possibility of collaboration with the other workmen, as, for example, where the press-corrector calls for changes in the composition while the work is going through the press.

This does not mean that parts of a volume may not have been printed in two different printing-houses, by two compositors. Then, as now, long works were often distributed. Mr. McKerrow has worked out from a study of differences in make-up of the parts of the second edition of Nashe's *The Unfortunate Traveler* (1594) a probable scheme of division between two compositors.[38] The space needed for one half was underestimated and apparently the text was mutilated to shorten that part. An interesting makeshift to cover up an error due to the independent paging of the parts of a folio distributed to two printers is found in Smith's *General Historie of Virginia*, published July, 1624. Owing to miscalculation of space needed for the first part, or possibly to cancellation of something, there occurs a hiatus of ten folio pages. An attempt was made to fill this in with a reprint of some complimentary verses from *The Description of New England*, the lame apology being made, that there was "so much paper to spare" here, and that this was done that the reader might not be "altogether cloyed with so much prose."[39]

External evidence also may be found that work was divided among printers. Moseley apologizes, in the preface to the 1647 Folio of Beaumont and Fletcher:

"After the Comedies and Tragedies were wrought off, we were forced (for expedition) to send the Gentlemen's Verses to severall Printers, which was the occasion of their different Character."

The Work of the Corrector

Familiarity with compositors' errors is even more necessary as an equipment for the study of sixteenth and seventeenth century texts than for study of those of an earlier period, on account of the general decline in standards of typography. Some of the old scholarly printer-publishers acted as editors and corrected their own presses. Caxton and Aldus are examples of the scholar-printer. The letters of Aldus show that he considered the correction of every sheet one of his chief duties. It has been said that the Stephens of Paris hung up proofs on the doors of the printing-office, after correcting them, and offered rewards for the

---

[38] *Works of Thos. Nashe*, II, 190 ff. On distribution in reprints, see R. B. McKerrow, "Elizabethan Printers and the Composition of Reprints," *Tr. of the Bibliographical Society*, V. 4 (1925), 357–64.

[39] Arber's reprint, *Scholar's Library*, XVI, 491. Cf. also the make-up of the Shakespeare folio, in the matter of the gap left for *Troilus and Cressida* (J. Q. Adams, "Timon of Athens and the Irregularities in the First Folio," *Jo. Germ. Philol.*, VII 53–64); and Greg's article, "The First Edition of Every Man Out of His Humour," *Tr. of Bibliogr. Soc'y*, n.s. I, 3, p. 517.

detection of inaccuracies.⁴⁰ Caxton's prefaces testify to his love of accuracy—particularly the preface which expresses his desire to make amends to Chaucer for having printed an imperfect text of his *Canterbury Tales*, (in his 2d ed., *c.* 1484).

Early printers who did not correct their own proofs often employed learned men. One of the most illustrious of early press-correctors was Erasmus. Coverdale corrected the first English Bible and Testament. The profession of corrector in the infancy of printing was one of dignity and honor, the corrector's name often being added to that of the printer to lend prestige to an edition:⁴¹ so that men of learning—physicians, lawyers, even bishops and popes—were willing to correct for the press on occasion.

The high ideals of the early press correctors may be illustrated by the enthusiastic outburst of Jean Fontaine, corrector for the press of Pierre Schoeffer:

Les correcteurs attachés a sa célèbre imprimerie sont maître Francois et moi-même; non pas que j'y cherche un sordide gain; je ne veux que l'avantage et le bonheur de mes semblables. Oh! puissent-ils s'appliquer à purger le texte d'erreurs ceux qui dirigent l'imprimerie et ceux qui lisent les épreuves. Ils recevront, n'en doutez pas, pour leur recompense, la sainte couronne des docteurs; n'est-ce pas grâce aux livres qu'ils ont corrigés que des milliers de chaires instruisent les peuples.⁴²

If one were to judge by the requirements laid down by Moxon (*c.* 1677), one might suppose the same high standards of accuracy in composing to have continued up to his day:

A Correcter should (besides the English Tongue) be well skilled in Languages especially in those that are used to be Printed with us, *viz*, the Latin, Greek, Hebrew, Syriack, Caldae, French, Spanish, Italian, High Dutch, Saxon, Low Dutch, Welch, &c. neither ought my in-

---

[40] T. C. Hansard, *The Art of Printing*, p. 95.

[41] The corrector is recognized by name in Marville's *Mèlanges d'histoire*, 1472 (Lacroix, *Hist. de l'imprimerie*, 115); in the *Polyhistor*. of Solin, *c.* 1476; in Augustini Datti *orationes*, Paris, 1513 (Ph. Renouard, *Imprimeurs Parisiens*, 348).

[42] At the close of the Decretals of Gregory IX, 1473; translated by Madden, *Lettres d'un bibliographe*, III, 95 ff. A similar note in Schoeffer's *Institutes of Justinian* names Master Francis, 'whose Methodic Science is celebrated all over the world,' and speaks of incredible sums paid to learned correctors (*Ibid.*, 98).

numerating only these be a stint to his skill in the number of them, for many times several other Languages may happen to be Printed, of which the Author has perhaps no more skill than the bare knowledge of the Words and their Pronunciations, so that the Orthography (if the Corrector haue no knowledge of the Language) may not only be false to its Native Pronunciation, but the Words altered into other Words by a little wrong Spelling, and consequently the Sense made ridiculous, the purpose of it controvertible, and the meaning of the Author irretrievably lost to all that shall read it in Aftertimes.

He ought to be very knowing in Derivations and Etymologies of Words, very sagacious in Pointing, skilful in the Compositers whole Task & Obligation, and endowed with a quick Eye to espy the smallest Fault.[43]

And from the account that follows, of the actual work of the corrector, we should suppose him to have editorial duties that required both knowledge and judgment. So it is well to keep in mind, in studying seventeenth century texts, the probability that correctors were allowed considerable liberty in directing the composers as to matters of form. Moxon shows us the corrector at his work:

The Compositor either carries him a Proof, or sends the Boy with it to his Appartment, which is commonly some little Closet adjoyning to the Composing-room: And the Master-Printer appoints him someone that is well skilled in true and quick Reading, to Read the Copy to him, whom I shall call the Reader.

This Reader, as I said, Reads the Copy to him, and the Corrector gives attention; and at the same time carefully and vigilantly examines the Proof, and considers the Pointing, Italicking, Capitalling, or any error that may through mistake, or want of Judgement be committed by the Compositer....

If the Work be large Forms and small Letters, he has a second, and sometimes a third Proof, which he reads as the first. After the second or third Proof he has a Revise, which is also a Proof-Sheet: He examines in this Revise, Fault by Fault, if all the Faults he markt in the last Proof were carefully mended by the Compositer; if not, he marks them in the Revise.

Thus you see it behoves him to be very careful as well as skilful; and indeed it is his own interest to be both: For if by his neglect an Heap be spoiled, he is obliged to make Reparation.[44]

[43] *Mechanick Exercises* (De Vinne), II, 260.
[44] *Ibid.*, II, 264.

Neither compositor nor corrector, however, should be expected to make good the errors caused by the author's faulty manuscript. Moxon cautions the author,

"Although I have in the precedent Exercises shew'd the Accomplishments of a good Compositer, yet will not a curious Author trust either to his Care or Abilities in Printing, Italicking, Capitalling, Breaking, &c. Therefore it behoves an Author to examine his Copy very well e're he deliver it to the Printer and to Point it, and mark it so as the Compositer may know what Words to Set in Italick, English, Capitals, &c." The copy should be perfect; "for by no means he ought to hope to mend it in the Proof, the Compositer not being obliged to it; And it cannot reasonably be expected he should be so good Natured to take so much pains to mend such Alterations as the second Dictates of an Author may make, unless he be very well paid for it over and above what he agreed for with the Master-Printer."

De Vinne expresses a lively doubt as to whether any corrector permanently employed by these printers had half the accomplishments listed by Moxon.[45] It does seem unlikely, and still more so for the period 1580-1640. The decline of typographical accuracy was no doubt gradual: one could not expect a uniform decline in all printing-houses. But as early as 1537 Richard Grafton, pleading for protection, by privilege, for his English Bible against those who wished to reprint it and undersell him, deplored the competing printers' unwillingness to expend sufficient sums to secure learned correctors. He said his own issue of 1500 copies cost him £500. Others, he said, wished to print it as "a thing done to their hands."

And yet shall they not do it as they find it, but falsify the text; that I dare say, look how many sentences are in the Bible, even so many faults and errors shall be made therein. For their seeking is not to set it out to God's glory, and to the edifying of Christ's congregation (but for covetousness). And that may appear by the former Bibles that they have set forth; which hath neither good paper, letters, ink, nor correction. And even so shall they corrupt this work and wrap it up after their fashions, and then may they sell it for nought at their pleasures. Yea, and to make it more true than it is, therefore Dutchmen living within this realm, go about the printing of it; which can neither speak good English, nor yet write none. And they will be both the printers and correctors thereof: because of a little covetousness, they

[45] *Ibid.*, II, 424.

will not bestow twenty or forty pounds to a learned man to take pains in it, to have it well done.[46]

In 1578 Christopher Barker wrote to the Queen that he had been at great charge "in retayning Journeymen and three learned men for a long time for the printing of the said Bibles, and correcting such small faultes as had escaped in the former prints thereof." In 1582 he lamented the printer's inability to buy good tools for his trade and to employ learned men as correctors. He predicted that the poverty of the printer (as compared with the book-seller) would result in discredit to the profession. And in 1631 Robert Barker's work was very strongly discredited by the Archbishop of Canterbury in a Star Chamber suit for careless printing of the Bible. In this suit the good old times of printing with "good compositors and the best correctors, ...grave and learned men," are feelingly lamented by the Archbishop, in contrast with the degenerate days when "the paper is naught, the composers boyes, and the correctors unlearned."[47]

Proof-reading by the Author

The press corrector, as we have seen, did his work near the press, as a rule, and often required errors to be corrected at once. His accuracy in discovering and righting errors, and that of the compositor in following out his directions for revising are of very great importance for the state of the text.

But we must not suppose the whole burden of correction to have rested on the shoulders of the corrector of the press. The duty of the author in reading proofs has, until very recently, been often overlooked or absolutely denied. Many of the older writers assume that authors did not see their work through the press. Thus, Steevens says:

Let it be remembered that it was no more the practice of other writers than of Shakespeare, to correct the press for themselves. Ben Jonson only (who, being versed in the learned languages, had been taught the value of accuracy) appears to have superintended the publication of his own dramatic pieces.[48]

[46] Strype, *Memorials of Archbishop Cranmer*, appx., p. xx.
[47] *Supra*, p. 319.
[48] *Prolegomena*, 1786; repeated in the *Variorum* of 1821, II, 642.

The same idea was held by W. A. Wright as recently as 1891. In speaking of the work of Heminge and Condell on the Shakespeare Folio, he says:

> The "overseeing" of which they speak probably meant a revision of the MSS, not a correction of the press, for it does not appear that there were any proof sheets in those days sent either to author or editor. Indeed we consider it as certain that after a MS had been sent to press, it was seen only by the printers and one or more correctors of the press, regularly employed by the publishers for that purpose.[49]

Even so recently as 1900, Van Dam and Stoffel, in discussing the frequent line-shifting in dramatic texts, declare:

> We have here again proof positive that the author himself can never have read the proofs of such work.
>
> Had the author himself had anything to do with such a mode of printing, he would very probably have made certain lines longer or shorter, and would most certainly have shown himself more consistent ....
>
> We may draw still another inference. If the Elizabethan printers could go the length of cutting up the lines according to a pattern of their own, this proves that they were allowed complete liberty, and that authors *were not in the habit* of reading the proofs of their works themselves.[50]

Again, in 1914 Professor Wendelin Foerster declares:

> Und selbst wenn der autor seine zustimmung zum druck gegeben, die korrektur des druckes erfolgte damals ausschliesslich von seiten der druckerei (ohne mitwirkung des autors), die sogar die orthographie und bis zu gewissen grade die grammatik nach gut-dünken änderte.[51]

It is surprising that errors such as are noted by these writers should escape an author's eye; but, the more one reads Elizabethan and Jacobean texts that were seen through the press by the authors, the more deeply one is convinced that almost any sort of error might escape some authors' eyes. Nor can one hope to account reasonably for all these slips. Mr. Nicholson, writing for *Notes and Queries* (ser. 7, VII, 304), gives the comparative accuracy of Jonson's texts as evidence that he saw proofs, but feels obliged to account for such errors as do exist:

[49] *Works of Shakespeare*, (L. Macmillan, 1891), I, xxvii.
[50] *Wm. Shakespeare: Prosody and Text*, pp. 296–97.
[51] *Bericht über die XII. Haupt-versammlung des Sächsischen Neuphilologenverbands in Chemnitz.*

Certainly there are occasional, but very occasional, word errors, and more in the quartos than in the folios; but as to these I would remark that no one but those who have tried know [*sic*] how readily a press error may escape notice, and secondly, that Jonson was notoriously over-fond of liquor stronger than milk and water.

The tendency to see what one expects, instead of what the compositor made of it, is so strong that anyone who has written for publication will grant that, if Mr. Nicholson had the opportunity to read the proofs of this remark, he needs no strong defense for the little error that escaped him. Certainly, if we were to account for the word-errors that escaped the eyes of Elizabethan and Jacobean authors in such fashion as above, we should have to assume for the England of that day a joyful bibulousness that passes comprehension.

It is a mistake to assume that the presence of numerous typographical errors in a text is sufficient evidence that the author did not see his proofs. For, as we shall see, the standard of typographical accuracy held by authors was in general lower than it is today; and, besides, we can find numbers of texts that are poor and yet show external evidence of the authors' supervision—as, for example, in authors' or printers' prefaces. The frequent references in prefaces to the authors' seeing proofs make it surprising that so many writers have denied the custom. It is no hard task to gather many of these bits of evidence; so it will perhaps be sufficient if a few clear references to the custom are introduced, by way of illustration.

Erasmus wrote to William Budé, June 19, 1516, referring to a work printed at Basel:

I thought that they had some emendated copies at Basel, and when I was disappointed in this expectation, I was forced to correct beforehand the manuscripts which the printers were to use. Another thing: two fairly good scholars had been engaged to correct the press, one a lawyer, the other a theologian, who had besides some knowledge of Hebrew; but they, being unpractised in that employment, could not complete what they had undertaken, and I was obliged to take upon myself the revision of what they call the last proofs. The writing and printing of the book were going on at the same time, a sheet being completed every day .... Jerome was in the press at the same time, and I was firmly resolved either to die at the work or to get clear of that tread-mill before Easter.[52]

In 1523 a printing indenture was made between John Palsgrave and the printer Pynson for the printing of *l'Eclaircissement de la langue François* in which "a special clause was inserted that Palsgrave should deliver the copy from time to time duly corrected, and Pynson undertook to print one sheet daily."[53]

William Turner, in his preface dedicating his *Herbal* (1568) to Queen Elizabeth, suggests that he has read proofs as the work was being put out:

After that I had made an end of ye third part of my Herbal .... & had ouersene agayne my first parte and both corrected it and encreased it very muche and had also corrected the seconde parte: and the Printer had geuen me warninge there wanted nothinge to the setting out of my hole Herbal (sauing only a Preface wherein I might require some both mighty and learned Patron ....

Author's revisions of proofs are to be found in a Bodleian manuscript collated by Dean Church and Canon Paget in editing Keble's Hooker. With it is the printer's copy from which Book V of the *Ecclesiastical Polity* was printed, with Hooker's corrections in his own hand, Archbishop Whitgift's signature, and the printer's request, "Good Mr. Hooker, I pray you be so good as to send us the next leaf that followeth this, for I know not by what mischance this of ours is lost, which standeth upon the finishing of the book."[54]

Correspondence between the historian John Speed and Sir Robert Cotton (*c.* 1609 or 1610) concerning the *History of Great Britaine* shows that Speed stayed at the press and sent out proofs and revised proofs for second examination. He wrote to Cotton:

I have sent you a coppy of some part of that which you have already sene, because you left in writing at the Printers that with a fast eye you had overune it, and your leasure better affording that busines in the

---

[52] F. Nichols, *Epistles of Erasmus*, II, 281. The book referred to was perhaps the *Institution of a Prince*. See letter from Froben to Erasmus, p. 279.

[53] *Letters and Papers of* .... *Henry VIII*, vol. III, pt. 2, article 3680; vol. IV, pt. 1, art. 39.

[54] Clarendon Press, Oxford, 1888, preface, v–vi; cited by Ed. Marshall in "Were proofs seen by Elizabethan authors?" *N. & Q.*, ser. 7, VIII (July 27, 1889), p. 73.

contrey then here you had; this therefore hath caused me to send you as much as my Printer cane espare, besiching your Worshipe to read it more attentyvly, to place the Coynes, and what adicssions you will before you returne it; and I pray you to past a paper where you doe adde, and not to intirline the coppy, for somewhere we cannot read your Notes because the place geues your pene not rome to expresse your mynd .... so much therefore as you shall perfect I praye you send againe with as much speed as you can.[55]

When Heminge and Condell, in the Shakespeare folio of 1623, expressed the wish that Shakespeare "had lived to have set forth and overseen his own writing," correcting of press errors was no doubt one of the things they had in mind.

Apologies for the enforced absence of the author from the press are in themselves an evidence that the custom was, to attend the press and supervise correction.

In both printers' and authors' prefaces, we find frequent endeavors to shift the blame for errors. The author excuses himself for the oversights of the printer, and, conversely, the printer apologizes because the author has not done his part. In some cases such apologies may have been honest and sincere; but we cannot accept them all without investigation. The excuse is too easily imitated, and runs the risk of becoming a mere device for shifting blame.

Scot's *Hop-garden*, 1574, contains a note of apology from the publisher:

Forasmuch as Mr. Scot could not be present at the printing of this his Booke, whereby I might have used his advise in the correction of the same, and especiallie of the Figures and Portratures conteyned therein, whereof he delivered unto us such notes as I being unskilfull in the matter could not so thoroughly conceyve, nor so perfect expresse as .... the Authour ....

A similar excuse is offered by the printer at the end of Bishop Babington's *Exposition of the Lord's Prayer*, 1588:

If thou findest any other faultes either in wordes or distinctions troubling a perfect sence (Gentle Reader), helpe them by thine owne judgement, and excuse the presse by the Authors absence, who best was acquainted to reade his owne hande.

[55] *Original Letters of Eminent Literary Men*, (Camden Society, 1843), pp. 109 ff.

The printer of Brathwaite's *Strappado for the Diuell* says, concerning the *Errata*:

The intricacies of the copie, and the absence of the Author from many important proofes were occasion of these errors.[56]

Various reasons appear for authors' failure to read their proofs: indifference, or a willingness to trust correctors, enforced absence from the press by reason of illness, dread of the plague, engagement in business or travel abroad. Nicholas Breton remarks, at the end of *The Wil of Wit*, (*c.* 1599): "What faults are escaped in the printing, finde by discretion, and excuse the Author, by other worke that let him from attendance to the Presse; Non hà che non sà." Nashe's address, "To his Readers," in *Lenten Stuffe*, 1599, clearly implies the custom of attendance at the press: "Apply it for me for I am cald away to correct the faultes of the presse, that escaped in my absence from the Printing-house." In Gascoigne's *The Droome of Doomesday*, 1576, the printer apologizes for his errors as due to the attendance of an incompetent substitute for the author:

Understand (gentle Reader) that whiles this worke was in the press, it pleased God to visit the translatour thereof with sicknesse. So that being unable himselfe to attend the dayly proofes, he appoynted a servaunt of his to oversee the same. Who (being not so well acquainted with the matter as his maister was) there have passed some faultes much contrary unto both our meanings and desires. The which I have therefore collected into this Table.

In spite of the frequent apologies for the author's failure to attend the press, resulting in the escape of faults, it is evident that, on occasions, proofs were sent to authors. This seems to have been the case with the works of Palsgrave and Hooker mentioned above. And in Fletcher's *The Nice Valour*, (act IV, sc. 1) the custom of sending proofs to the author is treated as if it were common. Lapet cries,

> So. bring me the last proof; this is corrected.
> Look I have perfect books within this half-hour!

[56] Quoted by Mr. Nicholson, in "Were Proofs Seen by Elizabethan Authors?" *N. & Q.*, ser. 7, VII (April, 1889), p. 304. See also: Stanyhurst, *Translation of Virgil's Aeneid*, 1582; Smith, *True Relation*, 1608; *The Mastive or Young Whelp of the Olde-Dogge*, 1615; Brathwaite, *English Gentleman*, 1630.

Later Galoshio enters with a proof-sheet and a table, saying,

> Here's your last proof, sir,
> You shall have perfect books now in a twinkling.

And, though Nashe sometimes excuses errors by enforced absence from the press, for one work, at least, *Christ's Tears* (S. R., 1593), the proofs were evidently sent. The author was in the Isle of Wight during the publication; but in sheet M he corrected an error in sheet K; and there is a list of errata drawn up when the whole work save the last sheet was printed.[57]

In surreptitious printing, it would be safer, no doubt, for proofs to be sent to the author than for him to attend the press (unless the press were a concealed one). Evidence taken in an examination of Thomas Purslowe, Gregory Dexter, and William Taylor for printing a "scandalous pamphlet," *Instructions to Churchwardens*, shows that Wickens, Mr. Prynne's man, went to the printing-house and asked Dexter to take a proof to the house of Wickens's father, where Prynne would be. Prynne went into an inner room, read the proof, and returned it, to be taken to the printing-house with directions to burn the original copy when he had made one perfect proof.[58]

Very clear evidence of the custom of sending proofs and revised proofs to the author when possible may be found in the charges and counter-charges passed between Ralph Brooke, York Herald, and William Jaggard, who in 1619 published Brooke's *Catalogue of the Succession of the Kings ... of England*. Brooke's catalogue was criticised for inaccuracy by Augustine Vincent in his *A Discovery of Errors in the first Edition of the Catalogue of Nobility Published by Ralph Brooke, Yorke Herald, 1619, And Printed heerewith word for word, by Wm. Jaggard, 1622*. Brooke, meanwhile, hearing of the attack, hastened to get out a corrected edition, in which he laid the blame for the faults of the first upon the printer, saying that illness caused his absence from the press. Both Vincent and Jaggard replied to this excuse in prefaces to the *Discovery of Errors*. Vincent asked,

> Was there euer heard a more miserable refuge? As if untruths in the Historie, or falsifications in the Chronologie,......or the like materiall

[57] *Works of Nashe*, ed. McKerrow, V, 25.
[58] *S. P. Dom. Chas. I*, vol. CCLVII, art. 172.

errors, which I (his *Enuious Detractor*) onely stoope at, were the Printers negligences, and not his owne grosse ignorances. But for that point, I will turn the Printer loose to you, who (it seemes) though he be blinde, means not to swallow any such flies at your hands.

Jaggard replied more hotly to Brooke's charges:

Seeing then we haue with much inquirie sifted out, what tares they were, which the Printer sowed in Master Yorkes booke, it remaines, that we take notice of the time pickt out to sow these tares, which is a point of especiall consequence. And to say truth, what time could it be, but in Master Yorkes absence from the Presse, occasioned by his unfortunate sicknesse? who all the time before, while hee stood sentinell at the Presse, kept such strict and diligent guard there, as a letter could not passe out of his due ranke, but was instantly checkt and reduced into order: but his sicknesse, confining him to his chamber, and absenting him from the Presse, then was the time, that the Printer tooke, to bring in that Troiane horse of Barbarismes, and literall errours, which ouer-runne the whole volume of his Catalogue. Neither makes it to the purpose, that in the time of this his unhappy sicknesse, though hee came not in person to ouer-looke the Presse, yet the Proofe, and Reuiewes duly attended him, and he perused them (as is well to be justifyed) in the maner he did before. . . . . . (sig. ¶ 6ᵛ)

Jaggard went on to say:

Brooke borrowed most of his materiales out of other mens copies, and copied them commonly by his owne hand, it is probable his clerkship might fail him, either in reading the text, as Scogans scholer, who read *Butyrum et Caseum* for *Brutum et Cassium*, or in transcribing, as in a place of his, *Teste Rex apud Northampton* or where in steed of Nunnes Cistercians he writ them *Sister-sences* (as if there had beene but five sisters of the Order) and a number of the like, yet extant in his Copie, which if the Worke-men had bene so madly disposed to tye themselves too, and haue giuen him leaue to print his owne English (which they now repent they did not) hee would (they say) haue made his Reader as good sport in his Catalogue as euer Tarleton did his Audience, in a clownes part.

This defense of William Jaggard's is of special interest because of the possibility that the workmen mentioned here were those engaged on the Shakespeare Folio.

It is possible that the lack of a cheap and speedy postal service prevented the sending of proofs of small or unimportant works to absent authors. The advantages of having the author correct his proofs at the press at this period are obvious. Avoiding of delay alone would be a sufficient reason for the customary presence of the author.

GENERAL STANDARDS OF TYPOGRAPHICAL ACCURACY

An important consideration for the student of texts in any period is that of the general standards of typographical accuracy. In the period 1580-1640 we should consider the official attitude of the authorities in control of printing toward the quality of the work; the aims and ideals of the men who produced the text; and, finally, the attitude of the author toward the purity of his text.

We have seen that the Star Chamber regulations, cramping as they were in some respects, in others tended toward the conserving of good printing. For the limitation of the number of apprentices and master printers helped, more than anything else, to discourage the tendency toward an increase in the number of printers beyond that which the book market could support. And the necessity of having printing done openly and of getting copyright recorded indirectly conserved good workmanship by discouraging hasty and careless because surreptitious printing. Also, we find traces of a tendency on the part of universities,[59] church authorities, and state officials to hold stationers blameworthy for inaccurate typography. On 18 July, 1583, the Commissioners appointed to look into the patentee controversy incorporated in their report clause 9, against false printing, recommending that those who so offend "geue up their presses and live as other workmen until they be better skilled."[60] From 1630 to 1635 poor typography was thrust into prominence

---

[59] This is noticeable in the Middle Ages. In the University of Paris, a statute of 1323 provided for punishment of careless stationers and compelled them to correct their errors:

"Item nullus Stationarius exemplar locet antequam corrigatur et taxetur per universitatem. Item ordinavit Universitas quod quilibet Rector faciat proclamari per scholas, si quis inveniat exemplaria corrupta illa offerat publice coram Rectore et Procuratoribus, ut exemplaria corrigantur et Stationarii qui talia locant, judicio universitatis puniantur et scholaribus emendare cogantur." (Bulaeus, *Hist. Univ. Parisiensis*, IV, 202–04; quoted by Kirchhoff, *Die Handschriftenhändler des Mittel-Alters*, 164.) Cf. also a similar provision for great care in the text in the statute of 1275, Bulaeus, III, 499; Kirchhoff, *op. cit.*, 163.

[60] *S.R.*, II, 785.

as a symptom of the decline of ideals among printers of the day. It came up in connection with the investigations of the false printings of the Bible, some of which were intentional corruptions of the thought, and others accidental errors of form. It was brought out that in 1630 the King's printing-house employed four correctors, all masters of arts; and that the Archbishop felt that Barker should be held responsible for slipshod correcting of the Bible. In May, 1632 he was brought to trial by the Court of High Commission for the omission of *not* from the seventh commandment, and other errors. The case dragged on for years, apparently; for in the State Papers of Feb. 19, 1634-5, the Court records speak of the "certifying of the fines" of Barker (£200) and of Lucas (£200) for corrupt printing of the Bible as "respited till next day of investigation."[61] On July 11, 1637, measures were taken to improve textual accuracy in general. Clauses 17-18 of the orders for printing provide: (1) That workmen who spoil sheets bear the cost of paper, printing, etc. to reprint them; and (2) "That noe Master Printer shall hereafter permit or suffer, by themselves, or their Journeymen, any Girles, Boyes, or others to take off anie Sheetes from the Timpin of the Presse, but that hee that pulleth at the Presse shall take off every Sheete himself."[62]

This last is not a mere precaution against smearing or careless handling of sheets. The one who pulled off the sheets was expected to notice all obvious errors and see to their correction. Moxon says:

And though he [the pressman] every other Sheet overlook the Heap yet his Companion that Pulles by an habitual use casts his eye upon every single Sheet; yet rarely hinders his riddance by it, for while he is taking the sheet off the tympan, he gives a quick spreading glance upon it, and lays it down......unless he perceive somewhat to mend: For then he lets it lye on the tympan till he has mended what he saw amiss.[63]

The burden of responsibility for errors fell in part upon correctors of the press. This they sometimes felt as a hardship.

[61] For the beginning of this case, see *Cases in the Courts of Star Chamber* . . . ., (Camden Soc'y, 1886), pp. 296–97. And cf. *S. P. Dom. Chas. I*, 1634–35, Feb. 19. During the Civil War the Dutch-English Bibles were burned by order of an assembly of divines for three important errors deliberately inserted for sectarian reasons.

[62] *S. P. Dom.*, 1637, vol. CCCI, art. 105; and 1634, vol. CCLXXX (p. 407).

[63] *Mechanick Exercises*, ed. De Vinne, II, 333.

In 1634 the Correctors of the King's Print-house sent a petition to William Laud, Archbishop of Canterbury, saying, "They exact from your peticioners the reprinting [*i.e.* the cost and oversight] of such faults as escape."[64]

The state of the text was, of course, largely dependent upon the typographical ideals of the printer or publisher. It may be said in the beginning that most of the printers of the period, though they offered all sorts of excuses for their errors, did show a willingness to record them.[65] One notable complaint we have from Thomas Heywood, who had a very lively sense of authors' rights and more than once asserted his. He attaches to *An Apology for Actors*, printed by Nicholas Okes in 1612, a letter to that printer, his "approved good Friend," complaining of a former printer, William Jaggard, who, he says, refused to publish the *Errata*:

> The infinite faults escaped in my booke of Britaines Troy by the negligence of the printer, as the misquotations, mistaking of sillables, misplacing halfe lines, coining of strange and never heard of words, these being without number, when I would have taken a particular account of the *errata*, the printer answered me, hee would not publish his own disworkemanship, but rather let his owne fault lye upon the necke of the author. And being fearefull that others of his quality had beene of the same nature and condition, and finding you, on the contrary, so carefull and industrious, so serious and laborious to doe the author all the rights of the presse, I could not choose but gratulate your honest indeavours with this short remembrance.[66]

The attitude of Heywood's printer, Okes, on the matter of *errata* may be seen in his poetical address to the reader, in the

---

[64] *S. P. Dom.*, 1634–35, vol. CCLXXX, art. 17.

[65] Timperley, in his dictionary of printing, says that the first list of errata known is a two-page one in a Juvenal printed at Venice with the notes of Merula, by Gabrielis Petrus. I do not know whether this is in fact the earliest instance. Before *errata* came into general use, errors were simply corrected by hand before the work was put into circulation, if they were noted at all.

[66] It is interesting to compare these charges with the defense made by Jaggard against the charges of the herald, Brooke (see p. 355).

What looks like a suspicion of future trouble over William Jaggard's printing of *Britain's Troy* is the entry on the Stationers' Register: "5 Dec., 1608, William Jaggerd, A booke called Brytans Troye Provyded that yf any question or trouble grow hereof, Then he shall answere and discharge it at his owne Losse & Costes."

1610 edition of Arthur Hopton's *Baculum Geodæticum; or the Geodeticall Staffe,* which he printed for Simon Waterson:

> For errours past, or faults that 'scaped be,
> Let this collection give content to thee;
> A worke of art, the grounds to us unknowne,
> May cause us erre, though all our skill be showne.
> When points and letters, doe containe the sence,
> The wise may halt, yet doe no great offence:
> Then pardon here, such faults that do befall;
> The next edition makes amends for all.[67]

Forty-four lines of *errata* follow. No second edition has been noted.

The alleged attitude of William Jaggard in regard to publishing *errata* seems to have been an unusual one. There was a general willingness to print them, arising from a firm conviction that errors were inevitable and therefore easily excused. As it is put in Brathwaite's *The Penitent Pilgrim,* 1641:

> No place but is of Error's rife
> In labours, lectures, leafes, lines, life.

It was assumed by many printers, however, that *errata* were required only where the blunders were of such a nature as to spoil the sense. Even Edward Blount, who might be said to be a publisher of high ideals for his day, said, in his apology for errors in *Horae Subseciuae* (1620):

> Of such errours as have escaped in the presse, I haue thought good to collect only those, which may be supposed likely to trouble the reader in his way, the rest being few, and but literall, I hope shall eyther passe unobserued or excused.

Errors oviously typographical, if laid to the blame of the corrector or printer, need give no great concern. In the 1633 quarto of Shirley's *The Bird in a Cage,* the printer says to the reader, after naming a few *errata*:

> Many other errors (though for the most part literal) thou shalt meet, which thou canst not, with safety of thy own, interpret a defect in the author's judgment, since all books are subject to these misfortunes.[68]

[67] *Notes and Queries,* 4th Ser., IV, 449.

[68] Shirley himself says, in his ironical dedication of the work to Prynne, "Many faults have escaped the press, which your judgment will no sooner find, than your mercy correct, by which you shall teach others a charity to your own volumes, though they be all errata."

The same attitude appears in *Microcosmus*, printed by Richard Oulton for Charles Greene in 1637:

The errours escap't in the Presse are not such, but that the apparent oversight of the Correctour may prevent the taxing me of ignorance. I therefore have omitted to expresse them.

Readers are frequently admonished by printers to use their own judgment in correcting errors. It was because the printer trusted in the reader's ability and willingness to read faulty texts that the correction of errors was so often made in only a part of the copies. Thus, in Nabbes's *Hannibal and Scipio*, published in 1637, a note of *errata* reads:

I desire thee Reader to notice that some escapes have past the Presse; As Tuning for Tunny; dimacing for dimning; meane for meere; stand for share; &c. which notwithstanding are corrected in divers of the copies; where they are not, let thine owne judgement rectifie them, before thy rashness condemne me.

The apologies for errors are not merely cheerful; often they are frivolous. The *Ad lectorem* of Dekker's *Satiromastix* (Q. of 1602) exhorts him:

In steed of the Trumpets sounding thrice, before the Play begin: it shall not be amisse (for him that will read) first to beholde this short Comedy of Errors, and where the greatest enter, to giue them in steed of a hisse, a gentle Correction.

A natural reaction from the tendency toward conventionalism[69] in the apology for *errata* is the burlesque apology, which may be illustrated by the quibbling "Upon the Errata" in R. Brathwaite's *The English Gentleman*, 1630:

Truth is, Gentlemen, when you encounter with any Errors (as they are individuates to all Labours) you are to impute the error to the absence of the Author......He was call'd away from *Lawrence Jury*, by the impannell of a *Northerne Jury*, and pressed to attendance by an *Old Bayliffe* of the country, when his occasion lay for the Presse in the *old Bayly* neere the City. In a word, had not a *Nisi prius* interposed, these errors by a *Quest of inquiry* had beene prevented.

The conventionality and insincerity of the apology are seen in the fact that it is often repeated in new editions inappropriately,

---

[69] Moseley, in 1646, prefaces the Beaumont and Fletcher folio with the remark: "For literall Errours committed by the Printer, 'tis the fashion to aske pardon, and as much in fashion to take no notice of him that asks it."

even untruthfully. The conventionality of prefaces may be illustrated by the introductory remarks of Binneman, in his preface to Stanyhurst's translation of Virgil's *Æneid*, where the printer is obviously imitating the manner of the Hollander, John Pates, in the preface to his edition of the work. Obviously insincere, at least in all editions after the first, is the address, "To the Reader and Hearer," upon the *errata* in Edward Sharpham's play, *The Fleire*:

If you finde anie errors by me committed correct thē or neglect thē The Author is inuisible to me (viz: ith' Country) but whereabouts I cannot learne; yet I feare hee will see mee too soone, for I had of him before his departure an Epistle or Apological præamble (this being his first Minerua) directed unto you, which should haue bin in this Page diuulg'd, and (not to ieast with you because this booke plaies that part sufficiently) I haue lost it, remembering none of the Contentes. And therfore (kinde Readers) I doe presume thus to salute you.

This occurs first in the quarto of 1607, "printed by F. B. in Paules Churchyard, at the signe of the Flower de Luce & the Crown." Sharpham died in the spring of 1608, and his will was probated 9 May, 1608.[70] But in the editions of 1610, 1615, 1631, the printer continued gravely assuring the reader, "The Author is inuisible to me (viz: ith' Country) but whereabouts I cannot learne; Yet I feare hee will see mee too soone."

Throughout the period, however, there were some printers and publishers who took *errata* seriously. Because of his connection with the Shakespeare folio, the attitude of Edward Blount is of special interest. We have already seen that he regarded a few "literal" errors as excusable and hardly necessary to enumerate. The inevitability of errors he comments on again in part 2 of the 1623 folio, *Guzman de Alfarache*:

It were a hard taske and rarely to be performed, for any printer to undertake the printing of a booke of this bulke and nature, without some faults; yea, were his copy neuer so fayre, or his apprehension so quicke. It is a *decorum* in Guzman to commit many solecismes, whose life was so full of disorders. This life of his beinge 26. severall times printed in the Spanish tongue in a few years, did neuer appeare to the world, but with *errata*: which makes me the more presuming on your

[70] H. Nibbe, Life of Sharpham, in his edition of *The Fleire*, *Materialien z. K. d. ält. engl. Dramas*, 1912.

humane courtesie: and as in the first, so in this second part, vouchsafe with your pen, the amendment of these few faults, before you begin to read the rest of his life.[71]

After reading the many prefaces in which printers try to shift the blame for all the errors, it is a pleasure to come upon Blount's preface to the first part of this same folio, with its honest shouldering of his share of responsibility:

After so much as you haue read heere uttered in their just commendation [i.e. the author's and translator's] let it be my minute, to be heard in a line or two for my selfe: which is, that you would be pleased not to lay my faults on them. I will neither pretend badnesse of copy, or his absence whose prouince it was to correct it; but pray the amendment of these few escapes (as you finde them here-under noted,) before you begin to reade: with hope of your pardon, the rather, because it hath beene my care they should be no more.

The same attitude appears in his 1628 edition of *Microcosmographie*:

If any faults haue escap'd the presse (as few bookes can bee printed without) impose them not on the author, I entreat thee; but rather impute them to mine and the printers ouersight, who seriously promise in the re-impression thereof, by greater care and diligence for this our former default to make thee ample satisfaction.

That Blount is one of the highest-minded publishers of his day appears not only from his attitude toward mere errata, but from the spirit of his remarks on the whole duty of the publisher. His conception of the relations between publishers and authors may be inferred from his dedication of the 1598 edition of Marlowe's *Hero and Leander*, which shows sincere admiration and pity for the author and a genuine desire to carry out his probable wishes. He regarded himself as executor to the "unhappily deceased author" of the poem:

The impression of the man that hath been dear unto us, living an after-life in our memory,......putteth us in mind of farther obsequies due unto the deceased; and namely of the performance of whatsoever we may judge, shall make to his living credit and to the effecting of his determinations prevented by the stroke of death.

There is a play-preface which is interesting because of the expectation expressed that the text will be progressively purified

[71] Noted by Bolton Corney, *Notes and Queries*, ser. 2, III, 8.

in succeeding editions—an ideal which, we must admit, was very seldom realized in the books of the period. *Philaster* appeared in quarto form, 1620, as printed for Thomas Walkley, and again for the same publisher in 1622. Walkley disclaimed for himself and his printer the blame for the great corruption of the first quarto, and credited himself with reforming the second. He may have got hold of a better text, from Fletcher or a friend of his. The third quarto, 1628, contains an interesting notice from "the stationer [Richard Hawkins] to the understanding gentry." It begins by stating that the play "hath received (as appears by the copious vent of two editions) no less acceptance with improvement of you likewise the readers, albeit the first impression swarmed with errors, proving itself like pure gold, which, the more it hath been tried and refined, the better is esteemed. The best poems of this kind in the first presentation resemble that all-tempting mineral newly digged up, the actors being only the labouring miners, but you the skilful triers and refiners."[72] It should be observed, however, that the third quarto does not differ greatly from the second.

It would be impracticable to attempt to illustrate all the varying ideals of individual printers and publishers toward purity of text. There were then, as now, good printers and bad. What stands out conspicuously from the printers' prefaces is this: that mere typographical inaccuracies were not by most printers regarded as nearly so serious a blemish as they are today—that the standard of accuracy in the text was very much lower than it is now, lower even than it had been in the early history of printing, owing to the commercializing of the profession and the excessive competition of the too numerous and too needy printers. It was an age of quick production—not only for trade reasons but because of the very spirit of the age. In a period characterized by such manifold expressions of creative genius, is it any wonder that the critical faculty lagged somewhat behind—that the joy of making something new was held dearer than the more sober satisfaction of making over and perfecting?

We now know positively that, under normal circumstances, the author had a chance to read his proofs. That the printers or

---

[72] See *Works of Beaumont and Fletcher*, Variorum, I, 118 and 134.

publishers might resent large revisions in the course of printing, we can readily believe: it is the case today with some publishers, though the matter has now been put upon a definite business basis by a plan for sharing costs of revision beyond a maximum allowance. But the authors of 1580-1640, we shall see, often showed something like the printers' attitude of cheerful tolerance of such errors as were not destructive of the sense. Indeed, we may question whether the printer's indifference to textual error is not often a reflection of the author's carelessness either about attending the press or about correcting typographical errors. A printer-publisher finds it a rather thankless task to be more concerned over the accuracy of a text than is the living author of it.

There are not wanting expressions, by authors, of their anxiety for perfect texts, or complaints (even complaints printed by the erring printers themselves) of the inaccuracies to be charged to printers' carelessness. Some authors are so meticulously careful as to long for perfection in such details as spelling, punctuation, and so forth. On the back of the title of "The first Booke of the Preservation of King Henry the VII." in English "rhythmical hexameters," printed in London, by R. B., 1599, is this advice from the author to the printer:

Print with a good letter, this booke and carefully Printer;
Print each word legibill, not a word nor sillabil alter:
Keepe points, and commas, periods, the parenthesis observe;
My credit and thy repute to defend, bothe safely to conserve.[73]

"T. M." shows a similar concern for details in his address "To the Reader," prefixed to *Father Hubbard's Tales*:

I swear, and that oath will be taken at any haberdasher's, I never wished this book better fortune than to fall into the hands of a true-spelling printer, and an honest-minded bookseller: and if honesty could be sold by the bushel like oysters, I had rather have one Bushel[74] of honesty than three of money.

One may find in prefaces by careful authors requests for corrections by the users of the books. Rather unusual regard for accuracy is shown in the preface "To the indifferent Reader" of Ralph Rabbard's translation of Ripley's *Compound of Alchymy*

[73] *Bookworm*, (2) III, 102.
[74] The allusion is to Thomas Bushell, printer of the first edition.

(1591). The errors he wishes corrected with the readers' aid are not alone the typographical ones, but errors in his interpretation of the manuscript. He says that Ripley's work has passed down, in several copies, for a hundred and fifty years. He hopes readers will not find it strange if he errs.

> Deciphering of this worke, by conference of many olde rude and ill written Copies, out of which the same with great travel and industry hath been gathered .... it was not possible for me to ground any certaintie [as to the various readings] if I had not happened on a most aunceint recorde thereof, and used the assurance of a most notable and experienced decipherer of olde and unperfect writing: and after conferred with many skilfull persons in this high Arte, praying thee if in reading hereof thou shalt note any fault in matter or forme: that thou wilt curteously note the same and send it unto me, or the house of Peter Bales in the Olde Bayly, to bee corrected uppon the next generall impression, there being but a small number of these Books imprinted.

Nashe occasionally complains of the bad form of his works. In the "private" epistle to Abel Jeffes, printer of the third (1592) edition of *Pierce Penilesse*, the author complains that the first edition, printed by Richard Jones, was abroad a fortnight before he knew it, "unfinished and uncorrected." He proceeds to criticise Jones's work, particularly with reference to the ostentatious title-page. The book was published while the author was absent, possibly because of the plague; but there is no good evidence that this was in any sense an unauthorized publication. It may have been a little premature. One has to take Nashe's remarks with a grain of salt, remembering his habit of making everything show to his own advantage. He is so careful not to seem to make many mistakes himself that he separates author's and printer's errors, in *Christ's Teares over Jerusalem*, 1593. Among the printer's errors is, "For Esau, read Cain," which is a possible but not a highly probable printer's error.

The authors who cannot attend the press send forth their frequent plaints. Thus, Samuel Hieron, in *The Spirituall Sonneship* (1611) addresses the "Christian Reader:"

> I have to desire of thee..... that if in the printing of these or any other of my publishings, thou hast met, or hereafter shalt meet with any errors, which may interrupt and stumble thee in thy passage, thou wouldest lay the fault wholly where it is: It hath much grieved me to

see the flawes, and maimes, in diuers of the things which I haue sent abroad, the falsifying of words, the misplacing of sentences, the dismembring of some, the confounding of other some clauses, by wrong pointing them;......I beseech thee make the best of these escapes, and let thy care and diligence to obserue my maine purpose in euery particular place, help these imperfections. My endeauor hath euer beene to put each thing perfect into the printers' hand; I dwelle farre off, and cannot attend their proceedings.....

Modbury in Deuon.[75]

The author's complaint of poor typography was sometimes contained in the very volume complained of, and printed by the printer criticised. Chapman, for example, in the address "To the Understander" before the 1598 quarto of *Achilles Shield* printed by John Windet (the printer of the *Seauen Bookes of the Iliades* issued the same year), apologizes: "Only the extreme false printing troubles my conscience, for fear of your deserved discouragement in the impair of your poet's sweetness." Chapman shows more regard for accuracy than the average writer of his day. One of his works, however, *The Widow's Tears*, of 1612, is full of faults. The copies vary so as to suggest revision in the course of printing.

The dramatic texts of the period are usually spoken of as if they were much inferior to those of contemporary works of other classes. I have not compared a sufficient number of texts to justify sweeping conclusions on this point; but my general impression is now that the typography of plays was, on the whole, somewhat lower than that of other literary works but not so much lower as it is usually said to be. It is, however, clear that stationers regarded plays as comparatively trifling ventures. Perhaps the market was uncertain because of whimsical variations in the public taste; or perhaps it was simply that the low selling-price of the play quarto prohibited large profits. In some cases the faulty state of the text is, of course, to be attributed to the irregular methods of acquiring manuscripts, resulting in the use of a poor version. But on the other hand, there are texts almost equally bad which were overseen by the authors and contain dedications and addresses by them. How shall we account for such carelessness of detail? With some dramatists there was perhaps a feeling that a play was a play,

[75] J. F. Mausergh, *Notes and Queries*, ser. 7, VI, 186.

rather than a bit of literature to print, and, if it were to be printed, the only real concern would be, to get the story before the public in a readable form. Marston, in the preface to his *The Malcontent*, shows no very lively concern over the formal errors arising from his inability to oversee the work:

> My inforced absence must much rely upon the Printer's discretion; but I shall intreat slight errors in orthography may be as slightly overpassed; and that the unhandsome shape which this trifle in reading presents, may be pardoned, for the pleasure it once afforded you, when it was presented with the soul of lively action.

We find, then, among authors, as varied attitudes toward accuracy of text as among printers. One will say frankly that errors are excusable because palatable to the ignorant and easily disposed of by the wise. Thus Gosson writes, in his *Schoole of Abuse (1579)*: "You which are gentlemen.... because you are learned, amende the faultes friendly which escaped the presse: the ignoraunt, I knowe, will swallow them downe and digest them with ease." Another will frankly own that he, and not the printer, is accountable for minor errors, but that he does not regard them as of serious importance. Perhaps he promises to do better in his next book, or (more rashly) in his next edition. Samuel Daniel prefaces his *Collection of the Historie of England* (1612-13) with the remarks:

> For the Faults committed herein, Charitable Reader, know they are not the Printers (who hath bin honestly carefull for his part), but meerly mine owne: freely confessing myselfe to be more an honorer then searcher of antiquities that be far off from us, and onely studious of the generall notions, which especially concerne the succession of affaires of action, which is the part I haue undertaken.....And (if I liue) after this primate impression, which is but of a few coppies for my friends, I will amend what is amisse in the publique.

But, according to Grosart,[76] the folios were not more accurate than the quarto.

A little thing like inaccuracy in historical writing seems not to have disturbed Daniel very much. He wrote in his preface to *The Collection of the History of England* (printed for Simon Waterson, 1626):

---

[76] *Works of Samuel Daniel*, (Spenser Society), V, 293.

Now for the errors herin committed, either by mine owne mistakings or the Printers ouer-sight, I must craue Pardon of course. It is a Fate Common to Bookes and Booke-men, and wee cannot auoyde it. For besides our owne faylings, we must heere take up many things upon other mens credits, which often come imperfect to our hands: As the summes of Monies, numbers of Souldiers, Shippes, the slayne in Battaile, Computation of Times, differences of Names & Titles, &c. Wherin our Authors agree not. And it were to be wished that we had more assured notes of these particulars then we haue, especially for summes of Monies (in regard it serues much for instruction) wherein I doubt many of our Collectors haue bin but ill Accountants, rekoning Markes for Pounds, and Pounds for Markes. The computation of Times is not of so great moment, figures are easily mistaken; the 10. of July and the 6. of August, with a yeare ouer or under, makes not a man the wiser in the businesse then done, which is onely that hee desires. But these things being but of the By, the understanding Reader will not much care to set at them.

The truth is that, like scholarly editors and translators, authors abundantly able to oversee the texts let slip gross errors. Archbishop Parker, for example, was a learned man, and he had the tools for printing and the workmen in his own house; so that he had every opportunity of oversight. Yet his text of the English history of Walsingham, *Historia Anglicana*, 1574, is very inaccurate. That he oversaw the printing appears from his notes on the margin of the manuscripts.[77] And some of the authors who make a great stir over printers' errors do not, apparently, take pains to do their share in improving the text. Heywood is a vehement protester against damage to his text. But note the errors that slip by him in two texts which he oversaw—*The Rape of Lucrece*, 1608, and *The Fair Maid of the West*, 1631.[78]

The remarks on faultiness of texts in the period 1580-1640 are numerous and lengthy. Over the *errata* arises a clamor of voices, of author, of printer, of publisher, from apologetic murmur to a hearty growl. What stands out unforgettably is, that the much mention of inaccuracy means little for the future of the text, in many cases; that, while *errata* are sometimes, indeed often, corrected in the next impression, as was promised,

---

[77] Hook, *Lives of the Archbishops*, IX, 499.

[78] See also W. W. Greg, "More Massinger Errors," *Tr. of the Bibliogr. Soc'y*, V, 1 (1924), 59–92.

almost as many new ones may occur, and even mistakes in the correction of the old. It seems that there was a growing sense of the desirability of accuracy of text, checked by an unwillingness to undertake the labor necessary to secure it.

Editing by Compositor, Corrector, and Publisher

The state of the text depended, to a considerable extent, upon the editorial functions exercised by compositors and publishers, as well as correctors of the press. On details of form, the compositor, at least in Moxon's time, was expected to use his judgment:

> By the Laws of Printing, a Compositer is strictly to follow his Copy, viz. to observe and do just so much and no more than his Copy will bear him out for; so that his Copy is to be his Rule and Authority: But the carelessness of some good Authors, and the ignorance of other Authors, has forc'd Printers to introduce a Custom, which among them is look'd upon as a task and duty incumbent on the Compositer, viz. to discern and amend the bad Spelling and Pointing of his Copy, if it be English; But if it be in any Forrain Language, the Author is wholy left to his own Skill and Judgment in Spelling and Pointing, &c his Copy, and Correcting the Prooves, unless they be Latine, Greek or Hebrew, for in those Languages there is generally a Corrector belongs to the Printing-House: And How well other Forrain Languages are Corrected by the Author, we may perceive by the English that is Printed in Forrain Countries.
>
> Therefore upon consideration of these accidental circumstances that attend Copy, it is necessary that a Compositer be a good English Schollar at least; and that he know the present traditional Spelling of all English Words, and that he have so much Sence and Reason, as to Point his Sentences properly: when to begin a Word with a Capital Letter, when (to render the Sence of the Author more intelligent to the Reader) to Set some Words or Sentences in Italick or English Letters &c.[79]

A rather amusing instance of a compositor's quandary when he knows the rule, to follow copy, and fears the result, is that of Henry Binneman, who in 1583 reprinted Richard Stanyhurst's translation of the first four books of the *Æneid*, first printed at Leyden, June, 1582. Now Stanyhurst had original ideas about orthography, particularly as representing quantity. The

---

[79] *Mechanick Exercises*, (De Vinne), II, 197–98.

Holland printer, John Pates, had already found the orthography puzzling and given voice to his troubles in his address "To Thee Curteous Reader:"

> I am too craue thy pacience and paynes (good reader) in bearing wyth such faultes as haue escapte in printing; and in correcting as wel such as are layd down heere too thy view, as al oother whereat thow shalt hap too stumble in perusing this treatise. Thee noʻoueltie of imprinting English in theese partes, and thee absence of the author from perusing soom proofes could not choose but breede errours. But for thee abridging of thy trauayle I wyl lay downe such faultes as are at this present found too bee of greatest importaunce. And as for thee wrong placing of an V for an N, or an N for an V, and in printing two EE for one E or one for two, and for thee mispoyncting of periods; thee correction of theese I must bee forced for this tyme too refer too thye friendlye paynes.

The next printer, Binneman, had Pates's errors, as well as Stanyhurst's spelling-scheme, to wrestle with. He and his conscience made a compromise:

> I am to craue thy pacience (good Reader) and thye friendly acceptance of my paines in printing this booke. The noueltye of the verse, and the absence of the Author put me halfe in a feare either to displease the gentleman that penned it, or not to please the gentlemen that reade it: if I should obserue the newe Ortographie used in the booke, (whether with the writer's mind, or the Printers fault, I know not) it might haue bred error in the understanding of many, and misliking in the judgement of most. And very loth I am to seeme vniurious to the Author, in straying any whit from his prescribed rules in writing, exactly obseruing the quantity of each syllable. If I haue here and there changed some one or other letter, My purpose was to giue more light to the matter, by that maner of spech, whereto our country men are most acquainted. The absence of any letter, which for the necessitie of the verse often falleth out, I haue noted with an Apostrophe thus (') for the placing of two oo and ee for one, and contrary one for two, which thou mayst often meete with in reading, I am to refer thee to the Authors Epistle at the beginning and generally to commend to thy curtesie my trauaile in so strange and unaccustomed a worke.[80]

Publishers seem often to have felt a responsibility for the tone, purpose, style, or even literary form of the works they brought out. "J. S.," the "printer and stationer," apologized for Middle-

---

[80] Arber's Reprint.

ton's use of couplets in *A Mad World, My Masters*, which he published in 1640, as being then out of fashion:

All that you can find in the perusal I will give you notice of beforehand, to prevent a censure that may arise in thy reading of this comedy, as also for the excuse of the author; and that is this: here and there you shall find some lines that do answer in metre; which I hope you will not prove so disdainful, whereby the book may be so much slighted as not to be read, or the author's judgment undervalued as of no worth. Consider, gentle reader, it is fully twenty years since it was written, (at which time metre was most in use, and showed well upon the conclusion of every act and scene.

Of more importance is the editorial attitude which led Richard Jones, apparently on æsthetic grounds, to omit some of the foolery from Marlowe's *Tamburlaine* (1592):

I have purposely omitted and left out some fond and frivolous gestures, digressing, and, in my poor opinion, far unmeet for the matter, which I thought might seem more tedious unto the wise than any way else to be regarded, though haply they have been of some vain-conceited fondlings greatly gaped at, what time they were shewed upon the stage in their graced deformities: nevertheless now to be mixtured in print with such matter of worth, it would prove a great disgrace to so honourable and stately a history. Great folly were it in me to commend unto your wisdoms either the eloquence of the author that writ them or the worthiness of the matter itself.[81]

Chettle seems to have believed in an extensive right of editing, in such matters as striking out passages, re-writing to change the tone, etc. In the preface to *Kind Hart's Dreame* (S. R., Dec., 1592)he states that the attack on certain "playmakers" in the *Groatsworth of Wit*, which he declares he bought from Robert Greene or his executors, has been ascribed to him. He first denies the authorship, and then defends himself as editor by posing as a pacifist:

How I have all the time of my conversing in printing hindred the bitter inveying against schollers, it hath been very well knowne, and how in that I dealt I can sufficiently proove,......as I have moderated the heate of living writers, and might have used my owne discretion (especially in such a case) the author beeing dead, that I did not .....For the first, whose learning I reverence, and, at the perusing of

[81] Cf. R. B.'s address to the Gentle Gentlewomen in *A Petite Palace of Pettie his Pleasure*, 1576.

Greene's booke, stroke out what then in conscience I thought that he in some displeasure writ, or, had it beene true, yet to publish it was intollerable, him I would wish to use me no worse than I deserve. I had onely in the copy this share: it was il written, as sometimes Greenes hand was none of the best; licensd it must be, ere it could bee printed, which could never be if it might not be reade: to be briefe, I writ it over, and, as neare as I could, followed the copy, only in that letter I put something out, but in the whole booke not a worde in, for I protest it was all Greenes, not mine, nor Master Nashes, as some unjustly have affirmed.

There can be no doubt that at times stationers omitted from and added to works they published, without consulting the author, and that they felt justified in doing so in the interests of their sales. Drayton, in the second part of his *Polyolbion*, scores the booksellers who handled the first part for omitting some introductory matter because the work did not sell fast enough. Editors interpolated or permitted interpolations to be made. Archbishop Parker, lover of learning though he was, added to and interpolated in Asser's life of Alfred, or at least permitted it to be done. He also "improved on" Matthew Paris by additions and alterations.[82]

Haste, carelessness, and crudity of style; youth, inexperience, and even wantonness of the author, are all acknowledged and apologized for by publishers of the period, who felt their responsibility.

Causes and Significance of Variant Readings

Probably the matter of greatest importance to the students of sixteenth and seventeenth century texts is, the multitude of variant readings. It was not so very long ago that the existence of the variants was regarded, even by critical writers, as a nuisance, rather than a source of interest and profit to a student of a text. Pope, apparently, would be relieved to see the Shakespeare variants on the dump-heap. He says, in prefacing his edition of Shakespeare's works, by way of comment on the Quartos, "And of some of these we meet with two or more editions by different printers, each of which has whole heaps of trash different from the other: which I should fancy was occasioned by their being taken from different copies belonging

---

[82] Hook, *Lives of the Archbishops*, IX, 501.

to different playhouses." But there is no evidence to support such a "fancy," and certainly no need usually for such an explanation of the variants; for different compositors, correctors, and publishers could and did produce widely varying results, though working from the same original. Indeed the same workmen, setting up a text anew, might be expected to produce variants by the introduction of new errors.

One cause of the many minute differences in texts was the multiplicity of editions. On Dec. 11, 1587, the standard number of books (in larger sized type than Brevier) in an edition was 1250. Exceptions were made for some books in great demand, such as proclamations, statutes, and almanacs. Four double impressions, of 2500 or 3000 copies each, were allowed annually for the grammar and accidence, primers, and catechisms.[83] These extensions were almost a necessity, in view of the quick sales of some of these works. The first edition of Lilly's almanac, *Merlinus Anglicus Junior*, is said to have sold in a week.[84] The size of the ordinary impression was raised from 1250 to 1500 or 2000 on Nov. 16, 1635.[85] It is the size of the ordinary impression that is of interest to the student of literature, as the extraordinary issues were of those reference books, devotional works, etc., that were in constant and large demand.

The significance of the printing regulation which limited the size of impressions lies not so much in the mere requirement of frequent new issues as in the necessity that these new issues be, as a rule, from new settings-up, in compliance with an order against standing forms. This order was intended to force the master printer to have copies newly set up, from time to time, so as to provide work for compositors and journeymen. The significance of new setting-up for the state of the text may be inferred from the differences between a reprint of a printed text and the original. One may find a good illustration in the two quartos of *Every Man Out of His Humour* by Holmes and Ling (1600) already referred to.

[83] *S.R.*, II, 883; 23.

[84] *S. P. Dom. Chas. I*, vol. DX, art. 112. A fortnight was said to have given time for the dispersion of Hayward's *History of Henry IV*, (*S. P. Dom.* 1595–97, preface, p. xix).

[85] *S.R.*, IV, 22. Larger editions were sometimes issued in piratical printing, as, for example, in the case of Wither's *Motto*, pirated in two issues of 3000 copies each, in 1621.

Not only the limitation of size of impressions, but, in conjunction with this, the rapidity of transfer of copyright from one stationer to another and the formation of new partnerships favored frequency of issues. We find among the copies of a work one with an imprint for one publisher, one with an imprint for a new publisher, or for the old one together with a new. This does not necessarily mean a new edition; for the new title-page may be only a cancel, with the insertion of a leaf or two in the old stock of printed books. Such seems to be the case with the copies of the *Tragedy of Caesar's Revenge* (*S. R.*, 1606, entered to Wright and Fosbrook). The undated edition which followed has in some copies the imprint "by G. E. for John Wright"; in others a cancelling of the original title-page and an insertion of a new one dated 1607, with the imprint "for Nathaniel Fosbrooke and John Wright."[86] Similarly, of seven copies of the 1632 Shakespeare Folio studied by Charles A. Herpick, and found to have "minute variations" in the texts, two had title-pages newly set up by the same printer for different publishers.[87] But if the title-page, in order to advertise the enterprise of the new owner or partner, makes a promise of fresh materials or real revision of the text, there must be at least a show of something new. Small changes, such as simple additions of a few items, might be made by insertions of a few pages, if there were old books in stock that could not be discarded. But, because of the order against standing forms,[88] any extensive improvement of the text undertaken to give new impetus to sales on the occasion of the venture of a new stationer meant a complete re-setting of the types. So here again, in the ambitions of stationers to exploit the copies they had acquired, by real changes (slight or large), we have a cause of variants in texts.

The differences that occur in successive issues of a text are of three general classes:

(1) Accidental changes of details in what are intended as mere reprints, or new issues.

(2) Intentional changes by printer, publisher, or editor, resulting in what may properly be called a new edition (unless the changes are so small and affect the text as a whole so slightly

---

[86] Malone Society, *Reprints*, 1911.
[87] *Notes and Queries*, ser. 9, X, September 6, 1902.
[88] The orders seem to have relaxed at a later period.

that *issue* defines the new production more accurately than *edition*).

(3) Intentional changes by the author in a new edition.

The steady degeneration of a text as it is reprinted from time to time may be illustrated by the quartos of Kyd's *Spanish Tragedy* after that put out for White, and also by the editions of Nashe's *Pierce Penilesse* (expecting that of 1595).[89] When an accidental corruption results in bad sense, there is a tendency on the part of compositor, corrector, or editor to make good the error in what appeals to him as a reasonable way. Thus, McKerrow notes a progressive corruption of a passage in *Pierce Penilesse*:

1592 ed., "The confutation of Citizens objections against players."
1593 ed., "The Confutation of Citizens against Players."
1595 ed., "Coniuration of Citizens against Players."

"Sense" has been editorially restored. A worse corruption by progression appears in the play, *The Bloody Brothers*, where the passage in II, i,"Oh power of tears dropt by a thorough woman" becomes, in the edition of 1639, "prayer dropt through by a woman," (*prayer* having been caught up, probably, from the line before), and in 1640 is still further disfigured as "paper dropt through by a woman."[90] Similarly in *Richard III.*, line 182, Q¹ reads, "What do I fear? myselfe? Later quartos have it, "What do I fear myselfe?" And the Folio, to restore the sense, makes it "What? do I feare myselfe?" As it happens, the change here is not so damaging as in the other instances. But the tendency to use printed texts as copy, when possible, gave opportunity for printer's errors upon printer's errors.

The supplying of accidental omissions, by new compositors or editors, to suit their own tastes, is one cause of variants. Thus, in the first scene (line 8) of *The Faithful Shepherdess*, the first quarto lacks two syllables of its line, closing with "and games." While Quarto 2 was being set up from Quarto 1, this was observed and "merry" was inserted before "games" in the copies not yet printed. Quarto 3 was probably set up from an un-

---

[89] See Schick's edition of *The Spanish Tragedy*, and McKerrow's edition of the works of Nashe, I, 143–45.
[90] Cited by Fleay, *Chronicle History* . . . . , I, 204.

corrected copy of Quarto 2, or else from 1, for it contains the insertion "jolly" before "games".[91]

A normal change in a new edition (though by no means of invariable occurrence) was the correction of *errata*, to please either author or stationer. The correction was often only imperfectly carried out.

Author's revision was, of course, an important source of variant readings in new editions, but a source very difficult to establish in particular cases, For example, many of the changes in the texts of Donne's poems *suggest* author's revision; so do some of Chapman's; so do the frequent changes of wording in Drayton's poems, 1608, 1610, 1613, 1619, 1628, 1630, 1637. As to the fact that authors revised texts for new editions there can no longer be any doubt; the only question is, did a particular set of changes originate with author, compositor, publisher, editor, or press-corrector? The answer is often only literary guess-work, to be safely indulged in only by scholars who are thoroughly familiar with the author's style and habits.

Quite as interesting to a student as the variant readings of editions and re-issues are the differences in copies of a single edition. These, again, are either accidental or intentional. The accidental variations here, however, are of minor importance, consisting chiefly of accidents which might occur in printing, such as shifting improperly wedged types in re-inking or printing or picking out a type here and there and replacing it wrongly. Such errors affect typographical accuracy, to be sure, but they do not so often become of major importance for the meaning of the text. Still, they should be kept in mind as a possible explanation of otherwise puzzling little differences in the typography of copies of the same edition.

Many differences between copies may be accounted for by the practice of stopping the press to correct errors as soon as they were noted, and allowing incorrectly and correctly printed sheets to be bound up together. The uncorrected sheets were not proof sheets, as some have supposed, but simply sheets printed before mistakes were noted, and kept because the printers felt they could not afford to waste them. The typographical ideals of the day, as we have seen, allowed the correction of errors in

---

[91] *Beaumont and Fletcher's Works, Variorum* (Bullen), III, 3–4.

"diuers of the copies."[92] Interesting examples of the binding up of corrected and uncorrected sheets in a volume may be found in the following texts: the Shakespeare Folios, and some of the Quartos, especially the 1608 *Lear* quarto which has the publisher's address; the 1639 *Wit without Money*; the 1609 *The Faithful Shepherdess*; the letters to noble ladies in the 1633 edition of Donne's *The Progresse of the Soule* (see Grierson's ed. of *Donne's Poems*, lix.).

The extent of the differences that may be found in copies of what might still be called a single edition is illustrated by Mr. McKerrow's note on variations in *The Return of Pasquill*, 1589.[93] Among seven copies he distinguishes three groups, according to such differences as spelling-changes, line-beginnings, paragraphing, and style of italic capitals. These differences are so radical as to indicate duplicate setting up for a part of the text. On comparison, the three groups show evidences of but two settings of types, in three combinations. This text offers an example of correction at the press which is unmistakable. A Guildhall copy has (B_7, 1.5) "ende at where it began." The British Museum and Bodleian copies show what might be guessed to be deliberate correction, "ende where it beganne," the change in spelling being probably intentional, for the sake of filling out the line. Mr. McKerrow has several times called attention to the use of new spellings by a compositor to shorten or extend the line to cover a correction or an error. That the change above noted is an intentional correction is made certain by the Lambeth copy, which has the word *at* crossed out in ink.

Variations in copies of the same issue may be due not only to revisions by the corrector of the press, but also to changes by the author. One might judge from Moxon's advice to the author that radical changes were not expected from him:

By no means he ought to hope to mend it in the Proofe, the Compositer not being obliged to it: and it cannot reasonably be expected he

---

[92] See Nabbes's preface to the *errata* in his *Hannibal and Scipio*, 1637, quoted on page 360.

[93] *Library*, n.s., IV, 385. For a fuller discussion of variants, see his "Notes on Bibliographical Evidence," (Bibliogr. Soc'y, 1914). Cf. also Lee's *Introduction to the Shakespeare Folio*, and his article, "Some Bibliographical Problems Connected with Elizabethan Drama," *Tr. of Bibliogr. Soc'y*, IV, 148-50; and C. A. Herpick, on 1632 Folios, *N. & Q.*, ser. 9, X, Sept. 6, 1902.

should be so good natured to take so much pains to mend such Alterations as the second Dictates of an Author may make, unless he be very well paid for it over and above what he agreed for with the Master-Printer.[94]

Authors clearly did expect and exercise the privilege of revising at the press their own, as well as the printers', errors. Nashe, Drayton, and Chapman, for example, seem to have revised their own work in the course of printing. Milton's objections to the necessity of inspection of the whole work before it could be licensed show that he regarded even extensive revision in the course of publication as the author's inalienable right:

And what if the author shall be one so copious of fancy, as to have many things well worth the adding, come into his mind after licensing, while the booke is yet under the press, which not seldom happens to the best and diligentest writers; and that perhaps a dozen times in one book. The printer dares not go beyond his licensed copy, so often then must the author trudge to his leave-giver, that those his new insertions may be viewed.[95]

It has been said that of the privately printed folio of the *De antiquitate Britannicæ ecclesiæ,* compiled under the direction of Archbishop Parker, 1572, no two copies have been found alike. The work was intended for private circulation by the editor, who said that "for the present he purposed to keep it by him, while he lived, to add and mend, as occasion should serve him, or utterly to suppress it, and to bren it." The copies show new setting-up of various pages. Space for addition is left in some copies, in the life of Parker, where p. 19 is printed only on one half, its verso also being blank. A copy in Christ Church has the addition, three unpaged leaves, the first the half-filled p. 19, then two extra leaves, then p. 20 as in other copies. The Christ Church copy has also a leaf after p. 24 that is lacking in most other copies. In works not privately printed, large material changes of this sort would probably not occur except in new editions.

Where minor variations occur in copies of one issue, the same problem confronts an editor as in the case of variants in editions, namely, what variants represent revisions by the author. No rules or principles of general application can be formulated:

[94] *Mechanick Exercises* (De Vinne), p. 266.
[95] *Areopagitica* (Lockwood), p. 93.

CAUSES AND SIGNIFICANCE OF VARIANT READINGS 379

the decision must be ruled by the editor's judgment and common-sense. Some cases are hard to determine; many will not be attempted by any cautious editor. Mr. H. R. Plomer, in presenting some variants in copies of the 1594 quarto of *Lucrece*, remarks:

> There is evidence that the work was corrected while passing through the press, by whom we do not know, although naturally one inclines to the belief that the corrections were made by the poet himself. Thus in the third line of the fifth stanza, one copy reads,
>
> What needeth then apologies be made,
>
> while in another we find
>
> What needeth then Appologie be made,
>
> and again, in the eighteenth stanza we have in one reading
>
> And everie one to rest themselves betake
> Save thieves, and cares, and troubled minds that wake
>
> and in the other,
>
> And everie one to rest himself betakes
> Save theeves, and cares, and troubled minds that wakes.

In the first example, one readily chooses the second reading as probably revised, and guesses that the *p* was doubled to preserve the spacing; but still the facts might not support the theory. In the second passage the syntax is equally distressing either way, from a modern point of view, and either spelling might serve for partially adjusting spaces. The rime obliges one false syntax or the other; and there is nothing to prove who made the choice, or why. It may be doubted whether the false reference of *themselves* (or, indeed, even the construction *minds that wakes*) would be especially distressing to an Elizabethan author. The revision is such as an author might make, if he cared to, but certainly such as an Elizabethan compositor or proof-corrector would not hesitate to make if he wished to do so.

Such puzzles have often been "solved" by editors to suit their own tastes in expression, or to accord with their conception of the author's tastes. Mr. R. B. McKerrow has called the attention of students of texts to the need of systematizing the adoption of preferred readings (those which are assumed to be corrections) by the introduction of a rational principle based on

[96] "Shakespeare Printers," *Bibliographer*, II (January–June, 1903), 174–88; 299–319.

the arrangement of pages in the sheet for printing. One must first determine whether a copy is a folio, quarto, octavo, or other form, and study out the paging and numbering accordingly. For example, in the quarto, the outside pages of the sheet would be $\begin{smallmatrix} ҭ & ϛ \\ 1 & 8 \end{smallmatrix}$, and the inner $\begin{smallmatrix} 9 & ɛ \\ 7 & 2 \end{smallmatrix}$. Then, if one feels bound to accept a reading on page 1 as a corrected reading, he cannot rationally reject as uncorrected pages 4, 5, 8. Similarly, the inner form must be accepted or rejected as a whole, so far as press corrections are concerned. The common practice of sewing folios in threes and fours must be kept in mind, and the real imposition of pages ascertained. One must remember that the inner form may be corrected, and the outside uncorrected, or *vice versa*. Mr. McKerrow's suggestion is entirely reasonable, and ought to be used by editors of these early texts whenever the textual problems are of sufficient importance to justify this expenditure of time.[97]

In gathering for binding, the directions by Moxon simply call for the taking of one sheet off every heap, beginning at the last heap (that is, at the left hand).[98] Though presentation copies were, in special cases, sometimes made up from carefully corrected sheets, there seems to be no evidence of any *habitual* care-taking in putting in one copy corrected or uncorrected sheets exclusively. That would indeed be impracticable, in view of the way of making corrections at the press; for one error might be discovered when only a few sheets had been printed; and, on another sheet, an error might escape notice till many copies had been pulled off. It is, therefore, usually unsafe to describe one copy as a more "correct" version on the whole, just because some of the variant readings contained in it happen to be distinctly preferable. Special presentation copies excepted, such "correct" versions would be only the result of chance. It is risky also to give weight to the number of copies giving a

---

[97] The best exposition of this method is in Mr. McKerrow's "Some Notes on Bibliographical Evidence," *Transactions of Bibliographical Soc'y*, 1914, p. 72 ff. and pp. 29–44. The method is applied in his editions of Nashe and of Barnes's *The Devil's Charter*.

[98] Mistakes in binding sometimes give, in single copies, leaves in duplicate showing variations, as in Massinger's *The Roman Actor* (Quarto of 1629) and *Holinshed's Chronicle* (1577), which has a duplicate leaf intended for a cancel.

single reading, as most of the copies of a sheet might happen to have been printed before an error was discovered. Examples of indiscriminate binding of corrected and uncorrected sheets are common enough. Two examples will serve for illustration: *The Faithful Shepherdess*, 1609, and *Wit without Money*, quarto of 1639. The number of combinations of corrected and uncorrected sheets possible in a given copy depends on the format and the number of pages; but even a folio of a few pages offers a variety of possibilities. The hopelessness of the task of determining Elizabethan and Jacobean texts absolutely where there are many variants is suggested by the author's frankly throwing up his hands and resigning the job of even listing all the *errata*. Burton says to the reader, in his farewell address concerning the *Anatomy of Melancholy* (1620), that there are "many letters mistaken, misplaced, added, omitted, as *i* for *y*, or *a* for *e* or *o*, false points, &c. which are in some copies only, not throughout (To point at each particular of which were to pick out the seedes of a foule bushell of corne)."

A consideration of the methods of correcting at the press and binding of sheets in volumes will inevitably lead to the conclusion that it is impossible to accept or reject, as wholes, individual copies of sixteenth or seventeenth century texts, where there are many variants, unless there is some more rational basis for a choice than the presence of a few obviously preferable readings.

A word may be said here about the possibility of detecting priority of editions and the use of one copy for setting up the other. In general, compositors preferred printed copies to manuscripts when they could secure them. As has been pointed out, this is of significance for degeneration of text by perpetuation of error, plus false correction of error, plus new error, and so on. Incidentally, the use of printed copies as exemplars enables one, in some cases, to determine the priority of undated copies and their relation of dependence. Indications of the use of a copy as exemplar are not, of course, always of the same sort: but there are two general classes of evidence to look for. The perpetuation of unusual typographical errors is suspicious. There is enough of this in the Ling quarto (1600) of *Every Man Out of His Humour* to warrant assumption that it was a reprint from Holmes's quarto of the same year (see pages 332ff.). Two quartos of Fletcher's *The Elder Brother*, in 1637, are seen to be related as exemplar and reprint, by the presence, in the former, of the word *young* (V.ii.72) after a pushed-up lead, and by the later compositor's interpretation of the leadmark as an apostrophe ('young).[99]

Slavish imitation of copy, when crossed by accident, often reveals itself by new errors in the reprint. When the pagination is for any reason lost, retention of a catch-word out of place would reveal unmistakably the relation of the texts. Schick used this method to establish the priority of a quarto of *The Spanish Tragedy*. The catch-word test has also shown that, of the two quartos of *Sir John Oldcastle*, the one with Skakespeare's name on the title-page is a later issue, and that there is no evidence of a cancellation in the other issue, as one might otherwise have been led to imagine.[100] But printers are not always so obliging as to leave these tracks behind them. As has been shown above, the efforts of a compositor to recover pagination or line-numbering, where it has been lost, may give unmistakable evidence of priority of text.[101]

Evidences of Surreptitious or Piratical Printing

In concluding this discussion of text, we may mention briefly the evidence which may be helpful in determining whether a given text is spurious, surreptitious, or piratical. The detection of falseness of date and imprint by composite photography of title-pages, with a printer's rule at the side to gauge minute differences of types and arrangement, was first successfully worked out by W. J. Neidig, with the aid of Professor J. M. Manly, for the purpose of establishing the spurious nature of the Shakespeare quartos dated 1600 and 1608 but really published by Jaggard in 1619.[102]

---

[99] *Beaumont and Fletcher's Works, Variorum*, ed. Bullen, II, p. 5.

[100] See *Sir John Oldcastle*, ed. for Malone Society, vol. 8. Cf. also Greg, "On Certain False Dates in Shakespearean Quartos," *Library*, n.s., IX (1908), 113, 381.

[101] On the detection of cancels in texts by studying the relation of chain-lines to each other and to the printing-lines, and by the position of the water-mark, see McKerrow's notes on a cancelled passage in Greene's *Quips for an Upstart Courtier, Gentleman's Magazine*, February 1906, and also his *Notes on Bibliographical Evidence*. . . . . (1914), pp. 81 ff.

[102] See W. J. Neidig, "The Shakespeare Quartos of 1619," *Mod. Philol.*, VIII, (1910), 145–65.

In surreptitiously printed books (as also in pirated) there is sometimes a peculiarity of imprint, such as omission of the date, the place of printing, or the printer's name. The author's name may be omitted. But, as we have seen, there were many reasons for anonymity, so that the omission of the author's name is no warrant for assuming that an issue was surreptitious, unauthorized, or pirated. Use of initials, or of reversed initials, was not then regarded as even anonymous publication, in all cases. Certainly it should not be regarded as any sure sign of unauthorized publication. Nor should we see in a title of such form as "Shakespeare's Sonnets" (as does Sir Sidney Lee)[103] an indication of piracy; for the form is a very common one and may be found in a number of works which were certainly authorized. The omission of one or all of the usual forms of imprint and title and signature is no *proof* of surreptitious or piratical printing. It merely creates a suspicion of irregularity, which must be confirmed by evidence of other kinds. The rigidity of the censorship has made us familiar with one sign which we incline to regard as a symptom of irregularity of one sort or another,—the mocking imprints of many books,—as if author or publisher were playfully defying the authorities, as in various products of the Cartwright press, *c.* 1572; *Martin Marprelate*, 1588; *Pasquil of England*, 1589, ("within a mile of an Oak"); *The Returne of ....Pasquil*, 1589 ("by Pepper Alley"); *Countercuff given to Martin, Jr.*, 1589 ("printed where I was"); *Pasquil's Apology*, 1590; *An Almond for a Parrot*; *Oh read ouer Dr. John Bridges*, 1589; *Vox Borealis*, 1641. False indication of place, in the imprint, was sometimes resorted to in piracies, as in Sparkes's edition of the Psalms, said to be printed at Cambridge (in *Cases in Star Chamber*, 1631, Camden Soc'y), and in the 1599 "Edinburgh" edition, by Waldegrave, of Sidney's *Arcadia*.

I have discussed elsewhere[104] the significance of the presence or absence of entry on the registers of the Stationers' Company for assumptions as to authority of texts. Mr. A. W. Pollard has made excellent application of this particular test in his sifting of "good" and "bad" Shakespeare quartos in his *Shakespeare Folios and Quartos*. As for the Elizabethan author's statements

---

[103] *Life of William Shakespeare*, 1916, p. 674.
[104] In *Authors' Rights and Copyright*, 1580–1640, ch. I, sec. 2.

that a particular edition was unauthorized, I have become so suspicious that I should always look for proof.

It remains to note that general typographical corruption, though tending to favor assumption of piracy or unlicensed printing, can not properly be used as proof. It has, of course, often been assumed that piracy means necessarily degeneration of text. Theoretically this is reasonable, but in fact, not every pirate is a poorer workman than his predecessor. Though Ling's reprint of Holmes's quarto of *Every Man Out of His Humor* is, perhaps, on the whole, worse than the original, it still contains a few improvements. And the "Allde for White" pirated quarto of *The Spanish Tragedy* is, as Schick has pointed out in his edition, better than the later copy by the rightful owner of the text and probably better than Jeffes' previous edition, which "swarmed with errors." A pirated text may usually be expected to be worse than an unpirated; but, if occasional better ones can be found, it is clear that corruption of text is no infallible proof of piracy.

It should be noted, in conclusion, that within the last decade there has been given a pronounced impetus to the application of strict bibliographical methods to the study of texts. This may be illustrated by the recent work of Pollard, Wilson, McKerrow, Greg, and others on texts of the sixteenth and seventeenth centuries. While the results in some cases are still open to discussion, it should be observed that the aim and spirit in this comparatively new method of approach are altogether wholesome, particularly as tending to substitute, wherever possible, scientific standards for personal impressions in the handling of problems of the text.[105]

[105] For a brief statement on the outlook for use of bibliographical aids in text problems, see A. W. Pollard, *Shakespeare's Fight with the Pirates* (1920), p. xxvii. An elaborate example of the application of critical bibliography to text problems is W. W. Greg, *Two Elizabethan Stage Abridgements*, Clarendon Press, 1923.

BIBLIOGRAPHICAL NOTE

Because of frequent recurrence, certain works are referred to in both my text and my notes by short titles. If not otherwise distinguished, all references to Murray, or Murray, *E. D. C.*, are to his *book, English Dramatic Companies*; those to Henslowe are to his *Diary*, edited by Greg; those to Rymer, are to Rymer's *Foedera*, etc., the full titles being given in the Bibliography which follows.

Titles transposed for economy in reference are:

S. R., Transcripts of the Registers of the Stationers' Company.

S. P., for all State Papers, separate collections being distinguished by the addition of *Dom.* for *Domestic*, or of *Foreign*, *Spanish*, *Venetian*, etc.

Hist. MSS Comm. stands for the general reports prepared by that Commission, the separate collections being entered under their names.

Cecil Papers and *Sidney Papers* are invented titles, explained under those entries in the Bibliography.

Alphabetical entries are by authors, agents, or editors, when possible; or, by a significant word of the title. Entries under such words as *Acts, Bulletins, Minutes, Transactions*, etc. have been discarded in favor of the names of the bodies, societies, or commissions concerned.

BIBLIOGRAPHY

ABBOTT, EDWIN A. Bacon and Essex. L. Seeley and Co., 1877.

ADAMS, JOSEPH Q., ed. Dramatic records of Sir Henry Herbert, Master of the Revels, 1623–73. New Haven. Yale Univ. Press, 1917.

———— Life of William Shakespeare. Boston. Houghton, 1923.

———— "Shakespeare, Heywood, and the Classics," Modern Language Notes, XXXIV (1919), 336–40.

———— "Timon of Athens and the irregularities in the first folio," Journal of English and Germanic Philology, VII (1907–08), 53–64.

———— "William Heminge and Shakespeare," Modern Philology, XII (1914–15), 51.

ADAMS, WILLIAM D. Dictionary of the drama: a guide to the plays, playwrights .... of the United Kingdom and America from the earliest times to the present. L. Chatto and Windus, 1904. Vol. I.

AIKIN, LUCY. Memoirs of the court of Charles I. Phila. Carey, Lea, and Blanchard, 1833. 2 v.
——— Memoirs of the court of Queen Elizabeth. 3d ed. L. 1819. 2 v.
ALBRIGHT, E. M. Author's rights and copyright, 1580–1640 (not yet published).
——— "Notes on the status of literary property, 1500–45," Modern Philology, XVII (1919), 439–55.
——— "To be staied," Publications of the Modern Language Association, XXX. 3 (1915), 474 ff.
ALDIS, HARRY G. "The book-trade, 1557–1625," the Cambridge History of English Literature, IV, ch. xviii.
——— The printed book. Cambridge University Press, 1916.
Alleyn Memoirs. Memoirs of Edward Alleyn, founder of Dulwich College; by J. P. Collier. L. Shakespeare Society, Pub., 1841.
Alleyn Papers. A collection of original documents illustrative of the life and times of Edward Alleyn and of the early English stage and drama. Ed. by J. P. Collier. L. Shakespeare Society, Pub., XVIII, 1843.
ALSTED, JOHANN H. Universal encyclopaedia. Herborn. [1610.] 1630. 2 v.
AMBLER, CHARLES. Cases in Chancery. Lib. Reg. 1770 B. fo. 35.
AMES, JOSEPH. Typographical antiquities: being an historical account of printing in England, with some memoirs of . . . . printers and a register of books. . . . . (1471–1600.) L. W. Faden, 1749.
——— Index to Ames's Typ. Antiq., by A. W. Pollard.
Ancient British Drama. Edited by Sir Walter Scott. L. 1810. 3 v.
ANDERS, H. R. D. Shakespeare's books. Schriften der deutschen Shakespeare-Gesellsch., I. Berlin. 1904.
ANDREWS, CLARENCE E. Richard Brome: a study of his life and works. Yale Studies in English, XLVI. N. Y. Holt, 1913.
Antiquaries' manuscripts. Catalogue of the manuscripts in the library of the Society of Antiquaries of London; compiled by Sir Henry Ellis. L. Bensley, 1816.
ARBER, EDWARD, ed. English reprints. [1869–.]
——— English scholars' library. 16 v.
——— Introductory sketch to the Martin Marprelate controversy. (English scholars' library, no. 8).
——— ed. Stationers' Registers, see London Stationers.
Archaeologia; or, miscellaneous tracts relating to antiquity, XXXI; 37. L. J. Nichols, 1773.
Archaeological Society, see British Arch. Soc'y.
Archiv für Stenographie: Monatshefte für die wissenschaftliche pflege der kurzschrift . . . . pub. by Curt Dewischeit. 1897–1914.
Archiv für Schrift-kunde: Offizielles organ des deutschen schriftmuseums zu Leipzig. Jahrg. I, 1914–1918. Lpz. K. F. Koehler, 1918.
ARONSTEIN, PH. "Thomas Heywood," Anglia, XXXVII, 2 ff.
ATKYNS, RICHARD. The original and growth of printing; collected out of history and the records of this kingdome. . . . . L. J. Streater, 1664.
BAILEY, JOHN E. "Timothy Bright." Phonetic Journal, 1875.
BAKER, DAVID E. Biographia dramatica; or, a companion to the playhouse . . . . historical and critical memoirs . . . . of British and Irish dramatic

writers .... also an alphabetical account of their works, and the dates when printed. 2d ed. L. 1782. (Continued by Isaac Reed, 1764–82.)

BAKER, GEORGE P. Elizabethan quartos: notes by G. W. Cole. 1910.

BAKER, G. P. Some bibliographical puzzles in Elizabethan quartos. Boston. Torch Press. Privately printed. (Also in Bibliographical Society, Proceedings, 1908–09.)

BAKER, HENRY B. The London stage: its history and traditions, 1576–1888. 1889. 2 v. Another ed., History of the London stage and its famous players, 1576–1903. 1904.

BALES, PETER. The writing school master; containing three books in one. The first, teaching swift writing, etc. January 1, 1590. T. Orwin.

BAMFORD, JOHN. Essays on the subject of mechanism and literature. L. Hamilton, 1838.

BANG, W., ed. Materialien zur kunde des älteren englischen dramas.

Barnavelt, Sir John van Olden: in Bullen, Old English plays, II.

Barnavelt, Tragedy of Sir John van Olden. Ed. by W. Frylinck. Amsterdam, 1922. (Not examined.)

BARNES, BARNABY. The devil's charter. Ed. by R. B. McKerrow, in Materialien zur kunde, etc., VI.

BARTLETT, HENRIETTA C. Catalogue of the exhibition of Shakespeariana held at the New York Public Library April 2–July 15, 1916. N. Y. Public Library. N. Y., 1917.

—— and Pollard, A. W. A census of Shakespeare quartos. (With introduction.) Yale Univ. Press, 1916.

—— Undescribed Shakespeare quartos (since the catalogue of 1916). London Times Lit. Sup., June 18, 1920. (Sir Geo. Holford's collection.)

BARWICK, G. F. "The laws regulating printing and publishing in France," Bibliographical Society, Transactions, XIV (1916), 69–107.

—— "The laws regulating printing and publishing in Spain." Bibliographical Society, Transactions, IV (1897), 47–55.

BATES, E. S. "Some foreigners in Shakespeare's England." Nineteenth Century, LXXII, 110 ff.

BAUGH, A. C. William Haughton's Englishmen for my money. Phila., 1917. U. of Pennsylvania diss.

—— "A seventeenth century play list," Modern Language Review XIII (1918), 401–11.

BAYFIELD, M. A. Study of Shakespeare's versification, with an inquiry into the trustworthiness of the early texts. An examination of the 1616 folio of Ben Jonson's works, and appendices, including a revised text of Antony and Cleopatra. Cambridge Univ. Press, 1920.

BEAUMONT, FRANCIS, and Fletcher, John.
Plays, 1625.
Comedies and tragedies never printed before and now published by the authors originall copies. L. Humphrey Robinson, 1647. F.
Fifty comedies and tragedies. 1679.
Works: with memoir by A. Dyce. L. 1843–46. 11 v.
Works. Variorum edition. Ed. by A. H. Bullen. L. 1904. 12 v.

Works. Cambridge Univ. Press, 1905–12. 10 v. (Notes and prefatory matter by A. R. Waller.)

BECKMANN, JOHANN. A history of inventions, discoveries, and origins. 4th ed. Translated by William Johnston. L. 1846. Vol. 2.

BELL, JOHN. London's remembrancer, 1665–66.

BELOE, REVEREND MR. WILLIAM. Anecdotes of literature and scarce books. L. F. Rivington, 1808–14. 6 v.

Bibliographical Society of London.
    Transactions.
    Publications, 1893–
    The Library: (indexed under authors of articles here.)

BIGMORE, EDWARD C., and Wyman, C. W. Bibliography of printing, with notes and illustrations. L. Quaritch, 1880. 3 v.

BIRCH, THOMAS. Memoirs of the reign of Queen Elizabeth, from 1581. L. 1754. 2 v.

BIRCH, W. DE G. Historical charters and constitutional documents of the city of London. L. 1887.

BLADES, WILLIAM. Books in chains, and other bibliographical papers. L. E. Stock, 1892.

—— "Common typographical errors, with especial reference to the text of Shakespeare." Athenaeum, Jan. 27, 1872, p. 114.

—— "The first printing-press in England," The Bookworm, October, 1869.

—— The Pentateuch of printing. (1877.) L. 1891. (With memoir of Blades.)

—— Shakespeare and typography; being an attempt to show Shakespeare's personal connection with and technical knowledge of the art of printing; also remarks upon some common typographical errors, with special reference to the text of Shakespeare. L. 1872.

—— "Water-marks," Library Journal, XIV (1889), 129–31.

BOAS, FREDERICK S. "A seventeenth century theatrical repertoire," The Library, VIII (1917), 225–40.

—— "Sources of Chapman's Conspiracy of Byron and The Revenge of Bussy d'Ambois," Athenaeum, Jan. 10, 1903.

—— "Stage censorship under Charles I," London Times Lit. Sup., Dec. 14, 1917, and Dec. 20, 1917.

—— "Stage censorship under Charles II: Sir Henry Herbert and *The Cheats*," London Times Lit. Sup., April 15 and 22, 1920.

Bodleian Library (Oxford). Catalogue of printed books and manuscripts of the Douce collection.

—— Catalogue of Shakespearian exhibition held at the Bodleian, 1916.

—— See also Malone Collection.

BOHN, H. G. Biography and bibliography of Shakespeare. (Miscellanies of the Philobiblon Society.) L. 1863. B.M. "Impression limited to forty copies for presentation to persons of wealth and rank." (This item is included for the more fortunate.)

BOHUN, EDMUND. The character of Queen Elizabeth . . . . , her policies, and . . . . methods. . . . . L. R. Chiswell, 1693.

BOSWELL, J., ed. Plays and poems of William Shakespeare; with corrections and illustrations of various commentators: comprehending a life of the poet and an enlarged history of the stage by the late E. Malone, with a new glossarial index. 1821. 21 vols. ("Third variorum," abbreviated as *Var.* in my notes.)

Boston Public Library. Catalogue of the Allen A. Brown collection.

———— A list of books on the history and art of printing and some related subjects in the Public Library of the city of Boston and the libraries of Harvard College and the Boston Athenaeum. Boston Public Library, 1906.

BOUCHOT, HENRI. Le livre. Paris.

BRACKETT, JAMES A. Theatrical law: legal rights of manager, artist, author, and public. Boston. C. M. Clark, 1907.

BRAND, JOHN. Popular antiquities of Great Britain. Edited by Ellis, 1902. Vol. 1.

BRASSINGTON, W. S. Hand-list of collective editions of Shakespeare's works published before the year 1800. Stratford-upon-Avon. J. Morgan, 1898.

BRATHWAITE, R. The English gentleman, 1630.

———— The penitent pilgrim, 1641.

BRETON, NICHOLAS. Complete works in prose and verse. Ed. by Alexander Grosart. 1877. 2 v. (Chertsey Worthies' Library.)

BREWER, J. S., editor. See State papers, Henry VIII.

BRIGGS, WILLIAM D. "Studies in Ben Jonson," Anglia, XXXVIII (1913–14), 101–20.

BRIGHT, TIMOTHE, M.D. Characterie. An arte of shorte, swifte, and secrete writing by character. L. I. Windet, 1588. Reprinted by J. Herbert Ford, 1888. (Not altogether accurate.)

BRIQUET, CHARLES M. De la valeur des filigranes du papier comme moyen de déterminer l'âge et la provenance de documents non datés. Genève. 1892.

British Archaeological Association. Journal, 1860. (Play lists.)

British Museum. Catalogue of books in the library of the British Museum printed in England, Scotland, and Ireland, and of books in English printed abroad to the year 1640; compiled by A. H. Bullen. 1884. 3 v.

———— Catalogue of Harleian manuscripts in the British Museum. L. R. and A. Taylor, 1813. Vols. 2 and 3.

———— Catalogue of Lansdowne manuscripts in the British Museum; with indexes. 1819.

———— Catalogue of printed books on Shakespeare; by G. Fortescue. L. Clowes, 1897. (232 columns of bibliography.)

———— List of bibliographical works in the reading-room of the British Museum; compiled by A. W. Pollard. 2d ed. 1889.

BROME, RICHARD. Dramatic Works. L. 1873. 3 v.

———— ———————————— Edinburgh, 1874.

———— Five new playes, 1653.

BROOK, C. F. TUCKER-, ed. Shakespeare Apocrypha: being a collection of fourteen plays which have been ascribed to Shakespeare; edited with introduction, notes, bibliography, and facsimiles of title-pages. Oxford. Clarendon Press, 1908.

BROOK, RUPERT. John Webster and the Elizabethan drama. N. Y. John Lane, 1916.

BROOKE, RALPH. Catalogue of the succession of the kings of England. William Jaggard, 1619.

——— A discoverie of certaine errours published in print in the much commended Britannia (1594). Very preiudiciall to the discentes and successions of the auncient nobilitie of this realme. By Yorke herault. L. 1596.
    Another edition, with Camden's answer, and Brooke's reply. L. 1724.

BROTANEK, R. Die englischen masken-spiele. Vienna. 1902.

BRUCE, JOHN. "Ben Jonson's supposed complicity in the Gunpowder Plot," Athenaeum, April 22, 1865.

———, ed. Correspondence of James VI of Scotland with Sir Robert Cecil and others in England during the reign of Elizabeth. Camden Society, XX (1860).

BUC, GEORGE. The third universitie of England, 1612; in Stowe's Annals, continued by Howe, 1615.

BULAEUS. Historia universitatis parisiensis, tom. III.

BULLEN, A. H. A collection of old English plays. L. 1882–85. 4 v.

BURN, JOHN SOUTHERNDEN. Court of High Commission. 1865.

BURTON, ROBERT. The anatomy of melancholy. Ed. by A. R. Shilleto. L. G. Bell, 1893.

BYRNE, M. ST. CLARE. "Anthony Mundy and his books," Bibliographical Society, Transactions, n.s. I, 4 (1921), 225–57.

Caesar's Revenge, Tragedy of. Malone Society reprints, 1911.

CALDERWOOD, DAVID. History of the Kirk of Scotland. Edinb., 1844–45.

Cambridge History of English Literature, vol. V, ch. xi, E. Walder, The text of Shakespeare; and ch. xiv, A. W. Ward, Some social and political aspects of the later Elizabethan and earlier Stewart period. Vol. VI, ch. x, Harold Child, The Elizabethan theatre; ch. xi, John M. Manly, The Children of the Chapel Royal, ch. xiv, J. Dover Wilson, The Puritan attack upon the stage, *et passim*.

CAMDEN, WILLIAM. Annales rerum anglicarum regnante Elisabetha, 1615–25.

——— Britannia (1594). 1806. 4 v.

CAMPBELL, DOUGLAS. The Puritan in Holland, England, and America. N. Y. 1892. 2 v.

CAMPBELL, JOHN. Shakespeare's legal acquirements considered. L. J. Murray, 1859.

CAMPBELL, JOHN C. Lives of the chancellors. . . . and chief-justices of England, Jersey City. 1881–85. 6 v. and Index.

CAMPBELL, WILLIAM. Materials for a history of the reign of Henry VII from documents in the Public Record Office. 1873–77. 2 v.

CARLTON, WILLIAM J. Timothe Bright, Doctour of Phisicke. L. Eliot Stock, 1911.

CARLETON, GUY M. "The Elizabethan Compositor," Columbia University, English Graduate Record, I–III (1905–07), pp. 7–24 (Jan.-Feb., 1906).

Cases in . . . . Star Chamber, *see* Gardiner, S., ed.

CASTELAIN, MAURICE. Ben Jonson: l'homme et l'œuvre. Paris. Hachette, 1907.

Catalogues listing plays (a partial list):

    Bellamy, B. P. General catalogue of all the English dramatic pieces I have been able to discover. Bath, 1834. 2 v.

Clavel. General catalogue of books, 1660–1700.

Feales, W. True and exact catalogue of all the plays and other dramatic pieces ever printed in the English tongue to April, 1732. L. 1732.

Kirkman, Francis. Exact catalogue of all the English stage plays printed till 1671. B.M. 643. d. 75.

King, T. Rare old plays and poetry. L. 1815.

Mears, W. A true and exact catalogue of all the plays that ever were yet printed in the English tongue. Printed for W. Mears. To 1713. Continued to 1715. B. M. 11903. f. 24.

The careless shepherdess: a tragicomedy . . . . with an alphabetical catalogue of all such plays that ever were printed. L. 1656.

Tom Tyler and his wife: with an exact catalogue of all the plays that were ever yet printed. 2d impression. L. 1661.

A true and perfect catalogue of all comedies, tragedies, and tragi-comedies, pastorals, masques, etc. ever yet printed and published to 1661. 1661. B. M. 641, g. 1.

A compleat catalogue of plays . . . . in the English language. 2d ed. 1726. B.M. 641, a. 15.

A true and exact catalogue of plays, 1732. B. M. 641, f. 18 (2).

Catalogue of curiosities chiefly theatrical . . . . 1748. B.M. 641, f. 18(5)

Boston Athenaeum Library catalogue.

Catalogue of Heber's collection of early English poetry, drama, ballads, broadsides, etc.; by J. P. Collier. L. 1834.

Catalogue of printed books in the library of the Faculty of Advocates. Edinburgh and L. 1860–69.

Catalogue of printed books, manuscripts, letters, etc. collected by the late Mr. Henry Huth. L. 1881. 5 v.

Catalogue of printed books and manuscripts in the John Rylands Library, Manchester. Manchester, 1899. 3 v.

See also: catalogues of the Allen Brown collection, Boston; of the Douce and Malone collections, Bodleian; of the Newberry Library, Chicago; and Foster, F. W. "Title-list of catalogues of Eng. plays," Notes and Queries, 5th Ser., XII (1879).

Cecil Papers. A collection of state papers relating to affairs in the reigns of King Henry VIII, King Edward VI, Queen Mary, and Queen Elizabeth . . . . transcribed from original letters by William Cecill Lord Burghley. 2 v. Vol. I, 1542–70, ed. by Samuel Haynes. L. 1740. Vol. 2, 1571–96, ed. by William Murdin. L. 1759.

CHALMERS, GEORGE. An apology for the believers in the Shakespeare-papers which were exhibited in Norfolk St. L. 1797.

────── Farther account of rise and progress of the English stage: in the Third Variorum of Shakespeare (1821).

────── A supplemental apology for the believers in the Shakespeare papers. (A reply to Mr. Malone's answer.) L. For Thomas Egerton. 1799.

CHAMBERLAIN, JOHN. Letters by John Chamberlain during the reign of Elizabeth. Edited by S. Williams. 1861.

CHAMBERS, EDMUND K. "Court performances before Queen Elizabeth," Modern Language Review, II, 1 (1906–07), 1–13.

—— "Court performances under James I," Modern Language Review, V (1909), 153–66.

—— "Elizabethan Lords Chamberlain," Malone Society, Collections, I, 1, pp. 31–43.

—— The Elizabethan Stage. Oxford University Press. 1923. 4 v.

—— The mediaeval stage. Oxford. Clarendon Press, 1903. 2 v.

—— Notes on the history of the Revels Office under the Tudors. L. A. H. Bullen, 1906. (Referred to as *Tudor Revels*.)

—— "Plays of the King's men in 1641," Malone Society, Collections, I, 4 and 5 (1911), 364–70.

CHAMBERS, E. K., and GREG, W. W., ed. "Dramatic records from the Lansdowne manuscripts (Burghley papers)," Malone Society, Collections, I, 2 (1908), 143 ff.

—— "Dramatic records from the patent rolls; company licenses," Malone Society, Collections, I, 3, pp. 260 ff.

—— "Dramatic records from the Privy Council register, 1603–42," Malone Society, Collections, I, 4 and 5, pp. 370 ff.

—— "Dramatic records of the city of London, The Remembrancia," Malone Society, Collections, I, 1, pp. 43–100.

CHAPMAN, GEORGE. Plays and poems. Edited by Thomas M. Parrott. L. G. Routledge, 1914.

—— Comedies and tragedies. L. J. Pearson, 1873.

—— The widow's tears (1612); in Dodsley's Old Plays, VI, 115 ff.

—— Achilles shield. J. Windet, 1598.

CHAPMAN, JOHN KEMBLE. Court theatre and royal dramatic record, being a history of theatrical entertainments . . . . from the time of Henry VIII. L. 1850.

CHETTLE, HENRY. Kind hart's dreame. . . . . L. For William Wright, 1593.

CHETWOOD, W. R. Select collection of old plays. Dublin. 1750.

—— General history of the stage. L. 1749.

CHEVILLIER, ANDRÉ. L'Origine de l'imprimerie de Paris. Paris. Laulne, 1694.

CHURCH, RICHARD W. Life of Edmund Spenser. N. Y. Harper, 1881.

CIBBER, COLLEY. Apology for the life of Colley Cibber. L. J. Watts, 1740.

CIRCUIT COURT of U. S. A., E.D. Pa., Phila. Reports, 4, Vol. XVII, 349.

CLARENCE, REGINALD. "The Stage" cyclopaedia; a bibliography of plays. L. 1909.

COBBETT, WILLIAM. Parliamentary history of England, 1066–1625. L. 1806.

COKE, ROGER. A detection of the court and state of England during the reigns of King James I, Charles I, Charles II, and James II. L. J. Brotherton and W. Meadows, 1719.

COLE, GEORGE W. "First folio of Shakespeare: a further word regarding the correct arrangement of its preliminary leaves." Bibliographical Society of America, Proceedings and papers, III, 65–83. 1909.

—— "Shakespeare quartos," Boston Transcript, August 25, 1909, p. 17.

Collection and selection of English prologues and epilogues. 1779. 4 v. (In the Newberry Library, Chicago.)

COLLES, WILLIAM N., and HARDY, HAROLD. Playright and copyright in all countries. L. Macmillan, 1906.

COLLIER, JOHN P. Annals of the English stage, to the Restoration; Vol. III of English dramatic poetry to the time of Shakespeare. L. J. Murray, 1831. 3 v.
―――― A bibliographical and critical account of the rarest books in the English language. L. 1865. 2 v.
―――― Book entries of the Stationers' Register relating to the drama and popular literature . . . . to 1586. Shakespeare Society, 1848–49. Continued to 1595, Notes and Queries, ser. 2, XII and ser. 3, i–iii.
――――, ed. Diary of Philip Henslowe, 1591–1609. Shakespeare Society, 1845.
―――― History of English dramatic poetry to the time of Shakespeare; and Annals of the stage to the Restoration. L. (1831.) 1879. 3 v.
―――― Memoirs of the principal actors in the plays of Shakespeare. Shakespeare Society, XIII (1846).
―――― Notes and emendations to the text of Shakespeare's plays, from early manuscript corrections in a copy of the folio of 1632 in the possession of J. P. C. 2d ed. L. Whittaker, 1853.
――――, see also Alleyn Memoirs, Alleyn Papers.
COLLINS, ARTHUR. See Sidney, Henry.
COLLINS, JOHN C. Studies in the text and prosody of Shakespeare. Westminster. A. Constable, 1904. Chapter VIII.
COOPER, CHARLES H. Annals of Cambridge. Cambridge, 1842–1908. 5 v.
―――― and Thompson. Athenæ Cantabrigienses [1500–1611]. 3 v.
CORYTON, JOHN. Stage-right: a compendium of the laws relating to dramatic authors. . . . . L. D. Nutt, 1873.
Court and times of Charles I, see Williams, Robert, ed.
Court and times of James I, see Williams, Robert, ed.
CREIGHTON, CHARLES. History of epidemics in Britain. Cambridge University Press, 1891–94. 2 v.
CREIGHTON, MANDELL. Queen Elizabeth. L. Longman, 1900.
CREIZENACH, WILHELM. Geschichte des neueren dramas. 2d ed. Halle. Max Niemeyer, 1911. Volumes IV and V.
―――― English drama in the age of Shakespeare; tr. from Geschichte, etc. Sidgwick and Jackson.
CRUICKSHANK, A. H. Philip Massinger. Oxford. Basil Blackwell, 1920.
CUNNINGHAM, PETER. Extracts from the accounts of the Revels at court, in the reigns of Queen Elizabeth and King James I, from the original office books of the Masters and Yeomen. Shakespeare Society, Pub., VII. L. 1842. (See Law, Some supposed Shakespeare forgeries; and a review of this in Athenaeum, June 3, 1911; and Charlotte C. Stopes, "Seventeenth century Revels books," London Times Lit. Sup., Dec. 3, 1920.)
CUTLER, EDWARD, SMITH, T. E., and WEATHERLY, F. E. Law of musical and dramatic copyright. L. Cassell, 1890.

DABORNE, ROBERT. Plays. Edited by A. E. H. Swaen. Anglia, XX (1898), 153–257, and XXI.
DAM, B. A. P. VAN, and STOFFEL, CORNELIS. "The authority of the Ben Jonson folio of 1616," Anglia, XXVI: 377.

―――― Chapters on English printing, prosody, and pronunciation, 1550–1700. Heidelberg, 1902. Cf. "High-handed ways of Elizabethan and Jacobean printers," Anglistische Forschungen, Heft 9.

DAM, B. A. P. VAN. William Shakespeare: prosody and text. Leyden. E. J. Brill, 1900.

DANIEL, SAMUEL. Complete works in prose and verse. Edited by Alexander Grosart. Spenser Society, 1896. 5 v.

―――― Collection of the history of England, 1613–18. Simon Waterson, 1626.

D'AVENANT, SIR WILLIAM. Dramatic works. Edited by J. Maidment and W. H. Logan. Edinburgh. 1872. 5 v.

DAVENPORT-ADAMS, W. A dictionary of the drama. 1904. Vol. 1.

DAY, JOHN. Works. Edited by A. H. Bullen. 1881. 2 v.

―――― Ile of Guls. 1606.

DEGROOT, H. Hamlet, its textual history. Amsterdam. 1923.

DEKKER, THOMAS. Dramatic works. L. J. Pearson, 1873. 4 v.

―――― Plays. Mermaid Series. L. T. F. Unwin, 1894.

DEVEREUX, WALTER B., ed. Lives and letters of the Devereux, Earls of Essex. L. 1853. 2 v.

DESLANDES, VENANCIO. Documentos para a historia da typogr. portugueza (16th and 17th c.) Lisboa. 1881–82.

DE VINNE, THEODORE L. The invention of printing. (L. 1877). 2d ed. 1878.

―――― Notable printers of Italy during the fifteenth century. N. Y. Grolier Club, 1910.

―――― The practice of typography: a treatise on plain printing types. 2d ed. 1902.

―――― Title-pages as seen by a printer: numerous illustrations in facsimile and some observations on the early and ancient printing of books. N. Y. Grolier Club, 1901.

D'EWES, SIR SIMONDS. A compleat journal of the votes, speeches, and debates, both of the House of Lords and House of Commons throughout the whole reign of Elizabeth. 2d ed. L. For J. Robinson, 1693.

DEWISCHEIT, CURT. "Shakespeare und Stenographie," Shakespeare Jahrbuch, XXXIV: 186.

DIBDIN, CHARLES. Complete history of the English stage. L. For the author. 1800. 5 v.

DIBDIN, JAMES C. The annals of the Edinburgh stage. Edinburgh. R. Cameron, 1888.

DIBDIN, THOMAS F. Typographical antiquities . . . . , 1471–1600 . . . . begun by . . . . Joseph Ames, considerably augmented by William Herbert, and now greatly enlarged, with copious notes, ... L. W. Miller, 1810–19. 4 v.

DIGGES, SIR DUDLEY. The compleat ambassador. L. Bedell, 1655.

DILKE, SIR C. W. Old English plays: being a continuation of Dodsley's collection. (1814-15.) 1816. 6 v.

D'ISRAELI, ISAAC. Commentaries on the life and reign of Charles I. L. Henry Colburn, 1851. 2 v.

DITCHFIELD, P. H. Books fatal to their authors. L. E. Stock, 1895.

DIX, HENRY. A new art of brachygraphy. 1633.

DOBELL, BERTRAM. "Newly discovered documents of the Elizabethan and Jacobean periods," Athenaeum, March 23 and 30, and April 6 and 13, 1901.

DODSLEY, ROBERT. A select collection of old English plays (1744). 4th ed., with notes by Hazlitt, 1874–76. 15 v. (V. 1 contains James Wright, Historia histrionica.)

DODSLEY, R. and J. Theatrical records: or, an account of the English dramatic authors and their works. L. 1756.

DONNE, JOHN. Poems. Ed. by H. J. Grierson. Oxford. 1912. 2 v.

—— Life and letters of John Donne. Ed. by Edmund Gosse. N. Y. Dodd, Mead, 1899. 2 v.

Douce collection, Bodleian, *see* Halliwell-Phillips.

DOWNES, JOHN. Roscius Auglicanus: or, an historical review of the stage from 1600 to 1706. L. 1886.

DUNN, S. G. "A Jonson copyright." London Times Lit. Sup., July 29, 1921.

DURHAM, F. HERMIA. "The relations of the crown to trade under James I." Royal Historical Soc'y, Trans., n.s. XIII (1899).

Early English Drama Society, Publications. Edited by J. S. Farmer, 1906.

EGERTON, JOHN. Egerton's theatrical remembrancer, containing a complete list of all the dramatic performances in the English language, ... editions, ... dates, ... theatres . . . . where originally performed: . . . . an account of those . . . . acted and . . . . unpublished (Elizabethan to 1787). L. T. and J. Egerton, 1788. (Continued. 1803.)

Elizabeth, Letters of, to James VI of Scotland, *see* Camden Society, Pub., Vol. XLVI.

Elizabethan bibliography, *see* Studies in Philology (U. of N. Car.), April, 1918, and various other issues, especially April, 1924.

Elizabethan Studies, second series, Ed. by Edwin Greenlaw. Univ. of North Carolina, Chapel Hill, N. Ca.

ELLIS. (Bookseller, 29 New Bond St., London.) Catalogue of books of the Tudor and Stuart period down to 1640. 3 pts. No. 162.

ELLIS, SIR HENRY, ed. Original letters illustrative of English history. 2d ed. L. Harding, 1825. 3 v.

—— Original letters of eminent literary men of the 16th, 17th, and 18th centuries. L. For the Camden Society. J. B. Nichols, 1843.

English Association, of England, *see* Year's work in English; *and see* bulletins of the Association (Modern Humanities Research Ass'n).

English drama and stage, 1543–1664, illustrated by documents, treatises, and poems. Roxburghe library. 1869.

ERASMUS. The epistles of Erasmus. Edited by Francis M. Nichols. L. Longmans, Green, 1901–04. 2 v.

FALKENSTEIN, KARL. Geschichte der buchdruckerkunst in ihrer entstehung und ausbildung. Lpz. Teubner, 1840.

FARMER, JOHN S., ed. Early English dramatists, 1st ser., 1905–08. 13 v.

—— Tudor facsimile texts of old English plays, 1907–14.

—— Hand-list to the Tudor facsimile texts. L. J. S. Farmer, 1914.

FARR, HARRY. "Notes on Shakespeare's printers and publishers, with special reference to the poems and Hamlet," Bibliogr. Soc'y, Tr., n. ser., III, 4, pp. 225–60.

FARRER, J. A. Books condemned to be burnt. L. 1892.
FAULMANN, KARL. Geschichte und litteratur der stenographie. Wien (1894). 1895.
FEASEY, EVELINE I. "Licensing of the Mirror for Magistrates," The Library, n.s. III, 3 (1922), pp. 177–93.
FEUILLERAT, ALBERT. Le bureau des menus-plaisirs et la mise en scène à la cour d'Elizabeth. Louvain. A. Uystpruyst, 1910.
—— Documents relating to the revels at court in the time of King Edward VI and Queen Mary . . . . (the Loseley manuscripts). Ed. with notes and indexes. Louvain. A. Uystpruyst. (Materialien zur kunde, etc., Bd. 44.) (Referred to as *Revels*, etc.)
—— Documents relating to the office of the revels in the time of Queen Elizabeth. 1908. (Materialien zur kunde, etc., Bd. 21.) (Referred to as *Revels*, etc.)
—— JOHN LYLY: Contribution à l'histoire de la Renaissance en Angleterre. Cambridge University Press, 1910.
FLEAY, FREDERICK G. "Annals of the careers of James and Henry Shirley," Anglia, VIII, 405 ff.
—— A biographical chronicle of the English drama, 1559–1642. L. Reeves and Turner, 1891. 2 v.
—— A chronicle history of the London stage, 1559–1642. 1890.
—— A chronicle history of the life and work of William Shakespeare. L. J. C. Nimmo, 1886.
—— Tabular view of the quarto editions of Shakespeare's works, 1593–1630. New Shakespeare Society, Trans., pt. 1, 40–50. L. 1874.
FLEMING, WILLIAM H. A bibliography of the First Folio in New York. In Shakespeariana, V (March, 1888), 102–17.
FLETCHER, GILES. Of the Russe common wealth . . . . with the manners and fashions of the people. . . . . Edited by E. A. Bond. Hakluyt Society, Vol. XX. L. 1856.
FLETCHER, JOHN. Nice Valour; in Beaumont and Fletcher folio, 1647.
—— see Beaumont.
FOLKINGHAM, W. Brachigraphy, post-writ, or the art of short-writing. 1618.
FORBES, JOHN. Certaine records touching the estate of Scotland since the Reformation. Edinburgh. 1846.
FORD, JOHN. Works. Edited by A. Dyce (1869). 1895.
—— Dramatische werke; in Materialien zur kunde, etc., Vol. 23. 1908.
FORMAN, SIMON. The booke of plaies and notes therof per formans. Shakespeare Society, Trans., 1875–76.
FORSYTHE, ROBERT S. The relations of Shirley's plays to the Elizabethan drama. N. Y. Columbia University Press. 1914.
FOWELL, FRANK, and PALMER, FRANK. Censorship in England. L. Frank Palmer, 1913.
FOXE, JOHN. Actes and monumentes, 1563.
—— Acts and monuments, with life, by Rev. Mr. George Townsend. L. Seeley, 1846. 8 v. and index.
—— Ecclesiastical history, conteyning the Actes and monumentes of martyrs. L. 1576. 2 v.

FRERE, W. H. The English church in the reigns of Elizabeth and James I (1553–1625); in W. Hunt and W. R. Stephens, History of the English church, 1904, vol. V.

FRIEDRICH, PAUL E. Studien zur englischen stenographie im zeitalter Shakespeares: Timothe Brights Characterie . . . . mit einem anhang: Neue gesichtspunkte für stenographische untersuchungen von Shakespeare quartos, dargelegt an der ersten Q. der Merry Wives of Windsor, 1602. Lpz. K. F. Koehler, 1914.

FROUDE, J. A. History of England from the fall of Wolsey to the defeat of the Spanish Armada. 1856–70. (Vols. VII–XII.)

FULLER, THOMAS. History of the University of Cambridge. Edited by Prickett and Wright. 1840.

FURNESS, H. H., editor, see Shakespeare.

GARDINER, SAMUEL R. History of England, 1624–28. L. Longmans, Green, 1875. 2 v.

——— History of England from the accession of James I . . . . to the Civil War (1603–42). 1893. 10 v.

——— "Political elements in Massinger," New Shakespeare Society, Trans., 1876, pp. 314–332. (Reprinted from Contemporary Review, Aug., 1876.)

——— Reports of cases in the Courts of Star Chamber and High Commission. Camden Society, Pub., n.s., vol. 39. 1886.

GAYLEY, CHARLES M. Francis Beaumont, dramatist. N. Y. Century Co., 1914.

——— Shakespeare and the founders of liberty in America. N. Y. Macmillan.

GEE, H. The Elizabethan clergy and the settlement of religion. 1898.

George à Greene, the Pinner of Wakefield (1599). Edited by J. C. Collins. 1905.

GILDERSLEEVE, VIRGINIA. Government regulation of the Elizabethan drama. N. Y. 1908. Columbia Univ. Studies in English, ser. 2, v. 4, no. 1.

GLAPTHORNE, HENRY. Plays and poems. In Bullen's Old plays, II. 1874.

GOFFLOT, L. V. Le theatre au collège du moyen âge a nos jours, avec bibliographie. Le Cercle français de l'Université Harvard. Paris, 1907.

GOLLANCZ, ISRAEL, ed., see Shakespeare (Book of homage).

GOSSE, EDMUND, see Donne, John.

GOSSON, STEPHEN. Plays confuted in five actions (1582).

——— The schoole of abuse . . . . against poets, pipers, players, etc. (1579.) Arber, English Reprints, no. 3.

GRAVES, THORNTON S. The court and the London theatres during the reign of Queen Elizabeth. Menasha, Wisconsin. Banta, 1913.

——— "Jonson's Epicoene and Lady Arabella Stuart," Modern Philology, XIV, 141.

——— "Political use of the stage during the reign of James I," Anglia, XXXVIII (1914), 137–56.

——— "Some allusions to religious and political plays," Modern Philology, IX, 545–54.

GRAY, G. J., compiler, see Hazlitt, W. C., Bibliographical Collections.

GRAY, HENRY D. "The first quarto of Hamlet," Modern Language Review. X (1915), 171–180.

GREENE, ROBERT. Life and complete works, in prose and verse. Edited by Alexander Grosart. L. 1881-1886. 15 v.
—— A Groatsworth of wit. 1592.
—— History of Orlando Furioso, 1594. Edited by W. W. Greg. Malone Society, Reprints, 1907.
—— Scottish history of James the Fourth . . . .entermixed with a pleasant comedie, presented by Oboram King of Fayeries. 1598.
GREENSTREET, JAMES. Documents relating to the players at the Red Bull, Clerkenwell, and the Cockpit in Drury Lane in the time of James 1. New Shakespeare Society, Pub., ser. 1, L. 1885. (Cf. Transactions, no. 10, 1880-86, pt. 3, pp. 459-508. 1886.)
—— "Hamlet quartos," London Times Lit. Sup., Apr. 10, 1919.
—— "The Whitefriars Theatre in the time of Shakespeare." New Shakespeare Society, Pub., ser. 1 (Tr.)1888, pp. 269-285.
GREG, WALTER W. "Autograph plays of A. Munday," Modern Language Review, VIII (1913), pp. 89-90.
—— "The bakings of Betsy," The Library, II (1911), 225-59.
—— "The bibliographical history of the First Folio," Library, n.s. IV (1903), 258-286.
—— Descriptive catalogue of the early editions of the works of Shakespeare preserved in the library of Eton College. L. Oxford University Press, 1909.
—— "On certain false dates in Shakespearian quartos," Library, n.s. IX (1908), pp. 113-131; and 381; cf. X, 208-211; 3 d ser. I, 36-53; Athenaeum, May 2, 1908; p. 544 and May 9, p. 574; and May 30, pp. 669-670; Nation, May 21, 1908, p. 462 and June 4, p. 510, and Nov. 12, p. 459.
—— "The first edition of *Every man out of his humour*," Bibliographical Society, Transactions, n.s. I, no. 3 (1920), 153-61.
—— "An Elizabethan printer and his copy," *Ibid.*, n.s. IV, no. 2 (1923), 102-118.
—— A list of English plays written before 1643 and printed before 1700. Blades. For the Bibliographical Society. L. 1900.
—— "Massinger's autograph corrections in *The duke of Milan*," Bibliographical Society, Trans., n.s. IV, no. 3 (1923), 207-218.
—— A list of masques, pageants, etc., supplementary to A list of English plays. L. Bibliographical Society. 1902.
—— "More Massinger corrections," Bibliographical Society, Trans., n.s. V, no. 1 (1924), 59-91.
—— "Notes on dramatic bibliographers," Malone Society, Collections, I (1911), pts. 4 and 5, pp. 324-341.
—— Pastoral poetry and pastoral drama. 1906
—— "The printing of the Beaumont and Fletcher folio of 1647," Bibliographical Society, Trans., n.s. II, no. 2 (1921), 109-115.
—— "Prompt copies, private transcripts, and the 'playhouse scrivener,' " Bibliographical Society, Trans., n.s. VI. no. 2 (1925), 148-156.
—— "*The Spanish Tragedy*—A leading case?" Bibliographical Society, Trans., n.s. VI. no. 1 (1925), 47-56.
—— "On transcription in the pirated plays of Shakespeare," London Times

Lit. Sup., May 20, 1920. (Cf. J. D. Fitzgerald, *Ibid.*, May 13, June 3, 1920.)

——- Two Elizabethan stage abridgements. Oxford. Clarendon Press, 1923.

—— "The two issues of Day's *Isle of Gulls*, 1606," Bibliographical Society, Trans., n.s. III, no. 4 (1923), 307–309.

——— editor. See Henslowe papers; Henslowe's diary; Merry Wives; More, Sir Thomas. See also Chambers, E. K., and Greg, Dramatic Records.

Grolier Club, N. Y. Catalogue of original and early editions of some of the poetical and prose works of English writers from Langland to Wither . . . . being a contribution to the bibliography of English literature. New York. For the Grolier Club, 1905.

GUENIN, LOUIS P. Histoire de la sténographie dans l'antiquité et au moyen-âge. Paris. Hachette, 1908.

HAAS, LORENZ. Verleger und drucker der werke Shakespeares bis zum Jahre 1640. Erlangen diss. Junge, 1904.

HALES, JOHN W. "King Richard the Second." Reprinted from The Academy, Nov. 20, 1875, in Notes and essays on Shakespeare. L. G. Bell, 1884. (pp. 205–209).

HALLIWELL-PHILLIPS, JAMES O. A brief hand-list of books, manuscripts, etc. illustrative of the life and writings of Shakespeare, collected between the years 1842 and 1859. L. 1859.

—— A brief skeleton hand-list of the early quarto editions of the plays of Shakespeare . . . .L. 1860.

—— A catalogue of the Shakespeare-study books in the immediate library of J. O. Halliwell-Phillips. L. Privately printed by J. E. Adlard. 1876.

—— A collection of ancient documents respecting the office of the Master of the Revels, and other papers relating to the early English theatre, from the original manuscripts formerly in the Haslewood collection. L. 1870 (Sometimes referred to by its running title, as Dramatic records.). 11 copies. (One in B. M., one in Birmingham Lib., one in Lib. of U. of Pennsylvania).

—— A dictionary of misprints, found in printed books of the sixteenth and seventeenth centuries . . . .Brighton, 1887. 94 pp. (An alphabetical list of errors,—not of great value).

—— A dictionary of old English plays in print or in manuscript (to the close of the seventeenth century). L. J. R. Smith, 1860.

—— Handlist of early English literature preserved in the Douce collection in the Bodleian. L. 1860.

—— A hand-list of upwards of one thousand volumes of Shakespeariana added to the three previous collections by J. O. H.–P.– L. 1862.

—— Illustrations of the life of Shakespeare. L. 1874.

—— Outlines of the life of Shakespeare. L. 1882.

—— Shakespeariana: an account of early editions . . . .and commentaries, etc. L. J. R. Smith. 1841.

—— Visits of Shakespeare's company of actors to the provincial cities and towns of England. Brighton, 1887.

HALPIN, N. J. Oberon's vision illustrated by a comparison with Lyly's Endymion. Shakespeare Society, 1843.

HANSARD, THOMAS C. Typographia: an historical sketch of the origin and progress of printing. L. 1825.

HARDY, SIR THOMAS DUFFUS, continuator. Fasti ecclesiae anglicanae, or, a calendar of the principal ecclesiastical dignitaries in England and Wales, and of other chief officers in the universities of Oxford and Cambridge,...(to 1715). Compiled by John Le Neve, and corrected and continued ....by T. D. Hardy. 1854.

—— compiler. See Rymer, *Foedera*, Syllabus of, in English.

Harleian Miscellany: A collection of scarce, curious, and entertaining pamphlets and tracts. L. 1811. 12v.

HARRIS, WILLIAM. An historical and critical account of the lives and writings of James I and Charles I (from originals and state papers). L. F. and J. Rivington. 1814. 5v.

HART, WILLIAM H. Index expurgatorius Anglicanus, or a descriptive catalogue of the principal books printed or published in England, which have been suppressed or burnt by the common hangman, or censured, or for which the authors, printers or publishers have been prosecuted. Parts 1–5. London, 1872–1878. (Incomplete).

Hatfield MSS, *see* Salisbury.

HATCHER, ORIE L. JOHN FLETCHER, Chicago, Scott, Foresman, 1905.

HAYNES and MURDIN, ed., *see* Cecil Papers.

HAZLITT, WILLIAM C. Bibliographical collections and notes, 1474–1700. L. 1876–1886. Ser. 2, 1882. Ser. 3, 1876, 1882, 1887. Supplements, 1889, 1892. Ser. 4, Bibliographical collections and notes made 1893–1903. L. 1903. (Index, by G. J. Gray, 1893).

—— The English drama and stage, under the Tudor and Stuart princes, 1543–1664; illustrated by a series of documents, treatises, and poems. L. For Roxburghe Library, 1869.

—— Handbook to the popular, poetical, and dramatic literature of Great Britain, from the invention of printing to the Restoration. L. J. R. Smith, 1867. (Continued by his Collections and notes).

—— General index to Hazlitt's Handbook and his Bibliographical collections, 1867–1889. By G. J. Gray. Edited by W. C. Hazlitt. L. B. Quaritch, 1893.

—— A manual for the collector and amateur of old English plays. L. 1892.

—— Prefaces, dedications, and epistles selected from early English books, 1540–1701. Printed for private circulation. 1874.

——, editor, *see also* Dodsley, Robert.

HEATH, THOMAS. Stenography. L. 1634.

HENSLOWE, PHILIP. Henslowe papers: being documents supplementary to Henslowe's Diary. Edited by W. W. Greg. L. A. H. Bullen, 1907.

—— Henslowe's diary. Edited by W. W. Greg. L. Bullen, 1904–1908. 2v.

HERBERT, SIR HENRY, Master of the Revels, *see* Adams, J. Q.

HERBERT, WILLIAM. Typographical antiquities ....1471–1600 ....begun by ....Joseph Ames ....considerably augmented by William Herbert. L. Printed for the editor, 1785–1790. 3 v.

—— A sketch of the history of English drama in its social aspects. 1881.

Herford, C. H. The first quarto edition of Hamlet, 1603. L. 1880.

―――― A sketch of recent Shakespearean investigation. L. Blackie, 1923.
HERPICK, C. A. "Shakespeare folios" (1632). Notes and Queries, ser. 9, X, Sept. 6, 1902.
HEYWOOD. THOMAS. Dramatic works, with a life of the poet, by J. P. Collier. L. Shakespeare Society, Publications, nos. 3, 13, 30, 42, 44–46.
―――― Works, with introduction by J. A. Symonds. Edited by A. W. Verity. Vizetelly, 1888.
―――― An apology for actors, 1612. Reprinted, Shakespeare Society, 1841.
―――― Two historical plays on the life of Queen Elizabeth [If you know not me, etc.] Shakespeare Society. 1851.
―――― Loves maistresse: or The Queens masque. L. R. Raworth for J. Crouch, 1636. Cf. 2d ed., 1640.
―――― Pleasant dialogues and dramas. 1637.
―――― Rape of Lucrece. 1608.
―――― Troia Britannica. William Jaggard, 1609.
―――― Life of Thomas Heywood, by F. W. Fairholt. Percy Society, Pub., vol. 20. 1856.
―――― See also Bates, Katherine, A woman killed with kindness, and The fair maid of the west, (Belles Lettres series), Heath, 1917. Introduction.
HIGGS, GRIFFIN. An account of the Christmas Prince as it was exhibited at the University of Oxford in 1607. Miscellanea antiqua anglicana. L. 1816. vol. 1, no. 3..
Historia histrionica, *see* Wright, James.
Historical Manuscripts Commission. Reports. L. 1871–1883.
HOE, RICHARD M. The literature of printing. L. 1877.
―――― Short history of the printing-press and of the improvements in printing machinery from the time of Gutenberg up to the present. N. Y. For R. Hoe, 1902.
HOLINSHED, RAPHAEL. Chronicles of England, Scotland, and Ireland. (1577). Ed. of 1587, in 6 vols., 1807–8.
HOOK, WALTER F. The lives of the archbishops of Canterbury. (1845–1852). L. 1860–1884. 12 v.
Hooker, Keble's; Ed. by Dean Church and Canon Paget. Oxford, Clarendon Press, 1888. (Preface, pt. 2, bk. 5). 3 v.
HORSEY, SIR JEROME. Travels of Sir Jerome Horsey in Russia at the close of the 16th century. Edited by Sir E. A. Bond. Hakluyt Society, vol. 20. 1856.
House of Commons, *see* Parliament.
House of Lords, *see* Parliament.
"Household Ordinances": A collection of ordinances and regulations for the government of the royal household, made in divers reigns from King Edward III to King William and Queen Mary. Society of Antiquaries of London. L. 1790.
HOWELL, JAMES. Epistolae Ho-Elianae. 1645.
HOWELL, T. B., and T. J. Complete collection of state trials and proceedings for high treason . . . .to 1820. 5th ed. L. 1816–26. 33v.
HUBBARD, FRANK G. The first quarto edition of Shakespeare's Hamlet. Madison. 1920. Univ. of Wisconsin Studies in Lang. and Lit., no. 8.

―――― "The 'Marcellus' theory of the first quarto of Hamlet," Modern Language Notes, XXXIII (1918), 73–79.
―――― "The Readings of the first quarto of *Hamlet*," P. M. L. A., XXXVIII (1923), 792-822.
HUDSON, WILLIAM. Treatise of the court of Star Chamber; in Francis Hargrave, Collectanea juridica, vol. II, pt. 1.
HUME, MARTIN A. S. The Courtships of Queen Elizabeth. L. T. F. Unwin, 1896.
HUNT, MARY L. Thomas Dekker. Columbia Univ. diss. N. Y. 1911.
HUTH, A. H. "On the supposed false dates in certain Shakespeare quartos," The Library, 3d ser., I (1910), pp. 36–46.

JACOBI, CHARLES T. "Printing inks," The Library, n.s. VII, 70–77.
JAGGARD, WILLIAM. "False dates in Shakespeare quartos," The Library, n.s. X (1909), 208–212.
―――― Shakespeare's publishers: notes on the Tudor-Stuart period of the Jaggard press. Jaggard Company, 1907. (Correcting D. N. B.)
―――― *See also* Shakespeare, Bibliography.
James I. of England.
   History and life of King James the Sext: an account of affairs in Scotland, 1566–1596 (anon.). Pub. by the Bannatyne Club.
   Letters of James VI. of Scotland, see Camden Soc'y, vols. 20 and 46.
   Secret history of the court of James I. Edited by Sir Walter Scott. Edinburgh, 1811. 2 v.
JAMES, THOMAS. (Bodleian Library). Index generalis librorum prohibitorum a pontificiis. 1627.
JEAFFRESON, J. C., ed. Manuscripts of W. M. Molyneux. Historical Manuscripts Commission, Seventh report. 1879. Appx.
JENKINSON, HILARY. Elizabethan handwriting. Bibliographical Society, Trans., n.s. III (1922), 1–34.
JOHNEN, CHR. Geschichte der stenographie. Berlin, 1911.
―――― "John Willis' Lehrbuch und system vom jahre 1602," Archiv für stenographie, 1908, p. 9 ff.
JONSON, BEN. Works, Edited by Gifford. L. 1816. 9 v.
―――― Works, Ed. by Cunningham, with memoir by Gifford. 1904. 3 v.
―――― Every man out of his humour, reprinted from Holmes's quarto of 1600, by W. Bang and W. W. Greg, Materialien zur kunde, etc., vol. XVI (1907).
―――― Every man out of his humour, reprinted from Ling's quarto of 1600, by W. Bang and W. W. Greg, Materialien zur kunde, etc., vol. XVII (1907). Cf. Anglia, XXVI, p. 377.
―――― Sejanus. Edited by W. D. Briggs. Heath, 1911. (Belles Lettres series).
JONSON, CHAPMAN, and MARSTON. Eastward Hoe. Edited by Felix Schelling. Heath. n.d. (Belles Lettres series).

KELLY, WILLIAM. Notices illustrative of the drama and other popular amusements chiefly in the 16th and 17th centuries . . . .; extracted from the Chamberlain's accounts; intr. and notes. L. J. R. Smith, 1865.

KELLNER, LEON. Restoring Shakespeare: a critical analysis of misreadings in Shakespeare's works. L. Allen and Unwin, 1925. (Reviewed, W. W. Greg, Review of Eng. Studies, I, 4; 463–78).

KEMPE, A. J., ed. Manuscripts and documents . . . .from the reign of Henry VIII to that of James I, preserved in the Muniment Room at Loseley House. 1835,

KENNEDY, WILLIAM. Annals of Aberdeen. 1812. 2v.

KIRCHHOFF, ALBRECHT. Die handschriftenhändler des mittelalters. 2d ed. Lpz. 1853.

KIRKMAN, FRANCIS. Exact catalogue of all the English stage plays printed till 1671. B. M. 643 d. 75.

KITCHIN, GEORGE. Sir Roger L'Estrange: a contribution to the history of the press in the 17th century. L. K. Paul, 1913.

KITTREDGE, G. L. "King James I and The devil is an ass," Modern Philology, IX (1911–1912), 195.

KLEIN, ARTHUR J. Intolerance in the reign of Queen Elizabeth. Boston. Houghton, Mifflin, 1917.

KLEIN, J. L. Geschicte des dramas. Lpz. 1865–1886. vols. XII and XIII.

KNIGHT, SAMUEL. Life of John Colet (1724). 1823.

KOCH, F. Ferrex und Porrex. Eine litterarhistor. untersuchung. Halle, 1881.

KÜHNELT, A. P. Über die geschwindschrift der alten. 1872.

KYD, THOMAS. Works. Edited from the original texts by F. S. Boas. Oxford. 1901.

——— The Spanish tragedy. A critical text, edited by J. Schick. Berlin. 1901.

LACROIX, PAUL; FOURNIER, EDOUARD; and SERÉ, FERDINAND. Le livre d'or des métiers. Histoire de l'imprimerie et des arts et professions qui se rattachent a la typographie, calligraphie, etc.

LAMBERT, D. H. A chronological catalogue of extant evidence relating to the life and works of Shakespeare. 1904.

Lanching of the Mary. In Bullen, Old English plays.

LANG, ANDREW. Social England illustrated: a collection of 17th century tracts. In Arber, English Garner. Westminster. 1903.

Lansdowne manuscripts, see British Museum.

LANGBAINE, GERARD. An account of the English dramatic poets. Oxford. By L. L. for G. West, 1691. (Based on his New catalogue of English plays, 1688, an unauthorized ed. of which had appeared a month before as *Momus triumphans*.)

——— Momus triumphans: or, The plagiaries of the English stage; exposed in a catalogue of all the comedies, tragicomedies, masques, and tragedies, opera's, pastorals, interludes, etc. both ancient and modern that were ever yet printed in English. The names of their known and supposed authors. Their several volumes and editions, etc. L. 1688.

———, and Gildon, Charles, The lives and characters of the English dramatic poets. Also an exact account of all the plays that were ever yet printed in the English tongue, etc. L. 1699.

LAW, ERNEST. More about Shakespeare "forgeries." Bell.

—— "On Shakespeare's plays in the Revels accounts", London Times Lit. Sup., Feb. 27, 1921. Cf. Times Index for further discussions.

LAW, THOMAS GRAVES. A co-operative catalogue of English literature up to 1640. The Library, V (1893), 97–102.

—— Essays and reviews. 1904.

LAWRENCE, W. J. "Assembled texts in the First Folio," London Times Lit. Sup., Jan. 12, 1922, p. 28.

LAWSON, ROBB. The story of the Scots stage. Paisley. Gardner.

LEACH, ARTHUR F. English plays and players, 1220–1548. In An English miscellany, presented to Dr. Furnivall. 1901.

—— "The Schoolboys' Feast," Fortnightly Review, n.s. LIX (1896), 128 ff.

LEE, SIR SIDNEY. "An Elizabethan bookseller," Bibliographica, I (1895), 474–498.

—— "Elizabethan England and the Jews," New Shakespeare Society, Trans., 1887–1892, pt. 2, pp. 143–167.

—— Facsimile of the First Folio edition of Shakespeare's plays, (1623). Oxford. Clarendon Press, 1902.

—— A life of William Shakespeare. 1898. Rewritten and enlarged. N. Y. Macmillan, 1916. New ed., 1923.

—— Notes and additions to the census of copies of the Shakespeare First Folio. 1906.

—— "The original of Shylock," Gentleman's Magazine, Feb., 1880.

—— "Shakespeare quartos," Athenaeum, 1908, p. 574.

—— "Shakespeare's company on tour," London Times Lit. Sup., May 5, 1921.

—— "Some bibliographical problems connected with Elizabethan drama: Summary." Bibliographical Society, Trans., IV (1896–8), 148–150.

—— "The topical side of the Elizabethan drama," New Shakespeare Society, Trans., 1887–1892, pt. 1, pp. 1–37.

——, editor. The year's work in English studies, 1919–20; 1920–21. For the English Association. L. Oxford Univ. Press, 1921–2.

L'ESTRANGE, SIR ROGER. A seasonable memorial in some historical notes upon the liberties of the presse and pulpit.

LEVY, MATHIAS. Shakespeare and shorthand. L. 1884.

—— William Shakespeare and Timothy Bright. L. 1910.

Life and death of Jacke Strawe, a notable rebell in England. 1593.

LODGE, EDMUND. Illustrations of British history, biography, and manners (Henry VIII to Chas. I.) (1791). L. 1838. 3 v.

LODGE, THOMAS. Complete works. Hunterian Club. 1875–1888. 4v.

London, Records of Corporation of, see Remembrancia.

London, Stationers Company of. Transcripts of the registers of the Company of Stationers of London 1554–1646. Edited by Edward Arber. 5 vols., with index.

London Times Literary Supplement. See index for many short papers of importance in this field.

Loseley manuscripts, see Kempe, Alfred J., editor.

LOUNSBURY, T. R. The text of Shakespeare: its history from the publication of

the quartos and folios to and including the editions of Pope and Theobald. N. Y. Scribner, 1906.
LOWE, ROBERT W. A bibliographical account of English theatrical literature from the earliest times to the present. L. Nimmo, 1888.
LOWNDES, W. H. The bibliographer's manual of English literature. H. G. Bohn, 1883–1885. 6v.
LUCKOMBE, PHILIP. Concise history of the origin and progress of printing. Adlard and Browne, 1770.
LUMMERT, AUG. Die orthographie der ersten folio-ausgabe.
LYLY, JOHN. Sixe court comedies. L. 1632.
———— Dramatic works, ed. Fairholt. 1858. 2v.
———— Complete works, ed. by R. W. Bond. Oxford. 1902. 3v.
———— Endymion, Arber, English Reprints.
————, see Feuillerat, Albert.
LYSONS, DANIEL. Environs of London. L. 1800–1811. 7v.
LÜHR, WILHELM. Die drei Cambridgen spiele vom Parnass, 1598–1603 in ihren litterarischen Beziehungen. Kiel. 1900.

MAAS, HERMANN. Äussere geschichte der englischen theatertruppen in dem zeitraum von 1559 bis 1642. Louvain. 1907. (Little fresh material).
MACRAY, WILLIAM D., editor. The pilgrimage to Parnassus, with the two parts of The return from Parnassus: three comedies performed in St. Johns College, Cambridge, 1597–1601. Clarendon Press, 1886. Cf. The return from Parnassus (1606), edited by Edward Arber. L. 1879.
MADAN, FALCONER. Books in manuscript: a short introduction to their study and use, with a chapter in records. L. Kegan Paul, 1893. Appendix, A list of printed catalogues of manuscripts in European languages. Revised, 1922. (See, on scribal blunders).
———— "Early representations of the printing press," Bibliographica, I, 223–249.
MADDEN, D. H. Shakespeare and his fellows. N. Y. E. P. Dutton, 1916.
MADDEN, JOHN P. A. Lettres d'un bibliographe. 1–6 séries. Versailles. Aubert, 1868–1886. 6v. in 5.
MALLINCKRODT, BERNARD VON. De ortu ac progressu artis typographicae dissertatio historica....Coloniae Agrippinae. J. Kinchwin, 1639.
MALONE, EDMOND, Collector. Catalogue of early English poetry and other miscellaneous works, illustrative of the British drama, collected by Edmond Malone and now preserved in the Bodleian Library. Oxford Univ. Press, 1836.
————, stage history, see Shakespeare, Variorum of 1821.
Malone Society. Collections, 1907—. Publications, 1906—.
MANLY, JOHN MATTHEWS. "The Children of the Chapel Royal and their masters," Camb. Hist. of Eng. Lit., VI (1910), pt. 2, ch. XI.
———— "Cuts and insertions in Shakespeare's plays," Studies in Philology, XIV (1917), 123 ff.
MANTZIUS, KARL. A history of theatrical art in ancient and modern times; translated by Louise von Cossell. 1904. vol. 3.
MARLOWE, CHRISTOPHER. Works. Edited by A. H. Bullen. L. 1885. 3v.
———— Edited by A. Dyce. 1850. 3v.

────── Edited by C. F. T. Brooke, 1910.

────── See also Ingram, J. H., Christopher Marlowe and his associates, 1904; and "Marlowe and Kyd," Lond. Times Lit. Sup., July 1, 1921.

MARSTON, JOHN. Works: reprinted from the original editions, with notes and life by J. O. Halliwell-Phillips. L. 1856. 3v.

────── Works. Edited by A. H. Bullen. 1887. 3v.

MARTIN, JOHN. Bibliographical catalogue of privately printed books. L. J. A. Arch, 1834.

Massachusetts Reports, 133 (p. 32).

MASSINGER, PHILIP. Believe as you list. Edited by T. C. Croker. Percy Society Pub., XXVII. L. 1849.

────── Plays. Ed. by F. Cunningham. 1868.

────── Best plays. Edited by A. Symons. (Mermaid Series). L. 1889. 2v.

──────, and Ford, John. Dramatic works. Edited by Hartley Coleridge. L. E. Moxon 1839–1840.

MASSON, DAVID. Life of John Milton . . . .in conection with the political, ecclesiastical, and literary history of the time. L. Macmillan, (1859). 1880. 6v.

Materialien zur kunde des älteren Englischen dramas. Edited by W. Bang. Bd. 1, 1902––.

MAWD, RICHARD. Semen Brachigraphia or the Academy of short writing. 1635.

MAY, THOMAS. The Heir. Q. 1633.

MELLOTTÉE, PAUL. Histoire èconomique de l'imprimerie. Paris. 1905.

MENTZ, DR. ARTHUR. Geschichte der stenographie. Lpz. 1910.

METCALFE, THEOPHILUS. Radio-stenography, or short-writing. 1635.

Middlesex County records. Edited by John C. Jeaffreson. L. Middlesex County Records Society, 1886.

MIDDLETON, THOMAS. Works. Edited by A. H. Bullen. L. 1885–6. 8v.

MILTON, JOHN. Areopagitica. Arber reprints. 1868–9.

Molyneux papers, *see* Jeaffreson.

MORE, SIR THOMAS. Edited by A. Dyce. Shakespeare Society, Pub., vol. XXIII. L. 1844.

────── "The book of Sir Thomas More," Edited by W. W. Greg, Malone Society reprints, 1911.

────── ────── Tudor facsimile text, 1910.

────── On the possibility of Shakespeare's hand in the MS, see under Shakespeare's hand, *infra*.

MORGAN, JAMES A. Digesta Shakespereana: a topical index of printed matter relating to Shakespeare, to the year 1886. N. Y. Shakespeare Society, 1886–1887.

────── The law of literature . . . .N.Y. J. Cockcroft. (1875). 1886–7. 2v.

MORLEY, H. Memoirs of Bartholomew Fair. 1859.

MOTLEY, JOHN. Life of John of Barneveld, Advocate of Holland. N. Y. Harper, 1902. 2v.

MOXON, JOSEPH. Mechanick exercises: or, The doctrine of handy-works applied to the art of printing; a literal reprint . . . .of the ed. of 1683, with preface and notes by T. L. DeVinne. N. Y. Typothetae, 1896.

MUMBY, FRANK A. The romance of bookselling: A history from the earliest times to the twentieth century. L. Chapman and Hall, 1910.
MUNDAY, ANTHONY, *see* More, Sir Thomas; *and see* Byrne.
MURCH, H. S. Beaumont and Fletcher's Knight of the burning pestle. Yale Studies in English, no. 33. N. Y. 1908.
MURRAY, JOHN TUCKER. English dramatic companies, 1558–1642. Boston. Houghton, Mifflin, 1910. 2 v. (Referred to as E. D. C.)
—— "English dramatic companies in the towns outside of London, 1550–1600." Modern Philology, II (1905), 539.
MCKERROW, RONALD B. "Booksellers, printers, and stationers' trade" . . .In *Shakespeare's England*, Oxford Univ. Press, 1916. vol. II, ch. XXIII.
—— Dictionary of printers and booksellers in England, Scotland, and Ireland, and of foreign printers of English books, 1557-1640. L. Bibliographical Society. 1910.
—— Notes on bibliographical evidence for literary students and editors of English works of the 16th and 17th centuries. L. Bibliographical Society, Trans., XII. Also separately printed.
—— "Note on variations in certain copies of The Return of Pasquill," The Library, n.s. IV (1903), 384–392.
—— "Use of the galley in Elizabethan printing." Bibliographical Society, Trans., n.s. II, no. 2 (1921), pp. 97–109.
——, editor, *see* Nashe, Thomas.
M'CRIE, THOMAS. Life of Andrew Melville. Blackwood, 1856. 2v.

NABBES, THOMAS. Works. Edited by A. H. Bullen. 1887. 2v.
NASHE, THOMAS. Complete works. Edited by A. Grosart. L. 1883–1885. 6v.
—— Works of Thomas Nashe. Edited by R. B. McKerrow. 3v.
NASON, ARTHUR. James Shirley, dramatist: a biographical and critical study. N. Y. Nason, 1915.
NAUNTON, SIR ROBERT. Fragmenta regalia, or observations on the late Queen Elizabeth, her times, and her favorites. From the 3d ed., of 1653. Arber, English Reprints, 1895.
NAVARRE, ALBERT. Histoire générale de la sténographie et de l'écriture à travers les âges. Paris. Delagrave, 1909.
NEIDIG, WILLIAM J. "The Shakespeare quartos of 1619," Modern Philology, VIII (1910), 145–165. (Cf. "False dates on Shakespeare quartos", Century Mag., Oct., 1910, pp. 912–919.).
NEUENDORFF, B. Die englische volksbühne im zeitalter Shakespeares nach den bühnenanweisungen. Berlin. E. Felber. 1910.
New Shakespeare Society. Publications; and Transactions. See index.
Newberry Library, Chicago. Materials for the study of the English drama excluding Shakespeare: A selected list of books in the Newberry Library. Chicago. 1912. (89 pp.)
NICHOLS, FRANCIS M., ed., *see* Erasmus.
NICHOLS, JOHN. The progresses and public processions of Queen Elizabeth. L. 1788–1821. 4v. 2d ed., 1823. 3v.
—— Progresses, processions, and festivities of James I, his court, etc. 1828. 4v.
NICHOLAS, SIR HARRY, compiler, *see* Privy Council.

NISSEN, P. James Shirley; ein beitrag zur englischen literaturgeschichte. Hamburg, 1901.

NORTHBROOKE, JOHN. A treatise against dicing, dancing, plays, and interludes . . . . Edited by J. P. Collier from ed. 1, *c.* 1577. Shakespeare Society, XII, no. 2 (1843).

NORTON, GEORGE. Commentaries on the history, constitution, and chartered franchises of the city of London. 1828.

Notes and Queries. See indexes.

OLDCASTLE, SIR JOHN, Life of, Q. of 1600. Malone Society reprint no. 8. 1908.

OLDENBARNEVELD, JOAN VAN, *see* Barnavelt.

OLIPHANT, E. H. C. "Problems of authorship in Elizabethan dramatic literature," Modern Philology, VIII (1910–1911), 411 ff.

ONIONS, C. T., ed., *see* Shakespeare's England, 1916.

Original letters of eminent literary men, *see* Ellis, Sir Henry, ed.

ØSTERBERG, V. Studier over Hamlet-Teksterne, I. Copenhagen. Gyldendalske Boghandel. 1920.

OVERALL, W. H. and H. C., *see* Remembrancia.

PANCIROLI, GUIDO. Rerum memorabilium jam olim deperditarum et contra recens atque ingeniose inventarum. Ambergae, 1599–1602. 2v. Translated into English, with a new commentary from Salmuth's Annotations. 2d ed. L. 1727. 2v.

PAPE, OTTO (*i.e.*, RICHARD OTTO). Über die entstehung der ersten quarto von Shakespeares Richard III. Berlin. G. Reimer, 1906. Diss.

PARKER, ARCHBISHOP. De antiquitate Britanniae ecclesiae. 1572.

Parliament. House of Commons, Journals, 1547–.

——— House of Lords, Journals, 1509–1819. 45 vols.

Parnassus plays, *see* Macray, William, ed.

Patent rolls, at the Public Record Office of Great Britain.

PEDDIE, R. A. "Books on the practical side of printing, 1566–1750," Bibliographical Society, Trans. IX (1906), 1–4.

PEELE, GEORGE. Works. Edited by A. H. Bullen. 1888. 2v.

PENLEY, BELVILLE. The Bath stage: a history of dramatic representations in Bath. L. W. Lewis, 1892.

PENNIMAN, JOSIAH H. The war of the theatres. Boston. 1897. Pennsylvania Univ. Series in philology, literature, etc., IV, no. 3.

PETTIE, GEORGE. A petite pallace of Pettie his pleasure. L. Chatto and Windus. 1908.

PHILLIPS, EDWARD. Theatrum poetarum Anglicanorum . . . . to 1675. 3d ed. Geneva, 1824. Reprinted by Sir Egerton Brydges.

PLOMER, HENRY R. A dictionary of the booksellers and printers . . . . in England, Scotland, and Ireland, 1641–67. Bibliographical Society. 1907.

——— A dictionary of the printers and booksellers who were at work in England, Scotland and Ireland, 1668–1725. Bibliographical Society. 1922.

——— "Notices of printers and printing in the state papers," Bibliographica, II (1896), 204–57.

——— "The printers of Shakespeare's plays and poems," The Library, n.s. VII (1906), 149–167.

—— "Shakespeare printers," Bibliographer, II (1903), 174–188 and 299–319.
—— Short history of English printing, 1476–1898. L. 1900. Revised, c. 1921, for "1476–1900."
—— "Two law-suits of Richard Pynson," The Library, n.s. X (1909), 115–152.
POCKNELL, E. Thomas Bright. 1884.
POEL, WILLIAM. "Shakespeare's prompt-books," London Times Lit. Sup., Aug. 4 and 18, Sept. 8, 1921. See index to London Times on this subject.
POLLARD, ALFRED W. "False dates in Shakespeare quartos," The Library, 3d. ser., I, pp. 46–53, and II, pp. 101–113.
—— The foundations of Shakespeare's text. N. Y. Oxford Press. 1923.
—— Shakespeare folios and quartos: a study in the bibliography of Shakespeare's plays, 1594–1685. L. F. Methuen, 1909. (Extremely valuable.)
—— Shakespeare's fight with the pirates; and the problems of the transmission of his text. L. Alex. Moring, 1917. 1920.
——, ed. See Shakespeare, Richard II.
—— and Wilson, J. D. See indexes to London Times Lit. Sup. from 1919 on for a series of important articles on Shakespeare texts.
—— and Wilson, J. D., editors. Shakespeare's hand in the play of Sir Thomas More. Papers by A. W. Pollard, W. W. Greg, E. Maunde Thompson, J. D. Wilson, and R. W. Chambers. . . . Cambridge University Press, 1923.
PORTER, CHARLOTTE, ed., see Shakespeare, Richard III.
POTTER, ALFRED C. A bibliography of Beaumont and Fletcher. Cambridge, 1890.
PRICE, HEREWARD T. The Text of *Henry V*. Newcastle-under-Lyme. Mandley, 1920.
Printing-presses, Early, see Bibliographica, I, 224, 499; III, 474; and Bibliographical Society, Trans. III–IV (1895–98), p. 240.
Blades, William, Books in Chains (1892).
—— "The first printing-press in England," Bookworm, October, 1869.
—— The Pentateuch of printing. L. 1891.
—— Hansard, T. C. Typographia. L. 1825.
Privy Council of England. Acts, n.s. 1542–1604. Edited by J. R. Dasent. L. 1890–1907. 32 v.
—— Proceedings and ordinances. Edited by Sir Harris Nicolas.
Privy Council of Scotland, Registers, *passim*.
PRÖLSS, R. Geschichte d. neueren dramas. 1881–83. v. 2.
—— Von den ältesten drucken der dramen Shakespeares, und dem einflusse den die damaligen Londoner theater und ihre einrichtungen auf diese dramen ausgeübt haben. Lpz. Berger, 1905.
PRYNNE, WILLIAM. Histrio-mastix: The players scourge or actors tragoedie. L. For Michael Sparke, 1633.
Public Records, *see* Thomas, F. S. Handbook to the public records (Gt. Britain Public Record Office). 1853.
PUTNAM, GEORGE H. The censorship of the Church of Rome and its influence upon production and distribution of literature. N. Y. Putnam, 1907.
PUTTENHAM, RICHARD? (supposed author). "George Puttenham. The arte of English Poesie." 1589. Arber, English reprints. L. 1869.

RAINOLDS, JOHN. The overthrow of stage-playes by way of controversie betwixt D. Gager and D. Rainoldes. 2d ed. Oxford. E. Forrest and W. Webb, 1629.

RANDOLPH, THOMAS. Works. Edited by W. C. Hazlitt. L. 1875.

RAUMER, FRIEDRICH L. G. VON. Political history of England during the 16th, 17th, and 18th centuries. Illustrated by original documents. Tr. from the German by H. E. Lloyd. L. 1837. 2 vols. (To 1660).

RAWLINS, THOMAS. The rebellion, 1640. In Dodsley, Select collection of old English plays, ed. Hazlitt, vol. XIV.

REA, JOHN D. Volpone, or the fox; with introduction, notes, and glossary. Yale Univ. Press, 1919. Yale Studies in Eng., LIX.

REDGRAVE, G. R. "The Privy Council in its relation to literature and printing," Bibliographical Society, Trans. VII, 92–95.

REED, ARTHUR W. "Regulation of the book trade before the proclamation of 1538," Bibliographical Society, Trans. XV (1917–1919), 157–184.

REED, TALBOT B. History of the old English letter foundries, with notes, historical and bibliographical, on the rise and progress of English typography. L. E. Stock, 1887.

——— "List of books and papers on printers and printing," Bibliographical Society, Trans. III (1895), pt. 1, pp. 81–152. (Topographically classified).

REES, ABRAHAM. Cyclopaedia, or Universal dictionary of arts and sciences and literature. First American ed. n.d.

Remembrancia: copies of correspondence between sovereigns, ministers, Privy Council, lord mayors, etc., 1579–1664. By authority of the Corporation of London. L. E. J. Francis, 1878.

——— :Analytical index to the series of records known as Remembrancia, 1579–1664. Edited by W. H. and H. C. Overall. L. 1878.

RENNERT, H. A. The Spanish stage in the time of Lope de Vega. N. Y. 1909.

RENOUARD, PHILIPPE. Documents sur les imprimeurs, libraires, etc . . . . à Paris de 1450 à 1600. Paris. H. Champion, 1901.

——— Imprimeurs parisiens, fondeurs des caractères et correcteurs . . . . (1470–1600). Paris. Claudin, 1898.

REUSCH, FRANZ H. Index der verbotenen bücher. Bonn. Cohen, 1883–1885. 2v.

REYHER, P. Les masques anglais, 1512–1640. Paris. 1909.

RHODES, R. CROMPTON. The Stagery of Shakespeare. Birmingham. Cornish Brothers, 1922.

RICKERT, EDITH. "Political propaganda and satire in A Midsummer night's dream," Modern Philology, XXI, 1, (1923), 53–89, 133–155.

ROBERTSON, J. M. Problem of the Merry wives of Windsor. Shakespeare Association, 1917–1918.

——— Problem of Hamlet. 1919.

——— Shakespeare and Chapman. L. Unwin, 1917.

ROCKWELL, JULIUS. Teaching, practice, and literature of shorthand. Washington. Gov't, 1884–5. Circulars of Information of Bureau of Education, no. 2, pp. 8 ff.

ROGERS, R. V. "Some things about theatres," The Green Bag, VI, 259–265 and 321–327.

ROLLINS, HYDER. "The King's players at court in 1610," Modern Language Review, January, 1920.
Row, JOHN. Historie of the kirk of Scotland. Edinburgh, 1842.
ROWLANDS, SAMUEL. Works. Edited by Rimbault. Percy Society, Pub. IX.
RUSHWORTH, JOHN. Historical collections, containing the principal matters from the sixteenth year of King James to the death of Charles I. 1659–1701. 4 pts. in 7 vols.
——— Historical collections of private passages of state and weighty matters in law, 1618–1648. L. D. Browne, 1721–2. 8v.
RYE, W. B. England as seen by foreigners in the days of Elizabeth and James. 1865.
RYMER, THOMAS, and SANDERSON, ROBERT, editors. Foedera, conventiones, literae, et . . .acta publica (1101–1726). 2d ed. L. J. Tonson, 1726–1735. 20 v.
——— Syllabus of Rymer's Foedera in English, by Sir Thomas D. Hardy. L. 1873. 3v.
SACKVILLE, THOMAS, and NORTON, THOMAS. Gorboduc, or, Ferrex and Porrex (1565–6). 1570–1.
SALISBURY, JAMES E. Calendar of the manuscripts of the most Honorable the Marquis of Salisbury. L. Eyre and Spottiswoode. 1883–. Historical Manuscripts Commission, Reports, XLVIII.
SCHELLING, FELIX E. Elizabethan drama, 1558–1642. Boston. 1908. 2v.
——— ——— The English chronicle play. N. Y. Macmillan, 1902.
SCHEVILL, RUDOLPH. The dramatic art of Lope de Vega. Univ. of California Press, 1918.
SCARGILL-BIRD, SAMUEL R. Guide to the principal classes of documents preserved in the Public Record Office. 2d ed. L. Eyre and Spottiswoode, 1896.
SCHIPPER, J. James Shirley, sein leben und seine werke. Wien. 1911.
SCHÖTTNER, ADOLF. Über die mutmässliche stenographische entstehung der ersten quarto von Shakespeares Romeo und Juliet. Archiv für Schriftkunde, I (1914–1918). Lpz. 1918.
SCHÜCKING, LEVIN L. Character problems in Shakespeare's plays. Translated by W. H. Peters. N. Y. Holt, 1922.
Scotland, *see* Privy Council; *and see* State papers.
"Second Maiden's Tragedy," 1611. Malone Society reprints, no. 14. 1909.
SCOTT, SIR WALTER, ed. Ancient British Drama, 1810. 3v.
SEEBERGER, A. Zur entstehung der quartausgabe des First part of Jeronimo. Archiv für stenographie, Jahrg. 1908.
SELDEN, JOHN. Works. Edited by David Wilkins. (1726). 1895. 3v.
Serapeum: Zeitschrift für bibliothekswissenschaft. Lpz. 1840–1870.

SHAKESPEARE

Editions examined:
    First folio (1623). (On the Sibthorp copy, see Cornhill Mag., April, 1899, pp. 449–458. See also Athenaeum, Aug., 1899, p. 267.
    Works. Edited by Alexander Pope and G. Sewell. 1723–5. 7v.
    Plays. Edited by Theobald. L. 1733. 7v.
    Plays. Edited by Hanmer, 1744.

—— Warburton, W., and Pope, A. 1747.
—— Johnson, Samuel, 1765. 8v.
—— Steevens, George, (1766) 4v. 1803. 21 v.
—— Capell. 1768.
—— and poems of William Shakespeare in ten volumes; collated verbatim . . . .an historical account of the English stage, and notes by Edward Malone. L. J. Rivington, 1790. 10 v. in 11.
—— . . . ., comprehending a life of the poet and an enlarged history of the stage by the late E. Malone. Edited by J. Boswell. L. 1821. 21v. (Commonly referred to as the "third variorum," and the "1821 variorum"; here abbreviated as *Var*.).

Works, Edited by Knight, C. 1838–1842. 8v.
—— Collier, J. P. 1842–1844. 8v.
—— Halliwell-Phillips, J. O. 1853–1865. 16v.
—— Dyce, A. 1857. 6v.
—— White, R. G. 1857–1860. 12v.

Plays, Ed. by Furness, H. H., New Variorum, 1871—. Continued by H. H. Furness, Jr.

Works. Edited by Rolfe, W. J. 1871–1896. 40v.
—— Wright, W. A. L. Macmillan, 1891.
—— Gollancz, I. (Temple Shakespeare). 1894–5. 40v.

Plays. Ed. by Craig, W. J. Arden Shakespeare. 1899—.
—— Porter, C., and Clarke, H. A. First Folio ed. 1903.

Works. Edited by Neilson, William A. Boston, Houghton, Mifflin. 1906. (Cambridge edition).
—— Edited for the syndics of the Univ. Press by Sir Arthur Quiller-Couch and John Dover Wilson. In progress, 1921.—(Illustrates new bibliographical approach to text problems.)

Special texts used for certain plays:

Hamlet. Vietor's parallel text.
Henry V. Vietor's parallel text.
Merry Wives of Windsor (1602). Ed. by W. W. Greg. Oxford, Clarendon press, 1910. Cf. Friedrich, Paul.
Richard II. A new Shakespeare quarto; The tragedy of King Richard II. (Q3, 1598), facsimile. Edited by A. W. Pollard. Cf. Q^1 and F^1 versions.
Richard III. First folio ed., by Charlotte Porter.
Romeo and Juliet, Q1 and Q2, parallel texts. Edited by Daniel. New Shakespeare Society, 1874.

Text problems, articles on, not listed elsewhere:

POLLARD, A. W., and WILSON, J. D. "The 'Stolne and surreptitious' Shakepeare texts," London Times Lit. Sup., Jan. 16, 1919. Discussion of this: Stopes, Charlotte, Jan. 23, 1919; Pollard, A. W., Jan. 30; Salmon, David, Feb. 6.; Fitzgerald, J. D., Feb. 20; Greg, W. W., April 28; Lawrence, W. J., Aug. 21; Pollard, A. W., Aug. 8, 15, and 28; Spens, J., Sept. 18; O'Neill, James, Aug. 7, Dec. 4 and 31, 1919. See also articles on the First Folio in T. L. S., 1923.

FITZGERALD, J. D., "Transcription in the pirated plays of Shakespeare," London Times Lit. Sup., 13 May and 3 June, 1920. Cf.
GREG, W. W., same topic, 20 May, 1920.
POLLARD, A. W. "On variant spellings in Shakespeare quartos," London Times Lit. Sup., 10 Dec., 1920. (Cf. Oct. 21, and Nov. 11, 1920).
FRANZ, W. Grammatisches zu Shakespeare," Englische Studien, LIV, 1, pp. 69–79. (Punctuation).
GRAY, H. D., "Shakespeare's punctuation," London Times Lit. Sup., 14 July 1921.
SIMPSON, PERCY. Shakespearian punctuation. Oxford. Clarendon Press, 1911.
FIEDLER, H. G. "Shakespearian pronunciation," London Times Lit. Sup., 26 Oct., 1919.

Shakespeare bibliographies and catalogues (a partial list):

Bodleian Library, Catalogue of Shakespeare exhibition held at the Bodleian in 1916.
British Museum. Guide to MSS and books exhibited in . . . . the tercentenary of F^1. 77 pp. B. M.
Chicago Public Library. Special Shakespeare bulletin. 1904.
COHN, A. Shakespeare-Bibliographie. In Shakespeare Jahrbuch 1864–1899. Continued annually; by Richard Schroeder for 1900–1902, 1905–6; by Gustav Becker for 1903–4; by Hans Daffis for 1907—.
ESDAILE, A. J. K. "Shakespeare literature, 1901–5," The Library, 2d ser. VII (1906), 167–180.
JAGGARD, WILLIAM. Shakespeare bibliography: a dictionary of every known issue of the writings . . . .and of recorded opinion thereon . . . .in English . . . .historical introduction, facsimiles, portraits, etc. Stratford-on-Avon. Shakespeare Press, 1911.
MEYER, H. H. B. (Library of Congress). A brief guide to the literature of Shakespeare. Board of American Library Assiciation, 1915.
NORTHUP, CLARK S. Shakespeare bibliographies and reference lists; in Bibliographies of English philology. Pub. by the Bibliographical Society of America. (274 drama entries; 114 Shakespeare entries).
SHAW, A. C. Index to Shakespeare memorial library. Birmingham. 1900–3. 3pts.
The Shakespeare Tercentenary catalogues; see London Times Lit. Sup., Oct. 5, 1916; and Dec. 7, 1916.
WILSON, J. Shakespeariana. Catalogue of all the books, pamphlets, etc. relating to Shakespeare. 1827. Cf. entries under: Halliwell-Phillips, Morgan, J. A., Thimm, F.

Shakespeare Studies. See the publications of the universities for the year 1916, for essays on subjects related to Shakespeare and dramatic history (as, for example, volumes issued by Columbia University, Univ. of Texas, Univ. of Wisconsin, The Book of Homage to Shakespeare, ed. by Gollancz, etc.)
Shakespeare Association. Studies in the First Folio. Oxf. Univ. Press, 1924.
Shakespeare Society. Publications; and Transactions.
New Shakespeare Society. Publications.
Shakespeare Jahrbuch.

Shakespeare's England: . . . .an account of the life and manners of the age. Ed. by C. T. Onions. Oxf. Univ. Press, 1916. 2v.

Shakespeare's hand in the play of Sir Thomas More: papers by A. W. Pollard, W. W. Greg, E. Maunde Thompson, J. Dover Wilson, and R. W. Chambers. Cambr. Univ. Press, 1923. Cf. A. W. Pollard, "Date of . . . . Sir Thos. More," L. T. S., Nov. 8, 1923, p. 751; and L. L. Schücking, "Shakespeare and Sir Thos. More." Rev. of Eng. Studies, I, 40–60; and S. A. Tannenbaum, "Shakespeare's Unquestioned autographs and the addition to Sir Thos. More," Stud. in Phil. XXII (1925), 133–160; see E. M. Thompson, *infra*; L. T. S. 1919–23; and E. K. Chambers, Eliz. Stage, IV, 32–3.

SHARPHAM, EDWARD, The Fleire. Edited by H. Nibbe, Materialien zur kunde, etc., 1912.

SHEAVYN, PHOEBE. The literary profession in the Elizabethan age. Manchester University Press, 1909.

SHELTON, THOMAS. Short writing. 1630. (Bodleian Library)

SHIPHERD, H. ROBINSON, "Play publishing in Elizabethan times," Publications of the Modern Language Association, XXXIV (1919), 590–600.

SHIRLEY, JAMES. Dramatic works and poems. Edited by W. Gifford and the Rev. Mr. A. Dyce. L. J. Murray, 1833. 6v.

——— Best plays. Edited by E. Gosse. Mermaid Series, v.15.

SHORTT, J. The law relating to works of literature and art. L. 1884.

SIDNEY, SIR HENRY. Letters and memorials of state (in the reigns of Mary, Elizabeth, James and Charles) written and collected by Sir Henry Sidney, Sir Philip Sidney, and Sir Robert Sidney. Ed. by A. Collins. 1746. 2v. (Referred to as Sidney Papers).

SIDNEY, SIR PHILIP. An Apology for poetry, 1595.

SILVESTRE. Marques typographiques; ou, recueil des monogrammes, chiffres, etc. en France. (1470–1600). Paris. 1853–1867.

SIMPSON, PERCY, editor. Ben Jonson's Every man in his humour. Oxford, Clarendon Press, 1919.

——— "The play of Sir Thomas More and Shakespeare's hand in it," The Library, VIII (1917), 79–105.

SIMPSON, RICHARD. 'The political use of the stage in Shakespeare's time," New Shakespeare Society, Trans., ser. 1, pt. 2 (1874), 371–95.

——— "'The politics of Shakespere's historical plays," *Ibid.*, pp. 396–441.

SIR THOMAS MORE, Play on, *see* More.

Six old plays on which Shakespeare founded his Measure for measure, etc. 1779. 2v.

SKEEN, WILLIAM. Early typography: an essay on . . . .letter-press printing in the 15th century. Colombo, Ceylon. 1872.

SMALL, ROSCOE. The stage quarrel between Ben Jonson and the so-called poetasters. Forschungen zur englischen sprache und litteratur, I. Breslau, 1899.

SMITH, HENRY. Works. Edited by James Nichol; with life by Thomas Fuller. (1675). 1866.

SMITH, CAPTAIN JOHN. A true relation of occurrences in Virginia. In Works of John Smith; edited by E. Arber, Eng. Scholars' Lib'y, no. 16. 1895.

SMITH, SIR JOHN. Discourse on the forms and effects of divers sorts of weapons. 1590.

SMITH, W. The Hector of Germany. Edited by L. W. Paine. Pub. of the University of Pennsylvania, 1906.

Society of Antiquaries of London. A collection of ordinances and regulations for the government of the royal household. L. J. Nichols. 1790.

Somers tracts. 2d ed. . . . . by Sir Walter Scott. Cadell, 1809–15.

SPECHT, FRITZ. Die schrift und ihre entwicklung zur modernen stenographie. Berlin. F. Schulze, 1909.

SPEDDING, JAMES. Letters and life of Francis Bacon. L. Longman, 1890. 7v.

SPOTTISWOOD, JAMES. (Bp. of Clogher, 1567–1644). History of the church and state of Scotland. 4th ed. L. 1677.

STÄHLIN, K. Sir Francis Walsingham und seine zeit. vol. 1. Heidelberg, 1908.

STANYHURST, RICHARD. Translation of Virgil's Aeneid, Bks. I–IV. 1583. Arber, English Scholar's Library, 1880.

Star Chamber cases. L. For John Grove, 1630.

Star Chamber cases, *see also* Gardiner, Samuel.

State papers of Great Britain.

Calendar of state papers, domestic series, of the reigns of Edward VI, Mary, Elizabeth, and James I preserved in the Public Record Office (1547–1625). Edited by R. Lemon and M. A. E. Green. L. 1856–1872. 12v.

Calendar of state papers, domestic series, of the reign of Charles I, 1625–1649. Edited by J. Bruce and W. D. Hamilton. L. 1858–1897. 23 vols.

Calendar of letters and papers, foreign and domestic, of the reign of Henry VIII, Edited by J. S. Brewer *et al.* L. 1862–.

State Papers, Miscellaneous, 1501–1776. Ed. by P. Yorke, Earl of Hardwicke. 1778. v. 1.

State papers of Scotland.

State papers, Spanish.

State papers, Venetian.

State trials, *see* Howell, T. B., compiler.

Stationers' Company, *see* London Stationers.

Statutes of the realm (Gt. Britain). Record Commission. L. 1810–1828. 9v. in 10.

STEELE, ROBERT. Bibliography of royal proclamations of Tudor and Stuart sovereigns, 1485–1714: in Crawford, J. L. Bibliotheca Lindesiana, Oxford, Clarendon Press, 1910. Vols. 5 and 6.

STEEVENS, GEORGE. Advertisement, *see* Shakespeare, Variorum of 1821.

STOLL, E. E. John Webster: the periods of his work. Boston. A. Mudge, 1905.

STOPES, MRS. CHARLOTTE C. "Dramatic records from the Privy Council registers," Shakespeare Jahrbuch, XLVIII, 103.

——— The life of Henry, third Earl of Southampton, Shakespeare's patron. Cambridge University Press, 1922.

——— "Shakespeare's fellows and followers . . . .from the Lord Chamberlain's papers," Shakespeare Jahrbuch, XLVI, 92–105.

────── "Seventeenth century revels books," London Times Lit. Sup., 3 Dec., 1920, and 24 Feb., 1921. Cf. other articles on this: 23 Dec., 30 Dec., 24 Feb., 1921.

────── William Hunnis and the revels of the Chapel Royal . . . .Louvain, 1910.

STOW, JOHN. Annales: or A generall chronicle of England, continued to 1631 by Edmund Howes. L. R. Meighen, 1631.

────── Summaries of the chronicles of England. L. 1575.

────── A survey of the cities of London and Westminster (1698). Edited by C. L. Kingsford. Oxford. Clarendon Press, 1908. 2 v.

STRANGE, EDWARD F. "The writing-books of the 16th century," Bibliographical Society, Trans., III–IV (1895–8), 41–71.

STRICKLAND, AGNES. Lives of the Queens of England. L. G. Bell, 1888–91. v. 3

STRUTT, J. The sports and pastimes of the people of England (1810). Edited by W. Hone. 1833.

STRYPE, JOHN. Annals of the Reformation and establishment of religion . . . . Queen Elizabeth. Oxford. Clarendon Press, 1824. 4v. in 7.

────── Ecclesiastical memorials, relating chiefly to religion . . . .(Henry VIII, Edward VI, and Mary I). Oxford. Clarendon Press, 1822. 3v.

────── Life of Aylmer.

────── Life and acts of Matthew Parker. Oxford. Clarendon Press, 1821.

────── Life of Sir Thomas Smith. Oxford. Clarendon Press, 1820.

────── Life and acts of John Whitgift. Oxford. Clarendon Press, 1822.

────── Memorials of . . . .Thomas Cranmer, Archbp . . . .L. Routledge, 1853.

STUBBES, PHILIP. The anatomie of abuses, (1583). Edited by F. J. Furnivall. New Shakespeare Society, ser. vi, 1877–1882. 2v.

SULLIVAN, MARY. Court masques . . . .of James I. G. H. Putnam, 1913.

SUMMERS, MONTAGUE. "A Restoration prompt-book," London Times Lit. Sup., 24 June, 1920, p. 400.

SYMMES, H. S. Les débuts de la critique dramatique en Angleterre. Paris. 1903.

TAILOR, ROBERT. The hog hath lost his pearl. In Select collection of old English plays: edited by Dodsley. 1874–6. vol. 11.

Term reports, Durnford and East.

THALER, ALWIN. Finance and business management of the Elizabethan theatre. Harvard dissertation, 1918. (unpublished?)

────── "The free-list and theatre tickets in Shakespeare's time and after," Modern Language Review, April, 1920.

────── "Playwrights' benefits and 'interior gathering' in the Elizabethan theatre," Studies in Philology, XVI (1919), no. 2, pp. 187–197.

────── Shakespeare to Sheridan. Cambridge. Harvard University Press.

────── "Shakespeare's income," Studies in Philology, XV (1918), no. 2, pp. 82–97.

────── "Strolling players . . . .after Shakespeare," Publications of the Modern Language Association, June, 1922.

────── "Travelling players in Shakespeare's England," Modern Philology, XVII (1920), 121–146.

THIMM, FRANZ. Shakespeariana from 1564 to 1864. An account of the Shakespearian literature of England, Germany, France, and other European countries during three centuries; with bibliographical introductions. L. Thimm, 1872.

THOMPSON, EDWARD MAUNDE. Shakespeare's handwriting. Oxford. Clarendon Press, 1916.

―― "Shakespeare's handwriting," *see* Shakespeare's England, Oxford Univ. Press, 1916, I, 284–311.

―― "Autograph MSS of A. Mundy," Bibliogr. Socy, *Trans.* XIV (1915–17), 325–57.

―― "Two pretended autographs of Shakespeare," The Library, July, 1917, pp. 193 ff.

THOMPSON, ELBERT N. S. The controversy between the Puritans and the stage. Yale Studies in English, XX. N. Y. Holt, 1903.

―― "Elizabethan dramatic co-operation," Englische Studien, XL (1908), 30 ff.

THORNDIKE, ASHLEY H. Shakespeare's theatre. N. Y. Macmillan.

Times, London; see Palmer's index to the Literary supplement for numerous short articles on drama and text problems.

TIMPERLEY, CHARLES H. Dictionary of printers and printing . . . .ancient and modern, ...to 1838. L. H. Johnson, 1839. (Re–issued as Encyclopaedia of literary and typographical anecdote)

TOURNEUR, CYRIL. Plays and poems. L. 1878.

―― Plays. Mermaid Series. L. 1888.

Tudor facsimiles, *see* Farmer, J., editor.

UDALL, JOHN. The state of the church of England. 1588. Arber, English Scholar's Library, no. 5.

Variorum of 1821, *see* Shakespeare, Editions of

VINCENT, AUGUSTINE. A discoverie of errours in the first edition of the catalogue of nobility published by Ralph Brooke, York Herald, 1619. William Jaggard, 1622.

VOYNICH, WILLIAM. Catalogue of rare books printed in the 15th, 16th, and 17th centuries, not to be found in the British Museum. n.d.

WAGNER, A. "Eine sammlung von Shakespeare-quartos in Deutschland (1600–1619)," Anglia, XXV, 518.

WAKEMAN, H. O. The church and the Puritans, 1570–1660. (1887). New ed., 1902.

WALLACE, C. W. The Children of the Chapel at Blackfriars, 1597–1603. Lincoln, Nebraska, 1908. Univ. of Nebraska Studies, VIII, nos. 2 and 3. Also separately printed.

―― "Discussions of the Globe and Blackfriars systems of finance," London Times Lit. Sup., Oct. 2 and 9, 1909.

―― The evolution of the English drama up to Shakespeare; with a history of the first Blackfriars theatre. Berlin. G. Reimer, 1912.

―― "New Shakespeare discoveries," Harper's Magazine, March, 1910.

―― "Shakespeare and the Blackfriars," Century, LXXX, (1910), 5 ff.

―― Shakespeare and his London associates as revealed in recently discovered documents. Lincoln, Nebr. 1910. Univ. of Nebraska Studies, X, no. 4.

────── "The Swan theatre and the Earl of Pembroke's servants," Englische Studien, XLIII (1911), 340–95.
WANDELL, SAMUEL H. The law of the theatre: a treatise on the legal relations of actors, managers, and audiences. Albany, N. Y., 1891.
WARD, A. W. History of English dramatic literature to the death of Queen Anne. L. 1899. 3v..
────── "Some political and social aspects of the later Elizabethan and earlier Stuart period," Cambridge History of English Literature, V, ch. xiv.
WARNER, REBECCA. Epistolary curiosities: series the first, consisting of unpublished letters, of the seventeenth century, illustrative of the Herbert family. L. 1818.
WARTON, THOMAS. History of English poetry. (1775–1781). 1871. 4v.
WATSON, F. The English grammar schools to 1660: their curriculum and practice. Cambridge. 1908.
WEBSTER, JOHN. Dramatic works. Edited by W. Hazlitt. L. 1897. 4v.
────── Works. Edited by A. Dyce. 1830. 4v.
WEBSTER, JOHN, and TOURNEUR, CYRIL. Plays. With introduction by A. H. Thorndike. N. Y. American Book Co., 1912. (Masterpieces of the English drama; ed by Felix Schelling.)
WEISE, DR. D. Schrift und buchwesen in alter und neuer zeit. Lpz. Teubner, 1899.
WELDON, SIR ANTHONY. Court and character of King James. L. Printed by R. J., 1650.
WESTBY–GIBSON, JOHN. Bibliography of short-hand. L. I. Pitman and Sons. 1887.
────── Early short–hand systems: with illustrations, pt. 1. L. J. Wade, 1882.
WHEATLEY, H. B. Notes on the life of J. P. Collier, with a complete list of his works and an account of such Shakespeare documents as are believed to be spurious. 1884. Reprinted from The Bibliographer, V, 108 ff.
────── "Shakespeare's editors from 1623 to the twentieth century," Bibliographical Society, Trans., XIV (1915–1917), 145–175.
────── "Shakespeare's choice of printers:" see "The Stationers' Registers," pt. 2, in The Bibliographer, I, 171–175.
WHITE, R. G. Works of William Shakespeare. Boston. Little and Brown, 1898.
WHITELOCKE, SIR BULSTRODE. Memorials of the English affairs . . . .to the end of the reign of King James I. L. (1682). (1709.) 1853.
────── Memorials of the English affairs from Charles I to Charles II. L. 1682.
WILKINS, DAVID. Life of John Selden; in Works of John Selden, 1726. (3v.)
WILLIAMS, ROBERT F., editor. Court and times of Charles I, illustrated by authentic and confidential letters from various public and private collections; with introduction and notes. L. H. Colburn, 1848. 2v.
────── Court and times of James I. L. H. Colburn. 1848. 2v.
WILLIS, EDMUND. An abbreviation of short writing by character.
WILLIS, JOHN. The art of stenographie . . . .L. Cuthbert Burby, 1602. (Copies at B. M., Bodleian, and Corpus Christi College, Oxford).
WILSON, ARTHUR. History of Great Britain: being the life and reign of King James the First. L. R. Lownds, 1653.

WILSON, J. DOVER. The copy for Hamlet, 1603. L. De la More Press. Reprinted from The Library, ser. 3, IX (1918), 153–186.

———— "Dramatic and bibliographical problems in Hamlet," Modern Language Review, XV. 163–66.

———— The Hamlet Transcript, 1593. De la More Press. Reprinted from The Library, ser. 3, IX (1918). 217–47.

———— John Lyly. Cambridge. Macmillan and Bowes, 1905.

———— "The Puritan attack on the stage," Cambridge History of English Literature, vol. VI.

WILSON, J. D., and POLLARD, A. W. "How some of Shakespeare's plays were pirated," London Times Lit. Sup., Jan. 17, 1919, p. 30.

WINWOOD, SIR RALPH. Memorials of affairs of state in the reigns of Queen Elizabeth and King James I. Edited by Edmund Sawyer. L. 1725. 3v.

WITHER, GEORGE. Schollers' purgatorie (1625). Percy Society.

WOOD, ANTHONY à. Athenae oxonienses: an exact history of all writers and bishops who have had their education in the University of Oxford. 2d ed., by P. Bliss. 1813–1820. 4v.

WOTTON, HENRY. Reliquiae Wottonianae. 1685.

———— ———— Life and Letters. Ed. by Logan Smith. 1907. 2v.

WRIGHT, JAMES. Historia histrionica: in Hazlitt's Dodsley, XV.

———— The second generation of English professional actors, 1625–1670. (From Historia histrionica, 1699). Edited by A. Lang, in English Garner: Social England illustrated, XXII (1903).

WRIGHT, THOMAS. Queen Elizabeth and her times: a series of original letters, selected from . . . .inedited private correspondence (Burghley, Leicester, Walsingham, Smith, Hatton, et al). L. H. Colburn, 1838, 2 v.

Year's Work in English Studies, 1919–1920. Edited for the English Association by Sir Sidney Lee. Oxford Univ. Press.

———— for 1920–1921.

ZEIBIG, JULIUS WALDEMAR. Geschichte und literatur der geschwindschreibkunst. Dresden. 1878.

ZELTNER, J. C. Correctorum in typographiis eruditorum centuria: speciminis loco collecta Norimbergae 1716. Ed. 2, Theatrum virorum eruditorum.

ZIMMERMAN, J. A. Geschichte der stenographie vom klassischen alterthum bis zur gegenwart. Wien. Hartleben, 1897.

INDEX

Abbott, George, 65.
Actors, companies of, 6; patronage of, 7–8; children, 6; women, 20–21; contracts of, with Henslowe, 10; pay of, 10–11; social status of, 6–11, 31; strolling, 7–8; in provinces, 12 ff.; in Scotland, 156ff.; irresponsible behavior of, 17–19; professional objections to, 31; attitude of, toward play publication, 4,211; leading, as heads of companies, 13, and as owners of plays, 224ff.; before Privy Council for plays, 166 *et passim*; before Justices of the Peace, 173; imprisoned for *Isle of Dogs*, 181; roles of, censored, 191; blamed for plays, 182, 195; cutting plays, 293–94; interpolating, 299; names of, in texts, 298; roles of, as source of text, 309; as pirates of texts, 300ff.
Adams, Joseph Quincy, 43, 52, 53, 55n., 189, 191, 344.
Admiral's men, imprisoned for *Isle of Dogs*, 181; relations with Strange's and Chamberlain's men, 268ff., 278, 279, with Pembroke's, 279.
Admonition to the Parliament, condemned, 69, 89.
Aldermen, licensing players and performances, 30, 32; ridiculed in plays, 174–75.
Aldus, typographical ideals, of, 344–5.
Aliens, satirized in drama, 148ff.; as craftsmen, satirized, 29, 105, 131. See Dutch, French, Spanish, Scottish.
Alleyn, Edward, actor and play owner, 224ff., 227, 282.
All Fools (Chapman), why published, 211.
Alsted, Johann, 328.
Alva, Duke of, 68.

Amboyna massacre, dramatized, 171.
Ames, Joseph, 71.
Anabaptists, 68n., 73.
Anagnostes, 328.
d'Ancre, Marquis, French favorite, in English plays, 163–64.
Anjou, Duke of, 75.
Anne, Queen of England, Catholicism of, in *A Game at Chess*, 165.
Antipodes, The (Brome), ownership of, 235.
Apprentices' riots, dramatization of, dangerous, 131.
Archbishop, as censor of literature, 62-ff., 86, 101. See Bishop, Censor, and Ecclesiastical.
Astley, John, 43.
Author, name of, to be printed, 27; name omitted, 383; use of initials of, 383; collaboration in plays, 202ff.; attitude of, toward publication, 2, 322; dedication or preface by, as sign of authorization, 288; reading proofs, 348ff.; standards of accuracy of, in texts, 341n., 349–50, 354, 364, 366, 367–8; excusing absence from press, 352ff., 365; revising texts in new edition, 376; revising single sheets at press, 377–78. See Playwright.
d'Aubigné, Esmé Stuart, Lord, patron of Jonson and Chapman, 145–147ff., 162.
Aylmer, John, Bp. of London, 64, 89.

Bales, Peter, *The Art of Brachygraphy*, 316.
Ball, The, censored for satirizing noblemen, 180.
Ballad, to be censored by parish clerk, 85; censored as political, 70, 85; as indecent, 71, 86; as sacrilegious, 85.

Bancroft, Richard, Bishop, 65; opposed to satires, 83; against James's claim to English throne, 153; in favor with James as King, 154.
Barker, Christopher, 348.
Barker, Robert, 348.
Barnavelt, censored, 65, 127, 183ff.; a playhouse manuscript, 296.
Barry, Lodowick, *Ram Alley*, 100n., 148.
Bartholomew Fair (Jonson), induction of, ridicules interpreters, 199.
Barwick. G. F., 66.
Basilicon Doron, 28 stationers fined for printing, 70.
Bates, E. S., 97.
Beckmann, Johann, 60n.
Beaumont, French ambassador, report of, on English plays, 117–18.
Beaumont, Francis, and Fletcher, John, *Cupid's Revenge*, censored? 117n., *Faire Maide of the Inne*, 171 n.; satirize suppression of contemporary discussion, *Knight of the Burning Pestle*, 200–01; *The Lover's Progress*, 263; *Philaster*, 284–5; *The Honest Man's Fortune*, a 'fair copy' for licenser extant, 294; playhouse manuscripts of *The Custom of the Country*, *Love's Pilgrimage*, and *The Spanish Curate*? 296; on the audience of the printed play, 214–15; the Folio from authors' manuscripts, 293; distribution of Folio printing, 344; Moseley on *errata* of Folio, 360.
Beeston, Christopher, 235; as head of King's and Queen's young co., imprisoned for acting unlicensed play, 188; has Chamberlain protect stage rights in 45 plays, 231; significance of this for stage right, 237; not opposed to publication of plays, 238.
Believe as You List (Massinger), license refused because of Spanish matters; remodeled and licensed, 169; a playhouse manuscript, 296.

Bell, John, 269.
Benefit performances for authors, 222.
Benger, Sir Thomas, 41.
Bibles, printing of, 347–48, 357n.; suit for false printing of, 319; printed by Dutchmen, 347; Geneva, forbidden, 91.
Bibliographical approach to study of text, 384 *et passim*.
Binding, gathering for, 378–81; corrected and uncorrected sheets together, *ibid*.
Biron, allusion to, 198.
Bishop, attitude of, toward plays, 20, 22, 23; as censor of literature, 62–3, 65, 67, 69, 73; censor of Barnavelt, 187. *See* Archbishop, Ecclesiastical, High Commission.
Blackfriars, *see* Children.
Blades, William, 331n., 338–39.
Blind Beggar of Alexandria (Chapman), 267.
Blount, Edward, 285; attitude toward *errata*, 359, 361–62.
Boas, F. S., 172, 296n.
Boccaccio, *Decameron*, forbidden, 86.
Boderie, M. de la, French ambassador, 75, 160, 178.
Bodleian collection of forbidden books, 91.
Bondman, The (Massinger), 125.
Books, forbidden, demand for, 89ff.; index of forbidden, 91; effect of imported, on English trade, 320.
Book-keeper, of acting company (Mr. Knight), 91, 292.
Book-sellers, number of, 320; rise of, *vs.* authors and *vs.* printers, 318–19.
Boy Bishop, The, 39.
Brakin, Francis, Cambridge Recorder, satirized in university play, 177.
Brathwaite, Richard, on *errata*, 360.
Brazen Age, The (Heywood), 208–09.
Breton, Nicholas, 353.
Bright, Timothy, *Characterie*, 316.

Brome, Richard, apology for offense in *The English Moor*, 197; ownership of *The Antipodes*, 235; contracts of, and stage right, 220, 234ff.; not to publish without consent of company, 235.
Brooke, C. F. Tucker, 130.
Brooke, Ralph, 354.
Browne, Robert, "seditious and schismatical," 73.
Browne, Robert, actor, part owner of plays, 225, 227.
Broughton, Hugh, censored, 69.
Bruce, Robert, opposes English actors in Scotland, 158.
Brushfield, T. N., 77n.
Buc, Sir George, Master of the Revels, 42, 43; as licenser of plays for print, 57; as censor, 122, 162, 163, 183ff., 190.
Bucer, Martin, *De honestibus ludis*, 28.
Buckingham, as favorite of James, in play of Massinger, 125–26; in play of Middleton, 165, 169.
Bullen, A. H., 168n., 183ff., 293., 296.
Burghley, William Cecil, Lord, 19, 23, 26, 30, 68–69, 76, 78, 80, 156–57; investigates Revels Office, 41; causes Philip II to be ridiculed in plays? 111; checks ridicule of Spain, 115; wishes a cozening case dramatized, 112; is appealed to in behalf of a Thomas Heywood, 113.
Burn, J. S., *Court of High Commission*, 77n., 88n.
Burton, Henry, *The Reconciler* and *Babel's no Bethel* censored, 74; *News from Ipswich* "scandalous", 91.
Burton, Robert, on the many errata in *The Anatomy of Melancholy*, 381.
Butter, Nathaniel, news publisher, 74, 81ff.
Byrne, Miss M. St. Clare, 131, 322.
Byron, Conspiracy of, and *Tragedy of Charles, Duke of* (Chapman), 51, 146, 160–61; refused a license for print by Buc, 162; cut by censor, 163.

Calderwood, David, 153.
Cambridge University, plays of, satirizing city officials, 174n.; satirizing lawyers and the Recorder of Cambridge, 177.
Camden, William, and censorship, 76.
Campaspe, (Lyly), why published, 265.
Cancels indicated by chain-lines and water-marks, 382.
Capitalizing, the duty of the compositor, 369.
Carleton, Eng. ambassador at the Hague, on plays, *see* Chamberlain, John.
Carleton, Guy, 327.
Carpenter, F. I., 151.
Carter, William, hanged for seditious book, 74.
Cartwright, *Confutation of the Rhemish Testament* suppressed, 73, 87.
Catholic, censorship, 65, 72; propaganda in plays, 98–99; attack on England, 97; plot to crown Lord Strange, 112; patronage of players? 113, satirized in plays, 94, 95, 98, 165ff.; in epigram, 96. *See* Jesuit and Protestant.
Catholicism, dispensation for pretended renunciation of, 147.
Cawarden, Sir Thomas, Master of the Revels, 41, 45.
Caxton, William, standards of accuracy, 345.
Cecil, Robert, 173.
Cecil, William, *see* Burghley, Lord.
Censorship, aims of, 71ff.; officers of, 60ff.; in antiquity, 60; early ecclesiastical, 60; of particular topics, 72ff. and 94ff.; of religious discussion, 50, 91, 94ff.; of works inciting to disorder, 28; of matters of state, 50 *et passim;* example of method of, 128ff.; efficiency of, 87ff.; difficulty of, in plays, 162; by suppression, 87ff.; effect of, on literary output and content, 92ff.; authors' reactions on, 197ff.; actors' evasion of

by pantomime, 196, and by interpolation, 192, 299; methods of, summarized, 193.
Cervantes, *Don Quixote*, censored, 87.
Chain-lines and cancels, 382.
Chalmers, George, 43, 50, 51, 53.
Chamberlain, attitude of, toward plays, 26; as regulating dramatic performances, 19, 25, 47; overseer of the Revels, 23; between sovereign and Master of the Revels, 23–24; licenser of plays for performance, 24; licenser for publication, 25; censor of plays, 24, 25, 188; patron of dramatic company, 25, 27; suppressing companies, 24; hearing Children of the Chapel rehearse, 24; literary patron, 26; champion of playwrights, 25, 27, 179; appealed to by Ben Jonson, 145, and intervening in Middleton's trouble, 167; protecting stage rights in plays, 23, 231, 314; protecting copyright, 232, 237, 240.
Chamberlain, John, 120, 165, 171, 177n., 183, 187, 263.
Chamberlain's men, publication of plays of, 267ff., 284; relations of, to Strange's and Admiral's men, 278–279.
Chambers, E. K., 42n., 109, 243, 295n.
Chancellor and censorship, 97.
Chancellor of Exchequer and censorship, 67.
Chapman, George, 31; *A Humorous Day's Mirth*, 99; on royalty, in *The Gentleman Usher*, 128; on royal policy, in *Eastward Hoe*, *A Widow's Tears*, and *Monsieur D' Olive*, 139–140, 148; imprisoned for *Eastward Hoe*, 144; patronized by d'Aubigné, 146; a play by, on "Bengemens plot" (1598), 203; censored for French history in Biron plays, 160ff.; censored (with Shirley) for satire in *The Ball*, 180; oversees publication, 205, 211; fears piracy? 211; dedicates *The Widow's Tears*, 211; publishes short version of *The Blind Beggar of Alexandria*, 267; is careless as to text, 341n., but shows concern over others' carelessness, 366; early earnings of, 221.
Charles I, as prince, in Middleton's *A Game at Chess*, 165ff.; as king, satirized by Massinger, 127–28; censors Massinger's play, 127; is requested by D'Avenant to pass on profanity of *The Wits*, 192; journey of, criticised in play censored, 188.
Chaucer, *Canterbury Tales*, Caxton's text, 345.
Chettle as editor, 371–72.
Children, as actors, 6, *and see* Actors; of Blackfriars, punished for satirizing James I, 161; of the Chapel, 6n.; recite before the Chamberlain, 24; present contemporary satire, 108.; steal 'Jeronimo' from the King's men, 227–28; of the Revels, 18, 51; of Paul's, 116; dissolved, 1590–91, 265; effect of this on publication of plays, 265ff.
Christmas Revels, 38–40.
Churchyard, Thomas, 106.
Christ's Teares (Nashe), 198.
City, attitude of, toward plays, 20, 26, 30, 200. See Aldermen, London, Mayor.
City Shuffler, The, non-extant play, censored by Herbert, 181.
Cobham, Henry Brooke, Lord, 34, 172.
Cobham, William Brooke, Lord, 26, 172.
Coleman v. Wathen, 313.
Collaboration in play writing as affecting publication, 202–203.
Collier, J. P., 11, 30, 51, 101.
Come See a Wonder, 50.
Common law, *see* Manuscript and Stage-right and Copyright.
Companies of actors; number of companies, 11–12, 50; number of actors in companies, 13; licenses of companies, 11; 'strangers', 50; the

'Four United Companies', 11–12, 282; poverty, dissolution, and recombination of companies affecting publication of plays, 226ff., 230ff., 277ff., attitude of, toward publication of plays, 2, 224ff., 228, 235ff., 238ff., 240–41.

Compositor, boy used as, 319, but forbidden, 357; spelling by, 322, 323, 325–26; duties of, 325; as editor, 369–70; may depart from copy, 332–33; 369; setting up only part of a text, with others, 325, 343–44; setting up from dictation? 295–96, 326, 335, 338; preferred printed copy 326, 329, 332; setting by eye, 328; using *visorium*, 329–330; from auditory images, 331–333, 334, 340; his unit of memorizing and line-shifting, 340–41; common errors due to, 333–37; foul case, 337–39; substitution of synonyms and homonyms, 341–42, and familiar words, 342; journeymen, setting up at home? 343.

Concini, execution of, dramatized, 163.

Contemporary subjects in drama, 101ff.; forbidden by James, 161; preferred by Jonson, Chapman, Marston, Beaumont, *et al.*, 200–201.

Copyright in plays; well preserved by King's men, 233, 244; owned and sold by companies, 234; owned with stage rights by Moseley, 245; reserved by entry on the Stationers' Registers, 244ff. *See* Stage right.

Corrector of the press, work and duties of, 344ff.; high standards of the early, 344–45; qualifications of, 345–46; methods, 346; lack of learned, 318–19, 347–48, in the King's printing-house, 357; held responsible for errors, 358.

Coryton, John, *Stage-right*, 4, 237.

Costume, realism of, in presenting contemporary characters, 165; in history play, 121–22.

Cotton, Robert, 351–52.

Courcelles, French ambassador to Scotland, 154.

Court, satirized, 137.

Court plays and masques, contemporary topics in, 106.

Court of High Commission, *see* High Commission and Ecclesiastical.

Court of Star Chamber, *see* Star Chamber.

Cowell, Dr. John, *The Interpreter*, censored as to political theory, 82.

Craftsmen, alien, attacked in plays, 29, 105, 131, 133ff.

Crane, Ralph, scrivener, copying plays for King's company, 294.

Creighton, C., 269.

Cromwell, Thomas, Life and Death of Lord, 104.

Cunningham, Peter, 43, 230.

Cupid's Revenge (Beaumont and Fletcher, censored? 117n.

Custom of the Country (Beaumont and Fletcher), playhouse manuscript? 296.

Cynthia's Revels (Jonson), personal satire in, 176.

Daborne, Robert, *The Poor Man's Comfort*, 100, *Machiavel*, 292.

Daniel, Samuel, licenses plays for a company, 51, 183; before the Privy Council for *Philotas*, 182, 213–14; on errors, 367.

D'Avenant, Sir William, *The Wits*, 21; censored for profanity, 190; *Playhouse to be Let*, 166; oversees publication, 205; and playbooks of King's men, 246n.

Day, John, *Isle of Gulls*, satire in, discussed in House of Commons, 116–17; prologue disclaims satire on lawyers and libel, 177, 180; oversees publication, 205; revises *Parliament of Bees*, 299.

Dedication of plays, "out of fashion" (1639), 206; significance of, for text 288–89.

Defence of Coney-Catching, A, 222–23, 278.

Dekker, Thomas, *If this be not a good play*, 100n., 105; *The Whore of Babylon*, 97, objected to, 108; personal satire in *Satiromastix*, 176; (and Chettle), *Sebastian of Portugal*, 170; early earnings of Dekker, 221.

Derby, *see* Strange, Lord, and Stanley.

Devereux, W. B., 150.

Devil's Law Case, The (Webster), 171.

De Vinne, T., 324, 325, 327, 347.

Dibdin, J. C., 12, 158.

Dobell, Bertram, 141ff., 148, 162.

"Doleman's book", (Parsons?), 152.

Donne, John, 67.

Drayton, Michael, *The Harmony of the Church*, suppressed, 88; *Psalms*, objected to, 88; *Polyolbion* and the booksellers, 372.

Drummond, William, 140, 142, 146, 195.

Dumb Knight, The (Markham and Machin), 177; why published, 214.

Dumb show, *see* Pantomime.

Dutch, dialect in plays, 148; craftsmen, antipathy toward, in *Sir Thomas More*, 132; relations with English, in a play, 171–72.

Dutch Courtesan, The (Marston), trouble-making, 89, 147.

Duty on wines, discussed in play, 175.

Dymock, Edward, suit against, for libel and slander in play, 180.

East India Companies, dramatization of English and Dutch relations in play, suppressed, 171; defense of English company in play, censored, 171.

Eastward Hoe, (Chapman, Jonson, Marston), 51; censored for contemporary satire, 139ff.; ridicules choice of old subjects, 200.

Ecclesiastical Commission, 22, 63ff., 67, 73–4, 90, 91, 192.

Ecclesiastical, control of drama, 22, 28; licensing of plays, 23, 48–50, 56–57, 61ff., and of literature, 63ff.; and *see* Bishop, and Archbishop, and High Commission.

Editing of texts by compositor, corrector, publisher, 369ff., 371–72, 375–6; by modern editors, choosing preferred readings, 379–80.

Editions, number and size of, 373; priority of, 381–82.

Editorial ideals, 365, 371–72.

Edward the First, King (Longshanks), 264n.

Elegies, censored, 83.

Elizabeth, Queen of England, marriage plans of, discussed in literature, 75, 109–111; her skill in deciphering allegory, 110–111; satirized in French book, 76; compared with James by French ambassador, 118; attacked in Jesuit play, 97; a character in English ballad, 85; favorite of, in a play, 196; issues proclamation forbidding discussion of religion and politics in plays, 95, and of her own times in plays, 108–109, 113; connives in ridiculing foreign nations in masque and play, 111, 114, 115. *See also* Sovereign.

Emperor of the East, The (Massinger), 176.

Endymion (Lyly), why published, 265.

England's Joy, 108.

English Traveler, The (Heywood), alleged attempt at unauthorized publication of, 210, 238.

Epigrams, censored, 83.

Erasmus, corrector of the press, 350.

Errata, kinds and causes of, 334ff.; shifting of blame for, 352, 354–55, 358, 361, 365; the printer acknowledging, 359; lightly excused, 359–60, 368; omitted because obvious, 360; left to the reader, 360–62; corrected on some sheets; seriously treated by publisher, 361ff.; corrected in new edition? 363.

Essex, Robert, second Earl of, figured in Daniel's *Philotas*, 82; alluded to in sermons, 197.

Every Man Out of His Humour, Greg on first ed. of, 344n.; texts of Ling's and Holmes' quartos of 1600, 332, 335–38, 340, 342.

Fair Quarrel, A (Middleton and Rowley), 285.
Faire Maide of the Inne (Beaumont and Fletcher), 171.
Fairs, European, and books, 66.
Faithful Shepherdess, The (Fletcher), why published, 215.
Falstaff, 172.
"Family of Love", objected to, 73.
Family of Love (Middleton), 284.
Favorites, royal: English, satirized by Massinger, 125–126; by Jonson, 143; French, in English play, 163.
Fayre Fowle One, The, 51.
Feast of Fools, 37.
Fenner, George, 114.
Feuillerat, A., 40, 42–44, 46, 53, 108 *et passim*.
Field, N., *Amends for Ladies*, 172.
Fleay, F. G., 56, 65, 132, 159, 180, 269, 272–73, *et passim*.
Fletcher, Giles, *The Russe Commonwealth*, censored, 79ff., 198.
Fletcher, John, *Rule a Wife, and Have a Wife*, 168ff.; *The Woman's Prize* censored for profanity and ribaldry, 189, to be revised in actors' roles, 191, 292; *The Faithful Shepherdess*, why published, 215; *Monsieur Thomas* not appreciated on stage, 216; *Cupid's Revenge*, 287; *The Wildgoose Chase*, lost manuscript advertised for, 293; (and Massinger), *Thierry and Theodoret*, 163.
Fletcher, Lawrence, English actor, favored by James in Scotland, 156, 158–59; wins freedom of Aberdeen, 159.
Foerster, Wendelin, 204, 349.
Fontaine, John, corrector, ideals of, 345.
Forbidden books, *see* Books.

Ford, John, oversees publication, 205; opposes professionalism, 207; on the worth of the printed play, 211.
Format of book, in relation to text problems, 379–80.
Four Prentices of London (Heywood), apologies for publication of, 209.
Fowell, Frank, and Palmer, Frank, 137, 217.
Foxe, John, 61n.; *Acts and Monuments* refused a license, 87.
France, licensing and censorship in, 66; Queen of, ridiculed in *Byron*, 160, 163ff.; Ambassador from, reports on English plays, 117; ambassador (Boderie) acts against *Byron*, 160. *See* French.
Freedom of speech, plea for, in a play, 124.
French, dialect of, parodied in plays, 148; workmen, antipathy toward, in *Sir Thomas More*, censored, 132, 135–36.
Freylinck, Miss W., 184.
Friar Bacon and Friar Bungay (Greene), 278.
Fuller, Thomas, 60n.
Furness, H. H., 326, 333; on dictating to compositors, 326–27.

Galathea (Lyly), why published, 265.
Game and Play of the Chesse, The, 165n., 273.
Game at Chess, A (Middleton), satirizing Spain, and, James, 111; censored, 21, 165ff.; popular, 166; antiquated and silenced, 167–68; an uncensored version extant? 68.
Gardiner, S. R., 169, 170.
Gascoigne, George, 353; *Ferdinando Jeronimo*, censored for slander, 83; *Posies*, censored for indecency, 86.
Gayley, C. M., 147n.
Gentleman Usher, The (Chapman), 128.
George a Greene, the Pinner of Wakefield, problem of text of, 298.
Gerschow, Friedrich, 107.

Gildersleeve, Virginia, 101, 218.
Glapthorne, Henry, *The Lady Mother*, manuscript play provisionally licensed, 193; oversees publication, 205.
Golden Age, The (Heywood), 208.
Gondomar, Spanish ambassador, satirized in English plays and ballads, 164ff., in *A Game at Chess*, 165ff.
Gorboduc (Sackville and Norton), 110.
Gosson, Stephen, *The Schoole of Abuse*, 90.
Gowry conspiracy, dramatization of, 120.
Grafton, Richard, 347.
Graves, T. S., 178.
Gray, D. H., on *Hamlet*, Q^1, 306ff.
Great Duke of Florence, The (Massinger), 126.
Greene, Robert, 147, 149; charged with double sale of *Orlando Furioso*, 222–23; 278; ownership of *Friar Bacon and Friar Bungay*, 278; edited by Chettle, 371–72.
Greene's Tu Quoque, (Cooke), 209.
Greenstreet, J., 239.
Greg, W. W., 128ff., 137, 223, 269, 285, 292, 295n., 300, 301, 333, 335n., 368n., 382, 384.
Grindal, Edmund, Archbishop, 64.
Guilpin, Edward, satires of, censored, 83.
Guise, Duke of, represented in a play, 107.
Guzman de Alfarache, Folio of 1623, 361.

"Hack poet" as text pirate, 307ff.
Hall, Joseph, censored for satires, 83, 88.
Halliwell-Phillips, J. O., 32, 33, 43, 53, 56, 173.
Hamlet (Shakespeare), Gray's theory on first quarto, 306ff., 315; Hubbard on first quarto, 288, 315.
Handwriting, in relation to text problems, 321, 322, 330, 335–6, 347, 352, 365. *See* Manuscript.

Harington, Sir John, in disfavor for satire, 84; *A Brief Apologie of Poetry*, 107.
Harvey, Gabriel, censored for personal satire, 83.
Haughton, William, *The English Fugitives*, non-extant play, on the house of Suffolk, 188.
Hayward, Edward, 54, 58.
Hayward, John, *Historie of . . . . Henry IV*, suppressed, and censored, 373.
Hazlitt, W. C., 90n., 286.
Heminge and Condell, 224, 352.
Henry IV (Shakespeare), censored, 34, 172–73.
Henry V (Shakespeare), 267–68, Pollard and Wilson on text of, 309ff.
Henry VI, Pt. III, actors' names in text of, 298.
Henry VIII, divorce of, a forbidden topic; 130; objectionably portrayed in *Sir Thomas More*, 136.
Henry VIII, (*All is True*), 121–22.
Henslowe, Philip, 273, 275; contracts with actors, 10; significance of his business for stage rights, 221; *Diary* of, 55, 56, 202–203, 236, 264, 270ff., 278, 280–281; 292 *et passim*.
Herbert, Sir Henry, Master of the Revels, 43, 51–56; 270ff., licenses plays for press, 57–58, 193; licenses non-dramatic literature, 67; burns plays, 87; censors plays, 127; is called before Council for licensing anti-Spanish play, 165–67; refuses license for anti-Spanish play, 169; censors play on East India Co., 171; refuses license for *A Tale of a Tub*, 179; censors *The Ball*, 180; stays *The City Shuffler*, 181; punishes Beeston for having unlicensed play acted, 188; censors for impropriety, 189; holds up *The Young Admiral* as model, 189; requires actors' roles to be revised, 191, 192; censors for profanity, 190; disagrees with Charles I. as to oaths in *The Wits*,

192; forbids Red Bull company to act some Shakespeare plays, 218, 230; preserves repertoire of Red Bull company, 233; orders "fair copy" of play from company bookkeeper, 292.

Herbert, Philip, see Pembroke, Earl of.

Herbert, William, see Pembroke, Earl of.

Heresy, censorship of, 60–65; 68n., 73.

Herpick, C. A., 374.

Heywood, Thomas, *Edward IV*, 105; *If you know not me*, 109, pirated by stenography, 113, 207; *Apology for Actors*, 113n; part author of over 200 plays, 203; oversees publication, 205; pretends to dislike publication, 207ff., 211; apologizes for publication of *The Three Ages*, 208; pretends forced publication of *Four Prentices of London*, 209, and *The English Traveler*, and *The Rape of Lucrece*, 210; declares his own modesty, 210, 238; approves his *Fair Maid of the West*, 210; *Rape of Lucrece* reissued, 285-86; *Funeral Elegy upon James I*, 113; complains of piracy by stenography and oral report, 315; attitude of, toward text and *errata*, 312, 358, 368.

Heywood, Mr. Thomas, Jesuit, 113.

High Commission, Court of, 88, 91, 192. See Archbishop, Bishop, Ecclesiastical.

History, censored, 76ff.

History plays, of past, 102–104; of contemporary topics, 102, *et passim*.

History of the Duchess of Suffolk, nonextant play, censored, 55, 188.

Histriomastix, 226.

Hoby, Sir Edward, 117.

Hog hath Lost His Pearl, The (R. Tailor), play satirizing London mayor, interrupted by sheriff, 174ff., 199.

Holinshed's Chronicles, censored, ordered suppressed, 76.

Holland, printing in, 319: presses in Holland and the Low Countries, 325.

Holland's Leaguer, censored, 70.

Honest Man's Fortune, 52.

Hooker, Richard, 351.

Horsey, Sir Jerome, 80.

Howard, Lord Charles, and plays, 26.

Hubbard, F. G., 288, 315.

Hunsdon, George Carey, first Lord, 26; as Chamberlain and literary patron, 26, 268.

Hunsdon, Henry Carey, second Lord, 26.

Hunt, Mary, 70.

If You Know not Me, (Play of Queen Elizabeth, by Heywood), pirated by stenography, 207.

Image of Love, The, censored, 62.

Imprint, false, 90, 382; irregular, 383.

Impropriety and indecency, censoring for, 188ff.

Induction hinting at trouble over play, 174, 175, 181. See Prologue, Preface.

Inking of types, 323, 324n.

Insurrection in plays dangerous, 134.

Interpolations, responsibility for, in plays, 194–95. See Actors, Censorship.

Interpreters, decipherers, and reporters of plays objected to, 197ff.

Introduction to a Devout Life, recalled, 88.

Isle of Dogs (Nashe), 34; "seditious and slanderous", 181ff.

Isle of Gulls (Day), censored, 117, 177n.

Italicising, by compositor, 369.

Jack Drum's Entertainment, personal satire in, 176.

Jack Straw, Life and Death of, 104.

Jaggard, William, attitude of, toward *errata*, 354–55; complained of by Heywood, 358; piratical reprints of 1619, 382–83.

James I. of England, favors English players in Scotland, 20 and 156ff.; censors sermons, 75; suppresses political theory, 82; prohibits discussion of affairs of state, 119, 161; asks for suppression of *The Faerie Queene*, 150ff., 154; his claims to English throne, 151, 153; his absolutism, 185–86; cowardice and instability, 154–56; satirized by Raleigh? 77; by Riche? 150; by William Leonard, 150; freely satirized in Eng. plays, 117–19, 157–58; ridiculed for cowardice in Brussels farce, 119–20; and for pretensions to throne, etc., in *A Midsummer Night's Dream?* 159; for policies, by Massinger, 124–25, 127; by Chapman, Jonson, Marston, *et al.* for favors to Scots, 139–40; for hunting, profanity, drunkenness, 161; for his use of Scotch mines, 161; by Middleton, in *A Game at Chess*, 165ff.; for absolutism and relations with Parliament? 184–86; conspiracy against, dramatized, 120; enjoys Cambridge satire on lawyers 177; suppresses companies for satire on himself, the Scotch, the French, 161; declares comedies shall cease, 161; acts against Chapman and Jonson, 148–49; acts against the players of *A Game at Chess*, 166; but relents towards the King's Company, 168.

James, Thomas, *Index generalis librorum prohibitorum* . . . ., 91.

Jeffes, Abel, 86.

Jealous Lovers, The (Randolph), to be immortal in print, 216.

Jenkinson, Hilary, 322.

"*Jeronimo*", stage right in, 227.

Jesuit, play in France against England, 97ff.; plot to crown Lord Strange King of England, 112–13. *See* Catholic.

Jew, satirized in drama, 99.

Jigs and dances forbidden, 35.

Jones, Inigo, designer and architect, satirized by Jonson, 179ff.

Jones, Richard, actor, owner of plays, 224ff., 227.

Jones, Richard, editing of Marlowe by, 371.

Jonson, Ben, 103; patronized by William Herbert, 26; collaborates with unknown author in *Sejanus*, 141, and with Chapman in unknown play, 203; and with Chapman and Marston, 176; imprisoned with Chapman for *Eastward Hoe*, 139ff., 195, 200; accused of popery and treason for *Sejanus*, 141ff.; is apologetic to James, 142, 197; serves in tracing Gunpowder Plot, 142; his relation to Catholicism, 142–43; enmity with Northampton, 140, 143; imprisonments of, 144–45; *Bartholomew Fair*, 99–100, its digs at censors and decipherers, 175, 192, 199; satire on decipherers in dedication to *Volpone*; 198–99; alleged insult to Lady Arabella Stuart in *Epicœne*, 177–78, and Jonson's protest against libel hunters, in dedication and second prologue, 178, 199; personal satire in *The Case is Altered*, 100, 176; *The Alchemist*, 100, 196; satire in *Cynthia's Revels* and *The Poetaster*, 176, and denial of satire in Address to Reader of *Poetaster*, and *Dialogue between Horace and Trebatius*, 177; five satires on Inigo Jones, 179; *Neptune's Triumph*, masque, rejected and Jonson out of favor for anti-Spanish matter, 164; in trouble over Nashe's *The Isle of Dogs*, 182; his *The Magnetic Lady* censored for interpolated oaths, 192; ridicules censorship for profanity, 192, 199; signs name to first folio, 205; oversees publication, 205; publishes *The New Inn* because unappreciated, 214; his Folio, 215; collects plays from many companies, 234.

INDEX

Journeymen printers and seditious and irregular printing, 321.
Justices of the peace, to forbid plays satirizing great people, 173.

Keene v. Wheatley and Clarke, 313.
Kellner, Leon, 322.
Kelly, William, 12, 49, 275–76.
Kempe, A. J., 44n.
Kempe, William, actor, personates alderman, 174; interpolates, 196.
Kennedy, William, *Annals of Aberdeen*, 159.
Kildare, Earl of, resents satire on ancestor in play, 173.
King, *see* Sovereign.
King and Subject, (Massinger), censored, 21, 127.
King's Company, 51; in trouble, 121, 166; satirize Spain, 168; restrained from acting, 189; steal *Malcontent* from Children, 227; protect stage right in plays through Master of Revels, 230, and copyright through Chamberlain and Stationers' Co., 240–42; preserve stage rights many years, 243; not opposed to publication, 241, 243.
Knack to Know a Knave, A, 99, 285.
Knight, Mr., book-keeper of actors' company, 292.
Knight of the Burning Pestle (Beaumont and Fletcher), satirizing prohibition of contemporary topics, 200–201.
Knox, John, censored, 72.
Kyd, Thomas, *Spanish Tragedy*, text of, 375.

Lady Mother, The, corrected before licensing, 51.
Lagus, Conrad, sixteenth century lawyer, on authors' rights, 314.
Lanchinge of the Mary (William Methold), manuscript play censored for profanity, etc., 171, 190, 292; playhouse version? 296.
Larum for London, A, 105.

Late Lanchashire Witches, The (Heywood and R. Brome), 235.
Laud, William, Archbishop of Canterbury, 65, 75.
Lawrence, W. J., 130, 139.
Lawyers, satirized in Jonson's *Poetaster*, in Cambridge play *Ignoramus*, Day's *Isle of Gulls*, Markham's *The Dumb Knight*, 176–77.
Lear, King (Shakespeare), A. W. Pollard on publication of, 283–84.
Lectures, unauthorized publication of, protested by Lagus in 1544, 314.
Lee, Sir Sidney, 2, 99, 204, 211, 286, 289, 291–2, 294.
Legal protection, *see* Play-right, Copyright, Lagus, Star Chamber.
Leighton, Alexander, censored for sedition, 68.
"Le Prince" censured for scandal against Queen Elizabeth, 76.
Lenten Stuffe (Nashe), 198.
L'Estrange, Roger, as censor, 92.
Libel in plays, 178, 180.
Liberty, civil, plea for, in a play, censored, 186.
License, of play for press at end of manuscript, 58, 167, 169, 193; provisional, 193–94; of old plays when revived, 191, 246.
Licensing, of actors, 14, 18, abused system of, 18–19; of traveling companies, 47; of plays, 51–52, 83; delays in, 87; Milton on injustice of, 378; Act of 1637, 194; *See* Censoring, Chamberlain, Ecclesiastical, High Commission, Master of the Revels, Mayor, and Sovereign.
Lincoln, Earl of, brings libel suit against Edward Dymocke for slander in a play, 180.
Line-shifting in poetical texts, 340–41.
Locke, letter to Carleton, 187.
London Stationers' Company, licensing plays for the press, 56, 57, 63, 69–71; destroying satires, epigrams, and elegies, 83; checking indecency, 85–86; recalling books, 88; pro-

tecting plays from unauthorized publication, 232ff., 240ff., 243, 266-67; significance of entry on the Registers, 289.
Longshanks, see Peele, *Edward I.*
Looking-Glass for London, A, 95.
Lope de Vega, *see* Vega
Lord of Misrule, 37–38.
Loves Maistresse, (Heywood), 210.
Love's Pilgrimage (Beaumont and Fletcher), playhouse manuscript? 296.
Lover's Melancholy, The (Ford), 207.
Lover's Progress, The (Beaumont and Fletcher), revival of, 263.
Lyly, John, 100, 101; his *Midas*, 95, 109, 116; *Endymion*, 110; *Campaspe*, 110, *Sappho and Phao*, 110; Folio, 215; publication of plays affected by dissolution of Paul's, 265; his *Sixe Court Comedies*, 285.

Machin, Lewes (and Markham), *The Dumb Knight*, why published, 214.
Madan, Falconer, 329.
Mad Couple, The (R. Brome), 235–36.
Madden, D. H., 288.
Madden, J. P. A., 327–28, 330.
Magnetic Lady, The (Jonson), actors punished for interpolations in, 192.
Maid of Honor, The (Massinger), 125–26.
Malcontent, The (Marston), why published, 198; 211–12; theft of, and stage rights, 227; editions, 228.
Malone, E., 2, 12, 43, 241, 245, *et passim.*
Manly, John Matthews, iii, 6, 338, 382.
Manuscript, of play, guarded? 4; theft of, actionable at common law, 314ff.; circulation of plays in, 290, 293–94, 295n.; author's autograph, 170, 293–95; private transcripts, 3, 292, 294; plays extant in, 122, 130, 138, 168, 169, 171, 183, 193, 293–95 *et passim. See also* Handwriting, Playhouse manuscripts, Prompt copies.

Marcellus, actor of, in *Hamlet*, as text pirate? 307ff.
Markham, Gervase, *The Dumb Knight*, satirizing lawyers, 177.
Marlowe, Christopher, *The Massacre at Paris*, 106-107; interpolations in *Doctor Faustus* (1616), 209; editing of, by Richard Jones, 371; *Edward II*, 280–82.
Marston, John, satires censored, 83–84; trouble over *Eastward Hoe*, 141ff., 147; satire in *What You Will*, 176; misconstruction of *The Malcontent* complained of, 198; *The Malcontent* stolen from one company by another, 227; oversees publications, 205, 211, 212–13; fears censors and critics more than pirates, 212; shirks editorial work, 212–13; thinks plays best on stage, 213.
Martin Marprelate controversy, 32–33, 73–74, 87, 100.
Mary, Queen of England, 63.
Mary, Queen of Scots, satire on as Duessa in *The Faerie Queene*, objected to by James, 150ff., 154; other slander on (1595), and a book on (1598) censored, 152.
Massinger, Philip, interest in contemporary problems, 123ff.; *The Roman Actor*, 123; *The Maid of Honor*, 125; *The Bondman*, 125; *King and Subject*, censored, 21, 127. *Believe as You List*, refused license, 169; autograph manuscript of *Believe as You List*, 170, 295; oversees publication, 205; declares dedications obsolete, 206; *errata* in the texts of, 368n.
Master of the Revels, *see* Revels, Master of the
Mayor, control of drama by, 11, 15, 17, 28; licenses actors, 30; licenses performances, 27, 29; supervises content of plays, 28, 30, 32, 48–49, 68; objects to performances, 20, 28, 29, 32; restrains from playing, 265;

entertains with pageants, 29; attitude of, toward drama, 30, 31; objects to dramatizing riots, 131; a mayor of London satirized for wine monopoly, 174.

Melanchthon, *Epistles*, suppressed, 72.

Melville, Andrew, 96, 97, 153.

Memorizing of play texts for publication, 310ff.; in Spanish theatre, 311-13; in American theatres illegal by 18th century, 313.

Merchant of Venice (Shakespeare), provisional license for publication of, 244.

Merry Devil of Edmonton, The, stage rights in, 217.

Merry Wives of Windsor, The (Shakespeare), theories on source of text of, 300 ff.

Midas (Lyly), 95, 109, 116; why published, 265.

Middleton, Edward, appears before Privy Council in place of Thomas Middleton with reference to *A Game at Chess*, 168.

Middleton, Thomas, ridicules Spanish ambassador and King James in *A Game at Chess*, 21, 111n., 124, 164ff., 273; to be called before Privy Council, 167; pageant of, *The Triumph of Honor and Industry*, ridiculing a Spanish ambassador, 196; *The Chaste Maid of Cheapside*, 100; *The Family of Love*, 284; oversees publications, 205; recovers manuscript of *The Witch* for publication, 293; (and Rowley) *A Fair Quarrel*, 285.

Midsummer Night's Dream, A, satirizing James's pretensions, 159.

Military policy, criticism of, censored, 78.

Milton, John, *Areopagitica*, 93; on author's right to revise during publication, 378.

Misrule, *see* Lord of Misrule.

Moldavia, Prince of, in Jonson's *Epicoene*, 177.

Monarchy attacked in *Barnavelt*, 186-87.

Monopolies, printing, effect of, on quality of work, 317, 321.

Monopolies, general, criticised in plays by Heywood, 105, by Dekker, 106, by Chapman, 148, by Tailor, 174, 175.

Monsieur d'Olive (Chapman), criticises royal policy, 148.

Monsieur Thomas (Fletcher), unappreciated on stage, 216.

Montgomery, Philip Herbert, Earl of (and of Pembroke), *see* Pembroke.

More, Sir Thomas, *see* Sir Thomas More.

Morgan, J. A., on unsatisfactoriness of damage suits for violation of stage rights, 220.

Moseley, Humphrey, 27n., 244.

Motto, (Wither), 70.

Moxon, Joseph, 324-25; 329-30, 337-38, 340, 345-46; 357, 369, 377-78, 380.

Mucedorus, 284.

Much Ado about Nothing (Shakespeare), Furness on text of, 326, 333; on actors' names in text of 1600 quarto, 298.

Munday, Anthony, 131; autograph manuscripts of *John à Kent and John à Comber* and of part of *Sir Thomas More*, 295. See *Sir Thomas More*.

Murray, Sir James, enmity against Jonson, 140.

Murray, J. T., 6, 7, 11, 13, 159, 226, 230, 270ff., 275n., 278, 280 *et passim*.

M'Crie, Thomas, 75n., 97, 147.

McKerrow, R. B., 60, 80n., 198, 325, 326, 333, 343-44, 375, 377, 379-80, 382, 384.

Nashe, Thomas, 79, 80, 353-54; sedition and slander in *Isle of Dogs*, 34, 117, 162n., 181ff., censored for satire, 83; Marprelate controversy,

100–101; *Almond for a Parrot*, 116; refers to trouble over *Isle of Dogs*, in *Summer's Last Will and Testament*, 197; satirizes decipherer and interpreter in *Strange Newes, Christs Teares*, and *Lenten Stuffe*, 198; text of, 365, 375; setting up of *The Unfortunate Traveler*, 343–44.
Neidig, W. J., 382.
Neilson, W. A., 327n.
New Inne, The (Jonson), published for better audience, 214.
News sheets censored, 81ff.
Nichols, John, 264n.
Nicoll, Allardyce, 245–46n.
Nixon, Anthony, *The Black Year*, 147.
Nobility, satires on, censored, 119, 122, 180 *et passim*.
Northbroke, John, 274–75.
Northern Lass, The (Brome), 235.
Norton, Thomas (Sackville and), *Gorboduc*, 110.

Oaths, *see* Profanity, Censoring, Buc, Herbert, Revels.
Oldcastle, Sir John (Lord Cobham) 61; name of Oldcastle cut from Shakespeare's *Henry IV*, 172.
Oldcastle, Sir John, a play, see *Sir John Oldcastle*.
Orange, Prince of, portrayed in Barnavelt, 184ff.
Orlando Furioso, 147, 149; sale to two companies, 222–23; stage right, 223, 278; Alleyn's title role in, 292.
Ovid declared immoral, 83; cancelled entry of publication in England, 86.
Ownership of plays, 217ff, 239ff. *See* Stage-right, Copyright.

Palsgrave, John, 351.
Pantomime, offensive, added to innocent play texts, 196–97.
Parasitaster, or The Faun (Marston) 212–13.
Parker, Matthew, Archbishop, 64, 378; attitude toward accuracy of text, 368.

Parliament, censorship by, 75; relations of, with King glanced at in play, 185; to be appealed to by Lady Arabella Stuart for Jonson's alleged satire on her, 178.
Parry's treason dramatized, 113.
Parsons, Father, Jesuit, 76.
Patentees, and unprivileged printers, 317, 320; and concern for good texts, 321.
Patents, *see* Monopolies, for satire in plays.
Patient Grissell, publication of, "stayed", 244, 266.
Patron, dedication of play to, 206; noble, using plays for politics, *see* Political.
Paul's, Children of, suppressed, 33; play *Midas*, 116.
Peele, George, *Edward III*, 149: *Edward I*, 264n.
Pembroke, William Herbert, Earl of, as Chamberlain and literary patron, 26; appealed to by Jonson, 145; sympathized with actors in Middleton's trouble, 167. *See* Chamberlain.
Pembroke and Montgomery, Philip Herbert, Earl of, as Chamberlain, 26; protects plays of King's and Queen's young boys from unauthorized publication, 233; directs Stationers' Co. to protect copyright of King's men, 240ff., 272ff. *See* Chamberlain.
Pembroke's men, effect of poverty of, on publication of plays, (1593–94), 280; relations with Chamberlain's men, and with Admiral's, 279, 281.
Penniman, J. H., 176.
Penry, John, executed for seditious book, 74.
Personal satire, *see* Satire.
Philaster (Beaumont and Fletcher), 284–85; text of, 363.
Philip II of Spain, ridiculed in court plays, 111, on public stage, 115, 166ff.; subject of play, *Philip of*

Spain, 170. *See also* Lyly, Middleton, and Queen Elizabeth.
Philip of Spain, 170.
Philotas, Tragedy of (S. Daniel), censored as referring to Essex, 182–83, 213–14.
Photography, composite, in detection of pirated texts, 382.
Piracy and unauthorized publication of plays, 2, 208–209, 210–211, 282–83; of playhouse versions: by "traitor-actor"? 300ff., 314; by memorizer, 310; by stenographer, 301, 315–16, but no case of stenographic piracy of play in this period proved, 316; by "hack poet" as aid? 307ff.; by playhouse transcripts, 310; indicated by corrupt text? 286–87; temptations to piratical printing, arising from trade conditions, 321; evidences of, 382ff.
Plagiarism, threat of law suit for, in 1544, 314.
Plague, affecting acting of plays, 15–16; 19, 29; affecting publication of plays, 262, 269–273, 275.
Play of Cards, A, contemporary satire in, 107–108.
Playhouse, *see* Theatre.
Playhouse manuscripts, characteristics, 296-98; how pirated, 300ff. *See* Manuscripts, Piracy, Text.
Play-right, *see* Stage-right, Plays, and Copyright.
Plays; objections to, by town and city, 15–18, 31, 35, by Mayors, and aldermen, 29, 30–33; by Master of the Revels, 189 *et passim*, by Bishops, 22, by Bucer, 28, by Privy Council, 28, 34, 36, 182, *et passim*; by sovereign, 33, 36; defense of, Lodge's, 90; limitations of number of performances, 33–35; subjects of, old or contemporary? 200–201; made over, 202, 285; old plays preferred at court, 263–64; revivals of, must be licensed, 51–52; 83, 285; stage life of, 263; published while good for stage, 249ff.; revised to keep up with stage versions, 285ff., 299; demand for printed plays, 2; worthiness of printed plays, 287; proportion of, published, 202; produced in collaboration, 202ff.; and in haste, 203; pay for, 221; ownership of, 217ff.; copyright in, by purchase, 289; sale of, and stage right, 220ff.; loss of manuscripts of, 228; texts inferior to other literary texts? 366–67. *See* Stage right, Copyright.
Playwright, attitude of, toward publication of plays, 204, 205, 236, 239; overseeing publication, 205ff.; attitude toward purity of text, 312; pay of, 221–22; benefits for, 222; loyal to sovereign? 102–03, 124, 141–45; satirizing other authors, 176; reacting against censorship, 197ff. *See* Author,
Plomer, H. R., 317.
Poetaster, The (Jonson), personal satire in, 176–77, 180.
Political discussion, forbidden in plays, 95, 118; in plays patronized by noblemen, 112, 114; influenced by family patron? 126. *See* Contemporary and Censoring.
Pollard, A. W., iii, 276, 283, 288, 295, 308, 383–84.
Pope, Alexander, 288; attitude toward variants in Shakespeare text, 372.
Porter, Charlotte, 205, 286–87.
Porter, Henry, imprisonment of, for his part in Nashe's *Isle of Dogs*, 182.
Precisian, *see* Puritan.
Preface, indicating trouble over a play, 141. *See* Prologue, Induction.
Presses, printing, 324–25; on cuts of early, 324n., 329; defects in text due to crudity of, 325.
Printed copy as exemplar preferred by compositor, 381–82.
Printers, poverty of, 318–20; number of, 320; foreign, 320; journeymen,

and irregular printing, seditious and piratical, 320–21. *See* Publishers.

Printing, commercializing of, 317; regulation of, by state, 317; by journeymen, 320, piratical and unlicensed, 321; crudity of equipment for, 323ff.; inking of types, 323; press, 324–25; composition, 325ff.

Privy Council, 11, 19, 22, 27, 28, 33–34, 36, 39, 49–51, 68–69, 72, 75, 81, 83, 97, 100–101, 124, 131, 141, 153, 163, 166–67, 171, 173–75, 181, 182, 266, 268.

Proctors satirized in a play, 175.

Profanity, statute forbidding, 190; objected to in *The Tamer Tamed*, or *The Woman's Prize*, 189; in the "*Second Maiden's Tragedy*", *A Plantation of Virginia*, *The Lanchinge of the Mary*, *The Magnetic Lady*, 192 ff.; defined by Herbert, 192; passed on by High Commission, for Jonson, and by King Charles for D'Avenant, 192ff.

Professionalism of playwrights, *see* Playwright and Author.

Prohibition of plays, 135. For cases, see Censorship, Master of the Revels, Privy Council, Bishop, Archbishop, High Commission, Ecclesiastical, Mayor, Sovereign, King, Queen.

Prologue showing trouble over plays, 170, 178, 181, 197, 198–99, 207. *See* Induction, Preface.

Prompt copies, 292n. 294. *See* Playhouse manuscripts.

Proof-reading by authors, 348ff.; proofs sent to author, 353–55; 358, 360.

Propriety, standards of, in allowance of literary works, 85.

Protestant censorship under Elizabeth, 68n., 73ff. *See* Catholic.

Provincial companies, on visits, 12; licensing of, 14, 47; treatment of, in towns, 15–17; in plague time, 15–16, 274–75.

Prynne, William, *Histriomastix*, censored, 20, 67; *Antithesis of the Church of England*, censored, 33; on the popularity of printed plays, 286.

Publication of plays: demand for, 2, 236, 284–85; compared with number produced, 286; in folios, 215ff.; fluctuating, 269; in large groups, 266, 276ff.; motives for, 204ff., 216, 283; staling plays for the stage? 236ff., 238ff., 247, 249ff., 262–63; of unacted plays, 215; playwrights' attitudes toward, 231ff.; jointly owned, by one sharer, forbidden, 240; encouraging violation of stage-right? 231ff.; affected by plague? 262; by prohibitions from playing? 264, 268; by poverty, dissolution, and re-combination of companies, 226ff., 230ff., 273, 277–80, 282; in 1594, 277; unauthorized, means of guarding against, 240–41; for sale at theatre, 248n. *See* Chamberlain, London Stationers, Piracy, Printing, Revels, Master of.

Publishers, ideals of, illustrated by Edward Blount, 361–62; by Richard Jones, 371; editorial attitudes of, 369, 370–72; partnerships of publishers, booksellers, and printers, as affecting issues and editions, 374.

Punctuation, author concerned over, 364; commonly done by compositor, 369.

Puritaine, The, 100.

Puritans, censored for opinion, 73, 74; objections to plays, 31; attacks on stage by Puritans and city authorities, 31, 172–73, 189ff.; character of, satirized in plays, 99–100; restraints of playing due to, and the effect on publication, 265–66.

Putnam, G. H., 65.

Queen's Men and Beeston's Boys, owner of plays, 231.

INDEX

Quin, Walter, answers *The Faerie Queene* for King James, 151; courts James's favor by proving his title to England, 151.

Rabelais, circulation objected to, 87.
Raleigh, Walter, history suppressed, 77.
Ramírez, Luis, memorizer of Spanish plays, 311–313.
Randolph, Thomas, *The Muses' Looking-Glass*, 100n.; *The Jealous Lovers*, 216.
Rape of Lucrece (Heywood), alleged unauthorized publication of, 210–211.
Raumer, F. von, 120.
Ravenscroft, *The Anatomist, or the Sham Doctor*, sold at theatre in 1697, 248n.
Reade, Charles, 4.
Reader in printing office, reading to corrector, 346. *See also* Anagnostes, and Compositor.
Red Bull Company, restrained from acting plays of Shakespeare, 218, 230; file list of their plays with Master of the Revels, 233.
Reed, A. W., 61n.
Religion, satires on, forbidden, 95, 101.
Religious works, censorship of, 72ff. *See* Censorship, Catholic, Protestant, Heresy.
Remembrancia, 270ff. *et passim*.
Rennert, H. A., 311, 313.
Reusch, F., 65, 87.
Revels, at universities and inns of court, 39; at court, 39.
Revels, Master of the: office of, 19, 52–54; fees of, 55; under the Chamberlain, 23–24; history of office of, 37ff.; names of masters, 40ff.; qualifications and duties, 44–48; planning entertainments and masques, 24, 45–46, 48; licensing playhouses, 48; licensing plays, 32, 49; licensing players, 46–47; licensing plays for press, 56; licensing other literature? 67; licensing revised plays, 199; fitness for censoring, 59; examples of censoring by, 94, 188, *et passim*; protecting copyright, 25–26, 233, 246; protecting stage-right, 25–26, 218, 230, 246, 314. *See* Buc, Tilney, Herbert.
Richard II (Shakespeare), cut and censored, 159; "old" in 1601, 263.
Riche, Barnabe, satirizes James I in *Farewell to the Military Profession?* 150.
Rickert, Edith, 159.
Riot, 33. *See* Apprentices.
Roberts, James, 307; provisional entry of *Merchant of Venice*, 244.
Roles of actors, 292.
Roman Actor, The (Massinger), political, 123, 126.
Romeo and Juliet (Shakespeare), actors' names in text of, 298.
Rowlands, Samuel, *Letting of Humor's Blood in the Head Vein* suppressed, 89.
Rowley, Samuel, *When You See Me, You Know Me*, 96; *The Noble Soldier*, 100.
Royal Master, The (Shirley), printed before being acted in England, 262.
Royal prerogative and absolutism, in plays, *see* Massinger, *Barnavelt*, Chapman, Sovereign, and James I.
Rule a Wife, and Have a Wife (Fletcher), 168–69.
Rushworth, John, 18.
Russia, satirized, 79–80, 198; Emperor of, satirized in play, 111.
Rymer, Thomas, *Fœdera*, 194, 269 *et passim*.

Sackville, Thomas (and Norton), *Gorboduc*, 110.
Sacrilege, in privately performed play, suit for, 180.
Sappho and Phao (Lyly), why published, 265.

Satires, censored, 71, 83; of courtiers, 84; ineffectively suppressed, 88; personal, in plays, 119, 172, 196; of fellow playwrights, 176ff., 179, 180; of professions, 172; of foreign nations, 148. *See* Censorship, Scotch, Dutch, French.

Satiromastix (Dekker), personal satire in, 176.

Schevill, R., 311–13.

Schoeffer, Pierre, presswork of, 345.

Scotch, relations of, with English, 1594–1601, 149ff., 159; satirized in plays, 117, 149ff., 156; knights, created by James in England, satirized, 139ff.; satire on, resented by James, 149–151; antipathy toward, shown by Greene, Peele, Dekker, Shakespeare, Jonson, Chapman, Marston, 149 *et passim*.

Scotland, English players touring, 156–57; books printed in, competing with English books, 320.

Scourge of Villainy, personal satire in 176.

Scrivener, in relation to play text, 291–92, 294; Ralph Crane, for King's company, 294.

Sebastian of Portugal (Dekker and Chettle), 170.

"*Second Maiden's Tragedy*", censored, 122, 189–90.

Secret printing, *see* Printing and Surreptitious and Piracy.

Sedition, censoring for, 68, 71, 73, 74, 75, 85n., 181ff.

Sejanus (Jonson), trouble over, 141ff.; contemporary analogy in? 143.

Selden, John, history of, censored, 77, 93.

Sermons, pirated by stenography, 315; on contemporary affairs, 17, censored, 75; alluding to forbidden topics, 197.

Shakespeare, William, *Twelfth Night*, 100; *A Midsummer Night's Dream*, 103, 149, 159, 267; *Henry IV*, censored, 172, 283; *King John* and *Love's Labour's Lost* topical? 283; *Richard II*, censored and cut, 159, text of, 295; *Henry V*, 149, 159, 267, text of, 309; *Henry VIII*, 122; *Hamlet*, text of, 288ff., 306ff.; *Merry Wives of Windsor*, text of, 300, 301ff.; *Troilus and Cressida*, "never staled with the stage", 238; *King Lear*, why published, 283; *Merchant of Venice*, provisionally entered for publication, 244, 267; *Richard III*, 283; *Romeo and Juliet*, pirated, 283, 26; *A Winter's Tale*, re-licensed for revival, in 1623, 246; publication of his plays, 2–3, in 1600, 266–67; from autograph manuscripts? 295ff.; dedication of first Folio, 1; setting up of Folio text, 344; Folios and quartos, 377; Folio of 1632, 374; the quartos "all surreptitious", 2–4; piratical reprints of 1619, 267, 382; the "bad quartos", 288ff.; actors' names in *Romeo and Juliet*, *Much Ado*, Pt. III of *Henry VI*, 298; Red Bull Company restrained from acting plays by, owned by King's men, 218, 230; textual variants, 372–73.

Sharpham, Edward, 361.

Sheavyn, Phoebe, 218n., 284, 290, 326.

Shipherd, H. R., 211, 242.

Shirley, James, 216; oversees publication, 205; on *errata*, 359; *The Royal Master* printed before being acted in England, 262; *The Young Admiral* Herbert's model of propriety, 189; (and Chapman), *The Ball*, censored for satirizing noblemen, 180.

Shorthand, *see* Stenography.

Sidney, Robert, 106.

Sir John Oldcastle, 95

Sir Thomas More, 128ff.

Sisson, C. J., 322.

Slaughter, Martin, actor and sharer in plays, 225, 227, 282.

Small, Roscoe, 176.

Smith, Captain John, *General Historie of Virginia*, setting up of, 344.
Smith, Sir John, criticism of military policies by, 78.
Smith, W., *Hector of Germanie*, 120–22.
Southampton, Henry, third Earl of, patron to Heywood? 113.
Sovereign, encouraging drama, 20, 34, 35; regulating drama, 19; licensing plays, 21, 36; licensing performances, 27; censoring plays, 21; prohibiting plays, 33, 35; censoring literature, 67, 78; and city, power of, over plays, 31; satirized in history, 20; attitudes of playwrights toward, 102–103, 106, 120, 166; presentation of, on stage forbidden, 106–107, 120, 166; satirized in plays, 20, 116ff.; 122ff.; marriage of, dramatized, 121; pomp of, presented in *Henry VIII*, 121–22; relation of, to subject, in Massinger's plays, 21, 123ff.; as tyrant, 126; lustful, 136; policies of, in plays, 128; relations with Parliament touched? 184; only mortal, 137; his divine right attacked, 184. See names of rulers also.
Spain, licensing and censorship in, 66.
Spanish relations with England affecting literature, 51, 82, 94, 100, 105; 108, 109, 111, 114–116, 164, 168–170; English forbidden to meddle in, 164; Spanish ambassador, 110–111, 114, 115; Coloma acts against *A Game at Chess*, 149, 165; ambassador ridiculed in *The Triumphs of Honour and Industry*, by Middleton, 196. See Jonson, Lyly, Massinger, Middleton, Fletcher.
Spanish Curate, The (Beaumont and Fletcher), playhouse manuscript? 296.
Spanish Tragedy, The (Kyd), texts of, 384.

Spanish Viceroy, The, played without license, 51, 127, 169.
Sparagus Garden (R. Brome), 235.
Sparke, Michael, 90.
Speed, John, 351.
Spelling and punctuation, by compositor, 369–70.; varieties of spelling, 322–27, 333n.
Spenser, Edmund, *The Faerie Queene*, King James of Scotland wishes suppressed because of satire on his mother as Duessa, 150ff.; the work "not privileged", 151.
Stage directions in manuscripts, 297. *See* Playhouse manuscripts.
"Stage quarrel, The", 176ff.
Stage-right, basis of, before statutes, 217; indicated by sales system, 220, 280, and by Henslowe's bargains, 221ff., by Brome's contracts, 220ff., by contemporary condemnation of sale of play to two companies, 222–23, 278; by contemporary criticism of appropriating lost plays, 227–28; not dependent on guarding the copy, 218ff., 227–29, 290; maintained without keeping plays out of print, 218ff., 232ff., 237, 290ff.; and without resorting to special intervention of Master of the Revels, 218, 229, or of the Chamberlain, 231ff.; proved violations of, extremely rare, 217ff., 223; law-suits on, unprofitable in any age, 219–20; statutory protection of, often poor, 313–14; affected by joint ownership by actors, 225, 230, 239ff., and by ownership by actor-manager, 225ff., and by shifting personnel of companies, 226ff.: in relation to copyright in plays, 3, 204, 233ff., 280; owned with copyright by Moseley, 233ff., 245; double sale of stage-right and copyright condemned by Heywood, 211, 213, 234ff.; stage-right occasionally split off from copyright by separate sale? 280.

440   INDEX

Stanley, William, Earl of Derby, 'penning comedies for common players,' 114. His family, 112–113.
Stanyhurst, Richard, 369–70.
Star Chamber, 319; decrees of, (1566 and 1586), 63, 93; acts on censorship, 67, 68, 73, 76, 91; judges a ballad, 85; case in, 357. Burghley wishes a cozening case in, dramatized, 112.
Stationers' Company, *see* London Stationers' Co.
"Staying" of plays, 244, 266.
Steele, Robert, 27, 270ff.
Steevens, George, 348.
Stenography, common use of in sixteenth and seventeenth centuries, 315; systems of, 315; securing play texts by? 2, 3, 113, 207, 223, 301, 307, 315; no play text yet proved to originate thus, 316; such piracy forbidden in 18th century in America, 313.
Stephens printing house, ideals of, 344–45.
Stopes, Mrs. C. C., 27n., 77n., 173.
Stow, John, 74, 270ff.
Strange, Ferdinando, Lord, 112.
Strange Newes (Nashe), 198.
Strange's men, and Admiral's, and Chamberlain's, 278, and Pembroke's, 279.
Strype, John, 63, 64, 69, 74, 76n., 89n., *et passim*.
Stubbs, John, *A Gaping Gulf* censored, 68, 75–76.
Stuhlweisenberg, sack of, dramatized in contemporary play, 107.
Succession, plays concerning the, 110, 139ff., 149ff., 188ff.; books on, 151–52, 188n., *et passim*.
Suffolk, History of the Duchess of, a "dangerous" play censored, 188.
Suffolk, Duchess of, in Haughton, *The English Fugitives* (non-extant),188n.
Surreptitious printing and publication, 87, 90. See Publishing, Piracy, Printing.

Sweden, Courtship of King of, ridiculed in court masque, 111.
Swinnerton, Sir John, Mayor of London, satirized as wine-monopolist, 105, 174.
Synonyms, substitution of, by compositor, 341–42.

Tailor, Robert, *The Hog Hath Lost his Pearl*, satire on London Mayor, interrupted by sheriff, 105, 174.
Tale of a Tub, A (Jonson), censored for satire on Inigo Jones, 179–80.
Tamer Tamed, The (Fletcher's *Woman's Prize*), *see* Fletcher.
Taming of a Shrew, 280.
Tarleton, Richard, actor, interpolation of, 196.
Tax situation criticised in play, 104.
Tell-Tale, The, private transcript of, 294.
Text, summary of causes of errors in, 325; affected by: monopolies, 317; large patents, 321; competition, 318; number of printers, and their poverty, 317–320; poor equipment, 318, 323, 325; low standards of printers, 319; faulty manuscripts, 293, 295–96, 321; lack of good correctors, 318; author's pretended piracies, 322; compositors' methods, 319, 322–23, 325–32, 333–34; use of printed copy as exemplar, 326, 332ff.; treatment of *errata* by authors, 349ff., by printers and publishers, 354ff., 358ff.; standards of typography held by state officials, 357; editing by compositor, corrector, and printer or publisher, 369–72, 375–76; corrections at the press, 377; author's revision, 299, 376; binding corrected and uncorrected sheets miscellaneously, 376–77; correcting by sheets or sides of sheets only, 379–80, resulting in no copies more "correct" unless by chance, 380; variant readings, 372; accidents while printing, 376; quick

transfers of copyright, and partnerships, 374; number of editions and issues, 373–74; requirements against standing forms, 373–74; degeneration in reprinting, 374–75: priority of editions, signs of, 332–33: sources of play texts, 288, 317; signs of legitimacy, 288–89; author's manuscript, 293–95; Shakespeare's autograph manuscripts? 295–96; acquisition of copy by purchase, 289; illegitimate acquisition of copy, 289ff.; cuts, additions, interpolations, 299; ways of pirating playhouse versions, 300ff.; lost and stolen manuscripts, 290, discarded manuscripts, 291–93; scriveners' copies, 291–92, 294; actors' roles, 292; playhouse manuscripts, 296–98; corrupt text not necessarily pirated, 384.

Thaler, Alwin, 11, 13, 222n., 276n.

Theatres, closing of, 33, 182; ordered pulled down, 34; number of, limited, 34, 266; location of, favoring disorder, 30; licensing of, 48; *et passim*.

Theobald, Lewis, 1.

Thierry and Theodoret, Tragedy of (Fletcher and Massinger?), 163.

Thompson, Sir E. Maunde, 131, 295, 322.

Thompson, E. N. S., 99.

Tilney, Edmund, Master of the Revels, 42, 48, 49, 53, 55; censor of *Sir Thomas More*, 131ff., 137.

Titus Andronicus, copyright and stage-right of, 281.

Tompkins, *v.* Thos. Hallock, 313.

"Torrismont", a play not to be printed for twelve months, by contract of joint owners, 240.

Townshend, Aurelian, to furnish masques when Jonson was out of favor, 179.

Trade problems dramatized, 171.

Tragedy of the Plantation of Virginia, censored for profanity, 190.

Treason in plays, 181ff. See Jonson, *Sejanus*.

Treasurer, regulating drama, 19, 23; recalling objectionable works, 69, 78, *et passim;* protecting copyright, 69. See Burghley.

Tourneur, Cyril, *The Atheist's Tragedy*, 100n.

Triumphs of Honour and Industry (Middleton's pageant), ridiculing a Spanish ambassador, 196.

Troilus and Cressida (Shakespeare), publication of, 238.

True Tragedy of Richard, Duke of York, The, 280.

Turkish affairs dramatized, 107.

Turner, William, 351.

Turquet, Lewes de Mayerne, censored, 76.

Two Plays in One, (Yarington), playhouse manuscript? 297.

Tyndale, the *New Testament* of, objectionable, 72.

Types, hasty distribution of, a source of error, 337; setting of, *see* Compositor.

Typographical ideals, 317ff.; 344–45, 356, 376; effect of regulation of printing on, 356. See Compositor, Printing, Text, Publication, Plays.

Udall, John, 64n., censored, 74.

United Companies, The Four, of players, 282.

University, attitude of, toward drama, 35, 36ff.; the university towns to be protected from common plays by Privy Council, 266.

Usurer satirized, 175.

VanDam, B. A. P., 341n., 342, 349.

Variant readings, significance of, 372ff.; in different copies of an edition, 376–78. See Text.

Vega, Lope de, plays of, pirated by a memorizer, 311–13.

Venetian ambassador, report of, on English plays, 164, 166n., 178.

Vennar, Richard, 108.
Verneuil, Madame de, in English play, 163.
Vincent, Augustine, 354–55.
Virgin Martyr, The, 52.
Visorium, copy-holder, 329–30.
Volpone (Jonson), dedication of, satirizing decipherers, 198–99.

Waldegrave, and the Marpelate controversy, 71, 74; and Quin's defense of James's title to English throne, 151–52.
Walder, Ernest, 3–4, 211–12.
Wallace, C. W., 11, 220, 234.
Walsingham, Francis, 107.
Ward, A. W., 102.
Warner, Rebecca, 53.
Water-mark, and cancel, 382.
Webster, John, *The Duchess of Malfi*, 98; oversees publications, 205; reason for publication of *The White Devil*, 214; readers the best judges, 217n.
Welsh, parodied in plays, 148.
What You Will (Marston), personal satire in, 176.
White, Edward, fined, 86.
White, R. G., 334, 339.
Whitefriars Theatre, contract of sharers in plays, 224ff., 239.
Whitgift, John, 63–64; opposed to satire, 83.
Whore, New Vamped, The, a "scandalous and libelous" play, suppressed, 175.

Widows Tears, The (Chapman), dedication of, on the worth of printed plays, 211.
Willis, John, *The Arte of Stenographie*, 316.
Willobie, "Avisa" suppressed, 84.
Wilson, J. Dover, 276, 295, 308ff., 384.
Wilson, Robert, *Three Ladies of London*, 105, 131.
Winter's Tale, A (Shakespeare), 51.
Winwood, Sir Ralph, 107, 111.
Wither, *The Motto*, 319n.; size of pirated edition, 373.
Wits, The (D'Avenant), censored for profanity, 21.
Wolsey, play on, objected to, 173.
Woman's Prize (Fletcher), censored as *The Tamer Tamed*, for profanity and ribaldry, 189, 191; Herbert orders the company book-keeper, Knight, to purge the actors' parts, 192.
Women, character of, assailed in plays, 187.
Wonder of a Kingdom, 50.
Worcester, Earl of, Catholic patron of dramatists, 113.
Wotton, Sir Henry, 119, 121, 174–75, 185.
Wright, W. A., 349.
Wycliffites censored, 61.

Yarington, Robert, *Two Plays in One*, playhouse manuscript? 297.

Zeltner, Conrad, 327–28, 330.